HISTORICAL
VIEWPOINTS

© 1970, 1971 by American Heritage Publishing Co., Inc.
All articles have appeared in American Heritage, The Magazine of History,
some under different titles. All rights reserved.
Copyright acknowledgments on pages 631–632.
Library of Congress Catalog Card Number: 78–141365
SBN: 8281–0167–1

HISTORICAL VIEWPOINTS

NOTABLE ARTICLES FROM

AMERICAN HERITAGE   *The Magazine of History*

Editor

JOHN A. GARRATY   *Columbia University*

American Heritage Publishing Co., Inc. New York

Harper & Row, Publishers

New York, Evanston, San Francisco, London

Introduction

There are almost as many kinds of history as there are historians. In addition to the differences between political history and the social, economic, and cultural varieties, the discipline lends itself to such classifications as analytical, narrative, statistical, impressionistic, local, comparative, philosophical, synthetic, and many others. Often the distinctions between one and another kind of history are overemphasized. No one can write good political history without some consideration of social, economic, and cultural questions; narrative history requires analysis to be meaningful; impressionistic treatments of past events are, in a way, statistical histories based on very tiny samples. Nevertheless, the types exist and serve different purposes. Each focuses on part of the total human experience and sees it from a particular perspective; each, when well done, adds its own contribution to the total record. It is therefore foolish to argue that any kind of historical approach is inherently better than all the others. Some are perhaps more generally useful (that is, more interesting to a wider segment of the population) or more suggestive at a particular time and place than others, but the distinctions are like those between a miniature and a mural, a sonnet and an epic poem. No one would suggest that "The Moonlight Sonata" was a waste of Beethoven's time because he was capable of producing the *Choral* symphony, or that Mozart should not have written "Eine Kleine Nachtmusik" because he had within him *Don Giovanni,* and in the same way a monograph or an article of twenty pages can be as well worth doing and as satisfying to read as Edward Gibbon's *Decline and Fall of the Roman Empire.*

The most useless and confusing distinction commonly drawn between varieties of history is that separating "scholarly" from "popular" history. These terms came into existence during the latter half of the nineteenth century. Before that time, all history was popular in the sense that those who wrote it, viewing themselves as possessors of special information acquired through scholarship or through having observed firsthand the events they described, aimed to transmit that knowledge to anyone interested in the subject. But when history became "scientific" and professionalized, historians began to write primarily for other historians. They assumed that nonspecialists had no interest in their work or were incapable of understanding it, and even argued that to write history for the general reader was to prostitute one's talents. Therefore, although with many notable exceptions, the best-trained and most knowledgeable and intelligent historians tended to forswear the task of transmitting their scholarly findings to ordinary readers.

Of course popular history continued to be written and read, but most of it was produced by amateurs, and thus its quality varied greatly. The scholarly prejudice against "popularizers" had a solid basis in fact. Too often popular history was—and still is—shallow, error-ridden, out-of-date before publication, a mere rehash of already written books, an exasperating mixture, as one critic has said, of "something we all knew before" and "something which is not so." Much of it was written by journalists and novelists who often lacked the patience, the professional skills, and the knowledge of sources that are as necessary for the writing of good history as narrative power, imagination, and lucidity of style.

It was chiefly with the hope of encouraging professional historians to broaden their perspectives that, beginning in the 1930's, a group of historians led by Professor Allan Nevins of Columbia University began to think of founding a general circulation magazine of American history. Their aim was a magazine in which solidly researched and significant articles would be presented in a way that would interest and educate readers who were not professional students of the past. Nevins himself, one of the great historians of the twentieth century, epitomized the combination these men sought to produce. He was a prodigious scholar, author of dozens of learned volumes, and trainer of literally hundreds of graduate students, but he was also a fluent and graceful writer whose work was widely read and appreciated. Nevins' books won Pulitzer Prizes as well as academic renown.

The example provided by Nevins and a few other outstanding historians of his generation, such as Samuel Eliot Morison, undoubtedly influenced the gradual revival of concern for popular history that has occurred in recent times on the part of professional academic scholars. So did the increasing sophistication of the general reading public, which made it less difficult for these experts to write this type of history without sacrificing their intellectual standards. In any case, in 1954 the Nevins group—the Society of American Historians—joined the American Association for State and Local History in sponsoring the hard-cover magazine they had envisioned: *American Heritage*.

The success of *American Heritage* was rapid and substantial. It achieved a wide circulation, and a galaxy of the best professional historians began to publish in its pages. Its articles, at their best, have been authoritative, interesting, significant, and a pleasure to read. They have ranged over the whole course of American history from the pre-colonial era to the present, and have dealt with every aspect of American development from politics to painting and from economics to architecture.

The present selection from among the hundreds of essays and book excerpts that have appeared in *American Heritage* since 1954 does not pretend to offer "the best" of these articles, although any such collection would undoubtedly include many of those I have chosen. It seeks rather to provide a balanced assortment of articles to supplement and enrich general college courses in American history. Keeping in mind the structure of these courses and the topics they tend to emphasize, I have reprinted here articles which, in my opinion, will add depth and breadth to the student's understanding.

This is—by definition—popular history, but it is also history written by experts. The articles differ in purpose and approach. Some present new findings, some re-examine old questions from a fresh point of view, others magisterially distill and synthesize masses of facts and ideas. From the total the reader may extract, along with the specifics of the individual essays, a sense of the variety and richness of historical literature. He will observe how forty-odd historians (and not all of them academic scholars) have faced the task of presenting knowledge not to other historians alone but to an audience of intelligent and interested general readers. Since most of the students enrolled in college history courses are not specialists—even those who intend to become professional historians stand at the very beginning of their training—this approach seems to me ideally adapted to their needs. Many, though by no means all, of the subjects treated in these essays have also been covered in articles in professional historical periodicals, often written by the same historians. But as here presented, without sacrifice of intellectual standards, the material is not so much easier to grasp as it is more meaningful. Details are clearly related to larger issues; historical characters are delineated in the round, not presented as stick figures or automatons; too much previous knowledge is not assumed. I once read the draft of an essay on the history of the Arabs which contained the sentence, "The life and philosophy of Mohammed are well-known," and which then went on to other less universally understood topics. Such essays no doubt have their place, but that place is not in collections designed for beginners, whatever the subject.

Finally, I believe that at least some of the essays I have included here illustrate the truth that history is, at its best, an art as well as a science. After all, the ancients gave history its own Muse, Clio. From reading the following pages, I hope and expect that students will come to realize that history is a form of literature, that it can be *enjoyed,* not merely assimilated. Even those who see college history courses exclusively as training grounds for future professionals surely will not object if their students enjoy these readings while they learn.

John A. Garraty
Columbia University
August, 1969

Contents

Perils of the Sea of Darkness, *by sixteenth-century Flemish engraver Theodore de Bry, combines truth and fantasy to symbolize the Old World's fascination with the new.*

Part
One

A
NEW
WORLD

Oliver La Farge

Myths That Hide The American Indian

As Oliver La Farge explains in this essay, the true character of the civilization of the American Indian has, from the time of Columbus, been shrouded in myth. White men have seen the Indians as they wished to see them, not as they were. Naturally, there are good reasons for this as well as bad: the tribes left no written records; they were scattered and isolated over a vast continent; and they differed one from another greatly in culture and social structure.

Years of patient research by archaeologists, anthropologists, and other students have gone into the work of reconstructing their way of life. As La Farge's essay shows, that task, if not completed, has been substantially advanced. Its importance, of course, is enormous, and not merely because of our interest in the first settlers of America. Only by understanding the Indians can the early history of the European in the New World be fully grasped.

An anthropologist by training, La Farge was an admirable exemplar of the role of the specialist in writing history for the general public. Besides his many scientific works, and a Pulitzer Prize winning novel, Laughing Boy, *in articles like this one he brought to thousands of readers objective and yet moving portraits of Indian life.*

*E*ver since the white men first fell upon them the Indians of what is now the United States have been hidden from white men's view by a number of conflicting myths. The oldest of these is the myth of the Noble Red Man or the Child of Nature, who is credited either with a habit of flowery oratory of implacable dullness or else with an imbecilic inability to converse in anything more than grunts and monosyllables.

That first myth was inconvenient. White men soon found their purposes better served by the myth of ruthless, faithless savages, and later, when the "savages" had been broken, of drunken, lazy good-for-nothings. All three myths coexist today, sometimes curiously blended in a schizophrenic confusion such as one often sees in the moving pictures. Through the centuries the mythical figure has been variously equipped; today he wears a feather headdress, is clothed in beaded buckskin, dwells in a tepee, and all but lives on horseback.

It was in the earliest period of the Noble Red Man concept that the Indians probably exerted their most important influence upon Western civilization. The theory has been best formulated by the late Felix S. Cohen, who, as a profound student of law concerning Indians, delved into early white-Indian relations, Indian political economy, and the white men's view of it. According to this theory, with which the present writer agrees, the French and English of the early seventeenth century encountered, along the East Coast of North America from Virginia southward, fairly advanced tribes whose semi-hereditary rulers depended upon the acquiescence of their people for the continuance of their rule. The explorers and first settlers interpreted these rulers as kings, their people as subjects. They found that even the commonest subjects were endowed with many rights and freedoms, that the nobility was fluid, and that commoners existed in a state of remarkable equality.

Constitutional monarchy was coming into being in England, but the divine right of kings remained firm doctrine. All European society was stratified in many classes. A somewhat romanticized observation of Indian society and government, coupled with the idea of the Child of Nature, led to the formulation, especially by French philosophers, of the theories of inherent rights in all men, and of the people as the source of the sovereign's authority. The latter was stated in the phrase, "consent of the governed." Both were carried over by Jefferson into our Declaration of Independence in the statement that "all men are created equal, that they are endowed by their Creator with certain unalienable Rights" and that governments derive "their just powers from the consent of the governed. . . ."

Thus, early observations of the rather simple, democratic organization of the more advanced coastal tribes, filtered through and enlarged by the minds of European philosophers whose thinking was ripe for just such material, at least influenced the formulation of a doctrine, or pair of doctrines, that furnished the intellectual base for two great revolutions and profoundly affected the history of mankind.

In the last paragraph I speak of "the more advanced" tribes.

Two of the myths attached to the American Indian are on view in these nineteenth-century engravings: the wild, bloodthirsty savage (right) and the drunken wastrel (left).

Part of the myth about the first Americans is that all of them, or most of them, had one culture and were at the same stage of advancement. The tribes and nations that occupied North America varied enormously, and their condition was anything but static. The advent of the white men put a sudden end to a phase of increasingly rapid cultural evolution, much as if a race of people, vastly superior in numbers, in civilization, and above all in weapons, had overrun and conquered all of Europe in Minoan times. Had that happened, also, the conquerors would undoubtedly have concluded, as so many white men like to conclude about Indians, that that peculiar race of light-skinned people was obviously inferior to their own.

Human beings had been in the New World for at least 15,000 years. During much of that time, as was the case in the beginning everywhere, they advanced but little from a Palaeolithic hunting culture. Somewhere around 2,500 B.C. farming began with the domestication of corn either in Peru or in Meso-America* in the vicinity of western Guatemala. Farming brought about the sedentary life and the increased food supply necessary for cultural progress. By the time of the birth of Christ, the influence of the high cultures, soon to become true civilizations, in Meso-America was beginning to reach into the present United States. Within the next 1,500 years the Indians of parts of North America progressed dramatically. When the white men first landed, there were three major centers of high culture: the Southeast-Mississippi Valley, the Southwest, and the Northwest Coast. None of the peoples of these regions, incidentally, knew about war bonnets or lived in tepees.

The Southeast-Mississippi Valley peoples (for brevity, I shall refer to the area hereafter simply as ''Southeast'') seem to have had the

* Meso-America denotes the area in which the highest civilizations north of Peru developed, extending from a little north of Mexico City into Honduras.

strongest influences from Meso-America, probably in part by land along the coast of Texas, in part by sea across the Gulf of Mexico, whether direct from Mexico or secondhand through the peoples of the West Indies. There is a striking resemblance between some of their great earthen mounds, shaped like flat-topped pyramids, with their wood-and-thatch temples on top, and the stone-and-mortar, temple-topped pyramids of Meso-America. Some of their carvings and engravings strongly suggest that the artists had actually seen Meso-American sculptures. The list of similarities is convincingly long.

There grew up along the Mississippi Valley, reaching far to the north, and reaching also eastwards in the far south, the high culture generally called "Mound Builder." It produced a really impressive art, especially in carving and modeling, by far the finest that ever existed in North America. The history of advancing civilization in the New World is like that of the Old—a people develops a high culture, then barbarians come smashing in, set the clock part way back, absorb much of the older culture, and carry it on to new heights. A series of invasions of this sort seems to have struck the Mound Builders in late prehistoric times, when they were overrun by tribes mainly of Muskhogean and Iroquoian linguistic stock. Chief among these were the ancestors of the well-known Five Civilized Tribes—the Seminoles, Creeks, Choctaws, Chickasaws, and Cherokees. When white men first met them, their culture was somewhat lower than that of the earlier period in the land they occupied. Nonetheless, they maintained, in Florida, Alabama, Mississippi, Louisiana, and Georgia, the highest level east of the Rockies. A late movement of Iroquoian tribes, close relatives of the Cherokees, among them the Iroquois themselves, carried a simpler form of the same culture into Pennsylvania, New York, Ohio, and into the edge of Canada.

All of these people farmed heavily, their fields stretching for miles. They were few in a vast land—the whole population of the present United States was probably not over a million. Hunting and fishing, therefore, were excellent, and no reasonable people would drop an easy source of abundant meat. The development of their farming was held in check quantitatively by the supply of fish and game. They farmed the choice land, and if the fields began to be exhausted, they could move. They moved their habitations somewhat more freely than do we, but they were anything but nomadic. The southern tribesmen lived neither in wigwams nor tepees, but in houses with thatched roofs, which in the extreme south often had no walls. They had an elaborate social structure with class distinctions. Because of their size, the white men called their settlements "towns." The state of their high chiefs was kingly. They were a people well on the road toward civilization.

The Natchez of Mississippi had a true king, and a curious, elaborate social system. The king had absolute power and was known as the Sun. No ordinary man could speak to him except from a distance, shouting and making obeisances. When he went out, he was carried on a litter, as the royal and sacred foot could not be allowed to touch the ground. The Natchez nation was divided into two groups, or moieties: the aristocracy and the common people. The higher group was subdivided into Suns (the royal family), Nobles, and Honored Ones. The common people were known simply as Stinkers. A Stinker could marry anyone he pleased, but all the aristocrats had to marry out of their moiety, that is, marry Stinkers. When a female aristocrat married a Stinker man, her children belonged to her class; thus, when a Sun woman married a Stinker, her children were Suns. The children of the men, however, were lowered one class, so that the children of a Sun man, even of the Sun himself, became Nobles, while the children of an Honored One became lowly Stinkers.

This system in time, if nothing intervened, would lead to an overwhelming preponderance of aristocrats. The Natchez, however, for all their near-civilization, their temples, their fine crafts and arts, were chronically warlike. Those captives they did not torture to death they adopted, thus constantly replenishing the supply of Stinkers (a foreigner could become nothing else, but his grandchildren, if his son struck a royal fancy, might be Suns).

The Indians of the Southeast knew the Mexican-West Indian art of feather weaving, by means of which they made brilliant, soft cloaks. The Sun also wore a crown of an elaborate arrangement of feathers, quite unlike a war bonnet. In cloak and crown, carried shoulder-high on a litter, surrounded by his retainers, his majesty looked far more like something out of the Orient than anything we think of ordinarily when we hear the word "Indian."

The Natchez were warlike. All of the southeasterners were warlike. War was a man's proper occupation. Their fighting was deadly, ferocious, stealthy if possible, for the purpose of killing—men, women, or children, so long as one killed—and taking captives, especially strong males whom one could enjoy torturing to death. It is among these tribes and their simpler relatives, the Iroquois, that we find the bloodthirsty savage of fiction, but the trouble is that he is not a savage. He is a man well on the road toward civilization.

With the Iroquois, they shared a curious pattern of cruelty. A warrior expected to be tortured if captured, although he could, instead, be adopted, before torture or at any time before he had been crippled. He entered into it as if it were a contest, which he would win if his captors failed to wring a sign of pain from him and if he kept taunting them so long as he was conscious. Some of the accounts of such torture among the Iroquois, when the victim was a member of a tribe speaking the same language and holding to the same customs, are filled with a quality of mutual affection. In at least one case, when a noted enemy proved to have been too badly wounded before his capture to be eligible for adoption, the chief, who had hoped that the man would replace his own son, killed in battle, wept as he assigned him to his fate. At intervals between torments so sickening that one can hardly make one's self read through the tale of them, prisoner and captors exchanged news of friends and expressions of mutual esteem. Naturally, when tribes who did not hold to these customs, including white men, were subjected to this treatment it was not well received.

This pattern may have come into North America from a yet more advanced, truly civilized source. The Mexicans—the Aztecs and their neighbors—expected to be sacrificed if they were captured, and on occasion might insist upon it if their captors were inclined to spare them. They were not tortured, properly speaking, as a general rule, but some of the methods of putting them to death were not quick. What we find in North America may have been a debasement of the Mexican practices developed into an almost psychopathic pleasure among people otherwise just as capable of love, of kindness, of nobility, and of lofty thought as any anywhere—or what the conquistadores found in Mexico may have been a civilized softening of earlier, yet more fearful ways. The Aztecs tore fantastic numbers of hearts from living victims, and like the people of the Southeast, when not at war said "We are idle." They were artists, singers, dancers, poets, and great lovers of flowers and birds.

The Iroquois and Muskhogeans had a real mental sophistication. We observe it chiefly in their social order and what we know of their religions. The Iroquois did not have the royalty and marked divisions of classes that we find farther south, but their well-organized, firmly knit tribes were what enabled them, although few in numbers, to dominate the Algonkians who surrounded them. The Iroquois came nearer to having the matriarchy that popular fable looks for among primitive people than any other American tribe. Actual office was held by the men, but the women's power was great, and strongly influenced the selection of the officers.

Five of the Iroquois tribes achieved something unique in North America, rare anywhere, when in the sixteenth century they formed the League of the Five Nations—Senecas, Onondagas, Mohawks, Cayugas, and Oneidas—to which, later, the Tuscaroras were added. The league remained united and powerful until after the American Revolution, and exists in shadowy form to this day. It struck a neat balance between sovereignty retained by each tribe and sovereignty sacrificed to the league, and as so durable and effective a union was studied by the authors of our Constitution.

The league was founded by the great leader Iliawatha. Any resemblance between the fictional hero of Longfellow's poem and this real, dead person is purely coincidental. Longfellow got hold of the name and applied it to some Chippewa legends, which he rewrote thoroughly to produce some of the purest rot and the most heavy-footed verse ever to be inflicted upon a school child.

The Iroquois lived in "long houses," which looked like extended Quonset huts sheathed in bark. Smaller versions of these, and similarly covered, domed or conical structures, are "wigwams," the typical housing of the Northeast. Many people use the word "wigwam" as synonymous with "tepee," which is incorrect. A tepee, the typical dwelling of the Plains Indians of a later period, is a functional tent, usually covered with hides or, in recent years, canvas, and one of its essential features is that it is the shelter of constantly mobile people.

A tepee, incidentally, is about the most comfortable tent ever invented, winter or summer—provided you have two or three strong, competent women to attend to setting it up and striking it.

The great tribes we have been discussing showed their sophistication in a new way in their response to contact with Europeans. Their tribal organizations became tighter and firmer. From south to north they held the balance of power. The British success in establishing good relations with many of them was the key to driving the French out of the Mississippi area; to win the Revolution, the Americans had to defeat the Iroquois, whose favor up to then had determined who should dominate the Northeast. The southern tribes radically changed their costume, and quickly took over cattle, slaves, and many arts. By the time Andrew Jackson was ready to force their removal, the Cherokees had a stable government under a written constitution, with a bicameral parliament, an alphabet for writing their language, printing presses, a newspaper, schools, and churches.

Had it not been for the white men's insatiable greed and utter lawlessness, this remarkable nation would have ended with a unique demonstration of how, without being conquered, a "primitive" people could adapt itself to a new civilization on its own initiative. They would have become a very rare example of how aborigines could receive solid profit from the coming of the white men.

After the five Civilized Tribes were driven to Oklahoma, they formed a union and once again set up their governments and their public schools. Of course we could not let them have what we had promised them; it turned out that we ourselves wanted that part of Oklahoma after all, so once again we tore up the treaties and destroyed their system. Nonetheless, to this day they are a political power in the state, and when one of their principal chiefs speaks up, the congressmen do well to listen.

The tribes discussed until now and their predecessors in the same general area formed a means of transmission of higher culture to others, east and west. Their influence reached hardly at all to the northwards, as north of the Iroquois farming with native plants was difficult or impossible. On the Atlantic Coast of the United States the tribes were all more or less affected. Farming was of great importance. Even in New England, the status of chiefs was definite and fairly high. Confederacies and hegemonies, such as that of the Narragansetts over many of the Massachusetts tribes, occurred, of which more primitive people are incapable. Farther south, the state of such a chief as Powhatan was royal enough for Europeans to regard him as a king and his daughter as a true princess.

To the westward, the pattern of farming and sedentary villages extended roughly to the line that runs irregularly through Nebraska and Kansas, west of which the mean annual rainfall is below twenty inches. In wet cycles, there were prehistoric attempts to farm farther west, and in historic times the Apaches raised fair crops in the eastern foothills of the southern tip of the Rockies, but only the white men combined the mechanical equipment and the stupidity to break the turf and exhaust the soil of the dry, high plains.

An essay as short as this on so large a subject is inevitably filled with almost indefensible generalizations. I am stressing similarities, as in the case of the Iroquois-Southeast tribes, ignoring great unlikenesses. Generalizing again, we may say that the western farmers, whose cultures in fact differed enormously, also lived in fairly fixed villages. In the southern part, they built large houses covered with grass thatch. At the northwestern tip of the farming zone we find the Mandans, Hidatsa, and Crows, who lived in semi-subterranean lodges of heavy poles covered with earth, so big that later, when horses came to them, they kept their choice mounts inside. These three related, Siouan-speaking tribes living on the edge of the Plains are the first we have come to whose native costume, when white men first observed them, included the war bonnet. That was in the early nineteenth century; what they wore in 1600, no one knows.

The western farmers had their permanent lodges; they also had tepees. Immediately at hand was the country of the bison, awkward game for men on foot to hunt with lance and bow, but too fine a source of meat to ignore. On their hunting expeditions they took the conical tents. The size of the tepees was limited, for the heavy covers and the long poles had to be dragged either by the women or by dogs. Tepee life at that time was desirable only for a short time, when one roughed it.

The second area of Meso-American influence was the Southwest, as anthropologists define it—the present states of New Mexico and Arizona, a little of the adjacent part of Mexico, and various extensions at different times to the north, west, and east. We do not find here the striking resemblances to Meso-America in numbers of culture traits we find in the Southeast; the influence must have been much more indirect, ideas and objects passing in the course of trade from tribe to tribe over the thousand miles or so of desert northern Mexico.

In the last few thousand years the Southwest has been pretty dry, although not as dry as it is today. A dry climate and a sandy soil make an archaeologist's paradise. We can trace to some extent the actual transition from hunting and gathering to hunting plus farming, the appearance of the first permanent dwellings, the beginning of pottery-making, at least the latter part of the transition from twining and basketry to true weaving. Anthropologists argue over the very use of the term "Southwest" to denote a single area, because of the enormous variety of the cultures found within it. There is a certain unity, nonetheless, centering around beans, corn, squashes, tobacco, cotton, democracy, and a preference for peace. Admitting the diversity, the vast differences between, say, the Hopi and Pima farmers, we can still think of it as a single area, and for purposes of this essay concentrate on the best-studied of its cultures, the Pueblos.

The name "Pueblo" is the Spanish for "village," and was given to that people because they lived—and live—in compact, defensible settlements of houses with walls of stone laid up with adobe mortar or entirely of adobe. Since the Spanish taught them how to make rectangular bricks, pure adobe construction has become the commoner type. They already had worked out the same roofing as was usual in Asia Minor and around the Mediterranean in ancient times. A modern Pueblo house corresponds almost exactly to the construction of buildings dating back at least as far as 600 B.C. in Asia Minor.

The Pueblos, and their neighbors, the Navahos, have become well enough known in recent years to create some exception to the popular stereotype of Indians. It is generally recognized that they do not wear feathers and that they possess many arts, and that the Pueblos are sedentary farmers.

Farming has long been large in their pattern of living, and hunting perhaps less important than with any people outside the Southwest. Their society is genuinely classless, in contrast to that of the Southeast. Before the Spanish conquest, they were governed by a theocracy. Each tribe was tightly organized, every individual placed in his niche. The power of the theocracy was, and in some Pueblos still is, tyrannical in appearance. Physical punishment was used to suppress the rebellious; now more often a dissident member is subjected to a form of being sent to Coventry. If he be a member of the tribal council, anything he says at meetings is pointedly ignored. If he has some ceremonial function, he performs it, but otherwise he is left in isolation. I have seen a once self-assertive man, who for a time had been a strong leader in his tribe, subjected to this treatment for several years. By my estimation, he lost some thirty pounds, and he became a quiet conformist.

The power of the theocracy was great, but it rested on the consent of the governed. No man could overstep his authority, no one man had final authority. It went hard with the individual dissident, but the will of the people controlled all.

The Pueblos had many arts, most of which still continue. They wove cotton, made handsome pottery, did fine work in shell. Their ceremonies were spectacular and beautiful. They had no system of torture and no cult of warfare. A good warrior was respected, but what they wanted was peace.

The tight organization of the Pueblo tribes and the absolute authority over individuals continues now among only a few of them. The loosening is in part the result of contact with whites, in part for the reason that more and more they are building their houses outside of the old, solid blocks of the villages, simply because they are no longer under constant, urgent need for defense.

It is irony that the peace-loving southwestern farmers were surrounded by the worst raiders of all the wild tribes of North America. Around A.D. 1100 or 1200 there began filtering in among them bands of primitives, possessors of a very simple culture, who spoke languages of the Athabascan stock. These people had drifted down from western Canada. In the course of time they became the Navahos and the Apaches. For all their poverty, they possessed a sinew-backed bow of Asiatic type that was superior to any missile weapon known to the Southwest. They traded with the Pueblos, learned from them, stole from them, raided them. As they grew stronger, they became pests. The Navahos and the northeastern branch of the Apaches, called Jicarilla Apaches, learned farming. The Navahos in time became artists, above all the finest of weavers, but they did not give up their raiding habits.

These Athabascans did not glorify war. They made a business of it. Killing enemies was incidental; in fact, a man who killed an enemy had to be purified afterwards. They fought for profit, and they were about the only North Americans whose attitude toward war resembled professional soldiers'. This did not make them any less troublesome.

The last high culture area occupied a narrow strip along the Pacific Coast, from northern California across British Columbia to southern Alaska, the Northwest Coast culture. There was no Meso-American influence here, nor was there any farming. The hunting and fishing were so rich, the supply of edible wild plants so adequate, that there was no need for farming—for which in any case the climate was unfavorable. The prerequisite for cultural progress is a food supply so lavish that either all men have spare time, or some men can specialize in non-food-producing activities while others feed them. This condition obtained on the Northwest Coast, where men caught the water creatures from whales to salmon, and hunted deer, mountain sheep, and other game animals.

The area was heavily forested with the most desirable kinds of lumber. Hence wood and bark entered largely into the culture. Bark was shredded and woven into clothing, twined into nets, used for padding. Houses, chests, dishes, spoons, canoes, and boats were made of wood. The people became carvers and woodworkers, then carried their carving over onto bone and horn. They painted their houses, boats, chests, and their elaborate wooden masks. They made wooden armor, including visored helmets, and deadly wooden clubs. In a wet climate, they made raincloaks of bark and wore basketry hats, on the top of which could be placed one or more cylinders, according to the wearer's rank. The chiefs placed carvings in front of their houses that related their lineage, tracing back ultimately to some sacred being such as Raven or Bear—the famous, so-called totem poles.

I have said that the finest prehistoric art of North America was that of the Mound Builders; in fact, no Indian work since has quite equaled it—but that is, of course, a matter of taste. The greatest historic Indian art was that of the Northwest Coast. Their carvings, like the Mound Builder sculptures, demand comparison with our own work. Their art was highly stylized, but vigorous and fresh. As for all Indians, the coming of the white men meant ruin in the end, but at first it meant metal tools, the possession of which resulted in a great artistic outburst.

Socially they were divided into chiefs, commoners, and slaves. Slaves were obtained by capture, and slave-raiding was one of the principal causes of war. Generosity was the pattern with most Indians, although in the dry Southwest we find some who made a virtue of thrift. In the main, a man was respected because he gave, not because he possessed. The Northwest Coast chiefs patterned generosity into an ugliness. A chief would invite a rival to a great feast, the famous potlatch. At the feast he would shower his rival and other guests with gifts, especially copper disks and blankets woven of mountain sheep wool, which were the highest units of value. He might further show his lavishness by burning some possessions, even partially destroy a copper disk, and, as like as not, kill a few slaves.

If within a reasonable time the other chief did not reply with an even larger feast, at which he gave away or destroyed double what his rival had got rid of, he was finished as a chief—but if he did respond in proper form, he might be beggared, and also finished. That was the purpose of the show. Potlatches were given for other purposes, such as to authenticate the accession of the heir to a former chief, or to buy a higher status, but ruinous rivalry was constant. They seem to have been a rather disagreeable, invidious, touchy people. The cruelty of the southeasterners is revolting, but there is something especially unpleasant about proving one's generosity and carelessness of possessions by killing a slave—with a club made for that special purpose and known as a "slave-killer."

The Meso-American culture could spread, changing beyond recognition as it did so, because it carried its food supply with it. The Northwest Coast culture could not, because its food supply was restricted to its place of origin.

North and east of the Northwest Coast area stretched the sub-Arctic and the plains of Canada, areas incapable of primitive farming. To the south and east were mountains and the region between the Rockies and the Coastal ranges called the Great Basin. Within it are large stretches of true desert; most of it is arid. Early on, Pueblo influences reached into the southern part, in Utah and Nevada, but as the climate grew drier, they died away. It was a land to be occupied by little bands of simple hunters and gatherers of seeds and roots, not strong enough to force their way into anywhere richer.

In only one other area was there a natural food supply to compare with the Northwest Coast's, and that was in the bison range of the Great Plains. But, as already noted, for men without horses or rifles, hunting bison was a tricky and hazardous business. Take the year 1600, when the Spanish were already established in New Mexico and the English and French almost ready to make settlements on the East Coast, and look for the famous Plains tribes. They are not there. Some are in the mountains, some in the woodlands to the northeast, some farming to the eastward, within the zone of ample rainfall. Instead we find scattered bands of Athabascans occupying an area no one else wanted.

Then the white men turned everything upside down. Three elements were most important in the early influence: the dislodgment of eastern tribes, the introduction of the horse, and metal tools and firearms. Let us look first at the impact on the centers of high culture.

White men came late to the Northwest Coast, and at first only as traders. As already noted, early contact with them enriched the life of the Indians and brought about a cultural spurt. Then came settlers. The most advanced, best organized tribes stood up fairly well against them for a time, and they are by no means extinct, but of their old culture there are now only remnants, with the strongest survivals being in the arts. Today, those Indians who are in the "Indian business," making money from tourists, dress in fringed buckskin and war bonnets, because otherwise the tourists will not accept them as genuine.

The tribes of the Atlantic Coast were quickly dislodged or wiped out. The more advanced groups farther inland held out all through colonial times and on into the 1830's, making fairly successful adjustments to the changed situation, retaining their sovereignty, and enriching their culture with wholesale taking over of European elements, including, in the South, the ownership of Negro slaves. Finally, as already noted, they were forcibly removed to Oklahoma, and in the end their sovereignty was destroyed. They remain numerous, and although some are extremely poor and backward, others, still holding to their tribal affiliations, have merged successfully into the general life of the state, holding positions as high as chief justice of the state supreme court. The Iroquois still hold out in New York and in Canada on remnants of their original reservations. Many of them have had remarkable success in adapting themselves to white American life while retaining considerable elements of their old culture. Adherents to the old religion are many, and the rituals continue vigorously.

The British invaders of the New World, and to a lesser degree the French, came to colonize. They came in thousands, to occupy the land. They were, therefore, in direct competition with the Indians and acted accordingly, despite their verbal adherence to fine principles of justice and fair dealing. The Spanish came quite frankly to conquer, to Christianize, and to exploit, all by force of arms. They did not shilly-shally about Indian title to the land or Indian sovereignty, they simply took over, then granted the Indians titles deriving from the Spanish crown. They came in small numbers—only around 3,000 settled in the Southwest—and the Indian labor force was essential to their aims. Therefore they did not dislodge or exterminate the Indians, and they had notable success in modifying Indian culture for survival within their regime and contribution to it.

In the Southwest the few Spaniards, cut off from the main body in Mexico by many miles of difficult, wild country, could not have survived alone against the wild tribes that shortly began to harry them. They needed the Pueblo Indians and the Pueblos needed them. The Christian Pueblos were made secure in their lands and in their local self-government. They approached social and political equality. During the period when New Mexico was under the Mexican Republic, for two years a Taos Indian, braids, blanket, and all, was governor of the territory. Eighteen pueblos survive to this day, with a population now approaching 19,000, in addition to nearly 4,000 Hopis, whose culture is Pueblo, in Arizona. They are conservative progressives, prosperous on the whole, with an excellent chance of

Alfred Jacob Miller's painting of a
Plains warrior—the myth still endures.

surviving as a distinctive group for many generations to come. It was in the house of a Pueblo priest, a man deeply versed in the old religion as well as a devout Catholic, that I first saw color television.

The Spanish, then, did not set populations in motion. That was done chiefly from the east. The great Spanish contribution was loosing the horses. They did not intend to; in fact, they made every possible effort to prevent Indians from acquiring horses or learning to ride. But the animals multiplied and ran wild; they spread north from California into Oregon; they spread into the wonderful grazing land of the high Plains, a country beautifully suited to horses.

From the east, the tribes were pressing against the tribes farther west. Everything was in unhappy motion, and the tribes nearest to the white men had firearms. So the Chippewas, carrying muskets, pushed westward into Minnesota, driving the reluctant Dakotas, the Sioux tribes, out of the wooded country into the Plains as the horses spread north. At first the Dakotas hunted and ate the strange animals, then they learned to ride them, and they were off.

The Sioux were mounted. So were the Blackfeet. The semi-civilized Cheyennes swung into the saddle and moved out of the farming country onto the bison range. The Kiowas moved from near the Yellowstone to the Panhandle; the Comanches came down out of the Rocky Mountains; the Arapahos, the Crows, abandoning their cornfields, and the Piegans, the great fighting names, all followed the bison. They built their life around the great animals. They ate meat lavishly all year round; their tepees, carried or dragged now by horses, became commodious. A new culture, a horse-and-bison culture, sprang up overnight. The participants in it had a wonderful time. They feasted, they roved, they hunted, they played. Over a serious issue, such as the invasion of one tribe's territory by another, they could fight deadly battles, but otherwise even war was a game in which shooting an enemy was an act earning but little esteem, but touching one with one's bare hand or with a stick was the height of military achievement.

This influx of powerful tribes drove the last of the Athabascans into the Southwest. There the Apaches and the Navahos were also mounted and on the go, developing their special, deadly pattern of war as a business. In the Panhandle country, the Kiowas and Comanches looked westward to the Spanish and Pueblo settlements, where totally alien peoples offered rich plunder. The Pueblos, as we have seen, desired to live at peace. The original Spanish came to conquer; their descendants, becoming Spanish-Americans, were content to hold what they had, farm their fields, and graze their flocks. To the north of the two groups were Apaches and Utes; to the east, Kiowas and Comanches; to the south, what seemed like unlimited Apaches; and to the west the Navahos, of whom there were several thousands by the middle of the seventeenth century.

The tribes named above, other than the Kiowas and Comanches, did not share in the Plains efflorescence. The Navahos staged a different cultural spurt of their own, combining extensive farming with constant horseback plundering, which in turn enabled them to become herdsmen, and from the captured wool develop their remarkable weaving industry. The sheep, of course, which became important in their economy, also derived from the white men. Their prosperity and their arts were superimposed on a simple camp life. With this prosperity, they also developed elaborate rituals and an astoundingly rich, poetic mythology.

The Dakotas first saw horses in 1722, which makes a convenient peg date for the beginning of the great Plains culture. A little over a hundred years later, when Catlin visited the Mandans, it was going full blast. The memory of a time before horses had grown dim. By 1860 the Plains tribes were hard-pressed to stand the white men off; by 1880 the whole pattern was broken and the bison were gone. At its height, Plains Indian culture was brittle. Materially, it depended absolutely on a single source of food and skins; in other aspects, it required the absolute independence of the various tribes. When these two factors were eliminated, the content was destroyed. Some Indians may still live in tepees, wear at times their traditional clothing, maintain here and there their arts and some of their rituals, but these are little more than fringe survivals.

While the Plains culture died, the myth of it spread and grew to become embedded in our folklore. Not only the Northwest Coast Indians but many others as unlikely wear imitations of Plains Indian costume and put on "war dances," to satisfy the believers in the myth. As it exists today in the public mind, it still contains the mutually incongruous elements of the Noble Red Man and the Bloodthirsty Savage that first came into being three centuries and a half ago, before any white man had ever seen a war bonnet or a tepee, or any Indian had ridden a horse.

Samuel Eliot Morison

Christopher Columbus, Mariner

America's astronauts have been rightly venerated for their achievements, and perhaps their adventures are indeed as significant as those of Columbus, with whom they have been repeatedly compared. Yet, in the perspective of history, as courageous explorers they seem but pale copies of the great Admiral of the Ocean Sea, who ventured into what was truly unknown at the mercy of the capricious elements, separating himself totally from his familiar world. Furthermore, for all their skills and determination, the astronauts, once launched, were irretrievably committed. Columbus, at every stage of his adventure, from the time he first conceived it, had to overcome the doubts and frailties of kings and crew members, as well as his own. His was a courage and determination without parallel in history.

The epic of Columbus has often been described, but never so convincingly and poetically as by Samuel Eliot Morison, emeritus professor of history at Harvard University. In the following section of his book, Christopher Columbus: Mariner, *he tells the story of the early life of Columbus, of his great vision and his struggles to make it a reality, and then, with gripping detail, of his first amazing voyage to America.*

Christopher Columbus, Discoverer of the New World, was first and foremost a sailor. Born and raised in Genoa, one of the oldest European seafaring communities, as a youth he made several voyages in the Mediterranean, where the greatest mariners of antiquity were bred. At the age of twenty-four, by a lucky chance he was thrown into Lisbon, center of European oceanic enterprise; and there, while employed partly in making charts and partly on long voyages under the Portuguese flag, he conceived the great enterprise that few but a sailor would have planned, and none but a sailor could have executed. That enterprise was simply to reach "The Indies"—Eastern Asia—by sailing west. It took him about ten years to obtain support for this idea, and he never did execute it, because a vast continent stood in the way. America was discovered by Columbus purely by accident and was named for a man who had nothing to do with it; we now honor Columbus for doing something that he never intended to do, and never knew that he had done. Yet we are right in so honoring him, because no other sailor had the persistence, the knowledge and the sheer guts to sail thousands of miles into the unknown ocean until he found land.

This was the most spectacular and most far-reaching geographical discovery in recorded human history. Moreover, apart from the magnitude of his achievement, Columbus was a highly interesting character. Born at the crossroads between the Middle Ages and the Renaissance, he showed the qualities of both eras. He had the firm religious faith, the a-priori reasoning and the close communion with the Unseen typical of the early Christian centuries. Yet he also had the scientific curiosity, the zest for life, the feeling for beauty and the striving for novelty that we associate with the advancement of learning. And he was one of the greatest seamen of all time.

The little we know about the Discoverer's childhood and early youth can be quickly told. Born at Genoa in the fall of 1451 into a family of wool weavers, he had very little formal schooling, spoke the Genoese dialect, which was almost unintelligible to other Italians, and never learned to read and write until he went to Portugal. As everyone who described him in later life said that he had a long face, an aquiline nose, ruddy complexion and red hair, we can picture him as a little, freckled-faced redhead with blue eyes. One imagines that he was a dreamy little boy and very religious for one of his age, and he must have disliked working in his father's loom shed, as he took every opportunity to go to sea.

In later life Columbus said that he first went to sea in 1461 when he was ten years old. Probably his seafaring at that age did not amount to much; maybe his father let him sail with a neighbor to Portofino to load dried fish, or even over to Corsica, which would have seemed like a foreign voyage to a little boy. What sailor can forget his first cruise? Every incident, every turn of wind, every vessel or person you meet stays in your memory for years. What pride and joy to be given the tiller while the skipper goes below and the mate snoozes on the sunny side of the deck! What a thrill to sight five mountains above the horizon, to watch them rise, spread out and merge into one as you approach! Then, to go ashore, to swap your jackknife for a curiosity, to see the island gradually sink below the horizon on the homeward passage, and to swagger ashore feeling you are a real old salt! Such things a sailor never forgets.

It is probable that for a period of about eight years, between ages fifteen and twenty-three, Christopher made several long voyages in the Mediterranean but spent most of his time ashore helping his father. He also made at least one voyage to Chios in the Aegean, in a ship owned by Genoese merchants, who had the monopoly of trade with that island.

In May 1476, in his twenty-fifth year, came the adventure that changed the course of Christopher's life. Genoa organized an armed convoy to carry a valuable cargo to Northern Europe, and in this convoy Christopher sailed as seaman in a Flemish vessel named *Bechalla*. On August 13, when it had passed the Strait of Gibraltar and was off the southern coast of Portugal, the fleet was attacked by a French task force. The battle raged all day, and by nightfall three Genoese ships and four of the enemy's had gone down. *Bechalla* was one of the casualties. Christopher, though wounded, managed to grasp a floating sweep and, by alternately kicking it ahead and resting on it, reached the shore six miles distant. The people of Lagos, near which he landed, treated him kindly, and on learning that his younger brother Bartholomew was living at Lisbon, sent him thither as soon as he could travel. That was one of the best things that could have happened to Christopher Columbus.

Portugal was then the liveliest and most progressive country in Europe, and Lisbon the center for exploration and discovery. Lisbon, moreover, was a learned city where it was easy for a new-comer like Columbus to learn Latin and modern languages, and to acquire books that increased his knowledge of the world. Bartholo-mew, who had already joined the Genoese community there, was em-ployed in one of the chart-making establishments, where he got a job for Christopher, and before long the Columbus brothers had a thriving chart business of their own. That put them in close touch with master mariners and the like, for all charts at that time were based on information and rough sketches that seamen brought home. The two brothers would manage to be on hand whenever a ship returned from Africa or the Western Islands to invite the master or pilot to dine or drink with them, and would extract from him all the data they could for correcting their charts of known countries or extending those of the African coast. It may well be that in one of these conferences a grizzled captain, looking at a chart of the known world, remarked, "I'm sick of sailing along the fever-stricken Guinea coast, chaffering with local chiefs for a cargo of blackamoors; why can't we sail due west beyond the Azores, till we hit the Golden East, and make a real killing?"

Why not, indeed? People had been talking of doing that since the days of the Roman Empire, but nobody had tried it within the memory of man. The ocean was reputed too broad, winds too uncertain; the ships could not carry enough cargo to feed their crews for several months, and the sailors themselves had acquired deep respect for that dark and turbulent waste, the North Atlantic, and would not engage in such an enterprise. That it was theoretically possible to reach the Orient by sailing west every educated man would admit, since every educated man knew the earth to be a sphere, but nobody had done anything to test the theory.

Exactly when and how he got the idea we do not know. It may have been put to him, as we suggest, by a shipmaster impatient of the dangers and disappointments of the Guinea trade. It may have come to him in a rush of religious emotion at Mass, when he heard Psalm 19, "The Heavens declare the Glory of God"; for a Genoa compatriot remarked that Christopher fulfilled the prophecy of the fourth verse, "And their words unto the ends of the world." He may have read that prophecy of Seneca in the *Medea*, "A time will come when the chains of the Ocean will fall apart, and a vast continent be revealed; when a pilot will discover new worlds and Thule no longer be the ultimate." That prophecy, too, was fulfilled by him, as his son Ferdinand duly noted in his copy of Seneca. We do not know how Columbus came by the idea of sailing west to reach the East, but once he had it, that was the truth for him; he was the sort of man in whom action is the complement of a dream. He *knew* the truth, but he could not rest until it was proved, until the word became flesh. And, let us admit, his combination of creative imagination with obstinate assurance, his impatience with all who were slow to be convinced and contempt for those who withstood him, made Columbus a fool in the eyes of some men and a bore to most. Like the pioneers of aviation, he was considered a little touched in the head: one who would fly in the face of God. And the worst of it was that he had to persuade stupid people in high places that his Enterprise of the Indies, as he called it, was plausible, because he wanted money, men and equipment to carry it out.

European knowledge of China at that time was slight and inaccurate. The Spanish Sovereigns, as their letter of introduction furnished to Columbus indicates, thought that the Mongol dynasty of Kubla Khan still reigned in the Celestial Empire, although the Ming dynasty had supplanted it as far back as 1368. Most of the information (and misinformation) that Europe had about China came from *The Book of Ser Marco Polo*, the Venetian who spent about three years in China around the turn of the fourteenth century. This account of his experiences was circulated in countless manuscript copies and was one of the earliest books to be printed. Marco Polo not only confirmed the rumors that Chinese emperors were rolling in wealth, but he wrote a highly embellished account of an even wealthier island kingdom named Cipangu (Japan) which, he said, lay 1500 miles off the coast of China.

We must constantly keep in mind that nobody in Europe had any conception or suspicion of the existence of the continent that we

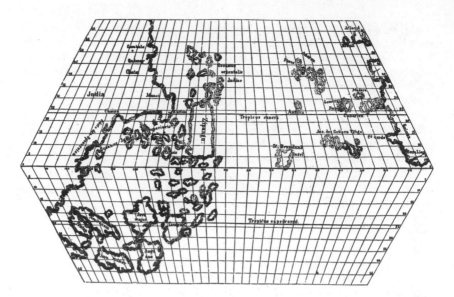

Columbus did not come to his geographical reckonings unaided. His position was supported by the learned Florentine Paolo Toscanelli, whose map (above) placed "Zipangu" (Japan) near where America was to be discovered.

call America. The voyages of the Northmen in the eleventh century to a part of the east coast of the future Canada or New England, which they called Vinland, were either unknown or forgotten in Southern Europe; and if Columbus had heard about them on his voyage to Iceland, they were of no interest to him, since he was not interested in wild grapes, pine trees and codfish, but in gold and spices. Everyone regarded the Ocean Sea as one and indivisible, flowing around Europe, Asia and Africa, which formed, as it were, one big island in one big ocean. The great questions before Columbus, and before the various monarchs and officials who must decide whether or not to support him, were, "How far west *is* the Far East? How many miles lie between Spain and China or Japan? How long would the voyage take? And is such a voyage practicable?"

Everyone, we repeat, admitted that the Earth was a sphere, and the convention of dividing a circle or sphere into 360 degrees had been arrived at by the Greeks. But how long was a degree? On your answer to that depended your estimate of the size of the Earth. Ptolemy of Alexandria, whose book was the geographical Bible of Columbus's day, said that it was 50 nautical miles long—the correct measure is 60. Alfragan, a Moslem geographer of the ninth century, said the degree measured 66 nautical miles, but Columbus misread him and decided that Alfragan's degree was 45 miles long and that Alfragan, not Ptolemy, was right. In other words, he underestimated the size of the world by 25 per cent.

Besides this mistake on the size of the globe, Columbus made another colossal error in reckoning how far eastward Asia stretched. The actual combined length of Europe and Asia is roughly 130 degrees from Cape St. Vincent to Peiping, or 150 degrees to Tokyo. Ptolemy guessed that it was 180 degrees, which was half the circumference of the globe. Marinus of Tyre, an earlier authority whom Columbus naturally preferred, stretched out this land mass to 225 degrees. Marco Polo, who took two or three years to cross Asia by land, made some rough calculations and tacked on 28 degrees more for China and 30 degrees additional for Japan; this, added to Marinus's 225 degrees, would place Tokyo on the meridian that runs through Western Cuba, Chattanooga, Grand Rapids and Western Ontario! Moreover, as Columbus proposed to jump off from the western Canary Islands, which lie on a parallel 9 degrees west of Cape St. Vincent, he figured he would have only 68 degrees of westing to make before hitting the coast of Japan. Combining that gross miscalculation with his underestimate of the length of a degree, he figured that the length of the ocean voyage from the Canaries to Japan would be 2400 nautical miles. The actual air-line distance is 10,600 miles!

In 1484 he made his first effort to interest a prince—John II, King of Portugal, a nephew of Henry the Navigator who was intensely interested in new discoveries. According to the contemporary Portuguese historians and chroniclers, the Columbian project was exactly the same then as later—to reach Japan by sailing west and to discover other islands en route. "The King," says one of the historians, "as he observed this *Christovão Colom* to be a big talker and boastful . . . and full of fancy and imagination with his Isle *Cypango* [Japan] . . . gave him small credit." Nevertheless, the King committed the project to a junta consisting of a prominent churchman and two Jewish physicians of reputed skill in celestial navigation. They turned it down, flat. Their reasons for so doing are not recorded, but we may assume that they had a more accurate idea of the distance to be covered than did Columbus.

The same year that the Portuguese committee turned him down, his wife Dona Felipa died at Lisbon. That broke his strongest tie with Portugal. Nobody there would stake him if the King would not, so Columbus decided to try his luck in Spain. He knew no one there except a sister of his late wife who was married to a Spaniard in Huelva, so to that part of Spain, adjoining Portugal, Columbus took ship with his five-year-old son Diego.

As his ship rounded into the Rio Tinto, he observed on a bluff the buildings of the Franciscan friary of La Rábida. That suggested a solution to his problem of what to do with Diego, as the Franciscans were known to take "boarders." So, after landing at Palos, he walked with his little son four miles to the friary, knocked at the gate and asked the porter for a drink of water and some bread for the boy. Fortunately, Antonio de Marchena, a highly intelligent Franciscan who had studied astronomy, came to the gate and got into conversation with Columbus. He invited both father and son to stay, accepted Diego as a pupil and introduced Columbus to the Count of Medina Celi, a grandee of Spain and also an important shipowner of Cadiz.

Medina Celi, of whom Columbus asked "three or four well-equipped caravels, and no more," had almost decided to underwrite the enterprise when it occurred to him to ask permission of the Queen. He did so, and Isabella refused, believing that so important an enterprise as that of Columbus should be conducted by the crown. But this transfer from Count to Queen postponed Columbus's voyage some six years.

About nine months elapsed before Columbus could obtain an audience with the Queen, because the court was traveling from city to city in central and northern Spain, and he had no funds to follow.

On May Day 1486, almost a year from the time he had first set foot in Spain, Columbus was received by the Queen in the Alcazar that still stands at Cordova. Isabella the Catholic was one of the ablest European sovereigns in an age of strong kings. She had an intuitive faculty for choosing the right man for a job, and for doing the right thing at the right time. She was very close to Columbus's age and similar to him in temperament, and in coloring—blue eyes and auburn hair. Her marriage with Ferdinand of Aragon had united all "the Spains," excepting Portugal, to which she was allied, and the remnant of the Moorish Caliphate of Cordova, which she had resolved to conquer. Some spark of understanding evidently passed between Christopher and Isabella at their first meeting, and although she turned down his enterprise more than once, he found that he could count on her in the end. On this occasion she appointed a special commission under Hernando de Talavera, her confessor, to examine the Great Project and recommend whether she should accept or reject it, or allow Medina Celi to back it.

Then began a period of almost six years, the most unhappy in Columbus's entire life. He had to sustain a continual battle against prejudice, contumely and sheer indifference. A proud, sensitive man who *knew* that his project was feasible and that it would open new pathways to maritime achievement and opportunity, he had to endure clownish witticisms and crackpot jests by ignorant courtiers, to be treated worse than a beggar, and at times actually to suffer want.

Not until late in 1490 did the Talavera commission issue its report, and it was unfavorable. The experts advised the Queen that the West-to-the-Orient project "rested on weak foundations"; that its attainment seemed "uncertain and impossible to any educated person"; that the proposed voyage to Asia would require three years' time, even if the ships could return, which they judged doubtful; that the Ocean was infinitely larger than Columbus supposed, and much of it unnavigable. And finally, it was not likely that God would have allowed any uninhabited lands of real value to be concealed from His people for so many centuries. Rejection could not have been more flat, and we must admit that all the commission's arguments, save the last, were sound. Suppose there had been no America, no ship then built, however resolute her master and crew, or frugal in provision, could have made the ten-thousand-mile voyage from Spain to Japan.

Apparently a complete deadlock. Columbus knew he could do it; the experts were certain he could not. It needed something as powerful as feminine intuition to break the log jam.

For the present, all the Queen would do was to give Columbus fresh hope. He could apply again, said she, when the war with the Moors was over.

At about Christmas time 1491, Columbus again appeared at court, which was then being held in the fortified camp of Sante Fe during the siege of Granada. A new commission was appointed, and the Royal Council reviewed their findings. The exact details are not known, but it seems probable that the commission, reading the Queen's mind, recommended that Columbus be allowed to try this project, and that the Council rejected it because of the price he asked. For this extraordinary man, despite poverty, delays and discouragement, had actually raised his demands. In 1485 he had been willing to sail west for Medina Celi on an expense-account basis, without any particular honors or emoluments. Now he demanded not only ennoblement and the title of Admiral, but also that he be made governor and viceroy of any new lands he might discover, that both titles be hereditary in his family, and that he and his heirs be given a ten per cent cut on the trade. He had suffered so many outrages and insults during his long residence in Spain that—by San Fernando!—he would not glorify Spain for nothing. If the Sovereigns would grant him, contingent on his success, such rank, titles and property that he and his issue could hold up their heads with Spanish grandees, well and good; but no more bargaining. Take it, Your Majesties, or leave it.

Leave it they did, in January 1492, immediately after the fall of Granada. Ferdinand and Isabella told him this at an audience that the King, at least, intended to be final. Columbus saddled his mule, packed the saddlebags with his charts and other exhibits, and started for Seville with his faithful friend Juan Pérez, intending to take ship for France and join Bartholomew in a fresh appeal to Charles VIII.

Just as, in Oriental bargaining, a storekeeper will often run after a departing customer to accept his last offer, so it happened here. Luis de Santangel, keeper of King Ferdinand's privy purse, called on the Queen the very day that Columbus left Sante Fe and urged her to meet Columbus's terms. The expedition, he pointed out, would not cost as much as a week's entertainment of a fellow sovereign, and he would undertake to raise the money himself. As for the honors and emoluments, Columbus asked only for a promise of them in the event of his success, and if he did succeed, they would be a small price to pay for the discovery of new islands and a western route to the Indies. Isabella, who had probably felt that way all along, jumped at this, her really last chance. She even proposed to pledge her crown jewels for the expenses, but Santangel said that would not be necessary. And she sent a messenger who overtook Columbus at a village four miles from Sante Fe, and brought him back.

Although it was now settled in principle, the success of the Enterprise depended on an infinite number of practical details. First, it was decided to fit out the fleet and recruit the men at Palos, the little port in the Niebla where Columbus had first set foot in Spain, and for several reasons. Columbus had made friends there of the Pinzón family, leading shipowners and master mariners; both ships and sailors were available. And Palos had committed some municipal misdemeanor for which the Queen conveniently fined her two well-equipped caravels. Columbus made a public appearance in the Church of St. George, Palos, on May 23, 1492, with his friend Fray Juan Pérez, while a notary read the royal order that "within ten days" the two caravels were to be provided and crews recruited, with four months' advance pay.

Ten days, of course, was preposterous, and it actually took about three months for Columbus to get to sea. He had been promised three caravels, not two, but it so happened that a ship from Galicia, owned and captained by Juan de la Cosa, was then in port, and Columbus chartered her as his flagship.

Santa María, as this ship was called, is the most famous of Columbus's ships. She left her bones on a reef off Hispaniola, and no picture or model of her has survived, but several conjectural models have been made and two full-size "replicas" have been constructed in Spain. The original *Santa María* was probably of about 100 tons' burthen, which meant that her cargo capacity was 100 "tuns" or double hogsheads of wine. Her rig was the conventional one of the period, when ships were just emerging from the one-big-mast type of the Middle Ages: a mainmast higher than she was long, a main yard as long as the keel, carrying an immense square sail—the main course—which was counted on to do most of the driving. Above the main course was spread a small main topsail. The foremast, little more than half the height of the mainmast, carried only a square fore course or foresail. The mizzenmast, stepped on the high poop, carried a small lateen-rigged sail, and under the bowsprit, which pointed up from the bows at a sharp angle, was spread a small square sail called the spritsail, which performed rather inefficiently the function of the modern jib.

A Spanish ship in those days had an official name, usually that of a saint, and a nickname which the sailors used; *Santa María* was *La Gallega,* "The Galician." One of the two caravels provided by the town of Palos was named *Santa Clara,* but she is universally known by her nickname *Niña,* so given because she belonged to the Niño family of Palos. *Niña* was Columbus's favorite. She carried him safely home from his First Voyage, took him to western Cuba and back to Spain on the Second, and made another voyage to Hispaniola. She measured about 60 tons, her length was not over 70 feet, and at the

An engraving done in 1621 shows the three caravels setting sail from Palos, Spain, with Ferdinand and Isabella bidding them farewell.

start she was rigged with three lateen sails, like a Portuguese caravel, but in the Canaries Columbus had her re-rigged square like *Santa María*, because square sails are much handier than lateen rig when running before the wind.

Pinta, also a locally built caravel, was probably a little larger than *Niña*, and square-rigged from the first. Her real name we do not know; *Pinta* probably was derived from a former owner named Pinto. She was a smart sailer; the New World was first sighted from her deck and she was first home to Spain.

All vessels carried inside stone ballast. They were fastened mostly with wooden trunnels or pins, such as one sees in the frames of old American houses; their sides were painted gay colors above the waterline and, below it, payed with pitch, which was supposed to discourage barnacles and teredos. Crosses and heraldic devices were emblazoned on the sails, and the ships carried a variety of large, brightly colored flags which were flown on entering and leaving port. Queen Isabella's royal ensign, quartering the castles and lions of Castile and Leon, was hoisted on the main truck, and on the foremast or mizzen was displayed the special banner of the expedition: a green cross on a white field, with a crown on each arm—a concession to Aragon. All three vessels carried a little crude artillery, to repel possible pirates or other unwelcome boarders, but they were in no sense combatant ships, and carried neither soldiers nor gunners.

By the second day of August, 1492, everything at last was ready.

That night every man and boy of the fleet confessed his sins, received absolution and made his communion at the church of Palos, which by happy coincidence was dedicated to Saint George, patron saint of Genoa. Columbus went on board his flagship in the small hours of Friday the third and gave the signal to get under way. Before the sun rose, all three vessels had anchors aweigh, and with sails hanging limp from their yards were floating down the Rio Tinto on the morning ebb, using their long sweeps to maintain steerageway. As they swung into the Saltés and passed La Rábida close aboard, they could hear the friars chanting the ancient hymn *Iam lucis orto sidere* with its haunting refrain *Et nunc et in perpetuum*, which we render "Evermore and evermore."

Columbus's plan for the voyage was simple, and its simplicity insured his success. Not for him the boisterous head winds, the monstrous seas and the dark, unbridled waters of the North Atlantic, which had already baffled so many Portuguese. He would run south before the prevailing northerlies to the Canary Islands, and there make, as it were, a right-angle turn; for he had observed on his African voyages that the winter winds in the latitude of the Canaries blew from the east, and that the ocean around them, more often than not, was calm as a millpond. An even better reason to take his departure from the Canaries was their position astride latitude 28 degrees North, which, he believed, cut Japan, passing en route the mythical Isle of Antilia, which would make a good break in the westward passage. Until about a hundred years ago when chronometers became generally available to find longitude, sailors always tried to find the latitude of their destination and then would "run their westing" (or easting) down until they hit it. That is what Columbus proposed to do with respect to Japan, which he had figured out to be only 2400 nautical miles due west of the Canaries.

The first leg of the voyage was made in less than a week. Then, within sight of the Grand Canary, the fleet ran into a calm that lasted two or three days. Columbus decided to send *Pinta* into Las Palmas for some needed repairs while *Santa María* and *Niña* went to Gomera, westernmost of the Canaries that the Spaniards had wrested from their native inhabitants. At Gomera the Captain General (as we should call Columbus on this voyage before he made Admiral) sent men ashore to fill extra water casks, buy breadstuffs and cheese, and put a supply of native beef in pickle. He then sailed to Las Palmas to superintend *Pinta's* repairs and returned with her to Gomera.

On September 2 all three ships were anchored off San Sebastián, the port of that island. Columbus then met for the first time Doña Beatriz de Bobadilla, widow of the former captain of the island. Beatriz was a beautiful lady still under thirty, and Columbus is said to have fallen in love with her; but if that is true, he did not love her warmly enough to tarry to the next full moon. Additional ship's stores were quickly hoisted on board and struck below, and on September 6, 1492, the fleet weighed anchor for the last time in the Old World. By nightfall September 9, every trace of land had sunk below the

Fifteenth-century sailors feared such monsters as the one depicted above from Olaus Magnus' Historia de Gentibus Septentrionalibus, *or in* English, A History of the Northern Nations.

eastern horizon, and the three vessels were alone on an uncharted ocean. Columbus himself gave out the course: "West; nothing to the north, nothing to the south."

Before going into the details of the voyage, let us see how those vessels were navigated, and how a day was passed at sea. Celestial navigation was then in its infancy, but rough estimates of latitude could be made from the height of the North Star above the horizon and its relation to the two outer stars (the "Guards") of the Little Dipper. A meridian altitude of the sun, applied to available tables of the sun's declination, also gave latitude, by a simple formula. But the instruments of observation—a solid wood or brass quadrant and the seaman's astrolabe—were so crude, and the movement of a ship threw them off to such an extent, that most navigators took their latitude sights ashore. Columbus relied almost completely on "dead reckoning," which means plotting your course and position on a chart from the three elements of direction, time and distance.

The direction he had from one or more compasses which were dry-card jobs, similar to those used in small craft until recently. Time was measured by a half-hour glass which hung from a beam so the sand could flow freely from the upper to the lower half. Distance was the most variable of these three elements. Columbus had no chip log or other method of measuring the speed of his vessels. He and the watch officers merely estimated it and noted it down. By carefully checking Columbus's Journal of his First Voyage, Captain J. W. McElroy ascertained that he made an average 9 per cent overestimate of his distance. This did not prevent his finding the way home, because the mistake was constant, and time and course were correct. It only resulted in Columbus placing the islands of his discovery farther west than they really were.

Comforts and conveniences were almost totally lacking. Cooking was done on deck over a bed of sand in a wooden firebox protected from the wind by a hood. The diet was a monotonous one of salt meat, hardtack and dried peas. For drink they had wine, while it lasted, and water in casks, which often went bad. Only the Captain General and the ships' captains had cabins with bunks; the others slept where they could, in their clothes.

During the first ten days (September 9 to 18), the easterly trade wind blew steadily, and the fleet made 1163 nautical miles' westing. This was the honeymoon of the voyage. *Que era plazer grande el gusto de las mañanas*—''What a delight was the savor of the mornings!'' wrote Columbus in his Journal. That entry speaks to the heart of anyone who has sailed in the trades; it recalls the beauty of the dawn, kindling clouds and sails rose color, the smell of dew drying on a wooden deck, and, something Columbus didn't have, the first cup of coffee. Since his ships were at the northern edge of the northeast trades, where the wind first strikes the water, the sea was smooth, and the air, remarked the Captain General in his Journal, was ''like April in Andalusia; the only thing wanting was to hear the song of the nightingale.'' But there were plenty of other birds following the ships: the little Mother Carey's chickens, dabbling for plankton in the bow waves and wakes; the boatswain bird, so called (as old seamen used to say) because it carries a marlinspike in its tail; the man-of-war or frigate bird, ''thou ship of the air that never furl'st thy sails,'' as Walt Whitman wrote; and when the fleet passed beyond the range of these birds, the big Jaeger gulls gave it a call. During this period the fleet encountered its first field of sargassum or gulfweed and found that it was no hindrance to navigation. ''Saw plenty weed'' was an almost daily notation in the Captain General's log. The gulfweed bothered him much less than observing a westerly variation of the compass, for in European waters the variation is always easterly.

On September 19, only ten days out from Ferro, the fleet temporarily ran into an area of variable winds and rain. During the next five days only 234 miles were made good. During this spell of moderate weather it was easy to converse from ship to ship. In the middle of one of these colloquies, a seaman of *Pinta* gave the ''Land Ho!'' and everyone thought he saw an island against the setting sun. Columbus fell on his knees to thank God, ordered *Gloria in excelsis Deo* to be sung by all hands, and set a course for the island. But at dawn no island was visible; there was none. It was simply a cloud bank above the western horizon resembling land, a common phenomenon at sea. Martín Alonso Pinzón apparently wished to beat about and search for this island, but Columbus refused, because, he said, ''his object was to reach the Indies, and if he delayed, it would not have made sense.''

The trade wind now returned, but moderately, and during the six days September 26 to October 1, the fleet made only 382 miles. Under these circumstances the people began to mutter and grumble. Three weeks was probably more than they had ever been outside sight of land before. They were all getting on each other's nerves, as happens even nowadays on a long voyage to a known destination. There was nothing for the men to do in the light wind except to follow the ship's routine, and troll for fish. Grievances, real or imaginary, were blown up; cliques were formed; Spain was farther away every minute, and what lay ahead? Probably nothing, except in the eye of that cursed Genoese. Let's make him turn back, or throw him overboard!

On the first day of October the wind increased, and in five days (October 2 to 6) the fleet made 710 miles. On the sixth, when they had passed longitude 65 degrees West and actually lay directly north of Puerto Rico, Martín Alonso Pinzón shot his agile *Pinta* under the flagship's stern and shouted, "Alter course, sir, to southwest by west . . . Japan!" Columbus did not understand whether Martín Alonso meant that he thought they had missed Japan and should steer southwest by west for China, or that Japan lay in that direction; but he knew and Pinzón knew that the fleet had sailed more than the 2400 miles which, according to their calculations, lay between the Canaries and Japan. Naturally Columbus was uneasy, but he held to the west course magnetic, which, owing to the variation for which he did not allow, was about west by south, true.

On October 7, when there was another false landfall, great flocks of birds passed over the ships, flying westsouthwest; this was the autumn migration from eastern North America to the West Indies. Columbus decided that he had better follow the birds rather than his chart, and changed course accordingly that evening. That was "good joss"; it was his shortest course to the nearest land. Now, every night, the men were heartened by seeing against the moon (full on October 5) flocks of birds flying their way. But by the tenth, mutiny flared up again. No land for thirty-one days. Even by the phony reckoning which Columbus gave out they had sailed much farther west than anyone had expected. Enough of this nonsense, sailing west to nowhere; let the Captain General turn back or else ! Columbus, says the record, "cheered them as best he could, holding out good hope of the advantages they might gain; and, he added, it was useless to complain, *since he had come to go to the Indies, and so had to continue until he found them, with Our Lord's help.*"

That was typical of Columbus's determination. Yet even he, conscious of divine guidance, could not have kept on indefinitely without the support of his captains and officers. According to one account, it was Martín Alonso Pinzón who cheered him by shouting, *Adelante! Adelante!* which an American poet has translated, "Sail on! Sail on!" But, according to Oviedo, one of the earliest historians who talked with the participants, it was Columbus alone who persuaded the Pinzóns and La Cosa to sail on, with the promise that if land were not found within three days, he would turn back. If this version is correct, as I believe it is, the Captain General's promise to his captains was made on October 9. Next day the trade wind blew fresher, sending the fleet along at 7 knots; it so continued on the eleventh, with a heavy following sea. But signs of land, such as branches of trees with green leaves and flowers, became so frequent that the people were content with their Captain General's decision, and the mutinous mutterings died out in the keen anticipation of making a landfall in the Indies.

As the sun set under a clear horizon October 11, the northeast trade breezed up to gale force, and the three ships tore along at 9 knots. But Columbus refused to shorten sail, since his promised time was running out. He signaled everyone to keep a particularly sharp watch, and offered extra rewards for first landfall in addition to the year's pay promised by the Sovereigns. That night of destiny was clear and beautiful with a late rising moon, but the sea was the roughest of the entire passage. The men were tense and expectant, the officers testy and anxious, the Captain General serene in the confidence that presently God would reveal to him the promised Indies.

At 10 P.M., an hour before moonrise, Columbus and a seaman, almost simultaneously, thought they saw a light "like a little wax candle rising and falling." Others said they saw it too, but most did not; and after a few minutes it disappeared. Volumes have been written to explain what this light was or might have been. To a seaman it requires no explanation. It was an illusion, created by overtense watchfulness. When uncertain of your exact position, and straining to make a night landfall, you are apt to see imaginary lights and flashes and to hear nonexistent bells and breakers.

On rush the ships, pitching, rolling, throwing spray—white waves at their bows and white wakes reflecting the moon. *Pinta* is perhaps half a mile in the lead, *Santa María* on her port quarter, *Niña* on the other side. Now one, now another forges ahead, but they are all making the greatest speed of which they are capable. With the sixth glass of the night watch, the last sands are running out of an era that began with the dawn of history. A few minutes now and destiny will turn up a glass the flow of whose sands we are still watching. Not since the birth of Christ has there been a night so full of meaning for the human race.

At 2 A.M., October 12, Rodrigo de Triana, lookout on *Pinta*, sees something like a white cliff shining in the moonlight, and sings out, *Tierra! tierra!* "Land! land!" Captain Pinzón verifies the landfall, fires a gun as agreed, and shortens sail to allow the flagship to catch up. As *Santa María* approaches, the Captain General shouts across the rushing waters, "Señor Martín Alonso, you *did* find land! Five thousand maravedis for you as a bonus!"

Yes, land it was this time, a little island of the Bahamas group. The fleet was headed for the sand cliffs on its windward side and would have been wrecked had it held course. But these seamen were too expert to allow that to happen. The Captain General ordered sail to be shortened and the fleet to jog off and on until daylight, which was equivalent to a southwesterly drift clear of the island. At dawn they made full sail, passed the southern point of the island and sought an opening on the west coast, through the barrier reef. Before noon they found it, sailed into the shallow bay now called Long or Fernandez, and anchored in the lee of the land, in five fathoms.

Here on a gleaming beach of white coral occurred the famous first landing of Columbus. The Captain General (now by general consent called Admiral) went ashore in the flagship's boat with the royal standard of Castile displayed, the two Captains Pinzón in their boats, flying the banner of the Expedition—the green crowned cross on a white field. "And, all having rendered thanks to Our Lord, kneeling on the ground, embracing it with tears of joy for the immeasurable mercy of having reached it, the Admiral rose and gave this island the name *San Salvador*"—Holy Saviour.

Herrera's engraving after a woodcut by de Bry shows Columbus planting the Cross and receiving treasure from the Indians on landing at the island of San Salvador.

A. L. Rowse

America and the Elizabethan Imagination

The history of America has often been explained in terms of the impact of a virgin continent upon European, African, and other immigrants, an impact at once physical and psychological. Less frequently stressed, but equally significant, was the impact of that continent, with all its wonders, on those peoples, especially the western Europeans, who did not migrate to the New World. The effects of America on Europe were staggering, and not confined to the obvious political, economic, and social aspects of life. True enough, the wealth of the New World provided a tremendous stimulus to Europe. But in some ways America's most profound effects were upon the imaginations of creative men and women.

The British historian, A. L. Rowse of Oxford University, treats this subject in the following essay, part of his general study of The Elizabethans and America. *He mentions the impact of the humble potato on England and Ireland, but his main concern is with the reactions of poets, philosophers, political thinkers, scientists, and other intellectuals. The stimulation that America provided undoubtedly helped produce the great flowering of Elizabethan culture that we associate with the age of Shakespeare; Professor Rowse, for example, shows how extensively contemporary information about the New World influenced* The Tempest. *Moreover, he makes clear, the effects were pervasive. America kindled the imagination of the Elizabethans and in countless ways contributed to one of the greatest outpourings of creative activity in all history.*

*D*uring the reign of Elizabeth I, as the interest in and knowledge of America gathered momentum, so their reverberation in literature and the arts became louder, more frequent, and more varied. On the one hand, there were the writings and reports of those who had been there, as collected by Hakluyt and Purchas; the books written by people like Captain Smith and Morton and Strachey; the histories and journals of Bradford and Winthrop; the numerous tracts and sermons devoted to the subject. On the other, there is the reflection of America in the mirror of the imagination, in the poetry and prose of Spenser and Sidney, Raleigh and Chapman, Shakespeare and Drayton, Bacon and Donne. Sometimes these things run into one another: in the case of Raleigh, for example, who always straddles all fences. But it is fascinating to observe how not only the content of the voyagers' accounts but their very phrases will appear in the lines of the poets; how the words of Raleigh's sea captain, Barlow, take wing in the verse of his master or reappear in Drayton's ode "To the Virginian Voyage," or how Strachey's account of the hurricane off Bermuda is echoed in *The Tempest*.

The transition from the factual world of translations and reports to the realm of the imagination may be seen first in the circle of Philip Sidney, to whom Hakluyt dedicated his *Divers Voyages*. When we read Sidney's *Arcadia*, whose author was so much interested in America and several times thought of coming here, we recognize the atmosphere of the voyages. It begins with a shipwreck, with the wrack floating in a sea of very rich things and "many chests which might promise no less." The capture of prizes dominates the first chapters, with the arrival of Musidorus in a strange country, having lost his friend Pyrocles, who subsequently turns up. It is like the beginning of *The Tempest*, or episodes of *A Winter's Tale* and *Pericles*. The influence of the voyages speaks in them all, inciting the imagination to strange scenes and countries across the seas.

The atmosphere of *Arcadia* is quite like that of *The Faërie Queene* —the dreamlike timelessness of a fairy world of romance. Spenser was a friend of both Sidney and Raleigh, and the introductory stanzas to Book II acknowledge the impulse of the expansion:

> *But let that man with better sense advise*
> *That of the world least part to us is red;*
> *And daily how through hardy enterprise*
> *Many great regions are discovered,*
> *Which to late age were never mentioned.*
> *Who ever heard of th' Indian Peru?*
> *Or who in venturous vessel measured*
> *The Amazon huge river now found true?*
> *Or fruitfullest Virginia who did ever view?*
>
> *Yet all these were men no man did them know,*
> *Yet have from wisest ages hidden been;*
> *And later times things more unknown shall show.*

DIVERS

voyages touching the difcouerie of America, *and the Ilands adiacent* vnto the fame, made firſt of all by our *Engliſhmen, and afterward by the French-men and Britons:*

And certaine notes of aduertifements for obferuations, neceſſarie for ſuch as ſhall heereafter make the like attempt,

With two mappes annexed heereunto foʒ the plainer vnderſtanding of the whole matter.

Imprinted at Lon-don for Thomas VVoodcocke, *dwelling in paules Church-yard,* at the ſigne of the blacke beare.

1582.

The title page from Hakluyt's 1582 edition of Divers Voyages.

In the Old World, America was regarded as overflowing with gold as some still believe it to be. Marlowe has several references to this in *Tamburlaine:*

> *Desire of gold, great sir?*
> *That's to be gotten in the Western Ind:*

The thought is expressed by Greene, Peele, Lyly, Massinger, Chapman. It appears in Shakespeare, where sooner or later everything gets expression. We must remember that America, in this connotation, often appears as India, with or without the adjective "Western." This is made sufficiently clear by the dominant association with "mines." "As bountiful as mines of India," he writes. Henry VIII's meeting with Francis I at the Field of the Cloth of Gold

> *Made Britain India; every man that stood*
> *Showed like a mine.*

In *Twelfth Night,* when Maria appears to lay down the letter that entraps Malvolio, Sir Toby belches, "How now, my metal of India," *i.e.*, piece of gold. When Malvolio falls into the trap and is utterly bemused, Maria reports, "He does smile his face into more lines than is in the new map with the augmentation of the Indies." That was the map that went with the first volume of the enlarged edition of Hakluyt published in 1598. Shakespeare derived inspiration and profit from reading Hakluyt. The theme of digging for gold is an important element in *Timon*—at a time, too, when the Jamestown colony was temporarily given over to a frantic search for it. One writer declared in 1608 that there was then "no talk, no hope, no work but to dig gold, wash gold, refine gold, load gold." And this was about the date when *Timon* was written. The combination of the gold theme with digging for roots for subsistence comes straight from the voyages.

The theme is extended in the scenes that Chapman, Raleigh's poet, contributed to Ben Jonson and John Marston's *Eastward Ho!* The absurd Sir Petronel Flash's money is bestowed on a ship bound for Virginia. Security comments: "We have too few such knight adventurers: who would not sell away competent certainties to purchase, with any danger, excellent uncertainties?" This was precisely what many did for Virginia, and New England too. Seagull helps with a lot of mariners' tales about Virginia to gull the public. "Come, boys," he says, "Virginia longs till we share the rest of her maidenhead." That was a regular phrase with the voyagers— Raleigh's phrase for Guiana.

On this Spendall asks: "Why, is she inhabited already with any English?" Seagull: "A whole country of English is there, man, bred of those that were left there in '79." (Actually the date was '87; but we do not go to dramatists for dates any more than to historians for dramatics.) "They have married with the Indians and make 'em bring forth as beautiful faces as any we have in England, and therefore the Indians are so in love with 'em that all the treasure they have they lay at their feet." Scapethrift: "But is there such treasure there, captain, as I have heard?" Seagull: "I tell thee, gold is more plentiful there than copper is with us; and for as much red copper as I can bring, I'll have thrice the weight in gold. Why, man, all their dripping pans and their chamber pots are pure gold; and all the chains with which they chain up their streets are massy gold; all the prisoners they take are fettered in gold; and for rubies and diamonds they go forth on holidays and gather 'em by the seashore . . ." Scapethrift asks, "And is it a pleasant country withal?" Captain Seagull replies: "As ever the sun shined on: temperate and full of all sorts of excellent viands."

These leads—Spenser, Marlowe, Chapman—all point to Raleigh, as they were all his friends; he stands at the crossroads in literature, as he did in these actions. The captains he sent to reconnoiter Virginia in 1584 reported as follows:

The second of July we found shoal water, where we smelt so sweet and so strong a smell as if we had been in the midst of some delicate garden abounding with all kind of odoriferous flowers, by which we were assured that the land could not be far distant . . . We viewed the land about us, being, whereas we first landed, very sandy and low towards the water's side, but so full of grapes as the very beating and surge of the sea overflowed them; of which we found such plenty, as well on every little shrub as also climbing towards the tops of high cedars that I think in all the world the like abundance is not to be found. Under the bank or hill whereon we stood, we beheld the valleys replenished with goodly cedar trees.

In the poem Raleigh was writing some years later to recover the Queen's favor (but never finished), *Cynthia, the Lady of the Sea*, we read:

On highest mountains where those cedars grow
Against whose banks the troubled ocean bet
And were the marks to find thy hoped port
Into a soil far off themselves remove.

And when we come to Drayton's ode, "To the Virginian Voyage," we find:

When as the luscious smell
Of that delicious land
Above the sea that flows
The clear wind throws,
Your hearts to swell
Approaching the dear strand.
And the ambitious vine
Crowns with his purple mass
The cedar reaching high
To kiss the sky,
The cypress, pine,
And useful sassafras.

Of the motives that could lead men to leave home Raleigh speaks, in his own case:

My hopes clean out of sight with forced wind
To kingdoms strange, to lands far off addressed . . .

And he sums them all up in one famous line:

To seek new worlds for gold, for praise, for glory.

There was a whole succession of literary men who went as officials to Virginia: William Strachey, John Pory, Christopher Davison, George Sandys. Donne, who was hard up before he condescended to enter the Church, sought to be made secretary. Strachey, a Cambridge man, moved in a literary and dramatic circle in London. He was a shareholder in the Children of the Queen's Revels and so came to Blackfriars two or three times a week, where he would meet Shake-

In 1609 Sea Venture *was wrecked in a hurricane off Bermuda. On board was William Strachey, whose recounting of the adventure provided Shakespeare with the plot for* The Tempest.

speare. In 1609 he went out with Gates and Somers in the *Sea Venture,* which was famously wrecked on Bermuda, though all were saved and spent an agreeable winter there. The extraordinary happening made a strong impression on people's minds at home, and several accounts of it appeared, the most detailed being Strachey's letter to a noble lady, which circulated in manuscript. It is not surprising that the most impressionable mind in that circle was struck by it, for this was the germ of *The Tempest.*

It is somehow right that, just as More's *Utopia* provides the first expression of genius of the New World in our period, so *The Tempest* provides the last; that these two transcendent minds should have risen to the full height of the theme. For there is far more of the New World in Shakespeare's play than the original suggestion from Strachey's letter: the storm with its veracious details, St. Elmo's fire flaming amazement along the mainmast: the wreck and not a hair of the people hurt; the enchanted island full of noises, for Bermuda was believed to be haunted by evil spirits. The whole play sings of the sea; the loveliest songs are of the sea:

> *Full fathom five thy father lies,*
> *Of his bones are coral made;*
> *Those are pearls that were his eyes:*
> *Nothing of him that doth fade*
> *But doth suffer a sea-change*
> *Into something rich and strange.*

Not only that, but with the creation of Caliban, the primitive savage, possessor of the island, and his relation to Prospero, the very civilized and lordly person who dispossesses him, the whole question of what happens when civilization makes its impact upon primitive society is placed before us in a way we can never forget. Our sympathies are not with Prospero—and perhaps in the subconscious corridors of the mind we think of what happened to the redskins. There is something deeply affecting about Caliban:

> *. . . When thou camest first,*
> *Thou strok'dst me and mad'st much of me: would'st give me*
> *Water with berries in't and teach me how*
> *To name the bigger light, and how the less.*
> *That burn by day and night . . .*

This is what had happened time and again, generation after generation, with tribe after tribe, all along the coasts of America when the Indians came in contact with the white men and their superior knowledge. We read in Hakluyt and Captain Smith with what avidity they learned about the stars and the firmament, watched the white men's instruments, were impressed by lodestone and magnet, optic glass and clock.

> *. . . and then I lov'd thee*
> *And show'd thee all the qualities o' the isle,*
> *The fresh springs, brine-pits, barren place, and fertile.*

That, too, had often happened—we remember how Squanto showed the Pilgrims where best to take their fish and how to set Indian corn, and enabled them to subsist through the hard first years. In one sense the Indians were quick to learn; in another, they never learned—the gulf between their primitive cast of mind and that of the white man was too deep to bridge. And so the red man lost in the struggle for existence. Nor did he profit from his knowledge, in spite of his experiences at the hand of the white man. After Prospero comes the drunken Stephano:

> CALIBAN: *I prithee, let me bring thee where crabs grow;*
> *And I with my long nails will dig thee pig-nuts;*
> *Show thee a jay's nest and instruct thee how*
> *To snare the nimble marmozet; I'll bring thee*
> *To clust'ring filberts and sometimes I'll get thee*
> *Young scamels from the rocks . . .*

In spite of what he has suffered at the hand of Prospero, Caliban now wants Stephano to be his god:

> *I'll show thee every fertile inch o' the island;*
> *And I will kiss thy foot: I prithee, be my god.*

We are reminded of the native Californians who embarrassed Drake and his men by taking them for gods.

The idea of an original state of nature was to have an important development in political speculation and theorizing about society, and it was given immense impetus by what men discovered in the New World. It was brought home vividly to me years ago when I saw John Locke's library as it had come down in the possession of his representatives: we take it for granted that he was a generalizing and abstract thinker, as he was, but his library was full of the American voyages. There, made visible, was an example of the way early anthropology went into political theory.

Tudor folk were fascinated by the trappings of Indian life and the spectacle of Indians, from the time Cabot brought some back to the streets of Westminster, and a Brazilian chief was presented at the court of Henry VIII. In 1614—when the great Virginian venture was much in mind—two masques were given by the Inns of Court. Bacon's *Masque of Flowers* argued the merits and demerits of Virginia's chief product, tobacco, before the antitobacconist James I. Chapman's masque, a much grander affair dressed by Inigo Jones, had the masquers attired in Indian costume, "with high sprigged feathers on their heads, hair black and large waving down to their shoulders." The musicians were attired like Virginian "priests"—no doubt from John White's drawing. But the serious-minded Chapman addressed himself to a searching theme, the problem posed by the diversity of religion revealed by a new world, of which Holy Scripture, which held the key to all human history, had no knowledge. The orthodox poet spoke through Eunomia, representing civilized order:

> *Virginian princes, you must now renounce*
> *Your superstitious worship of these Suns,*
> *Subject to cloudy darkenings and descents,*
> *And of your fit devotions turn the event*
> *To this our British Phoebus, whose bright sky*
> *(Enlightened with a Christian piety)*
> *Is never subject to black error's night,*
> *And hath already offered heaven's true light*
> *To your dark region.*

There were people, even then, who speculated sensibly whether the American Indians had not come across the narrow divide of the Bering Strait from Asia. Some reflection of these speculations may be seen in Bacon's *jeu d'esprit, The New Atlantis*. Naturally the influence of the voyages and of reading Hakluyt is apparent, and Bacon had a direct interest in colonization by this time: he was one of the Council for Newfoundland. Bacon's utopian island was in the Pacific, which might still have islands and continents not yet come to light— Australia was yet to come out of it. But he refers to the inundation of an Atlantic continent, and the shrinking Atlantic shelf of America. Hence the American Indians were but remnants of a people: "Marvel you not at the thin population of America, nor at the rudeness and ignorance of the people; for you must accept your inhabitants of America as a young people: younger a thousand years, at the least, than the rest of the world."

The mind of the poet Donne was markedly stimulated by the geographical curiosity of the time. This is reflected in the unexpected images he reaches out for on the subject of love:

Let sea-discoverers to new worlds have gone,
Let maps to others worlds on worlds have shown,
Let us possess one world, each hath one and is one.

Where we can find two better hemispheres
Without sharp North, without declining West?

Or in addressing his mistress, going to bed, in somewhat unusual terms:

O my America! my new-found-land,
My kingdom, safeliest when with one man manned!

Many were the sermons that were preached to speed the Virginia enterprise; but Donne's sermon is the finest specimen of the class, in which it is elevated to literature. As we should expect, he raised the issues presented by colonization to a higher plane. He warned those going against seeking independence or exemption from the laws of England. "If those that govern there would establish such a government as should not depend upon this, or if those that go thither propose to themselves an exemption from laws to live at their liberty, this is to . . . divest allegiance and be under no man." And Donne had something to say which is very much to the point in the modern discussion about colonialism. The law of nations ordains "that every man improve that which he hath . . . the whole world, all mankind must take care that all places be improved as far as may be to the best advantage of mankind in general."

With a New World being discovered, there was not only an immense extension of geographical knowledge, but a comparable impetus to improve its quality and techniques. England was backward in this art, as in so much else; but now her geographers profited from their contacts with these leaders of thought, while they made use of the information gathered by the English voyagers in constructing their maps—Ortelius, of Anthony Jenkinson, for Russia and Persia; Mercator, of Drake, for America and the Pacific. Though English map makers in this field were not yet comparable, they were beginning. Frobisher's and Gilbert's voyages to North America led to a considerable increase of information about the northern areas, reflected in the maps of Michael Lok and Thomas Best. A number of John Dee's maps of these regions remain, and illustrate, as everything about him does, his curious mixture of shrewd criticism and crazy credulity. His map of North America based on Gilbert's explorations, for example, has a proper realization of the width of the continent across Canada; but theorist that he was, he had no compunction in tracing a waterway right across, to debouch with the Colorado into Southern California. By the end of the century, much more exact and useful contributions were being made to navigation

John Smith's Generall Historie *(1624), the title page of which is reproduced here, attracted wide interest in England. The portraits are those of Elizabeth, James I, and Charles I.*

and cosmography by such men as John Davis and Edward Wright.

Hariot appears as the most complete, all-round scientist of that time, with his interest alike in mathematics and astronomy, anthropology and navigation. He set forth a model of first-class scientific method with his *Brief and True Report of the new found land of Virginia*. It is the work of a superior mind; no Elizabethan quaintness in this; no fancy, let alone fantasy; all is in due order based on close observation, accurately brought into correlation with existing categories. It gives an account of the flora and fauna: the commodities of the country with their qualities and uses; methods of agriculture and properties of the soil, plants and fruits and roots; the beasts, fowl, and fish; ending with the nature and manners of the people, for Hariot had learned enough of their language to communicate with them about their notions and beliefs.

This concise little work, important as it is, is only a fragment of the materials collected by Hariot and John White at Roanoke. White was similarly engaged in mapping the coasts and sounds and rendering the life of the place in his water colors of the plants and fishes, the characters and ways of the natives. But after the hurricane that decided the colony to leave, many of their maps and papers were lost in the sea in the hurried transfer of their goods to Drake's ships. Others of White's papers left on Roanoke were spoiled by the Indians. But what remains is considerable.

The impact of America upon natural history in general, and botany in particular, was no less exciting. A wide range of new plants and animals provided continuing stimulus to the scientific curiosity, as well as the fancy, of naturalists in England as elsewhere. And this is reflected in their books. From the New World came the giant sunflower, nasturtium, Michaelmas daisy, lobelia, evening primrose, and so on. But by far the most important introductions were tobacco and the potato: these affected history.

The medicinal properties of tobacco were considered valuable. Hariot reported that it "purgeth superfluous phlegm and other gross humours, and openeth all the pores and passages of the body: by which means the use thereof not only preserveth the body from obstructions, but also (if any be, so that they have not been of too long continuance) breaketh them."

The habit of smoking spread rapidly among the courtiers and the upper class, popularized by Raleigh and those in touch with the colonies. It was noted as a piece of arrogance on Raleigh's part that "he took a pipe of tobacco before he went to the scaffold"; it is more likely to have been to steady his nerves, or as a last pleasure on earth. Even before the end of the Queen's reign, the habit was spreading to the lower orders. All this was good for Virginia: it put the colony on its feet and enabled it to survive.

The potato has had even more effect in history. In *The History and Social Influence of the Potato*, Redcliffe N. Salaman writes: "The introduction of the potato has proved to be one of the major events in man's recent history, but, at the time, it was a matter of relatively little moment and called forth no immediate public comment.'' To the Elizabethans the innocuous potato was not only sustaining, but stimulating to lust. We remember that when Falstaff, with the worst intentions, gets Mistress Ford and Mistress Page to come in to him, he calls on the sky to rain potatoes. Amid so much that is earthy, not to say murky, about this root, Dr. Salaman thinks it quite probable that Raleigh did introduce the growing of potatoes into Ireland—one more of the many things he has to answer for. This certainly had remote and far-reaching consequences, setting in motion the cycle that ultimately led to the mass migration of the Irish, during and after the Famine, to America.

It was from Ireland, too, that John White's drawings of American life turned up, having long ago disappeared from view. In the end, it is through such things as these—Powhatan's mantle, a wampum girdle or a shell necklace, the things the Elizabethans held in their hands and brought home, the flotsam and jetsam of time—that we are most directly in touch with that early American life, as well as through those fragments of memory that have entered into folklore, the unforgotten impression that Pocahontas made on the English people in her day—still alive in the famous inn sign, ''La Belle Sauvage.'' I write these words not far from a village in Cornwall still called after her, Indian Queen's. For what enters into the unconscious life of the mind and is carried on in folklore is the best evidence of the strength of common memories, common affections, and common ancestry.

Fox hunting was a passion which colonial gentry gladly indulged. This rendering of a hunting party is a detail from an overmantel painting of the late seventeenth century.

Part
Two

COLONIAL
LIFE

Marshall Fishwick

William Byrd II of Virginia

Whether William Byrd II was actually as unique a person as he seems can never be known, for it is only because of his marvelously candid diary that we know him as well as we do. Perhaps if others among the privileged but hard-working tobacco planters of eighteenth century Virginia had left similar records we would have had to conclude that Byrd was merely typical. In any case, Byrd the historical figure is important not because of his personal qualities, fascinating as these were, but because of what the story of his life tells us about the society of colonial Virginia.

If Byrd was, as Professor Marshall Fishwick, director of the American Studies Institute, Lincoln University, notes in the following essay, a "Renaissance man," he was one no doubt in part because the world he inhabited demanded versatility and rewarded achievement. His career helps explain the extraordinary self-confidence, imagination, and energy of several generations of Americans, not only his own but even more those which immediately followed, and which, in the single case of his native Virginia, produced Washington, Jefferson, Madison, Patrick Henry, and a host of others—the great Virginia leaders of the American Revolution.

*H*e could never resist an old book, a young girl, or a fresh idea. He lived splendidly, planned extensively, and was perpetually in debt. Believing perhaps, like Leonardo, that future generations would be more willing to know him than was his own, he wrote his delicious, detailed diaries in code. Only now that they have been translated, and time has put his era in perspective, do we see what William Byrd of Westover was: one of the half-dozen leading wits and stylists of colonial America.

In the popular imagination, to be an American hero means to rise from rags to riches. William Byrd reversed the pattern, as he did so many other things: born to wealth, he never seemed able to hold on to it. His father, William Byrd I (1653–1704), was one of the most powerful and venerated men of his generation. Not only had he inherited valuable land on both sides of the James River, he had also won the hand of Mary Horsmanden, and a very dainty and wealthy hand it was, too. Some of the bold and red knight-errant blood of the Elizabethans flowed through the veins of William Byrd I. He had the same knack as did Captain John Smith (in whom that blood fairly bubbled) for getting in and out of scrapes. For example, William Byrd I joined Nathaniel Bacon in subduing the Indians, but stopped short of joining the rebellion against Governor William Berkeley, withdrawing in time to save his reputation and his neck. Later on he became receiver-general and auditor of Virginia, a member of the Council of State, and the colony's leading authority on Indians. The important 1685 treaty with the Iroquois bore his signature. Death cut short his brilliant career soon after his fiftieth birthday, and suddenly thrust his son and namesake into the center of the colonial stage. The boy, who had spent much of his time in England getting an education and, later, as an agent for Virginia, must now return to America and assume the duties of a man.

No one can read the story of young Will Byrd's early years, and his transformation, without thinking of Will Shakespeare's Prince Hal. If ever a young Virginian behaved scandalously in London, it was Will Byrd. "Never did the sun shine upon a Swain who had more combustible matter in his constitution," Byrd wrote of himself. Love broke out upon him "before my beard." Louis Wright, to whose editing of Byrd's diaries we are indebted for much of our knowledge of the man, says that he was notoriously promiscuous, frequenting the boudoirs of highborn and lowborn alike. Indeed, as his diary shows, he was not above taking to the grass with a *fille de joie* whom he might encounter on a London street.

Once, when he arrived for a rendezvous with a certain Mrs. A-l-n, the lady wasn't home, so he seduced the chambermaid. Just as he was coming down the steps Mrs. A-l-n came in the front door. Then Will Byrd and Mrs. A-l-n went back up the stairs together. Several hours later, he went home and ate a plum cake.

On his favorites he lavished neoclassic pseudonyms and some of the era's most sparkling prose. One such lady (called "Facetia" and believed to have been Lady Elizabeth Cromwell) was his preoccupation during 1703. When she left him to visit friends in Ireland, Will Byrd let her know she would be missed:

> The instant your coach drove away, madam, my heart felt as if it had been torn up by the very roots, and the rest of my body as if severed limb from limb. . . . Could I at that time have considered that the only pleasure I had in the world was leaving me, I had hung upon your coach and had been torn in pieces sooner than have suffered myself to be taken from you.

Having said all the proper things, he moved on to relate, in a later letter, some of the juicier bits of London gossip. Mrs. Brownlow had finally agreed to marry Lord Guilford—"and the gods alone can tell what will be produced by the conjunction of such fat and good humour!" The image is Falstaffian, as were many of Byrd's friends. But with news of his father's death he must, like Prince Hal, scorn his dissolute friends and assume new duties. With both Hal and Will the metamorphosis was difficult and partial, but nonetheless memorable.

The Virginia to which in 1705 William Byrd II returned—the oldest permanent English settlement in the New World and the first link in the chain that would one day be known as the British Empire —was a combination of elegance and crudity, enlightenment and superstition. While some of his Virginia neighbors discussed the most advanced political theories of Europe, others argued about how to dispose of a witch who was said to have crossed over to Currituck Sound in an eggshell. In 1706, the same year that Byrd was settling down in Virginia after his long stay in England, a Virginia court was instructing "as many Ansient and Knowing women as possible . . . to search her Carefully For teats spotts and marks about her body." When certain mysterious marks were indeed found, the obvious conclusion was drawn, and the poor woman languished in ye common gaol. Finally released, she lived to be eighty and died a natural death.

Other Virginia ladies faced problems (including, on occasions, Will Byrd) that were far older than the colony or the witch scare. A good example was Martha Burwell, a Williamsburg belle, who rejected the suit of Sir Francis Nicholson, the governor, so she might marry a man more to her liking. If she did so, swore the enraged Nicholson, he would cut the throat of the bridegroom, the clergyman, and the issuing justice. Unaware that females are members of the weaker sex, Martha refused to give in—even when Nicholson threw in half a dozen more throats, including those of her father and brothers. She married her true love. No throats were cut—but visitors to the Governor's palace in Williamsburg observed that His Excellency made "a Roaring Noise."

In those days Tidewater Virginia was governed by benevolent paternalists. The aristocrats intermarried, and the essential jobs— sheriff, vestryman, justice of the peace, colonel of militia—stayed in the family. The support of the gentry was the prerequisite to social and political advancement. Wealth, status, and privilege were the Tidewater trinity, and it was a case of three in one: wealth guaranteed status; status conveyed privilege; and privilege insured wealth.

Will Byrd both understood and mastered the world to which he had returned. He retained the seat in the House of Burgesses which he had won before going to England, and turned his attention to finding a suitable wife. Like many of his contemporaries, he confined "romantic love" to extracurricular affairs, and called on common sense to help him in matrimony. Both Washington and Jefferson married rich widows. Ambitious young men found they could love a rich girl more than a poor one, and the colonial newspapers reported their marriages with an honesty that bordered on impropriety. One reads, for example, that twenty-three-year-old William Carter married Madam Sarah Ellson, widow of eighty-five, "a sprightly old Tit, with three thousand pounds fortune."

Will Byrd's choice was the eligible but fiery Lucy Parke, daughter of the gallant rake Daniel Parke, who had fought with Marlborough on the Continent and brought the news of Blenheim to Queen Anne. Many a subsequent battle was fought between Lucy Parke and William Byrd after their marriage in 1706, though neither side was entirely vanquished. Byrd was quick to record his victories, such as the one noted in his diary for February 5, 1711: "My wife and I quarrelled about her pulling her brows. She threatened she would not go to Williamsburg if she might not pull them; I refused, however, and got the better of her and maintained my authority."

That Mrs. Byrd had as many good excuses for her fits of temper and violence as any other lady in Virginia seems plain—not only from her accusations, but from her husband's admissions. From his diary entry of November 2, 1709, for example, we get this graphic picture of life among the planters:

> In the evening I went to Dr. [Barrett's], where my wife came this afternoon. Here I found Mrs. Chiswell, my sister Custis, and other ladies. We sat and talked till about 11 o'clock and then retired to our chambers. I played at [r-m] with Mrs. Chiswell and kissed her on the bed till she was angry and my wife also was uneasy about it, and cried as soon as the company was gone. I neglected to say my prayers which I should not have done, because I ought to beg pardon for the lust I had for another man's wife. However I had good health, good thoughts, and good humor, thanks be to God Almighty.

As we read on, we begin to realize that we are confronting a Renaissance man in colonial America—a writer with the frankness of Montaigne and the zest of Rabelais. Philosopher, linguist, doctor, scientist, stylist, planter, churchman, William Byrd II saw and reported as much as any American who died before our Revolution.

Here was a man who, burdened for most of his life with the responsibility of thousands of acres and hundreds of slaves, never became narrow or provincial. Neither his mind, nor his tongue, nor his pen—the last possibly because he wrote the diaries in code—was restrained by his circumstances, and no one at home or abroad was immune from the barbs of his wit. When we read Byrd, we know just what Dean Swift meant when he said: "We call a spade a spade."

One of Byrd's most remarkable achievements, and one not nearly well enough known and appreciated, is his sketch of himself, attached to a letter dated February 21, 1722. For honesty and perception, and for the balance that the eighteenth century enthroned, it has few American counterparts.

> Poor Inamorato [as Byrd calls himself] had too much mercury to fix to one thing. His Brain was too hot to jogg on eternally in the same dull road. He liv'd more by the lively moment of his Passions, than by the cold and unromantick dictates of Reason . . . He pay'd his Court more to obscure merit, than to corrupt Greatness. He never cou'd flatter any body, no not himself, which were two invincible bars to all preferment. . . . His religion is more in substance than in form, and he is more forward to practice vertue than profess it . . . He knows the World perfectly well, and thinks himself a citizen of it without the . . . distinctions of kindred sect or Country.

He goes on to explain why, for most of his life, he began his day by reading ancient classics, and frowned upon morning interruptions:

> A constant hurry of visits & conversations gives a man a habit of inadvertency, which betrays him into faults without measure & without end. For this reason, he commonly reserv'd the morning to himself, and bestow'd the rest upon his business and his friends.

The reason for his own candor is clearly stated:

> He Lov'd to undress wickedness of all its paint, and disguise, that he might loath its deformity.

The extent of his philosophizing and his admitted heresy is made clear by this remarkable passage:

> He wishes every body so perfect, that he overlooks the impossibility of reaching it in this World. He wou'd have men Angells before their time, and wou'd bring down that perfection upon Earth which is the peculiar priviledge of Heaven.

Byrd left us a scattered and largely unavailable body of literature —vers de société, historical essays, character sketches, epitaphs, letters, poems, translations, and humorous satires. Of this work Maude Woodfin, one of the few scholars to delve adequately into Byrd's work, wrote:

"There is a distinctly American quality in these writings of the latter half of Byrd's life, in direct contrast to the exclusively English quality in the writings of his earlier years. Further study and time will doubtless argue that his literary work in the Virginia period from 1726 on, with its colonial scene and theme, has greater literary merit than his work in the London period."

Byrd has a place in our architectural history as well. His manor

This portrait of William Byrd was painted in London by Sir Godfrey Kneller between 1715 and 1720 when the aristocratic Virginian was in his prime.

house, Westover, is in many ways the finest Georgian mansion in the nation. Triumphant architectural solutions never came quickly or easily: only first-rate minds can conjure up first-rate houses. In the spring of 1709, we know from Byrd's diary, he had workmen constructing brick. Five years later, stonecutters from Williamsburg were erecting the library chimney. There were interruptions, delays, faulty shipments, workmen to be trained. But gradually a masterpiece—noble in symmetry, proportion, and balance—emerged.

Built on a little rise a hundred yards from the James River, Westover has not changed much over the generations. The north and south façades are as solid and rhythmical as a well-wrought fugue, and the beautiful doorways would have pleased Palladio himself. Although the manor is derived from English standards (especially William Salmon's *Palladio Londinensis*), Westover makes such superb use of the local materials and landscape that some European critics have adjudged it esthetically more satisfying than most of the contemporary homes in England.

Like other buildings of the period, Westover was planned from the outside in. The main hallway, eighteen feet wide and off center, goes the full length of the house. The stairway has three runs and a balustrade of richly turned mahogany. The handsomely paneled walls of the downstairs rooms support gilded ceilings. Underneath the house is a complete series of rooms, converging at the subterranean passage leading to the river. Two underground chambers, which could be used as hiding places, are reached through a dry well. Since he liked nothing less than the idea of being dry, William Byrd kept both chambers stocked with claret and Madeira.

Westover takes its place in the succession of remarkable Virginia manors that remain one of the glories of the American past. It was completed probably by 1736, after Stratford Hall, with its masculine vigor, and Rosewell, with its mahogany balustrade from San Domingo. Westover would be followed by Brandon, with chaste cornices and fine simplicity; Gunston Hall, with cut-stone quoins and coziness; Sabine Hall, so reminiscent of Horace's villa at Tivoli; and Pacatone, with its wonderful entrance and its legendary ghosts.

These places were more than houses. They were little worlds in themselves, part of a universe that existed within the boundaries of Virginia. The planters lavished their energy and their lives on such worlds. They were proud of their crops, their horses, their libraries, their gardens. Byrd, for example, tells us about the iris, crocus, thyme, marjoram, phlox, larkspur, and jasmine in his formal two-acre garden.

At Westover one might find the Carters from Shirley, the Lees from Stratford, the Harrisons from Randolph, or the Spotswoods from Germanna. So might one encounter Byrd's brother-in-law, that ardent woman-hater, John Custis, from Arlington. Surely the ghost of William Byrd would not want any tale of Westover to omit a short tribute to Custis' irascible memory.

While other founding fathers left immortal lines about life and liberty to stir our blood, Custis left words to warm henpecked hearts. With his highhanded lady he got on monstrous poor.

After one argument Custis turned and drove his carriage into the Chesapeake Bay. When his wife asked where he was going, he shouted, "To Hell, Madam." "Drive on," she said imperiously. "Any place is better than Arlington!" So that he might have the last word, Custis composed his own epitaph, and made his son execute it on pain of being disinherited:

UNDER THIS MARBLE TOMB LIES THE BODY
OF THE HON. JOHN CUSTIS, ESQ.,
* * * *
AGE 71 YEARS, AND YET LIVED BUT SEVEN YEARS,
WHICH WAS THE SPACE OF TIME HE KEPT
A BACHELOR'S HOME AT ARLINGTON
ON THE EASTERN SHORE OF VIRGINIA.

Still Custis came to Westover, like all others who could, to enjoy the fairs, balls, parlor games, barbecues—but above all, the conversation.

One should not conclude that entertaining friends was the main occupation of William Byrd. As soon as he awoke he read Latin, Greek, or Hebrew before breakfast. His favorite room was not the parlor but the library, in which were collected over 3,600 volumes dealing with philosophy, theology, drama, history, law, and science. Byrd's own writings prove his intimate knowledge of the great thinkers and writers of the past.

Of those works, none except his diary is as interesting as his *History of the Dividing Line*. On his fifty-third birthday, in 1727, Byrd was appointed one of the Virginia commissioners to survey the disputed Virginia–North Carolina boundary; the next spring saw the group ready to embark on their task. Byrd's *History*, which proves he was one of the day's ablest masters of English prose, is a thing of delight. For days comedy and tragedy alternated for supremacy. Indians stole their food. Bad weather and poor luck caused Byrd to swear like a trooper in His Majesty's Guards. To mend matters, Byrd's companions arranged a party around a cheerful bowl, and invited a country bumpkin to attend. She must have remembered the party for a long time: ". . . they examined all her hidden Charms and play'd a great many gay Pranks," noted Byrd, who seems to have disapproved of the whole affair. "The poor Damsel was disabled from making any resistance by the Lameness of her Hand."

Whenever matters got too bad, the party's chaplain "rubbed up" his aristocratic swamp-evaders with a seasonable sermon; and we must adjudge all the hardships a small price to pay for the *History*. This was followed by *A Journey to Eden*, which tells of Byrd's trip to survey twenty thousand acres of bottom land. On September 19, 1733, Byrd decided to stake out two large cities: "one at Shacco's, to be called Richmond, and the other at the point of the Appomattuck River, to be called Petersburg."

It is a generally accepted belief that only in politics did eighteenth-century America reach real distinction. But as we look more closely at our colonial literature and architecture, and apply our own criteria rather than those imposed upon us by the English, we find that this may not be so. How, for example, could we have underestimated William Byrd's importance all these years? There are several answers. He never pretended to be a serious writer (no gentleman of his time and place would), any more than Jefferson would have set himself up as a professional architect. But at least we have Jefferson's magnificent buildings to refute the notion that he was a mere dabbler, and for years we had little of Byrd's prose. Because he did "call a spade a spade," many of his contemporaries, and even more of their descendants, have not wanted his work and allusions made public. Byrd had been dead almost a century when Edmund Ruffin published fragments of his writings in the *Virginia Farmers' Register*. Only in our own generation have the diaries been deciphered: not until 1941 did a major publisher undertake to see part of them into print; not until 1958 did we have *The London Diary* (1717–21); not even now can we read all that Byrd left for us.

No amount of reappraisal can turn Byrd into a figure of the highest magnitude. What it might do is to reveal a man who for candor, self-analysis, and wit is unsurpassed—this in an age that produced Washington, Adams, Franklin, Henry, and Jefferson. Could any other colonial American, for example, have written such a delightful and ribald satire on women as "The Female Creed," which has an eighteenth-century lady profess: "I believe in astrologers, coffee-casters, and Fortune-tellers of every denomination, whether they profess to read the Ladys destiny in their faces, in their palms or like those of China in their fair posteriors."

Nor will one often encounter in a colonial writer the desire to exhume his father's corpse, and then to report: "He was so wasted there was not one thing to be distinguished. I ate fish for dinner."

When William Byrd II died in the summer of 1744, the pre-Revolutionary ethos and attitudes were dying too. They have not attracted historians and novelists as have the earlier adventurous days of settlement or the later days that tried men's souls. The period from 1700 to 1750 remains the forgotten one in American history and literature, despite much excellent but rather specialized work in it since 1930.

When we know more of that important and colorful half century, William Byrd's reputation will rise. In him we shall find the most complete expression of a man who lived with us but belongs to the world. In his work we shall see, more clearly than in that of his contemporaries, the emerging differences between England and the American colonies destined to grow into their own nationhood. Beside him, the so-called Connecticut Wits of the late eighteenth century seem to be lacking half their title. Compared to his prose, the tedious sermonizing of the Puritan and Anglican ministers seems like copybook work in an understaffed grammar school. Not that William Byrd was a saint, or a model husband—as he would have been the first to point out. But as with the saints, we admire him all the more because he tells us about his faults and lets us tabulate the virtues for ourselves. All told, we can say of him what Abraham Lincoln supposedly said when he saw Walt Whitman far down the corridors of a building: "There goes a man." William Byrd of Westover would have settled for this.

The Latin motto of William Byrd's coat of arms reads, appropriately enough, "No guilt to make one pale."

Ray Allen Billington

The Frontier
and the
American Character

New ways of looking at the past, called "interpretations," are a constant source of stimulation and controversy among historians. Most interpretations are produced not so much by the discovery of new facts as by present-mindedness; current events cause us to see the past in a new light, or, to put it differently, our search for the causes of contemporary events often leads us to change our understanding of the effects of past events.

Of all interpretations of American history, none has been more provocative of research and controversy than Frederick Jackson Turner's "frontier thesis." In a paper published in 1893, Turner argued that the whole character of American civilization had been shaped from earliest colonial times by the existence of undeveloped land and resources, and by their exploitation by pioneers. At a time when Americans were becoming aware that the western frontier was disappearing, this idea proved enormously persuasive; for years the Turner thesis dominated the writing of American history. Eventually, however, a new generation of scholars began to uncover its weaknesses and contradictions, and today the interpretation seems only one among many. The role of the frontier is generally accepted as having been important, but it is not seen as "explaining" American development, as Turner suggested.

The leading modern expert on the history of the frontier is Ray Allen Billington, Senior Research Fellow at the Huntington Library. Billington is currently completing a biography of Turner and is master of the complex and voluminous literature on the Turner thesis that has been published in this century. In this essay he sums up and balances this continuing discussion of Turner's ideas. If this is not the last word that will be written about the effects of the frontier on America, it is the best and fairest general judgment of the subject that we have.

*S*ince the dawn days of historical writing in the United States, historians have labored mightily, and usually in vain, to answer the famous question posed by Hector St. John de Crèvecœur in the eighteenth century: "What then is the American, this new man?" Was that composite figure actually a "new man" with unique traits that distinguished him from his Old World ancestors? Or was he merely a transplanted European? The most widely accepted—and bitterly disputed—answer was advanced by a young Wisconsin historian named Frederick Jackson Turner in 1893. The American was a new man, he held, who owed his distinctive characteristics and institutions to the unusual New World environment—characterized by the availability of free land and an ever-receding frontier—in which his civilization had grown to maturity. This environmental theory, accepted for a generation after its enunciation, has been vigorously attacked and vehemently defended during the past two decades. How has it fared in this battle of words? Is it still a valid key to the meaning of American history?

Turner's own background provides a clue to the answer. Born in Portage, Wisconsin, in 1861 of pioneer parents from upper New York state, he was reared in a land fringed by the interminable forest and still stamped with the mark of youth. There he mingled with pioneers who had trapped beaver or hunted Indians or cleared the virgin wilderness; from them he learned something of the free and easy democratic values prevailing among those who judged men by their own accomplishments rather than those of their ancestors. At the University of Wisconsin Turner's faith in cultural democracy was deepened, while his intellectual vistas were widened through contact with teachers who led him into that wonderland of adventure where scientific techniques were being applied to social problems, where Darwin's evolutionary hypothesis was awakening scholars to the continuity of progress, and where searchers after truth were beginning to realize the multiplicity of forces responsible for human behavior. The young student showed how well he had learned these lessons in his master's essay on "The Character and Influence of the Fur Trade in Wisconsin"; he emphasized the evolution of institutions from simple to complex forms.

From Wisconsin Turner journeyed to Johns Hopkins University, as did many eager young scholars of that day, only to meet stubborn opposition for the historical theories already taking shape in his mind. His principal professor, Herbert Baxter Adams, viewed mankind's development in evolutionary terms, but held that environment had no place in the equation; American institutions could be understood only as outgrowths of European "germs" that had originated among Teutonic tribes in the forests of medieval Germany. To Turner this explanation was unsatisfactory. The "germ theory" explained the similarities between Europe and America, but what of the many differences? This problem was still much in his mind when he returned to the University of Wisconsin as an instructor in 1889. In two remarkable papers prepared during the next few years he set forth his answer.

Frederick Jackson Turner,
photographed about 1890.

The first, "The Significance of History," reiterated his belief in what historians call "multiple causation"; to understand man's complex nature, he insisted, one needed not only a knowledge of past politics, but a familiarity with social, economic, and cultural forces as well. The second, "Problems in American History," attempted to isolate those forces most influential in explaining the unique features of American development. Among these Turner believed that the most important was the need for institutions to "adapt themselves to the changes of a remarkably developing, expanding people."

This was the theory that was expanded into a full-blown historical hypothesis in the famous essay on "The Significance of the Frontier in American History," read at a conference of historians held in connection with the World Fair in Chicago in 1893. The differences between European and American civilization, Turner stated in that monumental work, were in part the product of the distinctive environment of the New World. The most unusual features of that environment were "the existence of an area of free land, its continuous recession, and the advance of American settlement westward." This free land served as a magnet to draw men westward, attracted by the hope of economic gain or adventure. They came as Europeans or easterners, but they soon realized that the wilderness environment was ill-adapted to the habits, institutions, and cultural baggage of the stratified societies they had left behind. Complex political institutions were unnecessary in a tiny frontier outpost; traditional economic practices were useless in an isolated community geared to an economy of self-sufficiency; rigid social customs were outmoded in a land where prestige depended on skill with the axe or rifle rather than on hereditary glories; cultural pursuits were unessential in a land where so many material tasks awaited doing. Hence in each pioneer settlement there occurred a rapid reversion to the primitive. What little government was necessary was provided by simple associations of settlers; each man looked after his family without reliance on his fellows; social hierarchies disintegrated, and cultural progress came to a halt. As the newcomers moved backward along the scale of civilization, the habits and customs of their traditional cultures were forgotten.

Gradually, however, newcomers drifted in, and as the man-land ratio increased, the community began a slow climb back toward civilization. Governmental controls were tightened and extended, economic specialization began, social stratification set in, and cultural activities quickened. But the new society that eventually emerged differed from the old from which it had sprung. The abandonment of cultural baggage during the migrations, the borrowings from the many cultures represented in each pioneer settlement, the deviations natural in separate evolutions, and the impact of the environment all played their parts in creating a unique social organism similar to but differing from those in the East. An ''Americanization'' of men and their institutions had taken place.

Turner believed that many of the characteristics associated with the American people were traceable to their experience, during the three centuries required to settle the continent, of constantly ''beginning over again.'' Their mobility, their optimism, their inventiveness and willingness to accept innovation, their materialism, their exploitive wastefulness—these were frontier traits; for the pioneer, accustomed to repeated moves as he drifted westward, viewed the world through rose-colored glasses as he dreamed of a better future, experimented constantly as he adapted artifacts and customs to his peculiar environment, scorned culture as a deterrent to the practical tasks that bulked so large in his life, and squandered seemingly inexhaustible natural resources with abandon. Turner also ascribed America's distinctive brand of individualism, with its dislike of governmental interference in economic functions, to the experience of pioneers who wanted no hindrance from society as they exploited nature's riches. Similarly, he traced the exaggerated nationalism of the United States to its roots among frontiersmen who looked to the national government for land, transportation outlets, and protection against the Indians. And he believed that America's faith in democracy had stemmed from a pioneering experience in which the leveling influence of poverty and the uniqueness of local problems encouraged majority self-rule. He pointed out that these characteristics, prominent among frontiersmen, had persisted long after the frontier itself was no more.

This was Turner's famous ''frontier hypothesis.'' For a generation after its enunciation its persuasive logic won uncritical acceptance among historians, but beginning in the late 1920's, and increasingly after Turner's death in 1932, an avalanche of criticism steadily mounted. His theories, critics said, were contradictory, his generalizations unsupported, his assumptions inadequately based; what empirical proof could he advance, they asked, to prove that the frontier experience was responsible for American individualism, mobility, or wastefulness? He was damned as a romanticist for his claim that democracy sprang from the forest environment of the United States and as an isolationist for failing to recognize the continuing impact of Europe on America. As the ''bait-Turner'' vogue gained popularity among younger scholars of the 1930's with their international, semi-

Marxian views of history, the criticisms of the frontier theory became as irrational as the earlier support given by overenthusiastic advocates.

During the past decade, however, a healthy reaction has slowly and unspectacularly gained momentum. Today's scholars, gradually realizing that Turner was advancing a hypothesis rather than proving a theory, have shown a healthy tendency to abandon fruitless haggling over the meaning of his phrases and to concentrate instead on testing his assumptions. They have directed their efforts primarily toward re-examining his hypothesis in the light of criticisms directed against it and applying it to frontier areas beyond the borders of the United States. Their findings have modified many of the views expressed by Turner but have gone far toward proving that the frontier hypothesis remains one essential tool—albeit not the only one—for interpreting American history.

That Turner was guilty of oversimplifying both the nature and the causes of the migration process was certainly true. He pictured settlers as moving westward in an orderly procession—fur trappers, cattlemen, miners, pioneer farmers, and equipped farmers—with each group playing its part in the transmutation of a wilderness into a civilization. Free land was the magnet that lured them onward, he believed, and this operated most effectively in periods of depression, when the displaced workers of the East sought a refuge from economic storms amidst nature's abundance in the West. "The wilderness ever opened the gate of escape to the poor, the discontented and oppressed," Turner wrote at one time. "If social conditions tended to crystallize in the east, beyond the Alleghenies there was freedom."

No one of these assumptions can be substantiated in the simplified form in which Turner stated it. His vision of an "orderly procession of civilization, marching single file westward" failed to account for deviations that were almost as important as the norm; as essential to the conquest of the forest as trappers or farmers were soldiers, mill-operators, distillers, artisans, storekeepers, merchants, lawyers, editors, speculators, and town dwellers. All played their role, and all contributed to a complex frontier social order that bore little resemblance to the primitive societies Turner pictured. This was especially the case with the early town builders. The hamlets that sprang up adjacent to each pioneer settlement were products of the environment as truly as were the cattlemen or Indian fighters; each evolved economic functions geared to the needs of the primitive area surrounding it, and, in the tight public controls maintained over such essential functions as grist-milling or retail selling, each mirrored the frontiersmen's community-oriented views. In these villages, too, the equalitarian influence of the West was reflected in thoroughly democratic governments, with popularly elected councils supreme and the mayor reduced to a mere figurehead.

The pioneers who marched westward in this disorganized procession were not attracted by the magnet of "free land," for Turner's assumption that before 1862 the public domain was open to all who could pay $1.25 an acre, or that acreage was free after the Homestead Act was passed in that year, has been completely disproved. Turner failed to recognize the presence in the procession to the frontier of that omnipresent profit-seeker, the speculator. Jobbers were always ahead of farmers in the advance westward, buying up likely town sites or appropriating the best farm lands, where the soil was good and transportation outlets available. When the settler arrived his choice was between paying the speculator's price or accepting an inferior site. Even the Homestead Act failed to lessen speculative activity. Capitalizing on generous government grants to railroads and state educational institutions (which did not want to be bothered with sales to individuals), or buying bonus script from soldiers, or securing Indian lands as the reservations were contracted, or seizing on faulty features of congressional acts for the disposal of swampland and timberland, jobbers managed to engross most of the Far West's arable acreage: for every newcomer who obtained a homestead from the government, six or seven purchased farms from speculators.

Those who made these purchases were not, as Turner believed, displaced eastern workers fleeing periodic industrial depressions. Few city-dwelling artisans had the skills or inclination, and almost none the capital, to escape to the frontier. Land prices of $1.25 an acre may seem low today, but they were prohibitive for laborers earning only a dollar a day. Moreover, needed farm machinery, animals, and housing added about $1,000 to the cost of starting a farm in the 1850's, while the cheapest travel rate from New York to St. Louis was about $13 a person. Because these sums were always beyond the reach of factory workers (in bad times they deterred migration even from the rural East), the frontier never served as a "safety valve" for laborers in the sense that Turner employed the term. Instead, the American frontiers were pushed westward largely by younger sons from adjacent farm areas who migrated in periods of prosperity. While these generalizations apply to the pre-Civil War era that was Turner's principal interest, they are even more applicable to the late nineteenth century. During that period the major population shifts were from country to city rather than vice versa; for every worker who left the factory to move to the farm, twenty persons moved from farm to factory. If a safety valve did exist at that time, it was a rural safety valve, drawing off surplus farm labor and thus lessening agrarian discontent during the Granger and Populist eras.

Admitting that the procession to the frontier was more complex than Turner realized, that good lands were seldom free, and that a safety valve never operated to drain the dispossessed and the malcontented from industrial centers, does this mean that his conclusions concerning the migration process have been completely discredited? The opposite is emphatically true. A more divergent group than Turner realized felt the frontier's impact, but that does not minimize the extent of the impact. Too, while lands in the West were almost never free, they were relatively cheaper than those in Europe or the East, and this differential did serve as an attracting force. Nor can pages of statistics disprove the fact that, at least until the Civil War, the frontier served as an indirect safety valve by attracting displaced eastern farmers who would otherwise have moved into industrial cities; thousands who left New England or New York for the Old Northwest in the 1830's and 1840's, when the "rural decay" of the Northeast was beginning, would have sought factory jobs had no western outlet existed.

The effect of their exodus is made clear by comparing the political philosophies of the United States with those of another frontier country, Australia. There, lands lying beyond the coastal mountains were closed to pioneers by the aridity of the soil and by great sheep ranchers who were first on the scene. Australia, as a result, developed an urban civilization and an industrialized population relatively sooner than did the United States; and it had labor unions, labor-dominated governments, and political philosophies that would be viewed as radical in America. Without the safety valve of its own West, feeble though it may have been, such a course might have been followed in the United States.

Frederick Jackson Turner's conclusions concerning the influence of the frontier on Americans have also been questioned, debated, and modified since he advanced his hypothesis, but they have not been seriously altered. This is true even of one of his statements that has been more vigorously disputed than any other: "American democracy was born of no theorist's dream; it was not carried in the *Susan Constant* to Virginia, nor in the *Mayflower* to Plymouth. It came out of the American forest, and it gained a new strength each time it touched a new frontier." When he penned those oft-quoted words, Turner wrote as a propagandist against the "germ theory" school of history; in a less emotional and more thoughtful moment, he ascribed America's democratic institutions not to "imitation, or simple borrowing," but to "the evolution and adaptation of organs in response to changed environment." Even this moderate theory has aroused critical venom. Democracy, according to anti-Turnerians, was well advanced in Europe and *was* transported to America on the *Susan Constant* and the *Mayflower*; within this country democratic practices have multiplied most rapidly as a result of eastern lower-class pressures and have only been imitated in the West. If, critics ask, some mystical forest influence was responsible for such practices as manhood suffrage, increased authority for legislatures at the expense of executives, equitable legislative representation, and women's political rights, why did they not evolve in frontier areas outside the United States—in Russia, Latin America, and Canada, for example—exactly as they did here?

The answer, of course, is that democratic theory and institutions were imported from England, but that the frontier environment tended to make them, in practice, even more democratic. Two conditions common in pioneer communities made this inevitable. One was the wide diffusion of land ownership; this created an independent outlook and led to a demand for political participation on the part of those who had a stake in society. The other was the common

A contemporary etching of a wagon train encampment along the Laramie River.

social and economic level and the absence, characteristic of all primitive communities, of any prior leadership structure. The lack of any national or external controls made self-rule a hard necessity, and the frontiersmen, with their experience in community co-operation at cabin-raisings, logrollings, corn-huskings, and road or school building, accepted simple democratic practices as natural and inevitable. These practices, originating on the grass roots level, were expanded and extended in the recurring process of government-building that marked the westward movement of civilization. Each new territory that was organized—there were 31 in all—required a frame of government; this was drafted by relatively poor recent arrivals or by a minority of upper-class leaders, all of whom were committed to democratic ideals through their frontier community experiences. The result was a constant democratization of institutions and practices as constitution-makers adopted the most liberal features of older frames of government with which they were familiar.

This was true even in frontier lands outside the United States, for wherever there were frontiers, existing practices were modified in the direction of greater equality and a wider popular participation in governmental affairs. The results were never identical, of course, for both the environment and the nature of the imported institutions varied too greatly from country to country. In Russia, for instance, even though it promised no democracy comparable to that of the United States, the eastward-moving Siberian frontier, the haven of some seven million peasants during the nineteenth and early twentieth centuries, was notable for its lack of guilds, authoritarian churches, and all-powerful nobility. An official visiting there in 1910 was alarmed by the "enormous, rudely democratic country" evolving under the influence of the small homesteads that were the normal living units; he feared that czarism and European Russia would soon be "throttled" by the egalitarian currents developing on the frontier.

That the frontier accentuated the spirit of nationalism and individualism in the United States, as Turner maintained, was also true. Every page of the country's history, from the War of 1812 through the era of Manifest Destiny to today's bitter conflicts with Russia, demonstrates that the American attitude toward the world has been far more nationalistic than that of non-frontier countries and that this attitude has been strongest in the newest regions. Similarly, the pioneering experience converted settlers into individualists, although through a somewhat different process than Turner envisaged. His emphasis on a desire for freedom as a primary force luring men westward and his belief that pioneers developed an attitude of self-sufficiency in their lone battle against nature have been questioned, and with justice. Hoped-for gain was the magnet that attracted most migrants to the cheaper lands of the West, while once there they lived in units where co-operative enterprise—for protection against the Indians, for cabin-raising, law enforcement, and the like—was more essential than in the better established towns of the East. Yet the fact remains that the abundant resources and the greater social mobility of frontier areas did instill into frontiersmen a uniquely American form of individualism. Even though they may be sheeplike in following the decrees of social arbiters or fashion dictators, Americans today, like their pioneer ancestors, dislike governmental interference in their affairs. "Rugged individualism" did not originate on the frontier any more than democracy or nationalism did, but each concept was deepened and sharpened by frontier conditions.

His opponents have also cast doubt on Turner's assertion that American inventiveness and willingness to adopt innovations are traits inherited from pioneer ancestors who constantly devised new techniques and artifacts to cope with an unfamiliar environment. The critics insist that each mechanical improvement needed for the conquest of the frontier, from plows to barbed-wire fencing, originated in the East; when frontiersmen faced such an incomprehensible task as conquering the Great Plains they proved so tradition-bound that their advance halted until eastern inventors provided them with the tools needed to subdue grasslands. Unassailable as this argument may be, it ignores the fact that the recurring demand for implements and methods needed in the frontier advance did put a premium on inventiveness by Americans, whether they lived in the East or West. That even today they are less bound by tradition than other peoples is due in part to their pioneer heritage.

The anti-intellectualism and materialism which are national traits can also be traced to the frontier experience. There was little in pioneer life to attract the timid, the cultivated, or the aesthetically sensitive. In the boisterous western borderlands, book learning and intellectual speculation were suspect among those dedicated to the material tasks necessary to subdue a continent. Americans today reflect their background in placing the "intellectual" well below the "practical businessman" in their scale of heroes. Yet the frontiersman, as Turner recognized, was an idealist as well as a materialist. He admired material objects not only as symbols of advancing civilization but as the substance of his hopes for a better future. Given economic success he would be able to afford the aesthetic and intellectual pursuits that he felt were his due, even though he was not quite able to appreciate them. This spirit inspired the cultural activities—literary societies, debating clubs, "thespian groups," libraries, schools, camp meetings—that thrived in the most primitive western communities. It also helped nurture in the pioneers an infinite faith in the future. The belief in progress, both material and intellectual, that is part of modern America's creed was strengthened by the frontier experience.

Frederick Jackson Turner, then, was not far wrong when he maintained that frontiersmen did develop unique traits and that these, perpetuated, form the principal distinguishing characteristics of the American people today. To a degree unknown among Europeans, Americans do display a restless energy, a versatility, a practical ingenuity, an earthy practicality. They do squander their natural resources with an abandon unknown elsewhere; they have developed a mobility both social and physical that marks them as a people apart. In few other lands is the democratic ideal worshiped so intensely, or nationalism carried to such extremes of isolationism or international arrogance. Rarely do other peoples display such indifference toward intellectualism or aesthetic values; seldom in comparable cultural areas do they cling so tenaciously to the shibboleth of rugged individualism. Nor do residents of non-frontier lands experience to the same degree the heady optimism, the rosy faith in the future, the belief in the inevitability of progress that form part of the American creed. These are pioneer traits, and they have become a part of the national heritage.

Yet if the frontier wrought such a transformation within the United States, why did it not have a similar effect on other countries with frontiers? If the pioneering experience was responsible for our democracy and nationalism and individualism, why have the peoples of Africa, Latin America, Canada, and Russia failed to develop identical characteristics? The answer is obvious: in few nations of the world has the sort of frontier that Turner described existed. For he saw the frontier not as a borderland between unsettled and settled lands, but as an accessible area in which a low man-land ratio and abundant natural resources provided an unusual opportunity for the individual to better himself. Where autocratic governments controlled population movements, where resources were lacking, or where conditions prohibited ordinary individuals from exploiting nature's virgin riches, a frontier in the Turnerian sense could not be said to exist.

The areas of the world that have been occupied since the beginning of the age of discovery contain remarkably few frontiers of the American kind. In Africa the few Europeans were so outnumbered by relatively uncivilized native inhabitants that the need for protection transcended any impulses toward democracy or individualism. In Latin America the rugged terrain and steaming jungles restricted areas exploitable by individuals to the Brazilian plains and the Argentine pampas; these did attract frontiersmen, although in Argentina the prior occupation of most good lands by government-favored cattle growers kept small farmers out until railroads penetrated the region. In Canada the path westward was blocked by the Laurentian Shield, a tangled mass of hills and sterile, brush-choked soil covering the country north and west of the St. Lawrence Valley. When railroads finally penetrated this barrier in the late nineteenth century, they carried pioneers directly from the East to the prairie provinces of the West; the newcomers, with no prior pioneering experience, simply adapted to their new situation the eastern institutions with which they were familiar. Among the world's frontier nations only Russia provided a physical environment comparable to that of the United States, and there the pioneers were too accustomed to rigid feudal and monarchic controls to respond as Americans did.

Further proof that the westward expansion of the United States has been a powerful formative force has been provided by the problems facing the nation in the present century. During the past fifty years the American people have been adjusting their lives and institutions to existence in a frontierless land, for while the superintendent of the census was decidedly premature when he announced in 1890 that the country's "unsettled area has been so broken into by isolated bodies of settlement that there can hardly be said to be a frontier line" remaining, the era of cheap land was rapidly drawing to a close. In attempting to adjust the country to its new, expansionless future, statesmen have frequently called upon the frontier hypothesis to justify everything from rugged individualism to the welfare state, and from isolationism to world domination.

Political opinion has divided sharply on the necessity of altering the nation's governmental philosophy and techniques in response to the changed environment. Some statesmen and scholars have rebelled against what they call Turner's "Space Concept of History," with all that it implies concerning the lack of opportunity for the individual in an expansionless land. They insist that modern technology has created a whole host of new "frontiers"—of intensive farming, electronics, mechanics, manufacturing, nuclear fission, and the like—which offer such diverse outlets to individual talents that governmental interference in the nation's economic activities is unjustified. On the other hand, equally competent spokesmen argue that these newer "frontiers" offer little opportunity to the individual—as distinguished from the corporation or the capitalist—and hence cannot duplicate the function of the frontier of free land. The government, they insist, must provide the people with the security and opportunity that vanished when escape to the West became impossible. This school's most eloquent spokesman, Franklin D. Roosevelt, declared: "Our last frontier has long since been reached. . . . Equality of opportunity as we have known it no longer exists. . . . Our task now is not the discovery or exploitation of natural resources or necessarily producing more goods. It is the sober, less dramatic business of administering resources and plants already in hand, of seeking to re-establish foreign markets for our surplus production, of meeting the problem of under-consumption, of adjusting production to consumption, of distributing wealth and products more equitably, of adapting existing economic organizations to the service of the people. The day of enlightened administration has come." To Roosevelt, and to thousands like him, the passing of the frontier created a new era in history which demanded a new philosophy of government.

Diplomats have also found in the frontier hypothesis justification for many of their moves, from imperialist expansion to the restriction of immigration. Harking back to Turner's statement that the perennial rebirth of society was necessary to keep alive the democratic spirit, expansionists have argued through the twentieth century for an extension of American power and territories. During the Spanish-American War imperialists preached such a doctrine, adding the argument that Spain's lands were needed to provide a population outlet for a people who could no longer escape to their own frontier. Idealists such as Woodrow Wilson could agree with materialists like J. P. Morgan that the extension of American authority abroad, either through territorial acquisitions or economic penetration, would be good for both business and democracy. Later, Franklin D. Roosevelt favored a similar expansion of the American democratic ideal as a necessary prelude to the better world that he hoped would emerge from World War II. His successor, Harry Truman, envisaged his "Truman Doctrine" as a device to extend and defend the frontiers of democracy throughout the globe. While popular belief in the superiority of America's political institutions was far older than Turner, that belief rested partly on the frontier experience of the United States.

These practical applications of the frontier hypothesis, as well as its demonstrated influence on the nation's development, suggest that its critics have been unable to destroy the theory's effectiveness as a key to understanding American history. The recurring rebirth of society in the United States over a period of three hundred years did endow the people with characteristics and institutions that distinguish them from the inhabitants of other nations. It is obviously untrue that the frontier experience alone accounts for the unique features of American civilization; that civilization can be understood only as the product of the interplay of the Old World heritage and New World conditions. But among those conditions none has bulked larger than the operation of the frontier process.

Daniel P. Mannix
and
Malcolm Cowley

The
Middle
Passage

To men like William Byrd, America offered an environment of
unparalleled freedom and stimulation; for those of lesser fortune, as
the historical record shows, it supplied only somewhat less opportunity
for self-expression and improvement. But for black men—roughly ten
per cent of all the colonists by the middle of the eighteenth century—
America meant the crushing degradation of slavery. Until recently,
without excusing or justifying slavery, most historians have tended
not so much to ignore as to compartmentalize (one is almost tempted
to say "segregate") the history of the Negro from the general stream
of American development. When generalizing about American "free
institutions," "opportunity," and "equality," the phrase "except for
black men" needs always to be added if the truth is to be told.

Historical arguments have developed about the condition of slaves
in America, about the differences between the British-American and
Latin American slave systems, and about other aspects of the history
of the Negro in the New World. But there has been only unanimity
among historians about the horrors associated with the capture of
blacks in Africa and with the dread "middle passage" over which the
bondsmen were shipped to the Americas. In this essay the literary
critic Malcolm Cowley and the historian Daniel P. Mannix combine
their talents to describe what it meant to be wrenched from one's
home and native soil, herded in chains into the foul hold of a slave
ship, and dispatched across the torrid mid-Atlantic into the hell of
slavery.

*L*ong before Europeans appeared on the African coast, the merchants of Timbuktu were exporting slaves to the Moorish kingdoms north of the Sahara. Even the transatlantic slave trade had a long history. There were Negroes in Santo Domingo as early as 1503, and the first twenty slaves were sold in Jamestown, Virginia, about the last week of August, 1619, only twelve years after the colony was founded. But the flush days of the trade were in the eighteenth century, when vast supplies of labor were needed for the sugar plantations in the West Indies and the tobacco and rice plantations on the mainland. From 1700 to 1807, when the trade was legally abolished by Great Britain and the United States, more than seventy thousand Negroes were carried across the Atlantic in any normal year. The trade was interrupted by wars, notably by the American Revolution, but the total New World importation for the century may have amounted to five million enslaved persons.

Most of the slaves were carried on shipboard at some point along the four thousand miles of West African coastline that extend in a dog's leg from the Sahara on the north to the southern desert. Known as the Guinea Coast, it was feared by eighteenth-century mariners, who died there by hundreds and thousands every year.

Contrary to popular opinion, very few of the slaves—possibly one or two out of a hundred—were free Africans kidnapped by Europeans. The slaving captains had, as a rule, no moral prejudice against man-stealing, but they usually refrained from it on the ground of its being a dangerous business practice. A vessel suspected of man-stealing might be "cut off" by the natives, its crew killed, and its cargo of slaves offered for sale to other vessels.

The vast majority of the Negroes brought to America had been enslaved and sold to the whites by other Africans. There were coastal tribes and states, like the Efik kingdom of Calabar, that based their whole economy on the slave trade. The slaves might be prisoners of war, they might have been kidnapped by gangs of black marauders, or they might have been sold with their whole families for such high crimes as adultery, impiety, or, as in one instance, stealing a tobacco pipe. Intertribal wars, the principal source of slaves, were in many cases no more than large-scale kidnapping expeditions. Often they were fomented by Europeans, who supplied both sides with muskets and gunpowder so many muskets or so much powder for each slave that they promised to deliver on shipboard.

The ships were English, French, Dutch, Danish, Portuguese, or American. London, Bristol, and finally Liverpool were the great English slaving ports. By 1790 Liverpool had engrossed five eighths of the English trade and three sevenths of the slave trade of all Europe. Its French rival, Nantes, would soon be ruined by the Napoleonic wars. During the last years of legal slaving, Liverpool's only serious competitors were the Yankee captains of Newport and Bristol, Rhode Island.

Profits from a slaving voyage, which averaged nine or ten months, were reckoned at thirty per cent, after deducting sales commissions, insurance premiums, and all other expenses. The Liverpool merchants became so rich from the slave trade that they invested heavily in mills, factories, mines, canals, and railways. That process was repeated in New England, and the slave trade provided much of the capital that was needed for the industrial revolution.

A slaving voyage was triangular. English textiles, notions, cutlery, and firearms were carried to the Guinea Coast, where they were exchanged for slaves. These were sold in America or the West Indies, and part of the proceeds was invested in colonial products, notably sugar and rice, which were carried back to England on the third leg of the voyage. If the vessel sailed from a New England port, its usual cargo was casks of rum from a Massachusetts distillery. The rum was exchanged in Africa for slaves—often at the rate of two hundred gallons per man—and the slaves were exchanged in the West Indies for molasses, which was carried back to New England to be distilled into rum. A slave ship or Guineaman was expected to show a profit for each leg of its triangular course. But the base of the triangle, the so-called Middle Passage from Africa to the New World with a black cargo, was the most profitable part of the voyage, at the highest cost in human suffering. Let us see what happened in the passage during the flush days of the slave trade.

As soon as an assortment of naked slaves was carried aboard a Guineaman, the men were shackled two by two, the right wrist and ankle of one to the left wrist and ankle of another; then they were sent below. The women—usually regarded as fair prey for the sailors —were allowed to wander by day almost anywhere on the vessel, though they spent the night between decks, in a space partitioned off from that of the men. All the slaves were forced to sleep without covering on bare wooden floors, which were often constructed of unplaned boards. In a stormy passage the skin over their elbows might be worn away to the bare bones.

William Bosman says, writing in 1701, "You would really wonder to see how these slaves live on board; for though their number sometimes amounts to six or seven hundred, yet by the careful management of our masters of ships"—the Dutch masters, in this case—"they are so regulated that it seems incredible: And in this particular our nation exceeds all other Europeans; for as the French, Portuguese and English slave-ships, are always foul and stinking; on the contrary ours are for the most part clean and neat."

Slavers of every nation insisted that their own vessels were the best in the trade. Thus, James Barbot, Jr., who sailed on an English ship to the Congo in 1700, was highly critical of the Portuguese. He admits that they made a great point of baptizing the slaves before taking them on board, but then, "It is pitiful," he says, "to see how they crowd those poor wretches, six hundred and fifty or seven hundred in a ship, the men standing in the hold ty'd to stakes, the women between decks and those that are with child in the great cabin and the children in the steeridge which in that hot climate occasions an intolerable stench." Barbot adds, however, that the Portuguese provided the slaves with coarse thick mats, which were "softer for the poor wretches to lie upon than the bare decks . . . and it would be prudent to imitate the Portuguese in this point." The English, however, did not display that sort of prudence.

There were two schools of thought among the English slaving captains, the "loose-packers" and the "tight-packers." The former argued that by giving the slaves a little more room, better food, and a certain amount of liberty, they reduced the death rate and received a better price for each slave in the West Indies. The tight-packers answered that although the loss of life might be greater on each of their voyages, so too were the net receipts from a larger cargo. If many of the survivors were weak and emaciated, as was often the case, they could be fattened up in a West Indian slave yard before being offered for sale.

The argument between the two schools continued as long as the trade itself, but for many years after 1750 the tight-packers were in the ascendant. So great was the profit on each slave landed alive that hardly a captain refrained from loading his vessel to its utmost capacity. Says the Reverend John Newton, who was a slaving captain before he became a clergyman:

> The cargo of a vessel of a hundred tons or a little more is calculated to purchase from 220 to 250 slaves. Their lodging rooms below the deck which are three (for the men, the boys, and the women) besides a place for the sick, are sometimes more than five feet high and sometimes less; and this height is divided toward the middle for the slaves to lie in two rows, one above the other, on each side of the ship, close to each other like books upon a shelf. I have known them so close that the shelf would not easily contain one more.
>
> The poor creatures, thus cramped, are likewise in irons for the most part which makes it difficult for them to turn or move or attempt to rise or to lie down without hurting themselves or each other. Every morning, perhaps, more instances than one are found of the living and the dead fastened together.

This diagram is a typical example of the "tight packing" techniques of many slavers.

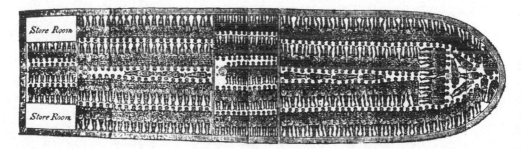

Newton was writing in 1788, shortly before a famous parliamentary investigation of the slave trade that lasted four years. One among hundreds of witnesses was Dr. Alexander Falconbridge, who had made four slaving voyages as a surgeon. Falconbridge testified that "he made the most of the room," in stowing the slaves, "and wedged them in. They had not so much room as a man in his coffin either in length or breadth. When he had to enter the slave deck, he took off his shoes to avoid crushing the slaves as he was forced to crawl over them." Falconbridge "had the marks on his feet where the slaves bit and pinched him."

Captain Parrey of the Royal Navy was sent to measure the slave ships at Liverpool and make a report to the House of Commons. That was also in 1788. Parrey discovered that the captains of many slavers possessed a chart showing the dimensions of the half deck, lower deck, hold, platforms, gunroom, orlop, and great cabin, in fact of every crevice into which slaves might be wedged. Miniature black figures were drawn on some of the charts to illustrate the most effective method of packing in the cargo.

On the *Brookes*, which Parrey considered to be typical, every man was allowed a space six feet long by sixteen inches wide (and usually about two feet seven inches high) ; every woman, a space five feet ten inches long by sixteen inches wide; every boy, five feet by fourteen inches; every girl, four feet six inches by twelve inches. The *Brookes* was a vessel of 320 tons. By a new law passed in 1788 it was permitted to carry 454 slaves, and the chart, which later became famous, showed where 451 of them could be stowed away. Parrey failed to see how the captain could find room for three more. Nevertheless, Parliament was told by reliable witnesses, including Dr. Thomas Trotter, formerly surgeon of the *Brookes,* that before the new law she had carried 600 slaves on one voyage and 609 on another.

Taking on slaves was a process that might be completed in a month or two by vessels trading in Lower Guinea, east and south of the Niger delta. In Upper Guinea, west and north of the delta, the process was longer. It might last from six months to a year or more on the Gold Coast, which supplied the slaves most in demand by the English colonies. Meanwhile the captain was buying Negroes, sometimes one or two a day, sometimes a hundred or more in a single lot, while haggling over each purchase.

Those months when a slaver lay at anchor off the malarial coast-line were the most dangerous part of her voyage. Not only was her crew exposed to African fevers and the revenge of angry natives; not only was there the chance of her being taken by pirates or by a hostile man-of-war; but there was also the constant threat of a slave mutiny. Captain Thomas Phillips says, in his account of a voyage made in 1693–94 :

When our slaves are aboard we shackle the men two and two, while we lie in port, and in sight of their own country, for 'tis then they attempt to make their escape, and mutiny; to prevent which we always keep centinels upon the hatchways, and have a chest full of small arms, ready loaden and prim'd, constantly lying at hand upon the quarter-deck, together with some granada shells; and two of our quarter-deck guns, pointing on the deck thence, and two more out of the steerage, the door of which is always kept shut, and well barr'd; they are fed twice a day, at 10 in the morning, and 4 in the evening, which is the time they are aptest to mutiny, being all upon the deck; therefore all that time, what of our men are not employ'd in distributing their victuals to them, and settling them, stand to their arms, and some with lighted matches at the great guns that yaun upon them, loaden with partridge, till they have done and gone down to their kennels between decks.

In spite of such precautions, mutinies were frequent on the Coast, and some of them were successful. Even a mutiny that failed might lead to heavy losses among the slaves and the sailors. Thus, we read in the Newport, Rhode Island, *Mercury* of November 18, 1765:

By letters from Capt. Hopkins in a Brig belonging to Providence arrived here from Antigua from the Coast of Africa we learn That soon after he left the Coast, the number of his Men being reduced by Sickness, he was obliged to permit some of the Slaves to come upon Deck to assist the People: These Slaves contrived to release the others, and the whole rose upon the People, and endeavoured to get Possession of the Vessel; but was happily prevented by the Captain and his Men, who killed, wounded and forced overboard, Eighty of them, which obliged the rest to submit.

There are scores of similar items in the colonial newspapers.

William Richardson, a young sailor who shipped on an English Guineaman in 1790, tells of going to the help of a French vessel on which the slaves had risen while it was at anchor. The English seamen jumped into the boats and pulled hard for the Frenchman, but by the time they reached it there were "a hundred slaves in possession of the deck and others tumbling up from below." The slaves put up a desperate resistance. "I could not but admire," Richardson says, "the courage of a fine young black who, though his partner in irons lay dead at his feet, would not surrender but fought with his billet of wood until a ball finished his existence. The others fought as well as they could but what could they do against fire-arms?"

There are fairly detailed accounts of fifty-five mutinies on slavers from 1699 to 1845, not to mention passing references to more than a hundred others. The list of ships "cut off" by the natives—often in revenge for the kidnapping of free Africans—is almost as long. On the record it does not seem that Africans submitted tamely to being carried across the Atlantic like chained beasts. Edward Long, the Jamaica planter and historian, justified the cruel punishments inflicted on slaves by saying, "The many acts of violence they

In 1839 some 53 captives revolted aboard the slaver Amistad. *They were recaptured but later freed in a case that reached the Supreme Court.*

have committed by murdering whole crews and destroying ships when they had it in their power to do so have made these rigors wholly chargeable on their own bloody and malicious disposition which calls for the same confinement as if they were wolves or wild boars.'' For ''wolves or wild boars'' a modern reader might substitute ''men who would rather die than be enslaved.''

With the loading of the slaves, the captain, for his part, had finished what he regarded as the most difficult part of his voyage. Now he had to face only the ordinary perils of the sea, most of which were covered by his owners' insurance against fire, shipwreck, pirates and rovers, letters of mart and counter-mart, barratry, jettison, and foreign men-of-war. Among the risks not covered by insurance, the greatest was that of the cargo's being swept away by disease. The underwriters refused to issue such policies, arguing that they would expose the captain to an unholy temptation. If insured against disease among his slaves, he might take no precautions against it and might try to make his profit out of the insurance.

The more days at sea, the more deaths among his cargo, and so the captain tried to cut short the next leg of his voyage. If he had shipped his slaves at Bonny, Old Calabar, or any port to the southward, he might call at one of the Portuguese islands in the Gulf of Guinea for an additional supply of food and fresh water, usually enough, with what he had already, to last for three months. If he had traded to the northward, he made straight for the West Indies. Usually he had from four to five thousand nautical miles to sail—or even more, if the passage was from Angola to Virginia. The shortest passage—that from the Gambia River to Barbados—might be made in as little as three weeks, with favoring winds. If the course was much longer, and if the ship was becalmed in the doldrums or driven back by storms, the voyage might take more than three months, and slaves and sailors would be put on short rations long before the end of the Middle Passage.

On a canvas of heroic size, Thomas Stothard, Esquire, of the Royal Academy, depicted *The Voyage of the Sable Venus from Angola to the West Indies*. His painting is handsomely reproduced in the second volume of Bryan Edwards' *History of the British Colonies in the West Indies* (1793), where it appears beside a poem on the same allegorical subject by an unnamed Jamaican author, perhaps Edwards himself.

The joint message of the poem and the painting is simple to the point of coarseness: that slave women are preferable to English girls at night, being passionate and accessible; but the message is embellished with classical details, to show the painter's learning.

Meanwhile the Sable Venus, if she was a living woman carried from Angola to the West Indies, was roaming the deck of a ship that stank of excrement; as was said of any slaver, "You could smell it five miles down wind." She had been torn from her husband and her children, she had been branded on the left buttock, and she had been carried to the ship bound hand and foot, lying in the bilge at the bottom of a dugout canoe. Now she was the prey of the ship's officers.

Here is how she and her shipmates spent the day.

If the weather was clear, they were brought on deck at eight o'clock in the morning. The men were attached by their leg irons to the great chain that ran along the bulwarks on both sides of the ship; the women and half-grown boys were allowed to wander at will. About nine o'clock the slaves were served their first meal of the day. If they were from the Windward Coast—roughly, the shoreline of present-day Liberia and Sierra Leone—the fare was boiled rice, millet, or corn meal, sometimes cooked with a few lumps of salt beef abstracted from the sailors' rations. If they were from the Bight of Biafra, at the east end of the Gulf of Guinea, they were fed stewed yams, but the Congos and the Angolas preferred manioc or plantains. With the food they were all given half a pint of water, served out in a pannikin.

After the morning meal came a joyless ceremony called "dancing the slaves." "Those who were in irons," says Dr. Thomas Trotter, surgeon of the *Brookes* in 1783, "were ordered to stand up and make what motions they could, leaving a passage for such as were out of irons to dance around the deck." Dancing was prescribed as a therapeutic measure, a specific against suicidal melancholy, and also against scurvy—although in the latter case is was a useless torture for men with swollen limbs. While sailors paraded the deck, each with a cat-o'-nine-tails in his right hand, the men slaves "jumped in their irons" until their ankles were bleeding flesh. Music was provided by a slave thumping on a broken drum or an upturned kettle, or by an African banjo, if there was one aboard, or perhaps by a sailor with a bagpipe or a fiddle. Slaving captains sometimes advertised for "A person that can play on the Bagpipes, for a Guinea ship." The slaves were also told to sing. Said Dr. Claxton after his voyage in the *Young Hero*, "They sing, but not for their amusement. The captain ordered them to sing, and they sang songs of sorrow. Their sickness, fear of being beaten, their hunger, and the memory of their country, etc., are the usual subjects."

While some of the sailors were dancing the slaves, others were sent below to scrape and swab out the sleeping rooms. It was a sickening task, and it was not well performed unless the captain imposed an iron discipline. James Barbot, Sr., was proud of the discipline maintained on the *Albion-Frigate*. "We were very nice," he says, "in keeping the places where the slaves lay clean and neat, appointing some of the ship's crew to do that office constantly and thrice a week we perfumed betwixt decks with a quantity of good vinegar in pails, and red-hot iron bullets in them, to expel the bad air, after the place had been well washed and scrubbed with brooms." Captain Hugh Crow, the last legal English slaver, was famous for his housekeeping. "I always took great pains," he says, "to promote the health and comfort of all on board, by proper diet, regularity, exercise, and cleanliness, for I considered that on keeping the ship clean and orderly, which was always my hobby, the success of our voyage mainly depended." Certainly he lost fewer slaves in the Middle Passage than the other captains, some of whom had the filth in the hold cleaned out only once a week.

At three or four in the afternoon the slaves were fed their second meal, often a repetition of the first. Sometimes, instead of African food, they were given horse beans, the cheapest provender from Europe. The beans were boiled to a pulp, then covered with a mixture of palm oil, flour, water, and red pepper, which the sailors called "slabber sauce." Most of the slaves detested horse beans, especially if they were used to eating yams or manioc. Instead of eating the pulp, they would, unless carefully watched, pick it up by handfuls and throw it in each other's faces.

That second meal was the end of their day. As soon as it was finished they were sent below, under the guard of sailors charged with stowing them away on their bare floors and platforms. The tallest men were placed amidships, where the vessel was widest; the shorter ones were tumbled into the stern. Usually there was only room for them to sleep on their sides, "spoon fashion." Captain William Littleton told Parliament that slaves in the ships on which he sailed might lie on their backs if they wished—"though perhaps," he conceded, "it might be difficult all at the same time."

After stowing their cargo, the sailors climbed out of the hatchway, each clutching his cat-o'-nine-tails; then the hatchway gratings were closed and barred. Sometimes in the night, as the sailors lay on deck and tried to sleep, they heard from below "an howling melancholy noise, expressive of extreme anguish." When Dr. Trotter told his interpreter, a slave woman, to inquire about the cause of the noise, "she discovered it to be owing to their having dreamt they were in their own country, and finding themselves when awake, in the hold of a slave ship."

More often the noise heard by the sailors was that of quarreling among the slaves. The usual occasion for quarrels was their problem of reaching the latrines. These were inadequate in size and number, and hard to find in the darkness of the crowded hold, especially by men who were ironed together in pairs.

In squalls or rainy weather, the slaves were never brought on deck. They were served their two meals in the hold, where the air became too thick and poisonous to breathe. Dr. Falconbridge writes:

For the purpose of admitting fresh air, most of the ships in the slave-trade are provided, between the decks, with five or six air-ports on each side of the ship, of about six inches in length and four in breadth; in addition to which, some few ships, but not one in twenty, have what they denominate wind-sails [funnels made of canvas and so placed as to direct a current of air into the hold]. But whenever the sea is rough and the rain heavy, it becomes necessary to shut these and every other conveyance by which the air is admitted. . . . The negroes' rooms very soon become intolerably hot. The confined air, rendered noxious by the effluvia exhaled from their bodies and by being repeatedly breathed, soon produces fevers and fluxes which generally carry off great numbers of them.

Dr. Trotter says that when tarpaulins were thrown over the gratings, the slaves would cry, "Kickeraboo, kickeraboo, we are dying, we are dying." Falconbridge gives one instance of their sufferings:

Some wet and blowing weather having occasioned the portholes to be shut and the grating to be covered, fluxes and fevers among the negroes ensued. While they were in this situation, I frequently went down among them till at length their rooms became so extremely hot as to be only bearable for a very short time. But the excessive heat was not the only thing that rendered their situation intolerable. The deck, that is, the floor of their rooms, was so covered with the blood and mucus which had proceeded from them in consequence of the flux, that it resembled a slaughter-house.

While the slaves were on deck they had to be watched at all times to keep them from committing suicide. Says Captain Phillips of the *Hannibal*, "We had about 12 negroes did wilfully drown themselves, and others starv'd themselves to death; for," he explained, " 'tis their belief that when they die they return home to their own country and friends again."

This belief was reported from various regions, at various periods of the trade, but it seems to have been especially strong among the Ibos of eastern Nigeria. In 1788, nearly a hundred years after the *Hannibal's* voyage, Dr. Ecroide Claxton was the surgeon who attended a shipload of Ibos. Some, he testified,

wished to die on an idea that they should then get back to their own country. The captain in order to obviate this idea, thought of an expedient viz. to cut off the heads of those who died intimating to them that if determined to go, they must return without heads. The slaves were accordingly brought up to witness the operation. One of them by a violent exertion got loose and flying to the place where the nettings had been unloosed in order to empty the tubs, he darted overboard. The ship brought to, a man was placed in the main chains to catch him which he perceiving, made signs which words cannot express expressive of his happiness in escaping. He then went down and was seen no more.

Dr. Isaac Wilson, a surgeon in the Royal Navy, made a Guinea voyage on the *Elizabeth*, captain John Smith, who was said to be very humane. Nevertheless, Wilson was assigned the duty of flogging the slaves. "Even in the act of chastisement," Wilson says, "I have seen them look up at me with a smile, and, in their own language, say 'presently we shall be no more.' " One woman on the *Elizabeth* found some rope yarn, which she tied to the armorer's vise; she fastened the other end round her neck and was found dead in the morning.

On the *Brookes* when Thomas Trotter was her surgeon, there was a man who, after being accused of witchcraft, had been sold into slavery with all his family. During the first night on shipboard he tried to cut his throat. Dr. Trotter sewed up the wound, but on the following night the man not only tore out the stitches but tried to cut his throat on the other side. From the ragged edges of the wound and the blood on his fingers, he seemed to have used his nails as the only available instrument. His hands were then tied together, but he refused all food, and he died of hunger in eight or ten days.

Besides the propensity for suicide, another deadly scourge of the Guinea cargoes was a phenomenon called "fixed melancholy." Even slaves who were well fed, treated with kindness, and kept under relatively sanitary conditions would often die, one after another, for no apparent reason; they had simply lost the will to live. Dr. Wilson believed that fixed melancholy was responsible for the loss of two thirds of the slaves who died on the *Elizabeth*. "No one who had it was ever cured," he says, "whereas those who had it not and yet were ill, recovered. The symptoms are a lowness of spirits and despondency. Hence they refuse food. This only increases the symptoms. The stomach afterwards got weak. Hence the belly ached, fluxes ensued, and they were carried off." But in spite of the real losses from despair, the high death rate on Guineamen was due to somatic more than to psychic afflictions.

Along with their human cargoes, crowded, filthy, undernourished, and terrified out of the wish to live, the ships also carried an invisible cargo of microbes, bacilli, spirochetes, viruses, and intestinal worms from one continent to another; the Middle Passage was a crossroad and market place of diseases. From Europe came smallpox, measles (somewhat less deadly to Africans than to American Indians), gonorrhea, and syphilis (which last Columbus' sailors had carried from America to Europe). The African diseases were yellow fever (to which the natives were resistant), dengue, blackwater fever, and malaria (which was not specifically African, but which most of the slaves carried in their blood streams). If anopheles mosquitoes were present, malaria spread from the slaves through any new territories to which they were carried. Other African diseases were amoebic and bacillary dysentery (known as "the bloody flux"), Guinea worms, hookworm (possibly African in origin, but soon endemic in the warmer parts of the New World), yaws, elephantiasis, and leprosy.

The particular affliction of the white sailors after escaping from the fevers of the Guinea Coast was scurvy, a deficiency disease to which they were exposed by their monotonous rations of salt beef and sea biscuits. The daily tot of lime juice (originally lemon juice) that prevented scurvy was almost never served on merchantmen during the days of the legal slave trade, and in fact was not prescribed in the Royal Navy until 1795. Although the slaves were also subject to scurvy, they fared better in this respect than the sailors, partly because they made only one leg of the triangular voyage and partly because their rough diet was sometimes richer in vitamins. But sailors and slaves alike were swept away by smallpox and "the bloody flux," and sometimes whole shiploads went blind from what seems to have been trachoma.

Smallpox was feared more than other diseases, since the surgeons had no way of curing it. One man with smallpox infected a whole vessel, unless—as sometimes happened—he was tossed overboard when the first scabs appeared. Captain Wilson of the *Briton* lost more than half his cargo of 375 slaves by not listening to his surgeon. It was the last slave on board who had the disease, says Henry Ellison, who made the voyage. "The doctor told Mr. Wilson it was the small-pox," Ellison continues. "He would not believe it, but said he would keep him, as he was a fine man. It soon broke out amongst the slaves. I have seen the platform one continued scab. We hauled up eight or ten slaves dead of a morning. The flesh and skin peeled off their wrists when taken hold of, being entirely mortified."

But dysentery, though not so much feared, probably caused more deaths in the aggregate. Ellison testified that he made two voyages on the *Nightingale*. On the first voyage the slaves were so crowded that thirty boys "messed and slept in the long boat all through the Middle Passage, there being no room below"; and still the vessel lost only five or six slaves in all, out of a cargo of 270. On the second voyage, however, the *Nightingale* buried "about 150, chiefly of fevers and flux. We had 250 when we left the coast."

The average mortality in the Middle Passage is impossible to state accurately from the surviving records. Some famous voyages were made without the loss of a single slave. On one group of nine voyages between 1766 and 1780, selected at random, the vessels carried 2,362 slaves and there were no epidemics of disease. The total loss of slaves was 154, or about six and one-half per cent. That figure is to be compared with the losses on a list of twenty voyages compiled by Thomas Clarkson, the abolitionist, in which the vessels carried 7,904 slaves with a mortality of 2,053, or twenty-six per cent. Balancing high and low figures together, the English Privy Council in 1789 arrived at an estimate of twelve and one-half per cent for the average mortality among slaves in the Middle Passage. To this figure it added four and one-half per cent for the deaths of slaves in harbors before they were sold, and thirty-three per cent for deaths in the so-called "seasoning" or acclimatizing process, making a total of fifty per cent. If these figures are correct, only one slave was added to the New World labor

In April of 1860 these despondent and emaciated slaves reached Key West in the bark Wildfire. *From an etching published in* Harper's Weekly.

force for every two purchased on the Guinea Coast.

To keep the figures in perspective, it might be said that the mortality among slaves in the Middle Passage was possibly no greater than that of white indentured servants or even of free Irish, Scottish, and German immigrants in the North Atlantic crossing. On the better-commanded Guineamen it was probably less, and for a simple economic reason. There was no profit on a slaving voyage until the Negroes were landed alive and sold; therefore the better captains took care of their cargoes. It was different on the North Atlantic crossing, where even the hold and steerage passengers paid their fares before coming aboard, and where the captain cared little whether they lived or died.

After leaving the Portuguese island of São Tomé—if he had watered there—a slaving captain bore westward along the equator for a thousand miles, and then northwestward toward the Cape Verde Islands. This was the tedious part of the Middle Passage. "On leaving the Gulf of Guinea," says the author of a *Universal Geography* published in the early nineteenth century, ". . . that part of the ocean must be traversed, so fatal to navigators, where long calms detain the ships under a sky charged with electric clouds, pouring down by torrents of rain and of fire. This *sea of thunder*, being a focus of mortal diseases, is avoided as much as possible, both in approaching the coasts of Africa and those of America." It was not until reaching the latitude of the Cape Verde Islands that the vessel fell in with the northeast trades and was able to make a swift passage to the West Indies.

Dr. Claxton's ship, the *Young Hero*, was one of those delayed for weeks before reaching the trade winds. "We were so streightened for provisions," he testified, "that if we had been ten more days at sea, we must either have eaten the slaves that died, or have made the living slaves *walk the plank*," a term, he explained, that was widely used by Guinea captains. There are no authenticated records of cannibalism in the Middle Passage, but there are many accounts of slaves killed for various reasons. English captains believed that French vessels carried poison in their medicine chests, "with which they can destroy their negroes in a calm, contagious sickness, or short provisions." They told the story of a Frenchman from Brest who had a long passage and had to poison his slaves; only twenty of them reached Haiti out of five hundred. Even the cruelest English captains regarded this practice as Latin, depraved, and uncovered by their insurance policies. In an emergency they simply jettisoned part of their cargo.

Often a slave ship came to grief in the last few days of the Middle Passage. It might be taken by a French privateer out of Martinique, or it might disappear in a tropical hurricane, or it might be wrecked on a shoal almost in sight of its harbor. On a few ships there was an epidemic of suicide at the last moment.

These, however, were exceptional disasters, recounted as horror stories in the newspapers of the time. Usually the last two or three days of the passage were a comparatively happy period. All the slaves, or all but a few, might be released from their irons. When there was a remaining stock of provisions, the slaves were given bigger meals—to fatten them for market—and as much water as they could drink. Sometimes on the last day—if the ship was commanded by an easy-going captain—there was a sort of costume party on deck, with the women slaves dancing in the sailors' castoff clothing. Then the captain was rowed ashore, to arrange for the disposition of his cargo.

This was a problem solved in various fashions. In Virginia, if the vessel was small, it might sail up and down the tidal rivers, bartering slaves for tobacco at private wharves. There were also public auctions of newly imported slaves, usually at Hampton, Yorktown, or Bermuda Hundred. In South Carolina, which was the great mainland slave market, the cargo was usually consigned to a commission merchant, who disposed of the slaves at auction, then had the vessel loaded with rice or indigo for its voyage back to England.

In the smaller West Indian islands, the captain sometimes took charge of selling his own slaves. In this case he ferried them ashore, had them drawn up in a ragged line of march, and paraded them through town with bagpipes playing, before exposing them to buyers in the public square. In the larger islands, commission merchants took charge of the cargo, and the usual method of selling the slaves at retail was a combination of the ''scramble''—to be described in a moment—with the vendue or public auction ''by inch of candle.''

First the captain, with the commission merchant at his side, went over the cargo and picked out the slaves who were maimed or diseased. These were carried to a tavern and auctioned off, with a lighted candle before the auctioneer; bids were received until an inch of candle had burned. The price of so-called ''refuse'' slaves sold at auction was usually less than half of that paid for a healthy Negro. ''I was informed by a mulatto woman,'' Dr. Falconbridge says, ''that she purchased a sick slave at Grenada, upon speculation, for the small sum of one dollar, as the poor wretch was apparently dying of the flux.'' There were some slaves so diseased and emaciated that they could not be sold for even a dollar, and these might be left to die on the wharves.

The healthy slaves remaining after the auction were sold by ''scramble,'' that is, at standard prices for each man, each woman, each boy, and each girl in the cargo. The prices were agreed upon with the purchasers, who then scrambled for their pick of the slaves. During his four voyages Falconbridge was present at a number of scrambles. ''In the *Emilia*,'' he says,

> at Jamaica, the ship was darkened with sails, and covered round. The men slaves were placed on the main deck, and the women on the quarter deck. The purchasers on shore were informed a gun would be fired when they were ready to open the sale. A great number of people came on board with tallies or cards in their hands, with their own names upon them, and rushed through the barricado door with the ferocity of brutes. Some had three or four handkerchiefs tied together, to encircle as many as they thought fit for their purposes.

For the slaves, many of whom believed that they were about to be eaten, it was the terrifying climax of a terrifying voyage.

The parliamentary investigations of 1788–1791 presented a complete picture of the Middle Passage, with testimony from everyone concerned except the slaves, and it horrified the English public. Powerful interests in Parliament, especially those representing the Liverpool merchants and the West Indian planters, prevented the passage of restrictive legislation at that time. But the Middle Passage was not forgotten, and in 1807 Parliament passed a law forbidding any slaver to sail from a British port after May 1 of that year. At about the same time, Congress prohibited the importation of slaves into American territory from and after January 1, 1808. All the countries of Europe followed the British and American example, if with some delay. During the next half century, however, reformers would learn that the trade was difficult to abolish in fact as well as in law, and that illegal slaving would continue as long as slavery itself was allowed to flourish.

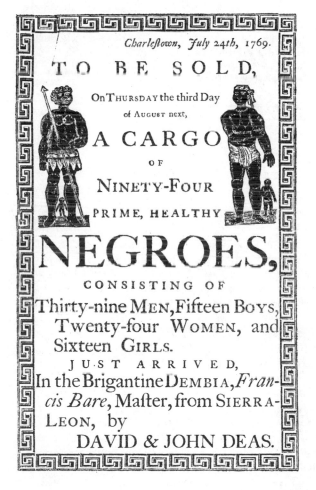

Charleſtown, July 24th, 1769.

TO BE SOLD,

On THURSDAY the third Day of AUGUST next,

A CARGO

OF

NINETY-FOUR

PRIME, HEALTHY

NEGROES,

CONSISTING OF

Thirty-nine MEN, Fifteen BOYS, Twenty-four WOMEN, and Sixteen GIRLS.

JUST ARRIVED,

In the Brigantine DEMBIA, *Francis Bare*, Maſter, from SIERRA-LEON, by

DAVID & JOHN DEAS.

This 1769 broadside is typical of those posted in southern ports to advertise the arrival of slave ships from Africa's west coast.

Perry Miller

The Old
Testament in
Colonial America

*While it is beyond argument that the primary motive driving
most colonists to settle in the New World was economic, large numbers
of them, especially those who came to New England, migrated for
religious and spiritual reasons as well. In such people religious and
material objectives tended to reinforce each other; the opportunity
to fashion a better life on earth was related in their minds to the
task of preparing themselves for a better hereafter. The Puritans
particularly, with their deep concern for Old Testament values, saw
America as the Promised Land, England as Egypt. They spoke of
New England as God's American Israel.*

*This essay by the late Professor Perry Miller of Harvard Uni-
versity shows how extensively Old Testament imagery affected the
thinking of the colonists and how far into postcolonial history their
way of looking at America persisted. Professor Miller, one of the
greatest of American intellectual historians, was, as this essay demonstrates, both a master of the sources and a superb re-creator of the
mind and point of view of a bygone age.*

"**P**olly certainly missed her vocation when she was trained for a servant," says Miss Mehitable in Harriet Beecher Stowe's *Oldtown Folks*. "She is a born professor of theology. She is so circumstantial about all that took place at the time the angels fell, and when the covenant was made with Adam in the Garden of Eden, that I sometimes question whether she really might not have been there personally."

Mrs. Stowe published this delicious piece of cultural history in 1869, purporting to describe a New England of about 1790; actually, she was pushing back into an eighteenth-century setting everything she remembered (and she remembered everything) about the world of her childhood, in Litchfield, Connecticut, around 1820. In New England, but also in every intensely Protestant community within the United States—which is to say, as of that date, virtually all American communities—there were innumerable Pollys. . . . They could all be as circumstantial about the Garden of Eden or the pit into which Joseph was thrust as about Deacon Badger's meadow—probably more circumstantial. . . .

Scenes and themes from Hebrew history are so pervasive in the literature—from Captain Ahab down to Mrs. Lydia Sigourney's *Aaron on Mount Hor*—that one can only stand today in speechless amazement at what a large intimacy with the Old Testament writers could assume as a matter of course among their readers:

> *But then, as Moses raised*
> *The mystic breastplate, and that dying eye*
> *Caught the last radiance of those precious stones,*
> *By whose oracular and fearful light*
> *Jehovah had so oft his will reveal'd*
> *Unto the chosen tribes, whom Aaron loved,*
> *In all their wanderings—but whose promised land*
> *He might not look upon—he sadly laid*
> *His head upon the mountain's turfy breast,*
> *And with one prayer, half wrapp'd in stifled groans,*
> *Gave up the ghost.*

One might well suppose that Lydia Sigourney also had been there personally! Her myriad admirers had no difficulty accepting on her say-so the botanical fact that Mount Hor was "turfy."

The Old Testament is truly so omnipresent in the American culture of 1800 or 1820 that historians have as much difficulty taking cognizance of it as of the air the people breathed. But as soon as you pause to ask the reason for this preoccupation with the Old Testament by a people intensely concerned about securing for themselves the salvation promised in the New, you find yourself in the realm of those intangibles which are the warp and woof of history, upon which politics and even economics are comparatively surface embellishments. But the deeper irony of the situation is the fact that in these very decades which produced in folk art and in popular literature the greatest efflorescence of the Hebraic imagination, Protestant piety was turning steadily away from the Old Testament toward an ecstatic rediscovery of the New. Such poems as Mrs. Sigourney's or such panels as Mary Ann Willson's *Prodigal Son* are not harbingers of the nineteenth century: they are the last lingering rays from a sun that set with the eighteenth century. If these creations are to be properly characterized, they should be called not "primitives" but the end products of a sophisticated culture that was receding before the onslaught of a new primitivism, that of the camp meeting.

It was this revolution in Protestant piety, with its communal shouting to the Lord for a mass salvation, that gradually shifted attention away from the Old Testament. However, in a curious way, the political Revolution of 1776 delayed the change. The Great Awakening of 1740, that which George Whitefield ignited, pointed the way to a surging emotionalism that might have washed out the traditional churchly standards of doctrine and practice, but as it subsided the "Old Lights" regained so much ground that their Biblicism was still vivid enough to provide symbolic parallels to the cause of the patriots. Though we think of the Revolution as led by rationalists like Jefferson or Franklin, who based the cause on scientific nature and common sense rather than on the example of Israel, still among the masses the Hebraic analogy was at least as powerful an incentive as the declaration of inalienable rights. "My dear countrymen," begins a typical communication in the Boston *Gazette* for May 6, 1782, "my sincere wish and prayer to God is, that our Israel may be saved from the rapacious jaws of a tyrant."

After the victory, in 1785, Timothy Dwight published what he conceived to be a native American epic, *The Conquest of Canaan*. This is as full of gore and battle and savage exultation as the most inveterate student of the Old Testament could desire; the hero, the "Leader," is Joshua, but the book is dedicated to "George Washington, Esquire," thus tactfully but emphatically making the point that a colossal retelling of the Jewish conquest of Canaan was in fact a narrative of Washington's conquest of America.

The fixation of colonial Protestantism upon the Old Testament— a phenomenon to be noted in every settlement—has one obvious explanation: bands of European immigrants seemed, to themselves at least, the modern equivalents of a chosen people taking possession of the promised land. It was natural, indeed inevitable, for William Bradford, looking back to the landing at Plymouth in the harsh December of 1620 and reviewing the desperate predicament, to cry out, even in his old age, "What could now sustain them but the Spirit of God and His Grace?" and then to answer his rhetorical question by quotations not from the Sermon on the Mount but by quotations from Deuteronomy and the Psalms. In 1648 Thomas Shepard had to defend the Bay Colony against the charge then being made in England by the Puritans who had stayed home and fought the Cavaliers, that the New Englanders had fled from the post of danger. Shepard went immediately to Hebrew precedent: "What shall we say of the singular providence of God bringing so many shiploads of His people, through so many dangers, as

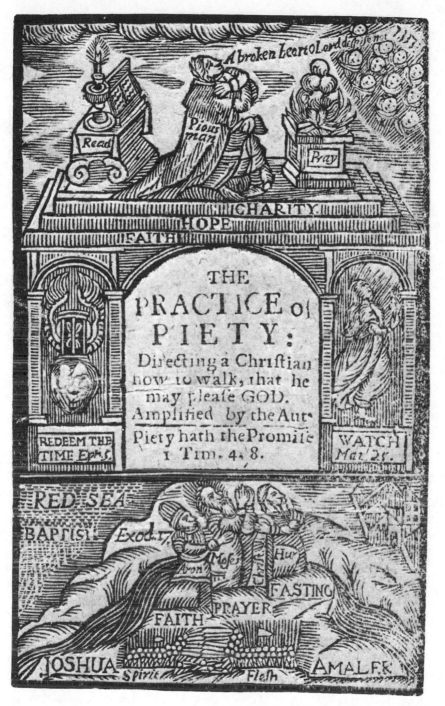

James Franklin's 1718 engraving shows the edifice of piety resting on Old Testament lore.

upon eagles' wings, with so much safety from year to year?" Thereupon he bolstered his thesis with attestations from Exodus and Micah.

Furthermore, the Calvinist elements among the settlers—this applies to Presbyterians in the middle colonies and even to the original pioneers of Virginia as well as to the Puritans of New England—had still a further reason to think of themselves as Israel: even before they reached these shores, their theology had been considerably recast into the terminology of the covenant. To secure a perspective on themselves and their place in universal history, they had elaborated the "federal" doctrine that the covenant made with Abraham was that Covenant of Grace which replaced the Covenant of Works that God made with Adam—that first covenant on which Miss Mehitable's Polly was so circumstantial. The covenant of Abraham had, according to this theology, extended unbroken from the children of Abraham to the present church, and was most binding on those churches that were then reforming the abuses of Antichrist. The effect was to give the migrants a deep sense of their being directly connected with the histories of Jacob, Noah and Moses.

"Thus stands the cause between God and us," Governor John Winthrop preached to the Great Migration in 1630, even before it reached the coast of Massachusetts. "We are entered into a covenant with Him for this work, we have taken out a commission; the Lord hath given us leave to draw our own articles, we have professed to enterprise these actions upon these and these ends." To make clear his meaning, the Governor invoked three passages from the Old Testament—Leviticus, I. Samuel, and Micah—and only one from Ephesians. The great crime of Roger Williams, in the eyes of the orthodox, was not so much that he advocated religious liberty but that he came to this heresy out of a previous and more shocking heresy; he denied that the covenant made with Abraham had continued unbroken down to the covenant of God with the Commonwealth of Massachusetts Bay. He repudiated the hold of the Old Testament upon the churches of Christ, with the result that the orthodox the more vigorously reaffirmed their allegiance to it. Thus from Rhode Island in 1676 could come the jibe of Benjamin Franklin's grandfather, Peter Folger:

> *New England they are like the Jews,*
> *as like as like can be.*

The dreadful experience of English Calvinism with the "sectaries" of the English civil wars has always to be kept in mind as the factor which sealed its Hebraism, a state of mind that would persist for another century and a half. Long after the Levellers and Anabaptists had gone, long after Roger Williams' "typology" was forgotten, the churches shuddered at the memory of these radicals. Far from London, on the frontier outpost of Concord in Massachusetts, Peter Bulkeley preached upon *The Gospel-Covenant,* his manuscript being sent home for publication in 1651, so that Englishmen could heed this American warning:

*And yet now some are risen up, renewing again that vile doc-
trine in these days of grace, teaching us to cast aside the
scriptures of the Old Testament, as if they were like a bond
cancelled and out of date. O Lord, whither will our deluded
hearts carry us, if thou, Lord, keepest us not in the way of
thy truth!*

By keeping resolutely in the way of the Lord's truth as set forth in
both Testaments, but by reading the New always in the light of the
more dramatic Old, American Protestants grew to regard themselves
as so like the Jews that every anecdote in the tribal history seemed a
part of their own recollection. They proclaimed, says Harriet Beecher
Stowe, a religion of asceticism, but they would never have achieved the
tremendous success of pushing the frontier steadily back or of sailing
and trafficking in the seven seas had they not added to this asceticism
"the spirit of the Old Testament, in which material prosperity is
always spoken of as the lawful reward of piety, in which marriage is
an honor, and a numerous posterity a thing to be desired." By its
isolation and its homogeneity New England seemed most close to the
pattern of Israel, but the archetype was almost as present to the imagination of Kentucky pioneers. Describing the migration in 1780 of
his parents, James B. Finley could remark: "Like ancient Israel, who,
while rebuilding the temple in troublous times, had to bear about
them the weapons of war, so the ministers of the Gospel at that day
were obliged to carry carnal as well as spiritual weapons." Thus
they felt a kinship with Joshua and Hiram, closer than any relationship to their cousins in Europe, and named their numerous posterity
Samuel, Benjamin, Eli, Mehitable, Judith, Abraham, and Peleg.

Consequently, by the time of the Revolution a mentality had long
been sustained and perfected that made easy an identification of the
new nation with the children of Abraham. This secularizing of
the covenant, as it might be called, was so natural and so unconscious a maneuver that it was enacted without anyone's being particularly aware that it had happened, let alone appreciating its
implications. It became, as is obvious, one of the sources, perhaps
the principal one, for American exceptionalism. For a long time,
well into the nineteenth century, the image could be constantly
invoked by nationalistic writers. Thus Herman Melville, arguing in
1850 that this nation should give up the barbarous custom of flogging
in its navy whether or not Britain retained it, exhorted: "Escaped
from the house of bondage, Israel of old did not follow after the ways
of the Egyptians." Melville could shamelessly assert: "We Americans
are the peculiar, chosen people—the Israel of our time; we bear the
ark of the liberties of the world."

Yet all during these decades from 1800 to 1850 the continuous, self-
renewing revival that historians call the Second Great Awakening
. . . was exciting a new sort of piety which put aside the legalistic covenant and focused the Christian life entirely on the orgy
of conversion. The orthodoxy of the seventeenth and eighteenth

centuries was theological, logical, metaphysical; therefore it could devise and elaborate such a complex conception as the covenant. The new revival was everywhere anti-intellectual. Whether they were Methodists or Baptists or Campbellites, the motto of all these exhorters was in effect Wesley's "I know, because I feel." As one convert said of Parson John Ingersoll, "He made salvation seem so plain, so easy, I wanted to take it to my heart without delays." Few may have gone to quite such extremes as Alexander Campbell, but he was representative in so stressing the New Testament that the remaining adherents of the older Protestantism could accuse him of "throwing away the Old Testament." To generalize—not too sweepingly—one may say that by the end of the century the most popular presentations of Protestantism in this country dwelt comparatively little on the stories of Noah or the Prodigal Son. . . .

Therefore the survival into the early nineteenth century of such a recalcitrant Hebraism . . . is to be found mainly in older settlements where pastoral conditions still reinforced the analogy with Israel, or where the more complex (and conservative) theory of pristine Calvinism resisted the emotionalism of the frontier and the city. Mrs. Stowe was herself one who moved with the century further and further from the intellectuality of her heritage. *Uncle Tom's Cabin* was effective because it spoke the language of revived pietism, and Uncle Tom was made a sentimentalized Christ-figure, not an Israelite in bondage. *Oldtown Folks* is in part a bitter attack upon what she called the "tragedy" of New England life: this, she says, consisted of a "constant wrestling of thought with infinite problems which could not be avoided, and which saddened the days of almost every one who grew up under it." Yet at the same time she looked back with an irresistible nostalgia to a grandeur that had, with the softening of doctrine, been lost. And the heart of this magnificence, she explicitly realized, had been that people then lived in constant face-to-face intimacy with Hebrew literature. The dramas of the Old Testament were their own dramas, the ordeals were theirs and the triumphs.

Just as a child brought up under the shadow of a cathedral, Mrs. Stowe mused, would have his mind stocked with legends of saints and angels which he could not understand, "so this wonderful old cathedral book insensibly wrought a sort of mystical poetry into the otherwise hard and sterile life of New England." She was undoubtedly speaking out of her own experience when she had her hero remark that, "although in details relating to human crime and vice, the Old Bible is the most plain-spoken book conceivable, it never violated the chastity of a child's mind, or stimulated an improper curiosity." To her dismay, she says through her alias, she was in later years astonished to learn the real meaning of passages she had formerly listened to "with innocent gravity." Harriet thus reveals, as no social historian can, why the colonial acceptance of the Old Testament gave way, however reluctantly, to the pragmatic pietism of the revival: she and her generation could no longer stand up to the violence in the Old Testament which their grandparents had taken in stride, not as pertaining to the record of a distant and exotic people in Palestine, but as the axiomatic premise of their own existence.

Indeed, as Harriet continues, she casts more and more light onto . . . a civilization that was steadily being transformed during her lifetime and that she could describe in 1869 as utterly vanished. The hero remarks that his grandfather's prayers were completely Hebraistic: "They spoke of Zion and Jerusalem, of the God of Israel, the God of Jacob, as much as if my grandfather had been a veritable Jew; and except for the closing phrase, 'for the sake of thy Son, our Saviour,' might all have been uttered in Palestine by a well-trained Jew in the time of David."

Henry Adams, searching at the beginning of *The Education* to indicate how remote the time in which he wrote was from the world into which, in 1838, he had been born, instinctively compared his status as an Adams to that of one "born in Jerusalem under the shadow of the Temple and circumcised in the Synagogue by his uncle the high priest, under the name of Israel Cohen." Just that real, just that tangible, just that comprehensible had the Old Testament been to the primitive American mind. Though the mood of the culture has undergone many changes since then, and no doubt will move even further from the original, still the stamp of this long period of Hebraistic imagination will always be impressed upon it. . . .

This rendition of Moses in the Bulrushes (c. 1815) is attributed to one Eunice Pinney.

In Daniel Berger's 1784 engraving, defiant Bostonians burn newspapers and documents carrying the stamp demanded by the act of 1765.

Part
Three

THE BIRTH
OF A
NATION

J. H. Plumb

George III, Our Last King

One of the most difficult tasks of the historian is to deal fairly with failure, with incompetence—even with evil. He must try to honor Othello's plea and speak of men (and institutions) as they actually were—"nothing extenuate, nor set down aught in malice." In this essay one of England's premier historians, Professor J. H. Plumb of Cambridge University, succeeds brilliantly in achieving this objective.

Professor Plumb's analysis of America's last king, the unfortunate and much-maligned George III, lays bare the monarch's inadequacies but describes him with sympathy and understanding. As a result, we learn a great deal not only about George III but also about eighteenth-century British politics, and thus about the causes of the American Revolution. George III is easy to caricature or to portray as the Devil incarnate, and as Plumb points out, historians have done both these things repeatedly. Their accounts have often been entertaining, but they have explained very little about the man and his times. By treating him as he has, however, Plumb makes George III and the tragic events of the early years of his long reign plausible, and thus meaningful.

Professor Plumb has written, among many books, The First Four Georges, England in the Eighteenth Century: 1714–1815, and two volumes of a definitive biography of Sir Robert Walpole.

*P*oor George III still gets a bad press. In a famous television talk in London, the Prime Minister of Great Britain suggested to the President of the United States that the kind of colonial policy associated with the name of George III still distorted the American view of the nature and function of the British Empire, and Mr. Eisenhower smilingly agreed. It is not surprising. Since Jefferson's great philippic in the Declaration of Independence, few historians, English or American, have had many good words to say for him. True, he has been excused direct responsibility for many items of the catalogue of enormities that Jefferson went on to lay at his door, but to the ordinary man he remains one of England's disastrous kings, like John or the two Jameses.

Actually, . . . toward the end of his life and immediately after it his reputation improved, and even the writers of American school textbooks did not at first hold him personally responsible for the disasters that led to independence. They held his ministers responsible. It was after the publication of Horace Walpole's *Memoirs* in 1845 that George III began to be blamed. Walpole's gossip appeared to give substance to Burke's allegations that the King deliberately attempted to subvert the British constitution by packing ministries and Parliament with his personal party—the King's friends—a collection of corrupt politicians bought with place and with pension.

Later historians held that these Tory incompetents, bent on personal government for their master, pursued a ruinous policy that ended only with the breakup of the first British Empire and a return of the Whigs to power. Historians reminded themselves not only of the disasters in America, but the failure of parliamentary reform in England, of the oppressions of the Irish, the Catholics, the Dissenters; they remembered the treatment of radicals at the time of the French Revolution; they recalled the merciless suppression of trade unions; the violent opposition to the abolition of slavery. It all added up to a huge indictment of George III and a magnificent justification for Whig doctrine. Here and there a scholar urged caution, but was little heeded. What the great historians formulated, the textbook writers cribbed. When English historians found so much to condemn, why should Americans lag behind? In 1954, two American historians—Leon Canfield and Howard Wilder—could write:

> In 1760, George III mounted the throne. A young man of twenty-two, he was unwilling to accept the idea that the King's power should be limited. His mother had always said to him: "George, be King!" When he became ruler this obstinate young man put his mother's advice into swift action. He set out to get his way not by ignoring Parliament but by building up a personal following. He made free use of bribes and appointments, and presently the King's friends were strong in Parliament.
>
> The increase in royal power drove the wedge of misunderstanding deeper between England and the colonies.

The young George III was portrayed in his coronation robes by court painter Allan Ramsay.

In 1959, an English historian, Jack Lindsay, was still writing in much the same vein. These views, however, are no longer fashionable. The greatest living English historian of the eighteenth century, Sir Lewis Namier, has hammered at them for thirty years. His friend, Romney Sedgwick, with a more caustic pen and no less scholarship, has subjected them to ridicule in review after review, sinking his verbal darts into reputations as skillfully as a savage at his blowpipe. Professor Herbert Butterfield has not only traced the origins of the myths of George III's tyranny but has also shown how the now-fashionable view of George III was held by historians and textbook writers long, long ago in the early nineteenth century. So the wheel has come full circle. Will it turn again? Or will blame and justification give way simply to understanding? Shall we at last have a balanced portrait of America's last king?

On one thing historians are agreed. To understand the part played by George III in the great tragedy of his reign, one must begin with the King's own personality and with the environment in which he was reared. David and Absalom provided the pattern of family relationship of European monarchs and their sons and heirs in the eighteenth century, except that most of the monarchs were less controlled than David. Peter the Great of Russia had his son Alexis executed—slowly and painfully. The Elector of Prussia, Frederick William, insisted that his son, whom he had kept in close confinement, watch the death of his dearest friend for what only a madman could call treason. So it is not surprising to learn that George III's grandmother wished that her son, Frederick, father of George III, were in the bottommost pit of hell or that she became almost hysterical on her deathbed when she thought he might inherit some of her personal possessions. The

James Gillray did this caricature of the penny-wise and pound-foolish monarch in 1791.

Lord Chancellor had to be sent for to lull her fears.

George II's opinion of his own lackluster son matched his wife's. He quite simply hated him as he had hated his own father, who, at one time, had put him under house arrest and removed his children. (It had required all the persuasive powers of the Cabinet to get him released.) This fantastic antagonism between father and son that went on from generation to generation found a situation in English politics that fitted it like a glove. The House of Commons always harbored a number of disappointed politicians who were so hated by the ministers in power that they had few prospects of immediate advancement. But as Sir Robert Walpole bluntly phrased it: "Everybody who could get no ready money had rather have a bad promissory note than nothing." So they made their court to the heir, who found them jobs in his household, and plotted the political changes that they would make when Father died. So throughout the century a Prince of Wales as soon as he was grown up became the leader of the Opposition. At times the Opposition made such a nuisance of itself that the monarch and his ministry decided to buy it off by giving jobs to the leaders, and the astonished heir apparent found his friends deserting him with alacrity. This happened both to George III and to his father. The politics of hatred and the politics of betrayal, therefore, became a part of the environment of the adolescence and early manhood of the Hanoverian kings.

It was in an atmosphere of faction that George III was born; an environment that might have taxed the most gifted of men. Unfortunately George III was as unlucky in his heredity as in his environment. Neither George II nor his Queen, Caroline, was devoid of character or without some gifts above the commonplace. Her intelligence and his memory were unusual in monarchs, and their hatred of their son was tinged with genuine disappointment. Frederick, George III's father, was known to posterity as "Poor Fred," and the epithet was not unjust. He possessed a small talent for music, a mild interest in games, particularly cricket, and little else. The unsympathetic Lord Shelburne described his life as a "tissue of childishness and falsehood"; and his friends as well as his enemies despised him. George II married his son to Princess Augusta of Saxe-Gotha simply because there was no one else. The other Protestant princesses of sufficiently high birth had madness in their families, and George II rejected them, for as he said, "I did not think ingrafting my half-witted coxcomb upon a madwoman would mend the breed." As it turned out, it could not have made matters much worse, for an astonishing number of Princess Augusta's children and grandchildren turned out to be congenital idiots, or subject to fits of insanity, or mentally unbalanced, or blind; the rest were odd or wicked or both.

In some ways George III can be described as the best of the bunch. He was very stupid, really stupid. Had he been born in different circumstances it is unlikely that he could have earned a living except as an unskilled manual laborer. He was eleven before he could read, and he never mastered grammar or spelling or punctuation. He was lethargic, apathetic, childish, a clod of a boy whom no one could teach. His major response to life was a doting love for his brother, Edward. In late adolescence he began to wake up, largely because of a passionately romantic attachment to Lord Bute, the close friend and confidant of his mother.* Somehow Bute made the young prince conscious not only of his destiny but also of his shortcomings. The Prince promised time and time again to throw off his lethargy so that he could accomplish great things for Bute's sake. Naturally the greatest of things was to get rid of his grandfather's evil ministers and to install Bute in a position of power. The ill-spelt, ungrammatical, childish, heartfelt notes that he sent to Bute make pathetic reading. They are charged with a sense of inadequacy, a feeling of hopelessness before the immensity of the burden which destiny had laid on his shoulders, and with an anxious need for help that is almost neurotic in its intensity.

Every year his reverence for the concept of kingship grew stronger; nothing illustrates his regard more than his behavior over Lady Sarah Lennox. This charming girl of fifteen swept him off his feet just before he succeeded to the throne. He longed to marry her. Bute said no, and George III wrote that "he [*i.e.*, Bute] has thoroughly convinced me of the impropriety of marrying a country woman; the interest of my country ever shall be my first care, my own inclinations shall ever submit to it." And submit he did and married a dull, plain, German Protestant princess who bore him the huge family that was to plague his days.

---

* The public thought she was his mistress. Almost certainly she was not. The slander deeply distressed George III and made his attachment to Bute firmer.

A sexually timid, if nonetheless passionate man, George may have found it easier to take Bute's advice than many have thought. Lady Sarah attracted lovers as a candle moths, and George, conscious of his faults and of his inadequacies, must have realized that he cut a poor figure amidst *her* brilliant courtiers. His Queen, Charlotte, attracted no one. And yet sacrifice there was, and George paid for it. Shortly after his marriage he experienced his first bout of insanity. Later in life these periods of madness grew longer. It was only during these attacks that his thoughts escaped from his strict concept of marriage, and rioted in adultery. Then, and then only, was it unsafe for a lady of his court to be alone with him.

During these years of delayed adolescence George III learned, too, that kings had to make other sacrifices. Men powerfully backed in the Lords and Commons, and with an experience of a lifetime's politics behind them, could not easily be dismissed. The great Whig families had ruled since the Hanoverian accession in 1714. They had filled the court of the Georges, monopolized the great offices of state, controlled the Cabinet, dominated the House of Lords, managed the Commons, and run the war with France which had lasted more or less for twenty years. The Duke of Newcastle, George II's Secretary of State, had held an important position in government since he had reached his majority. The Dukes of Devonshire took their high offices as if they belonged to them by hereditary right. Even the Whig career politicians, such as the Lord Chancellor Hardwicke, had been in power for so long that they had come to regard themselves as practically irreplaceable.

These men were not to be easily swept away and replaced by Bute; they possessed too much cunning, too much political experience, too many followers whom they had gratified with places. They doubted Bute's capacity to survive. And still time was on George III's side. The great Whig leaders were old men; indeed their party was known as the Old Corps. And in their long lives they had made plenty of enemies. They had disappointed some members of Parliament, made others impatient, and many disapproved of their policy. Chatham, that hawk-eyed man of destiny who had been responsible more than any other man for the sweeping English victories in the Seven Years' War, deplored their caution, ignored their advice, and treated them, as one of his colleagues grumbled, "as inferior animals." And behind Chatham was the restless brood of Grenvilles, his relations by marriage—difficult, disloyal, able and ambitious men. There was yet another powerful group, led by the immensely rich Duke of Bedford, who thought it high time for the old Whigs to retire, and let them enjoy the rich pastures of court patronage.

The King's intentions, of course, were known to all these groups in 1760. His aversion to Newcastle and to Chatham, whom he labeled "the blackest of hearts," was common court gossip. And after all, he was a young king with old ministers; many time-serving politicians thought that it might be wise to trim their sails and wait for the new breeze, from whatever quarter it might blow. Of course the old

Whigs, and even Chatham, realized they had to accept Bute and somehow or other please the King, if they were to survive. They soon had the measure of Bute. He lacked a personal following, felt unequal to the supreme task of ruling the country and running the war. His dependable allies in the House of Commons were few. He faltered; he hesitated; he failed to force a showdown and kick out the old Whigs. True, Chatham resigned in a huff because, knowing the King's pacific sentiments, the Cabinet refused to go along with him and declare war on Spain and seize her trade. Instead, as Chatham forecast, Spain declared war on England.

But Chatham gone did little to strengthen Bute. By the end of January, 1763, the consummate skill of those hoary old politicians Newcastle and Hardwicke had so undermined Bute's confidence that he was little better than a nervous wreck. He told George III that even the Angel Gabriel would find it difficult to govern England; that his own life was rendered intolerable by infamous scenes and blackened by ingratitude and that he felt himself on the brink of a precipice. George III was too young, too inept, too unpracticed in the arts of politics to help Bute, and so Bute resigned. George III tried to keep him as a private and secret adviser; the politicians would not let him. They grumbled, they nagged, they bullied. The King had to face his future on his own.

He was most reluctant to do so. Although peace had been achieved in 1763—he had ardently desired this—he soon found himself in the thick of problems which he felt too vast for his poor comprehension. Yet he knew that the fate of his people and his Empire was *his* responsibility to God. He felt so young, so hopeless, so desperately in need of help for someone who thought as he did on men and affairs yet was strong enough to force his will on the warring political factions. Although the old Whig empire had broken up under the strain of Chatham's resignation and the Treaty of Paris, yet the King found no stability. The King's necessity drove him back to Chatham. Chatham prided himself on being above party. The King's need, the nation's need, required men of ability, not politicians; sentiments that thrilled George III. But unfortunately Chatham's mental health was far from good, and no sooner had he become Prime Minister than the strain of office sent him off his head. He shut himself up, would speak to no one, and had his meals served through a trap door. The King waited and waited for him to recover for two long years, during which a leaderless ministry drove his country nearer to ruin. Chatham recovered only to resign and became a passionate supporter of the American cause and so, once more, the object of George III's hate. The ministries that followed earned neither the country's confidence nor the King's.

Thus the first ten years of George III's reign passed in political chaos; slowly, however, he learned the devious ways of politics, the price of men, and above all the necessity for a man who could manage the Commons in *his* interest. In 1770 he discovered Lord North, the eldest son of the Earl of Guilford; North, whose association with the

King was to prove so disastrous for England and so fortunate for America, was an odd character. An excellent administrator, a witty and practiced debater, full of good humor and charm, he always pleased and soothed the members of the Commons; nevertheless his soft, fat, rounded body and full, piglike face bespoke an indolence that bordered on disease, a physical incapacity that made his laborious days an intolerable burden on his spirit. Time and time again he begged the King to release him from office. The King would not, for North reverenced as he did the mystical power of monarchy and thought as he did on the two grave political problems which vexed his country—Wilkes and America.

Without North, he could see only ruin for himself and his people. The constantly changing ministries and the bitter factional strife of George III's first ten years had bedeviled both problems. John Wilkes, wit, libertine, master tactician, raised fundamental issues concerning the liberty of the British subject. None of the cases in which he was involved was clear-cut; in each the ministerial cause was handled with massive ineptitude. Wilkes divided the Whig groups in Parliament as effectively as he united the discontented in London. George hated "that devil Wilkes," and let this hatred be known to all and sundry. Thus Wilkes's supporters could talk of royal despotism and get others to believe them. In America Wilkes's name became a byword for liberty and for resistance to royal tyranny from Boston down the seaboard to Charleston.

America proved a graver problem than Wilkes; and the effect of ministerial changes far worse. After the great war with France which, through the Treaty of Paris, deprived her of Canada, the majority of Englishmen, and, indeed, many colonists, felt that some of the expenses of the conflict should be borne by the Americans. Each ministry from 1760–70 differed in its views as to how this should be done, and each had a separate solution for assuaging the bitterness aroused in the Americans by the inept attempts to get revenue. Acts passed by

George III's closest adviser, Frederick Lord North, from a mezzotint published in 1775.

one ministry were repealed by its successor, and party maneuver became more important than the fate of America. Nor was it the question of revenue alone that infuriated the colonists—the British constantly betrayed their ignorance of American needs and American aspirations. They tried to restrict settlement beyond the Allegheny Mountains, took Indian affairs into their own hands, attempted to suppress paper currency, renovated oppressive customs laws, and restricted trade with the West Indies. No Englishman realized that the American colonies were moving toward a rapid expansion in trade, wealth, and power, just as no American could conceive of the huge expense of war that arose from Britain's vast imperial connections.

By the late 1760's, hope for compromise was probably a delusive dream of men of good will such as Chatham and Franklin. But whether it had a chance or not, there can be no doubt that the known attitude of the King made matters worse. George III revered, naturally enough, the concept of kingship. Kings were God's immediate servants. Their duties were clear—to pass on all the rights, obligations, powers, territories, undiminished, to their heirs. The constitution was sacrosanct and unchangeable. And so absolutely did George III identify himself with the English Crown that any criticism of monarchical powers, any suggestion of reform or change, he regarded as a personal affront.

The King was so stupid that he could not distinguish between himself as a person and his constitutional position as ruler. Although he accepted the American policies—either of compromise or coercion—with which his ministers presented him, placing his signature first on the Stamp Act and then on its repeal, his heart was always with the physical-force party, and he moved with uttermost reluctance to the idea of compromise, which, he thought, would infuriate as well as ruin Britain.* Those politicians, therefore, who were prepared to bring the "American rebels," as the King called them, to their senses were the recipients of his warmhearted loyalty and devotion. In the small world of English political society, the King's views did not go for nothing. He was the fountain of patronage, the ultimate executive authority, the man who could make and break ministers and ministries. In consequence, the King's attitude began to polarize new attitudes in politics. He became the symbol of conservatism and reaction; his opponents, the men who thought that the liberties for which Wilkes and the Americans fought were essential, too, for all Englishmen, began to take a more radical attitude not only to the

---

* As may be seen from his letter to North of January 31, 1776: "You will remember that before the recess, I strongly advised you not to bind yourself to bring forward a proposition for restoring tranquillity to North America, not from any absurd ideas of unconditional submission my mind never harboured; but from foreseeing that whatever can be proposed, will be liable, not to bring America back to a sense of attachment to the Mother Country, yet to dissatisfy this Country, which has in the most handsome manner cheerfully carried on the contest, and therefore has a right to have the struggle continued, until convinced that it is in vain."

Crown but also to the very structure of English society. Naturally, the first effect of this was to disrupt the old political alignments; Whiggery began to break up into two groups, a right and a left wing; the Tories, who had been in opposition since 1714, now felt that they could support George III body and soul. It took many years for these new forces to push their way through into public consciousness, redefined, but George III's own personality—his meddling interference and his blind, obstinate conservatism—sharpened many men's intention to reduce the powers of the Crown even further.

The first twenty years of George III's reign were a public and a personal failure. He had done his duty conscientiously. He had tried, according to his lights, to put the government in the hands of tried and able men. The ills which assailed his country, he sincerely believed, were not of his making. Scarcely a man pitied him; the majority thought he had only himself to blame when disaster came. Yorktown ended his hopes that the tide might turn, and finished North.

During the long years of British defeat, the Old Corps of Whigs, now led by the Marquis of Rockingham, had developed a new view of the role of kingship; and their great publicist and philosopher, Edmund Burke, had persuasively pleaded for a new attitude to party and to politics. When, at last, the failures in America led the independent members of the Commons to desert North, and thereby compelled the King to send for Rockingham to take over the reins of government, George found Rockingham's terms hard to accept: freedom for America, peace with France, and hardest of all, no say in the appointment of his ministers, which he regarded as the darling prerogative of the Crown.

The King, despite himself, now had to accept what the Whigs offered him—a revolutionary action that cut at the root of royal power. He had been broken by forces that his poor brain could not understand. And, perhaps not without justice, he was held to blame for England's defeat in America by contemporaries in both countries, and by generations of historians, though justice would also demand that the shortsighted, quarrelsome, ignorant, power-seeking politicians who had made policy toward America as changeable as the British climate should be held equally responsible. We, at least, can feel pity for him —ignorant, stupid, conscientious, prejudiced, a victim of his own inadequate temperament. . . .

His motives were honorable; he gave all of his pitifully small abilities to the defense of what he thought to be the vital interests and essential rights of the British nation. Had he been as wise as Solomon, Britain and America would have gone their separate ways. The forces that crushed him would have crushed greater men. As it is, he remained a pathetic figure of tragicomedy; and, as the years passed, he acquired even a certain grandeur. There had been many worse kings to exercise rule over America and Britain. If he is to be blamed, it must be not for what he did but for what he was—an unbalanced man of low intelligence. And if he is to be praised, it is because he attempted to discharge honorably tasks that were beyond his powers.

Richard B. Morris

James Otis and the Writs of Assistance

Professor Richard B. Morris of Columbia University, author of this essay on the paradoxical figure James Otis and his fight against the British policy of issuing general search warrants in the years before the Revolution, is particularly well qualified to deal with this difficult and technical subject. He has devoted his scholarly life to the era of the Revolution and to American legal history. His many works include The Peacemakers, *a dramatic account of the negotiations that produced the Treaty of Paris ending the Revolution, and* Government and Labor in Early America, *a study of the laws regulating labor and working conditions during the colonial era.*

Besides describing a difficult subject and a complex man clearly, Morris' essay also demonstrates how effective history can be in throwing light on later events and current problems. He shows—always keeping the nuances of the question in mind—how the conflict between the rights of the individual and the rights of government (which represents the collective rights of all citizens) always exists in a state of dynamic tension. With fine balance he explains not only why Americans objected to the writs of assistance but also why, from the British viewpoint, such writs seemed perfectly reasonable. In addition, he delineates the relationship between this controversy and present-day arguments over the legitimacy of wire tapping and other "bugging" devices.

*F*ew freedoms are more fundamental to our way of life—and few so clearly differentiate our democracy from the rival system which seeks to bury it—than the freedom from the midnight knock on the door, from the arbitrary invasion of a man's home by soldiery or police. Enshrined in the Fourth Amendment to the Constitution, the right is nevertheless still a matter of contention: almost every year that passes sees cases based upon it coming before the United States Supreme Court. Given the almost inevitable conflict between the legitimate demands of civil authority and the equally legitimate demands of individual freedom, it is likely that the controversy will be always with us.

What one famous Supreme Court justice called "the right most valued by civilized man," the right to be let alone, is a venerable one in America: long before the Revolution, violation of it by representatives of the king rankled deeply in the hearts of his American subjects; it was, indeed, one of the major reasons they eventually decided they could no longer serve him.

The issue was first expounded in the course of an extraordinary forensic argument made in the year 1761 before five scarlet-robed judges in the council chamber of the Town-house in Boston. The speaker was James Otis, Jr., then thirty-six years old, born in nearby West Barnstable and considered the ablest young lawyer at the Boston bar.

His plea for the right of privacy was at once significant and poignant. It was significant because without the burning moral issue thus precipitated, it might have been possible for the cynical to dismiss the forthcoming Revolution as a mere squabble between colonies and mother country over taxation. The poignancy of Otis' plea derives from the brilliant young lawyer's subsequent curious conduct: while many of his friends became leaders in the fight for independence, he followed a mysterious zigzag course that unfortunately, in the eyes of some of his contemporaries, cast doubt upon his loyalty to the cause of freedom.

The specific occasion of Otis' appearance was an application to the Superior Court of Massachusetts Bay by Charles Paxton, Surveyor of Customs for the Port of Boston, for writs of assistance. These were general warrants which, as they were commonly interpreted, empowered customs officers under police protection arbitrarily to enter—if necessary, to break into—warehouses, stores, or homes to search for smuggled goods. The intruders were not even required to present any grounds for suspecting the presence of the illicit items. Such writs had been authorized in England—where they were issued by the Court of Exchequer—since the time of Charles II, but nothing like them had been used in the colonies prior to the French and Indian War. The only writs theretofore procurable had been specific search warrants issued by the regular common-law courts; but these had authorized search only in places specified in the warrants and only upon specific information, supported by oath, that smuggled goods were hidden there. True, an act of King William III regulating colonial trade had given the customs officers in America the same rights of search as their opposite numbers in England enjoyed. But it was a new question whether the royal order extended to colonial courts the same authority to issue the writs that the Court of Exchequer exercised in the mother country.

During the final phase of the Second Hundred Years' War between Britain and France, however, writs of assistance had been issued in Massachusetts to facilitate the feverish if futile efforts of customs officers to stamp out illegal trade between the colonists and the enemy— in Canada and the French West Indies. These writs had been issued in the name of King George II, but that monarch died in October, 1760, and his grandson succeeded to the throne as George III. According to law, the old writs expired six months after the death of a sovereign, and new ones had to be issued in the name of his successor. Now, in February of 1761, while the issue hung in the balance—George III would not be crowned until September—Surveyor Paxton's case came to trial.

Sixty-three prominent Boston merchants joined to oppose him, retaining the brilliant, impassioned, unstable Otis—and his amiable and temperate associate, Oxenbridge Thacher—to represent them. In order to take their case, Otis resigned his office as Advocate General of the Vice-Admiralty Court, in which capacity he would have been expected to represent the Crown and present the other side of the argument. That task was now assigned to Jeremiah Gridley, a leader of the Boston bar, who appeared as counsel for the customs officers.

Behind Otis' resignation lay deep personal animosities that added drama to the legal battle. Not long before, the chief justiceship of the Superior Court—which would hear the arguments on the writs of assistance and render a decision—had fallen vacant. William Shirley, then governor of the colony, had promised the post to Otis' father, but Shirley's successor, Francis Bernard, had ignored the commitment and instead named his lieutenant governor, Thomas Hutchinson. Already the target of colonists who resented his nepotistic use of the lieutenant governorship, Hutchinson now earned additional criticism for holding two offices at the same time. And his appointment of course precipitated a feud with the influential Otises; young James, according to rumor, declared "he would set the province in flames, if he perished by the fire."

Nevertheless Hutchinson, attired in his new judicial robes, took his seat in the great Town-house council chamber as the trial opened on February 24. With him on the bench were Justices Lynde, Cushing, Oliver, and Russell. Gridley opened for the Crown. He argued that such general writs were being issued in England by the Court of Exchequer, which had the statutory authority to issue them; the province law of 1699, he continued, had granted the Superior Court jurisdiction in Massachusetts "generally" over matters which the courts of King's Bench, Common Pleas, and Exchequer "have or ought to have."

Thacher replied first. Addressing himself largely to technical issues, he denied that the Superior Court could exercise the right of the Court of Exchequer in England to issue such writs. Then Otis arose to speak. One contemporary critic described him as "a plump, round-faced, smooth skinned, short-necked, eagle-eyed politician,'' but to John Adams—who attended the trial, reported it in his diary, and was to write an account of it more than fifty years later—''Otis was a flame of fire.''

He had prepared his argument with care. Although his oration covered some four or five hours and was not taken down stenographically, it left on Adams an indelible impression. With a "profusion of legal authorities," Adams tells us, "a prophetic glance of his eye into futurity, and a torrent of impetuous eloquence, he hurried away every thing before him." Adams continued: "Every man of a crowded audience appeared to me to go away, as I did, ready to take arms against writs of assistance." And he concluded: "Then and there the child Independence was born."

More important than the electrifying effect of Otis' argument upon his auditors was its revolutionary tenor. Anticipating ideas that would be set forth in the Declaration of Independence fifteen years later, Otis argued that the rights to life, liberty, and property were derived from nature and implied the guarantee of privacy, without which individual liberty could not survive. (Venturing beyond the immediate issue, Otis declared that liberty should be granted to all men regardless of color—an abolitionist note that startled even the sympathetic Adams.)

Relying on English lawbooks to prove that only special warrants were legal, Otis attacked the writs as "instruments of slavery," which he swore to oppose to his dying day with all the powers and faculties God had given him. Defending the right of privacy, he pointed out that the power to issue general search warrants placed "the. liberty of every man in the hands of every petty officer." The freedom of one's house, he contended, was "one of the most essential branches of English liberty." In perhaps his most moving passage he was reported to have declared:

A man's house is his castle, and whilst he is quiet he is as well guarded as a prince in his castle. This writ, if it should be declared legal, would totally annihilate this privilege. Customhouse officers may enter our houses when they please; we are commanded to permit their entry. Their menial servants may enter, may break locks, bars, and everything in their way; and whether they break through malice or revenge, no man, no court, can inquire. Bare suspicion without oath is sufficient. This wanton exercise of this power is not a chimerical suggestion of a heated brain. . . . What a scene does this open! Every man, prompted by revenge, ill humor, or wantonness to inspect the inside of his neighbor's house, may get a writ of assistance. Others will ask it from self-defense; one arbitrary exertion will provoke another, until society be involved in tumult and blood.

With remarkable prescience Otis' words captured the mood of the midnight visitation by totalitarian police which would terrify a later era less sensitive to individual freedom.

At right is Joseph Blackburn's portrait of the brilliant but unstable attorney James Otis.

Otis then proceeded to denounce the Navigation Acts, which had regulated the trade of the empire since the time of Cromwell, exposing their nuisance aspects with great wit. By implication he acknowledged the widespread existence of smuggling, and went so far as to contend that "if the King of Great Britain in person were encamped on Boston Common, at the head of twenty thousand men, with all his navy on our coast, he would not be able to execute these laws. They would be resisted or eluded." Turning to the similarly unenforceable Molasses Act, passed by Parliament in 1733 to protect the British West Indies planters from the competition of the foreign West Indies, he charged that the law was enacted "by a foreign legislature, without our consent, and by a legislature who had no feeling for us, and whose interest prompted them to tax us to the quick."

The nub of Otis' argument was that, even if the writs of assistance had been authorized by an Act of Parliament, "an act against the Constitution is void. An act against natural equity is void; and if an act of Parliament should be made, in the very words of this petition, it would be void. The executive courts* must pass such acts into disuse." This contention—that Parliament was not omnipotent and could be restrained by the unwritten Constitution and a higher law—was a notion soon to be pushed further by John Adams and other members of the Massachusetts bar: the argument became familiar in the colonies well before the Declaration of Independence was adopted.

Measured by its effect on its auditors and its immediate impact on the majority of the court, Otis' speech ranks among the most memorable in American history, alongside Patrick Henry's fiery oration protest-

---

* By "executive courts" he meant the regular courts of law as distinguished from the Massachusetts legislature, known as the General Court. Otis' argument presaged a special and unique role for the United States Supreme Court, the exercise of the power to declare laws unconstitutional.

This portrait of Chief Justice Thomas Hutchinson is attributed to John Singleton Copley.

ing the Stamp Act, Fisher Ames' memorable defense of Jay's Treaty in the House of Representatives, and Daniel Webster's classic reply to Hayne. Had a decision been rendered on the spot, Otis and Thacher would have won, for all the judges save Thomas Hutchinson were against the writs; even from *his* opinion, carefully worded, opponents of the writs could take comfort: "The Court has considered the subject of writs of assistance," the chief justice announced, "and can see no foundation for such a writ: but as the practice in England is not known [owing to the interregnum], it has been thought best to continue the question to the next term, and that in the meantime opportunity may be given to know the result." But the crafty chief justice, aware that he stood alone among his colleagues, was merely buying precious time.

Another hearing was held in November, 1761. This time Robert Auchmuty joined Gridley in defense of the writs. The arguments lasted "the whole day and evening," covering much the same ground as the previous hearing. But the court had now before it information that under the new monarch, George III, writs of assistance were being issued in the mother country by the Court of Exchequer; the Massachusetts judges accordingly felt that they could no longer refuse to issue them too. Writing years later, John Adams recounted that "the Court clandestinely granted them."

Thomas Hutchinson had won a pyrrhic victory. It was he who had talked the rest of the court into agreeing to a delay to learn what the English practice was and he who was chiefly responsible for granting the writs. He was to pay dearly in personal popularity. Moreover, at the younger Otis' prompting, the legislature manifested its displeasure with the decision not only by reducing the salary of the judges of the Superior Court, but by cutting out entirely Hutchinson's allowance as chief justice. And that was only the beginning. During the riots in Boston in 1765 over the passage of the Stamp Act, Hutchinson's mansion was sacked and his library and papers scattered—out of revenge, Governor Bernard claimed, for his connection with the writs. Henceforward, Hutchinson was to be the leader of the Court party and a frank advocate of coercion to secure colonial obedience to Parliament.

As for James Otis, his initial attack upon the writs had made him the darling of the populace of Boston and the leader of the radical party. Taking the issue to the people at once—in May of 1761—he won election to the Massachusetts General Court. When the news of it reached Worcester, Brigadier Timothy Ruggles, then chief justice of the common pleas court and later a Tory exile, declared at a dinner party in John Adams' presence, "Out of this election will arise a damned faction, which will shake this province to its foundation."

Ruggles' gloomy forebodings proved even more accurate than he could have expected, for the year 1761 triggered the Revolutionary movement, and the Otises, father and son, set off the chain reaction. That same year the father was re-elected Speaker of the House. Together they succeeded in pushing through an act forbidding the courts to issue any writ that did not specify under oath the person and place to be searched. On the advice of the justices of the Superior Court, Governor Bernard refused to approve the legislation; overoptimistically he stigmatized it as a "last effort of the confederacy against the customhouse and laws of trade."

The constitutional views which Otis first expounded in the writs of assistance case were given more elaborate formulation in a forceful political tract, "A Vindication of the Conduct of the House of Representatives," which he published in 1762. Therein he enunciated the Whig view that all men are naturally equal, and that kings are made to serve the people, not people the ends of kings.

It would be gratifying to report that the man who had made a political career out of his opposition to the writs was in the forefront of the Revolution when the fighting actually got under way. Regrettably, he was not. Quick-tempered and tense, increasingly eccentric and even abusive, Otis simply was not cast in the heroic mold. Whether from self-interest, fear, expediency, irresponsibility, or family friction (his wife was a high Tory and a shrew), or from a combination of all five, Otis now followed a vacillating course that branded him a recreant to his own principles, loathed by his foes, deserted by his followers.

It all started with what looked suspiciously like a deal. In 1764 Governor Bernard appointed Otis Senior chief justice of the Court of Common Pleas and judge of probate in Barnstable County. In that same year the son issued his "Rights of the British Colonies Asserted and Proved," the most influential American pamphlet published prior to John Dickinson's "Letters from a Farmer in Pennsylvania." Written in opposition to the Sugar Act, Otis' tract took the position that Parliament had no right to tax the colonies and that taxation was "absolutely irreconcilable" with the rights of the colonists as British subjects—indeed, as human beings. Nevertheless, it gave comfort to the Court party by affirming the subordination of the colonies to Great Britain and the right of Parliament to legislate for them in matters other than taxation. Hailed by the Whigs in England, the pamphlet elicited a grudging compliment from Lord Mansfield, who quickly pounced on Otis' concession of the supremacy of the Crown. When someone said that Otis was mad, Mansfield rejoiced that in all popular assemblies "madness is catching." The evidence that the younger Otis' more conciliatory tone was the *quid pro quo* for his father's appointment is at best circumstantial, but informed people felt that the connection was obvious.

Otis pursued his irresolute, even self-contradictory course during the Stamp Act controversy. In his "Vindication of the British Colonies" he reversed his earlier position: Parliament *did* have the authority to impose taxes, he said, though he questioned whether the taxes imposed were fair. In two subsequent tracts he again shifted his ground. Arguing against the writs of assistance, he had decried laws enacted "by a foreign legislature, without our consent." Now he even accepted the theory of "virtual representation"—the fiction that the colonies were virtually represented in Parliament, in the sense that the interests of all Englishmen were theoretically represented by the whole body of Parliament—though propertyless subjects could not vote, though many Members represented "rotten boroughs," and though many English cities had no Member at all. "Representation," Otis conceded, "is now no longer a matter of right but of indulgence only." But in the second tract he swung completely around again, denied the right of taxation without representation, and demanded actual representation in Parliament.

Considering his erratic and equivocal wanderings, it is little wonder that when Otis ran again for the House he was attacked in a bit of doggerel appearing in the Boston *Evening Post* and attributed to a customs official not noted for his sobriety:

> *So Jemmy rail'd at* upper folks *while Jemmy's Dad was out,*
> *But Jemmy's Dad has now* a place, *so Jemmy's turn'd about....*
> *And Jemmy is a silly dog, and Jemmy is a tool,*
> *And Jemmy is a stupid cur, and Jemmy is a fool....*

The attack outraged the voters' sense of decency and "Jemmy" was elected to the House by a small majority. When he had thought himself ruined, Otis ruefully admitted, "the song of a drunkard saved me."

Sent as a Massachusetts delegate to the Stamp Act Congress in New York in 1765, Otis had the satisfaction of seeing his constitutional doctrine of no taxation without representation embodied in the Resolves adopted by that body. But the radical leaders refused to incorporate his demand for actual representation of the colonies in the House of Commons. Most of them were wary of a trap, for a grant of token representation to the colonies could not have checked the anti-colonial course of the majority in Parliament.

Although far more moderate on the Stamp Act issue than either Patrick Henry or Daniel Dulany, Otis plucked up his courage and under the pseudonym "John Hampden" published in the Boston press a sweeping denial of Parliament's right to tax the colonies. But by now his waverings had placed him under suspicion. Forced to defend himself at a Boston town meeting held in the spring of 1766, and to deny charges that his behavior was the result of "weak nerves" or "cowardice," he offered to meet George Grenville in single combat on the floor of Faneuil Hall to settle the whole issue. Again returned to the House with his popularity temporarily restored, Jemmy was humiliated when Governor Bernard vetoed his selection by his colleagues as Speaker as simply "impossible." Thenceforward for several years he collaborated with Sam Adams in directing the radical party in the House.

In February, 1768, Sam Adams drew up a circular letter denouncing Lord Townshend's external tax measures—import duties on such items as glass, lead, paper, and tea—enacted by Parliament. Lord Hillsborough, Secretary of State for the colonies, promptly denounced Adams' letter, ordered the Massachusetts legislature to rescind it, and instructed the colonial governors that the assemblies of other colonies be prevented, by dissolution if necessary, from endorsing it. Otis launched into an abusive two-hour tirade against Hillsborough, ridiculing king's ministers who, like Hillsborough, had been educated by travel on the European continent as "the very frippery and foppery of France, the mere outside of monkeys." Although he withheld criticism of George III, he delivered an encomium on Oliver Cromwell and defended the execution of Charles I. That same year, following the arrival in Boston of two regiments of redcoats, Otis wrote to an English correspondent:

> You may ruin yourselves, but you cannot in the end ruin the colonies. Our fathers were a good people. We have been a free people, and if you will not let us remain so any longer, we shall be a great people, and the present measures can have no tendency but to hasten [with] great rapidity, events which every good and honest man would wish delayed for ages, if possible, prevented forever.

Unfortunately for his continued effectiveness as a political leader, no checkrein could be placed on Otis' abusive conduct toward others. "If Bedlamism is a talent, he has it in perfection," commented Tory Judge Peter Oliver, and even friendly critics agreed that Otis was unbalanced. The dispatch of troops to Boston heightened tempers. In 1769 Otis got into a coffeehouse brawl with John Robinson, a customs official. It is charitable to conclude that the caning he received accelerated his mental disintegration. In any event, two years later his family and friends requested he be examined by a sanity commission; as judge of probate, his old foe, Hutchinson, had the satisfaction of appointing its members, who found Otis to be a lunatic. Although he had intermittent lucid spells thereafter, he played no role at all during the Revolution. Instead, it was his brother Joseph who fought at Bunker Hill. James' death was appropriately dramatic. On May 23, 1783, he was standing in the doorway of a farmhouse in Andover when he was struck down by lightning. "He has been good as his word," commented Hutchinson. "Set the province in a flame and perished in the attempt."

A whole generation passed before John Adams, in a series of letters to the newspapers in 1818, established the legend of James Otis' heroic role. Even Virginians came to speak reverently of the "god-like Otis," and perhaps it is only fitting that he should be judged by his most brilliant and seminal achievement rather than by the sadder years when darkness fell upon him. It is only proper, too, that we recognize the writs of assistance case for what it was in fact—first of a series of crises which culminated at Lexington and Concord.

The attack against the writs, initiated by Otis, developed into a notable series of legal battles, fought not only in Massachusetts but throughout the colonies. Local justices of the peace in the Bay Colony refused in 1765 to grant them on the ground that they were repugnant to the common law. They continued to be issued by that province's Superior Court, but individuals sometimes managed to defy them: in 1766 a merchant named Daniel Malcolm, presumably on the advice if not the instigation of Otis, refused to admit the customs officials into part of his cellar, even though they were armed with writs of assistance, and warned them that he would take legal action against them if they entered. The customs men backed down.

Meantime opposition to the writs was spreading to other colonies. In 1766 the customs collector of New London, Connecticut, sought legal advice as to his power of search and seizure, but the judges at New Haven felt that in the absence of a colonial statute they could make no determination. The collector referred the matter to the Commissioner of Customs in England, who in turn asked the advice of Attorney General William de Grey. His opinion came as a shock to the customs officials, for he found that the Courts of Exchequer in England "do not send their Processes into the Plantations, nor is there any Process in the plantations that corresponds with the description in the act of K[ing] W[illiam]."

Aware that the ground was now cut from under them, the Lords of Treasury saw to it that the Townshend Acts passed in 1767 contained a clause specifically authorizing superior or supreme courts in the colonies to grant writs of assistance. Significantly, the American Board of Commissioners of Customs set up under the act sought between 1767 and 1773 to obtain writs in each of the thirteen colonies, but succeeded fully only in Massachusetts and New Hampshire. But as late as 1772 charges were made in Boston that "our houses and even our bed chambers are exposed to be ransacked, our boxes, chests, and trunks broke open, ravaged and plundered by wretches, whom no prudent man would venture to employ even as menial servants."

In other colonies the issue was stubbornly fought out in the courts. New York's Supreme Court granted the writs when the customs officers first applied for them in 1768, though not in the form the applications demanded; finally, the court flatly refused to issue the writs at all. In Pennsylvania the Tory Chief Justice, William Allen, refused also on the ground that it would be "of dangerous consequence and was not warranted by law." The writs were denied, too, in every southern colony save South Carolina, which finally capitulated and issued them in 1773. Significantly, the courts, though often manned by royal appointees, based their denials on the grounds advanced by Otis in the original Paxton case, going so far as to stigmatize the writs as unconstitutional.

What is important to remember throughout the controversy in which Otis played so large a part is that the colonists were seeking to define personal liberties—freedom of speech, the press, and religion—which even in England, right up to the eve of the American Revolution, were not firmly enshrined in law. Indeed, the issues of whether a person could be arrested under a general warrant or committed to prison on any charge by a privy councillor were not settled until the 1760's. Then Lord Camden took a strong stand for freedom from police intrusion. Less dramatically perhaps than in the colonies, similar issues of civil liberties were being thrashed out in the mother country, but in the colonies this struggle laid the groundwork upon which the new Revolutionary states, and later the federal government, built their safeguards for civil liberties.

In Virginia, where the issue was contested most bitterly, writs of assistance were condemned in the Bill of Rights of June 12, 1776, as "grievous and oppressive." Condemnation was also reflected in the clauses in the Declaration of Independence denouncing the King because he had made judges dependent for their tenure and their salaries upon his will alone. Five other states soon followed Virginia in outlawing the writs. Of these, Massachusetts in her constitution of 1780 provided the most explicit safeguards. The relevant section of the state constitution, notable because it served as the basis for Madison's later incorporation of such a guarantee in the federal Bill of Rights, reads as follows:

> XIV. Every subject has a right to be secure from all unreasonable searches and seizures of his person, his houses, his papers and all his possessions. All warrants, therefore, are contrary to this right, if the cause or foundation of them be not previously supported by oath or affirmation; and if the order in the warrant to a civil officer, to make search in suspected places, or to arrest one or more suspected persons, or to seize their property, be not accompanied with a special designation of the persons or objects of search, arrest, or seizure; and no warrant ought to be issued but in cases, and with the formalities prescribed by the laws.

John Adams, who wrote that constitution, had remembered his lessons very well indeed.

More succinctly than the guarantee in the Massachusetts constitution, the Fourth Amendment to the federal Constitution affirmed "the right of the people to be secure in their persons, houses, papers, and effects, against unreasonable searches and seizures," and declared that "no warrants shall issue, but upon probable cause, supported by oath or affirmation, and particularly describing the place to be searched, and the persons or things to be seized."

In our own day, several members of a Supreme Court heavily preoccupied with safeguarding personal liberty have conspicuously defended the guarantees in the Fourth Amendment. It was the late Justice Louis Brandeis who, in his dissenting opinion in a wire-tapping decision of 1928 (*Olmstead v. U.S.*) opposing police intrusion without a search warrant, championed "the right to be let alone—the most comprehensive of rights and the right most valued by civilized man. . . . To protect that right," he asserted, "every unjustifiable intrusion by the Government upon the privacy of the individual, whatever the means employed, must be deemed a violation of the Fourth Amendment."

More recently Justice Felix Frankfurter has opposed searches conducted as an incident to a warrant of arrest. In a notable dissent (*Harris v. U.S.*, 1946) he pointed out that the decision turned "on whether one gives the [Fourth] Amendment a place second to none in the Bill of Rights, or considers it on the whole a kind of nuisance, a serious impediment in the war against crime. . . . How can there be freedom of thought or freedom of speech or freedom of religion," he asked, "if the police can, without warrant, search your house and mine from garret to cellar merely because they are executing a warrant of arrest?" He went on to warn: "Yesterday the justifying document was an illicit ration book, tomorrow it may be some suspect piece of literature." Again, in a more recent case (*United States v. Rabinowitz*, 1950), Justice Frankfurter dissented from a decision authorizing federal officers to seize forged postage stamps without search warrant but as an incident to arrest. He said pointedly:

It makes all the difference in the world whether one recognizes the central fact about the Fourth Amendment, namely, that it was a safeguard against recurrence of abuses so deeply felt by the Colonies as to be one of the potent causes of the Revolution, or whether one thinks of it as merely a requirement for a piece of paper.*

Once it was a powerful monarch concerned about securing every shilling of customs revenue. Today it is a great republic legitimately concerned about the nation's security. Once it was the knock on the door. Today it is wire tapping or other electronic devices. The circumstances and techniques may differ; the issue remains the same.

* In 1957 Mrs. Dollree Mapp of Cleveland, Ohio, was arrested for possessing obscene literature seized in her home by police, apparently without a warrant. Her subsequent conviction was upheld by two state appeal courts, but on June 19, 1961, the Supreme Court reversed the conviction, declaring that evidence obtained by search and seizure in violation of the Fourth Amendment is inadmissible in a state court, as it is in a Federal court. But, in the case of Burton N. Pugach of New York City, accused of conspiring to maim the girl who had rejected him, the Supreme Court on February 27, 1961, had upheld the right of state officials and state courts to use evidence obtained by wire tapping, which many feel also violates a citizen's privacy. So the historic conflict between private right and the public good goes on.

Robert Cecil

Reflections on the American Revolution

Every nation tends to see history too much from its own perspective—to employ its past as a device for building national pride. Americans, being a relatively young people lacking in ancient traditions, have been particularly prone to using their history in this way, making up in intensity for what they lack in volume. The relative success of the United States in the world—seen in its rapid expansion, general prosperity, and widely admired institutions—has further encouraged this tendency to see American history from within, and as an unbroken series of righteous triumphs. There is nothing wrong in being proud of one's national past, but of course self-congratulation should not be the only or even the chief purpose for studying history. The best perspective comes from looking at history from many points of view, thus approaching truth by a kind of triangulation.

English diplomat Robert Cecil's reflections on the American Revolution and its aftermath provide an excellent example of the value of such an approach. While Cecil clearly admires America and believes the Revolution to have been necessary and proper, he treats the subject dispassionately and at the same time offers explanations of the British position that add to our overall understanding of what happened and why it occurred.

*I*n one way an Englishman's view of the Revolutionary War does not greatly differ from an American's. Our historians, in the main, agree with yours that the American colonies were lost through the mistakes and obstinacy of George III and Lord North and that the whole episode, whether regarded politically or militarily, is one of the most depressing in British history.

It is at this point that the historians, and even more the ordinary readers, tend to part company. The Englishman, if he overcomes his reluctance to study the period at all, looks at it soberly and objectively and observes how hardly the imperial lesson was learned. Americans, on the other hand, very naturally regard the Revolution with the greatest enthusiasm as the starting point in a series of developments that led to the foundation of a federal republic unique in constitutional history, and to the remarkable political and economic expansion of the nineteenth century. The extraordinary later success of the United States, both in the economic and political sense, has to some extent led Americans to read their history backward and find in the Revolutionary War more signs and portents of a splendid future than were at that time apparent. This provides admirable material for July Fourth oratory, but stretches at places the fabric of history. After all, history is more than an ornamental garden, laid out with hindsight by teachers and historians; it is rather a jungle where living forces were once at work, and the reconstruction of this jungle is our real business if we wish to understand the past.

The first point that I want to suggest is that the conventional picture of the American colonists as a band of gallant pioneers oppressed by a tyrannous government in London is a true one only if looked at through the eyes of a nineteenth or twentieth century democrat. The eighteenth century could have no inkling that the course of history would dictate that colonies in general should become self-administering and finally independent; indeed it was the shock of the American Revolutionary War that first began to teach that lesson. The eighteenth century regarded colonies as existing for the benefit of the mother country, with which, of course, the well-being of the colonies themselves was identified. Adam Smith, no enemy of the colonists, was the classic proponent of this theory. It is sometimes overlooked that the mother country accepted restraints on her own trade or agriculture in the interests of the colony, even if these restraints were of a less onerous character. For example, tobacco growing, although possible, was forbidden in Britain. Foreign produce, which was shipped via Britain, was cheap in the colonies, as duty had been paid by the British taxpayer. Adam Smith commented: "Parliament, in attempting to exercise its supposed right of taxing the Colonies, has never hitherto demanded of them anything which even approached to a just proportion to what was paid by their fellow subjects at home." To this very day, the British subject in the United Kingdom pays taxes at a much higher rate than any resident of the modern British colonies pays to his local administration.

Take next the question of defense. I quote again from Adam

Smith: "If any of the provinces of the British Empire cannot be made to contribute towards the support of the whole Empire, it is surely time that Great Britain should free herself from the expense of defending those provinces in time of war . . ." The peace of 1763 had freed the colonists from the fear of attack by the French or Indians, and they naturally felt a greater degree of independence from the mother country. In Britain, however, the legacy of victory was a burden of debt and a strong feeling of dissatisfaction with the meager contribution, in men and money, that the colonists had made to their own defense. There was angry talk of contraband trade with the French in time of war. A particular grievance was that most colonies were reluctant even to provide adequate quarters for the British troops. This grievance had emerged even before the suspicion that the troops were more likely to be used against the colonists themselves.

When all this has been said, the fact remains that the British government acted with extraordinary stupidity. There was no settled policy of trying either to conciliate the colonists or to exert sufficient force to coerce them while it was still possible. The point I have tried to establish, however, is that the British acted within the framework of the accepted political and economic theory of the day and not out of some feeling of special animosity or desire to oppress the colonists. It is true that "no taxation without representation" was a political principle that many Britons had given their lives to affirm; but here again we are in danger of using hindsight in our interpretation of the word "representation."

England in the eighteenth century was not a democracy; it was an oligarchy, in which no practical politician, however liberal, seriously considered that all men had an equal right to elect the government that ostensibly represented them. A say in the government of the country was the privilege of those whose ownership of property and contribution to its greatness justified their claim. From this point of view a rotten borough in the hand of a great landowner was a way of ensuring that his contribution to the political and economic life of the nation received its due weight.

In the age of the Whig oligarchy and the rotten borough, there was little to convince Englishmen that the American colonists were being unjustly treated by not being represented at Westminster. It is clear to us today; it was a very debatable point in the eighteenth century. As a matter of fact, the colonists themselves, except the Pennsylvanians, did not take a very liberal view of the franchise for a good many years after the Revolutionary War. The British have never been strong on political theory; they could hardly be expected to realize that across the Atlantic the doctrine of John Locke and the Glorious Revolution of 1688 was believed more literally. Even less could they gaze into the future and divine that the course of the history of the next two centuries would vindicate the judgment of the American colonists. What they saw was a contumacious colony which paid less in taxes than they did, but would neither stand in arms to defend itself, nor pay for the mother country to do so.

Naturally the Americans objected to being taxed; we all do. They fought against the duties levied under the Sugar Act of 1764; the "non-importation" movement boycotted many English goods. The colonists objected even more strongly to an internal (that is, direct) tax, the Stamp Act of 1765, and justification for their position was found on constitutional grounds. The Townshend Acts then, in 1767, imposed a strong external (or indirect) tax, and this was resisted with equal, indeed memorable, vigor. What are we to say of the tea that was hurled into Boston Harbor? The tea had been exempted from the one shilling duty previously payable on transshipment in England and was taxed only threepence in the colonies. The same tea that cost an Englishman six shillings a pound cost the American only three. Yet John Adams wrote of the Boston Tea Party (1773): "Many persons wish that as many dead carcases were floating in the harbour as there are chests of tea." This is not the language of an oppressed people; it is the language of aggressive independence.

The plain fact is that the colonists believed (and events proved them right) that they were fully capable of managing their own affairs; they did not want any control, financial or otherwise. They were equally opposed to any restriction on the way in which they colonized the American continent. They had been made deeply apprehensive by the Royal Proclamation of 1763, which emphasized trade with the Indians and sought to protect them from the territorial encroachment of the whites. But the colonists themselves wished to colonize. Nobody had yet coined the phrase "manifest destiny," but the idea was there. If Britain was opposed, then freedom from Britain must be achieved.

This determination of the colonists to be free was scarcely under-

The Boston Tea Party was much resented by Britons, who paid a tax on tea double that paid by Americans.

stood in Britain; indeed their rapidly growing capacity to determine their own fate was lamentably underestimated in London. This explains the failure of the British government either to prepare for war or to make a settlement acceptable to the Americans. For it is probable that up to a very late hour a loose federation with George III as titular sovereign would have been acceptable to the Americans, provided that it carried with it full self-government.

Meanwhile the British made no serious preparation. In 1774, at a time when General Thomas Gage in Boston was asking for twenty thousand men, there were actually reductions both in the Army and Navy. In 1775, General William Howe and his brother Admiral Lord Howe were given the incompatible functions of Commissioners of Conciliation as well as commanders in chief. Inevitably the attack was not vigorously pressed for fear of prejudicing the conciliation; this at a time when George Washington was complaining of the spirit of the men under his command and the totally insufficient arrangements for supplying them. In 1776, Sir Guy Carleton with superior numbers trapped the American forces that had invaded Canada, but deliberately allowed them to escape, believing that a display of magnanimity might show them, as he put it, that "the way to mercy is not yet shut." Though the British were already making use of the Loyalists and the restless frontier Indians, who had long regarded the colonists as their principal enemy, the fighting continued to have some of the characteristics of a civil war; but this first phase was fast coming to an end. By July, 1776, German mercenaries were reaching New York in substantial numbers, and Jefferson, busy with his draft of the Declaration of Independence, referred with horror to their coming.

Meanwhile, in Paris, Silas Deane—and Benjamin Franklin not long after—was negotiating with the old enemy, the Catholic King of France. Lord Stormont, the British ambassador, had a shrewd idea of what was going on, but could not intervene openly. A steady stream of French, German, and Swiss volunteers was crossing in French vessels to the support of the American forces, while French loans and shipments of arms kept the new republic going during the desperate winters of 1776–77 and 1777–78, the winter of Valley Forge. That winter, even after the American forces that had taken part in the defeat of Burgoyne at Saratoga had joined Washington, the General estimated (in December, 1777) that he had only 8,200 fit men under his command. General Howe was unaccustomed, like all who learnt war in the European theater, to campaigning during the winter. He failed to realize that this was the decisive moment—before the French were finally committed to open intervention. Nothing was done and, in effect, the war was lost. It was lost because the limited, colonial war had become a renewal of the worldwide war with France that had merely been suspended in 1763. The French had used the interval to build up their fleet, and they were now able to concentrate it in Atlantic waters. Even before Spain with her Navy joined the Franco-American alliance in 1779, the British had virtually lost command

*The American army survived the bitter winter
at Valley Forge, depicted here in a nineteenth-
century bank note engraving, because of French
money as well as the superb leadership of
Washington and the determination of his troops.*

of the sea, and this was bound to prove fatal.

In the first place, it was proving more and more difficult to protect trade and transport men and supplies to the American theater of war. Before the official French intervention took place in 1778, the depredation of American privateers, operating mainly from French ports, had already cost Britain 560 ships and losses equivalent to more than £1,800,000 at rates then current. In 1777, stores that had left England in March did not reach Howe till the end of May, and the summer campaign did not begin till August. Secondly, for their mobility the British forces in America relied to a very great extent on transport by water. Only on rare occasions were they able to operate effectively more than fifteen miles from navigable water. Now all their movements were endangered. In 1778, when Clinton was evacuating Philadelphia, his entire army was almost intercepted at sea by a superior French fleet under D'Estaing. The sealing of Cornwallis' escape routes by the French fleet under De Grasse in 1781 was only the culmination. The capitulation of Yorktown that followed had been written on the wall three years before, for everyone but George III to see.

The retirement of General Howe in 1778 introduced a new handicap. While he was collaborating with his brother, Admiral Howe, relations between Army and Navy had been reasonably good. Afterward, however, old rivalries reasserted themselves. The British Navy was more interested in Rodney's operations in the Caribbean than in transport duty off the American coast. Howe's successor, General Clinton, quarreled with Admiral Marriot Arbuthnot, who had taken up command of the North American station in August, 1778. A British army officer bitterly observed of his brother naval officers: "They do not seem to think that saving the Army is an object of such material consequence." Cornwallis showed an incapacity for combined operations. Significantly enough, he later proved himself a capable general during the land struggle in India.

It is, of course, a truism that generals fight only as well as their opponents permit them to, and we must make every allowance for the genius of Washington, who not only kept his army together in the face of every difficulty but excelled in fighting the defensive war that circumstances imposed on him. He was one of the great leaders of irregular forces. Yet even so, the British generals were strangely inept. A contemporary commented: "This is an unpopular war and men of ability do not choose to risk their reputation." A shrewd contemporary observer regarded Benedict Arnold, in command of British forces, as superior to the *British* generals. The latter had been trained in the European school of set maneuver and siege warfare. Even their rigid discipline put them at the mercy of an irregular force, in which every man was his own company commander, if not his own colonel. The heavy equipment of the regulars immobilized them in the face of lightly equipped forces living off the land—their own land. The American terrain, thickly wooded and crisscrossed with streams and bogs, was unfamiliar to the British, and they failed notably to adapt themselves to it. Washington turned all these failings to good account.

What of the results of this internecine struggle? In the first place, of course, it welded the colonies into a union and equipped them with executive and legislative machinery and the means of defending themselves. This could have been accomplished so rapidly only under the pressure of war. The United States were now free not only to expand their commerce with any part of the world, but to populate the rich lands beyond the Alleghenies. In spite of a generous peace (1783), which astonished the French, relations with Britain did not fulfill the hopes of those in Britain who had always opposed exacerbation of the conflict. The War of 1812 reopened old wounds, and, as the nineteenth century continued, the scars still showed—more clearly perhaps in the United States than in the United Kingdom. I myself believe that some overemotional and unhistorical presentations of the struggle constituted a real hindrance to harmonious Anglo-American relations. It is for consideration whether, even today, a fresh look should not be taken at some of the history textbooks of our two countries.

However that may be, any British view of the Revolutionary War must take into account what future generations of British statesmen learnt from it. Admittedly a generous offer of self-government in 1776, or even early in 1777, might conceivably have brought the war to an end while it could still be regarded as primarily a civil war; but the British did not formulate such an offer until too late. In February, 1778, Lord North was prepared to renounce the right to tax the colonists and to give them virtual autonomy in their own affairs; but by then the Continental Congress was unanimous for independence, and in May, 1778, the treaty with France was ratified. George III had clung too long to the contemporary idea of empire and his own concept of where his royal duty lay. Even a loose commonwealth connection might not have survived the strains and stresses of the Napoleonic Wars and Britain's blockade of Europe.

Leaving the field of speculation, we can be grateful that the American revolutionaries endowed with victory their great federal, republican experiment, without which the world would have been immeasurably poorer. We can rejoice, too, that Britain's failure in her first colonizing venture led thinking men to review the imperial relationship. Can anyone doubt that anything less than defeat could have caused the abandonment of Adam Smith's mercantile system, as applied to colonial territories? And but for this change of heart, the gradual transformation of a colonial empire into a commonwealth of self-governing, independent states could never have been accomplished.

Alden T. Vaughan

Shays' Rebellion

The American Revolution has been rightly praised for its essentially conservative character; for once, a people rose against an oppressive government without losing their respect for government itself, or for law. The American revolutionaries sought drastic change, but pursued it, as Jefferson put it in the Declaration of Independence, with "a decent respect to the opinions of mankind." However, the dislocations that the Revolution produced were severe, and in the years after Yorktown the young nation had its full share of social and economic problems, some of which threatened to destroy the respect of the people for legally established authority. Whether this was truly a "critical period" has long been debated; the current opinion of historians seems to be that conditions, in the main, were not as bad as they have sometimes been pictured. But the new national government did lack many important powers, and many of the state governments displayed insufficient will and confidence and thus failed to assume responsibility for governing with the force and determination that critical times require.

In this essay Professor Alden T. Vaughan of Columbia University describes the difficulties that plagued Massachusetts in the 1780's and produced what is known as Shays' Rebellion. How the fundamental conservatism and respect for democratic values of the citizens of Massachusetts eventually resolved this conflict is the theme of his narrative, although he also weighs the influence of the affair on the Constitutional Convention at Philadelphia, which followed closely upon it.

OCTOBER, 1786: "Are your people . . . mad?" thundered the usually calm George Washington to a Massachusetts correspondent. Recent events in the Bay State had convinced the General, who was living the life of a country squire at Mount Vernon, that the United States was "fast verging to anarchy and confusion!" Would the nation that had so recently humbled the British Empire now succumb to internal dissension and die in its infancy? To many Americans in the fall of 1786 it seemed quite possible, for while Washington was writing frantic notes to his friends, several thousand insurgents under the nominal leadership of a Revolutionary War veteran named Daniel Shays were closing courts with impunity, defying the state militia, and threatening to revamp the state government.

The uprising in Massachusetts was serious in itself, but more frightening was the prospect that it could spread to the other states. It had, in fact, already tainted Rhode Island, Vermont, and New Hampshire, and it showed some danger of infecting Connecticut and New York as well. By the spring of 1787, American spokesmen from Maine to Georgia were alarmed, Congress had been induced to raise troops for possible deployment against the rebels, and observers on both sides of the Atlantic voiced concern for the future of the nation. Even John Adams in London and Thomas Jefferson in Paris took time from their critical diplomatic duties to comment—the former, as might be expected, pessimistically; the latter with his usual optimism—on the causes and consequences of Shays' Rebellion. And well they might: the Massachusetts uprising of 1786-87 was to make a lasting contribution to the future of the United States by magnifying the demand for a stronger central government to replace the one created by the Articles of Confederation—a demand that reached fruition in the drafting and ratification of the Constitution in 1787-88. From the vantage point of the twentieth century, the rebellion of Daniel Shays stands—with the exception of the Civil War—as the nation's most famous and most important domestic revolt.

The root of the trouble in Massachusetts lay in the economic chaos that accompanied political independence. The successful war against Great Britain had left the thirteen former colonies free to rule themselves, but it had also left them without the commercial ties that had done so much to promote colonial prosperity. While American producers, merchants, and shippers scurried after new goods and new markets to replace the old, the ill effects of economic independence crept across the nation.

Of all the American states, perhaps none felt the postwar slump so grievously as did Massachusetts. Its $14 million debt was staggering, as was its shortage of specie. Day Staters once again swapped wheat for shoes, and cordwood for help with the plowing. They suffered too from the ruinous inflation that afflicted the entire nation as the value of Continental currency fell in the three years after 1777 to a ridiculous low of four thousand dollars in paper money to one dollar in silver or gold. But in addition, Massachusetts caught the full brunt of

England's decision—vengeful, the Americans considered it—to curtail trade between the United States and the British West Indies. To New Englanders, more than half of whom lived in Massachusetts, the new British policy threatened economic disaster. Gone was their dominance of the carrying trade, gone the booms in shipbuilding, in distilling, in food and lumber exporting, and in the slave trade. Gone too was New England's chief source of hard cash, for the West Indies had been the one place with which New England merchants enjoyed a favorable balance of trade.

Most residents of Massachusetts were probably unaware of the seriousness of their plight until it came close to home. By the early 1780's the signs were unmistakable. Men in debt—and debt was epidemic in the late seventies and eighties—saw their farms confiscated by the state and sold for as little as a third of what they considered to be the true value. Others, less fortunate, found themselves in the dark and filthy county jails, waiting helplessly for sympathetic friends or embarrassed relatives to bail them out of debtors' prison. As the economic crisis worsened, a gloomy pessimism spread among the farmers and tradesmen in the central and western parts of the state.

The economic problems of Massachusetts were difficult, but probably not insoluble. At least they could have been lessened by a wise and considerate state government. Unfortunately for the Bay Staters, good government was as scarce as good money in the early 1780's. After creating a fundamentally sound framework of government in the state constitution of 1780, the voters of Massachusetts failed to staff it with farsighted and dedicated servants of the people. "Thieves, knaves, and robbers," snorted one disgruntled citizen. With mounting grievances and apathetic legislators, the people increasingly took matters into their own hands.

As early as February, 1782, trouble broke out in Pittsfield in the Berkshires, and before the year was over, mob actions had disrupted the tranquillity of several other towns in the western part of the state. The immediate target of the Pittsfield agitators was the local court, which they temporarily closed by barring the door to members of the bench. A court that did not sit could not process foreclosures, pass judgments on debts, or confiscate property for defaulted taxes. In April, violence broke out at Northampton, where a former Connecticut clergyman named Samuel Ely—branded by one early historian as "a vehement, brazen-faced declaimer, abounding in hypocritical pretensions to piety, and an industrious sower of discord"—led the attack on the judges. Ely harangued a Northampton crowd to "go to the woodpile and get clubs enough, and knock their grey wigs off, and send them out of the world in an instant." Ely was promptly arrested and sentenced to six months in prison, but a mob soon freed him from the Springfield jail. The ex-parson found refuge in Vermont.

Instead of recognizing the validity of such protests, the Massachusetts legislature countered with a temporary suspension of habeas corpus and imposed new and higher court costs as well. And while the government did bend to the extent of authorizing certain foodstuffs and lumber to be used in lieu of money, the net effect of its measures was to rub salt into wounds already smarting. Currency remained dear, foreclosures mounted, the shadow of debtors' prison continued to cast a pall, and the state's legal system remained unduly complicated and expensive. Many citizens of western Massachusetts now began to question the benefits of independence; a few even concluded that the patriot leaders of 1776 had deluded them, and cheers for King George III were heard once again in towns that a few years before had cursed his name. And unrest continued to spread. In May, 1783, a mob tried to prevent the opening of the spring session of the Hampshire County Court at Springfield.

Perhaps the major outbreak of 1786 would have occurred a year or so sooner had it not been for a fortuitous combination of events that made the years 1784 and 1785 relatively easy to bear. In 1784 came news that a final peace had been signed with England; in 1785 Massachusetts farmers enjoyed their best harvest in several years, while the legislature, in one of its conciliatory if vagrant moods, refrained from levying a state tax. Although tempers continued to simmer, no serious outbreaks marred the period from early 1783 to midsummer 1786.

The episodes of 1782–83 and those that followed held a particular appeal for veterans of the Revolution. Even more than their civilian neighbors, the former soldiers nursed grievances that they could attribute to incompetent, if not dishonest, government. They had left their farms and shops to fight the hated redcoats, but they could not even depend on the paltry sums their services had earned for them. Inflation had made their Continental currency almost worthless, and now the government set up by the Articles of Confederation was delaying payment of overdue wages and retracting its promises of lifetime pensions to officers.

One lesson of the Revolution not lost on the Massachusetts veterans was that in times of necessity the people could reform an insensitive government by force of arms, and many of them still had in their possession the weapons they had used so effectively against the British and Hessian troops. Old habits and old weapons increasingly took on new meaning to the men of Massachusetts as the economic and political crisis of the 1780's deepened. The veterans of the Bay State knew where to find leadership, too, for among those hardpressed by the economic problems of the decade were many who had served as officers during the War for Independence.

By 1786 several of these officers had emerged as acknowledged leaders in their own localities, although not until the final stages of the rebellion would any single commander claim the allegiance of more than a few hundred men at most.

In the eastern part of the state the most prominent leader was Captain Job Shattuck of Groton, a veteran of the French and Indian War as well as of the Revolution. Now in his fifties, Shattuck had been protesting vehemently, and sometimes violently, since 1781. His principal lieutenant in Middlesex County was Nathan Smith of Shirley, a tough veteran of both wartime and peacetime conflict—with a patch over one eye as testimony to his involvement in the latter. It was the burly Smith who on one occasion gave his hearers the unhappy choice of joining his band or being run out of town.

Farther west the rebels looked to other leaders. In Springfield and neighboring towns it was to Luke Day, said by some to be "the master spirit of the insurrection." A former brevet major in the Continental Army, Day seems to have had the inclination as well as the experience necessary to command a rebellion. In the dismal eighties he was often found grumbling his discontent in West Springfield's Old Stebbin's Tavern or drilling his followers on the town common.

But it was not upon Shattuck or Smith or Day that the final leadership devolved, with its mixed portions of glory and infamy, but on Captain Daniel Shays of Pelham. In some respects Shays was an improbable leader for a popular revolt, for he seems to have been a reluctant rebel in the first place; as late as the fall of 1786 he insisted: "I at their head! I am not." And even after he had assumed command of the bulk of the rebel army, he expressed eagerness to accept a pardon. But at the same time, Shays had attributes that made him a likely prospect for gaining the loyalty of the insurgents. Unlike the others, Shays presented a calm moderation that inspired confidence and respect. He also had a penchant for military courtesy and protocol, a quality that would have undoubtedly been repugnant to the veterans if overdone, but one that was essential if the "mobbers," as they were often called, were to acquire the discipline and organization necessary to resist the forces of government.

Daniel Shays also attracted confidence through his impressive Revolutionary War record. Joining the Continental Army at the outbreak of hostilities, he fought bravely at Bunker Hill (where his courage earned him a promotion to sergeant), served under Ethan Allen at Ticonderoga, helped thwart Gentleman Johnny Burgoyne at Saratoga, and stormed Stony Point with Mad Anthony Wayne. For recruiting a company of volunteers in Massachusetts Shays ultimately received a commission as their captain, a position he seems to have filled adequately if not outstandingly. And before leaving the service, Shays suffered at least one wound in battle.

Shays resigned from the army in 1780 and turned his hand to farming in the small town of Pelham, a few miles east of the Connecticut River. There his popularity, undoubtedly enhanced by his military reputation, won him election to various local offices. At the same time, Shays learned at first hand the problems that can beset a returned veteran. He had already sold for cash the handsome ceremonial sword that the Marquis de Lafayette had presented to him in honor of the victory at Saratoga. On long winter evenings at Conkey's Tavern, Daniel Shays listened to his neighbors' tales of distress. In 1784 he was himself sued for a debt of twelve dollars; by 1786 he was deeply involved in the insurrection. Like so many other men in western and central Massachusetts, Shays had been maneuvered by events of the postwar period into actions that he would hardly have contemplated a few years earlier.

The relative calm that followed the outbreaks of 1782–83 was abruptly shattered in 1786. To make up for the low revenue of the previous year, the legislature in the spring of 1786 imposed unusually heavy poll and property taxes, amounting to one third of the total income of the people. In 1774 taxes had been fifteen cents per capita; in 1786 they leaped to $1.75—a hefty sum for heads of families in frontier areas where a skilled laborer earned thirty to fifty cents a day. Protested one poor cobbler, "The constable keeps at us for rates, rates, rates!" Besides, the new tax schedule was notorious for its inequity, placing heavy duties on land without regard to its value—a palpable discrimination against the poorer farmers. The new schedule also worked injury on the least affluent classes by seeking almost forty per cent of its revenue through a head tax, asking equal amounts from pauper and merchant prince. As court and jail records poignantly testify, many people in the central and western parts of the state could not pay both the new taxes and their old debts. Worcester County, for example, had four thousand suits for debt in 1785–86 (double the total of the preceding two years), and the number of persons imprisoned for debt jumped from seven to seventy-two during that period. In 1786 debtors outnumbered all other criminals in Worcester County prisons 3 to 1.

The new taxes would probably have caused considerable anger by themselves, but when added to old grievances they were sure to bring trouble. During the summer of 1786, conventions met in several western counties—in Worcester, in Hampshire, in Berkshire—and even as far east as Middlesex, only a few miles from Boston. From these quasi-legal meetings came resolutions to the Massachusetts legislature calling for a variety of reforms: reduction of court and lawyers' fees, reduction of salaries for state officials, issuance of paper money, removal of the state capital from Boston (where it was deemed too susceptible to the influence of eastern commercial interests), reduction of taxes, redistribution of the tax load, and many similar changes. A few protests called for still more drastic reforms, such as abolition of the state senate and curtailment of the governor's appointive power, while some petitioners insisted on a state-wide convention to amend the constitution of 1780, now barely six years old. But on the whole the petitions demanded evolution, not revolution. This was a tempered and healthy challenge to an administration that had shown itself insensitive and incompetent.

In the protests about the government, two categories of citizens were singled out for criticism by the petitioners. First were the merchants and professional men, who enjoyed an unfair advantage within the tax system. Second were the lawyers, who seemed to be conspiring with judges and creditors to force the debtor still further into obligation. Perhaps not all lawyers were so harshly judged, but the condemnation was certainly meant to apply to those whom John Adams called "the dirty dabblers in the law," men who often created more litigation than they resolved. In contrast to the turbulent days before the Revolution, the new era in Massachusetts did not find lawyers in the vanguard of the movement for reform.

But in one respect, at least, the 1780's bore resemblance to the years before Lexington: peaceful protest soon gave way to more forceful action. In late August, following a Hampshire County convention at Hatfield, a mob of 1,500 men "armed with guns, swords, and other deadly weapons, and with drums beating and fifes playing" took command of the county courthouse at Northampton and forced the judges of the Court of Common Pleas and General Sessions of the Peace to adjourn sine die. During the next few months, similar conventions with similar results took place in Middlesex, Bristol, and Worcester counties. By early fall, mobs armed with muskets or hickory clubs and often sporting sprigs of hemlock in their hats as a sign of allegiance to the rebel cause moved at will through the interior counties.

Farmers threatened with foreclosure seize a Massachusetts court, depicted in 1884 by the noted illustrator, Howard Pyle.

The rebels did not go unopposed. In each county there were some citizens who looked askance at the growing anarchy and did their best to thwart it. In Worcester, seat of Worcester County, Judge Artemas Ward showed the mettle of those who would not succumb to mob rule. When on the fifth of September two hundred armed men blocked his path to the courthouse, the aging but still impressive ex-general defied the bayonets that pierced his judicial robes and for two hours lectured the crowd on the dangers of anarchy and the meaning of treason. A heavy downpour finally silenced the judge, though not until he had intoned a timely plea that "the sun never shine on rebellion in Massachusetts." But neither rain nor words had got the judge and his colleagues into the courthouse.

Elsewhere the story was much the same: a few citizens tried to stem the tide of rebellion but in the end were swept aside. At Great Barrington, in Berkshire County, a mob of 800 stopped the court, broke open the jail and released its prisoners, and abused the judges who protested. At Springfield, Daniel Shays and Luke Day made sure that the courthouse doors remained shut, while at Concord, less than twenty miles from Boston, Job Shattuck, aided by Nathan Smith and his brother Sylvanus, prevented the sitting of the Middlesex County court. Only at Taunton, in Bristol County, did a sizable mob meet its match. There Chief Justice (and former general) David Cobb was ready with a field piece, thirty volunteers, and a determination to "sit as a judge or die as a general." The Bristol court met as scheduled.

Governor James Bowdoin and the legislature responded to the latest outbreaks with a confusing mixture of sternness, concession, and indecision. In early September, the Governor issued his first proclamation, condemning the mobbers' flirtation with "riot, anarchy and confusion." In October the legislature suspended habeas corpus, but it also authorized some categories of goods as legal tender for specified kinds of public and private debts, and it offered full pardon to all rebels who would take an oath of allegiance before the end of the year. Yet the government failed to find solutions to the major complaints. No significant reforms were made in court procedures, the tax load was not reduced, officials' salaries were not lowered, the capital was not moved, and no curbs were placed on lawyers' machinations.

As mob violence continued through the fall of 1786, spokesmen in the Bay State and elsewhere voiced a growing fear that the anarchy of Massachusetts might infect the entire nation. Several months earlier John Jay had predicted a crisis—"something I cannot foresee or conjecture. I am uneasy and apprehensive; more so than during the war." Now Secretary of War Henry Knox, Massachusetts statesman Rufus King, and others began to have similar apprehensions. They wrote frantic letters to one another, asking for news and predicting disaster. Abigail Adams, then in London, bristled at the "ignorant and wrestless desperadoes," while reports of the uprising helped prod her husband John into writing his ponderous *Defence of the Constitutions*. Even General Washington lost his equanimity. "[For] God's sake, tell me," he wrote to his former aide-de-camp, David Humphreys, in October, "what is the cause of all these commotions? Do they proceed from licentiousness, British influence disseminated by the tories, or real grievances which admit of redress? If the latter, why were they delayed 'till the public mind had been so much agitated? If the former, why are not the powers of Government tried at once?"

Fearful that the powers of state government would not be sufficient to thwart the rebellion, Governor Bowdoin and Secretary of War Knox hatched a scheme for employing federal troops should the need arise. Knox discussed the matter with Congress: the outcome was a call for 1,340 volunteers for the federal army (which then numbered only 700), most of them to be raised in Massachusetts and Connecticut. The additional troops were ostensibly to be used against the Indians of the Northwest, but in secret session Congress acknowledged the possibility that they might be sent instead against the self-styled "regulators" in New England, and that they might be needed to protect the federal arsenal in Springfield—a likely target for the rebellious veterans. Meanwhile the Massachusetts Council authorized a state army of 4,400 men and four regiments of artillery, to be drawn largely from the militia of the eastern counties.

Command of the state forces fell to Major General Benjamin Lincoln, a battle-tested veteran of the Revolution, and a man of tact and humanity as well as martial vigor. But before taking the field, Lincoln served a brief stint as fund-raiser for his own army, for the cost of a thirty-day campaign had been calculated at about £5,000, or about $20,000, and the impoverished state treasury could offer nothing but promises of eventual reimbursement to any who would lend cash to the government. In less than twenty-four hours General Lincoln collected contributions from 130 of Boston's wealthy citizens, including £250 from Governor Bowdoin.

By the time Lincoln's army was equipped for action, the rebellion was over in eastern Massachusetts. It had never been strong there, but in November of 1786 a mob tried to halt the Middlesex County court. This time the militia was alert. After a brief skirmish in which Job Shattuck received a crippling wound, the Groton leader and two of his lieutenants were captured. While Shattuck languished in the Boston jail, his followers drifted west to join other rebel groups.

The situation now grew alarming in Worcester, where the Supreme Court was scheduled to meet on December 5; by late November, mobs of armed men drifting into town had closed the Court of Common Pleas and made it obvious that no court could meet without an army to back it up. Local officials looked on helplessly. Even bold Sheriff Greenleaf, who offered to help alleviate the high court costs by hanging every rebel free of charge, was powerless in the face of such numbers, and he became a laughingstock to boot when he strode away from the courthouse one day unaware that someone had adorned his hat with the symbolic hemlock tuft.

At first the rebels at Worcester suffered from lack of a universally recognized leader. Then in early December Daniel Shays rode in from

Pelham, mounted on a white horse and followed by 350 men. He had not come to do battle if he could avoid it; to a friend he confided: "For God's sake, have matters settled peaceably: it was against my inclinations I undertook this business; importunity was used which I could not withstand, but I heartily wish it was well over." Still, as a showdown with the judges approached, Shays increasingly assumed the role of spokesman for the disparate forces. And it was just as well; with milling crowds of disgruntled veterans and a frightened and divided populace, violence might well have erupted. Instead, choosing wisdom as the better part of valor, the rebels put their energies into drafting a petition to the legislature for a redress of grievances and into several wordy defenses of their own actions. Violence was scrupulously avoided. And their immediate point, after all, had been won; the Worcester court gathered meekly in the Sun Tavern and adjourned until January 23. The insurgents then gave way before the more impressive force of winter blizzards and dispersed to the west. Friends of the rebels were not greatly heartened, however, for the basic grievances remained. Friends of the government rejoiced at the retreat of the rebels, and chanted:

> Says sober Bill, " Well Shays has fled,
> And peace returns to bless our days!"
> "Indeed," cries Ned, "I always said
> He'd prove at last a fall-back Shays,
> And those turned over and undone
> Call him a worthless Shays, to run!"

But Shays was only running to a new scene of action. The Hampshire County court, scheduled to meet in Springfield in late January, should be stopped. Besides, the federal arsenal in that town had the only cache of arms the rebels could hope to capture, and without weapons the rebellion must collapse.

General Lincoln was preparing to defend the January session of the Worcester court when news reached him of the crisis in Springfield. The arsenal there boasted a garrison of some 1,100 militia under General William Shepard, but surrounding the troops were three rebel forces: Daniel Shays commanded 1,200 men at Wilbraham, eight miles to the east; Eli Parson had 400 at Chicopee, three miles to the north; Luke Day led another 400 at West Springfield, just across the Connecticut River to the west. There was every reason to believe they could overwhelm Shepard's garrison if they were willing to risk some bloodshed. General Lincoln headed for Springfield on the double.

Had Shays and his cohorts carried out their original plan they would in all likelihood have had possession of the arsenal before Lincoln arrived with reinforcements. The attack had been set for January 25: Shays was to have led a frontal assault from the southeast while Day directed a flanking movement from the west. But at the last minute Day decided to wait until the twenty-sixth, and his note informing Shays of the change was intercepted by Shepard's men. When Shays moved forward on the afternoon of the twenty-fifth,

After Shays' followers were repulsed at the Springfield armory, as shown here, the rebellion quickly fell apart.

Shepard confidently grouped his full strength against the lone attack. But not much strength was needed. Shepard fired only three cannon shots. When two warning volleys failed to turn back the rebels, Shepard aimed the third into their midst. Three insurgents fell dead in the snow, a fourth lay mortally wounded. The remainder fled in confusion. It was a shattered band that Shays succeeded in regrouping a few miles from the scene of conflict.

At this point General Lincoln arrived and took position between Day and Shays. Both rebel armies at once broke camp and headed for safer territory—Day's men so hastily that they left pork and beans baking in their ovens and discarded knapsacks strewn along their route. The main force, under Shays, beat a rapid retreat to the northeast, passing through Ludlow, South Hadley, Amherst, and Pelham. Lincoln followed in close pursuit, moving overland after Shays, while General Shepard marched up the frozen Connecticut River to prevent a reunion of the rebel army's eastern and western wings.

At Hadley, General Lincoln halted his pursuit long enough to discuss surrender proposals with Shays. The rebel leader was willing to negotiate, but his insistence on an unconditional pardon for himself and his men was more than General Lincoln was authorized to grant. With no agreement likely, Shays suddenly shifted his men to the relative security of Petersham, a center of regulator sentiment which lay in terrain easier to defend. It was midwinter—an unusually cold and stormy winter—and deep snow blanketed the Connecticut Valley. Perhaps the militia would not bother to follow.

But Shays reckoned without General Lincoln. Ever since 1780, when he had surrendered Charleston, South Carolina, and its garrison of 5,400 men to the British in the most costly American defeat of the Revolution, Benjamin Lincoln had had to endure charges of cowardice and indecision. Although he had been officially exonerated, a few critics persisted; in a vigorous suppression of the Shaysites General Lincoln could perhaps fully restore himself in the public's esteem. With superb stamina and determination, Lincoln marched his men the thirty miles from Hadley to Petersham through a blinding snowstorm on the night of Saturday, February 3, arriving at Petersham early the next morning. Taken completely by surprise, the insurgents were routed: some 150 were captured; the rest, including Shays, escaped to the north. Lincoln then moved across the Connecticut River to disperse rebel nests in the Berkshires. By the end of February only scattered resistance remained. What the legislature had recently condemned as a "horrid and unnatural Rebellion and War . . . traiterously raised and levied against this Commonwealth" had come to an inglorious end.

While the militia crushed the remnants of rebellion, the state government drafted a series of regulations for punishing the insurgents. In mid-February, two weeks after Shays' dispersal at Petersham, it issued a stiff Disqualifying Act, offering pardons to privates and noncommissioned officers, but denying them for three years the right to vote, to serve on juries, and to be employed as schoolteachers, innkeepers, or liquor retailers. Massachusetts citizens would thus be shielded from the baneful influence of the Shaysites. Not included in the partial amnesty were the insurgent officers, citizens of other states who had joined the Massachusetts uprising, former state officers or members of the state legislature who had aided the rebels, and persons who had attended regulator conventions. Men in those categories would be tried for treason.

The government's vindictive measures aroused widespread protest, not only from those who had sympathized with the rebel cause but from many of its active opponents as well. General Lincoln, among others, believed that such harsh reprisals would further alienate the discontented, and he observed to General Washington that the disfranchisement of so many people would wholly deprive some towns of their representation in the legislature. New outbreaks, he argued, would then occur in areas that had no other way to voice their grievances. In token concession to its critics, the legislature in March, 1787, appointed a special commission of three men to determine the fate of rebels not covered by the Disqualifying Act. General Lincoln served on the commission, and under his moderating influence it eventually extended pardons to 790 persons. But in the meantime, county courts apprehended and tried whatever rebel leaders they could find. In Hampshire County, with Robert Treat Paine serving as prosecuting attorney, six men were sentenced to death and many others incurred fines or imprisonment. In Berkshire County eight men were sentenced to die for their part in the uprising .

Had the government of 1786–87 remained in office, more than a dozen lives would have been lost to the hangman, hundreds of other men would have suffered disqualifications, and the fundamental causes of Shays' Rebellion might have lingered on to trigger new outbreaks. But however strongly the regulators might complain of the legislative and judicial shortcomings of Massachusetts, they had cause to be thankful that its constitution required annual elections and that the franchise was broad enough to let popular sentiment determine the tenor of government. The result of the April election revealed the breadth and depth of the sympathy in which the regulators were held by the citizens and the extent of popular revulsion at the ineptitude of the government. In the gubernatorial contest, popular John Hancock, recently recovered from an illness that had caused him to resign the governorship early in 1785, overwhelmingly defeated Governor Bowdoin. Only 62 of the 222 members of the legislature and 11 members of the 24-man senate were returned to their seats. In some instances the voters chose men who had actively participated in the rebellion, including Josiah Whitney, who had recently served sixteen days in the Worcester jail.

Within the next few months the new legislature sharply mitigated both the causes of unrest and the punishments assigned to the rebels. It repealed the Disqualifying Act, reprieved all men under sentence of death—some on the very steps of the gallows—and by the following summer it had pardoned even Daniel Shays, though he and a few other leaders were still precluded from holding civil and military offices in the state. Equally important, it enacted long-range reforms— extending the law that permitted the use of certain personal and real property in payment of debts, imposing a lower and more equitable tax schedule, and releasing most debtors from prison.

Now in truth the rebellion was over. Peace, and soon prosperity, returned to the Massachusetts countryside. Differences of opinion still lingered, of course, as was made clear one Sunday when the church at Whately christened two infants—one named after Daniel Shays, the other after Benjamin Lincoln. But the Shaysites made no further trouble for Bay State authorities, and Daniel Shays, the reluctant leader, soon moved on to New York State, where he eked out a skimpy existence on his Revolutionary War pension until his death in 1825.

Americans of the 1780's drew various lessons from the affair in Massachusetts. Some, like Washington and Madison, appear to have misinterpreted the event and ascribed to the rebels a more drastic program than the majority of them had ever advocated. Others, like Mercy Warren, the lady historian, and Joseph Hawley, the Massachusetts patriot, detected the hand of Great Britain behind the uprising. Still others sensed that the true causes of Shays' Rebellion were local in origin and primarily the fault of the state government. Baron von Steuben had correctly surmised that "when a whole people complains . . . something must be wrong," while Thomas Jefferson, then American Minister to France, thought the rebellion of no dangerous importance and preferred to set it in a broader perspective than had most Americans. "We have had," wrote Jefferson, "13 states independent 11 years. There has been one rebellion. That comes to one rebellion in a century and a half for each state. What country before ever existed a century and a half without a rebellion? And what country can preserve its liberties if their rulers are not warned from time to time that the people preserve the spirit of resistance? . . . The tree of liberty must be refreshed from time to time with the blood of patriots and tyrants." But while observers were drawing these diverse conclusions from the episode in Massachusetts, an increasing number of Americans were concerned with how to make sure it would never happen again.

On May 25, 1787, less than four months after the rout at Petersham, the Constitutional Convention began its deliberations at Independence Hall, Philadelphia. Through a long hot summer the delegates proposed, argued, and compromised as they sought to construct a new and better form of government for the American nation. And among the knottiest problems they faced were several recently emphasized by Shays' Rebellion: problems of currency regulation, of debts and contracts, and of ways to thwart domestic insurrection. As the records of the federal Convention reveal, the recent uprising in Massachusetts lay heavily on the minds of the delegates. Although it is impossible to pinpoint the exact phrases in the final document that owed their wording to the fear of similar revolts, there is no doubt that the Constitution reflected the determination of the Founding Fathers to do all they could to prevent future rebellions and to make it easier for the new government to suppress them if they did occur. Significantly, the new polity forbade the states to issue paper money, strengthened the military powers of the executive branch, and authorized Congress to call up state militiamen to "suppress Insurrections" and enforce the laws of the land. Jefferson's first glimpse of the Constitution convinced him that "our Convention has been too much impressed by the insurrection of Massachusetts. . . ." Jefferson exaggerated, but it is clear that the movement for a stronger central government had gained immense momentum from the "horrid and unnatural Rebellion" of Daniel Shays.

By the summer of 1788 the requisite nine states had ratified the new Constitution, and in the following spring General Washington took the oath of office as President. In the prosperous and dynamic years that followed, the passions generated by the insurrection in Massachusetts were gradually extinguished. But the lesson and the impact of Shays' Rebellion are still with us. Because of it, important changes were made in the government of Massachusetts as well as in the government of the nation, changes that have stood the test of time. Perhaps this episode lends some ironic credence to Thomas Jefferson's suggestion that "the spirit of resistance to government is . . . valuable on certain occasions."

Henry Steele Commager

The Constitution: Was It an Economic Document?

When Charles A. Beard published An Economic Interpretation of the Constitution *in 1913, in which he argued that the personal economic interests of the Founding Fathers played a major role in the shaping of the Constitution, he roused a furor, and incidentally triggered a rash of studies designed to show how importantly material interests had influenced men's behavior throughout our history. Beard's line of reasoning was never accepted by all scholars, but for a long generation his basic approach came close to dominating the writing of American history. In recent times, however, the Beardian economic interpretation has been subjected to devastating attack (almost line by line) by such historians as Robert E. Brown and Forrest McDonald.*

In this essay Professor Henry Steele Commager of Amherst College takes a fresh look at this controversial subject, offering a thoughtful and objective evaluation of Beard's work and of the motives and actions of the Founding Fathers. Commager, a historian of wideranging interests, combines a detailed knowledge of constitutional history with a sensitive perception of the force of ideas in shaping events.

By June 26, 1787, tempers in the Federal Convention were already growing short, for gentlemen had come to the explosive question of representation in the upper chamber. Two days later Franklin moved to invoke divine guidance, and his motion was shunted aside only because there was no money with which to pay a chaplain and the members were unprepared to appeal to Heaven without an intermediary. It was not surprising that when James Madison spoke of representation in the proposed legislature, he was conscious of the solemnity of the occasion. We are, he said, framing a system "which we wish to last for ages" and one that might "decide forever the fate of Republican Government."

It was an awful thought, and when, a few days later, Gouverneur Morris spoke to the same subject he felt the occasion a most solemn one; even the irrepressible Morris could be solemn. "He came here," he observed (so Madison noted),

> as a Representative of America; he flattered himself he came here in some degree as a Representative of the whole human race; for the whole human race will be affected by the proceedings of this Convention. He wished gentlemen to extend their views beyond the present moment of time; beyond the narrow limits . . . from which they derive their political origin. . . .
>
> Much has been said of the sentiments of the people. They were unknown. They could not be known. All that we can infer is that if the plan we recommend be reasonable & right; all who have reasonable minds and sound intentions will embrace it . . .

These were by no means occasional sentiments only. They were sentiments that occurred again and again throughout the whole of that long hot summer, until they received their final, eloquent expression from the aged Franklin in that comment on the rising, not the setting, sun. Even during the most acrimonious debates members were aware that they were framing a constitution for ages to come, that they were creating a model for people everywhere on the globe; there was a lively sense of responsibility and even of destiny. Nor can we now, as we contemplate that Constitution which is the oldest written national constitution, and that federal system which is one of the oldest and the most successful in history, regard these appeals to posterity as merely rhetorical.

That men are not always conscious either of what they do or of the motives that animate them is a familiar rather than a cynical observation. Some 45 years ago Charles A. Beard propounded an economic interpretation of the Constitution—an interpretation which submitted that the Constitution was *essentially* (that is a crucial word) an economic document—and that it was carried through the Convention and the state ratifying conventions by interested economic groups for economic reasons. "The Constitution," Mr. Beard concluded, "was essentially an economic document based upon the concept

Independence Hall as it appeared in an engraving done just prior to the Revolution.

that the fundamental private rights of property are anterior to government and morally beyond the reach of popular majorities.''

At the time it was pronounced, that interpretation caused something of a sensation, and Mr. Beard was himself eventually to comment with justifiable indignation on the meanness and the vehemence of the attacks upon it—and him. Yet the remarkable thing about the economic interpretation is not the criticism it inspired but the support it commanded. For within a few years it had established itself as the new orthodoxy, and those who took exception to it were stamped either as professional patriots—perhaps secret Sons or Daughters of the Revolution—or naïve academicians who had never learned the facts of economic life.

The attraction that the economic interpretation had for the generation of the twenties and thirties—and that it still exerts—is one of the curiosities of our cultural history, but by no means an inexplicable one. To a generation of materialists Beard's thesis made clear that the stuff of history was material. To a generation disillusioned by the exploitations of big business it discovered that the past, too, had been ravaged by economic exploiters. To a generation that looked with skeptical eyes upon the claims of Wilsonian idealism and all but rejoiced in their frustration, it suggested that all earlier idealisms and patriotisms—even the idealism and patriotism of the framers—had been similarly flawed by selfishness and hypocrisy.

Yet may it not be said of *An Economic Interpretation of the Constitution* that it is not a conclusion but a point of departure? It

Thomas Rossiter's view of the signing of the Consti-tution was painted about 1850.

explains a great deal about the forces that went into the making of the Constitution, and a great deal, too, about the men who assembled in Philadelphia in 1787, but it tells us extraordinarily little about the document itself. And it tells us even less about the historical meaning of that document.

What were the objects of the Federal Convention? The immediate objects were to restore order; to strengthen the public credit; to enable the United States to make satisfactory commercial treaties and agreements; to provide conditions in which trade and commerce could flourish; to facilitate management of the western lands and of Indian affairs. All familiar enough. But what, in the light of history, were the grand objects of the Convention? What was it that gave Madison and Morris and Wilson and King and Washington himself a sense of destiny?

There were two grand objects objects inextricably interrelated. The first was to solve the problem of federalism, that is, the problem of the distribution of powers among governments. Upon the wisdom with which members of the Convention distinguished between powers of a general and powers of a local nature, and assigned these to their appropriate governments, would depend the success or failure of the new experiment.

But it was impossible for the children of the eighteenth century to talk or think of powers without thinking of power, and this was a healthy realism. No less troublesome—and more fundamental—than the problem of the distribution of powers, was the problem of sanctions. How were they to enforce the terms of the distribution and impose limits upon all the governments involved? It was one thing to work out the ideal distribution of general and local powers. It was another thing to see to it that the states abided by their obligations under the Articles of Union and that the national government respected the autonomy of states and liberty of individuals.

Those familiar with the Revolutionary era know that the second of these problems was more difficult than the first. Americans had learned how to limit government: the written constitutions, the bills of rights, the checks and balances. They had not yet learned (nor had anyone) how to "substitute the mild magistracy of the law for the cruel and violent magistracy of force." The phrase is Madison's.

Let us return to the *Economic Interpretation*. The correctness of Beard's analysis of the origins and backgrounds of the membership of the Convention, of the arguments in the Convention, and of the methods of assuring ratification, need not be debated. But these considerations are, in a sense, irrelevant and immaterial. For though they are designed to illuminate the document itself, in fact they illuminate only the processes of its manufacture.

The idea that property considerations were paramount in the minds of those assembled in Philadelphia is misleading and unsound and is borne out neither by the evidence of the debates in the Convention nor by the Constitution itself. The Constitution was not *essentially* an economic document. It was, and is, *essentially* a political document. It addresses itself to the great and fundamental question of the distribution of powers between governments. The Constitution was—and is—a document that attempts to provide sanctions behind that distribution; a document that sets up, through law, a standing rule to live by and provides legal machinery for the enforcement of that rule. These are political, not economic functions.

Not only were the principles that animated the framers political rather than economic; the solutions that they formulated to the great questions that confronted them were dictated by political, not by economic considerations.

Here are two fundamental challenges to the Beard interpretation: first, the Constitution is primarily a document in federalism; and second, the Constitution does not in fact confess or display the controlling influence of those who held that "the fundamental private rights of property are anterior to government and morally beyond the reach of popular majorities."

Let us look more closely at these two contentions. The first requires little elaboration or vindication, for it is clear to all students of the Revolutionary era that the one pervasive and over-branching problem of that generation was the problem of imperial organization. How to get the various parts of any empire to work together for common purposes? How to get central control—over war, for example, or commerce or money—without impairing local autonomy? How, on the other hand, preserve personal liberty and local self-government without impairing the effectiveness of the central government? This was one of the oldest problems in political science—as old as the history of the Greek city-states; as new as the recent debate over Federal aid to education or the Bricker amendment.

The British failed to solve the problem of imperial order; when pushed to the wall they had recourse to the hopelessly doctrinaire Declaratory Act, which was, in fact, a declaration of political bankruptcy; as Edmund Burke observed, no people is going to be argued into slavery. The Americans then took up the vexatious problem. The Articles of Confederation were satisfactory enough as far as the distribution of powers was concerned, but wholly wanting in sanctions. The absence of sanctions spelled the failure of the Articles—and this failure led to the Philadelphia Convention.

Now it will be readily conceded that many, if not most, of the questions connected with federalism were economic in character. Involved were such practical matters as taxation, the regulation of commerce, coinage, western lands, slavery, and so forth. The problem that presented itself to the framers was not whether goverment should exercise authority over such matters; it was *which* government should exercise such authority—and how should it be exercised?

There were, after all, no anarchists at the Federal Convention. Everyone agreed that *some* government had to have authority to tax, raise armies, regulate commerce, coin money, control contracts, enact bankruptcy legislation, regulate western territories, make treaties, and do all the things that government must do. But where should these authorities be lodged—with the state governments or with the national government they were about to erect, or with both?

This question was a political, not an economic, one. And the solution at which the framers arrived was based upon a sound understanding of politics, and need not be explained by reference to class attachments or security interests.

Certainly if the framers were concerned primarily or even largely with protecting property against popular majorities, they failed signally to carry out their purposes. It is at this point in our consideration of the *Economic Interpretation of the Constitution* that we need to employ what our literary friends call *explication du texte*. For the weakest link in the Beard interpretation is precisely the crucial one—the document itself. Mr. Beard makes amply clear that those who wrote the Constitution were members of the propertied classes,* and that many of them were personally involved in the out-

---

* "A majority of the members were lawyers by profession.

"Most of the members came from towns, on or near the coast, that is, from the regions in which personalty was largely concentrated.

"Not one member represented in his immediate personal economic interests the small farming or mechanic classes.

"The overwhelming majority of members, at least five-sixths, were immediately, directly, and personally interested in the outcome of their labors at Philadelphia, and were to a greater or less extent economic beneficiaries from the adoption of the Constitution."

Beard, *An Economic Interpretation of the Constitution.*

come of what they were about to do; he makes out a persuasive case that the division over the Constitution was along economic lines. What he does not make clear is how or where the Constitution itself reflects all these economic influences.

Much is made of the contract clause and the paper money clause of the Constitution. No state may impair the obligations of a contract—whatever those words mean, and they apparently did not mean to the framers quite what Chief Justice Marshall later said they meant in *Fletcher v. Peck* or *Dartmouth College v. Woodward*. No state may emit bills of credit or make anything but gold and silver coin legal tender in payment of debts.

These are formidable prohibitions, and clearly reflect the impatience of men of property with the malpractices of the states during the Confederation. Yet quite aside from what the states may or may not have done, who can doubt that these limitations upon the states followed a sound principle—the principle that control of coinage and money belonged to the central, not the local governments, and the principle that local jurisdictions should not be able to modify or overthrow contracts recognized throughout the Union?

What is most interesting in this connection is what is so often overlooked: that the framers did not write any comparable prohibitions upon the United States government. The United States was not forbidden to impair the obligation of its contracts, not at least in the Constitution as it came from the hands of its property-conscious framers. Possibly the Fifth Amendment may have squinted toward such a prohibition; we need not determine that now, for the Fifth Amendment was added by the *states* after the Constitution had been ratified. So, too, the emission of bills of credit and the making other than gold and silver legal tender were limitations on the states, but not on the national government. There was, in fact, a lively debate over the question of limiting the authority of the national government in the matter of bills of credit. When the question came up on August 16, Gouverneur Morris threatened that ''The Monied interest will oppose the plan of Government, if paper emissions be not prohibited.'' In the end the Convention dropped out a specific authorization to emit bills of credit, but pointedly did not prohibit such action. Just where this left the situation troubled Chief Justice Chase's Court briefly three quarters of a century later; the Court recovered its balance, and the sovereign power of the government over money was not again *successfully* challenged.

Nor were there other specific limitations of an economic character upon the powers of the new government that was being erected on the ruins of the old. The framers properly gave the Congress power to regulate commerce with foreign nations and among the states. The term commerce—as Hamilton and Adair (and Crosskey, too!) have made clear—was broadly meant, and the grant of authority, too, was broad. The framers gave Congress the power to levy taxes and, again, wrote no limitations into the Constitution except as to the apportionment of direct taxes; it remained for the most conservative of Courts peachments of Officers of the United States; to all cases of Admiralty and Maritime Jurisdiction; to Controversies between two or more States; (~~between a State and citizens of~~) ~~between a State and citizens of~~ another State, between citizens of different States, and between a State or the citizens thereof and foreign States, citizens or subjects. (In cases of Impeachment, cases affecting Ambassadors, other Public Ministers and Consuls, and those in which a State shall be party, ~~the jurisdiction shall be original.~~ In all the other cases beforementioned ~~the jurisdiction shall be on appeal,~~ with such exceptions and under such regulations as the Legislature shall make. The Legislature may assign any part of the jurisdiction abovementioned (except the trial of the President of the United States) in the manner and under the limitations which it shall think proper, to such Inferior Courts as it shall constitute from time to time.

Sect. 4. The trial of all criminal offences, (except in cases of impeachments) shall be in the State where they shall be committed; ~~and shall be by jury.~~

Sect. 5. Judgment, in cases of Impeachment, shall not extend further than to removal from office, and disqualification to hold and enjoy any office of honour, trust or profit under the United States. But the party convicted shall nevertheless be liable and subject to indictment, trial, judgment and punishment, according to law.

XII

No State shall coin money; nor grant letters of marque and reprisal; nor enter into any treaty, alliance, or confederation; nor grant any title of nobility.

XIII

No State, without the consent of the Legislature of the United States, shall lay imposts or duties on imports; nor keep troops or ships of war in time of peace; nor enter into any agreement or compact with another State, or with any foreign power; nor engage in any war, unless it shall be actually invaded by enemies, or the danger of invasion be so imminent, as not to admit of a delay, until the Legislature of the United States can be consulted.

XIIII

The citizens of each State shall be entitled to all privileges and immunities of citizens in the several States.

XV

Any person charged with treason, felony, or ~~high misdemeanor~~ in any State, who shall flee from justice, and shall be found in any other State, shall, on demand of the Executive Power of the State from which he fled, be delivered up and removed to the State having jurisdiction of the offence.

XVI

Full faith shall be given in each State to the acts of the Legislatures, and to the records, and judicial proceedings of the courts and magistrates of every other State.

XVII

Washington's working copy of a printed draft of the Constitution indicated approval of federal control over coinage and duties in Articles XII and XIII.

to reverse itself, and common sense, and discover that the framers had intended to forbid an income tax! Today, organizations that invoke the very term "constitutional" are agitating for an amendment placing a quantitative limit upon income taxes that may be levied; fortunately, Madison's generation understood better the true nature of governmental power.

The framers gave Congress—in ambiguous terms, to be sure—authority to make "all needful Rules and Regulations respecting the Territory or other Property" of the United States, and provided that "new states may be admitted." These evasive phrases gave little hint of the heated debates in the Convention over western lands. Those who delight to find narrow and undemocratic sentiments in the breasts of the framers never cease to quote a Gouverneur Morris or an Elbridge Gerry on the dangers of the West, and it is possible to compile a horrid catalogue of such statements. But what is significant is not what framers said, but what they did. They did not place any limits upon the disposition of western territory, or establish any barriers against the admission of western states.

The fact is that we look in vain *in the Constitution itself* for any really effective guarantee for property or any effective barriers against what Beard calls "the reach of popular majorities."

It will be argued, however, that what the framers feared was the *states*, and that the specific prohibitions against state action, together with the broad transfer of economic powers from state to nation, were deemed sufficient guarantee against state attacks upon property. As for the national government, care was taken to make that sufficiently aristocratic, sufficiently the representative of the propertied classes, and sufficiently checked and limited so that it would not threaten basic property interests.

It is at this juncture that the familiar principle of limitation on governmental authority commands our attention. Granted the wisest distribution of powers among governments, what guarantee was there that power would be properly exercised? What guarantees were there against the abuse of power? What assurance was there that the large states would not ride roughshod over the small, that majorities would not crush minorities or minorities abuse majorities? What protection was there against mobs, demagogues, dangerous combinations of interests or of states? What protection was there for the commercial interest, the planter interest, the slave interest, the securities interests, the land speculator interests?

It was Madison who most clearly saw the real character of this problem and who formulated its solution. It was not that the people as such were dangerous; "The truth was," he said on July 11, "that all men having power ought to be distrusted to a certain degree." Long before Lord Acton coined the aphorism, the Revolutionary leaders had discovered that power corrupts. They understood, too, the drive for power on the part of individuals and groups. All this is familiar to students of *The Federalist*, No. 10. It should be familiar to students of the debates in Philadelphia, for there, too, Madison set forth his theory and supported it with a wealth of argument. Listen to him on one of the early days of the Convention, June 6, when he is discussing the way to avoid abuses of republican liberty—abuses which "prevailed in the largest as well as the smallest [states] . . ."

> . . . And were we not thence admonished [he continued] to enlarge the sphere as far as the nature of the Government would admit. This was the only defence against the inconveniences of democracy *consistent with the democratic form of Government* [our italics]. All civilized Societies would be divided into different Sects, Factions & interests, as they happened to consist of rich & poor, debtors and creditors, the landed, the manufacturing, the commercial interests, the inhabitants of this district or that district, the followers of this political leader or that political leader, the disciples of this religious Sect or that religious Sect. In all cases where a majority are united by a common interest or passion, the rights of the minority are in danger. . . . In a Republican Govt. the Majority if united have always an opportunity [to oppress the minority. What is the remedy?] The only remedy is to enlarge the sphere, & thereby divide the community into so great a number of interests & parties, that in the first place a majority will not be likely at the same moment to have a common interest separate from that of the whole or of the minority; and in the second place, that in case they should have such an interest, they may not be apt to unite in the pursuit of it. It was incumbent on us then to try this remedy, and . . . to frame a republican system on such a scale & in such a form as will controul all the evils which have been experienced.

This long quotation is wonderfully eloquent of the attitude of the most sagacious of the framers. Madison, Wilson, Mason, Franklin, as well as Gerry, Morris, Pinckney, and Hamilton feared power. They feared power whether exercised by a monarch, an aristocracy, an army, or a majority, and they were one in their determination to write into fundamental law limitations on the arbitrary exercise of that power. To assume, as Beard so commonly does, that the fear of the misuse of power by majorities was either peculiar to the Federalists or more ardent with them than with their opponents, is mistaken. Indeed it was rather the anti-Federalists who were most deeply disturbed by the prospect of majority rule; they, rather than the Federalists, were the "men of little faith." Thus it was John Lansing, Jr., of New York (he who left the Convention rather than have any part in its dangerous work) who said that "all free constitutions are formed with two views—to deter the governed from crime, and the governors from tyranny." And the ardent Patrick Henry, who led the attack on the Constitution in the Virginia Convention—and almost defeated it complained not of too little democracy in that document, but too much.

The framers, to be sure, feared the powers of the majority, as they feared all power unless controlled. But they were insistent that, in the last analysis, there must be government by majority; even conservatives like Morris and Hamilton made this clear. Listen to Hamilton, for example, at the very close of the Convention. Elbridge Gerry, an opponent of the Constitution, had asked for a reconsideration of the provision for calling a constitutional convention, alleging that this opened the gate to a majority that could "bind the union to innovations that may subvert the State-Constitutions altogether." To this Hamilton replied that

> There was no greater evil in subjecting the people of the U.S. to the major voice than the people of a particular State. . . . It was equally desirable now that an easy mode should be established for supplying defects which will probably appear in the New System. . . . There could be no danger in giving this power, as the people would finally decide in the case.

. . . But we need not rely upon what men said; there it too much of making history by quotation anyway. Let us look rather at what men did. We can turn again to the Constitution itself. Granted the elaborate system of checks and balances: the separation of powers, the bicameral legislature, the executive veto, and so forth—checks found in the state constitutions as well, and in our own democratic era as in the earlier one—what provision did the framers make against majority tyranny? What provisions did they write into the Constitution against what Randolph called "democratic licentiousness"?

They granted equality of representation in the Senate. If this meant that conservative Delaware would have the same representation in the upper chamber as democratic Pennsylvania, it also meant that democratic Rhode Island would have the same representation as conservative South Carolina. But the decision for equality of representation was not dictated by considerations either economic or democratic, but rather by the recalcitrance of the small states. Indeed, though it is difficult to generalize here, on the whole it is true that it was the more ardent Federalists who favored proportional representation in both houses.

They elaborated a most complicated method of electing a Chief Executive, a method designed to prevent the easy expression of any majority will. Again the explanation is not simple. The fact was that the framers did not envision the possibility of direct votes for presidential candidates which would not conform to state lines and interests and thus lead to dissension and confusion. Some method, they thought, must be designated to overcome the force of state prejudices (or merely of parochialism) and get an election; the method they anticipated was a preliminary elimination contest by the electoral college and then eventual election by the House. This, said George Mason, was what would occur nineteen times out of twenty.* There is no

---

* It has happened twice: Jefferson vs. Burr (1801) and J. Q. Adams vs. Clay, Jackson, and Crawford (1825).

evidence in the debates that the complicated method finally hit upon for electing a President was designed either to frustrate popular majorities or to protect special economic interests; its purpose was to overcome state pride and particularism.

Senators and Presidents, then, would not be the creatures of democracy. But what guarantee was there that senators would be representatives of property interests, or that the President himself would recognize the "priority of property"? Most states had property qualifications for office holding, but there are none in the Federal Constitution. As far as the Constitution is concerned, the President, congressmen, and Supreme Court justices can all be paupers.

Both General Charles Cotesworth Pinckney and his young cousin Charles, of South Carolina, were worried about this. The latter proposed a property qualification of $100,000 (a tidy sum in those days) for the Presidency, half that for the judges, and substantial sums for members of Congress. Franklin rebuked him. He was distressed, he said, to hear anything "that tended to debase the spirit of the common people." More surprising was the rebuke from that stout conservative, John Dickinson. "He doubted," Madison reports, "the policy of interweaving into a Republican constitution a veneration for wealth. He had always understood that a veneration for poverty & virtue were the objects of republican encouragement." Pinckney's proposal was overwhelmingly rejected.

What of the members of the lower house? When Randolph opened "the main business" on May 29 he said the remedy for the crisis that men faced must be "the republican principle," and two days later members were discussing the fourth resolution, which provided for election to the lower house by the people. Roger Sherman of Connecticut thought that "the people should have as little to do as may be about the Government," and Gerry hastened to agree in words now well-worn from enthusiastic quotation that "The evils we experience flow from the excess of democracy." These voices were soon drowned out, however. Mason "argued strongly for an election . . . by the people. It was to be the grand depository of the democratic principle of the Govt." And the learned James Wilson, striking the note to which he was to recur again and again, made clear that he was for "raising the federal pyramid to a considerable altitude, and for that reason wished to give it as broad a basis as possible." He thought both branches of the legislature—and the President as well, for that matter—should be elected by the people. "The Legislature," he later observed, "ought to be the most exact transcript of the whole Society."

A further observation is unhappily relevant today. It was a maxim with John Adams that "where annual elections end, there tyranny begins," and the whole Revolutionary generation was committed to a frequent return to the source of authority. But the framers put into the Constitution no limits on the number of terms which Presidents or congressmen could serve. It was not that the question was ignored; it received elaborate attention. It was rather that the generation that wrote the Constitution was better grounded in political principles than is our own; that it did not confuse, as we so often do, quantitative and qualitative limitations; and that—in a curious way—it had more confidence in the intelligence and the good will of the people than we seem to have today. It is, in any event, our own generation that has the dubious distinction of writing into the Constitution the first quantitative limitation on the right of the majority to choose their President. It is not the generation of the framers that was undemocratic; it is our generation that is undemocratic.

It is relevant to note, too, that the Constitution contains no property qualification for voting. Most states, to be sure, had such qualifications—in general a freehold or its equivalent—and the Constitution assimilated such qualifications as states might establish. Yet the framers, whether for reasons practical or philosophical we need not determine, made no serious efforts to write any property qualifications for voting into the Constitution itself.

The question of popular control came up clearly in one other connection as well: the matter of ratification. Should the Constitution be ratified by state legislatures, or by conventions? The practical arguments for the two methods were nicely balanced. The decisive argument was not, however, one of expediency but of principle. "To the people with whom all power remains that has not been given up in the Constitutions derived from them" we must resort, said Mason. Madison put the matter on principle, too. "He considered the difference between a system founded on the Legislatures only, and one founded on the people, to be the true difference between a *league* or *treaty* and a *Constitution*." Ellsworth's motion to refer the Constitution to legislatures was defeated by a vote of eight to two, and the resolution to refer it to conventions passed with only Delaware in the negative.

Was the Constitution designed to place private property beyond the reach of majorities? If so, the framers did a very bad job. They failed to write into it the most elementary safeguards for property. They failed to write into it limitations on the tax power, or prohibitions against the abuse of the money power. They failed to provide for rule by those whom Adams was later to call the wise and the rich and the well-born. What they did succeed in doing was to create a system of checks and balances and adjustments and accommodations that would effectively prevent the suppression of most minorities by majorities. They took advantage of the complexity, the diversity, the pluralism, of American society and economy to encourage a balance of interests. They worked out sound and lasting political solutions to the problems of class, interest, section, race, religion, party.

Perhaps the most perspicacious comment on this whole question of the threat from turbulent popular majorities against property and order came, *mirabile dictu*, from the dashing young Charles Pinckney of South Carolina—he of the "lost" Pinckney Plan. On June 25 Pinckney made a major speech and thought it important enough to write out and give to Madison. The point of departure was the hackneyed one of the character of the second branch of the legislature, but the comments were an anticipation of De Tocqueville and Lord Bryce. We need not, Pinckney asserted, fear the rise of class conflicts in America, nor take precautions against them.

> The genius of the people, their mediocrity of situation & the prospects which are afforded their industry in a Country which must be a new one for centuries are unfavorable to the rapid distinction of ranks. . . . If equality is . . . the leading feature of the U. States [he asked], where then are the riches & wealth whose representation & protection is the peculiar province of this permanent body [the Senate]. Are they in the hands of the few who may be called rich; in the possession of less than a hundred citizens? certainly not. They are in the great body of the people . . . [There was no likelihood that a privileged body would ever develop in the United States, he added, either from the landed interest, the moneyed interest, or the mercantile.] Besides, Sir, I apprehend that on this point the policy of the U. States has been much mistaken. We have unwisely considered ourselves as the inhabitants of an old instead of a new country. We have adopted the maxims of a State full of people . . . The people of this country are not only very different from the inhabitants of any State we are acquainted with in the modern world; but I assert that their situation is distinct from either the people of Greece or of Rome . . . Our true situation appears to me to be this a new extensive Country containing within itself the materials for forming a Government capable of extending to its citizens all the blessings of civil & religious liberty—capable of making them happy at home. This is the great end of Republican Establishments. . . .

Not a government cunningly contrived to protect the interests of property, but one capable of extending to its citizens the blessings of liberty and happiness—was that not, after all, what the framers created?

An early nineteenth-century allegory by John A. Woodside is symptomatic of the nationalistic fervor of the period. The triumphant seaman, his fetters broken, treads on England's crown and scepter.

Part
Four

NATIONAL
GROWING
PAINS

Henry Steele Commager

The Search
for a
Usable Past

One of the most remarkable things about the American nation, as
Professor Commager points out in the following essay, is that it came
into being before its people really had much sense of their common
nationality. The word "American," used as a generalization for the
common set of values and traditions possessed by the inhabitants
of what is now the United States, did not exist before the middle of
the eighteenth century, a mere generation before these inhabitants
revolted against Great Britain and established the political organism
called the United States. This was the case for a number of reasons,
the most important probably being that most of the colonists came to
America without much sense of psychological alienation from the
mother country; they continued to think of themselves as Englishmen.
Furthermore, the decentralized political structure imposed upon the
colonies by Britain prevented for many decades the development of
a general, or American, point of view: if settlers did not consider
themselves primarily as Englishmen, they were likely to describe
themselves as New Yorkers, Virginians, Pennsylvanians, and so on.

Thus, when the Revolution occurred and the nation was "born,"
it was necessary to create a national spirit, a sense of common identity.
How this was accomplished is the theme of Commager's essay. This
type of historical writing demands a well-stocked, imaginative mind,
one that has ranged widely over the sources, exploring out-of-the-way
as well as obvious records of the past. How well Commager fulfills
these requirements is amply demonstrated in the following pages.

The United States was the first of the "new" nations. As the American colonies were the first to rebel against a European "mother country," so the American states were the first to create—we can use Lincoln's term, to bring forth—a new nation. Modern nationalism was inaugurated by the American, not the French, Revolution. But the new United States faced problems unknown to the new nations of nineteenth-century Europe—and twentieth. For in the Old World the nation came before the state; in America the state came before the nation. In the Old World nations grew out of well-prepared soil, built upon a foundation of history and traditions; in America the foundations were still to be laid, the seeds still to be planted, the traditions still to be formed.

The problem which confronted the new United States then was radically different from that which confronted, let us say, Belgium, Italy, Greece, or Germany in the nineteenth century, or Norway, Finland, Iceland, and Israel in the twentieth. These "new" states were already amply equipped with history, tradition, and memory—as well as with many of the other essential ingredients of nationalism except political independence. Of them it can be said that the nation was a product of history. But with the United States, history was rather a creation of the nation, and it is suggestive that in the New World the self-made nation was as familiar as the self-made man.

It is unnecessary to emphasize anything as familiar as the importance of history, tradition, and memory to successful nationalism. On this matter statesmen, historians, and philosophers of nationalism are all agreed. It was the very core of Edmund Burke's philosophy: the nation—society itself—is a partnership of past, present, and future; we (the English) "derive all we possess as an inheritance from our forefathers." It is indeed not merely the course of history but of nature itself. Thus Friedrich von Schlegel, trying to quicken a sense of nationalism in the Germans, urged that "nothing is so important as that the Germans . . . return to the course of their own language and poetry, and liberate from the old documents of their ancestral past that power of old, that noble spirit which . . . is sleeping in them." And Mazzini, in his struggle for the unification of Italy, was ever conscious that "the most important inspiration for nationalism is the awareness of past glories and past sufferings."

So, too, with the philosophers of nationalism, and the historians as well. Listen to Ernest Renan. In that famous lecture "What Is a Nation?" he emphasized "the common memories, sacrifices, glories, afflictions, and regrets," and submitted that the worthiest of all cults was "the cult of ancestors." So, too, with the hard-headed John Stuart Mill, across the Channel. "The strongest cause [for the feeling of nationality] is identity of political antecedents, the possession of a national history, and consequent community of recollections, collective pride and humiliation, pleasure and regret."

But if a historical past and a historical memory are indeed essential ingredients for a viable nationalism, what was the new United States to do in 1776, or in 1789, or for that matter at almost any time before the Civil War? How does a country without a past of her own acquire one, or how does she provide a substitute for it? Where could such a nation find the stuff for patriotism, for sentiment, for pride, for memory, for collective character? It was a question that came up very early, for Americans have always been somewhat uncomfortable about their lack of history and of antiquity, somewhat embarrassed about being historical *nouveaux riches.*

It was Henry James who put the question in most memorable form. I refer to the famous passage about the historical and intellectual environment in which the young Nathaniel Hawthorne found himself in 1840. It takes a great deal of history to make a little literature, said James, and how could Hawthorne make literature with a history so meager and so thin: "No state, in the European sense of the word, and indeed barely a specific national name. No sovereign, no court, no personal loyalty, no aristocracy, no church, no clergy, no army, no diplomatic service, no country gentlemen, no palaces, no castles, nor manors, nor old country houses, nor parsonages, nor thatched cottages, nor ivied ruins; no cathedrals, nor abbeys, nor little Norman churches; no great Universities, nor public schools, no Oxford nor Eton nor Harrow; no literature, no novels, no museums, no pictures, no political society, no sporting class—no Epsom nor Ascot!"

There is almost too much here; the indictment, as James himself remarked, is a lurid one, and he noted, too, with some satisfaction, that Hawthorne had not been wholly frustrated by the thinness of his materials—how he managed was, said James wryly, our private joke. It is suggestive that James' famous outburst was inspired by Hawthorne himself; he had, so he wrote, delighted in a place—his own dear native land—which had "no shadow, no antiquity, no mystery, no picturesque and gloomy wrong, nor anything but a commonplace prosperity, in broad and simple daylight, as is happily the case with my dear native land." It is worth dwelling on this for a moment, for this is from the author of *The Scarlet Letter,* and of *The House of Seven Gables,* and of a score of stories which did precisely dwell on shadows, antiquities, gloomy wrongs—witchcraft, for example. If a Hawthorne, who all his life felt it necessary to immerse himself in New England antiquities and inherited wrongs, could yet contrast his own dear native land with the Old World in these terms, think how unshadowed were the lives of most Americans—or how empty, if you want to adopt the James point of view.

A host of Americans had anticipated all this, but with different emphasis. Thus the poet Philip Freneau, introducing the abbé Robin's *New Travels in America:* "They who would saunter over half the Globe to copy the inscription on an antique column, to measure the altitude of a pyramid, or describe the ornaments on the Grand Seigneur's State Turban, will scarcely find anything in American Travels to gratify their taste. The works of art are there comparatively trivial and inconsiderable, the splendor of pageantry rather obscure, and consequently few or none but the admirers of simple Nature can either travel with pleasure themselves or read the travels of others with satisfaction, through this country." And half a century later James Fenimore Cooper, caught in that dilemma of New World innocence and Old World corruption so pervasive in the first century of our history, admitted that in America "there are no annals for the historian, no follies beyond the most vulgar and commonplace for the satirist; no manners for the dramatist; no obscure fictions for the writer of romance; no gross and hardy offenses against decorum for the moralist; nor any of the rich artificial auxiliaries of poetry."

But if there were "no annals for the historian," and if a historical past was necessary to nation-making, what were Americans to do?

Americans had, in fact, several courses open to them, and with characteristic self-confidence, took them all.

Over a century before the Revolution it had been observed of the Virginians that they had no need of ancestors, for they themselves were ancestors. The variations on this theme were infinite, but the theme was simple and familiar: that Americans had no need of a past because they were so sure of a future. Goethe had congratulated them on their good fortune in a famous but almost untranslatable poem: *Amerika, du hast es besser:* "no ruined castles, no venerable stones, no useless memories, no vain feuds [he said]. . . . May a kind providence preserve you from tales of knights and robber barons and ghosts."

Americans took up the refrain with enthusiasm. The romantic artist Thomas Cole observed that though American scenery was "destitute of the vestiges of antiquity" it had other features that were reassuring, for "American associations are not so much with the past as of the present and the future, and in looking over the uncultivated scene, the mind may travel far into futurity."

This theme runs like a red thread through early American literature and oratory, and finally connects itself triumphantly with Manifest Destiny. It began, appropriately enough, with Crèvecoeur: "I am sure I cannot be called a partial American when I say that the spectacle afforded by these pleasing scenes must be more entertaining and more philosophical than that which arises from beholding the musty ruins of Rome. Here everything would inspire the reflecting traveller with the most philanthropic ideas; his imagination, instead of submitting to the painful and useless retrospect of revolutions, desolations, and plagues, would, on the contrary, wisely spring forward to the anticipated fields of future cultivation and improvement, to the future extent of those generations which are to replenish and embellish this boundless continent." Washington Irving's friend and collaborator, James Paulding, entertained the same sentiment: "It is for the other nations to boast of what they have been, and, like garrulous age, muse over the history of their youthful exploits that only renders decrepitude more conspicuous. Ours is the more animating sentiment of hope, looking forward with prophetic eye."

Best of all is Cooper's John Cadwallader in *Notions of the Americans,* rebuking his travelling companion, the bachelor Count, for his unmanly longing for antiquity: "You complain of the absence of association to give its secret, and perhaps greatest charm which such a sight is capable of inspiring. You complain unjustly. The moral feeling with which a man of sentiment and knowledge looks upon the plains of your [Eastern] Hemisphere is connected with his recollections; here it should be mingled with his hopes. The same effort of the mind is as equal to the one as to the other."

The habit of looking forward instead of back blended readily enough with Manifest Destiny. Thus John Louis O'Sullivan, who all but invented Manifest Destiny, dismissed the past in favor of the future: "We have no interest in scenes of antiquity, only as lessons of avoidance of nearly all their examples. The expansive future is our arena. We are entering on its untrodden space with the truth of God in our minds, beneficent objects in our hearts, and with a clear conscience unsullied by the past. We are the nation of human progress, and who will, what can, set limits on our onward march? . . . The far-reaching, the boundless future will be the era of American greatness. . . ."

There was nothing surprising in Emerson's conclusion that America had no past. "All," he said, "has an outward and prospective look." For transcendentalism—the first genuine expression of the American temperament in philosophy, or New England's at least—was impatient with origins, put its confidence in inspiration, looked upon each day as a new epoch and each man as an Adam. It is difficult to exaggerate the impatience of the transcendentalists with the past. It was not so much that they were opposed to it as they found it irrelevant. And note that New England's major historians—Bancroft, Prescott, Ticknor, Motley, and Parkman—were all outside the mainstream of transcendentalism.

This was all very well, this confidence in the future. But it was, after all, pretty thin fare for nationalism to feed on at a time when other self-conscious nations were rejoicing in an ancient and romantic past. To be sure, the past became ancient and the future became present more rapidly in America than anywhere else: thus Thomas Jefferson could write from Paris in 1787 that much was to be said for keeping the "good, old, venerable, fabrick" of the six-year-old Articles of Confederation. And thus, too, John Randolph, in the Virginia ratifying convention, could "take farewell of the Confederation, with reverential respect, as an old benefactor."

Happily, there was a second formula to which Americans had recourse, and one no less convenient than the first: that America had, in fact, the most impressive of all pasts; *all* Europe was the American past. After all, we speak the tongue that Shakespeare spake—and for good measure, the tongues of Luther and Racine and Dante and Cervantes as well. Just because Americans had crossed the Atlantic Ocean did not mean that they had forfeited or repudiated their heritage. Americans enjoyed, in fact, the richest and most varied of all heritages. Other benighted peoples had only their past—the Danes a Danish, the Germans a German—but Americans had them all. Were we not in very truth a teeming nation of nations? Edward Everett asserted this as early as 1820: "We suppose that in proportion to our population Lord Byron and Walter Scott are more read in America

than in England, nor do we see why we are not entitled to our full
share of all that credit which does not rest . . . in the person of the
author. . . .'' Whitman made this the burden of "Thou Mother With
Thy Equal Brood":

Sail, sail thy best, ship of Democracy,
Of value is thy freight, 'tis not the Present only,
The Past is also stored in thee,
Thou holdest not the venture of thyself alone, not of the Western
*   Continent alone,*
Earth's résumé entire floats on thy keel O ship, is steadied by thy
*   spars, . . .*
Steer then with a good strong hand, and wary eye O helmsman,
*   thou carriest great companions,*
Venerable priestly Asia sails this day with thee,
And royal feudal Europe sails with thee.

All very well, but a risky business, this assimilation of the Old
World past. For could the Old World be trusted? Could the past be
trusted? We come here to one of the major themes of American
intellectual history, and one of the most troublesome of all the problems
in the creation of a usable past.

The theme of New World innocence and Old World corruption
emerged early, and persisted all through the nineteenth century: it is
a constant of American literature as of American politics, and if it no
longer haunts our literature, it still bedevils our politics and diplomacy.

How deeply they were shocked, these innocent Americans, by the
goings on in Europe! Benjamin Franklin, after a long residence in
England, could deprecate the notion of a reconciliation between the
Americans and the mother country on moral grounds: "I have not
heard what Objections were made to the Plan in the Congress, nor
would I make more than this one, that, when I consider the extreme
Corruption prevalent among all Orders of Men in this old rotten
State, and the glorious publick Virtue so predominant in our rising
Country, I cannot but apprehend more Mischief than Benefit from a
closer Union." Dr. Benjamin Rush, who had studied in Edinburgh
and in London, never ceased to preach the danger of contamination
from abroad. With Jefferson—surely the most cosmopolitan American
of his generation—New World innocence and Old World corruption
was almost an *idée fixe*. How illuminating, that famous letter to John
Banister about the education of his son. "Why send an American
youth to Europe for education? . . . Let us view the disadvantages.
. . . To enumerate them all, would require a volume. I will select a
few. If he goes to England, he learns drinking, horse racing, and box-
ing. These are the peculiarities of English education. The following
circumstances are common to education in that, and the other countries of Europe. He acquires a fondness for European luxury and dissipation, and a contempt for the simplicity of his own country; he is
fascinated with the privileges of the European aristocrats and sees,
with abhorrence, the lovely equality which the poor enjoy with the

rich, in his own country; he contracts a partiality for aristocracy or monarchy; he forms foreign friendships which will never be useful to him . . . he is led, by the strongest of all the human passions, into a spirit for female intrigue, destructive of his own and others' happiness, or a passion for whores, destructive of his health, and, in both cases, learns to consider fidelity to the marriage bed as an ungentlemanly practice. . . . It appears to me, then, that an American coming to Europe for education, loses in his knowledge, in his morals, in his health, in his habits, and in his happiness. . . .''

The theme, and the arguments, persisted. Hezekiah Niles wrote on the eve of the War of 1812 that ''the War, dreadful as it is, will not be without its benefits in . . . separating us from the *strumpet governments of Europe.*'' It is the most persistent theme in American literature from Crèvecoeur to Tocqueville, from Hawthorne's *Marble Faun* to James' *Daisy Miller* and *Portrait of a Lady,* from *Innocents Abroad* to *The Sun Also Rises.* Something of its complexity and difficulty can be seen in the position of the expatriate. Here Americans long maintained a double standard; it was taken for granted not only that European immigrants to the United States give up their nationality and identify themselves with their adopted country, but that they do so exuberantly. But for Americans to give up their nationality and identify themselves with a foreign country was another matter.

Needless to say, there are philosophical and psychological implications here which we ignore at our peril. For this concept of New World innocence and Old World corruption encouraged that sense of being a people apart which nature herself had already sufficiently dramatized. How characteristic that Jefferson should have combined nature and morality in his first inaugural: ''Kindly separated by nature from one quarter of the globe; too high-minded to endure the degradations of the others. . . .'' To this day Americans are inclined to think that they are outside the stream of history, exempt from its burden.

But quite aside from the theme of Old World corruption, the availability of the European past was not a simple matter of chronological assimilation or absorption. It was available, to be sure, but only on limited terms. It was there more for purposes of contrast than for enrichment; it pointed the moral of American superiority, and adorned the tale of American escape from contamination. It was there, too, as a museum, a curio shop, and a moral playground. But for practical purposes it contributed little to the juices of American Life.

Americans had a third choice: They could use what they had. ''We have not, like England and France, centuries of achievements and calamities to look back on,'' wrote the indefatigable diarist George Templeton Strong, ''but being without the eras that belong to older nationalities—Anglo-Saxon, Carolingian, Hohenstaufen, Ghibelline, and so forth—we dwell on the details of our little all of historic life and venerate every trivial fact about our first settlers and colonial governors and revolutionary heroes.'' Not all Americans struck so modest a pose. All their past lacked, after all, was antiquity, and antiquity was relative; in any event, this meant that the American past was better authenticated than the European.

Nothing in the history of American nationalism is more impressive than the speed and the lavishness with which Americans provided themselves with a usable past: history, legends, symbols, paintings, sculpture, monuments, shrines, holy days, ballads, patriotic songs, heroes, and—with some difficulty—villains. Henry James speaks of Emerson dwelling for fifty years "within the undecorated walls of his youth." To Emerson they did not seem undecorated, for he embellished them with a profusion of historical association and of memory: the author of "Concord Hymn" was not unaware of the past.

Not every American, to be sure, was as deeply rooted as Emerson, but even to newcomers America soon ceased to be undecorated. Uncle Sam was quite as good as John Bull, and certainly more democratic. The bald eagle (Franklin sensibly preferred the turkey, but was overruled) did not compare badly with the British lion and was at least somewhat more at home in America than the lion in Britain. The Stars and Stripes, if it did not fall straight out of heaven like Denmark's *Dannebrog,* soon had its own mythology, and it had, besides, one inestimable advantage over all other flags, in that it provided an adjustable key to geography and a visible evidence of growth. Soon it provided the stuff for one of the greatest of all national songs—the tune difficult but the sentiments elevated—and one becoming to a free people. The Declaration of Independence was easier to understand than Magna Carta, and parts of it could be memorized and recited— as Magna Carta could not. In addition it had a Liberty Bell to toll its fame, which was something the British never thought of. There were no less than two national mottoes—*E pluribus unum,* selected, so appropriately, by Franklin, Jefferson, and John Adams, and *Novus ordo seclorum,* with their classical origins. There were no antiquities, but there were shrines: Plymouth Rock, of course, and Independence Hall and Bunker Hill and Mount Vernon and Monticello; eventually there was to be the Log Cabin in which Lincoln was born, as indestructible as the hull of the *Mayflower.*

These were some of the insignia, as it were, the ostentatious manifestations of the possession of a historical past. The stuff of that past was crowded and rich; it is still astonishing that Americans managed to fill their historical canvas so elaborately in so short a time. The colonial era provided a remote past: Pocahontas saving John Smith; the Pilgrims landing on the sandy coast of Plymouth, and celebrating the first Thanksgiving; Roger Williams fleeing through the wintry storms to Narragansett Bay; William Penn treating with the Indians; Deerfield going up in flames, its captives trekking through the snow to Canada; Franklin walking the streets of Philadelphia, munching those "three great puffy rolls" that came to be permanent props.

The Revolution proved a veritable cornucopia of heroic episodes and memories: Washington crossing the Delaware; Washington dwelling at Valley Forge; the signing of the Declaration; Captain Parker at Lexington Common: "If they mean to have a war, let it begin here!"; Prescott at Bunker Hill: "Don't fire until you see the whites of their eyes!''; John Paul Jones closing with the *Serapis:* ''I have not yet begun to fight!''; Nathan Hale on the gallows: ''I only regret that I have but one life to lose for my country''; Tom Paine writing the first *Crisis* on the flat of a drum, by the flickering light of campfires; George Rogers Clark wading through the flooded Wabash bottom lands to capture Vincennes; Washington at Yorktown: ''The World Turned Upside Down''; Washington, again, fumbling for his glasses at Newburgh: ''I have grown gray in your service, and now find myself growing blind''; Washington even in Heaven, not a pagan Valhalla but a Christian Heaven, doubly authenticated by a parson and a historian—one person to be sure—the incomparable Parson Weems.

The War of 1812, for all its humiliations, made its own contributions to national pride. Americans conveniently forgot the humiliations and recalled the glories: Captain Lawrence off Boston Harbor: ''Don't

This painting of Washington's apotheosis was done in China about 1800 by an unknown artist.

give up the ship"; the *Constitution* riddling the *Guerrière;* Francis Scott Key peering through the night and the smoke to see if the flag was still there; Perry at Put-in-Bay: "We have met the enemy and they are ours"; the hunters of Kentucky repulsing Pakenham—

> *There stood John Bull in Martial pomp*
> *But here was old Kentucky.*

No wonder Old Hickory went straight to the White House.

The West, too—not one West but many—provided a continuous flow of memories and experiences and came to be, especially for immigrants, a great common denominator. There was the West of the Indian; of Washington at Fort Necessity; the West of Daniel Boone; of Lewis and Clark; of the Santa Fe Trail and the Oregon Trail and the California Gold Rush; the West of the miner and the cowboy; the West of the Union Pacific trail and the other transcontinentals. "If it be romance, if it be contrast, if it be heroism that we require," asked Robert Louis Stevenson, "what was Troytown to this?" What indeed?

And richest of all in its contribution to the storehouse of American memory was the Civil War, with its hero, Lincoln: it produced the best literature and the best songs of any modern war; it was packed with drama and with heroism. To one part of America it gave the common bond of defeat and tragedy, but a defeat that fed sentiment so powerful that it was metamorphosed into victory. It gave to the whole of America a dramatic sense of unity; to Negroes it associated national unity with freedom; and to all it gave the most appealing of national heroes, probably the only modern hero to rank with Alfred and Barbarossa and Joan of Arc. Certainly, of all modern heroes it is Lincoln who lends himself most readily to mythology; his birth humble and even mysterious; his youth gentle and simple; his speech pithy and wise; his wit homely and earthy; his counsels benign. He emerged briefly to save his nation and free the slaves, and died tragically as the lilacs bloomed; no wonder the poets and the myth-makers have exhausted themselves on this theme.

No less remarkable was the speed and comprehensiveness with which the new nation provided itself with an artistic record. From the beginning, to be sure, Americans had been fortunate in this realm; no other nation, it is safe to say, has had its entire history so abundantly recorded as the American, from the first contributions by Le Moyne and De Bry and John White to the realism of the Ash Can school of the early twentieth century. Never before in recorded history had anything excited the imagination like the discovery of the New World —O brave new world, O strange new world, new world that was Utopia and Paradise. Everything about it excited the explorers and conquerors: the Patagonian giants and the Amazons of Brazil and the pygmies of the Far North; the mountains that soared fifty miles into the clouds and the lakes as vast as continents and the caves of solid gold; the natives who were descended from the Chinese or the Jews or the Norwegians or the Welsh; the flora and fauna so strange they all but defied description. How to make clear the wonder and the terror of it all?

All the explorers were historians, to be sure; almost all of them were artists as well, and soon all Europe could share the wonder of those who had seen what men had never seen before. It was as if cartographers had given us maps of the voyages of the Phoenicians or of the Vikings; it was as if artists had pictured Hector and Agamemnon before the walls of Troy or Romulus founding the city that would bear his name, or Hengist and Horsa on the shores of Ebbsfleet!

Political independence brought with it artistic freedom, and an ardent preoccupation with the birth of the nation created the stirring political drama; the scenes of battle, lurid and triumphant; the Founding Fathers, grave, as became men occupying a sure place in history. In a generation when Franklin doubted the possibility and John Adams the propriety of art, a host of artists emerged, as if in defiance of counsels too sober; if they were not Rembrandts or Turners, they were better than anyone had any right to expect. It is not, however, their artistic merits that interest us, but their historical function. John Singleton Copley gave us a rich and crowded portrait gallery of colonial society in the process of becoming American—the merchants, the statesmen, the captains, and their ladies as well. John Trumbull regarded himself as the official painter of the Revolution and covered that chapter of history systematically though not comprehensively. Scarcely less impressive was the contribution of the versatile Charles Willson Peale, who left us a whole gallery of Founding Fathers as well as an academy of artistic sons, while the achievement of Gilbert Stuart in impressing on future generations his image of the Father of His Country is almost without parallel in the history of art. This school of artistic historians came to an end when its work was done, when it had provided posterity with artistic archives and monuments of its birth and its youth. Then the new nation, secure in the possession of an artistic record, could afford to indulge the romanticism of an Allston or a Cole, of the Hudson River school, or of genre painters like the puckish John Quidor—worthy companion to Washington Irving—or William Sidney Mount.

The celebration of independence and the founding of the republic was but one chapter in the history of the creation of an artistic image of the American past. Another school seized, almost instinctively, on the inexhaustible theme of the Indian and the winning of the West. Thus, while scores of American artists sailed for the Italian Arcadia, others, untrained, or trained in the irrelevant school of Düsseldorf, moved quite as confidently across the Alleghenies and on to the prairies and the plains and the mountains of the West. What a romantic group they were: the Swiss Carl Bodmer, who went with Prince Maximilian of Wied up the Missouri River in the early 1830's, and who gave us a crowded gallery of Sioux, Crees, Assiniboins, and Mandans; the indefatigable George Catlin with his hundreds of Indian portraits—surely the fullest artistic re-creation of the West before photography; Alfred Jacob Miller, who was the artist for Captain Stewart's explorations in the Far West and who sketched not only Indians but the landscape—Chimney Rock and Independence

Rock and the Tetons and the Wind River Mountains; the luckless John Mix Stanley, who was ubiquitous, from the lead mines of Galena to the Cherokee country, with Kearny on the Santa Fe Trail, one thousand miles by canoe up the Columbia, even to distant Hawaii—the work of a lifetime lost in the great Smithsonian fire of 1865.

Not all of these artists of the early West re-created the past for their own generation. Miller, for example, was not really known in his own day, nor was Stanley. Far more important in the creation of the popular image of America were two artist-ornithologists, Alexander Wilson and John James Audubon, who captured for all time the flora and fauna of America in its pastoral age. Wilson's nine-volume *American Ornithology* was perhaps the most ambitious work of science in the early republic. Soon came Audubon's *Birds of America*, less scientific than Wilson's *Ornithology* but more splendid, "the most magnificent monument" said Cuvier, "which art has ever raised to ornithology." And Audubon, of course, contributed more: his own extraordinary life and legend.

The sumptuous paintings of Wilson and Audubon reached the public only gradually, and in cheap reproductions. More effective was the impact of the almost forgotten school of panoramists. The hapless John Vanderlyn, who had dared display his nude *Ariadne* to an outraged public, introduced the panorama, in a specially built rotunda in New York's City Hall Park. But it was Versailles and Athens and Mexico which he chose to display; perhaps that is why he failed. His successors preferred to reveal America, and particularly the Father of Waters, which had the advantage of being almost the only object of nature longer than their paintings. One John Rowson Smith did a panorama of the Mississippi as early as 1844; when he displayed it at Saratoga Springs, New York, he took in twenty thousand dollars in six weeks. Soon there were a dozen rivals in the field: John Banvard, for example, who claimed that his Mississippi panorama was three miles long (actually it was only a quarter of a mile—a bad calculation, that). Poor John Stanley, who had so little luck with his Indian paintings, scored a tremendous success with a panorama of the *Western Wilds*, forty-two episodes, no less, requiring a minimum of two hours to view! Greatest of all the panoramists was Henry Lewis, who managed to cover almost three quarters of a mile of canvas with his paintings; his earnings from his great panorama enabled him to settle in Düsseldorf and learn to paint. Whatever their artistic merits, or demerits, the panoramas helped give a whole generation of Americans some feeling for the spaciousness and the beauty of the early West.

Writing in 1841, Emerson had lamented that "banks and tariffs, the newspaper and caucus, Methodism and Unitarianism, are flat and dull to dull people but rest on the same foundations of wonder as the town of Troy and the temple of Delphi. . . . Our logrolling, our stumps and their politics, our fisheries, our Negroes and Indians, our boasts and our repudiations . . . the northern trade, the southern planting, the western clearing, Oregon and Texas, are yet unsung. Yet America is a poem in our eyes; its ample geography dazzles the imagination.'' Poets and artists had responded, but none had quite encompassed American nature. Even Whitman and Winslow Homer could not quite do that. For nature played a special role in American history and in the process of creating a sense of history and a national consciousness. Since the seventeenth century, Europeans have not had to concern themselves energetically with the conquest of nature, for nature, like history, was given. For Americans, on the other hand, the relationship to nature was more personal, and more complex. They had an empty continent to settle and successive frontiers to conquer, and for them nature had always played a twofold role: her ruggedness was a challenge, and her richness a manifestation of divine favor. How suggestive it is that for over two hundred years Europeans could not make up their minds whether the New World was Paradise or an accursed place, whether its natives were Noble Savages or degenerate men without souls. But however nature was to be interpreted—and by the nineteenth century the paradisiacal interpretation had triumphed—it was, in a peculiar way, the great common denominator and the great common experience. Virginians, Pilgrims, and Quakers alike could rejoice in the abundance of nature, and generations of pioneers, even those who were not *Mayflower* descendants or FFV's, could cherish the common memory of hardship endured and overcome.

Because they had conquered nature, Americans came in time to think that they had created it and to display toward it a proprietary interest. The stupendous flow of Niagara, the luxuriance of the Bluegrass, the power and majesty of the Father of Waters, the limitless expanse of prairie and plain, the glory of the Rockies—all of these came to be regarded as national attributes, and failure to appreciate them, like failure to appreciate political attributes, an affront. How interesting that from ''Swanee River'' to ''Ol' Man River'' songs celebrating nature have usurped the place of formal patriotic music —''Dixie,'' for example, or ''My Old Kentucky Home,'' or ''On the Banks of the Wabash,'' or ''Home on the Range,'' or best of all, ''America, the Beautiful.''

And how interesting, too, that where in other countries topography is local, in America it is national. In the Old World, plains, valleys, and mountains belong to the people who happen to inhabit them, but in America the whole country, ''from sea to shining sea,'' belongs to the whole people. The Italians and Germans traditionally celebrate their own cities, their particular churches or bridges; the English write two-volume works on Fly-casting in the Dart, or Cricket in Lower Slaughter, but until recently there has been little of this local possessiveness about Americans. ''We have so much country that we have no country at all,'' Hawthorne lamented back in 1837, but Hawthorne was far from typical, and newcomers who could find little satisfaction in the slums of New York or the coal mines of Pennsylvania or the steel mills of Gary might yet rejoice in the Great Lakes and Yosemite. Movement, especially westward movement, is an essential ingredient in the American memory. When John F. Kennedy hit on the slogan, "Get America moving," he touched a responsive chord.

The task of providing themselves with a historical past was peculiarly difficult for Americans because it was not something that could be taken for granted, as with most peoples, or arranged once and for all. It was something that had to be done over and over again, for each new wave of newcomers, and that had to be kept up to date, as it were, continually reinvigorated and modernized. Above all, it had to be a past which contained an ample supply of easily grasped common denominators for a heterogeneous people, English and German, Irish and Norse, white and black, gentile and Jew, Protestant, Mormon, and Catholic, old stock and newcomer. Almost inevitably the common denominators tended to be pictorial and symbolic: the Pilgrims and Valley Forge, Washington and Lincoln, cowboy and Indian, and along with them ideas and institutions like Democracy, Liberty, Equality, the American Dream, and the American Way of Life.

One consequence of this emphasis on the simple, the symbolic, and the ideological is that American patriotism tended to be more artificial, labored, and ostentatious than that of most Old World peoples. It was almost inevitably calculated and artificial: after all, the process of drawing the juices of tradition for a German boy newly arrived in America was very different from that for a French or an English lad at home, where everything could be taken for granted, or left to nature. Tradition in America had to be labored, for it was not born into the young; it did not fill the horizon, as the glory of Joan of Arc or the fame of Nelson filled the horizons of French and English boys and girls. The American past could not be absorbed from childhood on in the art and architecture of every town and village, in song and story and nursery rhyme, in novel and history, in the names of streets and squares and towns. Growing up in Pittsburgh or Chicago was a very different experience, historically, from growing up in London or Edinburgh, Paris or Rome. And patriotism probably had to be ostentatious; in any event, it is. Ostentation characterizes new wealth, and new loyalties as well. This is doubtless one reason there is so much emphasis on the overt observance of patriotism in America. Americans dedicate a large number of days to ceremonial patriotism: the Fourth of July, Memorial Day, Confederate Memorial Day, Veterans Day, Washington's Birthday, Lincoln's Birthday, Columbus Day, Loyalty Day, and many others, and for good measure many states have their own special holidays—Patriots' Day in Massachusetts or Texas Independence Day. Americans require children to "pledge allegiance to the flag," impose loyalty oaths for every conceivable occasion, and march in "I Am an American Day" parades, and there is no W. S. Gilbert to satirize what so many take with passionate seriousness. Perhaps nowhere else in the Western world is loyalty such a touchstone as in the United States, perhaps nowhere else are there so many organizations dedicated to fostering patriotism: the Daughters of the American Revolution, the Sons of the American Revolution, the Colonial Dames, the United Daughters of the Confederacy, the Americanism committees of the great veterans' organizations, and, more recently, the Minute Women.

The process of acquiring a usable past was immensely facilitated by two extraordinary circumstances. The first was the eagerness of almost all newcomers from every part of the globe to slough off their pasts and take on an American habit, an eagerness so avid and so pervasive that it made nonsense of the compunctions and fears of native Americans from Fisher Ames to Thomas Bailey Aldrich a century later. Perhaps no other society in the process of transforming itself into a nation had more co-operative material to work with. The American newcomer, as he told us over and over again, was under both moral and practical compulsions to achieve acceptance for himself and for his children by becoming completely American as rapidly and as thoroughly as possible. Crèvecoeur, who saw so much, saw this, and so too the magisterial Tocqueville, but it is a lesson that has had to be relearned in every generation.

That it was *possible* for newcomers to become American overnight was the second circumstance. The explanation here lies in large part in the high degree of literacy that obtained in America, even in the eighteenth century, and the tradition of literacy and of education that flourished in that and the next century. Schools proved, in the long run, the most effective agencies for the creation and the transmission of an American memory. If they did not deliberately inculcate Americanism, that was because they did not need to: Noah Webster's Spellers, McGuffey's many Readers, Jedidiah Morse's Geographies and Peter Parley's Histories—these and scores of books like them conjured up an American past and provided, for generations of children, the common denominators, the stories and songs and poems, the memories and symbols. And it was the children, in turn, who educated the parents, for America is the only country where, as a matter of course, it is assumed that each new generation is wiser and more sophisticated than the old, and where parents adopt the standards of their children rather than children adopting those of their parents. For newcomers too old for school, and too inflexible to learn from their children, the work of providing an American past was carried on by voluntary organizations which have always performed the most miscellaneous of social tasks: churches, political parties, labor unions, lyceums, fraternal and filiopietistic organizations, and so forth.

What this meant was that the sentiment of American nationalism was, to an extraordinary degree, a literary creation, and that the national memory was a literary and, in a sense, a contrived memory. The contrast here with the Old World is sharp. There the image of the past was conjured up and sustained by a thousand testimonials: folklore and folk song, the vernacular and the patois, church music and architecture, monuments, paintings and murals, the pageantry of the court and of popular feasts and holidays. To be sure, literature —poetry and drama and formal histories—came to play a role, but only when it was quarried from cultural foundations that went deep. In America the image of the past was largely the creation of the poets and the storytellers, and chiefly of the New England-New York group who flourished between the War of 1812 and the War for the Union, that group familiar to an earlier generation through the amiable game of Authors: Irving, Cooper, and Bryant; Longfellow, Hawthorne, and Whittier; Emerson, Lowell, and Holmes. These were the Founding Fathers of American literary nationalism, and their achievement was scarcely less remarkable than that of the Founding Fathers of political nationalism.

In a single generation these men of letters gave Americans the dramas, the characters, the settings, which were to instruct and delight succeeding generations: Uncas and Deerslayer and Long Tom Coffin; Rip Van Winkle and the Headless Horseman; Miles Standish, Paul Revere, Evangeline, and Hiawatha; Goodman Brown, the Grey Champion, and Hester Prynne, as well as the Salem Customs House, the House of Seven Gables, the Old Manse, and the Great Stone Face; Skipper Ireson and Concord Bridge and Old Ironsides and the One-Hoss Shay and Hosea Biglow with all his Yankee company.

Note that this image of the past which the literary Founding Fathers created and imposed upon Americans was very largely a New England image, and much that was most distinctive about American nationalism was to be conditioned by this circumstance. It meant that Americans on Iowa prairies or the plains of Texas would sing *"I love thy rocks and rills, thy woods and templed hills"* with no sense of incongruity; that Plymouth would supplant Jamestown as the birthplace of America; that Thanksgiving Day would be a New England holiday; that Paul Revere would be the winged horseman of American history and Concord Bridge the American equivalent of the Rubicon; that Boston's Statehouse would vindicate its claim—or Holmes'—to be the "hub of the solar system." If all this was hard on the South, southerners had only themselves to blame for their indifference to their own men of letters. The most familiar of southern symbols came from the North: Harriet Beecher Stowe of New England gave us Uncle Tom and Little Eva and Topsy and Eliza, while it was Stephen Foster of Pittsburgh who sentimentalized the Old South, and even "Dixie" had northern origins.

The literary task of creating a usable past was largely performed by 1865; after that date perhaps only Mark Twain, Bret Harte, and Louisa May Alcott added anything substantial to the treasure house of historical memories. This was, in perspective, the most significant achievement of American literature and one almost without parallel in the literature of any other country in a comparable period. How interesting that a people supposed to be indifferent to literature—supposed by some to have no literature—should depend so largely upon literature for the nourishment of its historical self-consciousness. Certainly the speed and effectiveness with which Americans rallied their resources to supply themselves with a historical past cannot but excite astonishment. And what a past it was—splendid, varied, romantic, and all but blameless, in which there were heroes but no villains, victories but no defeats—a past that was all prologue to the Rising Glory of America.

John A. Garraty

Marbury
v. Madison

One of the most remarkable aspects of the Constitution of the United States (and the secret of its longevity) is its flexibility. A form of government designed to deal with the problems of a handful of farmers, merchants, and craftsmen scattered along a thousand miles of coastline, separated from one another by acres of forest and facing the trackless western wilderness, has endured with a minimum of changes through nearly two centuries, in which the nation has occupied a continental domain and become an urban-industrial behemoth.

A major reason for the flexibility of the Constitution has been the system of judicial review, which exists in the document largely by implication, but which has nonetheless functioned with enormous effectiveness. The following essay deals with one of the great landmarks in the development of the power of the Supreme Court to interpret the meaning of the Constitution and thus define the powers of both the federal government and the states. The case of Marbury v. Madison, like so many controversies that crucially affected the Constitution, was in itself of no importance. A minor federal official, deprived of his office by a technicality, was seeking redress from the Court. But in deciding his fate, the Court laid down a principle that altered the whole future of the country, shaping events that neither Marbury, nor Madison, nor the framers of the Constitution could possibly have anticipated.

*I*t was the evening of March 3, 1801, his last day in office, and President John Adams was in a black and bitter mood. Assailed by his enemies, betrayed by some of his most trusted friends, he and his Federalist party had gone down to defeat the previous November before the forces of Thomas Jefferson. His world seemed to have crumbled about his doughty shoulders.

Conservatives of Adams' persuasion were deeply convinced that Thomas Jefferson was a dangerous radical. He would, they thought, in the name of individual liberty and states' rights, import the worst excesses of the French Revolution, undermine the very foundations of American society, and bring the proud edifice of the national government, so laboriously erected under Washington and Adams, tumbling to the ground. Jefferson was a "visionary," Chief Justice Oliver Ellsworth had said. With him as President, "there would be no national energy." Ardent believers in a powerful central government like Secretary of State John Marshall feared that Jefferson would "sap the fundamental principles of government." Others went so far as to call him a "howling atheist."

Adams himself was not quite so disturbed as some, but he was deeply troubled. "What course is it we steer?" he had written despairingly to an old friend after the election. "To what harbor are we bound?" Now on the morrow Jefferson was to be inaugurated, and Adams was so disgruntled that he was unwilling to remain for the ceremonies, the first to be held in the new capital on the Potomac. At the moment, however, John Adams was still President of the United States, and not yet ready to abandon what he called "all virtuous exertion" in the pursuit of his duty. Sitting at his desk in the damp, drafty, still-unfinished sandstone mansion soon to be known as "the White House," he was writing his name on official papers in his large, quavering hand.

The documents he was signing were mostly commissions formally appointing various staunch Federalists to positions in the national judiciary, but the President did not consider his actions routine. On the contrary: he believed he was saving the republic itself. Jefferson was to be President and his Democratic-Republicans would control the Congress, but the courts, thank goodness, would be beyond his control: as soon as the extent of Jefferson's triumph was known, Adams had determined to make the judiciary a stronghold of Federalism. Responding enthusiastically to his request for expansion of the courts, the lame-duck Congress had established sixteen new circuit judgeships (and a host of marshals, attorneys, and clerks as well). It had also given Adams blanket authority to create as many justices of the peace for the new District of Columbia as he saw fit, and—to postpone the evil day when Jefferson would be able to put one of his sympathizers on the Supreme Court—it provided that when the next vacancy occurred, it should not be filled, thus reducing the Court from six justices to five. (The Constitution says nothing about the number of justices on the Court; its size is left to Congress. Originally six, the membership was enlarged to seven in 1807. The justices first numbered nine in 1837. Briefly during the Civil War the bench held ten; the number was set at seven again in 1866 and in 1869 returned to nine, where it has remained.)

In this same period between the election and the inauguration of the new President, Chief Justice Ellsworth, who was old and feeble, had resigned, and Adams had replaced him with Secretary of State Marshall. John Marshall was primarily a soldier and politician; he knew relatively little of the law. But he had a powerful mind, and, as Adams reflected, his "reading of the science" was "fresh in his head." He was also but forty-five years of age, and vigorous. Clearly a long life lay ahead of him, and a more forceful opponent of Jeffersonian principles would have been hard to find.

Marshall had been confirmed by the Senate on January 27, and without resigning as Secretary of State he had begun at once to help Adams strengthen the judicial branch of the government. They had worked rapidly, for time was short. The new courts were authorized by Congress on February 13; within two weeks Adams had submitted a full slate of officials for confirmation by the Senate. The new justices of the peace for the District of Columbia were authorized on February 27; within three days Adams had submitted for confirmation the names of no less than forty-two justices for the sparsely populated region. The Federalist Senate had done its part nobly, pushing through the various confirmations with great dispatch. Now, in the lamplight of his last night in Washington, John Adams was affixing his signature to the commissions of these "midnight justices," as the last-minute appointees were to become derisively known.

Working with his customary puritanical diligence, Adams completed his work by nine o'clock, and when he went off to bed for the last time as President of the United States, it was presumably with a clear conscience. The papers were carried to the State Department, where Secretary Marshall was to affix the Great Seal of the United States to each, and see to it that the commissions were then dispatched to the new appointees. But Marshall, a Virginian with something of the southerner's easygoing carelessness about detail, failed to complete this routine task.

All the important new circuit judgeships were taken care of, and most of the other appointments as well. But in the bustle of last-minute arrangements, the commissions of the new justices of the peace for the District of Columbia went astray. As a result of this trivial slip-up, and entirely without anyone's having planned it, a fundamental principle of the Constitution—affecting the lives of countless millions of future Americans—was to be established. Because *Secretary of State* Marshall made his last mistake, *Chief Justice* Marshall was soon to make one of the first—and in some respects the greatest—of his decisions.

It is still not entirely clear what happened to the missing commissions on the night of March 3. To help with the rush of work, Adams had borrowed two State Department clerks, Jacob Wagner and Daniel Brent. Brent prepared a list of the forty-two new justices and gave it to another clerk, who filled in the blank commissions. As fast as batches of these were made ready, Brent took them to Adams' office, where he turned them over to William Smith Shaw, the President's private secretary. After they were signed, Brent brought them back to the State Department, where Marshall was supposed to affix the Great Seal. Evidently he did seal these documents, but he did not trouble to make sure that they were delivered to the appointees. As he later said: "I did not send out the commissions because I apprehended such . . . to be completed when signed & sealed." Actually, he admitted, he would have sent them out in any case "but for the extreme hurry of the time & the absence of Mr. Wagner who had been called on by the President to act as his private secretary."

March 4 dawned and Jefferson, who apparently had not yet digested the significance of Adams' partisan appointments, prepared to take the oath of office and deliver his inaugural address. His mood, as the brilliant speech indicated, was friendly and conciliatory. He even asked Chief Justice Marshall, who administered the inaugural oath, to stay on briefly as Secretary of State while the new administration was getting established. That morning it would still have been possible to deliver the commissions. As a matter of fact, a few actually were delivered, although quite by chance.

Marshall's brother James (whom Adams had just made circuit judge for the District of Columbia) was disturbed by rumors that there was going to be a riot in Alexandria in connection with the inaugural festivities. Feeling the need of some justices of the peace in case trouble developed, he went to the State Department and personally picked up a number of the undelivered commissions. He signed a receipt for them, but "finding that he could not conveniently carry the whole," he returned several, crossing out the names of these from the receipt. Among the ones returned were those appointing William Harper and Robert Townsend Hooe. By failing to deliver these commissions, Judge James M. Marshall unknowingly enabled Harper and Hooe, obscure men, to win for themselves a small claim to legal immortality.

The new President was eager to mollify the Federalists, but when he realized the extent to which Adams had packed the judiciary with his "most ardent political enemies," he was indignant. Adams' behavior, he said at the time, was an "outrage on decency," and some years later, when passions had cooled a little, he wrote sorrowfully: "I can say with truth that one act of Mr. Adams' life, and one only, ever gave me a moment's personal displeasure. I did consider his last appointments to office as personally unkind." When he discovered the justice-of-the-peace commissions in the State Department, he decided at once not to allow them to be delivered.

James Madison, the Secretary of State, was not yet in Washington. Jefferson called in his Attorney General, a Massachusetts lawyer named Levi Lincoln, whom he had designated Acting Secretary. Giving Lincoln a new list of justices of the peace, he told him to put them "into a general commission" and notify the men of their selection.

Thomas Jefferson,
by Gilbert Stuart.

In truth, Jefferson acted with remarkable forbearance. He reduced the number of justices to thirty, fifteen for the federal District, fifteen for Alexandria County. But only seven of his appointees were his own men; the rest he chose from among the forty-two names originally submitted by Adams. Lincoln prepared two general commissions, one for each area, and notified the appointees. Then, almost certainly, he destroyed the original commissions signed by Adams.

For some time thereafter Jefferson did very little about the way Adams had packed the judiciary. Indeed, despite his much-criticized remark that office holders seldom die and never resign, he dismissed relatively few persons from the government service. For example, the State Department clerks, Wagner and Brent, were permitted to keep their jobs. The new President learned quickly how hard it was to institute basic changes in a going organization. "The great machine of society" could not easily be moved, he admitted, adding that it was impossible "to advance the notions of a whole people suddenly to ideal right." Soon some of his more impatient supporters, like John Randolph of Roanoke, were grumbling about the President's moderation.

But Jefferson was merely biding his time. Within a month of the inauguration he conferred with Madison at Monticello and made the basic decision to try to abolish the new system of circuit courts. Aside from removing the newly appointed marshals and attorneys, who served at the pleasure of the Chief Executive, little could be done until the new Congress met in December. Then, however, he struck. In his first annual message he urged the "contemplation" by Congress of the

Judiciary Act of 1801. To direct the lawmakers' thinking, he submitted a statistical report showing how few cases the federal courts had been called upon to deal with since 1789. In January, 1802, a repeal bill was introduced; after long debate it passed early in March, thus abolishing the jobs of the new circuit judges.

Some of those deposed petitioned Congress for "relief," but their plea was coldly rejected. Since these men had been appointed for life, the Federalists claimed that the repeal act was unconstitutional, but to prevent the Supreme Court from quickly so declaring, Congress passed another bill abolishing the June term of the Court and setting the second Monday of February, 1803, for its next session. By that time, the Jeffersonians reasoned, the old system would be dead beyond resurrection.

This powerful assault on the courts thoroughly alarmed the conservative Federalists; to them the foundations of stable government seemed threatened if the "independence" of the judiciary could be thus destroyed. No one was more disturbed than the new Chief Justice, John Marshall, nor was anyone better equipped by temperament and intellect to resist it. Headstrong but shrewd, contemptuous of detail and of abstractions but a powerful logician, he detested Jefferson (to whom he was distantly related), and the President fully returned his dislike.

In the developing conflict Marshall operated at a disadvantage that in modern times a Chief Justice would not have to face. The Supreme Court had none of the prestige and little of the accepted authority it now possesses. Few cases had come before it, and few of these were of any great importance. Before appointing Marshall, Adams had offered the Chief Justiceship to John Jay, the first man to hold the post, as an appointee of President Washington. Jay had resigned from the Court in 1795 to become governor of New York. He refused the reappointment, saying that the Court lacked "energy, weight, and dignity." A prominent newspaper of the day referred to the Chief Justiceship, with considerable truth, as a "sinecure." One of the reasons Marshall had accepted the post was his belief that it would afford him ample leisure for writing the biography of his hero, George Washington. Indeed, in the grandiose plans for the new capital, no thought had been given to housing the Supreme Court, so that when Marshall took office in 1801 the justices had to meet in the office of the clerk of the Senate, a small room on the first floor of what is now the north wing of the Capitol.

Nevertheless, Marshall struck out at every opportunity against the power and authority of the new President; but the opportunities were pitifully few. In one case, he refused to allow a presidential message to be read into the record on the ground that this would bring the President into the Court, in violation of the principle of separation of powers. In another, he ruled that Jefferson's decision in a prize case involving an American privateer was illegal. But these were matters of small importance.

When he tried to move more boldly, his colleagues would not sustain him. He was ready to declare the judicial repeal act unconstitutional, but none of the deposed circuit court judges would bring a case to court. Marshall also tried to persuade his associates that it was unconstitutional for Supreme Court justices to ride the circuit, as they were forced again to do by the abolishment of the lower courts. But although they agreed with his legal reasoning, they refused to go along —because, they said, years of acquiescence in the practice lent sanction to the old law requiring it. Thus frustrated, Marshall was eager for any chance to attack his enemy, and when a case that was to be known as *Marbury v. Madison* came before the Court in December, 1801, he took it up with gusto.

William Marbury, a forty-one-year-old Washingtonian, was one of the justices of the peace for the District of Columbia whose commissions Jefferson had held up. Originally from Annapolis, he had moved to Washington to work as an aide to the first Secretary of the Navy, Benjamin Stoddert. It was probably his service to this staunch Federalist that earned him the appointment by Adams. Together with one Dennis Ramsay and Messrs. Harper and Hooe, whose commissions James Marshall had *almost* delivered, Marbury was asking the Court to issue an order (a writ of mandamus) requiring Secretary of State Madison to hand over their "missing" commissions. Marshall willingly assumed jurisdiction and issued an order calling upon Madison to show cause at the next term of the Supreme Court why such a writ should not be issued. Here clearly was an opportunity to get at the President through one of his chief agents, to assert the authority of the Court over the executive branch of the government.

This small controversy quickly became a matter of great moment both to the administration and to Marshall. The decision to do away with the June term of the Court was made in part to give Madison more time before having to deal with Marshall's order. The abolition of the circuit courts and the postponement of the next Supreme Court session to February, 1803, made Marshall even more determined to use the Marbury case to attack Jefferson. Of course Marshall was personally and embarrassingly involved in this case, since his carelessness was the cause of its very existence. He ought to have disqualified himself, but his fighting spirit was aroused, and he was in no mood to back out.

On the other hand, the Jeffersonians used every conceivable means to obstruct judicial investigation of executive affairs. Madison ignored Marshall's order. When Marbury and Ramsay called on the Secretary to inquire whether their commissions had been duly signed (Hooe and Harper could count on the testimony of James Marshall to prove that theirs had been attended to), Madison gave them no satisfactory answer. When they asked to *see* the documents, Madison referred them to the clerk, Jacob Wagner. He, in turn, would only say that the commissions were not then in the State Department files.

Unless the plaintiffs could prove that Adams had appointed them, their case would collapse. Frustrated at the State Department, they turned to the Senate for help. A friendly senator introduced a motion calling upon the Secretary of the Senate to produce the record of the action in executive session on their nominations. But the motion was defeated, after an angry debate, on January 31, 1803. Thus, tempers were hot when the Court finally met on February 9 to deal with the case.

In addition to Marshall, only Justices Bushrod Washington (a nephew of the first President) and Samuel Chase were on the bench, and the Chief Justice dominated the proceedings. The almost childishly obstructive tactics of administration witnesses were no match for his fair but forthright management of the hearing. The plaintiffs' lawyer was Charles Lee, an able advocate and brother of "Light-Horse Harry" Lee; he had served as Attorney General under both Washington and Adams. He was a close friend of Marshall, and his dislike of Jefferson had been magnified by the repeal of the Judiciary Act of 1801, for he was another of the circuit court judges whose "midnight" appointments repeal had cancelled.

Lee's task was to prove that the commissions had been completed by Adams and Marshall, and to demonstrate that the Court had authority to compel Madison to issue them. He summoned Wagner and Brent, and when they objected to being sworn because "they were clerks in the Department of State, and not bound to disclose any facts relating to the business or transactions in the office," Lee argued that in addition to their "confidential" duties as agents of the President, the Secretary and his deputies had duties "of a public nature" delegated to them by Congress. They must testify about these public matters just as, in a suit involving property, a clerk in the land office could be compelled to state whether or not a particular land patent was on file.

Marshall agreed, and ordered the clerks to testify. They then disclosed many of the details of what had gone on in the presidential mansion and in the State Department on the evening of March 3, 1801, but they claimed to be unsure of what had become of the plaintiffs' commissions.

Next Lee called Attorney General Levi Lincoln. He too objected strenuously to testifying. He demanded that Lee submit his questions in writing so that he might consider carefully his obligations both to the Court and to the President before making up his mind. He also suggested that it might be necessary for him to exercise his constitutional right (under the Fifth Amendment) to refuse to give evidence that might, as he put it, "criminate" him. Lee then wrote out four questions. After studying them, Lincoln asked to be excused from answering, but the justices ruled against him. Still hesitant, the Attorney General asked for time to consider his position further, and Marshall agreed to an overnight adjournment.

The next day, the tenth of February, Lincoln offered to answer all Lee's questions but the last: What had he done with the commissions? He had seen "a considerable number of commissions" signed and sealed, but could not remember—he claimed—whether the plaintiffs' were among them. He did not know if Madison had ever seen these documents, but was certain that *he* had not given them to the Secretary. On the basis of this last statement, Marshall ruled that the embarrass-

John Marshall,
by Chester Harding.

ing question as to what Lincoln had done with the commissions was irrelevant; he excused Lincoln from answering it.

Despite these reluctant witnesses, Lee was able to show conclusively through affidavits submitted by another clerk and by James Marshall that the commissions had been signed and sealed. In his closing argument he stressed the significance of the case as a test of the principle of judicial independence. "The emoluments or the dignity of the office," he said, "are no objects with the applicants." This was undoubtedly true; the positions were unimportant, and two years of the five-year terms had already expired. As Jefferson later pointed out, the controversy itself had become "a moot case" by 1803. But Marshall saw it as a last-ditch fight against an administration campaign to make lackeys of all federal judges, while Jefferson looked at it as an attempt by the Federalist-dominated judiciary to usurp the power of the executive.

In this controversy over principle, Marshall and the Federalists were of necessity the aggressors. The administration boycotted the hearings. After Lee's summation, no government spokesman came forward to argue the other side, Attorney General Lincoln coldly announcing that he "had received no instructions to appear." With his control over Congress, Jefferson was content to wait for Marshall to act. If he overreached himself, the Chief Justice could be impeached. If he backed down, the already trifling prestige of his Court would be further reduced.

Marshall had acted throughout with characteristic boldness; quite possibly it was he who had persuaded the four aggrieved justices of the peace to press their suit in the first place. But now his combative temperament seemed to have driven him too far. As he considered the Marbury case after the close of the hearings, he must have realized this himself, for he was indeed in a fearful predicament. However sound his logic and just his cause, he was on very dangerous ground. Both political partisanship and his sense of justice prompted him to issue the writ sought by Marbury and his fellows, but what effect would the mandamus produce? Madison almost certainly would ignore it, and Jefferson would back him up. No power but public opinion could make the executive department obey an order of the Court. Since Jefferson was riding the crest of a wave of popularity, to issue the writ would be a futile act of defiance; it might even trigger impeachment proceedings against Marshall that, if successful, would destroy him and reduce the Court to servility.

Yet what was the alternative? To find against the petitioners would be to abandon all principle and surrender abjectly to Jefferson. This a man of Marshall's character could simply not consider. Either horn of the dilemma threatened utter disaster; that it was disaster essentially of his own making could only make the Chief Justice's discomfiture the more complete.

But at some point between the close of the hearings on February 14 and the announcement of his decision on the twenty-fourth, Marshall found a way out. It was an inspired solution, surely the cleverest of his long career. It provided a perfect escape from the dilemma, which probably explains why he was able to persuade the associate justices to agree to it despite the fact that it was based on the most questionable legal logic. The issue, Marshall saw, involved a conflict between the Court and the President, the problem being how to check the President without exposing the Court to his might. Marshall's solution was to state vigorously the justice of the plaintiffs' cause and to condemn the action of the Chief Executive, but to deny the Court's power to provide the plaintiffs with relief.

Marbury and his associates were legally entitled to their commissions, Marshall announced. In withholding them Madison was acting "in plain violation" of the law of the land. But the Supreme Court could not issue a writ of mandamus, because the provision of the Judiciary Act of 1789 authorizing the Court to issue such writs was unconstitutional. In other words, Congress did not have the legal right to give that power to the Court.

So far as it concerned the Judiciary Act, modern commentators agree that Marshall's decision was based on a very weak legal argument. Section 13 of the Act of 1789 stated that the Supreme Court could issue the writ to "persons holding office under the authority of the United States." This law had been framed by experts thoroughly familiar with the Constitution, including William Paterson, one of Marshall's associate justices. The Court had issued the writ in earlier cases without questioning Section 13 for a moment. But Marshall now claimed that the Court could not issue a mandamus except in cases that came to it *on appeal* from a lower court, since the Constitution, he said, granted original jurisdiction to the Court only in certain specified cases—those "affecting ambassadors, other public ministers and consuls, and those in which a state shall be a party." The Marbury case had *originated* in the Supreme Court; since it did not involve a diplomat or a state, any law that gave the Court the right to decide it was unauthorized.

This was shaky reasoning because the Constitution does not necessarily *limit* the Supreme Court's original jurisdiction to the cases it specifies. And even accepting Marshall's narrow view of the constitutional provision, his decision had a major weakness. As the Court's principal chronicler, Charles Warren, has written, "It seems plain, at the present time, that it would have been possible for Marshall, if he had been so inclined, to have construed the language of [Section 13 of the Act of 1789] which authorized writs of mandamus, in such a manner as to have enabled him to escape the necessity of declaring the section unconstitutional."

Marshall was on more solid ground when he went on to argue cogently the theory that "the constitution controls any legislative act repugnant to it," which he called "one of the fundamental principles of our society." The Constitution is "the *supreme* law of the land," he emphasized. Since it is the "duty of the judicial department to say what the law is," the Supreme Court must overturn any law of Congress that violates the Constitution. "A law repugnant to the Constitution," he concluded flatly, "is void." By this reasoning, Section 13 of the Act of 1789 simply ceased to exist, and without it the Court could not issue the writ of mandamus. By thus denying himself authority, Marshall found the means to flay his enemies without exposing himself to their wrath.

Although this was the first time the Court had declared an act of Congress unconstitutional, its right to do so had not been seriously challenged by most authorities. Even Jefferson accepted the principle, claiming only that the executive as well as the judiciary could decide questions of constitutionality. Jefferson was furious over what he called the "twistifications" of Marshall's gratuitous opinion in *Marbury v. Madison*, but his anger was directed at the Chief Justice's stinging criticisms of his behavior, not at the constitutional doctrine Marshall had enunciated.

Even in 1803, the idea of judicial review, which Professor E. S. Corwin has called "the most distinctive feature of the American constitutional system," had had a long history in America. The concept of natural law (the belief that certain principles of right and justice transcend the laws of mere men) was thoroughly established in American thinking. It is seen, for example, in Jefferson's statement in the immortal Declaration that men "are endowed by their Creator" with "unalienable" rights. Although not a direct precedent for Marshall's decision, the colonial practice of "disallowance," whereby various laws had been ruled void on the ground that local legislatures had exceeded their powers in passing them, illustrates the American belief that there is a limit to legislative power and that courts may say when it has been overstepped.

More specifically, Lord Coke, England's chief justice under James I, had declared early in the seventeenth century that "the common law will controul acts of Parliament." One of the American Revolution's chief statesmen and legal apologists, James Otis, had drawn upon this argument a century and a half later in his famous denunciation of the Writs of Assistance. And in the 1780's, courts in New Jersey, New York, Rhode Island, and North Carolina had exercised judicial review over the acts of local legislatures. The debates at the Constitutional Convention and some of the Federalist Papers (especially No 78) indicated that most of the Founding Fathers accepted the idea of judicial review as already established. The Supreme Court, in fact, had considered the constitutionality of a law of Congress before—when it upheld a federal tax law in 1796—and it had encountered little questioning of its right to do so. All these precedents—when taken together with the fact that the section of the Act of 1789 nullified by Marshall's decision was of minor importance—explain why no one paid much attention to this part of the decision.

Thus the "Case of the Missing Commissions" passed into history, seemingly a fracas of but slight significance. When it was over, Marbury and his colleagues returned to the obscurity whence they had arisen.* In the partisan struggle for power between Marshall and Jefferson, the incident was of secondary importance. The real showdown came later—in the impeachment proceedings against Justice Chase and the treason trial of Aaron Burr. In the long run, Marshall won his fight to preserve the independence and integrity of the federal judiciary, but generally speaking, the courts have not been able to exert as much influence over the appointive and dismissal powers of the President as Marshall had hoped to win for them in *Marbury v. Madison.* Even the enunciation of the Supreme Court's power to void acts of Congress wrought no immediate change in American life. Indeed, it was more than half a century before another was overturned.

Nevertheless, this trivial squabble over a few petty political plums was of vital importance for later American history. For with the expansion of the federal government into new areas of activity in more recent times, the power of the Supreme Court to nullify acts of Congress has been repeatedly employed, with profound effects. At various times legislation concerning the income tax, child labor, wages and hours, and many other aspects of our social, economic, and political life have been thrown out by the Court, and always, in the last analysis, its right to do so has depended upon the decision John Marshall handed down to escape from a dilemma of his own making.

*What happened to Marbury? According to his descendants, he became president of a Georgetown bank in 1814, reared a family, and died, uncommissioned, in 1835.

Irving Brant

Madison
and the
War of 1812

Historians, as Irving Brant writes in this essay, should "appraise,"
not "acquit or indict." That duty is often difficult to fulfill, especially
for political historians, who deal with controversial issues and with
men who were subject to sharp partisan attacks and showered with
equally distorting praise by their contemporaries. This essay is an
excellent example of how a good historian tries to solve the problem
of stripping away the blanket of prejudice that so often surrounds
his subject.

The War of 1812, which might well have been avoided and which
had no official results, has frequently been seen as a comic, and sometimes as a tragic, blunder. President James Madison has, with equal
frequency, been denounced and laughed at for his management of the
conflict. Brant, author of a multivolume life of Madison noted for
its meticulous research and its generally favorable interpretation of
the man, seeks here to rehabilitate Madison's reputation as a wartime
President and to demonstrate that the war was neither purposeless nor
inconclusive. How well he succeeded in doing so is an open question.
Like most biographers, his long years of study led him to become so
absorbed in his subject that he took on Madison's point of view almost
completely; in redressing the balance he may well in this case have
tipped it in the opposite direction. Nevertheless, Brant always supports
his argument with hard evidence. His essay reads like a lawyer's
brief, but like a good brief it bristles with facts and references to
authorities. Although not every reader will accept all of Brant's
conclusions, no one, having read the essay, can again see President
Madison as a weak-willed, ineffective old man overwhelmed by events.

O f all the major events in American history, the War of 1812 is least known to the most people. Its naval glories are exploited in popular narrative. Its military failures, formerly glossed over, are emphasized by more objective historians with something akin to pleasure. Least known of all is the part taken by President Madison, who by virtue of the Constitution was commander in chief of the Armed Forces, charged with the duty of "making" the war that Congress "declared."

Through the years, however, a picture of James Madison has been built up by the brushes or palette knives of historians and popular word-artists. He appears as a pacifistic little man overshadowed by the ample figure of his wife, Dolley; a great political philosopher overwhelmed by the responsibilities of a war into which he was projected, at the age of sixty-one, against his will and with no capacity for executive leadership.

The purpose of this article is to appraise, not to acquit or indict. But in the case of Madison, the adverse preconceptions are embedded so deeply that they stand in the way of a fair appraisal. Historians have rejected the Federalist charge that he carried the United States into war to help Napoleon master the Old World. But with few exceptions they have treated him as the dupe of the French Emperor, tricked into war with England by the apparent repeal by the French of the Berlin and Milan Decrees at a time when both countries were despoiling American commerce. As for his conduct of the war, Madison has received little credit for victories and plenty of blame for misfortunes. Finally, the Treaty of Ghent satisfied none of the grievances cited in the declaration of war, and the one decisive military victory— that of General Andrew Jackson at New Orleans was won two weeks after the signing of the peace treaty. It all adds up to the picture of a useless and costly conflict, saved by mere luck from being a disaster, and coming to an inconclusive end.

"Everybody knew" in 1812, just as everybody "knows" today, that Madison was timid, hesitant, ruled by stronger men. Everybody knew it, that is, except the foreign diplomats who were sent to overawe him. "Curt, spiteful, passionate," France's Louis Turreau called him. "Madison is now as obstinate as a mule," wrote England's "Copenhagen" Jackson (the Francis James Jackson who in 1807 had burned Denmark's capital) just before the President kicked him out of the country. Turreau's friendlier successor, Louis Sérurier, heard that the Chief of State was ruled by his Cabinet. He waited several months before he wrote to Paris: "Mr. Madison governs by himself."

Expelling an obnoxious minister was a civilian job. But how could Madison be anything of a war leader when "everybody knew" that he had been kicked into the war by Clay, Calhoun, Grundy, and other congressional War Hawks? There were certain things that "everybody" did not know. They did not know that in March, 1809, two weeks after he became President, Madison authorized British Minister David M. Erskine to inform his government that if she would relax her Orders in Council, he would ask Congress "to enter upon immediate measures of hostility against France."

They did not know of a simultaneous notice to France that if she ceased her commercial aggressions and Great Britian did not, "the President of the United States will advise to an immediate war with the latter." Neither Congress nor the public ever learned that when President Madison proclaimed nonintercourse with England on November 2, 1810, he informed General Turreau that continued interference with American trade by England "will necessarily lead to war"—as it did. The 1809 offer to join England against France brought gasps of astonishment in Congress when Madison revealed it in asking for the declaration of war against England. It brought no gasps of any sort from writers of history. It didn't fit their conception of Madison, so they disposed of it by silence.

England first, then France, was Madison's schedule of redress. In August, 1812, the moment he was notified that England had repealed her Orders in Council, he offered to settle the one remaining issue— impressment of seamen—by informal agreement. At the same time he wrote to his minister in Paris that if England made peace and France failed to repair American wrongs, war would be declared against France as soon as Congress convened, and that if England did not make peace he might even recommend a double war. Joel Barlow was directed to show that letter to the French government. As a result, Barlow was called to Poland to confer with Napoleon in the field and complete a treaty, but Napoleon's defeat at Berezina intervened, and Barlow died of pneumonia near Cracow on his way back to Paris. Madison's letter has been in print for nearly a hundred years, ignored even by historians who knew that it was described in the French foreign office as an ultimatum of war.

The same Federalist editors who jeered at "poor Madison" in 1812 denounced him as a dictator in 1814. They were free to do so. Open sedition and silent resistance forced the United States to fight the war with one arm—New England—tied behind her back. That was more crippling than incompetent generals, raw militia, and an empty treasury. Yet the President rejected every counsel that would have narrowed the constitutional liberties of those who gave vocal aid to the enemy. They would hang themselves, he said, and they did. Among all the words of praise addressed to him when he left office, he may have felt keenest pride in those of the Citizens' Committee of Washington:

> Power and national glory, sir, have often before been acquired by the sword; but rarely without the sacrifice of civil or political liberty. When we reflect that this sword was drawn under your guidance, we cannot resist offering you our own as well as a nation's thanks for the vigilance . . . the energy . . . and the safety with which you have wielded an armed force of 50,000 men . . . without infringing a political, civil or religious right.

It takes time, of course, for people to accept a portrait after a hundred years of caricature. At the risk of being abrupt, let us turn

James Madison was Jefferson's Secretary of State when Gilbert Stuart did this portrait.

to Madison's actions as war leader. Expecting hostilities with England, why did he not call for adequate preparations? He did, but in Congress a vote for taxes was looked on as political suicide. Madison's first action in national defense was to lay up most of President Jefferson's little gunboats as wasteful of men and money in proportion to gunpower and to order laid-up frigates refitted. Congress cut the requested appropriation and stopped the work. In September, 1811, Sérurier told his government that the President was stimulating a nationwide debate on the question of whether it suited the Republic to have a navy, and if so, should it not be "such as can make the American flag respected"? The proposition had to be presented "in this questioning and deferential form," said the Minister, to avoid exciting state jealousy of federal power.

At the ensuing session of Congress the administration asked for twelve seventy-four-gun ships and ten new frigates, and the repair or reconstruction of six of the ten existing frigates. The new construction was voted down and the reconditioning limited to three ships.

To prepare for the land war, which would have to be fought either on American or Canadian soil, the President wanted a quick build-up of military forces. Then, if the expected bad news came from England, the troops would be ready to march on weakly defended Montreal and Quebec before reinforcements could cross the ocean.

With an authorized personnel of ten thousand, the Army had only about four thousand. The President asked that the old regiments be filled up, that ten thousand additional regulars be recruited, and that provision be made for fifty thousand volunteers. Senator William Branch Giles of Virginia, leader of the anti-Madison Democrats, shook the roof as he decried these puny measures. He demanded thirty-five thousand regulars and five-year enlistments, making it necessary to build a large and costly officer corps before men could be recruited.

"The efforts of General [Senator Samuel] Smith and of Mr. Giles of Virginia," British Minister Augustus J. Foster reported, "have been added to those of the Federalists as a means to overthrow Mr. Madison and his administration." Congress talked most of the winter and Giles won. The bill for fifty thousand volunteers occasioned a lengthy constitutional harangue and a decision for state-appointed officers. The result, many believed, would be a militia that could refuse to go onto foreign soil. Skeptically, Madison signed the bills for the regulars and the volunteers.

His skepticism had warrant. On June 8 the number of recruits was estimated at five thousand, and there were few unbalky volunteers except in the West.

With England unyielding, the President on March 31 notified the House Committee on Foreign Relations that he was ready to ask for a shipping embargo—a prelude to war. But "the Executive will not take upon itself the responsibility of declaring that we are prepared for war." Congress must make the final decision with its eyes open. Four days later it did so, the embargo taking effect on April 4.

By that time, military and naval decisions were crowding in upon the Executive. In those fields, two stories are told which carry the suggestion that Madison was stupid, or at least indecisive. The fact that they are still in circulation proves that some writers have been a trifle credulous. One story says that the President decided to make an untrained civilian, Henry Clay, supreme military commander but was dissuaded by his Cabinet. The other is that Madison made up his mind to keep the American Navy tied up for harbor defense, but reversed himself on the pleas of Navy Captains Charles Stewart and William Bainbridge.

The story of the abortive appointment of Henry Clay reached full and rounded form in Calvin Colton's 1857 biography of Clay. It can be traced backward in print and manuscript, diminishing as it recedes —back to Colonel Isaac Cole's recollection, in 1838, of what he once heard from General John Mason, back to Mason's memory of what he was told by his brother-in-law, General Ben Howard. And that was: a group of Clay's friends suggested Clay's appointment to President Madison, who "assented to their opinion of [Clay's] fitness, etc., but said he could not be spared out of Congress." That was the molehill out of which the mountain grew.

The naval history was no third-hand, dry-land scuttlebutt. It came from Captain Stewart himself. As Stewart published the story in 1845, he and Captain Bainbridge went to the Navy Department on June 21, 1812, three days after the declaration of war, to solicit commands at sea. They were told by Secretary Paul Hamilton that the President and Cabinet had decided to keep the ships tied up. They protested, and the argument was continued before the President, who agreed with the captains but gave way to the Cabinet at a special meeting called that evening. Bainbridge and Stewart thereupon drafted a joint letter to the President, who overruled the Cabinet and ordered the Navy into action. Capping Stewart's story was his account of a great naval ball in the following December to which a courier brought news of Captain Stephen Decatur's victory over the frigate *Macedonian*. Whereupon President Madison told the assembled guests that if it had not been for Bainbridge and Stewart, the warships never would have gone to sea.

All rather convincing, unless you happen to know that Madison did not attend that December ball, that on June 23 Bainbridge wrote from Boston (he was not in Washington at all at the time) asking for a fighting command, and that all major warships ready for action were ordered to sea on the day war was declared. Stewart did not invent his 1845 story. It arose out of his muddled recollection and grandiose enlargement of a discussion held at the White House in February, 1812, some months before the declaration of war, in which the President sided with the captains against the Secretary of the Navy. Congress had just rejected the administration's request for twenty-two new warships. The captains, arguing with Hamilton, conceded that even if an American vessel were victorious it might, without reinforcements, be overwhelmed and captured by the enemy. To which Madison replied: "It is victories we want; if you give us them and lose your ships afterwards, they can be replaced by others."

The February discussion between the captains and the President was prophetic. For when Madison made his next request for greater sea power, in the closing weeks of 1812, it was dramatized by the *Constitution*'s victory over the *Guerrière* in August, the capture of the *Macedonian* by the *United States* in October, and especially by the gallant exploit of the sloop *Wasp*, which ran into exactly the kind of trouble Stewart and Bainbridge had predicted. Victorious over the *Frolic,* the *Wasp* was unable to hoist a sail when a lumbering British seventy-four came along and took both victor and prize to Bermuda. Captain Stewart, in this campaign for funds, furnished Secretary Hamilton with the technical arguments that helped persuade Congress to authorize four ships of the line, four heavy frigates, and as many sloops of war.

In one critical area the issue of naval power could not wait until the war began. In March, 1812, Stewart was called to Washington and offered a yet-uncreated command on the Great Lakes, controlled then by a few British armed vessels. The President intended to ask Congress for money to build a fleet; in the meantime enough would be scraped up for an eighteen-gun brig. Stewart refused; he was a deep-sea man.

The matter was given a new turn by Governor William Hull of Michigan Territory, a veteran of the Revolution. Offered a commission as brigadier general, he urged the building of lake squadrons. But with Stewart rejecting the command and Congress hostile to naval construction, Hull assured the President that he could lead an army across the Detroit River and down the north shore of Lake Erie to the Niagara River. That would restrain the northwestern Indians, deliver much of upper Canada into American hands, and win control of the lakes in less time and at less cost than building a fleet.

A Detroit campaign was being forced on the government anyway. Early operations against Montreal were made impossible by the dearth of regulars and the refusal of New England governors to furnish militia for federal service. On the other hand, western volunteers were so eager to break up the British-Indian alliance, Clay and others reported, that inaction might chill their spirit. Madison accepted Hull's promise of lake control by land action and thereby made the biggest strategic error of the war.

The appointment of Hull was a major blunder, but hardly a foreseeable one. Thirty years of peace with the Army almost nonexistent forced the President to choose his generals either from aging Revolutionary veterans with fighting experience and reputation, or from young regimental officers who had never seen action. Among the veterans called back, Hull had an unsurpassed Revolutionary record. Even Federalist editors applauded Madison's selection.

Hull commanded twenty-five hundred confident Kentuckians, Ohioans, regulars, and Michigan territorials. He crossed into Canada on July 12, 1812, skirmished with the vastly outnumbered enemy, and retreated to Fort Detroit. There, on August 16, without firing a shot, without consulting his officers, he surrendered his entire army to General Isaac Brock, who was advancing at the head of 330 British regulars and 400 Canadian militiamen, with several hundred Indians whooping in the woods.

Hull's claim that he was short of supplies was categorically denied by his officers but avidly accepted by the Federalist press, with a resultant impact on historians. His most startling assertion was that he had only one day's supply of powder. When he made the same remark to Sir George Prevost, the British commander handed him "the return of the large supply found in the fort; it did not create a blush." Those were the words of British Adjutant General Edward Baynes. Hull's actions, wrote another member of Prevost's staff, "stamp him either for a coward or a traitor." With such comments coming from the captors, it seems just a trifle severe to blame the surrender on either the President or the War Department.

Suppose, instead, we find out how the President reacted to the disaster. New land forces, he said, could be counted on to redeem the country's honor. The immediate necessity was to speed up the building of warships to gain control of the lakes—a method that would have been adopted at the outset "if the easy conquest of them by land held out to us [by Hull] had not misled our calculations." The strength of his feeling was recorded by Richard Rush, who wrote to John Adams the following June: "I know the President to be so convinced upon this subject that I heard him say last fall if the British build thirty frigates upon [the lakes] we ought to build forty."

Madison's insistence produced the warships with which Commodore Perry defeated and captured the British squadron on Lake Erie in September, 1813, changing the whole complexion of the war. He ordered the building of ship after ship on Lake Ontario. Superiority swung back and forth on that lake like reversing winds, but neither side could force a decision because each had protected bases—the British at York (now Toronto) and Kingston, the Americans at Sackets Harbor—to retire to when the other was ahead.

Far more important and more critical was the state of affairs in 1814 on Lake Champlain, the great sluice that opened a supply route northward to Montreal and southward to the Hudson River valley. By summer, more than twenty thousand seasoned veterans of the Peninsular War, released for transatlantic service by Napoleon's downfall, were crowding onto British transports bound for Canada, Chesapeake Bay, and New Orleans. On Lake Champlain, the American ship *Saratoga* was launched thirty-five days after the laying of her keel. Sailors were in short supply both there and on Lake Ontario. Madison ordered the crews filled up with soldiers and told the protesting Secretary of War that naval efficiency was essential even for land operations.

Then came news that the enemy was building a new vessel on Lake Champlain, the *Confiance,* far more powerful than the twenty-six-gun *Saratoga.* Loss of the lake might still be averted, Captain Thomas Macdonough believed, by the swifter building of a light brig. Navy Secretary William Jones, though far more vigorous and capable than his predecessor, said the limit of available funds had been reached.

Madison ordered the ship built anyhow. Its keel had been laid when Jones again drew back. "God knows where the money is to come from," he wrote. The President reaffirmed the order and obtained a pledge of the utmost speed. On July 15 the timbers of the twenty-gun *Eagle* were still standing in the forest. The vessel was launched on August 11 and furnished the margin of power that changed sure defeat into a victory which resounded from Washington to Ghent.

"The battle of Lake Champlain, more than any other incident of the War of 1812, merits the epithet 'decisive,'" wrote the distinguished naval historian Alfred Thayer Mahan many years later. Within earshot of the battle, many of them within sight, nearly fourteen thousand of Wellington's battle-hardened soldiers waited for the Royal Navy to open the way to Albany and New York. When the British fleet surrendered, the army of invasion marched back to Canada and never returned.

In naval affairs, Madison could rely on officers unsurpassed anywhere in the world for knowledge and ability. In army matters he had to learn by hard experience. His first Secretary of War, William Eustis, was a Massachusetts medical man of bustling energy who bore a tremendous load of work in a War Department consisting of himself and eight clerks. Eustis, even in the opinion of some congressmen who wanted him fired, outperformed what anybody had a right to expect in equipping the Army as war approached. But he had no more than a civilian's knowledge of military operations, did little to systematize the nation's defenses, and seemed unable to recognize incompetence in field officers before it was demonstrated in battle. The President shared this last fault. When Adjutant General Baynes visited Major General Henry Dearborn under a flag of truce, he saw at a glance that the

American commander lacked energy. Neither Madison nor Eustis sensed this, and the President couldn't see the deficiencies of Eustis. His resignation, after failures on the Niagara front followed the Hull catastrophe, was a concession to public opinion.

Brigadier General John Armstrong, who succeeded Eustis, was notorious for political intrigue but had enough of a military reputation to warrant his selection. The President chose him reluctantly, after Secretary of State James Monroe and Senator William Harris Crawford had refused the place.

During the next year and a half, until the burning of Washington forced him to resign, Armstrong performed his work with one eye on the war and the other on the 1816 presidential race. His good and bad traits showed up at once but not in equal measure. He drove the competent Andrew Jackson to fury and disobedience with a brusque, unappreciative dismissal of his temporary Tennessee volunteers in a distant wilderness. He removed the incompetent General Dearborn with a note even more callous. Both men wrote to the President, Jackson boiling with indignation, Dearborn heartbroken. Madison forced Armstrong to make amends to Jackson. He himself consoled Dearborn but affirmed the removal.

Armstrong's strategy to gain the presidential nomination paralleled that of his rival, James Monroe. Each hoped to be made a lieutenant general and win the war. Monroe's chance vanished when Armstrong took the War Department. Armstrong's opportunity seemed to open when the President, in June of 1813, was stricken with an almost fatal illness followed by several months' convalescence in Virginia. Freed of effective presidential supervision, Armstrong went north under the pretense of making an inspection trip and did not come back until Christmas. During the interval he assumed personal direction of a two-pronged campaign against Montreal, failed to co-ordinate the mishandled offensive movements, and ducked away to Albany to watch the approaching double fiasco as a detached observer.

Personal ambition and laziness turned Armstrong's strategic ideas, even when sound, into flashy gambits, without the preparation or drive required to follow through. Two weeks before the event that drove him out of office, he received a written rebuke from Madison that would have pierced the hide of a rhinoceros—though it did not penetrate his—for secretly exercising powers delegated by Congress to the President, ordering military operations without consultation, suppressing letters intended for the President, accepting the resignation of General William Henry Harrison without authority, and posing to Harrison's successor as the bestower of the appointment.

Nevertheless, Armstrong possessed capabilities that, combined with Madison's ability to thwart their misuse, gave a new look to the American Army. Both men recognized youthful talent, and Armstrong was ruthless enough to get rid of old incompetents.

Zebulon Pike, promoted to brigadier general, was killed in winning his first victory. Jacob Brown and George Izard, lately raised to the same rank, stood out in the Montreal campaign in contrast to their soon-to-be-ousted commanders, Major Generals James Wilkinson and Wade Hampton. Shining talents were displayed by Colonels E. P. Gaines and Winfield Scott; solid performance by Alexander Macomb, T. A. Smith, E. W. Ripley. Every one of these eight men was recommended by Armstrong for promotion, with the exception of Brown. He advised the President that for major generals, not a moment should be lost in promoting Brigadiers Izard and Thomas Flournoy.

Flournoy, a nobody at New Orleans! His promotion, by making Andrew Jackson his subordinate instead of his superior, would have knocked Jackson straight out of the military service—if not into apoplexy. But it also would have barricaded the upward path of Brown —the man most likely to stand in Armstrong's way if Armstrong succeeded in establishing the grade of lieutenant general—by filling all the major-generalships allowed by law.

The President nominated Izard—*and Brown*. It could almost be said that at that moment the Battle of New Orleans was won, although Jackson's appointment as major general still awaited a future vacancy. Also, the leadership was established that retrieved American prestige in the 1814 battles of the Niagara peninsula and helped persuade England that the time was ripe for peace.

The location of that Niagara campaign, illogical because of its limited objective, resulted from troop movements made by Armstrong without consulting the President. To remedy that feature, the Secretary sent a proposal to Madison at Montpelier that Brown's army bypass the peninsula and swing around Lake Ontario to Burlington and York. Madison imposed the same restriction that was to be recognized a hundred years later by Admiral Mahan: control of the lake must first be won to prevent the landing of an army in the American rear. The civilian commander in chief was learning the art of war. By a succession of decisions affecting strength, strategy, and leadership on Lake Champlain, at New Orleans, and on the Niagara front— overruling his subordinates in every instance—Madison went far to determine the outcome.

In spite of their conflicts over appointments, Armstrong and the President worked effectively together in a fundamental regeneration of the military command. On the day war was declared the United States Army had eight generals, most of them just appointed. Their average age was sixty years. Two years later all of them were out of service or assigned to quiescence. In the first half of 1814 nine generals were appointed or promoted—their average age was thirty-six— and these men turned raw American recruits into disciplined soldiers. When the war ended they had just begun to fight.

These redeeming events of 1814 are obscured in popular narrative and even in histories by the burning of Washington and the miserable failure of its defenders. For that occurrence President Madison bore an inescapable responsibility: constitutionally, he was commander in chief; physically, he was in Washington when the enemy approached. Why did he not foresee the attack; why didn't he guard against it?

*The burning of Washington in 1814 by
the British is the subject of this highly
dramatized contemporary engraving.*

The answer to the first question accentuates the second. On May 24, after reading a British proclamation calling for a general uprising of southern slaves, the President wrote to Armstrong that this presaged a campaign of ruthless devastation in which the national capital could not fail to be "a favorite target." On July 1, without dissent but with skepticism concerning the danger (so wrote Navy Secretary William Jones), the Cabinet approved Madison's proposal that ten thousand militiamen be drawn out to help guard the Washington-Baltimore area. When Brigadier General William H. Winder wished to summon them, Secretary Armstrong (the chief skeptic) made the fatal reply that the best mode of using militia "was upon the spur of the occasion." Nevertheless, the power and responsibility belonged to the President, and his own recorded foresight called for vigorous defensive measures. He intervened again and again, to overcome Armstrong's sloth and skepticism, but never forced action on a large enough scale.

Almost in another world is the popular word-picture of the Madisons at this time. It is a composite of Dolley saving the portrait of George Washington as the enemy approached, and of the President—as depicted by the scurrilous (and anonymous) versifier of "The Bladensburg Races"—galloping in terrified flight forty miles into Maryland.

The rhapsodic glee with which the versifier danced in the ashes of the Capitol and White House may not impeach his veracity, but his figurative observation post hardly matched the physical one of Sérurier, who had a panoramic view from the unmenaced Octagon House. The President, Sérurier wrote to Talleyrand two days before the battle, "has just gone to the camp to encourage, by his presence, the army to defend the capital." Madison returned to the White House from the actual battlefield (where Congreve rockets fell near him) after Dolley left the house. He remained there, the French minister said, until after the Georgetown and Washington militia streamed by in confused flight toward Frederick. The manner of his departure as described by Sérurier would be of little moment except that it emphasizes still further how different Madison's character was from the one history has bestowed on him:

It was then, my lord, that the President, who, in the midst of all this disorder, had displayed to stop it a firmness and constancy worthy of a better success . . . coolly mounted his horse, accompanied by some friends, and slowly gained the bridge that separates Washington from Virginia.

By the time the news of the burning of Washington reached London, the bellicosity and bad temper that had given rise to Admiral Alexander Cochrane's "treat 'em rough" instructions were things of the past. War weariness in England, fresh dangers emerging in chaotic Europe, and the sharp improvement in the American position, strength, and morale in the north, all helped produce a sudden reversal of British policy at Ghent. Peace was signed the day before Christmas, and the fighting ended on January 8, 1815, when two thousand British soldiers—a third of the entire assaulting army—fell dead or wounded at New Orleans.

The Treaty of Ghent left things as they were. Did the war itself leave them unchanged? Impressment and the Orders in Council both vanished before the treaty was signed. European peace removed them as immediate future hazards. If the war had lifted American prestige, no treaty was needed to abolish them forever. By that measurement the New Orleans victory was climax, not epilogue. In 1815, Justice Joseph Story weighed the results of the war and found them massive:

Never did a country occupy more lofty ground; we have stood the contest, single-handed, against the conqueror of Europe; and we are at peace, with all our blushing victories thick crowding on us. If I do not much mistake, we shall attain to a very high character abroad as well as crush domestic faction.

Domestic faction was crushed in the next election. Those who would fix the time at which the country attained international stature might ask themselves: Could there have been a Monroe Doctrine in 1823 without the War of 1812? It was under President James Madison that the struggling young republic won an equal position among the free nations of the world, and began its long climb to leadership.

Bray Hammond

Was Jackson Wise to Dismantle the Bank?

 The conflict waged by President Andrew Jackson against the Second Bank of the United States, one of the most dramatic political confrontations in American history, has produced over the years a wide variety of reactions. Jackson's Whig enemies presented him as a ruthless, dictatorial ignoramus striking out at the Bank in order to increase his own power; his friends described him as a noble crusader destroying the "monster," a monopolistic economic colossus that was extracting profits for its wealthy stockholders from "the people's money." In later years historians tended to accept one or the other of these views, usually without much understanding of the financial questions around which the "bank war" raged.

 This was the situation when the late Bray Hammond, then a retired governor of the Federal Reserve Board, wrote the following essay. In the 1940's a liberal young historian, Arthur M. Schlesinger, Jr., had published The Age of Jackson, *a widely read book which took an extremely pro-Jackson position in the controversy. Hammond, whose knowledge of banking and finance enabled him to grasp and explain the issues involved, disagreed with Schlesinger's interpretation. His researches also led to the uncovering of a great deal of new evidence about the attitudes and actions of Nicholas Biddle, president of the Bank, and of many of the state bankers who opposed him. Although the subject, like nearly all important historical questions, is still being debated, Hammond's thesis represents the dominant view at the present time.*

Relief, sir!" interrupted the President. "Come not to me, sir! Go to the monster. It is folly, sir, to talk to Andrew Jackson. The government will not bow to the monster. . . . Andrew Jackson yet lives to put his foot upon the head of the monster and crush him to the dust."

The monster, "a hydra of corruption," was known also as the Second Bank of the United States, chartered by Congress in 1816 as depository of the federal government, which was its principal stockholder and customer. The words were reported by a committee which called on President Jackson in the spring of 1834 to complain because he and Secretary of the Treasury Roger Taney had removed the federal deposits from the federal depository into what the Jacksonians called "selected banks" and others called "pet banks." The President was disgusted with the committee.

"Andrew Jackson," he exclaimed in the third person as before, "would never recharter that monster of corruption. Sooner than live in a country where such a power prevailed, he would seek an asylum in the wilds of Arabia."

In effect, he had already put his foot on the monster and crushed him in the dust. He had done so by vetoing a new charter for the Bank and removing the federal accounts from its books. So long as the federal Bank had the federal accounts, it had been regulator of the currency and of credit in general. Its power to regulate had derived from the fact that the federal Treasury was the largest single transactor in the economy and the largest bank depositor. Receiving the checks and notes of local banks deposited with it by government collectors of revenue, it had had constantly to come back on the local banks for settlements of the amounts which the checks and notes called for. It had had to do so because it made those amounts immediately available to the Treasury, wherever desired. Since settlement by the local banks was in specie, i.e. silver and gold coin, the pressure for settlement automatically regulated local bank lending, for the more the local banks lent, the larger the amount of their notes and checks in use and the larger the sums they had to settle in specie. This loss of specie reduced their power to lend.

All this had made the federal Bank the regulator not alone of the currency but of bank lending in general, the restraint it had exerted being fully as effective as that of the twelve Federal Reserve Banks at present, though by a different process. With its life now limited to two more years and the government accounts removed from its books, it was already crushed but still writhing.

The Jacksonian attack on the Bank is an affair respecting which posterity seems to have come to an opinion that is half hero worship and half discernment. In the words of Professor William G. Sumner, the affair was a struggle "between the democracy and the money power." Viewed in that light, Jackson's victory was a grand thing. But Sumner also observed—this was three quarters of a century ago— that since Jackson's victory the currency, which previously had owned no superior in the world, had never again been so good. More

Jackson slays the Bank, "the hydra of corruption," assisted by Van Buren (center) and a popular cartoon character of the day (right). Bank President Biddle is in the top hat.

recently Professor Lester V. Chandler, granting the Bank's imperfections, has said that its abolition without replacement by something to take over its functions was a "major blunder" which "ushered in a generation of banking anarchy and monetary disorder." So the affair stands, a triumph and a blunder.

During Andrew Jackson's lifetime three things had begun to alter prodigiously the economic life of Americans. These were steam, credit, and natural resources.

Steam had been lifting the lids of pots for thousands of years, and for a century or so it had been lifting water from coal mines. But only in recent years had it been turning spindles, propelling ships, drawing trains of cars, and multiplying incredibly the productive powers of man. For thousands of years money had been lent, but in most people's minds debt had signified distress—as it still did in Andrew Jackson's. Only now was its productive power, long known to merchants as a means of making one sum of money do the work of several, becoming popularly recognized by enterprising men for projects which required larger sums than could be assembled in coin. For three centuries or more America's resources had been crudely surmised, but only now were their variety, abundance, and accessibility becoming practical realities. And it was the union of these three, steam, credit, and natural resources, that was now turning Anglo-Saxon America from the modest agrarian interests that had preoccupied her for two centuries of European settlement to the dazzling possibilities of industrial exploitation.

In the presence of these possibilities, the democracy was becoming transformed from one that was Jeffersonian and agrarian to one that was financial and industrial. But it was still a democracy: its recruits were still men born and reared on farms, its vocabulary was still Jeffersonian, and its basic conceptions changed insensibly from the libertarianism of agrarians to that of *laissez faire*. When Andrew Jackson became President in 1829, boys born in log cabins were already becoming businessmen but with no notion of surrendering as bankers and manufacturers the freedom they might have enjoyed as farmers.

There followed a century of exploitation from which America emerged with the most wealthy and powerful economy there is, with her people the best fed, the best housed, the best clothed, and the best equipped on earth. But the loss and waste have long been apparent. The battle was only for the strong, and millions who lived in the midst of wealth never got to touch it. The age of the Robber Barons was scarcely a golden age. It was scarcely what Thomas Jefferson desired.

It could scarcely have been what Andrew Jackson desired either, for his ideals were more or less Jeffersonian by common inheritance, and the abuse of credit was one of the things he abominated. Yet no man ever did more to encourage the abuse of credit than he. For the one agency able to exert some restraint on credit was the federal Bank. In destroying it, he let speculation loose. Though a hard money devotee who hated banks and wanted no money but coin, he fostered the formation of swarms of banks and endowed the country with a filthy and depreciated paper currency which he believed to be unsound and unconstitutional and from which the Civil War delivered it in the Administration of Abraham Lincoln thirty years later.

This, of course, was not Andrew Jackson's fault, unless one believes he would have done what he did had his advisers been different. Though a resolute and decisive person, he also relied on his friends. He had his official cabinet, largely selected for political expediency, and he had his "kitchen cabinet" for informal counsel. Of those advisers most influential with him, all but two were either businessmen or closely associated with the business world. The two exceptions were Major William B. Lewis, a planter and neighbor from Tennessee who came to live with him in the White House; and James K. Polk, also of Tennessee, later President of the United States. These two, with Jackson himself, constituted the agrarian element in the Jacksonian Administration. Several of the others, however, were agrarian in the sense that they had started as poor farm boys.

Martin Van Buren, probably the ablest of Jackson's political associates, was a lawyer whose investments had made him rich. Amos Kendall, the ablest in a business and administrative sense, later made the telegraph one of the greatest of American business enterprises and himself a man of wealth. He provided the Jacksonians their watchword, "The world is governed too much." He said "our country-men are beginning to demand" that the government be content with "protecting their persons and property, leaving them to direct their labor and capital as they please, within the moral law; getting rich or remaining poor as may result from their own management or fortune." Kendall's views may be sound, but they are not what one expects to hear from the democracy when struggling with the money power.

Roger Taney, later Chief Justice, never got rich, but he liked banks and was a modest investor in bank stock. "There is perhaps no business," he said as Jackson's secretary of the treasury, "which yields a profit so certain and liberal as the business of banking and exchange; and it is proper that it should be open as far as practicable to the most free competition and its advantages shared by all classes of society." His own bank in Baltimore was one of the first of the pets in which he deposited government money.

David Henshaw, Jacksonian boss of Massachusetts, was a banker and industrialist whose advice in practical matters had direct influence in Washington. Henshaw projected a Jacksonian bank to take the place of the existing institution but to be bigger. (A similar project was got up by friends of Van Buren in New York and one of the two was mentioned favorably by Jackson in his veto message as a possible alternative to the existing United States Bank.) Samuel Ingham, Jackson's first secretary of the treasury, was a paper manufacturer in Pennsylvania and later a banker in New Jersey. Churchill C. Cambreleng, congressional leader of the attack on the Bank, was a New York businessman and former agent of John Jacob Astor. These are not all of the Jacksonians who were intent on the federal Bank's destruction, but they are typical.

There was a very cogent reason why these businessmen and their class generally wanted to kill the Bank of the United States. It interfered with easy money; it kept the state banks from lending as freely as they might otherwise and businessmen from borrowing.

New York, for example, was now the financial and commercial center of the country and its largest city, which Philadelphia formerly had been. The customs duties collected at its wharves and paid by its businessmen were far the largest of any American port, and customs duties were then the principal source of federal income. These duties were paid by New York businessmen with checks on New York banks. These checks were deposited by the federal collectors in the New York office of the Bank of the United States, whose headquarters were in Philadelphia and a majority of whose directors were Philadelphia businessmen. This, Amos Kendall observed, was a "wrong done to New York in depriving her of her natural advantages."

It was not merely a matter of prestige. As already noted, the United States Bank, receiving the checks of the New York businessmen, made the funds at once available to the secretary of the treasury. The Bank had therefore to call on the New York banks for the funds the checks represented. This meant that the New York banks, in order to pay the federal Bank, had to draw down their reserves; which meant that they had less money to lend; which meant that the New York business-men could not borrow as freely and cheaply as they might otherwise. All this because their money had gone to Philadelphia.

Actually the situation was not so bad as my simplified account makes it appear. For one thing, the goods imported at New York were sold elsewhere in the country, and more money came to New York in payment for them than went out of the city in duties paid the government. But I have described it in the bald, one-sided terms that appealed to the local politicians and to the businessmen prone to grumbling because money was not so easy as they would like. There was truth in what they said, but less than they made out.

New York's grievance was special because her customs receipts were so large and went to a vanquished rival. Otherwise the federal Bank's pressure on the local banks—all of which were state banks—was felt in some degree through the country at large. Wherever money was paid to a federal agency—for postage, for fines, for lands, for excise, for import duties—money was drawn from the local banks into the federal Bank. The flow of funds did not drain the local banks empty and leave them nothing to do, though they and the states' rights politicians talked as if that were the case. The federal Bank was simply their principal single creditor.

And though private business brought more money to New York and other commercial centers than it took away, the federal govern-ment took more away than it brought. For its largest payments were made elsewhere—to naval stations, army posts, Indian agents, owners of the public debt, largely foreign, and civilians in the government service throughout the country. In the normal flow of money pay-ments from hand to hand in the economy, those to the federal govern-ment and consequently to the federal Bank were so large and conspicuous that the state banks involved in making them were disagreeably conscious of their size and frequency.

These banks, of course, were mostly eastern and urban rather than western and rural, because it was in eastern cities that the federal government received most of its income. Accordingly, it was in the eastern business centers, Boston, New York, Baltimore, and Charleston, that resentment against Philadelphia and the federal Bank was strongest. This resentment was intensified by the fact that the federal Bank's branch offices were also competitors for private business in these and other cities, which the present Federal Reserve Banks, very wisely, are not.

General Jackson's accession to the presidency afforded an op-portunity to put an end to the federal Bank. Its charter would expire in seven years. The question of renewal was to be settled in that inter-val. Jackson was popular and politically powerful. His background and principles were agrarian. An attack on the Bank by him would be an attack "by the democracy on the money power." It would have, therefore, every political advantage.

The realities behind these words, however, were not what the words implied. The democracy till very recently had been agrarian because most of the population was agricultural. But the promoters of the assault on the Bank were neither agrarian in their current interests nor representative of what democracy implied.

In the western and rural regions, which were the most democratic in a traditional sense, dislike of the federal Bank persisted, though by 1829 it had less to feed on than formerly. Years before, under incompetent managers, the Bank had lent unwisely in the West, had been forced to harsh measures of self-preservation, and had made itself hated, with the help, as usual, of the state banks and states' rights politicians. But the West needed money, and though the Bank never provided enough it did provide some, and in the absence of new offenses disfavor had palpably subsided by the time Jackson became President.

There were also, in the same regions, vestiges or more of the traditional agrarian conviction that all banks were evil. This principle was still staunchly held by Andrew Jackson. He hated all banks, did so through a long life, and said so time after time. He thought they all violated the Constitution. But he was led by the men around him to focus his aversion on the federal Bank, which being the biggest must be the worst and whose regulatory pressure on the state banks must obviously be the oppression to be expected from a great, soulless corporation.

However, not all agrarian leaders went along with him. For many years the more intelligent had discriminated in favor of the federal Bank, recognizing that its operations reduced the tendency to inflation which, as a hard-money party, the agrarians deplored. Altogether, it was no longer to be expected that the agrarian democracy would initiate a vigorous attack on the federal Bank, though it was certainly to be expected that such an attack would receive very general agrarian support.

It was in the cities and within the business world that both the attack on the Bank and its defense would be principally conducted. For there the Bank had its strongest enemies and its strongest friends. Its friends were the more conservative houses that had dominated the old business world but had only a minor part in the new. It was a distinguished part, however, and influential. This influence, which arose from prestige and substantial wealth, combined with the strength which the federal Bank derived from the federal accounts to constitute what may tritely be called a "money power." But it was a disciplined, conservative money power and just what the economy needed.

But it was no longer *the* money power. It was rivaled, as Philadelphia was by New York, by the newer, more vigorous, more aggressive, and more democratic part of the business world.

The businessmen comprising the latter were a quite different lot from the old. The Industrial Revolution required more men to finance, to man, and manage its railways, factories, and other enterprises than the old business world, comprising a few rich merchants, could possibly provide. The Industrial Revolution was set to absorb the greater part of the population.

Yet when the new recruits, who yesterday were mechanics and farmers, offered themselves not only as laborers but as managers, owners, and entrepreneurs requiring capital, they met a response that was not always respectful. There was still the smell of the barnyard on their boots, and their hands were better adapted to hammer and nails than to quills and ink. The aristocrats were amused. They were also chary of lending to such borrowers; whereupon farmers' and mechanics' banks began to be set up. These banks found themselves hindered by the older banks and by the federal Bank. They and their borrowers were furious. They resisted the federal Bank in suits, encouraged by sympathetic states' rights politicians, and found themselves blocked by the federal courts.

Nor were their grievances merely material. They disliked being snubbed. Even when they became wealthy themselves, they still railed at "the capitalists" and "the aristocrats," as David Henshaw of Massachusetts did, meaning the old families, the Appletons and Lawrences whom he named, the business counterparts of the political figures that the Jacksonian revolution had replaced. Henshaw and his fellow Jacksonian leaders were full of virtue, rancor, and democracy. Their struggle was not merely to make money but to demonstrate what they already asserted, that they were as good as anyone, or more so. In their denunciation of the federal Bank, one finds them calling it again and again "an aristocracy" and its proprietors, other than the federal government, "aristocrats."

The Jacksonians, as distinct from Jackson himself, wanted a world where *laissez faire* prevailed; where, as Amos Kendall said, everyone would be free to get rich; where, as Roger Taney said, the benefits of banks would be open to all classes; where, as the enterprising exploiters of the land unanimously demanded, credit would be easy. To be sure, relatively few would be rich, and a good many already settling into an urban industrial class were beginning to realize it. But that consideration did not count with the Jacksonian leaders. They wanted a new order; they achieved the age of the Robber Barons.

The attack on the old order took the form of an attack on the federal Bank for a number of reasons which may be summed up in political expediency. A factor in the success of the attack was that the president of the Bank, Nicholas Biddle, was the pampered scion of capitalists and aristocrats. He was born to wealth and prominence. He was elegant, literary, intellectual, witty, and conscious of his own merits. When at the age of 37 he became head of the largest moneyed corporation in the world he was wholly without practical experience. In his new duties he had to rely on brains, self-confidence, and hard work. With these he did extraordinarily well. He had a remarkable grasp of productive and financial interrelations in the economy. The policies he formulated were sound. His management of the Bank, despite his inexperience, was efficient. His great weakness was naïveté, born of his ignorance of strife . . . .

Nicholas Biddle's response to the Jacksonian attack was inept. He was slow in recognizing that an attack was being made and ignored the warnings of his more astute friends. He expected the public to be moved by careful and learned explanations of what the Bank did. He broadcast copies of Jackson's veto message, one of the most popular and effective documents in American political history, with the expectation that people in general would agree with him that it was a piece of hollow demagogy. He entered a match for which he had no aptitude, impelled by a quixotic sense of duty and an inability to let his work be derogated. He engaged in a knock-down-drag-out fight with a group of experts as relentless as any American politics has ever known. The picture he presents is that of Little Lord Fauntleroy, lace on his shirt and good in his heart, running into those rough boys down the alley.

In his proper technical responsibilities Nicholas Biddle was a competent central banker performing a highly useful and beneficial task. It is a pity he had to be interrupted, both for him and for the economy. For him it meant demoralization. He lost track of what was going on in the Bank, he made blundering mistakes, he talked big. These things his opponents used tellingly against him. He turned from able direction of the central banking process to the hazardous business of making money, of which he knew nothing and for which his only knack lay in an enthusiastic appraisal of America's great economic future. In the end his Bank of the United States broke, he lost his fortune, he was tried on criminal charges (but released on a technicality), and he died a broken man.

This was personal misfortune, undeserved and severe. The more important victim was the American people. For with destruction of the United States Bank there was removed from an overexcitable economy the influence most effective in moderating its booms and depressions.

Andrew Jackson had vetoed recharter in 1832 and transferred the federal accounts to the pet banks in 1833 and 1834. The Bank's federal charter expired in 1836, though Nicholas Biddle obtained a charter from Pennsylvania and continued the organization as a state bank. The period was one of boom. Then in 1837 there was panic, all the banks in the country suspended, prices fell, and business collapsed. It was all Andrew Jackson's fault, his opponents declared, for killing the federal Bank. This was too generous. Jackson was not to blame for everything. The crisis was world-wide and induced by many forces. It would have happened anyway. Yet certainly Jackson's destruction of the Bank did not help. Instead it worsened the collapse. Had the Bank been allowed to continue the salutary performance of the years immediately preceding the attack upon it, and had it been supported rather than undermined by the Administration, the wild inflation which culminated in the collapse would have been curbed and the disaster diminished. Such a course would have been consistent with Jackson's convictions and professions. Instead he smote the Bank fatally at the moment of its best performance and in the course of trends against which it was needed most. Thereby he gave unhindered play to the speculation and inflation that he was always denouncing.

To a susceptible people the prospect was intoxicating. A continent abounding in varied resources and favorable to the maintenance of an immense population in the utmost comfort spread before the gaze of an energetic, ambitious, and clever race of men, who to exploit its wealth had two new instruments of miraculous potency: steam and credit. They rushed forward into the bright prospect, trampling, suffering, succeeding, failing. There was nothing to restrain them. For about a century the big rush lasted. Now it is over. And in a more critical mood we note that a number of things are missing or have gone wrong.

That critical mood was known to others than Jackson. Emerson, Hawthorne, and Thoreau felt it. So did an older and more experienced contemporary of theirs, Albert Gallatin, friend and aide in the past to Thomas Jefferson, and now president of a New York bank but loyal to Jeffersonian ideals.

"The energy of this nation," he wrote to an old friend toward the end of Andrew Jackson's Administration, "is not to be controlled; it is at present exclusively applied to the acquisition of wealth and to improvements of stupendous magnitude. Whatever has that tendency, and of course an immoderate expansion of credit, receives favor. The apparent prosperity and the progress of cultivation, population, commerce, and improvement are beyond expectation. But it seems to me as if general demoralization was the consequence; I doubt whether general happiness is increased; and I would have preferred a gradual, slower, and more secure progress. I am, however, an old man, and the young generation has a right to govern itself. . . ."

In these last words, Mr. Gallatin was echoing the remark of Thomas Jefferson that "the world belongs to the living." Neither Gallatin nor Jefferson, however, thought it should be stripped by the living. Yet nothing but the inadequacy of their powers seems to have kept those nineteenth-century generations from stripping it. And perhaps nothing else could.

But to the extent that credit multiplies man's economic powers, curbs upon credit extension are a means of conservation, and an important means. The Bank of the United States was such a means. Its career was short and it had imperfections. Nevertheless it worked. The evidence is in the protest of the bankers and entrepreneurs, the lenders and the borrowers, against its restraints. Their outcry against the oppressor was heard, and Andrew Jackson hurried to their rescue. Had he not, some other way of stopping its conservative and steadying influence could doubtless have been found. The appetite for credit is avid, as Andrew Jackson knew in his day and might have foretold for ours. But because he never meant to serve it, the credit for what happened goes rather to the clever advisers who led the old hero to the monster's lair and dutifully held his hat while he stamped on its head and crushed it in the dust.

Meanwhile, the new money power had curled up securely in Wall Street, where it has been at home ever since.

William Sidney Mount was a founder of the American school of genre art. In The Rustic Dance *(1830, detail), he portrayed antebellum society with lighthearted candor.*

*Part
Five*

ANTEBELLUM
SOCIETY

Bernard A. Weisberger

Religion

on

the Frontier

The following essay illustrates how exotic and colorful historical material can be presented in all its vigor without the historian surrendering his obligation to analyze and explain the significance of the subject he is describing. Indeed, in this case the discussion of the "meaning" of backwoods revivalism adds greatly to the verisimilitude of the strange events themselves. Portraits of the emotionally charged religious camp meetings of the nineteenth-century frontier easily degenerate into caricature. Bernard A. Weisberger studiously avoids this trap both by showing that the meetings were complex affairs (to which many kinds of people, driven by differing urges, came) and by pointing out the rational bases for the meetings and the emotional excesses they generated. He takes a relatively narrow subject, frontier religion, and relates it to a wide range of larger questions: American democracy; east-west conflicts; the nature of nationalism; human nature itself.

Dr. Weisberger, formerly a professor of history at Chicago, Rochester, and other universities, is currently devoting himself full time to historical research and writing. Among his books are They Gathered at the River, *a study of revivalism,* The American Newspaperman, *and* The New Industrial Society.

*T*he Great Revival in the West, or the Kentucky Revival of 1800, as it was sometimes called, was a landmark in American history. It was not some accidental outburst of religious hysteria that crackled through the clearings. Rather, it was one of many answers to a question on which America's destiny hung during Thomas Jefferson's Presidency. Which way would the West go? It was filling up fast in 1800, and yet it still remained isolated behind the mountain barriers, only thinly linked to the nation by a cranky, awkward, and dangerous transportation "system" of trails and rivers. Could it be held within the bounds of American institutions as they had developed over 175 colonial years? Would its raw energies pull it into some new orbit—say, an independent confederation? Or, if it stayed in the Union, would it send representatives swarming back eastward to crush old patterns under the weight of numbers?

No group asked this question more anxiously than eastern clergymen. For, in 1800, they saw that their particular pattern was being abandoned on the frontier. From Kentucky, Tennessee, the western Carolinas, and Virginia, reports came back of a world that was shaggy, vicious, and churchless. The hard-living men and women of the forest clearings were not raising temples to God. Their morals (to eastern eyes) were parlous. Corn liquor flowed freely; marriages were celebrated long after children had arrived; gun and rope settled far too many legal disputes. The West was crowded with Sabbath-breakers and profane swearers, thieves, murderers, and blasphemers, with neither courts of law nor public opinion to raise a rebuke. The whole region seemed "hair-hung and breeze-shaken" over Hell's vault. And this was a matter of life-or-death seriousness to the churches. It was clear even then that America's future lay beyond the mountains. And if the West grew up Godless, then the entire nation would one day turn from His ways, to its destruction. It was no wonder that pious folk of the seaboard dug into their pocketbooks to scrape up funds for "home missionary" societies aimed at paying the way of parsons traveling westward. Or that church assemblies warned of crises ahead and called for special days of fasting, humiliation, and prayer for the West.

Yet, for a fact, the easterners were wrong. They misjudged their pioneers. Western people wanted and needed the church just as badly as the church needed their support for survival. Religion had a part to play in the hard-driven lives of the frontier settlers. It was more than a mere foundation for morality. It offered the hope of a bright future, shining beyond the dirt-floored, hog-and-hominy present. It offered an emotional outlet for lives ringed with inhibition. It was a social thing, too, furnishing occasions on which to lay aside axe and gun and skillet and gather with neighbors, to sing, to weep, to pray, or simply to talk with others. The West had to have religion—but religion of its own special kind. The West was not "lost" in 1800, but on the verge of being saved. Only it was going to be saved the same way it did everything else: on its own individualistic terms.

The East found this hard to understand. The East had trouble taking stock of such a man as the father of the western revival, James McGready. McGready was an angular, black-eyed Scotch-Irishman, born on the Pennsylvania frontier. He came of a hard-working and pious stock that had filled the western stretches of the Colonies in the sixty years before the Revolution. McGready was true to the spirit of his Highland Calvinistic ancestors, who worked, prayed, and fought heartily. He grew to adolescence without becoming a swearer, drinker, or Sabbath-breaker, which made him something of a God-fearing rarity among frontier youth. So his family sent him to a private school conducted by a minister, where he wrestled with Scripture in the morning and did farm chores in the afternoon for his "tuition." In 1788, he was licensed to preach, and came down to western North Carolina's Guilford County, where his family had moved. Thus, McGready was a product of western Presbyterianism.

That was important. In the 1790's, the religious picture in the United States already showed considerable (and characteristic) variety. Episcopalianism was solidly rooted among the landed gentry of the South. The Dutch Reformed Church carried on the heritage established when the flag of Holland flapped over New York. Various shoots of Lutheranism pushed up out of the soil of German settlements. Baptism and Methodism were small but growing faiths. There were little wedges in the pie of church membership labeled "Quaker," "Catholic," and "Jewish." A few bold souls called themselves Deists. A few more were on the way to becoming Unitarians. American worship wore a coat of many colors. But in New England and the mid-Atlantic states, the Presbyterian and Congregational bodies were unquestionably in the forefront. Both were rooted in the preceding century's Puritanism. Both officially believed in "predestination" and "limited election"—God had chosen a few individuals to be saved from general damnation, and the list, made up from the beginning of eternity, was unchangeable. These chosen "saints" were born in sin, but in His own way God would convert them to holiness during their lifetimes. Meanwhile, the laws of God must be interpreted and explained to mankind. In order to do this, the Presbyterians and Congregationalists had raised up colleges to train their ministers, the most famous among them by 1800 being Harvard, Yale, and Princeton. Graduates of these schools thundered of Jehovah's wrath to their congregations in two-hour sermons rich with samples of their learning. During the week they warmed their study chairs ten hours a day, writing black-bound volumes of theology.

Religion of this sort lacked appeal for the Scotch-Irish migrants pushing into the frontier regions. They were Presbyterians in name. But their wild surroundings did something to them. They came to resent authority—whether exercised by excise collectors, land speculators, lawyers, or, finally, ministers. What was more, they wanted a little stronger assurance of salvation than a strict reading of limited election gave them. There was a need, in this fur-capped, bewhiskered Christian world, for more promise in life, and more passion too. Learned lectures might do for townspeople, but not for pioneers.

Among common folk, both East *and* West, a ferment of resentment against the "aristocratic" notion of election was at work. In the 1740's it had exploded in a revival called the Great Awakening. Baptist, Presbyterian, Congregationalist, Anglican, and Dutch-Reformed Christians were caught up in a common whirlwind of handclapping, shouting, and hosannaing. A good many new leaders, and a number of unpleasant schisms, had risen out of this storm. And in western Pennsylvania, revival-minded Presbyterians had founded a number of little academies to train their preachers. Derisively dubbed "log colleges" by the learned, they took the name proudly. Their graduates were short on Greek and exegesis but long on zeal. When the Great Awakening sputtered out before the Revolution, these colleges remained, helping to keep the sparks alive. Now, with the new nation established, the fire was ready to blaze again. McGready, himself a log-college graduate, was one of the first to blow on it.

McGready got to grips with the powers of darkness in North Carolina without wasting any time. He began to preach against the "formality and deadness" of the local churches. Besides that, he

Anabaptists of Hudson Falls, New York, attend a convert's immersion in the Hudson River.

demanded some concrete testimony of good living from his flock, and the particular evidence he asked for was highly exacting. The new preacher insisted that strong drink was a slippery path to Hell. In Guilford County this did not sit well. Frontiersmen saw no harm in lightening a hard life with a dram or two, and they wanted no lectures on the subject from men of the cloth. In point of fact, there was no cloth. Pioneer ministers wore buckskin, and took their turn with the next man at hoeing corn or splitting kindling. McGready got nowhere—at least nowhere in North Carolina. After a futile battle, he left to seek a more promising future in Kentucky—some said by request of the congregation.

In Kentucky, circumstances were riper for him. Despite eastern concern, a new Christian community was taking shape in that rugged, bear-and-savage-haunted wilderness province, where crude living went along with high dreaming. It was a community ready to be stirred into life, and McGready was the man to seize the stick. In Logan County, in the southwestern part of the state—a region well-known for unregenerate doings—he had three small congregations: at Red River, Gasper River, and Muddy River. He began to preach to these congregations, and he did not deal with such recondite matters as the doctrines contained in Matthew, or their applications. Instead he would "so describe Heaven" that his listeners would "see its glories and long to be there." Then he went on to "array hell and its horrors" so that the wicked would "tremble and quake, imagining a lake of fire and brimstone yawning to overwhelm them." With that brimstone smoking away in the background, McGready struck for bedrock. The whole point of Christianity, for him, was in the conversion of sinners to saints assured of eternal bliss. His question of questions was dagger-sharp: "If I were converted, would I feel it and know it?" A McGready parishioner was not going to be allowed to rest in self-satisfaction merely because he attended worship and avoided the grosser forms of indecency.

Under such spurring, results began to show among the faithful. In 1799, during a service at Gasper River, many fell to the ground and lay "powerless, groaning, praying and crying for mercy." Women began to scream. Big, tough men sobbed like hysterical children. What could explain this? Simply the fact that belly-deep fear was taking over. For it is well to remember that in those days conversion was the *only* token of salvation. No matter how young one was, no matter how blameless a life he had led, until the moment of transformation one was a sinner, bound for torment. If death stepped in before conversion was completed, babes and grandsires alike sank screaming into a lake of burning pitch—a lake that was not metaphorical, not symbolical, but *real* and eternal. And death on the frontier was always around the corner—in the unexpected arrow, the milk sickness, the carelessly felled tree, the leap of the wounded grizzly. Frontiersmen bottled up their fear. It was the price of sanity and survival. But when a religious service provided an acceptable excuse for breaking down the barriers, it was no wonder that men shivered and wept.

After shaking up the dry bones of the Gasper River settlement, McGready moved on in June of 1800 to Red River. He meant to hold a sacramental service, at the end of which church members would take the Lord's Supper together. What he got was something more uncontrolled. In a meetinghouse of undressed logs McGready shared his pulpit with three other Presbyterian ministers. A Methodist preacher was also present. That was not unusual. Frontier preachers were a small band. They knew each other well. A service was a social occasion, and therefore a treat, and several ministers often took part in order to draw it out.

The Presbyterian shepherds did their preaching, and what they said has not come down to us, but they must have dragged a harrow through the congregation's feelings. When John McGee, the Methodist, arose, an awesome hush had fallen on the house. McGee faced a problem. The Methodists were relative newcomers to America, officially on the scene only since 1766. They were frowned on by more established groups, mainly because they gave emotion free rein in their worship. It was not unusual at a Methodist meeting for women to faint, men to shout in strange tongues, and the minister himself to windmill his arms and bawl himself red-faced. For the more formal Presbyterians, such conduct was out of bounds. McGee knew this, and wanted to mind his ecclesiastical manners. But he knew a ripe audience when he saw one, too, and after an apparent debate with himself, he made his move. Rising, he shouted that everyone in the house should submit to "the Lord Omnipotent." Then he began to bounce from backless bench to backless bench, pleading, crying, shouting, shaking, and exhorting, "with all possible energy and ecstasy."

That broke the dam. The sinners of Red River had spent a lonely winter with pent-up terrors gnawing at them. McGee's appeal was irresistible. In a moment the floor was "covered with the slain; their screams for mercy pierced the heavens." Cursers, duelers, whiskey-swillers, and cardplayers lay next to little children of ten and eleven, rolling and crying in "agonies of distress" for salvation. It was a remarkable performance for a region "destitute of religion." When it was through, a new harvest of souls had been gathered for the Lord.

Word of the Red River meeting whisked through the territory. When McGready got to Muddy River, his next congregation, new scenes of excitement were enacted. During the meeting, sinners prayed and cried for mercy once again, and some of them, overwhelmed by feeling, bolted from the house and rushed in agony into the woods. Their cries and sobs could be heard ringing through the surrounding trees. And when this meeting had yielded up its quota of saved, the Kentucky Revival was not only a fact, but a well-known one. McGready announced another sacramental meeting for Gasper River, and before long, dozens, perhaps hundreds, of Kentuckians who did not belong to his district were threading the trails on their way to the service. Some came as far as a hundred miles, a hard week's trip in the back country. In wagons, on horseback, and on foot came the leather-shirted men, rifles balanced on their shoulders, and their pinched-looking, tired women, all looking for blessed assurance and a washing away of their sins.

At Gasper River, history was made. The cabins of the neighborhood could not hold the influx of visitors, so the newcomers came prepared to camp out. They brought tents—some of them—and cold pork, roasted hens, slabs of corn bread, and perhaps a little whiskey to hold them up through the rigors of a long vigil. The Gasper River meetinghouse was too small for the crowd, so the men got out their educated axes, and in a while the clop-clop of tree-felling formed an overture to the services. Split-log benches were dragged into place outdoors, and the worshipers adjourned to God's first temple. What was taking place was an outdoor religious exercise, meant to last two or three days, among people who camped on the spot. This was the camp meeting. Some claimed that Gasper River sheltered the very first of them. That claim has been challenged in the court of historical inquiry. But whether it stands up or not, the Gasper River meeting was something new in worship. It took its form from its western surroundings. Outsiders were a long time in understanding it, because they saw its crude outside and not its passionate heart.

The outside was raw enough. Once again McGready exhorted, and once again sinners fell prostrate to the ground. Night came on; inside the meetinghouse, candlelight threw grotesque, waving shadows on the walls. Outside, the darkness deepened the sense of mystery and of eternity's nearness. Preachers grew hoarse and exhausted, but insatiable worshipers gathered in knots to pray together, and to relieve their feelings by telling each other of "the sweet wonders which they saw in Christ." Hour followed hour, into dawn. For people who had to rise (and generally retire) with the sun each day of their lives, this alone was enough to make the meeting memorable for the rest of their lives. Lightheaded and hollow-eyed, the "mourners," or unconverted, listened alternately to threats of sulphur and promises of bliss, from Saturday until Monday. On Tuesday, after three throbbing days, they broke it up. Forty-five had professed salvation. Satan had gotten a thorough gouging.

Now the tide of camp-meeting revivalism began to roll northward. One of the visitors at the Logan County meetings was a young Presbyterian clergyman whose life was something of a copy of McGready's. Barton Warren Stone too had learned on the frontier to revere God Almighty and to farm well. He too had studied religion in a log college. But more than this, he was one of McGready's own converts, having fallen under the power of the older man's oratory in North Carolina. Stone liked what he observed in Logan County, and he took McGready's preaching methods and the camp-meeting idea back to his own congregations in Bourbon County, well to the north and east. Soon he too had imitators, among them Richard McNemar, who had small Presbyterian charges across the river in Ohio.

But it was Stone himself who touched off the monster camp meeting of the region's history. He set a sacramental service for August 6, 1801, at Cane Ridge, not far from the city of Lexington. Some unde-

*With the help of the Word, and sometimes of
the bottle, frontier camp meetings went on for
days and reaped rich harvests of converts.*

finable current of excitement running from cabin to cabin brought out every Kentuckian who could drop his earthly concerns and move, by horseflesh or shoe leather, toward the campground. Later on, some people estimated that 25,000 were on hand, but that figure is almost too fantastic for belief. In 1800, Kentucky had only a quarter of a million residents, and Lexington, the largest town, numbered under two thousand. But even a crowd of three or four thousand would have overwhelmed anything in the previous experience of the settlers.

Whatever the actual number, there was a sight to dazzle the eyes of the ministers who had come. Technically the meeting was Presbyterian, but Baptist and Methodist parsons had come along, and there was room for them, because no one man could hope to reach such a mob. Preaching stands built of logs were set up outdoors. One man remembered a typical scene—a crowd spilling out of the doors of the one meetinghouse, where two Presbyterian ministers were alternately holding forth, and three other groups scattered within a radius of a hundred yards. One cluster of sinners was gathered at the feet of a Presbyterian preacher, another gave ear to a Methodist exhorter, and lastly, a knot of Negroes was attending on the words of some orator of their own race. All over the campground, individual speakers had gathered little audiences to hear of *their* experiences. One observer said that there were as many as three hundred of these laymen "testifying."

So Cane Ridge was not really a meeting, but a series of meetings that gathered and broke up without any recognizable order. One Methodist brother who could not find a free preaching-stand ventured up the slanting trunk of a partly fallen tree. He found a flat spot, fifteen feet off the ground, and he spoke from this vantage point while a friend on the ground held up an umbrella on a long pole to shelter him from the weather. Within a few moments, this clergyman claimed, he had gathered an audience of thousands. Undoubtedly they stayed until lured away by some fresh address from a stump or the tail of a wagon. For the crowds were without form as they collected, listened, shouted "Amen!" and "Hallelujah!" and drifted off to find neighbors or refreshments or more preaching. The din can only be guessed at. The guilty were groaning and sometimes screaming at the top of their lungs, and those who felt that they were saved were clapping their hands, shouting hymns, and generally noising out their exultation. There were always hecklers at the meetings too, and some of them were no doubt shouting irreverent remarks at the faithful. Crying children added their bit, and tethered horses and oxen stamped, bawled, and whinnied to make the dissonance complete. Someone said that the meeting sounded from afar like the roar of Niagara. At night the campfires threw weird shadow-patterns of trees across the scene, and the whole moving, resounding gathering appeared to be tossing on the waves of some invisible storm. As if to etch the experience into men's memories, there were real rainstorms, and the drenched participants were thrown into fresh waves of screaming as thunder and lightning crashed around them.

All in all, a memorable enough episode. And yet still stranger things happened to put the brand of the Lord's sponsorship on Cane Ridge's mass excitement. Overwhelmed with their sensations, some men and women lay rigid and stiff on the ground for hours in a kind of catalepsy. One "blasphemer" who had come to scoff at the proceedings tumbled from his saddle unconscious and remained so for a day and a half. There was something incredibly compelling in what was going on. One remembered testimony came from a reasonably hardheaded young man named James Finley. Later in life Finley became a Methodist preacher, but in 1801 he was, except for a better-than-average education, a typical frontiersman. He had a small farm, a new wife, and a vigorous love of hunting. He had come to the Cane Ridge meeting out of curiosity, but as he looked on, he was taken with an uncontrollable trembling and feelings of suffocation. He left the campground, found a log tavern, and put away a glass of brandy to steady his nerves. But they were beyond steadying. All the way home he kept breaking out in irrational fits of laughter or tears. Many a spirit, returning from Cane Ridge, must have been moved in the same near-hysterical way.

A holy frenzy seemed to have taken hold of the West. Throughout the frontier communities, the ecstasy of conversion overflowed into the nervous system. At Cane Ridge, and at a hundred subsequent meetings, the worshipers behaved in ways that would be unbelievable if there were not plenty of good testimony to their truth. Some got the "jerks," a spasmodic twitching of the entire body. They were a fearful thing to behold. Some victims hopped from place to place like bouncing balls. Sometimes heads snapped from side to side so rapidly that faces became a blur, and handkerchiefs whipped off women's heads. One preacher saw women taken with the jerks at table, so that teacups went flying from their hands to splash against log walls. Churchmen disagreed about the meaning of these symptoms. Were they signs of conversion? Or demonstrations of the Lord's power, meant to convince doubters? Peter Cartwright, a famous evangelist of a slightly later era, believed the latter. He told of a skeptic at one of his meetings who was taken with the jerks and in a particularly vicious spasm snapped his neck. He died, a witness to the judgment of Omnipotence but gasping out to the last his "cursing and bitterness." Besides the jerks, there were strange seizures in which those at prayer broke into uncontrollable guffaws or intoned weird and wordless melodies or barked like dogs.

It was wild and shaggy, and very much a part of life in the clearings. Westerners wanted to feel religion in their bones. In their tough and violent lives intellectual exercises had no place, but howls and leaps were something that men who were "half-horse and half-alligator" understood. It was natural for the frontier to get religion with a mighty roar. Any other way would not have seemed homelike to people who, half in fun and half in sheer defensiveness, loved their brag, bluster, and bluff.

Yet there was something deeper than mere excitement underneath it all. Something fundamental was taking place, some kind of genuine religious revolution, bearing a made-in-America stamp. The East was unhappy with it. For one thing, camp-meeting wildness grated on the nerves of the educated clergy. All of this jigging and howling looked more like the work of Satan than of God. There were ugly rumors too, about unsanctified activities at the meetings. Some candidates for salvation showed up with cigars between their teeth. Despite official condemnation, liquor flowed free and white-hot on the outskirts of the gatherings. It might be that corn did more than its share in justifying God's ways to man. Then there were stories that would not down which told how, in the shadows around the clearing, excited men and women were carried away in the hysteria and, as the catch phrase had it, "begot more souls than were saved" at the meeting. All these tales might have had some partial truth, yet in themselves they did not prove much about frontier religion. As it happened, a part of every camp-meeting audience apparently consisted of loafers and rowdies who came for the show and who were quite capabie of any sin that a Presbyterian college graduate was likely to imagine.

Yet it was not the unscrubbed vigor of the meetings that really bothered conservatives in the Presbyterian Church. Their fundamental problem was in adjusting themselves and their faith to a new kind of democratic urge. Enemies of the revivals did not like the success of emotional preaching. What would happen to learning, and all that learning stood for, if a leather-lunged countryman with a gift for lurid word pictures could be a champion salvationist? And what would happen—what *had* happened—to the doctrine of election when the revival preacher shouted "Repent!" at overwrought thousands, seeming to say that any Tom, Dick, or Harry who felt moved by the Spirit might be receiving the promise of eternal bliss? Would mob enthusiasm replace God's careful winnowing of the flock to choose His lambs? The whole orderly scheme of life on earth, symbolized by a powerful church, an educated ministry, and a strait and narrow gate of salvation, stood in peril.

Nor were the conservatives wrong. In truth, when the McGreadys and Stones struck at "deadness" and "mechanical worship" in the older churches, they were going beyond theology. They were hitting out at a view of things that gave a plain and unlettered man little chance for a say in spiritual affairs. A church run by skilled theologians was apt to set rules that puzzled simple minds. A church which held that many were called, but few chosen, *was* aristocratic in a sense. The congregations of the western evangelists did not care for rules, particularly rules that were not immediately plain to anyone. In their view, the Bible alone was straightforward enough. Neither would they stand for anything resembling aristocracy, whatever form it might take. They wanted cheap land and the vote, and they were getting these things. They wanted salvation as well—or at least free and easy access to it—and they were bound to have that too. If longer-established congregations and their leaders back east did not like that notion, the time for a parting of the ways was at hand. In politics, such a parting is known as a revolution; in religion, it is schism. Neither word frightened the western revivalists very much.

The trouble did not take long to develop. In McGready's territory, a new Cumberland Presbytery, or subgroup, was organized in 1801. Before long it was in a battle with the Kentucky Synod, the next highest administrative body in the hierarchy. The specific issue was the licensing of certain "uneducated" candidates for the ministry. The root question was revivalism. The battle finally went up to the General Assembly, for Presbyterians a sort of combined Congress and Supreme Court. In 1809 the offending revivalistic presbytery was dissolved. Promptly, most of its congregations banded themselves into the separate Cumberland Presbyterian Church. Meanwhile, Barton Stone, Richard McNemar, and other members of the northern Kentucky wing of camp-meeting Presbyterianism were also in trouble. They founded a splinter group known as the "New Lights," and the Kentucky Synod, as might have been foreseen, lost little time in putting the New Lights out, via heresy proceedings. Next, they formed an independent Springfield Presbytery. But like all radicals, they found it easier to keep going than to apply the brakes. In 1804 the Springfield Presbytery fell apart. Stone and some of his friends joined with others in a new body, shorn of titles and formality, which carried the magnificently simple name of the Christian Church. Later on, Stone went over to the followers of Thomas and Alexander Campbell, who called themselves Disciples of Christ. Richard McNemar, after various spiritual adventures, became a Shaker. Thus, ten years after Cane Ridge, the score was depressing for Presbyterians. Revivalism had brought on innumerable arguments, split off whole presbyteries, and sent ministers and congregations flying into the arms of at least four other church groups. That splintering was a stronger indictment than any conservative could have invented to bring against Cane Ridge, or against its western child, the camp meeting.

A dead end appeared to have been reached. But it was only a second-act curtain. In the first act, religion in the West, given up for lost, had been saved by revivalism. In the second, grown strong and rambunctious, it had quarreled with its eastern parents. Now the time was at hand for a third-act resolution of the drama. Both sides would have to back down and compromise. For the lesson of history was already plain. In religious matters, as in all matters, East and West, metropolis and frontier, were not really warring opposites. Each nourished the other, and each had an impact on the other. Whatever emerged as "American" would carry some of the imprint of both, or it would perish.

On the part of the West, the retreat consisted of taming the camp meeting. Oddly enough, it was not the Presbyterians who did that. By 1812 or so, they had drawn back from it, afraid of its explosive qualities. But the Methodists were in an excellent position to make use of revivalism and all its trappings. They had, at that time at least, no educated conservative wing. They welcomed zealous backwood preachers, even if they were grammatically deficient. In fact, they worked such men into their organization and sent them, under the name of "circuit-riders," traveling tirelessly on horseback to every lonely settlement that the wilderness spawned. The result was that the Methodists were soon far in the lead in evangelizing the frontier. They did not have to worry about the claims of limited election either. Their formal theology did not recognize it. With a plain-spoken and far-reaching ministry freely offering salvation to all true believers, Methodism needed only some kind of official harvest season to count and bind together the converts. The camp meeting was the perfect answer. By 1811, the Methodists had held four or five hundred of them throughout the country; by 1820, they had held a thousand—by far the majority of all such gatherings in the nation.

But these meetings were not replicas of Cane Ridge. They were combed, washed, and made respectable. Permanent sites were picked, regular dates chosen, and preachers and flocks given ample time to prepare. When meeting time came, the arriving worshipers in their wagons were efficiently taken in charge, told where to park their vehicles and pasture their teams, and given a spot for their tents. Orderly rows of these tents surrounded a preaching area equipped with sturdy benches and preaching stands. The effect was something like that of a formal bivouac just before a general's inspection. Tight scheduling kept the worship moving according to plan—dawn prayers, eight o'clock sermons, eleven o'clock sermons, dinner breaks, afternoon prayers and sermons, meals again, and candlelight services. Years of experience tightened the schedules, and camp-meeting manuals embodied the fruits of practice. Regular hymns replaced the discordant bawling of the primitive era. Things took on a generally homelike look. There were Methodist ladies who did not hesitate to bring their best feather beds to spread in the tents, and meals tended to be planned and ample affairs. Hams, turkeys, gravies, biscuits, preserves, and melons produced contented worshipers and happy memories.

There were new rules to cope with disorderliness as well. Candles, lamps, and torches fixed to trees kept the area well lit and discouraged young converts from amorous ways. Guards patrolled the circumference of the camp, and heroic if sometimes losing battles were fought to keep whiskey out. In such almost decorous surroundings jerks, barks, dances and trances became infrequent and finally nonexistent.

Not that there was a total lack of enthusiasm. Hymns were still yelled and stamped as much as sung. Nor was it out of bounds for the audience to pepper the sermon with ejaculations of "Amen!" and "Glory!" Outsiders were still shocked by some things they saw. But they did not realize how far improvement had gone.

Eastern churchmen had to back down somewhat, too. Gradually, tentatively, they picked up the revival and made it part of their religious life. In small eastern towns it became regularized into an annual season of "ingathering," like the harvest or the election. Yet it could not be contained within neat, white-painted meetinghouses. Under the "sivilized" clothing, the tattered form of Twain's Pap Finn persisted. Certain things were taken for granted after a time.

The doctrine of election was bypassed and, in practice, allowed to wither away.

Moreover, a new kind of religious leader, the popular evangelist, took the stage. Men like Charles G. Finney in the 1830's, Dwight L. Moody in the 1870's, and Billy Sunday in the decade just preceding the First World War flashed into national prominence. Their meetings overflowed church buildings and spilled into convention halls, auditoriums, and specially built "tabernacles." As it happened, these men came from lay ranks into preaching. Finney was a lawyer, Moody a shoe salesman, and Sunday a baseball player. They spoke down-to-earth language to their massed listeners, reduced the Bible to basic axioms, and drew their parables from the courtroom, the market, and the barnyard. They made salvation the only goal of their service, and at the meeting's end they beckoned the penitents forward to acknowledge the receipt of grace. In short, they carried on the camp-meeting tradition. By the closing years of the nineteenth century, however, the old campgrounds for the most part were slowly abandoned. Growing cities swallowed them up, and rapid transportation destroyed the original reason for the prolonged camp-out. But the meetings were not dead. Mass revivalism had moved them indoors and made them a permanent part of American Protestantism.

All of this cost something in religious depth, religious learning, religious dignity. Yet there was not much choice. The American churches lacked the support of an all-powerful state or of age-old traditions. They had to move with the times. That is why their history is so checkered with schismatic movements—symptoms of the struggle to get in step with the parade. Hence, if the West in 1800 could not ignore religion, the rest of the country, in succeeding years, could not ignore the western notion of religion. One student of the camp meeting has said that it flourished "side by side with the militia muster, with the cabin raising and the political barbecue." That was true, and those institutions were already worked deeply into the American grain by 1840. They reflected a spirit of democracy, optimism, and impatience that would sweep us across a continent, sweep us into industrialism, sweep us into a civil war. That spirit demanded some religious expression, some promise of a millennium in which all could share.

The camp meeting was part of that religious expression, part of the whole revival system that channeled American impulses into churchgoing ways. In the home of the brave, piety was organized so that Satan got no breathing spells. Neither, for that matter, did anyone else.

Lewis Mumford

Ralph
Waldo
Emerson

Too often historians treat great individuals of the past only as reflections of their times, and draft from their lives and beliefs social blueprints or designs for the construction of large generalizations. All men, of course, are products of their surroundings; their ways of looking at the world, their basic values, even their language are to a large degree imposed upon them by the particular time and place in which they live. And the study of such men and their careers is indeed a fruitful way to approach the study of their world. Nevertheless, truly great men are not merely reflections of a special Zeitgeist, and as biographers from the earliest times have recognized, their lives are important to later generations as examples, as inspiration, and for a dozen other didactic purposes. Such was the life of Ralph Waldo Emerson, as Lewis Mumford so well demonstrates in this essay.

Emerson was surely a product of early nineteenth-century American culture, as many lesser historians have noted, and Mumford reminds us of this. But Mumford does not place any special importance on this "typical" Emerson; instead he portrays the unique genius of Emerson and uses his life to throw light not so much on the nineteenth century as on the twentieth. To write history in this way demands not only a great subject but a great author. Lewis Mumford, best known as an architectural critic, has over a long and richly productive career established his own claim to greatness, both through his trenchant analyses of modern urban problems and through his remarkable historical works, such as The Brown Decades, The City in History, and his biography of Herman Melville.

*T*he first twenty-five years of Ralph Waldo Emerson's life —from 1803 to 1828—were a struggle for bodily survival. He was threatened with the lethal disease of his day, tuberculosis, which two of his three younger brothers finally succumbed to; and he was poor. His father, minister of Boston's First Unitarian Church, died when he was eight, and the Emerson family lived in genteel penury, so poor that Emerson was forced to share a greatcoat with a brother during the grim Boston winters. Soon after marrying, his father had reported: "We are poor and cold and have little meal, and little wood, and little meat; but thank God, courage enough."

Armed with this family fortitude, Emerson, like his younger brothers, managed to get a Harvard education; and in the end the discipline of poverty underwrote his independence. By merely external pressures he could not be bullied or bribed. The fact that the outer world gave him so little during his growing period fostered his habit of living from within. But there his widowed mother had set him a good example: even in their neediest days, she withdrew for an hour after breakfast from the cares of the household, to meditate behind a closed door.

"A man must thank his defects," Emerson wrote in "Fate," "and stand in some terror of his talents." His original defects were a poor constitution, low vitality, shyness and awkwardness in company, a lack of outward warmth and responsiveness. It took him half a lifetime to compensate for these defects, if not entirely to overcome them, in acts of hospitality and friendly service and secret generosity. These acts touched not only those he loved, like Thomas Carlyle, Henry Thoreau, or Bronson Alcott, but passing strangers. Happily, Emerson's courtly manners softened his remoteness; and to the very end, as Walt Whitman noted on a final visit to him, he bore a cheerful and intelligent face, such a face as Emerson regarded as the ultimate proof and justification of culture.

If some of Emerson's essays, like those on Love and on Friendship, seem a little too toplofty, a little too rarefied, this is perhaps because during his early years he could survive only by keeping his actual environment—that bed of nails—at a distance, and countering it with ideal possibilities that existed only in his mind. His immunity to pain and grief, or at least his reluctance to give vent to them, was not a mark of stolid optimism; it was rather a psychological nerve block that enabled him to get on with his true work: his daily reading of nature and culture and the human soul, for the sake of catching some new illumination; for, as he noted in 1861, "A rush of thoughts is the only conceivable prosperity that can come to me." Fortunately, after his first marriage, in 1829, Emerson's economic circumstances improved, though he never escaped the pressure of supporting a large household.

The dividing line in Emerson's intellectual development was his first trip to Europe, in 1833; for he returned from this adventure, despite its physical ordeals, in robust health, with the old threat of tuberculosis overcome, and a kind of inner toughness that enabled him later, as a lecturer, to withstand the most gruelling journeys into the West, in crowded canal-boats, in sordid inhospitable taverns, over jolting icy roads; crossing the Mississippi on foot in the depth of winter, sometimes reaching his destination more dead than alive. To have endured these vulgar indignities, to have survived these misadventures, without a groan of self-pity, marks Emerson's iron discipline. Such a character could (as he put it) afford to write "Whim" over his door.

The first trip to Europe was an attempt to overcome two crises in Emerson's life. The personal crisis was occasioned by the death (in 1831) of his first wife, Ellen Tucker: a lovely, quietly impish, impassioned spirit, who had awakened an ardor and a love that he found himself unable adequately to express. ("I do not wish to hear of your prospects," she had said when Emerson had begun to preface a declaration of love with a summary of modest material expectations.) Her going left an empty niche in his life that his second wife, Lydia Jackson, a maturer woman, could never fill. It was surely with Ellen in mind that he wrote, in 1840: "I finish this morning transcribing my old essay on Love, but I see well its inadequateness. I, cold because I am hot—cold at the surface only, as a sort of guard and compensation for the fluid tenderness of the core—have much more experience than I have written there, more than I will, more than I can write."

Ellen's death was Emerson's first direct encounter with grief and desolation; and it was followed in a few years by the premature deaths of two younger brothers, one of whom, Charles Chauncy, he always regarded as having talent superior to his own. Even before this, some sobering premonition had made him write, on being engaged to Ellen, that he was "now as happy as it is safe in life to be."

The other crisis was a religious one, occasioned by his abandoning the calling he had struggled during the eighteen twenties to fit himself for: that of a duly qualified clergyman in the Unitarian Church. He had approached the duties of a minister with some repulsion for the homely routines of visitation, comfort for the dying, and moral suasion, with all their intrusive intimacies. But still more, he had come to realize that the God he had found in his consciousness had little need for either the dogmas or the rituals of an established church: even the Christ that moved him was not a God come to earth, but a singular being who had demonstrated while on earth the secret by which any man might become godlike. Emerson broke with his congregation at the Second Church of Boston over a single issue: his unwillingness to celebrate the Lord's Supper. But that break widened during the next decade into a total rejection of the church's whole institutional life and its claims to a unique revelation.

This parting of the ways removed the economic prop of Emerson's life and made it necessary for him to find an alternative mode of getting a living: that of a lecturer at the new lyceums that were springing up all over the country. For Emerson the lecture hall had become the living church of his day, spreading a many-tongued gospel that was destined to replace the "cant and snuffle of a dead Christianity."

This photograph of the aging Emerson captures with remarkable clarity his philosophy of self-reliance and courage.

Emerson's lectures, in reality soliloquies spoken aloud, were little different in texture from the notes in his Journals, where many parts of them were first recorded as scattered items.

In shaking himself loose from the Unitarian Church, Emerson had found his true vocation: that of being Emerson. This new mode of preaching turned out to be another blessing in disguise, for without the direct, face-to-face contact with mixed audiences of everyday people, in every part of the country except the South, Emerson would have lacked his sense of the more expansive and masculine America one associates with Audubon and Lincoln. New Englander that he was, he respected the uncouth vigor of the pioneers. And when Emerson met

President Lincoln face to face, Lincoln reminded him of what he had said about Kentuckians in an Illinois lecture: "A Kentuckian seems to say by his air and manners, 'Here am I; if you don't like me, the worse for you.'"

Emerson's difficulties did not come to an end with his marriage to Lidian—as he re-named his second wife—in 1835, and his settling down in a commodious house, surrounded by a few acres of usable land at the edge of Concord: for if he had a good garden, productive pear trees, willing servants, a tender and devoted wife, he all too soon had the shattering experience of losing his five-year-old son Waldo to scarlet fever, that son whose angelic qualities had won free access to Emerson's otherwise inviolate study. Well had he written earlier to his spiritual monitor, Aunt Mary Moody Emerson: "He has seen but half the Universe who has never been shown the house of pain." Even in the serene years before little Waldo's death Emerson had faced, no less than Herman Melville did, the evils that dog the human condition: "Now, for near five years," he wrote in 1840, "I have been indulged by the gracious Heaven in my long holiday in this goodly house of mine, entertaining and entertained by so many worthy and gifted friends, and all this time poor Nancy Barron, the mad-woman, has been screaming herself hoarse at the Poor-house across the brook and I still hear her whenever I open my window."

In the middle years, between 1835 and 1865, Emerson did the bulk of his work: the little book on Nature; the two trenchant series of essays—in every way his central work; the book on English Traits; the sometimes crabbed but authentic poems, rough-skinned, tart, like his own winter pears; and those maturer reflections on the Conduct of Life, which at least one contemporary thought more "pungent and piercing" than anything he had written before. During those same middle years, despite Emerson's original need for solitude, despite his resolute effort to free his days for communion with nature and his own mind, he took on all the demands of daily life. On settling in Concord, he accepted the ancient office of hogreeve—in charge of stray pigs; and as a husband and father, as a householder, a lyceum lecturer, and an editor of the *Dial*, he bore cheerfully, or if pressed, stoically, the duties of domestic and civic life. What he often characterized as his "indolence" was his need between whiles to recoup his energies for thought.

Whatever Emerson's reluctance to leave his study, his involvement in the political and social issues of his time, from the forties on, grew deeper: in the crises that culminated in the Civil War, his moral commitment was not only firm but passionate. Witness his protest to President Martin Van Buren over the scandalous chicane practiced by the federal government against the Cherokee Indians, his denunciation of slavery and the Fugitive Slave Law, his contempt for his one-time hero, Daniel Webster, the chief sponsor of that law; and not least his scalding attacks upon the infamous Mexican War, the Vietnam of his day, in his "Ode" inscribed to William Henry Channing.

In his mature years the aloof, self-contained, self-sufficient Emerson gave to society some of the allegiance he had once given too exclusively to solitude. For this was not only the period of his great friendships, with Carlyle, Arthur Hugh Clough, Bronson Alcott, Thoreau, Margaret Fuller, but also of the relaxing sociabilities of the Saturday Club, with its monthly luncheon meeting at the Parker House in Boston. There a more congenial Emerson appeared, one who horrified the elder Henry James by drinking wine and by covering his diffidence in company by smoking a cigar—as if a disembodied angel could enjoy a cigar!

By 1865 Emerson's main written work, with the exception of a few poems, was done; and when the war was over, his lecturing tapered off too, though he would still at intervals struggle painfully through old lectures, handicapped by lapses of memory, but sustained by sympathetic and indulgent audiences. Ironically, one of the last lectures he gave was on Memory—a lecture in which he redressed his original overemphasis upon the fresh and the newborn while dismissing the past: "Life only avails, not the having lived." Now he realized, belatedly, that the American, in the raw confidence of youth, had forgotten too much: that memory was "the thread on which the beads of man are strung, making the personal identity which is necessary to moral action. Without it all life and thought are an unrelated succession." He had lived long enough to realize, at last, that the "having lived" availed too.

Since Emerson still has much to give us—not because his method or his mood reflects that of our own times, but because it is so defiantly the opposite—there is no need to gloze over his deficiencies. His coldness and remoteness were almost constitutional qualities: they are hardly more a subject for reproach than his sloping shoulders, his narrow frame, his long nose. He himself "thought it a good remark" that "I always seemed to be on stilts. . . . Most of the persons whom I see in my own house, I see across a gulf, I cannot go to them nor they come to me."

With this coldness went, it would seem, not a failure of love—far from it—but a lack of strong sexual ardor. As late as the age of thirty-one, he could dismiss Boccaccio because he represented only the pleasure of appetite, "which only at rare intervals, a few times in a lifetime, are intense." Even by the standards of Puritan New England, that was a startling statement. The celebrations of sex in Walt Whitman's *Leaves of Grass* served, doubtless unconsciously, to fill in this omission in Emerson, whom Whitman revered as his master. But for all this quantitative lack of energy, Emerson had boxed the compass of life in a sense that none of his great American contemporaries had done: even sexually he was more mature than the fastidious but adolescent Thoreau, or the amative but unmarried Whitman. The sweet Emersonian smile, as on an archaic Greek face, was the witness of a complete, fully manifested life: he was "all there." And his work, though seemingly in fragments, was equally complete.

Perhaps one of the reasons for the pallid impression that Emerson left on a later generation is that he himself in his last fifteen years gradually faded out of the picture, ceasing after 1870 even to have the impulse to post in his Journals such stray thoughts as perhaps flickered through his mind. Yet no one could have met the disturbances of senescence with more smiling tranquillity, with more equable resignation. A little later, no longer able even to edit his unpublished papers, he left that task to his trusted friend, James Elliot Cabot, and his daughter, Ellen. Like a winter apple, still ruddy though mealy-ripe, he clung to the tree, safe from the worms and the wasps. When his thoughts no longer made sense, he had the sense to be silent. But the halo remained gay and bright; and today, against the addled counsels, the insensate threats, the artful, self-induced psychoses of our age, that halo has become gayer and brighter than ever, for it radiates from a poised and finely balanced personality. The sense of Emerson's luminous presence—that is what the reader will find on every page.

To understand the peculiar gifts of Emerson and the quality of his mind, one must realize that he was, primarily, neither a philosopher nor a didactic writer, still less a scholar or a scientist, but a poet: one who used the materials of other arts and disciplines to provide colors for his own palette. He did not regard himself as a great poet, but whatever he was, he told a friend, was of poet all through; yet he qualified this modestly, in another place, by saying that he was only half a poet. Yes; half a poet, if one thinks only of his verses: but what a half! Emerson nevertheless was a major poet, if one realizes that all his thought underwent a poetic transformation: an intensification, a distillation, a penetration that again and again would be crystallized in a perfect paragraph or poem. Emerson the poet remains present everywhere in his work, for all his thought is by its nature metaphoric and evocative, meant to excite a corresponding resonance directly in the reader's mind.

As a writer, Emerson stands on the level of the great essayists he admired—Michel de Montaigne and Francis Bacon: he has the same wide range of interests, the same sharp perceptions, the same gift for reducing a whole chapter of experience to a single sentence; and in addition, he has a crystalline freshness all his own, as of cool water bubbling upward from an underground spring. Though, like Montaigne, he ceaselessly read and often quoted old authors, he presents even old thoughts as if he were perceiving them anew and asking what, after all, they mean here and now.

If any one essay might be singled out to reveal Emerson's peculiar virtue and character as an American, it would probably be that on Self-Reliance; for there he spoke with the unmistakable voice of New World man, opening up and exploring a virgin continent of the mind, testing himself against nature, and finding out how much past knowledge and equipment he might need in order to survive and prosper.

In "Self-Reliance" Emerson established, better than anyone else had yet done, the central trait of the American character, at the moment when it became conscious of its special nature and its potential destiny. This sense was expressed in art by the aesthetic doctrines of the sculptor Horatio Greenough; in the novel by Cooper, Hawthorne, and Melville; in moral philosophy by Thoreau; in poetry by Whitman, as later in philosophy by William James and John Dewey; and it was not by accident that the most original of American architects, who bore indubitably the New World stamp, Frank Lloyd Wright, was more deeply devoted to Emerson than to any other writer. Emerson saw that if his country was to have free cultural intercourse with other countries, it must first have a character of its own. He realized that even the swagger and crudity of the Kentuckian or the Hoosier were better than a subservient colonialism that sought only to ape traditional Old World forms that had outlived their uses, or to keep up with the passing fashions of Paris and London.

This was the note Emerson struck repeatedly in *Nature,* in "Self-Reliance," and again in "The American Scholar." But neither Emerson nor those who were truly influenced by him could be trapped for long by an ingrowing provincial isolationism. If they had left Europe behind them, it was to take not only America but the whole world as their spiritual province. Before Whitman had composed his "Salut au Monde" and his "Passage to India," Emerson had made that same salute and traced the same passage himself, the latter with the aid of a small library of Oriental classics that some English friends had brought over to Concord. So deeply did Emerson immerse himself in the religion and philosophy of that elder Old World that some Hindus have taken his poem "Brahma," one of a half dozen perfect poems he wrote, as a true expression of the essential Hindu spirit.

So, when Emerson had swept away all the battered furniture and dusty heirlooms of the past, it was not for the purpose of conducting a miserable existence in an empty, cold, desolate chamber decorated only by a national flag, but in order to make better use of the space, and to provide it with more adequate furnishings. Some of the old belongings would come back again, not because they were old and respectable, but because they were still imperishably new. His "Away with the Dead!" meant "Hail to the Living!" He knew better than most that by regrouping old words one brings forth new thoughts. Past, present, and future, near and far, fused in his consciousness. "A true man belongs to no other time and place, but is the center of things." By the same token, once self-reliance was established, one might give and take aid freely, profiting the more by society because one was no longer dependent upon it.

Partly as a result of his temperamental remoteness and insulation, Emerson was more at home with Plato or Shakespeare than with his own contemporaries. As a young man he was an overcaptious critic even of those writers he admired, like Wordsworth, William Savage Landor, or Goethe. Most current novels seemed to him trivial and superficial: Jane Austen, Dickens, Thackeray, even Hawthorne, did not engage him. But he realized that Thoreau wrote an even meatier prose than his own, and almost alone he dared at once to acclaim Whitman's *Leaves of Grass* as the original work that it was. Yet it is not as a critic of literature that one turns to Emerson: he was primarily a critic of life, and he had a capacity to face bitter realities that his contemporaries flinched from.

"Great men, great nations," Emerson wrote, "have not been boasters and buffoons, but perceivers of the terror of life, and have manned themselves to face it." And again in the same essay on Fate he observed:

> We must see that the world is rough and surly, and will not mind drowning a man or a woman, but swallows your ship like a grain of dust. . . . The diseases, the elements, fortune, gravity, lightning, respect no persons. The way of Providence is a little rude. . . . The forms of the shark, the *labrus,* the jaw of the sea-wolf paved with crushing teeth, the weapons of the grampus and other warriors hidden in the sea, are hints of ferocity in the interiors of nature. Let us not deny it up and down. Providence has a wild, rough, incalculable road to its end, and it is of no use to try to whitewash its huge, mixed instrumentalities, or to dress up that terrific benefactor in the clean shirt and white neckcloth of a student in divinity.

Did Herman Melville ever indict the nature of things in harsher terms?

Yet there was a difference between Emerson and the Melville of *Moby Dick* and *Pierre,* not only in their respective visions of evil, but in their attitude as to how it should be treated. "What can we do in dark hours?" Emerson asked. And he answered: "We can abstain. In the bright hours we can impart." This is perhaps Emerson's final justification for his reserves, his inhibitions, his silences: he did not deny the existence of evil and pain, still less hide them from himself, but he answered them as his father had done when facing starvation: "We have, thank God, courage enough." If there is any central lesson to be learned from Emerson's thought, it is the lesson of heroism: *have courage!* And he might have drily added, looking around him at the screaming madwoman, the corrupt politicians, the whip-happy slavemongers, "You will need it."

Just because Emerson rejected none of the offices of the mind, he was, within the compass of his own experience, full of fresh perceptions, and he anticipated vividly, sometimes by a generation, sometimes by a whole century, the more studious efforts and discoveries of other men. As early as 1832 Emerson wrote: "Dreams and Beasts are two keys by which we are to find out the secrets of our own nature. All mystics use them. They are like comparative anatomy. They test objects; or we may say, that must be a good theory of the universe, that theory will bring a commanding claim to confidence, which explains these phenomena." The theory of Beasts is Darwin and evolution; the theory of Dreams is Freud and the unconscious. In Emerson, neither of these interests was haphazard or the result of a lucky stab. From the currents of evolutionary doctrine that flowed through the nineteenth century, after Buffon and Lamarck, Emerson realized in poetic phrase, well before Darwin, that "striving to be man, the worm mounts through all the spires of form." Man's life in nature includes every aspect of nature, however formidable, not only those that flatter or comfort man; yet nature, coming into consciousness in man, discloses purposes and ideal ends that transcend all previous evolutionary experience.

But if the theory of Beasts, that is, man's linkages with all organic nature, was important, this was tied up in Emerson's mind with that other mystery still to be penetrated, the mystery of Dreams; and in taking dreams seriously, not least his own, Emerson was well in advance of the thinkers of his own day who had, since the time of Descartes, regarded the inner life as the special province of religion. In this matter, Emerson was a better naturalist than most of his scientific contemporaries: he accepted dreams as a natural phenomenon which had some significance for man's own development. The fact that Emerson regarded sex, too, as one of the mysteries that needed further investigation—though he confined this recognition to his Journals— only shows how central, and in a sense how faithful to natural revelation, his essential thought was.

Emerson's attaching importance to beasts, dreams, and sex was an example of his devotion to the truths available to him through self-revelations rather than books, and this was connected with an even more central faith in the reality of God's presence and influence, disclosed in every manifestation of life. He would have nothing of the doctrine that supposed that revelation was something that happened long ago, was "given and gone, as if God were dead." God was tremendously alive for Emerson, as were the soul and the oversoul, the first immediate and individual, the second general and universal. This god was not the god of the churches; and it is only now, perhaps, that we can begin to see what Emerson was really talking about when he used the orthodox term "God" to express his new perception.

"There is a power above and behind us," wrote Emerson, "and we are the channel of its communication." If I am not deceived, Emerson had realized that a direct access to the unconscious was as important in opening one's eyes to reality as the pageant of the outer world—or even more important, since the unconscious bore within it the whole experience of the race, from the time before consciousness itself had emerged.

Emerson himself linked the experience of God with the operation of the unconscious, sometimes in so many words, as when he observed: "Blessed is the child; the unconscious is ever the act of God himself. Nobody can reflect upon his unconscious period; or any particular word or act in it, with regret or contempt." Or again, "The central fact is the super-human intelligence, pouring into us from the unknown fountain, to be received with religious awe and defended from any mixture of our will." When Emerson says, "Dare to love God without mediator or veil," he is saying, "Dare to respect and embrace and live openly with your unconscious."

In this poetic discovery of the role of the unconscious Emerson was not alone: the same discovery was made by Hawthorne and Melville, and this served as a secret link between those two souls, though as yet there was no name for the unconscious except the ancient one that Emerson loyally clung to: God. But as more than one religion had testified, this God has an almost equal counterpart and antagonist, Satan, whose exalted energies Milton and Blake had contemplated even before Melville had baptized Moby Dick in the name of the Devil. Through the exploration of dreams, fantasies, and psychal disorders that has gone on for the last half century and more, we now realize that both versions of the unconscious are true: this polarity plays an essential role in human creativity. Emerson's unconscious is mainly the luminous one, out of which love and brotherhood and justice and truth are born; while Melville's is the dark one, from which come forth murderous hate, satanic pride, insensate destruction—or demonic revelation. Neither version is to be trusted as an expression of cosmic and human potentialities without the other: but only when the luminous god gains the upper hand can life prosper.

At first, Emerson did not realize this ambivalent quality of the unconscious: when he was young, his private revelations were apparently so angelic and so well disciplined that he trusted them absolutely. Even in middle life he had said jauntily, in reply to an older friend who asked how he could be sure that his confident new revelation might not come from below rather than from above, "If I am the Devil's child, I will live then from the Devil." This was all very well as a youthful act of defiant integrity: but it is no answer if it happens that the Devil's disciple is not a staid, well-bred, firmly moralized young man, needing to discard his moral braces, but a Hitler or a Stalin, heeding every sadistic impulse and magnifying all the possibilities for human iniquity.

In later life Emerson corrected his youthful bias: he fervently blessed the yoke of men's opinions which he had once forsworn. In his poem "Grace," Emerson even thanked his "preventing God" for the defenses he had set around him: "example, custom, fear, occasion slow"—scorned bondmen who had served as parapet, keeping him from "the roaring gulf below." This again is one of those occasions when those who gauge Emerson's mind by this or that isolated expression fail to correct the momentary aberration by the full report of his life.

All this, and more, one will find in Emerson. But there is no use looking in his work for a closely ordered philosophic system; and to make Emerson into a mere Transcendentalist, as many have done, is to show little insight into either the scope or the depth of his thought, for he transcended Transcendentalism as decisively as he protested against Protestantism and dematerialized Materialism. The nearest Emerson ever came to presenting his philosophy as a unity was in his first work on Nature, where he laid out the four chief categories of his thought—commodity, beauty, language, and discipline. But if that were his sole credential as a seminal thinker, it would hardly meet his own criteria; for he kept on contemplating a more adequate expression of his metaphysics in a natural history of the mind, a work whose belated publication as an essay did not fulfill the hopes he had long nourished.

The fact is that Emerson's abortive efforts to produce a coherent philosophy were untrue to his own system-shattering openness. His mission was to examine crumbling foundations, to condemn unsound structures, to clear the site of lumber, to quarry new materials—not to instruct the would-be builders, nor to design a new structure. Repeatedly Emerson told Carlyle that he had no talent for construction. But what Emerson regarded as a defect was perhaps his essential virtue: his unwillingness to deny a truth because it was inconsistent in appearance or in logic with other equally reputable truths. What he retained, through this constitutional ineptitude, was a readiness to examine and even anticipate incredible new discoveries that system-mongers could not open the door to without acknowledging the insufficiency of their systems. George Edward Woodberry, an unsympathetic critic, said that in studying Emerson "one is reminded of the early sages of Greece." Precisely: for in both cases this originality and imperfection marked the embryonic expression of a new culture.

Such a description places Emerson's mind in its proper social setting: it does justice to his intellectual nakedness, his bright innocence, his sparkling richness of potentialities. Unburdened by past encrustations, untrammelled by future constraints, he was free to move in any direction. Emerson's, in short, was the most liberated mind that the West had produced in several centuries: as liberated as Shakespeare's. If Emerson "has no philosophy" it is because, like Shakespeare, his philosophy is as large as life, and cannot be reduced to an articulated skeleton without forfeiting its life.

"The day will come," Emerson prophesied, "when no badge or uniform or star will be worn." That day has not yet dawned; indeed, in our status-conscious, caste-bound America it seems further away now than ever. No such ungraded, fully individuated society as yet exists anywhere. So perhaps the high value of Emerson's thought for the present generation lies not only in the way it anticipated or marched ahead of the special discoveries of our time, as in the place it gave to the unconscious and the prerational processes of the mind, but even more in the way it radically differs from our current assumptions and challenges our practices: our conformity, our timidity, our docility —or those fashionable negative images of these same traits, our mindless anarchies, our drug-excited audacities, our aimless violence.

Certainly Emerson's America is not our present America: it is rather an older yet more youthful America, part achieved reality, part hopeful ideal, which we have lost. It is in Emerson's mind, more fully even than in Jefferson's, Whitman's, Thoreau's, or Lincoln's mind, that we can measure all that we have disowned or buried, and may, if we go further in the same direction, lose forever. And it is by entering Emerson's mind once more that we may recover at least a portion of our lost heritage, and gain courage—"courage enough!" —to seek a better life.

Arnold Welles

Samuel Slater Imports a Revolution

The transition of the United States from an agricultural to a predominantly industrial nation was one of the most important, and by the end of the period, most obvious developments of the nineteenth century. When Washington became President there was not a true factory in the entire country; when Theodore Roosevelt became President the United States was already the leading industrial nation of the world. Industrialization and the factory system are not absolutely synonymous terms, but factories are the basic structures in which the industrial process operates most effectively. And Samuel Slater, a young English immigrant, was the man who designed and built the first factory in America. What Slater did, a remarkable personal story as well as one of the key events in the economic and social history of the United States, is told in this essay by one of his great-great-grandsons, Arnold Welles, a successful businessman who is also a fine historian.

*F*eats of memory, particularly of the kind of memory derided as "photographic"—for all the cornucopias of wealth they sometimes pour over television contestants—are looked down on in modern times, but they have their role in history. Consider, for example, the story of Samuel Slater. It would be impolite to call him a spy, for he would not have considered himself one. Furthermore, he was a man of peace. Yet in his own time this cotton spinner's apprentice achieved with his prodigious memory an effect as great as or greater than any successful military espionage has brought about in our own. For he successfully transplanted the infant Industrial Revolution, which was in many ways an English monopoly, across an ocean to a new country.

To understand Slater's feat, one must look back to the economic situation of England and America in the days directly after the Colonies had achieved their independence. If Britain no longer ruled her former colonies, she clung tenaciously to her trade with them. Thanks to her flourishing new textile industry, she was able to sell large quantities of cotton goods in the United States at prices so low there was little incentive left for making cloth over here by the old-fashioned hand methods. To maintain this favorable dependency as long as possible, England went to fantastic lengths to guard the secrets that had mechanized her cotton industry, and so effective were these measures that America might well have continued solely as an agricultural nation for years, had it not been for Samuel Slater.

Slater was born in 1768 on his family's property, Holly House, in Derbyshire, England. His father, William Slater, was an educated, independent farmer and timber merchant, the close friend and neighbor of Jedediah Strutt, successively farmer, textile manufacturer, and partner of England's famous inventor, Sir Richard Arkwright, whose spinning frame had revolutionized the manufacture of cotton yarn. Three years after Samuel Slater's birth, Strutt had financed Arkwright's factory at Cromford—the world's earliest authentic cotton mill—where water power replaced humans and animals in moving the machinery, and where the whole operation of spinning yarn could be accomplished for the first time automatically under one roof. Within five years Arkwright's mills were employing over 5,000 workers, and England's factory system was launched.

It was in this atmosphere of industrial revolution that young Slater grew up. He showed signs of his future mechanical bent at a tender age by making himself a polished steel spindle with which to help wind worsted for his mother, and whenever he had the chance, he would walk over to nearby Cromford or Belper on the Derwent River to see the cotton mills which Strutt and Arkwright owned. In 1782 Strutt began to erect a large hosiery factory at Milford, a mile from the Slater property, and he asked William Slater's permission to engage his eldest son as clerk. Slater, who had noticed the ability and inclinations of his younger son, Samuel, recommended him instead, observing that he not only "wrote well and was good at figures" but was also of a decided mechanical bent.

Thus, at the age of fourteen, Samuel Slater went to live and work with Strutt. When William Slater died shortly afterward, in 1783, young Samuel Slater signed his own indenture to learn cotton spinning as an apprentice in Strutt's factory until the age of 21.

During the early days of his term the boy became so engrossed in the business that he would go for six months without seeing his family, despite the fact that they lived only a mile away, and he would frequently spend his only free day, Sunday, experimenting alone on machinery. In those days millowners had to build all their own machinery, and Slater acquired valuable experience in its design, as well as its operation, and in the processes of spinning yarn. Even before completing his term of indenture he was made superintendent of Strutt's new hosiery mill.

But Slater had become concerned about the chances for an independent career in England. Arkwright's patents having expired, factories had sprung up everywhere, and Slater could see that to launch out on his own he would need more and more capital to stay ahead of the technical improvements constantly taking place. His attention had been drawn to the United States by an article in a Philadelphia paper saying that a bounty of £100 had been granted by the Pennsylvania legislature to a man who had designed a textile machine. Young Slater made up his mind that he would go to the United States and introduce the Arkwright methods there. As his first step, even before his term with Strutt expired, Slater obtained his employer's permission to supervise the erection of the new cotton works Arkwright was then starting, and from this experience he gained valuable knowledge for the future.

There were, it was true, grave risks to consider. Britain still strictly forbade the export of textile machinery or the designs for it. With France entering a period of revolution which might unsettle the economy of the Old World, it was even more important that the large American market be safeguarded for British commerce. As a result, the Arkwright machines and techniques were nowhere in use in America at the time, and various attempts—in Pennsylvania, Massachusetts, Connecticut, Maryland, and South Carolina—to produce satisfactory cotton textiles had borne little fruit. Without Arkwright's inventions it was impossible to make cotton yarn strong enough for the warps needed in hand-loom weaving.

Enterprising Yankees undertook all kinds of ingenious attempts to smuggle out modern machines or drawings. Even the American minister to France was involved in some of them: machinery would be quietly purchased in England, dismantled, and sent in pieces to our Paris legation for transshipment to the United States in boxes labeled "glassware" or "farm implements." British agents and the Royal Navy managed to intercept almost all such shipments, however, and skilled workers who attempted to slip away with drawings or models were apprehended on the high seas and brought back. Passengers leaving England for American ports were thoroughly searched by customs agents before boarding ship.

This portrait of an eminently successful Samuel Slater includes in the background a view of his first cotton-spinning mill.

Slater knew of these handicaps and determined to take along nothing in writing save his indenture papers. . . . But he was carrying with him in a very remarkable memory the complete details of a modern cotton mill.

After a passage of 66 days, Slater's ship reached New York. He had originally intended to go to Philadelphia, but when he learned of the existence of the New York Manufacturing Company on Vesey Street in downtown Manhattan, he showed his indenture and got a job there instead. The company had recently been organized to make yarns and cloth, but the yarn was linen and the machinery, hand-operated, was copied from antiquated English models. This was a far cry from the factories Slater had supervised in Derbyshire.

Fortunately, about this time, the newcomer happened to meet the captain of a packet sailing between New York and Providence, Rhode Island, and from him learned of the interest in textile manufacturing shown by a wealthy, retired merchant of Providence, Moses Brown, later to become one of the founders of Brown University. A converted Quaker and a man of large imagination and business acumen, Brown had invested considerable cash in two rough, hand-operated spinning frames and a crude carding machine as well as in a couple of obsolete "jennies." But all his attempts to produce cotton yarns had ended in failure, and he could find little use for his expensive machinery. Such was the situation when he received a letter from Slater:

SIR,—   New York, December 2d, 1789

A few days ago I was informed that you wanted a manager
of *cotton spinning*, etc., in which business I flatter myself that
I can give the greatest satisfaction, in making machinery,
making good yarn, either for *stockings* or *twist*, as any that is
made in England; as I have had opportunity, and an oversight
of Sir Richard Arkwright's works, and in Mr. Strutt's mill
upwards of eight years. If you are not provided for, should be
glad to serve you; though I am in the New York manufactory,
and have been for three weeks since I arrived from England.
But we have but *one card, two machines*, two spinning jennies,
which I think are not worth using. *My intention* is to erect a
perpetual card and spinning. (Meaning the Arkwright patents).
If you please to drop a line respecting the amount of encouragement you wish to give, by favor of Captain Brown, you will
much oblige, sir, your most obedient humble servant.

SAMUEL SLATER

N.B.—Please to direct to me at No. 37, Golden Hill, New York.

Slater's letter fired the shrewd Quaker's imagination, and he
hastened to reply, declaring that he and his associates were "destitute
of a person acquainted with water-frame spinning" and offering Slater
all the profits from successful operation of their machinery over and
above interest on the capital invested and depreciation charges. His
invitation concluded: "If the present situation does not come up to
what thou wishes, and, from thy knowledge of the business, can be
ascertained of the advantages of the mills, so as to induce thee to
come and work ours, and have the *credit* as well as the advantage of
perfecting the first water-mill in America, we should be glad to engage thy care so long as they can be made profitable to both, and we
can agree."

Tempted and flattered, and assuming that the Providence operation needed only an experienced overseer to make it a success, Slater
decided to accept. He took a boat in January, 1790, reached Providence
on the eighteenth of the month, and immediately called on Moses
Brown.

The two men were in striking contrast. Slater, only 21, was nearly
six feet tall and powerfully built, with ruddy complexion and fair
hair. Moses Brown, in his soft, broad-brimmed Quaker hat, was well
past middle age, of small stature, with a pair of bright, bespectacled
eyes set in a benevolent face framed by flowing gray locks. Satisfied
from a glance at the Strutt indenture that his young caller was bona
fide, Brown took Slater in a sleigh to the little hamlet of Pawtucket, a
community consisting of a dozen or so cottages on both sides of the
Blackstone River, just outside Providence. They stopped at a small
clothier's shop on the river's bank, close by a bridge which linked
Rhode Island and Massachusetts. Here was assembled Brown's ill-
assorted machinery.

Slater took one look and shook his head, his disappointment obvious.

Compared to Strutt's splendid mill this was almost a caricature. He spoke bluntly: "These will not do; they are good for nothing in their present condition, nor can they be made to answer." Brown urged him to reconsider, to give the machines a try, but the young Englishman was not to be persuaded. At last, in desperation, the old merchant threw Slater a challenge:

"Thee said thee could make machinery. Why not do it?"

Reluctantly, Slater finally agreed to build a new mill, using such parts of the old as would answer, but only on one condition: that Brown provide a trusted mechanic to make the machinery which Slater would design and that the man be put under bond neither to disclose the nature of the work nor to copy it.

"If I don't make as good yarn as they do in England," Slater declared, "I will have nothing for my services, but will throw the whole of what I have attempted over the bridge!" Brown agreed, arranging in addition to pay Slater's living expenses.

Then the old merchant took his visitor to the cottage of Oziel Wilkinson, an ingenious ironmaster, with whom Slater could board. Wilkinson, also a Quaker, operated a small anchor forge using water power from the river, and there he turned out ships' chandlery, shovels, scythes, and other tools. As the young Englishman entered the Wilkinson home, his host's younger daughter shyly scampered out of sight, but Hannah, the elder, lingered in the doorway to look at the stranger. Slater fell in love with her. (Within two years they would be married, and Hannah Slater would later acquire fame in her own right as the discoverer of cotton sewing thread, which she first produced from the fine yarns her husband manufactured.) In the Wilkinson household young Slater found new parents who helped him overcome his homesickness and encouraged him in the first difficult months.

Part of that winter he spent experimenting with Moses Brown's crude carding machine, and he was able to improve the quality of cotton fleece it turned out. This, when spun by hand on the jennies, produced a better yarn, but one which was still too weak and uneven to be used as warp in the hand weaving of cloth. Slater was downhearted; he realized that he must build everything from scratch.

The rest of the winter he spent assembling the necessary materials for constructing the Arkwright machines and processes. He lacked even the tools with which to make the complicated equipment, and he was forced to make many of them himself before any building could commence. Furthermore, without models to copy, he had to work out his own computations for all measurements. One of the most ingenious elements of the Arkwright inventions was the variation in speeds of various parts of the machines. Mathematical tables for these were not available anywhere save in England; Slater had to rely on his own extraordinary memory. Nevertheless, by April, 1790, he was ready to sign a firm partnership agreement to build two carding machines, a drawing and roving frame, and two spinning frames, all to be run automatically by water power. He was to receive one dollar a day as wages, half-ownership in the machinery he built, and, in addition, one half of the mill's net profits after it was in operation. Moses Brown had turned over the supervision of his textile investments to William Almy, his son-in-law, and Smith Brown, his cousin, and these two men became Slater's new partners.

Now, behind shuttered windows in the little clothier's building on the riverbank, young Slater began to design the first successful cotton mill in America. As he drew the plans with chalk on wood, Sylvanus Brown, an experienced local wheelwright, cut out the parts from sturdy oak and fastened them together with wooden dowels. Young David Wilkinson, Slater's future brother-in-law and like his father a skilled ironworker, forged shafts for the spindles, rollers for the frames, and teeth in the cards which Pliny Earle, of Leicester, Massachusetts, prepared for the carding machines. Before iron gearwheels and card rims could be made, Slater and Wilkinson had to go to Mansfield, Massachusetts, to find suitable castings. By autumn, working sixteen hours a day, Slater had more than fulfilled his agreement: he had built not two but three carding machines, as well as the drawing and roving frame and the two spinning frames. At last he was ready for a trial.

Taking up a handful of raw cotton, Slater fed it into the carding machine, cranked by hand for the occasion by an elderly Negro. This engine was one of the most important elements of the Arkwright system, for in it the raw cotton was pulled across leather cards studded with small iron teeth which drew out and straightened the fibers, laid them side by side, and formed them into a long, narrow fleece called an "end," or "sliver." This was then placed on the drawing and roving frame to be further stretched, smoothed, and then twisted before being spun into yarn on the spinning frame. Before the cotton was run through the cards, the fibers lay in every direction, and it was essential that the carding be successful if the "end" was to be suitable for the subsequent steps. But when Slater fed the test cotton into his machine it only piled up on the cards. . . .

After a number of sleepless nights, Slater determined that the trouble arose from a faulty translation of his design into reality, for Pliny Earle had never before made cards of that description. Slater decided that the teeth stood too far apart, and that under pressure of the raw cotton they fell back from their proper places instead of standing firm and combing the cotton as it moved past. He pointed out the defect to Earle, and together, using a discarded piece of grindstone, they beat the teeth into the correct shape. Another test was made and the machine worked satisfactorily.

The final stage was now at hand. Almost a year had passed in preparation for this moment. Would the machinery operate automatically by water power? That was the miracle of the Arkwright techniques, which gave them their name, "perpetual spinning." A connection was made to the small water wheel which had been used by the clothier in whose little shop Slater's new machinery now stood. It was deep winter, and the Blackstone River was frozen over, so that Slater was obliged to crawl down and break up the ice around the wheel. When the wheel turned over, his machinery began to hum.

On December 20, 1790, Samuel Slater's mill produced the first cotton yarn ever made automatically in America. It was strong and of good quality, suitable for sheetings and other types of heavy cotton goods; soon Slater was turning out yarn fine enough to be woven into shirtings, checks, ginghams, and stockings, all of which had until then been imported from Europe. Good cotton cloth woven at home from English yarn had cost from forty to fifty cents per yard, but soon Slater brought the cost down as low as nine cents. For the remainder of that first winter, unable to get anyone else to do the job, Slater spent two or three hours each morning before breakfast breaking the river ice to start the water wheel. Daily it left him soaking wet and numb from exposure; his health was affected for the rest of his life.

The little mill started with four employees, but by the end of one month Slater had nine hands at work, most of them children. In this he was following the practice in England, where entire families were employed in the mills. Early English millowners had found children more agile and dexterous than adults, their quick fingers and small hands tending the moving parts more easily. Slater, like other pioneer millowners dealing with small working forces, was able to maintain a paternalistic attitude toward the young persons in his charge; until the coming of the factory system and absentee ownership, child labor was not the evil it later became. Slater introduced a number of social customs he had learned in the Arkwright and Strutt mills. For his workers he built the first Sunday school in New England and there provided instruction in reading, writing, and arithmetic, as well as in religion. Later he promoted common day schools for his mill hands, often paying the teachers' wages out of his own pocket.

About 1812 an unknown artist portrayed Slater's first mill, on Rhode Island's Blackstone River.

Proudly Slater sent a sample of his yarn back to Strutt in Derbyshire, who pronounced it excellent. Yet Americans hesitated to use it, preferring traditional hand-spun linen yarn or machine-made cotton yarn imported from England. Within four months Moses Brown was writing to the owners of a little factory in Beverly, Massachusetts, run by a relative, proposing a joint petition to Congress: Why not raise the duties on imported cotton goods? Some of the proceeds could be given to southern cotton farmers as a bounty for upgrading their raw cotton, and some could be presented to the infant textile industry as a subsidy.

Next, Brown arranged to transmit to Alexander Hamilton, secretary of the treasury and already known as a supporter of industry, a sample of Slater's yarn and of the first cotton check made from it, along with various suggestions for encouraging the new textile manufacturers. He reported to Hamilton that within a year machinery and mills could be erected to supply enough yarn for the entire nation. Two months later, when Hamilton presented to Congress his famous *Report on Manufactures*, he mentioned "the manufactory at Providence [which] has the merit of being the first in introducing into the United States the celebrated cotton mill."

By the end of their first ten months of operations, Almy, Brown & Slater had sold almost 8,000 yards of cloth produced by home weavers from their yarns. After twenty months the factory was turning out more yarn than the weavers in its immediate vicinity could use; a surplus of 2,000 pounds had piled up. Desperately, Moses Brown appealed to Slater, "Thee must shut down thy gates or thee will spin all my farms into cotton yarn."

It was at this point that the full force of Slater's revolutionary processes began to become apparent. To dispose of their surplus the partners began to employ agents in Salem, New York, Baltimore, and Philadelphia, and so encouraging were the sales that it became obvious to them that their potential market was enormous. In 1791, therefore, they closed the little mill and built nearby a more efficient factory designed to accommodate all the processes of yarn manufacturing under one roof. It was opened in 1793. (Now the Old Slater Mill Museum, the building still stands today.)

As of December, 1792, the partners' ledgers had shown a credit in Slater's name of £882, representing his share of the proceeds from the sale of yarn spun by his mill. From then on both he and the infant industry he had helped to create prospered rapidly. The factory was no longer a neighborhood affair but sought its markets in a wider world. When the War of 1812 had ended, there were 165 mills in Rhode Island, Massachusetts, and Connecticut alone, many of them started by former employees of Slater who had gone into business for themselves. By this time Slater, too, had branched out; he owned at least seven mills, either outright or in partnership. An important mill town in Rhode Island already bore the name of Slatersville. Around three new cotton, woolen, and thread mills which he built in Massachusetts, a new textile center sprang up which became the town of

Webster. Later, his far-reaching enterprise carried him to Amoskeag Falls on the Merrimac River; in 1822 he bought an interest in a small mill already established there, and in 1826 erected a new mill which became the famous Amoskeag Manufacturing Company, hub of an even greater textile center—Manchester, New Hampshire.

President James Monroe had come to Pawtucket in 1817 to visit the "Old Mill," which was then the largest cotton mill in the nation, containing 5,170 spindles. It had started with 72. Slater himself conducted his distinguished visitor through the factory and proudly showed him his original spinning frame, still running after 27 years. Some years later another President, Andrew Jackson, visited Pawtucket, and when he was told that Slater was confined to his house by rheumatism brought on from that first winter of breaking the ice on the Blackstone, Old Hickory went to pay his respects to the invalid. Courteously addressing Slater as "the Father of American Manufactures," General Jackson said:

"I understand you taught us how to spin, so as to rival Great Britain in her manufactures; you set all these thousands of spindles to work, which I have been delighted in viewing, and which have made so many happy, by a lucrative employment."

Slater thanked his visitor politely and with the dry wit for which he was well known replied:

"Yes, Sir, I suppose that I gave out the psalm, and they have been singing to the tune ever since."

By the time he died in 1835, Slater had become generally recognized as the country's leading textile industrialist. The industry he had founded 45 years earlier had shown phenomenal growth. In 1790 the estimated value of all American manufactured goods barely exceeded $20,000,000, and the domestic cotton crop was about 2,000,000 pounds. By 1835 cotton manufactured goods alone were valued in excess of $47,000,000, and that single industry was consuming almost 80,000,000 pounds of cotton annually. Few men in our history have lived to see such tremendous economic changes wrought in one lifetime by their own efforts.

The social changes which Samuel Slater witnessed and helped to further were even more far-reaching. When he arrived in 1789 America was a nation of small farmers and artisans. By the time he died, and to a considerable extent because of his accomplishments, many artisans had become mill hands.

Three years after Slater's mill began operations, a young Yale graduate named Eli Whitney, visiting a Georgia plantation, devised the cotton gin, and this, in combination with English cotton mills and American ones like Slater's in New England, enormously stimulated the cotton economy (and the slave-labor system) of the South. Simultaneously, and paradoxically, Slater and Whitney helped fasten on the North an industrial economy which would defeat the South when the long-standing economic conflict between the two sections flared out at last in civil war.

Carl N. Degler

There Was Another South

To uncover the meaning of complicated historical events, historians search for generalizations; they sift through the clutter of fact and opinion that makes up the sources and locate the common elements that show us the significance of the past. On the other hand, the process of generalization requires the discarding of "atypical" and "irrelevant" material, although what is put aside is obviously part of history too. The historian's constant problem is to find true generalizations without distorting truth. The broader his generalizations, the more likely they are to ignore part of the reality being described, yet the more the historian qualifies his conclusions in the interest of complete accuracy, the less meaningful his conclusions become.

In this essay, which deals with southern attitudes before, during, and immediately after the Civil War, Professor Carl N. Degler of Stanford University examines some important but overly broad generalizations. He shows with a convincing array of evidence that historians who write about "the South" and even about southern attitudes toward slavery and race relations before 1860 as though a common point of view pervaded the region are missing a large part of the story. His intention, however, is not to destroy the old generalizations or to supplant them with completely different ones. Rather his argument points up the complexity of history, which is one of its fascinations. From his account the reader can extract newer generalizations, less simple but more convincing since they conform to a large generalization about human nature, namely that in any large group uniformity of opinion is impossible.

*T*he stereotype of the South is as tenacious as it is familiar: a traditionally rebellious region which has made a dogma of states' rights and a religious order of the Democratic party. Here indeed is a monotonous and unchanging tapestry, with a pattern of magnolia blossoms, Spanish moss, and the inevitable old plantations running ceaselessly from border to border. To this depiction of almost willful backwardness, add the dark motif of the Negro problem, a few threads of poor white, and the picture is complete.

Such is the mythical image, and a highly inaccurate one it is, for the South is a region of immense variety. Its sprawling landscape ranges from the startlingly red soil of Virginia and North Carolina to the black, sticky clay of the Delta; from the wild and primitive mountain forests of eastern Kentucky to the lush, junglelike swamps of southern Louisiana; from the high, dry, wind-swept plains of the Texas Panhandle to the humid tidelands of the South Carolina coast. An environment so diverse can be expected to produce social and political differences to match, and in fact, it always has.

Today, with the South in ferment, we have come to recognize increasingly the wide variety of attitudes that exist in the region. But this denial of the southern stereotype is a relatively new development, even among historians. For too long the history of the region has been regarded as a kind of unbroken plain of uniform opinion. This is especially true of what has been written about the years before the Civil War; a belief in states' rights, the legality of secession, and the rightfulness of slavery has been accepted almost without question as typical of southern thought. In a sense, such catch phrases do represent what many southerners have believed; but at the same time there were many others who both denied the legality of secession and denounced slavery. It is time this "other South" was better known.

Let us begin with the story of those southerners who so cherished the Union that they refused to accept the doctrine of nullification and secession. They included not only humble farmers and remote mountain men, but some of the greatest names in the history of the South; their devotion to the Union was tested in several bitter clashes with states' righters during the ante-bellum decades. The first of these contests came over the question of the high protective tariffs which many southerners felt would hurt the cotton trade; the arguments advanced at the beginning set forth the basic lines of debate that were followed thereafter. South Carolina's *Exposition and Protest* of 1828, which John C. Calhoun wrote secretly in opposition to the tariff passed that year, embodied the classic defense of state sovereignty. In the *Exposition*, Calhoun contended that nullification of federal legislation by a state and even secession were constitutional—a doctrine rejected by many prominent southerners in 1828 and after.

Foremost among them was former President James Madison, the reputed "father of the Constitution." As a Jeffersonian in politics and a Virginian by birth and heritage, Madison was no friend of the protective tariff, and certainly not of the monstrous one of 1828, which had been promulgated by the Jacksonian faction in Congress in an effort to discredit the Adams administration. But he could not accept even that politically inspired tariff as sufficient reason for nullification. Indeed, he could not accept the constitutional doctrine of nullification on any grounds. It is worthwhile to consider briefly Madison's views on nullification, because virtually all subsequent southern defenses of the Union followed his line of thought; at the time, no man in the South carried more authority on the meaning and interpretation of the Constitution than the venerable Virginian, who celebrated his eightieth birthday in 1830, and was the last surviving signer of that document.

Many political leaders sought his views all through the tariff crisis of 1828–33, and to all of them Madison reiterated the same conclusions. The United States was a "mixed government" in which the states were supreme in some areas and the federal government in others. In the event of conflict between them, the Supreme Court was the intended arbiter under the Constitution; the Court, Madison wrote, was "so constituted as to be impartial as it could be made by the mode of appointment and responsibility of the judges."

If confidence were lacking in the objectivity of the judges, Madison continued, then there were further remedies: the impeachment of offending officials, election of a new government, or amendments to the Constitution. But neither nullification nor secession was legal, he tirelessly pointed out. Of course, if tyrannized sufficiently, a state could invoke its natural right to overthrow its oppressor; but that was a right of revolution, and not a constitutional right as Calhoun and his followers maintained.

As a southern Unionist, Madison did not stand alone, either at the time of the nullification crisis or later. In Calhoun's own state, in fact, the Unionists were a powerful and eloquent minority. Hugh S. Legare (pronounced Legree, curiously enough), Charleston aristocrat, intellectual, and one-time editor of the *Southern Review,* distinguished himself in defense of the Union, vigorously opposing Calhoun during the heated debates in Charleston in 1832. (Eleven years later, as United States Attorney General, Legare again differed with the majority of southerners when he offered the official opinion that free Negroes in the United States enjoyed the same civil rights as white men.)

James Petigru and Joel Poinsett (who, as minister to Mexico, gave his name to the Poinsettia) were two other prominent Charlestonians who would not accept the doctrine that a state could constitutionally withdraw from the Union. Unlike Legare and Poinsett, Petigru lived long enough to fight nullification and secession in South Carolina until that state left the Union. (When asked by a stranger in December, 1860, where the insane asylum was, he contemptuously pointed to the building where the secession convention was meeting.)

Andrew Jackson is often ignored by those who conceive of the South as a monolith of states' rights and secession. A Carolinian by birth and a Tennessean by choice, Jackson acted as an outspoken advocate of the Union when he threatened South Carolina with overwhelming force in the crisis of 1832–33. Jackson's fervently nationalistic proclamation

Charleston Unionist James Louis Petigru, by Thomas Sully.

to the people of the dissident state was at once a closely reasoned restatement of the Madisonian view that the United States was a "mixed government," and a highly emotional panegyric to the Union. Though there can be no question of Jackson's wholehearted acceptance of every patriotic syllable in that proclamation, it comes as no surprise to those acquainted with the limited literary abilities of Old Hickory that its composition was the work of an adviser. That adviser, it is worth noting, was a southerner, Secretary of State Edward Livingston of Louisiana.

There were few things on which Henry Clay of Kentucky and Andrew Jackson could agree, but the indissolubility of the Union was one of them. Clay never concurred with those southern leaders who accepted Calhoun's position that a state could nullify national legislation or secede from the Union. As a matter of fact, Henry Clay's Whig party was probably the most important stronghold of pro-Union sentiment in the ante-bellum South. Unlike the Democratic party, the Whigs never succumbed, in defending slavery, to the all-encompassing states' rights doctrine. Instead, they identified themselves with the national bank, internal improvements, the tariff, and opposition to the "tyranny" of Andrew Jackson. Despite the "unsouthern" sound of these principles to modern ears, the Whig party was both powerful and popular, capable of winning elections in any southern state. In the heyday of the Whigs, a solidly Democratic South was still unimaginable.

In 1846, the attempt of antislavery forces to prohibit slavery in the vast areas about to be acquired as a result of the Mexican War precipitated another bitter sectional struggle. But as much as they might support the "peculiar institution," the southern Whigs stood firm against Calhoun's efforts to commit the whole South to a states' rights position that once more threatened the existence of the Union. When, in 1849,

The daguerreotype of Henry Clay (left) dates from the late 1840's. Clay devoted himself to preserving the Union from the curse of "Secession Fever," as depicted in the contemporary newspaper cartoon at right.

Calhoun invited southern Congressmen to join his Southern Rights movement in order to strengthen resistance against northern demands, forty of the eighty-eight he approached refused to sign the call. Almost all of them were Whigs.

Throughout the Deep South in the state elections of 1851, Unionist Democrats and Whigs combined to stop the incipient secessionist movement in its tracks. In Georgia, Howell Cobb, the Unionist candidate for governor, received 56,261 votes to 37,472 for his opponent, a prominent Southern Rights man; in the legislature the Unionists captured 101 of the 127 seats. After the same election the congressional delegation of Alabama consisted of two secessionists and five Union supporters. In the Calhoun stronghold of Mississippi, where Jefferson Davis was the best-known spokesman for the Southern Rights movement, Davis was defeated for the governorship, 28,738 to 27,729, by his Unionist opponent, Henry S. Foote. Even in fire-eating South Carolina itself, the anti-Calhoun forces won overwhelmingly, 25,045 to 17,710.

By the time of the Kansas-Nebraska Act of 1854, the Whig party had all but disappeared, the victim of a widening sectional schism. Bereft of its traditional political organization, southern Unionism was, for the time, almost voiceless, but it was not dead. In the election of 1860, it reappeared in the shape of the Constitutional Union party. Its candidate was John Bell of Tennessee, an old-line Whig and staunch Unionist who, in order to prevent disruption of the nation, made his platform the Union itself. That year, in a four-party race, the Constitutional Unionists were the effective second party to the southern Democrats; for Stephen A. Douglas, the candidate of the northern Democrats, received few votes outside the border states, and Lincoln was not even on a ballot in ten of the fifteen slave states.

Deaf Man—I have got the Secession **Fever, and** it is making me deaf.

The Constitutional Unionists gave the dominant Democratic party a hot fight in every southern state. Of the upper southern states, Virginia, Kentucky, and Tennessee went to Bell outright, while Maryland gave him forty-five per cent and North Carolina forty-seven per cent of their votes.

Bell's showing in the Deep South was not as strong as in the upper South, but it nonetheless demonstrated that those southerners still willing to be counted for the Union were a large minority in almost all of the states. From the whole South, Bell received forty per cent of the popular vote to southern Democrat Breckinridge's forty-five.

A clear indication of the continuity of Unionism from the days of the Whigs to the election of 1860 is that Bell's support in the Deep South centered in the same general areas where the Whigs had been most powerful in the 1840's. Many of the delta counties along the Mississippi River—in Arkansas, Mississippi, and Louisiana—which were always strongholds of Whiggery, went for Bell. Whig votes had always been conspicuous in the black belt counties of central Alabama and Georgia, and so were Bell's in 1860.

Surprisingly enough, the wealthy, slaveholding counties of the South were more often Whig than Democratic in the years before the war. Ever since the days of Jackson, the Democracy had been predominantly the party of the small planter and non-slaveholder. Regardless of the serious threat to slavery posed by the Republican party in 1860, many slaveholders could still not bring themselves to violate their traditional political allegiances and vote for a Democratic candidate identified with states' rights.

A further test of southern Unionism was provided in the election of delegates to the state secession conventions in the winter of 1860–61. Unfortunately, the voting figures do not tell us as much as we would like to know. To most southerners at the time, the issue was not simply the Union versus the right of a state to secede; more often it was whether secession was expedient, with little thought about its constitutionality. Therefore, those delegates who favored a course other than immediate secession did not necessarily support the Union under all and every circumstance.

Nevertheless, these voting returns make clear that even on the verge of secession, tens of thousands in all the states of the Deep South were still opposed to a break with the Union. In Alabama, for example, 28,200 voted against immediate secession to 35,700 for; furthermore, one third of the delegates to the convention refused to sign the secession ordinance because it would not be submitted to the people. In Georgia, 37,123 were against secession to 50,243 in favor; in Louisiana the Unionists were an even larger minority: 17,296 against secession, 20,448 for. In Texas, despite much intimidation of Unionists, twenty-two per cent of the voters still opposed secession.

Before Sumter was fired upon and Lincoln called for volunteers, the states of the upper South refused to join the seceding states. Early in 1861, the people of Tennessee voted against having a secession convention, 68,282 to 59,449; the vote of the people of Arkansas against secession in February, 1861, was 22,000 to 17,000. North Carolina, in a popular vote, also turned down a call for a secession convention. As late as April 4, the Virginia convention voted down a proposal to draw up an ordinance of secession by an almost two-to-one majority. Even after Sumter, when the upper South states did secede, it is clear that loyalty to the Union was still a powerful sentiment.

Throughout the war southern Unionists were active in opposition to the Confederacy. Areas of strong Unionist feeling, like eastern Tennessee, western Virginia, northern Alabama, and the mountain counties of Arkansas, quickly come to mind. In eastern Tennessee, for example, Unionist sentiment was so widespread and deep-felt that for a large part of the war, the courts of the Confederacy in that area could not function without military support and not always even then. After the war broke out, Charles Galloway, a staunch Unionist who had opposed secession in Arkansas, led two companies of his fellow southerners to Springfield, Missouri, where they were mustered into the Union Army. Galloway then led his men back to Arkansas to fight the Confederates. Some 48,000 white southern Unionists, it has been estimated, served voluntarily in the Army of the United States. In northern Alabama and Georgia in 1863 and after, peace societies, replete with secret grips, passwords and elaborate security precautions, worked to encourage desertion from the Confederate Army.

A recent study of the Southern Claims Commission provides the most explicit and detailed evidence of the character of southern Unionism during the war. The commission was set up by the United States government at the end of hostilities in order to reimburse those southerners who had sustained certain kinds of property losses because of their loyalty to the Union. (Only actual material losses incurred by loyal southerners in behalf of the Union armies were to be honored;

acts of charity or mercy, or losses occasioned by Confederate action, for example, were not included.) Since all claimants first had to offer ironclad proof of loyalty before their losses could even be considered, those who did file claims may well be taken as the hard core of southern Unionism. There must have been thousands more who, because they lacked the opportunity or the substance to help the Union armies, went uncounted. Still others may not have been able to meet the high standards set for proof of loyalty, though their devotion to the Union was unquestioned. Under these circumstances, 22,298 claimants is an impressive number.

One of the striking facts that emerges from a study of the records of the commission is the great number of southern Unionists who were people of substance. The total amount of the claims was $22.5 million, and 701 claims were for losses of $10,000 or more—a very substantial sum in the 1860's. The wealthy claimants were mainly planters, owners of great plantations and large numbers of slaves. Despite their wealth, or perhaps because of it, they stood with the Union when the storm of secession broke upon them—though to do so often meant obloquy and harassment at the very least, and not infrequently confiscation of property and personal danger.

Southern Unionism also played its part in the complicated history of Reconstruction. Tennessee, for example, probably escaped radical congressional Reconstruction because of the large number of Unionists in the state. William "Parson" Brownlow, an old Whig and Unionist turned Republican, was able to gain control of the state after the war, and under his leadership Tennessee managed to avoid the military occupation that was the retribution visited upon its more recalcitrant neighbors.

In Louisiana, the first Republican governor, Michael Hahn, was also a lifelong Unionist, though originally a Democrat; he had opposed secession and during the war had refused to take a pledge of loyalty to the Confederacy. About a third of the members of the Mississippi legislature during Reconstruction were so-called scalawags; but far from being the disreputable persons usually associated with that label, most of them were actually respectable former Whig Unionists turned Republican.

This shift in allegiance from Whig to Republican—by no means a rarity in the Reconstruction South—is not so strange when it is recalled that Lincoln, the first Republican President, was once a confirmed Whig. Indeed, to many former southern Whigs it must have seemed that the Republican party—the party of business, national authority, sound money, and internal improvements—was a most fortunate reincarnation of Henry Clay's old organization. And now that slavery was no more, it seemed that southerners could once again divide politically as their interests dictated.

The opportunity, however, proved to be short-lived, for to resist effectively the excesses of the Radicals during Reconstruction, all southerners of consequence became Democrats as a matter of necessity. But though they may have been Democrats in name, in principles they were Whigs, and as such worked quite easily with northern Republicans to end Reconstruction and to bring new railroads and industry to the South in the 1880's.

Most Americans assume that between 1830 and 1860 all southerners favored slavery. This is not so. In the earlier years of the Republic, the great Virginians had not defended the institution but only excused it as an undeniable evil that was exceptionally difficult to eradicate. It was not until the 1830's that it began to be widely upheld as something to be proud of, a positive good. Here too, as in the nullification controversy, Calhoun's thought dominated the southern mind. He had been among the first prominent southerners to shake off the sense of guilt over slavery and to proclaim it a "great moral revolution." At the same time, however, many men and women in the South continued to doubt the utility, the wisdom, and the justice of slavery. These, too, constituted another South.

Although there were some southerners who opposed slavery for reasons of Christian ethics, many more decried it for economic and political reasons. Cassius Marcellus Clay of Kentucky, a cousin of the more famous Henry, was prominent among those who abominated slavery because it retarded the economic growth of the South. The son of a wealthy slaveholder, Clay was educated at Yale, where his future is supposed to have been decided by hearing William Lloyd Garrison present an abolitionist lecture. Regardless of the cause for Clay's subsequent antislavery views, he emancipated his slaves in 1833, soon after his graduation, and devoted himself to ridding his state of slavery. Despite his proclaimed hostile sentiments on the subject, Clay gained a large following in state and national politics.

Cassius Marcellus Clay, cousin of Henry, objected to slavery on economic grounds.

The nature of Clay's objections to slavery were made clear in a speech he delivered before the Kentucky legislature in 1841:

Gentlemen would import slaves "to clear up the forests of the Green River country." Take one day's ride from this capital and then go and tell them what you have seen. Tell them that you have looked upon the once most lovely and fertile lands that nature ever formed; and have seen it in fifty years worn to the rock . . . tell them of the depopulation of the country and the consequent ruin of the towns and villages; tell them that the white Kentuckian has been driven out by slaves, by the unequal competition of unpaid labor; tell them that the mass of our people are uneducated; tell them that you have heard the children of white Kentuckians crying for bread, whilst the children of the African was [sic] clothed, and fed, and laughed! And then ask them if they will have blacks to fell their forests.

The troublesome race question effectively prevented some anti-slavery southerners from taking any concrete steps to end slavery; others saw a threat in the possibility of a large free Negro population. To many, the return of former slaves to Africa seemed the necessary first step in any movement toward emancipation. Cassius Clay was both more radical and more realistic. He recognized that colonization was as illusory a solution to the evils of slavery and the Negro problem as it actually proved to be; many more Negroes were born each year than could possibly be sent to Liberia in a generation. Instead, Clay boldly advocated gradual emancipation, with the owners of the slaves being compensated by the state.

Hinton Rowan Helper is better known today as an antislavery southerner than Clay, though the latter was certainly the more prominent at the time. Helper was the son of a poor North Carolina farmer; with the publication of his book, *The Impending Crisis of the South,* in 1857, he became a nationally known figure. In an effort to demonstrate the material and cultural backwardness of the slave states, Helper brought together statistics from the Census of 1850 —compiled by that most indefatigable southern publicist, J. D. B. De Bow, and therefore unimpeachable in southern eyes—to show that in number of libraries, newspapers, and schools, as well as in wealth, manufactures, population, and commerce, the North far outdistanced the South. Helper pointed out that even in agriculture, the vaunted specialty of Dixie, northern production exceeded southern. Almost contemptuously, he observed that the value of the Cotton Kingdom's chief staple was surpassed by that of the North's lowly hay crop. The cause for all these discrepancies, Helper contended, was slavery.

Helper's indictment of slavery was sufficiently telling to arouse violent southern attacks. He also serves to illustrate the variety of motives underlying the southern antislavery movement. He was more disturbed about what slavery did to the poor white man than about what it did to the Negro. Many antislavery men felt the same, but

Helper went further; his concern for the white man was coupled with an almost pathological hatred of the black.

Not its economic disadvantages, but its essential incompatibility with the genius of America, was the more compelling argument against slavery for some southerners. The great Virginians of the eighteenth century—men like Washington, Marshall, Patrick Henry, Madison, Jefferson, and Monroe—all felt that it somehow contradicted their ideal of a new republic of freemen. Echoes of this view were heard by Frederick Law Olmsted when he traveled through the back country of the South in the 1850's. One mountain dweller told Olmsted that he "was afraid that there was many a man who had gone to the bad world, who wouldn't have gone if he hadn't had any slaves."

Though less moralistic in his conclusions, Henry Clay was of much the same opinion. "I am no friend to slavery," he wrote to an Alabaman in 1838. "I think it is an evil; but I believe it better that slaves should remain slaves than to be set loose as free men among us . . ." For Clay, as for many antislavery southerners, it was difficult to believe that emancipated Negroes and whites could live together peacefully in the same country. This deep-seated belief in the incompatibility of the two races constituted the great dilemma in the minds of antislavery southerners; often it paralyzed all action.

The effects of this dilemma were certainly evident in the course of the remarkable debate on slavery in the Virginia legislature in 1832.

The event which precipitated it was a brief but violent uprising of slaves in Southampton County on August 21, 1831. Led by Nat Turner, a slave preacher given to visions and prophecies, the insurrectionists deliberately killed some sixty white people, mainly women and children. But even the rapidity and efficiency with which the might of the white man had been mobilized against the runaway slaves did not assuage the fear that surged through the minds of southerners everywhere. And so it was that on January 11, 1832, there began one of the most searching debates on slavery ever held by the elected representatives of a slaveholding people. For two weeks the venerable institution was subjected to the frankest kind of criticism.

Three quarters of the members of the House of Delegates held slaves, yet more than half of that body spoke out against the institution in one fashion or another. In analyzing the statements and the notes of the members, one historian concluded that 60 of the 134 delegates were consistently antislavery, working for legislation that would eventually terminate Negro bondage in Virginia. Twelve more, whom he calls the compromisers, were antislavery in belief, but were not prepared to vote for any measure which would, at that time, commit the state to emancipation. It was this latter group, in league with the sixty or so defenders of the *status quo*, who defeated the efforts to initiate gradual emancipation in 1832.

Though individual opponents of slavery remained in the South right up to the Civil War, it is impossible to ascertain their numbers. However, a glimpse into the mind of one such southerner has been afforded by the publication of the diary of Mary Minor Blackford.

Mrs. Blackford lived in Fredericksburg, Virginia, across the street from a slave trader's house, a location which permitted her to see slavery at its worst. And it was slavery as a moral evil rather than as an economic fallacy which troubled her: how could people otherwise good and humane, kind and Christian, hold fellow human beings in bondage? For unlike some northern abolitionists, she knew slave owners too well to think them innately evil. Her answer was not surprising: material self-interest morally blinded them.

The tragedy of the South's history was woven into the fabric of Mary Minor Blackford's life. Despite her long opposition to slavery, she proudly saw five of her sons serve in the Confederate Army. Yet with its defeat, she could still write early in 1866: "A New Era has dawned since I last wrote in this book. Slavery has been abolished!!!"

Other individual opponents of slavery in the South could be cited, but perhaps it would be best to close by mentioning an antislavery organization. The American Colonization Society, founded in 1817 by southern and northern antislavery men, always included prominent southerners among its leaders. In the course of its half century of operations, the society managed to send more than six thousand Negroes to its African colony in Liberia.

The society was strongest in the South; indeed, it was anathema to the New England and middle western abolitionists. Though it is true that antislavery was never a popular cause in the South, it was never a dead one, either, so long as thousands of southerners refused to view slavery as anything but an evil for their region.

As we have seen, the South was even less united on nullification and secession than it was on the question of slavery. In fact, it is now clear that if a majority of southerners ever did support secession— and there is real doubt on this—it was never a big majority, and it was not achieved until the very eve of the Civil War. In short, the South, rather than being a monolith of undivided opinion, was not even of one mind on the two most vital issues of the thirty years that led up to the war.

Quite innocent of war, these Confederate volunteers struck bold poses before the First Battle of Bull Run in 1861.

CIVIL WAR
AND
RECONSTRUCTION

Allan Nevins

The
Needless
Conflict

The qualities that make Allan Nevins such an excellent example of the scholar-historian writing for a broad audience are all illustrated in this story of the tragic events that occurred in Kansas in the decade before the Civil War. Scholarship, a powerful narrative style, historical imagination, sound judgment, and a deep understanding of the fallible human beings whose story he tells combine to make this essay a model for future historians.

Nevins believes that the troubles in Kansas resulting from the opening up of that territory to slavery under the Kansas-Nebraska Act, troubles which, as he says, were central to the events that led to secession, could have been avoided. He does not hesitate to place the blame for what happened on the shoulders of particular individuals. Yet unlike some of the historians who have seen the Civil War as caused by "a blundering generation," Nevins is not an apologist for the South. He condemns slavery flatly and believes that it had to be destroyed.

Professor Nevins, a Senior Research Fellow at the Huntington Library, has written more works of history than any other living American. He is currently completing his massive, multivolume study, The Ordeal of the Union.

*W*hen James Buchanan, standing in a homespun suit before cheering crowds, took the oath of office on March 4, 1857, he seemed confident that the issues before the nation could be readily settled. He spoke about an army road to California, use of the Treasury surplus to pay all the national debt, and proper guardianship of the public lands. In Kansas, he declared, the path ahead was clear. The simple logical rule that the will of the people should determine the institutions of a territory had brought in sight a happy settlement. The inhabitants would declare for or against slavery as they pleased. Opinions differed as to the proper time for making such a decision; but Buchanan thought that "the appropriate period will be when the number of actual residents in the Territory shall justify the formation of a constitution with a view to its admission as a State." He trusted that the long strife between North and South was nearing its end, and that the sectional party which had almost elected Frémont would die a natural death.

Two days after the inaugural Buchanan took deep satisfaction in a decision by the Supreme Court of which he had improper foreknowledge: the Dred Scott decision handed down by Chief Justice Taney. Its vital element, so far as the nation's destiny was concerned, was the ruling that the Missouri Compromise restriction, by which slavery had been excluded north of the 36° 30′ line, was void; that on the contrary, every territory was open to slavery. Not merely was Congress without power to legislate *against* slavery, but by implication it should act to protect it. Much of the northern press denounced the decision fervently. But the country was prosperous; it was clear that time and political action might change the Supreme Court, bringing a new decision; and the explosion of wrath proved brief.

Buchanan had seen his view sustained; slavery might freely enter any territory, the inhabitants of which could not decide whether to keep it or drop it until they wrote their first constitution. In theory, the highway to national peace was as traversible as the Lancaster turnpike. To be sure, Kansas was rent between two bitter parties, proslavery and antislavery; from the moment Stephen A. Douglas' Kansas-Nebraska Act had thrown open the West to popular sovereignty three years earlier, it had been a theater of unrelenting conflict. Popular sovereignty had simply failed to work. In the spring of 1855 about five thousand invading Missourians, swamping the polls, had given Kansas a fanatically proslavery legislature which the free-soil settlers flatly refused to recognize. That fall a free-soil convention in Topeka had adopted a constitution which the slavery men in turn flatly rejected. Some bloody fighting had ensued. But could not all this be thrust into the past?

In theory, the President might now send out an impartial new governor; and if the people wanted statehood, an election might be held for a new constitutional convention. Then the voters could give the nation its sixteenth slave state or its seventeenth free state—everybody behaving quietly and reasonably. Serenity would prevail. Actually, the idea that the people of Kansas, so violently aroused, would show quiet reason, was about as tenable as the idea that Europeans would begin settling boundary quarrels by a quiet game of chess. Behind the two Kansas parties were grim southerners and determined northerners. ''Slavery will now yield a greater profit in Kansas,'' trumpeted a southern propagandist in *De Bow's Review,* ''either to hire out or cultivate the soil, than any other place.'' He wanted proslavery squatters. Meanwhile, Yankees were subsidizing their own settlers. ''I know people,'' said Emerson in a speech, ''who are making haste to reduce their expenses and pay their debts . . . to save and earn for the benefit of Kansas emigrants.''

Nor was reason in Kansas the only need. Impartiality in Congress, courage in the presidential chair, were also required. The stage was dressed for a brief, fateful melodrama, which more than anything else was to fix the position of James Buchanan and Stephen A. Douglas in history, was to shape the circumstances under which Lincoln made his first national reputation, and was to have more potency than any other single event in deciding whether North and South should remain brothers or fly at each other's throats. That melodrama was entitled ''Lecompton.'' Douglas was to go to his grave believing that, had Buchanan played an honest, resolute part in it, rebellion would have been killed in its incipiency. The role that Buchanan did play may be counted one of the signal failures of American statesmanship.

To hold that the Civil War could not have been averted by wise, firm, and timely action is to concede too much to determinism in history. Winston Churchill said that the Second World War should be called ''The Unnecessary War''; the same term might as justly be applied to our Civil War. Passionate unreason among large sections of the population was one ingredient in the broth of conflict. Accident, fortuity, fate, or sheer bad luck (these terms are interchangeable) was another; John Brown's raid, so malign in its effects on opinion, North and South, might justly be termed an accident. Nothing in the logic of forces or events required so crazy an act. But beyond these ingredients lies the further element of wretched leadership. Had the United States possessed three farseeing, imaginative, and resolute Presidents instead of Fillmore, Pierce, and Buchanan, the war might have been postponed until time and economic forces killed its roots. Buchanan was the weakest of the three, and the Lecompton affair lights up his incompetence like a play of lightning across a nocturnal storm front.

The melodrama had two stages, one in faraway, thinly settled Kansas, burning hot in summer, bitter cold in winter, and, though reputedly rich, really so poor that settlers were soon on the brink of starvation. Here the most curious fact was the disparity between the mean actors and the great results they effected. A handful of ignorant, reckless, semi-drunken settlers on the southern side, led by a few desperadoes of politics—the delegates of the Lecompton Constitutional Convention—actually had the power to make or mar the nation. The other stage was Washington. The participants here, representing great interests and ideas, had at least a dignity worthy of the scene and the consequences of their action. James Buchanan faced three main groups holding three divergent views of the sectional problem.

The proslavery group (that is, Robert Toombs, Alexander H. Stephens, Jefferson Davis, John Slidell, David Atchison, and many more) demanded that slavery be allowed to expand freely within the territories; soon they were asking also that such expansion be given federal protection against any hostile local action. This stand involved the principle that slavery was morally right, and socially and economically a positive good. Reverdy Johnson of Maryland, in the Dred Scott case, had vehemently argued the beneficence of slavery.

The popular sovereignty group, led by Douglas and particularly strong among northwestern Democrats, maintained that in any territory the issue of slavery or free soil should be determined *at all times* by the settlers therein. Douglas modified the Dred Scott doctrine: local police legislation and action, he said, could exclude slavery even before state-making took place. He sternly rejected the demand for federal protection against such action. His popular sovereignty view implied indifference to or rejection of any moral test of slavery. Whether the institution was socially and economically good or bad depended mainly on climate and soil, and moral ideas were irrelevant. He did not care whether slavery was voted up or voted down; the right to a fair vote was the all-important matter.

The free-soil group, led by Seward and Chase, but soon to find its best voice in Lincoln, held that slavery should be excluded from all territories present or future. They insisted that slavery was morally wrong, had been condemned as such by the Fathers, and was increasingly outlawed by the march of world civilization. It might be argued that the free-soil contention was superfluous, in that climate and aridity forbade a further extension of slavery anyhow. But in Lincoln's eyes this did not touch the heart of the matter. It might or might not be expansible. (Already it existed in Delaware and Missouri, and Cuba and Mexico might be conquered for it.) What was important was for America to accept the fact that, being morally wrong and socially an anachronism, it *ought* not to expand; it *ought* to be put in the way of ultimate eradication. Lincoln was a planner. Once the country accepted nonexpansion, it would thereby accept the idea of ultimate extinction. This crisis met and passed, it could sit down and decide when and how, in God's good time and with suitable compensation to slaveholders it might be ended.

The Buchanan who faced these three warring groups was victim of the mistaken belief among American politicians (like Pierce, Benjamin Harrison, and Warren G. Harding, for example) that it is better to be a poor President than to stick to honorable but lesser posts. He would have made a respectable diplomat or decent Cabinet officer under a really strong President. Sixty-six in 1857, the obese bachelor felt all his years. He had wound his devious way up through a succession of offices without once showing a flash of inspiration or an ounce of grim courage. James K. Polk had accurately characterized

Hedged in by his own circumspection and vacillation, President Buchanan was ill-equipped to surmount the growing national crisis.

him as an old woman—"It is one of his weaknesses that he takes on and magnifies small matters into great and undeserved importance." His principal characteristic was irresolution. "Even among close friends," remarked a southern senator, "he very rarely expressed his opinions at all upon disputed questions, except in language especially marked with a cautious circumspection almost amounting to timidity."

He was industrious, capable, and tactful, a well-read Christian gentleman; he had acquired from forty years of public life a rich fund of experience. But he was pedestrian, humorless, calculating, and pliable. He never made a witty remark, never wrote a memorable sentence, and never showed a touch of distinction. Above all (and this was the source of his irresolution) he had no strong convictions. Associating all his life with southern leaders in Washington, this Pennsylvanian leaned toward their views, but he never disclosed a deep adherence to any principle. Like other weak men, he could be stubborn; still oftener, he could show a petulant irascibility when events pushed him into a corner. And like other timid men, he would sometimes flare out in a sudden burst of anger, directed not against enemies who could hurt him but against friends or neutrals who would not. As the sectional crisis deepened, it became his dominant hope to stumble through it, somehow, and anyhow, so as to leave office with

Buchanan ran head on into Douglas, the "Little Giant." Convinced that he had "made" Buchanan President, Douglas vowed he would "unmake" him.

the Union yet intact. His successor could bear the storm.

This was the President who had to deal, in Kansas and Washington, with men of fierce conviction, stern courage and, all too often, ruthless methods.

In Kansas the proslavery leaders were determined to strike boldly and unscrupulously for a slave state. They maintained close communications with such southern chieftains in Washington as Senator Slidell, Speaker James L. Orr, and Howell Cobb and Jacob Thompson, Buchanan's secretaries of the Treasury and the Interior. Having gained control of the territorial legislature, they meant to keep and use this mastery. Just before Buchanan became President they passed a bill for a constitutional convention—and a more unfair measure was never put on paper. Nearly all county officers, selected not by popular vote but by the dishonestly chosen legislature, were proslavery men. The bill provided that the sheriffs and their deputies should in March, 1857, register the white residents; that the probate judges should then take from the sheriffs complete lists of qualified voters; and that the county commissioners should finally choose election judges.

Everyone knew that a heavy majority of the Kansas settlers were antislavery. Many, even of the southerners, who had migrated thither opposed the "peculiar institution" as retrogressive and crippling in character. Everybody also knew that Kansas, with hardly thirty thousand people, burdened with debts, and unsupplied with fit roads, schools, or courthouses, was not yet ready for statehood; it still needed the federal government's care. Most Kansans refused to recognize the "bogus" legislature. Yet this legislature was forcing a premature convention, and taking steps to see that the election of delegates was controlled by sheriffs, judges, and county commissioners who were mainly proslavery Democrats. Governor John W. Geary, himself a Democrat appointed by Pierce, indignantly vetoed the bill. But the legislature immediately repassed it over Geary's veto; and when threats against his life increased until citizens laid bets that he would be assassinated within forty days, he resigned in alarm and posted east to apprise the country of imminent perils.

Along the way to Washington, Geary paused to warn the press that a packed convention was about to drag fettered Kansas before Congress with a slavery constitution. This convention would have a free hand, for the bill just passed made no provision for a popular vote on the instrument. Indeed, one legislator admitted that the plan was to avoid popular submission, for he proposed inserting a clause to guard against the possibility that Congress might return the constitution for a referendum. Thus, commented the *Missouri Democrat*, "the felon legislature has provided as effectually for getting the desired result as Louis Napoleon did for getting himself elected Emperor." All this was an ironic commentary on Douglas' maxim: "Let the voice of the people rule."

And Douglas, watching the reckless course of the Kansas legislators with alarm, saw that his principles and his political future were at stake. When his Kansas-Nebraska Act was passed, he had given the North his solemn promise that a free, full, and fair election would decide the future of the two territories. No fraud, no sharp practice, no browbeating would be sanctioned; every male white citizen should have use of the ballot box. He had notified the South that Kansas was almost certain to be free soil. Now he professed confidence that President Buchanan would never permit a breach of fair procedure. He joined Buchanan in persuading one of the nation's ablest men, former Secretary of the Treasury Robert J. Walker, to go out to Kansas in Geary's place as governor. Douglas knew that if he consented to a betrayal of popular sovereignty he would be ruined forever politically in his own state of Illinois.

For a brief space in the spring of 1857 Buchanan seemed to stand firm. In his instructions to Governor Walker he engaged that the new constitution would be laid before the people; and "they must be protected in the exercise of their right of voting for or against that instrument, and the fair expression of the popular will must not be interrupted by fraud or violence."

It is not strange that the rash proslavery gamesters in Kansas prosecuted their designs despite all Buchanan's fair words and Walker's desperate efforts to stay them. They knew that with four fifths of the people already against them, and the odds growing greater every year, only brazen trickery could effect their end. They were aware that the South, which believed that a fair division would give Kansas to slavery and Nebraska to freedom, expected them to stand firm. They were egged on by the two reckless southern Cabinet members, Howell Cobb and Thompson, who sent an agent, H. L. Martin of Mississippi, out to the Kansas convention. This gathering in Lecompton, with 48 of the 60 members hailing from slave states, was the shabbiest conclave of its kind ever held on American soil. One of Buchanan's Kansas correspondents wrote that he had not supposed such a wild set could be found. The *Kansas News* termed them a body of "broken-down political hacks, demagogues, fire-eaters, perjurers, ruffians, ballot-box stuffers, and loafers." But before it broke up with the shout, "Now, boys, let's come and take a drink!" it had written a constitution.

This constitution, the work of a totally unrepresentative body, was a devious repudiation of all the principles Buchanan and Douglas had laid down. Although it contained numerous controversial provisions, such as a limitation of banking to one institution and a bar against free Negroes, the main document was not to be submitted to general vote at all. A nominal reference of the great cardinal question was indeed provided. Voters might cast their ballots for the "constitution with slavery" or the "constitution without slavery." But when closely examined this was seen to be actually a piece of chicanery. Whichever form was adopted, the 200 slaves in Kansas would remain, with a constitutional guarantee against interference. Whenever the proslavery party in Kansas could get control of the legislature, they might open the door wide for more slaves. The rigged convention had put its handiwork before the people with a rigged choice: "Heads I win, tails you lose."

Would Buchanan lay this impudent contrivance before Congress, and ask it to vote the admission of Kansas as a state? Or would he contemptuously spurn it? An intrepid man would not have hesitated an instant to take the honest course; he would not have needed the indignant outcry of the northern press, the outraged roar of Douglas, to inspirit him. But Buchanan quailed before the storm of passion into which proslavery extremists had worked themselves.

The hot blood of the South was now up. That section, grossly misinformed upon events in Kansas, believed that *it* was being cheated. The northern freesoilers had vowed that no new slave state (save by a partition of Texas) should ever be admitted. Southerners thought that in pursuance of this resolve, the Yankees had made unscrupulous use of their wealth and numbers to lay hands on Kansas. Did the North think itself entitled to every piece on the board—to take Kansas as well as California, Minnesota, Iowa, Nebraska, Oregon—to give southerners nothing? The Lecompton delegates, from this point of view, were dauntless champions of a wronged section. What if they did use sharp tactics? That was but a necessary response to northern arrogance. Jefferson Davis declared that his section trembled under a sense of insecurity. "You have made it a political war. We are on the defensive. How far are you to push us?'' Sharp threats of secession and battle mingled with the southern denunciations. ''Sir,'' Senator Alfred Iverson of Georgia was soon to assert, ''I believe that the time will come when the slave States will be compelled, in vindication of their rights, interests, and honor, to separate from the free States, and erect an independent confederacy; and I am not sure, sir, that the time is not at hand.''

Three southern members of the Cabinet, Cobb, Thompson, and John B. Floyd, had taken the measure of Buchanan's pusillanimity. They, with one northern sympathizer, Jeremiah Black, and several White House habitués like John Slidell of Louisiana, constituted a virtual Directory exercising control over the tremulous President. They played on Buchanan's fierce partisan hatred of Republicans, and his jealous dislike of Douglas. They played also on his legalistic cast of mind; after all, the Lecompton constitution was a legal instrument by a legal convention—outwardly. Above all, they played on his fears, his morbid sensitiveness, and his responsiveness to immediate pressures. They could do this the more easily because the threats of disruption and violence were real. Henry S. Foote, a former senator from Mississippi and an enemy of Jefferson Davis, who saw Lecompton in its true light and hurried to Washington to advise the President, writes:

''It was unfortunately of no avail that these efforts to reassure Mr. Buchanan were at that time essayed by myself and others; he had already become thoroughly *panic-stricken;* the howlings of the bulldog of secession had fairly frightened him out of his wits, and he ingloriously resolved to yield without further resistance to the decrial and villification to which he had been so acrimoniously subjected.''

And the well-informed Washington correspondent of the New Orleans *Picayune* a little later told just how aggressively the Chief Executive was bludgeoned into submission:

''The President was informed in November, 1857, that the States of Alabama, Mississippi, and South Carolina, and perhaps others, would hold conventions and secede from the Union if the Lecompton Constitution, which established slavery, should not be accepted by Congress. The reason was that these States, supposing that the South had been cheated out of Kansas, were, whether right or wrong, determined to revolt. The President believed this. Senator Hunter, of Virginia, to my knowledge, believed it. Many other eminent men did, and perhaps not without reason.''

Buchanan, without imagination as without nerve, began to yield to this southern storm in midsummer, and by November, 1857, he was surrendering completely. When Congress met in December his message upheld the Lecompton Constitution with a tissue of false and evasive statements. Seldom in American history has a chief magistrate made a greater error, or missed a larger opportunity. The astute secretary of his predecessor, Franklin Pierce, wrote: ''I had considerable hopes of Mr. Buchanan—I really thought he was a statesman—but

I have now come to the settled conclusion that he is just the damndest old fool that has ever occupied the presidential chair. He has deliberately walked overboard with his eyes open—let him drown, for he must.''

As Buchanan shrank from the lists, Douglas entered them with that *gaudium certaminis* which was one of his greatest qualities. The finest chapters of his life, his last great contests for the Union, were opening. Obviously he would have had to act under political necessity even if deaf to principle, for had he let popular sovereignty be torn to pieces, Illinois would not have sent him back to the Senate the following year; but he was not the man to turn his back on principle. His struggle against Lecompton was an exhibition of iron determination. The drama of that battle has given it an almost unique place in the record of our party controversies.

"By God, sir!" he exclaimed, "I made James Buchanan, and by God, sir, I will unmake him!" Friends told him that the southern Democrats meant to ruin him. "I have taken a through ticket," rejoined Douglas, "and checked my baggage." He lost no time in facing Buchanan in the White House and denouncing the Lecompton policy. When the President reminded him how Jackson had crushed two party rebels, he was ready with a stinging retort. Douglas was not to be overawed by a man he despised as a weakling. "Mr. President," he snorted, "I wish you to remember that General Jackson is dead."

As for the southern leaders, Douglas' scorn for the extremists who had coerced Buchanan was unbounded. He told the Washington correspondent of the Chicago *Journal* that he had begun his fight as a contest against a single bad measure. But his blow at Lecompton was a blow against slavery extension, and he at once had the whole "slave power" down on him like a pack of wolves. He added: "In making the fight against this power, I was enabled to stand off and view the men with whom I had been acting; I was ashamed I had ever been caught in such company; they are a set of unprincipled demagogues, bent upon perpetuating slavery, and by the exercise of that unequal and unfair power, to control the government or break up the Union; and I intend to prevent their doing either."

After a long, close, and acrid contest, on April 1, 1858, Lecompton was defeated. A coalition of Republicans, Douglasite Democrats, and Know-Nothings struck down the fraudulent constitution in the House, 120 to 112. When the vote was announced, a wild cheer rolled through the galleries. Old Francis P. Blair, Jackson's friend, carried the news to the dying Thomas Hart Benton, who had been intensely aroused by the crisis. Benton could barely speak, but his exultation was unbounded. "In energetic whispers," records Blair, "he told his visitor that the same men who had sought to destroy the republic in 1850 were at the bottom of this accursed Lecompton business. Among the greatest of his consolations in dying was the consciousness that the House of Representatives had baffled these treasonable schemes and put the heels of the people on the neck of the traitors."

The Administration covered its retreat by a hastily concocted measure, the English Bill, under which Kansas was kept waiting on the doorstep—sure in the end to enter a free state. The Kansas plotters, the Cobb-Thompson-Floyd clique in the Cabinet, and Buchanan had all been worsted. But the damage had been done. Southern secessionists had gained fresh strength and greater boldness from their success in coercing the Administration.

The Lecompton struggle left a varied and interesting set of after-effects. It lifted Stephen A. Douglas to a new plane; he had been a fighting Democratic strategist, but now he became a true national leader, thinking far less of party and more of country. It sharpened the issues which that summer and fall were to form the staple of the memorable Lincoln-Douglas debates in Illinois. At the same time, it deepened the schism which had been growing for some years between southern Democrats and northwestern Democrats, and helped pave the way to that disruption of the party which preceded and facilitated the disruption of the nation. It planted new seeds of dissension in Kansas—seeds which resulted in fresh conflicts between Kansas free-soilers or jayhawkers on one side and Missouri invaders or border ruffians on the other, and in a spirit of border lawlessness which was to give the Civil War some of its darkest pages. The Lecompton battle discredited Buchanan in the eyes of most decent northerners, strengthened southern conviction of his weakness, and left the Administration materially and morally weaker in dealing with the problems of the

Armed and disorderly border ruffians from Missouri head for Lawrence, Kansas, determined to win the entire territory for slaveholders.

next two and a half critical years.

For the full measure of Buchanan's failure, however, we must go deeper. Had he shown the courage that to an Adams, a Jackson, a Polk, or a Cleveland would have been second nature, the courage that springs from a deep integrity, he might have done the republic an immeasurable service by grappling with disunion when it was yet weak and unprepared. Ex-Senator Foote wrote later that he knew well that a scheme for destroying the Union "had long been on foot in the South." He knew that its leaders "were only waiting for the enfeebling of the Democratic Party in the North, and the general triumph of Free-soilism as a consequence thereof, to alarm the whole South into acquiescence in their policy." Buchanan's support of the unwise and corrupt Lecompton constitution thus played into the plotters' hands.

The same view was taken yet more emphatically by Douglas. He had inside information in 1857, he later told the Senate, that four states were threatening Buchanan with secession. Had that threat been met in the right Jacksonian spirit, had the bluff been called—for the four states were unprepared for secession and war—the leaders of the movement would have been utterly discredited. Their conspiracy would have collapsed, and they would have been so routed and humiliated in 1857 that the Democratic party schism in 1860 might never have taken place, and if it had, secession in 1861 would have been impossible.

The roots of the Civil War of course go deep; they go back beyond Douglas' impetuous Kansas-Nebraska Bill, back beyond the Mexican War, back beyond the Missouri Compromise. But the last good chance of averting secession and civil strife was perhaps lost in 1857. Even Zachary Taylor in 1850 had made it plain before his sudden death that he would use force, if necessary, to crush the secessionist tendencies which that year became so dangerous. A similar display of principle and resolution seven years later might well have left the disunionist chieftains of the Deep South so weakened in prestige that Yancey and his fellow plotters would have been helpless. The lessons of this failure in statesmanship, so plain to Douglas, ought not to be forgotten. The greatest mistake a nation can make is to put at its helm a man so pliable and unprincipled that he will palter with a clean-cut and momentous issue.

Bruce Catton

Soldiering in the Civil War

Surely one of the most "popular" of American historians is Bruce Catton, editor emeritus of American Heritage magazine, whose books about the Civil War have been read and enjoyed by hundreds of thousands of persons. Yet Catton is also among the most scholarly of historians; his work is based on meticulous research in archives and old attics, and his analyses of events and men have been widely praised by Civil War scholars.

One of the reasons for Catton's success has been his ability to understand the Civil War both in broad strategic terms and also as a very human conflict, full of tragedy, bravery, and humor. In this essay he draws a graphic portrait of the ordinary soldier, Union and Confederate. From dozens of anecdotes and small details one gathers a general impression, vivid yet with a sense of its universal applicability, of what it was like to fight in that epic struggle. At the same time—and it is one of the infallible marks of a good historian—Catton sees the "G.I." of the 1860's from a modern perspective and is thus able to explain why he acted and believed as he did.

The volunteer soldier in the American Civil War used a clumsy muzzle-loading rifle, lived chiefly on salt pork and hardtack, and retained to the very end a loose-jointed, informal attitude toward the army with which he had cast his lot. But despite all of the surface differences, he was at bottom blood brother to the G.I. Joe of modern days.

Which is to say that he was basically, and incurably, a civilian in arms. A volunteer, he was still a soldier because he had to be one, and he lived for the day when he could leave the army forever. His attitude toward discipline, toward his officers, and toward the whole spit-and-polish concept of military existence was essentially one of careless tolerance. He refused to hate his enemies—indeed, he often got along with them much better than with some of his own comrades—and his indoctrination was often so imperfect that what was sometimes despairingly said of the American soldier in World War II would apply equally to him: he seemed to be fighting chiefly so that he could some day get back to Mom's cooking.

What really set the Civil War soldier apart was the fact that he came from a less sophisticated society. He was no starry-eyed innocent, to be sure—or, if he was, the army quickly took care of that—but the America of the 1860's was less highly developed than modern America. It lacked the ineffable advantages of radio, television, and moving pictures. It was still essentially a rural nation; it had growing cities, but they were smaller and somehow less urban than today's cities; a much greater percentage of the population lived on farms or in country towns and villages than is the case now, and there was more of a backwoods, hay-seed-in-the-hair flavor to the people who came from them.

For example: every war finds some ardent youngsters who want to enlist despite the fact that they are under the military age limit of eighteen. Such a lad today simply goes to the recruiting station, swears that he is eighteen, and signs up. The lad of the 1860's saw it a little differently. He could not swear that he was eighteen when he was only sixteen; in his innocent way, he felt that to lie to his own government was just plain wrong. But he worked out a little dodge that got him into the army anyway. He would take a bit of paper, scribble the number *18* on it, and put it in the sole of his shoe. Then, when the recruiting officer asked him how old he was, he could truthfully say: "I am *over* eighteen." That was a common happening, early in the Civil War; one cannot possibly imagine it being tried today.

Similarly, the drill sergeants repeatedly found that among the raw recruits there were men so abysmally untaught that they did not know left from right, and hence could not step off on the left foot as all soldiers should. To teach these lads how to march, the sergeants would tie a wisp of hay to the left foot and a wisp of straw to the right; then, setting the men to march, they would chant, "Hay-foot, straw-foot, hay-foot, straw-foot"—and so on, until everybody had caught on. A common name for a green recruit in those days was "strawfoot."

On the drill field, when a squad was getting basic training, the men were as likely as not to intone a little rhythmic chant as they tramped across the sod—thus:

March! March! March old soldier march!
Hayfoot, strawfoot,
Belly-full of bean soup—
March old soldier march!

Because of his unsophistication, the ordinary soldier in the Civil War, North and South alike, usually joined up with very romantic ideas about soldiering. Army life rubbed the romance off just as rapidly then as it does now, but at the start every volunteer went into the army thinking that he was heading off to high adventure. Under everything else, he enlisted because he thought army life was going to be fun, and usually it took quite a few weeks in camp to disabuse him of this strange notion. Right at the start, soldiering had an almost idyllic quality; if this quality faded rapidly, the memory of it remained through all the rest of life.

Early days in camp simply cemented the idea. An Illinois recruit, writing home from training camp, confessed: "It is fun to lie around, face unwashed, hair uncombed, shirt unbuttoned and everything un-everythinged. It sure beats clerking." Another Illinois boy confessed: "I don't see why people will stay at home when they can get to soldiering. A year of it is worth getting shot for to any man." And a Massachusetts boy, recalling the early days of army life, wrote that "Our drill, as I remember it, consisted largely of running around the Old Westbury town hall, yelling like Devils and firing at an imaginary foe." One of the commonest discoveries that comes from a reading of Civil War diaries is that the chief worry, in training camp, was a fear that the war would be over before the ardent young recruits could get into it. It is only fair to say that most of the diarists looked back on this innocent worry, a year or so afterward, with rueful amusement.

There was a regiment recruited in northern Pennsylvania in 1861 —13th Pennsylvania Reserves officially, known to the rest of the Union Army as the Bucktails because the rookies decorated their caps with strips of fur from the carcass of a deer that was hanging in front of a butcher shop near their camp—and in mid-spring these youthful soldiers were ordered to rendezvous at Harrisburg. So they marched cross-country (along a road known today as the Bucktail Trail) to the north branch of the Susquehanna, where they built rafts. One raft, for the colonel, was made oversized with a stable; the colonel's horse had to ride, too. Then the Bucktails floated down the river, singing and firing their muskets and having a gay old time, camping out along the bank at night, and finally they got to Harrisburg; and they served through the worst of the war, getting badly shot up and losing most of their men to Confederate bullets, but they never forgot the picnic air of those first days of army life, when they drifted down a river through the forests, with a song in the air and the bright light of adventure shining just ahead. Men do not go to war that way nowadays.

*A haunting face from a lost generation: Georgia
Private Edwin Jennison, killed at Malvern Hill.*

Discipline in those early regiments was pretty sketchy. The big
catch was that most regiments were recruited locally—in one town, or
one county, or in one part of a city—and everybody more or less knew
everybody else. Particularly, the privates knew their officers—most of
whom were elected to their jobs by the enlisted men—and they never

saw any sense in being formal with them. Within reasonable limits, the Civil War private was willing to do what his company commander told him to do, but he saw little point in carrying it to extremes.

So an Indiana soldier wrote: "We had enlisted to put down the Rebellion, and had no patience with the red-tape tomfoolery of the regular service. The boys recognized no superiors, except in the line of legitimate duty. Shoulder straps waived, a private was ready at the drop of a hat to thrash his commander—a thing that occurred more than once." A New York regiment, drilling on a hot parade ground, heard a private address his company commander thus: "Say, Tom, let's quit this darn foolin' around and go over to the sutler's and get a drink." There was very little of the "Captain, sir" business in those armies. If a company or regimental officer got anything especial in the way of obedience, he got it because the enlisted men recognized him as a natural leader and superior and not just because he had a commission signed by Abraham Lincoln.

Odd rivalries developed between regiments. (It should be noted that the Civil War soldier's first loyalty went usually to his regiment, just as a navy man's loyalty goes to his ship; he liked to believe that his regiment was better than all others, and he would fight for it, any time and anywhere.) The army legends of those days tell of a Manhattan regiment, camped near Washington, whose nearest neighbor was a regiment from Brooklyn, with which the Manhattanites nursed a deep rivalry. Neither regiment had a chaplain; and there came to the Manhattan colonel one day a minister, who volunteered to hold religious services for the men in the ranks.

The colonel doubted that this would be a good idea. His men, he said, were rather irreligious, not to say godless, and he feared they would not give the reverend gentleman a respectful hearing. But the minister said he would take his chances; after all, he had just held services with the Brooklyn regiment, and the men there had been very quiet and devout. That was enough for the colonel. What the Brooklyn regiment could do, his regiment could do. He ordered the men paraded for divine worship, announcing that any man who talked, laughed, or even coughed would be summarily court-martialed.

So the clergyman held services, and everyone was attentive. At the end of the sermon, the minister asked if any of his hearers would care to step forward and make public profession of faith; in the Brooklyn regiment, he said, fourteen men had done this. Instantly the New York colonel was on his feet.

"Adjutant!" he bellowed. "We're not going to let that damn Brooklyn regiment beat us at anything. Detail twenty men and have them baptized at once!"

Each regiment seemed to have its own mythology, tales which may have been false but which, by their mere existence, reflected faithfully certain aspects of army life. The 48th New York, for instance, was said to have an unusually large number of ministers in its ranks, serving not as chaplains but as combat soldiers. The 48th, fairly early in the war, found itself posted in a swamp along the South Carolina coast, toiling mightily in semitropical heat, amid clouds of mosquitoes, to build fortifications, and it was noted that all hands became excessively profane, including the one-time clergymen. A visiting general, watching the regiment at work one day, recalled the legend and asked the regiment's lieutenant colonel if he himself was a minister in private life.

"Well, no, General," said the officer apologetically. "I can't say that I was a regularly ordained minister. I was just one of these —— —— local preachers."

Another story was hung on this same 48th New York. A Confederate ironclad gunboat was supposed to be ready to steam through channels in the swamp and attack the 48th's outposts, and elaborate plans were made to trap it with obstructions in the channel, a tangle of ropes to snarl the propellers, and so on. But it occurred to the colonel that even if the gunboat was trapped the soldiers could not get into it; it was sheathed in iron, all its ports would be closed, and men with axes could never chop their way into it. Then the colonel had an inspiration. Remembering that many of his men had been recruited from the less savory districts of New York City, he paraded the regiment and (according to legend) announced:

"Now men, you've been in this cursed swamp for two weeks—up to your ears in mud, no fun, no glory and blessed poor pay. Here's a chance. Let every man who has had experience as a cracksman or a safe-blower step to the front." To the last man, the regiment marched forward four paces and came expectantly to attention.

Not unlike this was the reputation of the 6th New York, which contained so many Bowery toughs that the rest of the army said a man had to be able to show that he had done time in prison in order to get into the regiment. It was about to leave for the South, and the colonel gave his men an inspirational talk. They were going, he said, to a land of wealthy plantation owners, where each Southerner had riches of which he could be despoiled; and he took out his own gold watch and held it up for all to see, remarking that any deserving soldier could easily get one like it, once they got down to plantation-land. Half an hour later, wishing to see what time it was, he felt for his watch . . . and it was gone.

If the Civil War army spun queer tales about itself, it had to face a reality which, in all of its aspects, was singularly unpleasant. One of the worst aspects had to do with food.

From first to last, the Civil War armies enlisted no men as cooks, and there were no cooks' and bakers' schools to help matters. Often enough, when in camp, a company would simply be issued a quantity of provisions flour, pork, beans, potatoes, and so on—and invited to prepare the stuff as best it could. Half a dozen men would form a mess, members would take turns with the cooking, and everybody had to eat what these amateurs prepared or go hungry. Later in the war, each company commander would usually detail two men to act as cooks for the company, and if either of the two happened to know anything about cooking the company was in luck. One army legend held that company officers usually detailed the least valuable soldiers to this job, on the theory that they would do less harm in the cook shack than anywhere else. One soldier, writing after the war, asserted flatly: "A company cook is a most peculiar being; he generally knows less about cooking than any other man in the company. Not being able to learn the drill, and too dirty to appear on inspection, he is sent to the cook house to get him out of the ranks."

When an army was on the march, the ration issue usually consisted of salt pork, hardtack, and coffee. (In the Confederate Army the coffee was often missing, and the hardtack was frequently replaced by corn bread; often enough the meal was not sifted, and stray bits of cob would appear in it.) The hardtack was good enough, if fresh, which was not always the case; with age it usually got infested with weevils, and veterans remarked that it was better to eat it in the dark.

In the Union Army, most of the time, the soldier could supplement his rations (if he had money) by buying extras from the sutler—the latter being a civilian merchant licensed to accompany the army, functioning somewhat as the regular post exchange functions nowadays. The sutler charged high prices and specialized in indigestibles like pies, canned lobster salad, and so on; and it was noted that men who patronized him regularly came down with stomach upsets. The Confederate Army had few sutlers, which helps to explain why the hungry Confederates were so delighted when they could capture a Yankee camp: to seize a sutler's tent meant high living for the captors, and the men in Lee's army were furious when, in the 1864 campaign, they learned that General Grant had ordered the Union Army to move without sutlers. Johnny Reb felt that Grant was really taking an unfair advantage by cutting off this possible source of supply.

If Civil War cooking arrangements were impromptu and imperfect, the same applied to its hospital system. The surgeons, usually, were good men by the standards of that day—which were low since no one on earth knew anything about germs or about how wounds became infected, and antisepsis in the operating room was a concept that had not yet come into existence; it is common to read of a surgeon whetting his scalpel on the sole of his shoe just before operating. But the hospital attendants, stretcher-bearers, and the like were chosen just as the company cooks were chosen; that is, they were detailed from the ranks, and the average officer selected the most worthless men he had simply because he wanted to get rid of men who could not be counted on in combat. As a result, sick or wounded men often got atrocious care.

A result of all of this—coupled with the fact that many men enlisted without being given any medical examinations—was that every Civil War regiment suffered a constant wastage from sickness. On paper, a regiment was supposed to have a strength ranging between 960 and 1,040 men; actually, no regiment ever got to the battlefield with anything like that strength, and since there was no established system for sending in replacements a veteran regiment that could muster 350 enlisted men present for duty was considered pretty solid. From first to last, approximately twice as many Civil War soldiers died of disease—typhoid, dysentery, and pneumonia were the great killers—as died in action; and in addition to those who died a great many more got medical discharges.

In its wisdom, the Northern government set up a number of base hospitals in Northern states, far from the battle fronts, on the theory that a man recovering from wounds or sickness would recuperate better back home. Unfortunately, the hospitals thus established were under local control, and the men in them were no longer under the orders of their own regiments or armies. As a result, thousands of men who were sent north for convalescence never returned to the army. Many were detailed for light work at the hospitals, and in these details they stayed because nobody had the authority to extract them and send them back to duty. Others, recovering their health, simply went home and stayed there. They were answerable to the hospital authorities, not to the army command, and the hospital authorities rarely cared very much whether they returned to duty or not. The whole system was ideally designed to make desertion easy.

On top of all of this, many men had very little understanding of the requirements of military discipline. A homesick boy often saw nothing wrong in leaving the army and going home to see the folks for a time. A man from a farm might slip off to go home and put in a crop. In neither case would the man look on himself as a deserter; he meant to return, he figured he would get back in time for any fighting that would take place, and in his own mind he was innocent of any wrongdoing. But in many cases the date of return would be postponed from week to week; the man might end as a deserter, even though he had not intended to be one when he left.

A drawing of Confederate soldiers carousing in camp typifies the casual discipline of both Northern and Southern soldiers.

Combat artist Alfred Waud made this sketch of the results of a foraging expedition by Northern troops in Virginia.

This merely reflected the loose discipline that prevailed in Civil War armies, which in turn reflected the underlying civilian-mindedness that pervaded the rank and file. The behavior of Northern armies on the march in Southern territory reflected the same thing—and, in the end, had a profound effect on the institution of chattel slavery.

Armies of occupation always tend to bear down hard on civilian property in enemy territory. Union armies in the Civil War, being imperfectly disciplined to begin with—and suffering, furthermore, from a highly defective rationing system—bore down with especial fervor. Chickens, hams, cornfields, anything edible that might be found on a Southern plantation, looked like fair game, and the loose fringe of stragglers that always trailed around the edges of a moving Union army looted with a fine disregard for civilian property rights.

This was made all the more pointed by the fact that the average Northern soldier, poorly indoctrinated though he was, had strong feelings about the evils of secession. To his mind, the Southerners who sought to set up a nation of their own were in rebellion against the best government mankind had ever known. Being rebels, they had forfeited their rights; if evil things happened to them that (as the average Northern soldier saw it) was no more than just retribution. This meant that even when the army command tried earnestly to prevent looting and individual foraging the officers at company and regimental levels seldom tried very hard to carry out the high command's orders.

William Tecumseh Sherman has come down in history as the very archetype of the Northern soldier who believed in pillage and looting; yet during the first years of the war Sherman resorted to all manner of ferocious punishments to keep his men from despoiling Southern property. He had looters tied up by the thumbs, ordered courts-martial, issued any number of stern orders—and all to very little effect. Long before he adopted the practice of commandeering or destroying Southern property as a war measure, his soldiers were practicing it against his will, partly because discipline was poor and partly because they saw nothing wrong with it.

It was common for a Union colonel, as his regiment made camp in a Southern state, to address his men, pointing to a nearby farm, and say: "Now, boys, that barn is full of nice fat pigs and chickens. I don't want to see any of you take any of them"—whereupon he would fold his arms and look sternly in the opposite direction. It was also common for a regimental commander to read, on parade, some ukase from higher authority forbidding foraging, and then to wink solemnly—a clear hint that he did not expect anyone to take the order seriously. One colonel, punishing some men who had robbed a chicken house, said angrily: "Boys, I want you to understand that I am not punishing you for stealing but for getting caught at it."

It is more than a century since that war was fought, and things look a little different now than they looked at the time. At this distance, it may be possible to look indulgently on the wholesale foraging in which Union armies indulged; to the Southern farmers who bore the brunt of it, the business looked very ugly indeed. Many a Southern family saw the foodstuffs needed for the winter swept away in an hour by grinning hoodlums who did not need and could not use a quarter of what they took. Among the foragers there were many lawless characters who took watches, jewels, and any other valuables they could find; it is recorded that a squad would now and then carry a piano out to the lawn, take it apart, and use the wires to hang pots and pans over the campfire. . . . The Civil War was really romantic only at a considerable distance.

Underneath his feeling that it was good to add chickens and hams to the army ration, and his belief that civilians in a state of secession could expect no better fate, the Union soldier also came to believe that to destroy Southern property was to help win the war. Under orders, he tore up railroads and burned warehouses; it was not long before he realized that anything that damaged the Confederate economy weakened the Confederate war effort, so he rationalized his looting and foraging by arguing that it was a step in breaking the Southern will to resist. It is at this point that the institution of human slavery enters the picture.

Most Northern soldiers had very little feeling against slavery as such, and very little sympathy for the Negro himself. They thought they were fighting to save the Union, not to end slavery, and except for New England troops most Union regiments contained very little abolition sentiment. Nevertheless, the soldiers moved energetically and effectively to destroy slavery, not because they especially intended to

Winslow Homer's sketch of Union troops on the firing line portrays the kind of mass formations vulnerable to the Civil War's improved weaponry.

but simply because they were out to do all the damage they could do. They were operating against Southern property—and the most obvious, important, and easily removable property of all was the slave. To help the slaves get away from the plantation was, clearly, to weaken Southern productive capacity, which in turn weakened Confederate armies. Hence the Union soldier, wherever he went, took the peculiar institution apart, chattel by chattel.

As a result, slavery had been fatally weakened long before the war itself came to an end. The mere act of fighting the war killed it. Of all institutions on earth, the institution of human slavery was the one least adapted to survive a war. It could not survive the presence of loose-jointed, heavy-handed armies of occupation. It may hardly be too much too say that the mere act of taking up arms in slavery's defense doomed slavery.

Above and beyond everything else, of course, the business of the Civil War soldier was to fight. He fought with weapons that look very crude to modern eyes, and he moved by an outmoded system of tactics, but the price he paid when he got into action was just as high as the price modern soldiers pay despite the almost infinite development of firepower since the 1860's.

Standard infantry weapon in the Civil War was the rifled Springfield—a muzzle-loader firing a conical lead bullet, usually of .54 caliber.

To load was rather laborious, and it took a good man to get off more than two shots a minute. The weapon had a range of nearly a mile, and its "effective range"—that is, the range at which it would hit often enough to make infantry fire truly effective—was figured at about 250 yards. Compared with a modern Garand, the old muzzle-loader is no better than a museum piece; but compared with all previous weapons—the weapons on which infantry tactics in the 1860's were still based—it was a fearfully destructive and efficient piece.

For the infantry of that day still moved and fought in formations dictated in the old days of smoothbore muskets, whose effective range was no more than 100 yards and which were wildly inaccurate at any distance. Armies using those weapons attacked in solid mass formations, the men standing, literally, elbow to elbow. They could get from effective range to hand-to-hand fighting in a very short time, and if they had a proper numerical advantage over the defensive line they could come to grips without losing too many men along the way. But in the Civil War the conditions had changed radically; men would be hit while the rival lines were still half a mile apart, and to advance in mass was simply to invite wholesale destruction. Tactics had not yet been adjusted to the new rifles; as a result, Civil War attacks could be fearfully costly, and when the defenders dug entrenchments and got some protection—as the men learned to do, very quickly—a direct frontal assault could be little better than a form of mass suicide.

It took the high command a long time to revise tactics to meet this changed situation, and Civil War battles ran up dreadful casualty lists. For an army to lose 25 per cent of its numbers in a major battle was by no means uncommon, and in some fights—the Confederate army at Gettysburg is an outstanding example—the percentage of loss ran close to one third of the total number engaged. Individual units were sometimes nearly wiped out. Some of the Union and Confederate regiments that fought at Gettysburg lost up to 80 per cent of their numbers; a regiment with such losses was usually wrecked, as an effective fighting force, for the rest of the war.

The point of all of which is that the discipline which took the Civil War soldier into action, while it may have been very sketchy by modern standards, was nevertheless highly effective on the field of battle. Any armies that could go through such battles as Antietam, Stone's River, Franklin or Chickamauga and come back for more had very little to learn about the business of fighting.

Perhaps the Confederate General D. H. Hill said it, once and for all. The battle of Malvern Hill, fought on the Virginia peninsula early in the summer of 1862, finished the famous Seven Days campaign, in which George B. McClellan's Army of the Potomac was driven back from in front of Richmond by Robert E. Lee's Army of Northern Virginia. At Malvern Hill, McClellan's men fought a rear-guard action—a bitter, confused fight which came at the end of a solid week of wearing, costly battles and forced marches. Federal artillery wrecked the Confederate assault columns, and at the end of the day Hill looked out over the battlefield, strewn with dead and wounded boys. Shaking his head, and reflecting on the valor in attack and in defense which the two armies had displayed, Hill never forgot about this. Looking back on it, long after the war was over, he declared, in substance:

"Give me Confederate infantry and Yankee artillery and I'll whip the world!"

James G. Randall and
R. N. Current

How Lincoln
Would Have
Rebuilt the Union

What would Lincoln have done after the Civil War had he not been assassinated? The sainthood that his foul murder brought to him distorted for decades his actual views. He was pictured as both the Great Emancipator of the blacks and as the binder of the nation's wounds, the man who, "with malice toward none," would have treated the former slaveholders with Christlike compassion. That he could not have been both an ardent champion of Negro rights and the forgiving friend of the former rebels eventually became clear, but a full understanding of his attitudes was only slowly uncovered by historians.

One of the historians who did most to throw light on Lincoln's policies was the late James G. Randall, whose four-volume Lincoln the President *is a model of lucid and painstaking scholarship. When Randall died before completing the last volume of this work, Richard N. Current, now professor of history at the University of North Carolina at Greensboro, took on the task of finishing it. In the following essay Randall and Current discuss Lincoln's approach to reconstructing the Union. As they admit, no one can say with total assurance how Lincoln would have acted if he had not been killed, or what the result would have been. But they demonstrate beyond argument that his policy was carefully thought out and based on close observation of conditions in the South.*

*I*n his annual message to Congress, delivered in December of 1863 in fulfillment of the provision of the Constitution requiring that the President shall "give to the Congress Information of the State of the Union," Lincoln addressed himself to the question of reconstruction. He did not deal in quibbles or generalities, but came up with a plan. Anyone who knew Lincoln would have known that his design for a restored Union would not be hateful and vindictive. It would not rule out the very spirit of reunion. His view had never been narrowly sectional. Born in the Southern state of Kentucky of Virginia-born parents, moving thence to Indiana and Illinois, he was part of that transit of culture by which Southern characteristics, human types, and thought patterns had taken hold in the West and Northwest. Though he was antislavery and of course antisecession, he was never anti-Southern.

He had said in his first inaugural: "Physically we cannot separate," and on various later occasions he had returned to this theme. As he wrote in his annual message of December 1, 1862, to "separate our common country into two nations" was to him intolerable. The people of the greater interior, he urged, "will not ask where a line of separation shall be, but will vow rather that there shall be no such line." The situation as he saw it, in "all its adaptations and aptitudes . . . demands union and abhors separation." It would ere long "force reunion, however much of blood and treasure the separation might cost."

Thus Lincoln's fundamental adherence to an unbroken Union was the point of departure for his reconstruction program. One could find, in the earlier part of his presidency, other indications bearing upon restoration. In an important letter to General G. F. Shepley, military governor of Louisiana (November 21, 1862), he advised strongly against what came to be known as "carpetbagger" policy. He did not want "Federal officers not citizens of Louisiana" to seek election as congressmen from that state. On this his language was emphatic: he considered it "disgusting and outrageous . . . to send a parcel of Northern men here as representatives, elected, as it would be understood (and perhaps really so), at the point of the bayonet."

While in this manner disallowing the idea of importing Northern politicians into a Southern state as pseudo-representatives in Congress, he also repudiated the opposite policy of Fernando Wood of New York which would accept Southerners in Congress prematurely—that is, before resistance to the United States was ended and loyalty assured. To mention another point, he had, in considering the formation of the new state of West Virginia, expressed his view that, in the pattern of the Union, only those who were loyal—i. e., who adhered to the United States—could be regarded as competent voters.

To these points—the indispensable Union, loyalty, and the unwisdom of carpetbaggism—one must add Lincoln's fundamental policy of emancipation and his non-vindictiveness in the matter of confiscation. Taking these factors together the historian has, before December, 1863, the ingredients of the President's reunion program.

In announcing that program on December 8, 1863, Lincoln issued two documents: a proclamation, and a message to Congress. In his proclamation, having the force of law, he set forth the conditions of a general pardon and the terms of restoring a Southern state to the Union. In his accompanying message he commented upon his plan, telling more fully what was in his mind and defending his course by reason and persuasion. The offer of pardon (with stated exceptions) and restoration of rights (except as to slaves) was given to anyone in a seceded state who would take and keep a simple oath. Phrased by the President, this oath constituted a solemn pledge to support the Constitution of the United States "and the union of the States thereunder." The oath-taker would also swear to abide by and faithfully support all the acts of Congress and all the proclamations of the President relating to slaves unless repealed, modified, or declared void by the Supreme Court.

So much for the oath, with pardon and restoration of rights. The next element in the proclamation was re-establishment of a state government. This again was intended to be simple and practical. Whenever, in a seceded state, a number not less than one tenth of those voting in 1860, should re-establish a republican government, such a government, according to Lincoln's proclamation, would "be recognized as the true government of the State."

Turning from the proclamation to the simultaneous message, we find Lincoln setting forth the reasons and conditions of his policy. In this he addressed himself to various questions that he knew would arise. What about the oath? Why the ten per cent? What about state laws touching freedmen? Why preserve the state as it was? How about state boundaries? Why was the President assuming the power of reconstruction as an executive function? He started with the obvious unwisdom and absurdity of protecting a revived state government constructed from the disloyal element. It was essential to have a test "so as to build only from the sound." He wanted that test to be liberal and to include "sworn recantation of . . . former unsoundness." As for laws and proclamations against slavery, they could not be abandoned. Retaining so far as possible the existing political framework in the state, as Lincoln saw it, would "save labor, and avoid confusion." He did not, of course, mean by this that the system in any state was to be permanently frozen for the future in unchangeable form.

As to the specific formula of ten per cent, he said little; yet his simile of a rallying point held the key. The important object was to get a movement started. Acceptance of an initial electorate of ten per cent did not signify that Lincoln was favoring minority rule. It was not his thought that any minority should usurp the rights of the majority. Within his pattern of loyalty, Union, non-dictatorial government, and emancipation, he was putting the formation of any new state government in the hands of the loyal people of the state. Government by the people was to him fundamental, but as a practical matter some loyal nucleus was essential; else time would pass, precious time, and nothing would be done.

In J.E. Baker's 1864 cartoon,
Andrew Johnson, who was
a tailor as a young man, and
Lincoln, the railsplitter,
labor to reunite the Union.

The whole situation, of course, was abnormal. All beginnings, or re-beginnings, are difficult, especially rebuilding after or during a war, taking up the shattered pieces of a disrupted social and political order and putting them partly together so that ultimately they could be fully restored. Lincoln was willing to accept informality in order to accomplish the main practical purpose which he considered imperative. He was unwilling to throw away the cause while futilely waiting for perfection. Reconstruction, as he saw it, was a matter of stages. His "ten per cent plan" was easy to criticize. Yet it was the first step.

Lincoln would take his first step in the most available manner. A few states could be rebuilt and restored. This was to be done during the war, indeed as an important factor in waging and ending the war. Let people see that Lincoln did not intend an ugly and vindictive policy, and Southerners themselves, the President hoped, would set their own houses in order. Let one or two states do this; they would serve as examples for others as the armies advanced and national authority was extended. In time of war, prepare for peace, was Lincoln's thought. On the other hand, let the months pass, and let the Southern people witness only carpetbaggism, Federal occupation, and a repressive attitude as to the future, and victory itself would lose much of its value. It was Lincoln's intent that policy associated with victory should envisage willing loyalty while leaving free play for self government.

Lincoln's plan of reunion was greeted with a mixed response. The Washington *Chronicle,* regarded as a Lincoln "organ," naturally praised the President's announcement. The editor noted that the President gave out his statement in a setting of military and naval success: our armies victorious, our navy in control of Southern coasts, our cause strengthened by increased friendship of foreign nations. His generous offering of pardon was interpreted by the *Chronicle* as evidence of his kindness and sympathy toward the people of the South.

An English gentleman friendly to the United States wrote: "We have just received the news of President Lincoln's message, accompanied with his amnesty; also the message of . . . [Jefferson] Davis. The two documents coming together are doing an immense amount of good for the right cause."

It is doubtful how many readers made the comparison of the two messages, but those who did must have noted a marked difference of tone. In general spirit Lincoln's message of December 8, 1863, was notable for its absence of war-engendered hatred toward the South, ending as it did on the note of "freedom disenthralled." In appealing for reunion the President was holding out the hand for genuine renewal of friendly relations. This attitude, however, was not reciprocated by the Confederate President. Though perhaps the comparison should not be overstressed, one finds quite the opposite note in the message (December 7, 1863) of Jefferson Davis to his Congress. After a depressing account of Confederate military reverses and of discouraging condition in foreign affairs and finance, the Southern Executive threw in bitter denunciations of the "barbarous policy" and "savage ferocity" of "our enemies." At one point he referred to them as "hardened by crime." (There were, of course, those in the North, though not Lincoln, who were saying equally hateful things of the South.) That enemy, wrote Davis, refused "even to listen to proposals . . . [of peace] of recognizing the impassable gulf which divides us." This expression, the orthodox attitude of Confederate officialdom, must be remembered along with Lincoln's other problems. If anyone doubted why the President, in his reconstruction plans and his wariness toward "peace negotiations," realized the hopelessness of expecting high Confederate officials to consider a peaceable restoration of the Union, the reading of this message of Davis would have been enough to dispel such doubt.

It was obvious from the start that the President's plan would not have smooth sailing, but on several fronts steps were taken to make it known and put it into operation. Army officers were instructed to take copies of the proclamation and distribute them so as to reach soldiers and inhabitants within Confederate-held territory. Aid and protection was to be extended to those who would declare loyalty. On the occasion of raids into enemy territory a number of men were to be detailed ''for the purpose of distributing the proclamation broadcast among rebel soldiers and people, and in the highways and byways.''

On the legal or prosecuting front the effect of the pardon policy was explained in an instruction from the office of the attorney general of the United States to district attorneys throughout the country. It was made known that the ''President's pardon of a person guilty of . . . rebellion . . . [would] relieve that person for the penalties'' of that crime. District attorneys were therefore directed to discontinue proceedings in United States courts whenever the accused should take the oath and comply with the stated conditions.

Such a statement would make it appear that the transition from a kind of rebellious guilt to complete relief from penalty was easy, automatic, and practically instantaneous, but it soon became evident that the matter was not so simple as that. Lincoln found that he had to make a distinction in applying his offer of pardon in return for the oath. What about Confederate soldiers held by Union authorities as prisoners of war? On this point the President issued a letter clarifying the proclamation, declaring that his pardon did not apply to men in custody or on parole as prisoners of war. It did apply, he explained, to persons yet at large (i.e., free from arrest) who would come forward and take the oath. It was also explained that those excluded from the general amnesty could apply to the President for clemency and their cases would have due consideration.

What it amounted to was that Lincoln himself was generous in the application of his pardon both to soldiers and civilians, and the same was true of the attorney general's office; but army officers were not prepared, in return for the oath, to deliver prisoners nor give up penalties for offences of various sorts, such as violation of rules of war. No one statement applies. Some enemies held as prisoners, on establishing loyalty, were discharged from custody by the President on assurance of good faith by three congressmen. This showed, as in many cases, that Lincoln's general rules were subject to individual exceptions.

With a scorn of fine-spun theories and an urgent wish to get ahead with the job of reconstruction, the President proceeded, so far as possible, to make restoration a reality whenever, and as soon as, any reasonable opportunity offered in the seceded South.

In Lincoln's plan of reconstruction the effort in Louisiana was of vital importance. From the time that New Orleans fell to Union arms on May 1, 1862, the President saw, in terms of Federal occupation, an early opportunity to make reconstruction a wartime reality. Let Louisiana be restored, he thought, let this be done in a reasonable manner with Washington approval, let it be seen that the plan would work, and other states would follow. To go into all the details of the Louisiana story, treating its complications month by month, would be a tedious process. It will be convenient to reduce this elaborate Louisiana story to four successive phases:

First Phase in Louisiana: Military Rule Under Butler and Shepley. The first phase was that of army rule under General B. F. Butler. Immediate adjustments were of course necessary from the moment when New Orleans, largest city of the South, together with a large portion of Louisiana, came under the Union flag. Governmental officials in the occupied region, including merely local functionaries in city or parish, were now under Federal authority—not in terms of any deliberation as to procedure by Congress or the Executive, but simply by the fortunes of war. Where men in local office stood ready to co-operate with the occupying power, they had a good chance of being retained; if un-cooperative, they were dismissed. For a time the mayor and council of New Orleans were continued in office subject to General Butler's authority with some relaxation of military pressure, but this situation did not last long. Within a month the mayor was deposed and imprisoned, and George F. Shepley, acting closely with Butler, took over mayoral functions. Then in June, 1862, Shepley became military governor of Louisiana; soon afterward he had the rank of brigadier general.

This was military occupation, and of course it was intended only as a temporary condition. It amounted to martial law which has been defined as the will of the military commander; this meant that the sometimes eccentric will of General Butler was paramount. If nothing offered in the form of a re-established and recognized state government, the abnormal and temporary regime would continue.

It thus came about that Federal rule in Louisiana, the first step toward what Lincoln regarded as restoration of loyalty and normal conditions, got off to a bad start. The name of "Beast Butler" became a hated byword in the South, with far-reaching complications in Federal-Confederate relations; it came as a considerable relief when President Lincoln removed him from his Louisiana command on December 16, 1862. His successor, as commander of the military forces stationed in Louisiana and Texas, was Major General Nathaniel P. Banks, with Shepley retaining his position as "military governor of Louisiana."

Under Butler little or nothing had been done toward wartime governmental reconstruction in the state, but this problem, dear to Lincoln's heart, was tackled under the President's urging during the Banks-Shepley regime.

A careful study of these matters reveals a problem as to top executive leadership locally applied—that is, the difficulty of achieving effectiveness in a particular area in terms of policy developed in Washington. Lincoln was President; he was the Chief; he made the appointments and formed decisions; presumably he would choose men to put his policies into operation. Yet so unpredictable were events and so complicated was the situation as to politicians' maneuvers that those who supposedly should have carried out Lincoln's purposes promoted their own factional and contrary schemes in such manner as to jeopardize the President's best laid plans.

George F. Shepley was a case in point. He had been a Maine Democrat, an appointee of Pierce and later of Buchanan as district attorney, and a supporter of Douglas in 1860. These factors in his background did not militate against him in Lincoln's view—the President often appointed Democrats—nor should they have been a drawback to successful service in Louisiana's reconstruction. There was, however, the further fact that Shepley became a Butlerite and a Radical; remaining after Butler's removal, he played the Radical game at a time when it was hoped that a more Lincolnian policy would be inaugurated. Thus Shepley stood as an obstacle to Lincoln's efforts to allay factionalism and to promote speedy and liberal restoration.

Toward the end of the Butler-Shepley period an election was held within the Union lines on December 3, 1862, for members of Congress from Louisiana. Two men of different outlook were elected: B. F. Flanders from New Hampshire, who was to become an instrument of the Radical faction; and Michael Hahn, a citizen of Louisiana born in Bavaria, who was more in tune with Lincoln's purposes. When the question of admitting these gentlemen as members of the House of Representatives was brought before that body (February 9, 1863) a species of dog fight ensued, a forerunner of the rough treatment in store for Lincoln's whole reunion program. Few were ready for frontal attack and sidestepping was more in evidence; the result was confusion, unrelated motions, and postponement. Finally, on February 17, 1863, the House voted, 92 to 44, to seat Flanders and Hahn. By that time that particular Congress, the Thirty-seventh, was about to pass out of existence.

Second Phase: Shepley and Durant versus Banks. In the next phase, while Banks was in top command in Louisiana with Shepley as military governor—i. e., governor as to civil affairs under military authority—certain groups in the state got to work, though at cross purposes, to seize control of the process of state remaking. It turned out to be a period of bickering and futility, a time of bitter disappointment to the President. Taking over the rebuilding task and attempting to do it in his own way, Governor Shepley proceeded to make a registry of voters, appointing T. J. Durant, a Radical like himself, as commissioner of registration. An oath of allegiance was required (this was before the presidentially prescribed oath of December 8, 1863) and the registration of whites who would take the oath was ordered. It was Durant's idea that ten loyal men in a parish, if no more could be registered, would be a sufficient basis for an election. This was a period when Banks was preoccupied with military command in the Port Hudson and Texas areas, while Shepley was also absent from Louisiana, spending a large part of the summer of 1863 in Washington. Lincoln approved the Shepley-Durant registration and wanted it pushed.

The President was trying to keep himself in the background, to avoid seeming to dictate, and to let things work themselves out as a Louisiana movement. Yet he soon found that a jurisdictional dispute or confusion as to control was spoiling everything. Shepley as military governor and Durant, his appointee, were claiming "that they were exclusively charged with the work of reconstruction in Louisiana," while Banks had "not felt authorized to interfere" with them. In a letter of December 16, 1863, Banks advised the President that he was "only in partial command," adding: "There are not less than *four* distinct governments here claiming . . . independent powers based upon instructions received directly from Washington, and recognizing no other authority than their own."

Though this unfortunate situation was due in large part to the activities of Radical groups, another factor may have been a bit of inadvertence on the part of the burdened President: he had supposed all the time that Banks was in chief command but had not made that point sufficiently clear. He now wrote a strong letter to Banks (December 24, 1863) with a fourfold repetition of the main theme: You are master. The President was seriously annoyed at the frustration and delay. Shepley, he wrote, was to "assist" Banks, not to "thwart" him. The desirable object, of course, was to have unity among pro-Union men and leaders, but a serious obstacle to such unity was the attitude of Shepley and his considerable faction. It became increasingly apparent that these Radicals were unwilling to co-operate with the man whom Lincoln had placed in chief authority and whom he had plainly designated as "master." Treating delay and factionalism as if things of the past, Lincoln wrote to Banks: "Give us a free State reorganization of Louisiana in the shortest possible time."

Third Phase: The Louisiana Constitution of 1864. Under Lincoln's spurring Banks went into action. In January and February of 1864 he issued proclamations for two kinds of elections: an election for governor under the old Louisiana constitution of 1853, and an election of delegates to a convention to make a new state constitution. In his proclamations, copies of which he sent to the President, Banks declared that officials then to be chosen were to govern unless they tried to change Federal statutes as to slavery. Voters were required to take the oath of allegiance to the United States.

Lincoln continued to prod and encourage. Proceed "with all possible dispatch," wrote the President. "Frame orders, and fix times and places for this and that. . . ." Recognition of the death of slavery in Louisiana was causing less difficulty than might have been expected. While the planter class wanted to keep the institution, they were in the minority; the majority of the people were ready to accept emancipation.

Both of the elections were a success from the standpoint of Banks and of Lincoln. Not that Lincoln considered the outcome perfect, but the whole point of Lincoln's policy was that he was not expecting perfection. He wanted steps to be taken, a "free" government set up; modifications and improvements could come later. The vote for state officials was held on February 22, 1864. In a total of 11,411 votes (over a fourth of the normal peacetime vote of Louisiana) Michael Hahn, the moderate Union candidate acceptable to Banks and Lincoln, received 6,183 votes and was elected; Flanders, candidate of the anti-Banks

Radical element, received 2,232 votes; J. Q. A. Fellows, nominated by the proslavery conservatives, received the disturbingly large vote of 2,996.

Next came the problem of constitution remaking. By Banks's proclamation an election was held on March 28, 1864, by which delegates were chosen (not a distinguished lot, but they represented the people rather than officials or politicians) to form a new instrument of government. From April to July the convention labored. Among its main acts was to abolish slavery by a vote of seventy to sixteen. Negro suffrage, then a new question and a difficult one, came harder. After voting it down, the convention reconsidered; it then "empowered" the legislature to grant the vote to colored persons; by the constitution it was provided that a militia be enrolled without distinction of color.

On September 5, 1864, the people of Louisiana voted to ratify the constitution (6,836–1,566); members of Congress were then chosen by popular election, after which the legislature set up under the new constitution chose two senators. If and when these men should be admitted by Congress—a big "if"—reconstruction for Louisiana, so far as essential political structure was concerned, would be complete. In the matter of preliminary steps—shaping up the situation so that Congress could act—the work of the executive branch for this pivotal state was done.

Fourth Phase: Trouble in Congress. Much water was to pass over the mill before one could know what Congress would do as to admitting Louisiana according to Lincoln's plan. The Radical clique in Louisiana had opposed the measures taken in 1864 looking toward a new state government. This element made a break with the Lincoln Administration, denounced the new constitution as null and void, and proceeded to make their influence felt in Congress. The Radical element in Congress was working strongly against Lincoln's program in any case, and it was no surprise that the decision of the solons at Washington concerning Louisiana reorganization was negative. A long period of Federal occupation and troublous abnormality was to ensue. There were a number of uneasy years after Lincoln's death before the state was, one should not say restored, but outfitted with a carpetbag government. After that there was to be further delay—nearly a decade—before that unworkable carpetbag regime collapsed.

As in Louisiana, so in other regions of the Confederate South, Lincoln did his best to promote reorganization measures so that state governments could supersede Federal military rule, but wartime conditions made for obstruction and progress was slow. In Tennessee, where secession had been strongly resisted and where Union victories came in February and April of 1862, it might have seemed that a choice opportunity was offered for early restoration of civil government under unionist auspices. The pro-Confederate regime in Tennessee was brief; it extended only from May 7, 1861 (legislative ratification of the military league with the Confederacy) to March 3, 1862, when Lincoln appointed Andrew Johnson military governor of the state, a period of ten months.

Johnson's attitude had been demonstrated by "violent opposition to slavery and secession" and by retention of his seat in the United States Senate. His unionism was unassailable, but he could only perform the functions of civil government on an emergency basis and Lincoln's hopes for instituting a more permanent and regular regime were repeatedly deferred. There was heavy fighting in 1862 and 1863. Guerrilla warfare, raids by Forrest, agitation among discordant pro-Union elements, puzzlement as to what was "regular" by the old code of the state (nothing could be strictly regular in those war times), lack of popular interest when elections were held, complications as to soldier voting and military influence, divided leadership as between Nashville and Washington—these were among the factors that caused continual delay.

Not until February, 1865, was an election held in Tennessee which had importance in terms of popular voting for fundamental state reorganization. After that there loomed, as always, the serious obstacle of congressional opposition. Tennessee was not to be admitted to the Union until 1866. Yet as early as September 11, 1863, Lincoln had written to Governor Johnson: "All Tennessee is now clear of armed insurrectionists." Insisting that "Not a moment should be lost" in "reinaugurating a loyal State government," the President insisted, as in Louisiana, that prudent steps be taken without delay. Discretion was left with Johnson and "co-operating friends" as to ways and means, with the presidential injunction that the reinauguration should not be allowed to slip into the hands of enemies of the Union, "driving its friends . . . into political exile." "It must not be so," wrote Lincoln. "You must have it otherwise."

In September, 1863, Andrew Johnson said to his people: "Here lies your State; a sick man in his bed, emaciated and exhausted . . . unable to walk alone. The physician comes. Don't quarrel about antecedents, but administer to his wants . . . as quickly as possible. . . . This is no . . . metaphysical question. It is a plain, common sense matter, and there is nothing in the way but obstinacy." Johnson's simile of the sick man and his suggestion as to the ineptness of those administering to him could have covered a great deal more territory than Tennessee.

Events of 1863 and early 1864 in Arkansas proceeded with little difficulty so far as that commonwealth itself was concerned. It was a sparsely settled state, with 435,000 inhabitants in 1860, of whom 111,115 were slaves. Illinois, of comparable area, had nearly four times the population. It was chiefly in the southeastern part, in the plantation area near the Mississippi River, that slaveholding was concentrated. Throughout most of the state there were few slaves, in the northern portion hardly any. People of the Ozark mountain region had little in common with the few cotton-growing magnates. To the vast majority of the people the abolition of slavery would produce no serious reordering of their lives and economy.

The state had avoided secession until swept away by the post-Sumter excitement; when secession was adopted it was done reluctantly. Even after secession, considerable Union sentiment remained.

According to a contemporary account, pertaining to the situation in 1863, "Citizens of distinction came forward to advocate the Union cause; among others, Brig.-Gen. E. W. Gantt, of the Confederate army, once held as a prisoner of war." The shift of General Gantt from Confederate to Union allegiance was, as he said, part of a popular movement; Union sentiment, he noted, was "manifesting itself on all sides and by every indication." For many who were of like mind with Gantt the open declaration of loyalty to the Federal government, especially after the Confederate surrender of Vicksburg, came naturally. It was like snapping out of an abnormal situation.

Military events provided a considerable impulse toward Union reorganization, especially the Union victories at Vicksburg and Port Hudson, and the Helena-Little Rock expedition of General Frederick Steele, U. S. A., against Sterling Price, C. S. A., which resulted in Confederate evacuation of Little Rock on September 10, 1863. With this Confederate reverse a large part of the state was brought under Union control.

Lincoln kept in touch with Arkansas affairs, notifying General Steele that he, as in the case of Banks in Louisiana, was "master" of the reorganization process. "Some single mind," wrote the President, "must be master, else there will be no agreement in anything." He had ample reason to realize the truth of this statement.

The pattern of the Arkansas movement reveals much as to Lincoln's plan in practical operation. Sentiment developed in meetings, with Union resolutions, in large parts of the state. Delegates were chosen in such meetings (by no more and no less authority than is usual in such popular movements under the stress of abnormal conditions) for a "convention" designed to make a new regime constitutional and legal. Lincoln encouraged the holding of the convention, welcoming it as a fulfillment of his plan as announced in December, 1863. On January 20, 1864, he indicated that the reorganization emanated from citizens of Arkansas petitioning for an election, and directed Steele to "order an election immediately" for March 28, 1864. When, on counting the votes for a Union-minded governor and for changes in the state constitution, the number should reach or exceed 5,406 (that being ten per cent of the Arkansas vote of 1860), Lincoln directed that the governor thus chosen should be declared qualified and that he should assume his duties under the modified state constitution. (As a minor detail, when it was found that the Union convention in Arkansas was planning the election for March 14, not March 28, the President quickly acquiesced in the convention plan.)

In the President's mind a milestone had been reached in Arkansas affairs with that election of March 14. By an overwhelming majority (12,179 to 226) the voters, having qualified by taking the Federal oath of allegiance, approved those changes in the state constitution which abolished slavery, declared secession void, and repudiated the Confederate debt. Isaac Murphy, already installed as provisional governor by the convention, was now elected governor by "more than double what the President had required." On April 11 the new state government under the modified constitution was inaugurated at Little Rock. The reconstructed legislature chose senators (William M. Fishbach and Elisha Baxter); three members of Congress had already been chosen in the March election.

Obstruction in House and Senate prevented the admission of these representatives and senators, and for long years Arkansas remained outside the pale so far as Congress was concerned. Lincoln's view, however, both as to practical matters and as to his own function in promoting them, was shown in his executive measures to get these important steps taken, and in his advice to Steele (June 29, 1864) that, despite congressional refusal to give these solons their seats at Washington, the new state government should have "the same support and protection that you would [have given] if the members had been admitted, because in no event . . . can this do any harm, while it will be the best you can do toward suppressing the rebellion."

A different type of situation presented itself in Florida, where the reconstruction effort was of a minor sort. Military accomplishment, so evident in Louisiana, Tennessee, and Arkansas, was lacking in this detached area, which was off the main line of strategy and unpromising as a field in which to commit any considerable body of troops. Aside from holding a few coastal points and maintaining the blockade, the United States paid little attention to the region of the St. John's, the St. Mary's, and the Suwannee. The only sizable engagement in the state during the war was the ill-starred "battle of Olustee," in the northeast corner, a short distance inward from Jacksonville, where a minor Union force under General Truman Seymour, U. S. A., was defeated by somewhat superior numbers, with advantage of defensive position, under General Joseph Finegan, C. S. A. This engagement, February 20, 1864, was the futile anticlimax of an army-navy expedition of Seymour, a subordinate of General Quincy A. Gillmore who was in command of the "Department of the South" with headquarters at Hilton Head, S. C.

Under these circumstances, though Union sentiment was held to be widespread in the state, the small-scale efforts to restore Florida were subject to the taunt that their motive was to give a plausible basis for sending pro-Lincoln delegates to the coming Republican convention; even the Seymour expedition was derided as a feature of the political campaign of 1864.

From Lincoln's standpoint the approach to reconstruction in Florida was like that in other Southern areas. On January 13, 1864, he wrote Gillmore advising that the general was to be "master" if differences should arise; in this letter the President urged that restoration be pushed "in the most speedy way possible," and that it be done within the range of the December proclamation. To handle some of the details John Hay was sent to Florida "with some blank-books [for recording oaths] and other blanks, to aid in the reconstruction." This trip of Hay's (February-March 1864) was not a brilliant success and the sum-total of the Florida gesture for reconstruction was far from impressive. Florida's "delegates," chosen by a few in Jacksonville, did turn up at the Republican convention in June, 1864, but not until after the war did the commonwealth proceed to the making of a new state constitution within the range of the Union; readmission to the Union—i.e., inauguration of carpetbag government—occurred in 1868; restoration of home rule—the throwing off of Radical Republican control—was deferred to 1877.

Small though it was, there was more in the Union effort in Florida than at first met the eye. One could treat the Seymour, or Gillmore-Seymour, expedition of 1864 as a sorry military enterprise, or as a disappointing phase of Lincoln's reconstruction plan, but in a realistic study one needs to enlarge the scope of inquiry. The episode must also be viewed in its relation to such subjects as the use of Negro troops (in which there was creditable performance), maneuvers in the pro-Chase sense, the opening of trade, and what has been called "carpetbag imperialism." In a detailed study George Winston Smith has pointed out that grandiose schemes or experiments were conjured up in connection with the Florida effort. There was, for example, the "extravagant plan" of Eli Thayer of Kansas emigrant fame—a well-intentioned plan to set up "soldier-colonists" and create model communities on the most approved New England pattern. The plan reached "only the blue-print stage," but it reveals much as to Yankee enterprise in the deep South. There was also injected into the wartime Florida scene the "machinations" of Lyman K. Stickney, "the most notorious of the early Florida carpetbaggers," who operated under Secretary Chase in the enforcement of a congressional act for collecting the Federal direct tax in the South. This law, writes Smith, was a "move to confiscate the real property of southern landholders" and was so administered as to become "an instrument of predatory corruption in Florida."

These factors need to be borne in mind in judging Lincoln's approach to reconstruction. It was a complicated problem of many facets, with idealistic motives combined with profit-seeking greed. Lincoln tried to keep restoration on the main track and keep it unmarred, but it was part of the history of the time—the prelude to the "Gilded Age"—that debased and uninspiring maneuvers would creep in. Florida was only an example. When one remembers such influences, he can realize with fuller force the significance of Lincoln's rejection of the whole drive and tendency toward carpetbaggism.

. . . In Lincoln's planning for a restored Union he kept his eye constantly on a highly important factor, that of unionism in the South. Of course it could have been said by critics that Lincoln was not bothering with the opposition, that he was requiring an oath of Union allegiance as a prerequisite for the right to vote on any state reorganization, and that he was thus stacking the cards in his favor, working only with friends of the Union. This seemed the more striking because of his willingness to depend on a Union-minded minimum of ten per cent (of 1860 voters) for the initial steps of reconstruction.

Yet on closer study it will be seen that success for any reunion movement was dependent upon popular support in the state. Always at some point there had to be an election, a popular choice of a constitutional convention to remake the state constitution, and a vote for state officials and members of Congress. People who voted in these initial elections had to take the Union oath; but no one was to be coerced into taking it, and if the number of oath-takers was too insignificant, the plan would not get very far. Lincoln was starting with a loyal minority, but the quality and extent of that minority was never unimportant. Furthermore, the President was planning for peace, for the long years ahead after the war ended.

At all times the President felt assured that his plan would work for the whole South. He could hardly have proceeded with such confidence unless he genuinely believed that unionists in the South were, for the long run and for normal times, in the majority. In fact the validity of Lincoln's basic political philosophy depended upon self rule by the people. To impose a government upon an unwilling state—even a benevolent government—would have been contrary to this fundamental philosophy. There was a risk involved in Lincoln's scheme but it was a calculated risk. When there would come the hazard of an election, that would not merely mean that people should vote because of having sworn allegiance. It meant that such allegiance was expected to prove justified in the type of government set up, the working out of labor adjustment, the choice of well disposed officials, the installing of honest government, and the like.

If these things went wrong even after the initial steps had been taken in compliance with the President's plan, the broad policy would fail. Lincoln's feeling of assurance that it would not fail must have been based on more than wishful thinking. It is therefore of importance to look into the matter and find the basis for this assurance—in other words, to discover some of the evidences of unionism in the South which were known to the President. To give the whole body of such evidence is obviously impracticable, but a few items may be mentioned with the understanding that they were typical of a large and impressive total.

There was the element of war-weariness in the South; people were sick and tired of the continued slaughter. A captured Union general, the famous Neal Dow, wrote to Lincoln from Libby Prison, Richmond, on November 12, 1863: ". . . I have seen much of Rebeldom, behind the curtain, and have talked with a great many soldiers, conscripts, deserters, officers, and citizens. The result of all is, to my mind, that . . . the masses are heartily . . . anxious for its [the war's] close on any terms. . . ." He went on to mention numerous Confederate desertions, soldier infirmities, general debility, the worthlessness of conscripts, depreciation of the currency, flour at $125 a barrel, and "everything in the provision line . . . [bearing] a corresponding price."

In Virginia the attitude of intelligent and patriotic unionists was typified by Alexander H. H. Stuart. Though not active against secession during the war, he had been fundamentally opposed to it as inexpedient. Stuart defined his wartime attitudes as follows:

"During the war, I abstained from all participation in public affairs, except on two or three occasions when I was called to address public meetings to urge contributions for the relief of the suffering soldiers and the prisoners going to as well as returning from the North.

"My age relieved me from the obligation to render military service, and all the assistance I gave to the Confederate cause was by feeding the hungry and clothing the naked and nursing the sick Confederate soldiers, and making myself and urging others to make liberal donations for their relief."

Another prominent Virginia unionist was the distinguished lawyer John Minor Botts. He had strongly opposed Southern Democratic disunionists, and, though disapproving also of abolitionists, had given support to the efforts of John Quincy Adams in the matter of anti-slavery petitions presented to Congress. When Lincoln was a Whig member of Congress from Illinois, Botts was a Whig member from Virginia (1847-49); indeed many of his views were similar to Lincoln's. Both in 1850 and in 1860 he was an earnest opponent of secession, his opposition to Jefferson Davis and to Governor Henry Wise of Virginia being especially marked. He greatly regretted the secession of his state in 1860, which he had tried to prevent. During the war he was so far out of sympathy with the Confederate government that he was arrested and confined for some months in jail. For the most part, however, he spent the war years in retirement. His later career showed the steadfastness of his Union loyalty.

The fact that certain Southern areas had never left the Union was, of course, significant. That was true of Kentucky. It was remarked that the mountainous districts of that border state were "with very few exceptions . . . thoroughly union." The same observer noted derisively that in the central part of the state "most of the large slave holders, . . . the gamblers . . . all the decayed chivalry . . . all the fast & fashionable ones & nearly all the original Breckinridge Democrats are bitter to secessionists."

Unionist voices were audible throughout the unhappy South. A clear sign of the times in Louisiana was the editorial of the *True Delta* of New Orleans (February 5, 1864) praising Lincoln, comparing him to Washington and Jackson, and favoring his re-election. In Mississippi a local judge wrote: "I have *first, last and all the time,* been a Union man." Secession, he reported, had been put over without the people understanding what was involved. In another report from Mississippi it was indicated that there were "thousands . . . who desire most ardently the restoration of the United States."

In North Carolina peace movements were rife and it was reported early in 1864 that troops from the Old North State were deserting rapidly and extensively from the Confederate service. In the previous year a group of North Carolina citizens had presented a petition to the President, asking him to "order an election day for this district for the purpose of electing a representative for the next Congress." These petitioners represented themselves as "loyal to the Constitution of our country anxious that it should be perpetuated."

As to Alabama it was predicted that if the question of returning to the Union were submitted to a vote, the people would "vote aye, *five to one.*" The President was given the following assurance: "Could you know how deep and universal is the returning love for the union among the people of Ala & Geo you would discharge your great responsibilities with a hymn of joy in your heart.''

These evidences, and more of the same, were available to Lincoln. Since his day further material has come to light tending to reveal the extent of Union sentiment in seceded states. Naturally, men and women of Union sympathies in the South found existing conditions difficult for any expression of loyalty in active, organized form. Yet their restricted attitude was significant as they maintained a kind of passive resistance, avoided voluntary measures against the government at Washington, opposed the Confederate draft, carried provisions and medicines to Union soldiers, contributed money for the welfare of blue-coats, attended boys in hospitals, and performed other friendly acts for Federal troops. Such acts incurred persecution, and the Southern unionist moved often in an atmosphere of scorn and hostility not unaccompanied by threats and acts of personal violence. Of course, in various respects he was compelled to act against his will when it was a matter of serving as conscript, subscribing to a Confederate loan, contributing cotton, paying taxes, or performing labor. Since Southern wartime history has been largely remembered and recorded in Confederate terms, these details are still somewhat obscure; at least their full force is not generally recognized.

No history of Lincoln, however, can ignore them. His reports from the South were a vital element in policy making. When he made his broad appeal in December, 1863, offering pardon, prescribing his simple oath, and opening the way for new state governments by genuine Southern effort looking toward peace with freedom and union, he had reason to know, at least in large part, the kind of support and fulfillment upon which he could count. His sense of his own function as leader was strengthened by his realization that Southern unionism did not signify willingness to accept the program and regime of congressional Radicals. On the contrary, such union-mindedness was oriented in Lincolnian terms. In taking on the responsibility of launching and promoting reconstruction, Lincoln saw an opportunity which needed to be seized while its most fruitful results were yet possible. . . .

The many-sided problem of reconstruction was a subject of continual debate in the North from 1863 on. After reaching a furious pitch in the summer of 1864, the debate had been toned down during the final weeks of the presidential campaign, to be renewed fitfully and shrilly as the final military victory approached. Lee's surrender brought the issue to a climax again. Then, temporarily at least, Lincoln and the Radicals found themselves even farther apart than before.

For a while, in early April, 1865, he seemed willing to readmit the Southern states on terms more generous than those he had announced in his ten per cent plan and in his amnesty proclamation of December, 1863. But the Radicals were prepared to demand terms even more rigorous than those they had embodied in the Wade-Davis bill, which Lincoln had refused to sign in July, 1864.

With a new sense of urgency the Radicals began to consult with one another and to speak out. On the day after Appomattox, in Washington, General Butler made a speech in which he recommended, on the one hand, that the leaders of the rebellion should be disfranchised and disqualified for public office and, on the other, that the masses including the Negroes should be given immediately all the rights of citizenship. The next evening, in Baltimore on court duty, Chief Justice Chase dined with Henry Winter Davis and other Maryland Radicals, then wrote a letter to the President. "It will be, hereafter, counted equally a crime and a folly," Chase said, "if the colored loyalists of the rebel states shall be left to the control of restored rebels, not likely, in that case, to be either wise or just, until taught both wisdom and justice by new calamities."

That same evening, April 11, Lincoln made his own, last contribution to the public debate when he addressed the crowd gathered on the White House grounds. After a few congratulatory words on Grant's recent victory, he proceeded to defend at some length his own reconstruction view.

The problem, as he saw it, was essentially one of re-establishing the national authority throughout the South. This problem was complicated by the fact that there was, in the South, "no authorized organ" to treat with. "Nor is it a small additional embarrassment that we, the loyal people, differ among ourselves as to the mode, manner, and means of reconstruction." He had been criticized, he said, because he did not seem to have a fixed opinion on the question "whether the seceded States, so called," were "in the Union or out of it." He dismissed that question as "a merely pernicious abstraction" and went on to declare: "We all agree that the seceded States, so called, are out of their proper practical relation with the Union; and that the sole object of the government, civil and military, in regard to those States is to again get them into that proper practical relation."

He had been criticized also for setting up and sustaining the new state government of Louisiana, which rested on the support of only ten per cent of the voters and did not give the franchise to the colored man. He confessed that the Louisiana government would be better if it rested on a larger electorate including the votes of Negroes —at least "the very intelligent" and those who had served as soldiers. "Concede that the new government of Louisiana is only to what it should be as the egg is to the fowl, we shall sooner have the fowl by hatching the egg than by smashing it?" The loyalists of the South would be encouraged and the Negroes themselves would be better off, Lincoln argued, if Louisiana were quickly readmitted to the Union. An additional ratification would be gained for the Thirteenth Amendment, the adoption of which would be "unquestioned and unquestionable" only if it were ratified by three fourths of *all* the states.

What Lincoln said of Louisiana, he applied also to the other states of the South. "And yet so great peculiarities pertain to each state; and such important and sudden changes occur in the same state; and, withal, so new and unprecedented is the whole case, that no exclusive, and inflexible plan can safely be prescribed as to details and colatterals." (Virginia was not mentioned.) In concluding, Lincoln said enigmatically that it might become his duty "to make some new announcement to the people of the South. I am considering, and shall not fail to act, when satisfied that action will be proper."

In Washington and throughout the country the speech aroused much speculation about Lincoln's undisclosed intentions, and it provoked mixed feelings about his general approach to reconstruction. The editor of the Philadelphia *Public Ledger* noted that the President had indicated his "feelings and wishes" rather than his "fixed opinions," then commended him for his lack of "passion or malignancy" toward the late rebels. The Washington correspondent of the Cincinnati *Gazette* believed that Lincoln's position was generally approved except among the Radical Republicans, who were saying that the rebel leaders must be punished and the rebel states subjected to "preliminary training" before being restored to their rights as members of the Union. "The desire of the people for a settlement—speedy and final—upon the easiest possible terms, will, it is believed, sustain the President in his policy foreshadowed in his speech."

Whatever the people might have approved, it was again made clear to Lincoln, when the Cabinet met on the morning of April 14 (with General Grant present), that some of his own advisers would not approve a settlement upon easy terms. Secretary Stanton came to the meeting with a project for military occupation as a preliminary step toward the reorganization of the Southern states, Virginia and North Carolina to be combined in a single military district. Secretary Welles objected to this arrangement on the grounds that it would destroy the individuality of the separate states. The President sustained Welles's objection but did not completely repudiate Stanton's plan. Instead, he suggested that Stanton revise it so as to deal with Virginia and North Carolina separately, and that he provide copies of the revised plan for the members of the Cabinet at their next meeting.

Before the Cabinet meeting adjourned, Lincoln said he was glad that Congress was not in session. The House and the Senate, he was aware, had the unquestioned right to accept or reject new members from the Southern states; he himself had nothing to do with that. Still, he believed, the President had the power to recognize and deal with the state governments themselves. He could collect taxes in the South, see that the mails were delivered there, and appoint Federal officials (though his appointments would have to be confirmed, of course, by the Senate). He knew that the congressional Radicals did not agree with him, but they were not in session to make official objection, and he could act to establish and recognize the new state governments before Congress met in December. He did not intend to call a special session before that time, as he told the Speaker of the House, Schuyler Colfax, later on the day of that final Cabinet meeting, as he was leaving to go to Ford's Theater.

When, in December, 1865, the regular session of Congress finally began, Andrew Johnson had been President for nearly eight months. At first, in the days of terror following Lincoln's assassination, Johnson talked like a good Radical. He also acted like one when he ordered the arrest of Jefferson Davis and other Confederate leaders on the charge of complicity in the assassination. But Johnson and the Radicals soon disagreed on reconstruction. During the summer he succeeded in the restoration of state governments according to a plan which required them only to abolish slavery, retract their ordinances of secession, and repudiate their debts accumulated in the Confederate cause. In December the Radicals in Congress refused to seat the Senators and Representatives from these restored states. After checking Johnson's program, the Radicals proceeded to undo it, while impeaching the President. Eventually they carried through their own program of military occupation, similar to the one Stanton had proposed at the Cabinet meeting of April 14, and they undertook to transfer political power from the old master class to the freedmen, as Chase and other Radicals long had advocated.

Whether Lincoln, if he had lived, would have done as Johnson did, is hard to say. Certainly Lincoln would not have hounded Jefferson Davis or other Confederate officials (but, then, the presupposition here is that there would have been no assassination to seem to justify it). To his Cabinet in April he had indicated his hope that there would be no persecution, no bloody work, with respect to any of the late enemy. "None need expect he would take any part in hanging or killing those men, even the worst of them," Welles paraphrased him. "Frighten them out of the country, open the gates, let down the bars, scare them off, said he, throwing up his hands as if scaring sheep."

As for the restoration of state governments, it is impossible to guess confidently what Lincoln would have done or tried to do, since the very essence of his planning was to have no fixed and uniform plan, and since he appeared to be changing his mind on some points shortly before he died. In the states already being reconstructed under his program of December, 1863, he doubtless would have continued to support that program, as he did to the last. In other states he might have tried other expedients.

Whether, if Lincoln had lived and had proceeded along Johnson's lines, he would have succeeded any better than Johnson, is another "iffy" question, impossible to answer. It seems likely that, with his superior talent for political management, Lincoln would have avoided the worst of Johnson's clashes with Congress. Yet he could scarcely have escaped the conflict itself, unless he had conceded much more to the Radicals than Johnson did.

Another poser is the question whether Lincoln's approach to peace, if he had lived and had carried it through, would have advanced the Negro toward equal citizenship more surely than did the Radical program, which degenerated into a rather cynical use of the Negro for party advantage. One is entitled to believe that Lincoln's policy would have been better in the long run for Negroes as well as for Southern whites and for the nation as a whole.

David Donald

Why They
Impeached
Andrew Johnson

The story of Presidential Reconstruction begun by Randall and Current in the last essay is completed in this one by Professor David Donald of Johns Hopkins University. Lincoln's approach to restoring the Union was cautious, practical, thoughtful—humane in every sense of the word. Because of his assassination, however, the evaluation of his policy has to be a study in the might-have-beens of history. The Reconstruction policy of his successor, Andrew Johnson, superficially similar to Lincoln's, was reckless, impractical, emotional, and politically absurd. While historians have differed in evaluating his purposes, they have been in unanimous agreement that his management of the problem was inept and that his policy was a total failure.

Professor Donald's essay provides an extended character study of Johnson, and it is not an attractive portrait. Donald believes that Johnson "threw away a magnificent opportunity" to smooth and speed the return of the Confederate states to a harmonious place in the Union. But he also shows how difficult Johnson's task was and to how great an extent southern white opinion was set against the full acceptance of Negro equality. Donald, a former student of James G. Randall, is best known for his revision and expansion of Randall's The Civil War and Reconstruction, *and for his own Pulitzer Prize winning* Charles Sumner and the Coming of the Civil War, *the first part of a soon-to-be-completed biography of the Massachusetts senator.*

Reconstruction after the Civil War posed some of the most discouraging problems that have ever faced American statesmen. The South was prostrate. Its defeated soldiers straggled homeward through a countryside desolated by war. Southern soil was untilled and exhausted; southern factories and railroads were worn out. The four billion dollars of southern capital invested in Negro slaves was wiped out by advancing Union armies, "the most stupendous act of sequestration in the history of Anglo-American jurisprudence." The white inhabitants of eleven states had somehow to be reclaimed from rebellion and restored to a firm loyalty to the United States. Their four million former slaves had simultaneously to be guided into a proper use of their new-found freedom.

For the victorious Union government there was no time for reflection. Immediate decisions had to be made. Thousands of destitute whites and Negroes had to be fed before long-range plans of rebuilding the southern economy could be drafted. Some kind of government had to be established in these former Confederate states, to preserve order and to direct the work of restoration.

A score of intricate questions must be answered: Should the defeated southerners be punished or pardoned? How should genuinely loyal southern Unionists be rewarded? What was to be the social, economic, and political status of the now free Negroes? What civil rights did they have? Ought they to have the ballot? Should they be given a freehold of property? Was Reconstruction to be controlled by the national government, or should the southern states work out their own salvation? If the federal government supervised the process, should the President or the Congress be in control?

Intricate as were the problems, in early April, 1865, they did not seem insuperable. President Abraham Lincoln was winning the peace as he had already won the war. He was careful to keep every detail of Reconstruction in his own hands; unwilling to be committed to any "exclusive, and inflexible plan," he was working out a pragmatic program of restoration not, perhaps, entirely satisfactory to any group, but reasonably acceptable to all sections. With his enormous prestige as commander of the victorious North and as victor in the 1864 election, he was able to promise freedom to the Negro, charity to the southern white, security to the North.

The blighting of these auspicious beginnings is one of the saddest stories in American history. The reconciliation of the sections, which seemed so imminent in 1865, was delayed for more than ten years. Northern magnanimity toward a fallen foe curdled into bitter distrust. Southern whites rejected moderate leaders, and inveterate racists spoke for the new South. The Negro, after serving as a political pawn for a decade, was relegated to a second-class citizenship, from which he is yet struggling to emerge. Rarely has democratic government so completely failed as during the Reconstruction decade.

The responsibility for this collapse of American statesmanship is, of course, complex. History is not a tale of deep-dyed villains or pure-as-snow heroes. Part of the blame must fall upon ex-Confederates who refused to recognize that the war was over: part upon freedmen who confused liberty with license and the ballot box with the lunch pail; part upon northern antislavery extremists who identified patriotism with loyalty to the Republican party; part upon the land speculators, treasury grafters, and railroad promoters who were unwilling to have a genuine peace lest it end their looting of the public till.

Yet these divisive forces were not bound to triumph. Their success was due to the failure of constructive statesmanship that could channel the magnanimous feelings shared by most Americans into a positive program of reconstruction. President Andrew Johnson was called upon for positive leadership, and he did not meet the challenge.

Andrew Johnson's greatest weakness was his insensitivity to public opinion. In contrast to Lincoln, who said, ''Public opinion in this country is everything,'' Johnson made a career of battling the popular will. A poor white, a runaway tailor's apprentice, a self-educated Tennessee politician, Johnson was a living defiance to the dominant southern belief that leadership belonged to the plantation aristocracy.

As senator from Tennessee, he defied the sentiment of his section in 1861 and refused to join the secessionist movement. When Lincoln later appointed him military governor of occupied Tennessee, Johnson found Nashville ''a furnace of treason,'' but he braved social ostracism and threats of assassination and discharged his duties with boldness and efficiency.

Such a man was temperamentally unable to understand the northern mood in 1865, much less to yield to it. For four years the northern people had been whipped into wartime frenzy by propaganda tales of Confederate atrocities. The assassination of Lincoln by a southern sympathizer confirmed their belief in southern brutality and heartlessness. Few northerners felt vindictive toward the South, but most felt that the rebellion they had crushed must never rise again. Johnson ignored this postwar psychosis gripping the North and plunged ahead with his program of rapidly restoring the southern states to the Union. In May, 1865, without any previous preparation of public opinion, he issued a proclamation of amnesty, granting forgiveness to nearly all the millions of former rebels and welcoming them back into peaceful fraternity. Some few Confederate leaders were excluded from his general amnesty, but even they could secure pardon by special petition. For weeks the White House corridors were thronged with ex-Confederate statesmen and former southern generals who daily received presidential forgiveness.

Ignoring public opinion by pardoning the former Confederates, Johnson actually entrusted the formation of new governments in the South to them. The provisional governments established by the President proceeded, with a good deal of reluctance, to rescind their secession ordinances, to abolish slavery, and to repudiate the Confederate debt. Then, with far more enthusiasm, they turned to electing governors, representatives, and senators. By December, 1865, the southern states had their delegations in Washington waiting for admission by Congress. Alexander H. Stephens, once vice president of the Con-

A Harper's Weekly cartoon depicts Johnson (left) and Thaddeus Stevens as engineers committed to a collision course.

federacy, was chosen senator from Georgia; not one of the North Carolina delegation could take a loyalty oath; and all of South Carolina's congressmen had "either held office under the Confederate States, or been in the army, or countenanced in some way the Rebellion."

Johnson himself was appalled, "There seems in many of the elections something like defiance, which is all out of place at this time." Yet on December 5 he strongly urged the Congress to seat these southern representatives "and thereby complete the work of reconstruction." But the southern states were omitted from the roll call.

Such open defiance of northern opinion was dangerous under the best of circumstances, but in Johnson's case it was little more than suicidal. The President seemed not to realize the weakness of his position. He was the representative of no major interest and had no genuine political following. He had been considered for the vice presidency in 1864 because, as a southerner and a former slaveholder, he could lend plausibility to the Republican pretension that the old parties were dead and that Lincoln was the nominee of a new, nonsectional National Union party.

A political accident, the new Vice President did little to endear himself to his countrymen. At Lincoln's second inauguration Johnson appeared before the Senate in an obviously inebriated state and made a long, intemperate harangue about his plebeian origins and his hard-won success. President, Cabinet, and senators were humiliated by the shameful display, and Charles Sumner felt that "the Senate should call upon him to resign." Historians now know that Andrew Johnson was not a heavy drinker. At the time of his inaugural display, he was just recovering from a severe attack of typhoid fever. Feeling ill just before he entered the Senate chamber, he asked for some liquor to steady his nerves, and either his weakened condition or abnormal sensitivity to alcohol betrayed him.

Lincoln reassured Republicans who were worried over the affair: "I have known Andy for many years; he made a bad slip the other day, but you need not be scared. Andy ain't a drunkard." Never again was Andrew Johnson seen under the influence of alcohol, but his reformation came too late. His performance on March 4, 1865, seriously undermined his political usefulness and permitted his opponents to discredit him as a pothouse politician. Johnson was catapulted into the presidency by John Wilkes Booth's bullet. From the outset his position was weak, but it was not necessarily untenable. The President's chronic lack of discretion made it so. Where common sense dictated that a chief executive in so disadvantageous a position should act with great caution, Johnson proceeded to imitate Old Hickory, Andrew Jackson, his political idol. If Congress crossed his will, he did not hesitate to defy it. Was he not "the Tribune of the People"?

Sure of his rectitude, Johnson was indifferent to prudence. He never learned that the President of the United States cannot afford to be a quarreler. Apprenticed in the rough-and-tumble politics of frontier Tennessee, where orators exchanged violent personalities, crude humor, and bitter denunciations, Johnson continued to make stump speeches from the White House. All too often he spoke extemporaneously, and he permitted hecklers in his audience to draw from him angry charges against his critics.

On Washington's birthday in 1866, against the advice of his more sober advisers, the President made an impromptu address to justify his Reconstruction policy. "I fought traitors and treason in the South," he told the crowd; "now when I turn around, and at the other end of the line find men—I care not by what name you call them— who will stand opposed to the restoration of the Union of these States, I am free to say to you that I am still in the field."

During the "great applause" which followed, a nameless voice shouted, "Give us the names at the other end. . . . Who are they?"

"You ask me who they are," Johnson retorted. "I say Thaddeus Stevens of Pennsylvania is one; I say Mr. Sumner is another; and Wendell Phillips is another." Applause urged him to continue. "Are those who want to destroy our institutions . . . not satisfied with the blood that has been shed? . . . Does not the blood of Lincoln appease the vengeance and wrath of the opponents of this government?"

The President's remarks were as untrue as they were impolitic. Not only was it manifestly false to assert that the leading Republican in the House and the most conspicuous Republican in the Senate were opposed to "the fundamental principles of this government" or that they had been responsible for Lincoln's assassination; it was incredible political folly to impute such actions to men with whom the President had to work daily. But Andrew Johnson never learned that the President of the United States must function as a party leader.

There was a temperamental coldness about this plain-featured, grave man that kept him from easy, intimate relations with even his political supporters. His massive head, dark, luxuriant hair, deep-set and piercing eyes, and cleft square chin seemed to Charles Dickens to indicate "courage, watchfulness, and certainly strength of purpose," but his was a grim face, with "no genial sunlight in it." The coldness and reserve that marked Johnson's public associations doubtless stemmed from a deep-seated feeling of insecurity; this self-educated tailor whose wife had taught him how to write could never expose himself by letting down his guard and relaxing.

Johnson knew none of the arts of managing men, and he seemed unaware that face-saving is important for a politician. When he became President, Johnson was besieged by advisers of all political complexions. To each he listened gravely and non-committally, raising no questions and by his silence seeming to give consent. With Radical Senator Sumner, already intent upon giving the freedmen both homesteads and the ballot, he had repeated interviews during the first month of his presidency. "His manner has been excellent, & even sympathetic," Sumner reported triumphantly. With Chief Justice Salmon P. Chase, Sumner urged Johnson to support immediate Negro suffrage and found the President was "well-disposed, & sees the rights & necessities of the case." In the middle of May, 1865, Sumner reassured a Republican caucus that the President was a true Radical; he had listened repeatedly to the Senator and had told him "there is no difference between us." Before the end of the month the rug was pulled from under Sumner's feet. Johnson issued his proclamation for the reconstruction of North Carolina, making no provisions for Negro suffrage. Sumner first learned about it through the newspapers.

While he was making up his mind, Johnson appeared silently receptive to all ideas; when he had made a decision, his mind was immovably closed, and he defended his course with all the obstinacy of a weak man. In December, alarmed by Johnson's Reconstruction proclamations, Sumner again sought an interview with the President. "No longer sympathetic, or even kindly," Sumner found, "he was harsh, petulant, and unreasonable." The Senator was depressed by Johnson's "prejudice, ignorance, and perversity" on the Negro suffrage issue. Far from listening amiably to Sumner's argument that the South was still torn by violence and not yet ready for readmission, Johnson attacked him with cheap analogies. "Are there no murders in Massachusetts?" the President asked.

"Unhappily yes," Sumner replied, "sometimes."

"Are there no assaults in Boston? Do not men there sometimes knock each other down, so that the police is obliged to interfere?"

"Unhappily yes."

"Would you consent that Massachusetts, on this account, should be excluded from Congress?" Johnson triumphantly queried. In the excitement the President unconsciously used Sumner's hat, which the Senator had placed on the floor beside his chair, as a spittoon!

Had Johnson been as resolute in action as he was in argument, he might conceivably have carried much of his party with him on his Reconstruction program. Promptness, publicity, and persuasion could have created a presidential following. Instead Johnson boggled. Though he talked boastfully of "kicking out" officers who failed to support his plan, he was slow to act. His own Cabinet, from the very beginning, contained members who disagreed with him, and his secretary of war, Edwin M. Stanton, was openly in league with the Republican elements most hostile to the President. For more than two years he impotently hoped that Stanton would resign; then in 1867, after Congress had passed the Tenure of Office Act, he tried to oust the Secretary. This belated firmness, against the letter of the law, led directly to Johnson's impeachment trial.

Instead of working with his party leaders and building up political support among Republicans, Johnson in 1866 undertook to organize his friends into a new party. In August a convention of white southerners, northern Democrats, moderate Republicans, and presidential appointees assembled in Philadelphia to endorse Johnson's policy. Union General Darius Couch of Massachusetts marched arm in arm down the convention aisle with Governor James L. Orr of South Carolina, to symbolize the states reunited under Johnson's rule. The convention produced fervid oratory, a dignified statement of principles —but not much else. Like most third-party reformist movements it lacked local support and grass-roots organization.

Johnson himself was unable to breathe life into his stillborn third party. Deciding to take his case to the people, he accepted an invitation to speak at a great Chicago memorial honoring Stephen A. Douglas. When his special train left Washington on August 28 for a "swing around the circle," the President was accompanied by a few Cabinet members who shared his views and by the war heroes Grant and Farragut.

At first all went well. There were some calculated political snubs to the President, but he managed at Philadelphia, New York, and Albany to present his ideas soberly and cogently to the people. But Johnson's friends were worried lest his tongue again get out of control. "In all frankness," a senator wrote him, do not "allow the excitement of the moment to draw from you any *extemporaneous speeches.*"

At St. Louis, when a Radical voice shouted that Johnson was a "Judas," the President flamed up in rage. "There was a Judas and he was one of the twelve apostles," he retorted. ". . . The twelve apostles had a Christ. . . . If I have played the Judas, who has been my Christ that I have played the Judas with? Was it Thad Stevens? Was it Wendell Phillips? Was it Charles Sumner?" Over mingled hisses and applause, he shouted, "These are the men that stop and compare themselves with the Saviour; and everybody that differs with them . . . is to be denounced as a Judas."

Johnson had played into his enemies' hands. His Radical foes denounced him as a "trickster," a "culprit," a man "touched with insanity, corrupted with lust, stimulated with drink." More serious in consequence was the reaction of northern moderates, such as James Russell Lowell, who wrote, "What an anti-Johnson lecturer we have in Johnson! Sumner has been right about the *cuss* from the first. . . ."

The fall elections were an overwhelming repudiation of the President and his Reconstruction policy.

Johnson's want of political sagacity strengthened the very elements in the Republican party which he most feared. In 1865 the Republicans had no clearly defined attitude toward Reconstruction. Moderates like Gideon Welles and Orville Browning wanted to see the southern states restored with a minimum of restrictions; Radicals like Sumner and Stevens demanded that the entire southern social system be revolutionized. Some Republicans were passionately concerned with the plight of the freedmen; others were more interested in maintaining the high tariff and land grant legislation enacted during the war. Many thought mostly of keeping themselves in office, and many genuinely believed, with Sumner, that "the Republican party, in its objects, is identical with country and with mankind." These diverse elements came slowly to adopt the idea of harsh Reconstruction, but Johnson's stubborn persistency in his policy left them no alternative. Every step the President took seemed to provide "a new encouragement to (1) the rebels at the South, (2) the Democrats at the North and (3) the discontented elements everywhere." Not many Republicans would agree with Sumner that Johnson's program was "a defiance to God and Truth," but there was genuine concern that the victory won by the war was being frittered away.

The provisional governments established by the President in the South seemed to be dubiously loyal. They were reluctant to rescind their secession ordinances and to repudiate the Confederate debt, and they chose high-ranking ex-Confederates to represent them in Congress. Northerners were even more alarmed when these southern governments began to legislate upon the Negro's civil rights. Some laws were necessary—in order to give former slaves the right to marry, to hold property, to sue and be sued, and the like—but the Johnson legislatures went far beyond these immediate needs. South Carolina, for example, enacted that no Negro could pursue the trade "of an artisan, mechanic, or shopkeeper, or any other trade or employment besides that of husbandry" without a special license. Alabama provided that "any stubborn or refractory servants" or "servants who loiter away their time" should be fined $50 and, if they could not pay, be hired out for six months' labor. Mississippi ordered that every Negro under eighteen years of age who was an orphan or not supported by his parents must be apprenticed to some white person, preferably the former owner of the slave. Such southern laws indicated a determination to keep the Negro in a state of peonage.

It was impossible to expect a newly emancipated race to be content with such a limping freedom. The thousands of Negroes who had served in the Union armies and had helped conquer their former Confederate masters were not willing to abandon their new-found liberty. In rural areas southern whites kept these Negroes under control through the Ku Klux Klan. But in southern cities white hegemony was less secure, and racial friction erupted in mob violence. In May, 1866, a quarrel between a Memphis Negro and a white teamster led to a riot in which the

JOHNSON'S LOVE FOR THE SOLDIER.

Black Soldier—Massa, I come for my Bounty of $300, under the bill signed by President Johnson.

Johnson Paymaster, All right, my brave man, here is your money.

White Soldier—I come for the EXTRA bounty of $100 which Congress voted to me.

Johnson Paymaster, I am very sorry, but the President says the brave black troops must be paid first.

This cartoon is an example of the virulence of the attacks on Johnson by his enemies.

city police and the poor whites raided the Negro quarters and burned and killed promiscuously. Far more serious was the disturbance in New Orleans two months later. The Republican party in Louisiana was split into pro-Johnson conservatives and Negro suffrage advocates. The latter group determined to hold a constitutional convention, of dubious legality, in New Orleans, in order to secure the ballot for the freedmen and the offices for themselves. Through imbecility in the War Department, the Federal troops occupying the city were left without orders, and the mayor of New Orleans, strongly opposed to Negro equality, had the responsibility for preserving order. There were acts of provocation on both sides, and finally, on July 30, a procession of Negroes marching toward the convention hall was attacked.

"A shot was fired . . . by a policeman, or some colored man in the procession," General Philip Sheridan reported. "This led to other shots, and a rush after the procession. On arrival at the front of the Institute [where the convention met], there was some throwing of brick-bats by both sides. The police . . . were vigorously marched to the scene of disorder. The procession entered the Institute with the flag, about six or eight remaining outside. A row occurred between a policeman and one of these colored men, and a shot was again fired by one of the parties, which led to an indiscriminate firing on the building, through the windows, by the policemen.

"This had been going on for a short time, when a white flag was displayed from the windows of the Institute, whereupon the firing ceased and the police rushed into the building. . . . The policemen opened an indiscriminate fire upon the audience until they had emptied their revolvers, when they retired, and those inside barricaded the doors. The door was broken in, and the firing again commenced when many of the colored and white people either escaped out of the door, or were passed out by the policemen inside, but as they came out, the policemen who formed the circle nearest the building fired upon them, and they were again fired upon by the citizens that formed the outer circle.''

Thirty-seven Negroes and three of their white friends were killed; 119 Negroes and seventeen of their white sympathizers were wounded. Of their assailants, ten were wounded and but one killed. President Johnson was, of course, horrified by these outbreaks, but the Memphis and New Orleans riots, together with the Black Codes, afforded a devastating illustration of how the President's policy actually operated. The southern states, it was clear, were not going to protect the Negroes' basic rights. They were only grudgingly going to accept the results of the war. Yet, with Johnson's blessing, these same states were expecting a stronger voice in Congress than ever. Before 1860, southern representation in Congress had been based upon the white population plus three fifths of the slaves; now the Negroes, though not permitted to vote, were to be counted like all other citizens, and southern states would be entitled to at least nine additional congressmen. Joining with the northern Copperheads, the southerners could easily regain at the next presidential election all that had been lost on the Civil War battlefield.

It was this political exigency, not misguided sentimentality nor vindictiveness, which united Republicans in opposition to the President.

Johnson's defenders have pictured Radical Reconstruction as the work of a fanatical minority, led by Sumner and Stevens, who drove their reluctant colleagues into adopting coercive measures against the South. In fact, every major piece of Radical legislation was adopted by the nearly unanimous vote of the entire Republican membership of Congress. Andrew Johnson had left them no other choice. Because he insisted upon rushing Confederate-dominated states back into the Union, Republicans moved to disqualify Confederate leaders under the Fourteenth Amendment. When, through Johnson's urging, the southern states rejected that amendment, the Republicans in Congress unwillingly came to see Negro suffrage as the only counterweight against Democratic majorities in the South. With the Reconstruction Acts of 1867 the way was open for a true Radical program toward the South, harsh and thorough.

Andrew Johnson became a cipher in the White House, futilely disapproving bills which were promptly passed over his veto. Through his failure to reckon with public opinion, his unwillingness to recognize his weak position, his inability to functon as a party leader, he had sacrificed all influence with the party which had elected him and had turned over its control to Radicals vindictively opposed to his policies. In March, 1868, Andrew Johnson was summoned before the Senate of the United States to be tried on eleven accusations of high crimes and misdemeanors. By a narrow margin the Senate failed to convict him, and historians have dismissed the charges as flimsy and false. Yet perhaps before the bar of history itself Andrew Johnson must be impeached with an even graver charge—that through political ineptitude he threw away a magnificent opportunity.

Alan F. Westin

Ride-in:
A Century of
Protest Begins

The last quarter of the nineteenth century—after the federal government relaxed its pressure on the southern states to deal fairly with their black citizens—has been called "the nadir" of the history of the Negro in America after emancipation. Some historians argue that the low point came somewhat later, during the early twentieth century, but few would disagree with the thesis that the period in question was indeed disastrous for American blacks. Although never really treated decently (in the North as well as in the South), Negroes had made important gains during Reconstruction; the Fourteenth and Fifteenth Amendments "guaranteed" their political and civil rights, and Congress passed stiff laws protecting these rights, including the Civil Rights Act of 1875, which outlawed discrimination in places of public accommodation.

After the so-called Compromise of 1877, however, these gains were gradually stripped away by a combination of southern pressure, northern indifference, and a series of crippling legal interpretations by the Supreme Court. In this essay Professor Alan F. Westin of Columbia University, an expert on constitutional history, describes one of the first and most significant of the Supreme Court decisions of the era, one which emasculated the Civil Rights Act of 1875. His story reads in some ways like an account of the civil rights struggles of the 1950's and 1960's, but with the terrible difference that freedom and justice were in this instance the losers, not the winners of the fight.

*I*t began one day early in January when a Negro named Robert Fox stepped aboard a streetcar in Louisville, Kentucky, dropped his coin into the fare box, and sat down in the white section of the car. Ordered to move, he refused, and the driver threw him off the car. Shortly after, Fox filed a charge of assault and battery against the streetcar company in the federal district court, claiming that separate seating policies were illegal and the driver's actions were therefore improper. The district judge instructed the jury that under federal law common carriers must serve all passengers equally without regard to race. So instructed, the jury found the company rules to be invalid and awarded damages of fifteen dollars (plus $72.80 in legal costs) to Mr. Fox.

Immediately there was sharp criticism of the Fox decision from the city and state administrations, both Democratic; the company defied the court's ruling and continued segregated seating. After several meetings with local federal officials and white attorneys co-operating with them, Louisville Negro leaders decided to launch a full-scale "ride-in." At 7 P.M. on May 12, a young Negro boy boarded a streetcar near the Willard Hotel, walked past the driver, and took a seat among the white passengers. The driver, under new company regulations, did not attempt to throw him off but simply stopped the car, lit a cigar, and refused to proceed until the Negro moved to "his place." While the governor, the Louisville chief of police, and other prominent citizens looked on from the sidewalks, a large crowd which included an increasingly noisy mob of jeering white teen-agers gathered around the streetcar.

Before long, there were shouts of "Put him out!" "Hit him!" "Kick him!" "Hang him!" Several white youths climbed into the car and began yelling insults in the face of the young Negro rider. He refused to answer—or to move. The youths dragged him from his seat, pulled him off the car, and began to beat him. Only when the Negro started to defend himself did the city police intervene: they arrested him for disturbing the peace and took him to jail.

This time the trial was held in Louisville city court, not the federal court. The magistrate ruled that streetcar companies were not under any obligation to treat Negroes exactly as they treated whites, and that any federal measures purporting to create such obligations would be "clearly invalid" under the constitutions of Kentucky and the United States. The defendant was fined, and the judge delivered a warning to Louisville Negroes that further ride-ins would be punished.

But the ride-in campaign was not halted that easily. In the following days, streetcar after streetcar was entered by Negroes who took seats in the white section. Now the drivers got off the cars entirely. On several occasions, the Negro riders drove the cars themselves, to the sound of cheers from Negro spectators. Then violence erupted. Bands of white youths and men began to throw Negro riders off the cars; windows were broken, cars were overturned, and for a time a general race riot threatened. Moderate Kentucky newspapers and many community leaders deplored the fighting; the Republican candidate for governor denounced the streetcar company's segregation policies and blamed the violence on Democratic encouragement of white extremists.

By this time, newspapers across the country were carrying reports of the conflict, and many editorials denounced the seating regulations. In Louisville, federal marshals and the United States attorney backed the rights of the Negro riders and stated that federal court action would be taken if necessary. There were even rumors that the President might send troops.

Under these threats, the streetcar company capitulated. Soon, all the city transit companies declared that "it was useless to try to resist or evade the enforcement by the United States authorities of the claim of Negroes to ride in the cars." To "avoid serious collisions," the company would thereafter allow all passengers to sit where they chose. Although a few disturbances took place in the following months, and some white intransigents boycotted the streetcars, mixed seating became a common practice. The Kentucky press soon pointed with pride to the spirit of conciliation and harmony which prevailed in travel facilities within the city, calling it a model for good race relations. Never again would Louisville streetcars be segregated.

The event may have a familiar ring, but it should not, for it occurred almost one hundred years ago, in 1871. The streetcars were horse-drawn. The President who considered ordering troops to Louisville was ex-General Grant, not ex-General Eisenhower. The Republican gubernatorial candidate who supported the Negro riders, John Marshall Harlan, was not a post-World War II leader of the G.O.P. but a former slaveholder from one of Kentucky's oldest and most famous political families. And the "new" Negroes who waged this ride-in were not members of the Congress of Racial Equality and the National Association for the Advancement of Colored People, or followers of Dr. Martin Luther King, but former slaves who were fighting for civil rights in their own time, and with widespread success.

And yet these dramatic sit-ins, ride-ins, and walk-ins of the 1870's are almost unknown to the American public today. The standard American histories do not mention them, providing only thumbnail references to "bayonet-enforced" racial contacts during Reconstruction. Most commentators view the Negro's resort to direct action as an invention of the last decade. Clearly, then, it is time that the civil-rights struggle of the 1870's and 1880's was rescued from newspaper files and court archives, not only because it is historically important but also because it has compelling relevance for our own era.

Contrary to common assumptions today, no state in the Union during the 1870's, including those south of the Mason-Dixon line, required separation of whites and Negroes in places of public accommodation. Admission and arrangement policies were up to individual owners. In the North and West, many theatres, hotels, restaurants, and public carriers served Negro patrons without hesitation or discrimination. Some accepted Negroes only in second-class accommodations, such as smoking cars on railroads or balconies in theatres, where they sat among whites who did not have first-class tickets. Other northern and

An 1875 Harper's Weekly *cartoon bore the caption, "Shall We Withdraw Our Troops?"*

western establishments, especially the more exclusive ones, refused Negro patronage entirely.

The situation was similar in the large cities of the southern and border states. Many establishments admitted Negroes to second-class facilities. Some gave first-class service to those of privileged social status—government officials, army officers, newspapermen, and clergymen. On the other hand, many places of public accommodation, particularly in the rural areas and smaller cities of the South, were closed to Negroes whatever their wealth or status.

From 1865 through the early 1880's, the general trend in the nation was toward wider acceptance of Negro patronage. The federal Civil Rights Act of 1866, with its guarantee to Negroes of "equal benefit of the laws," had set off a flurry of enforcement suits—for denying berths to Negroes on a Washington-New York train; for refusing to sell theatre tickets to Negroes in Boston; and for barring Negro women from the waiting rooms and parlor cars of railroads in Virginia, Illinois, and California. Ratification of the Fourteenth Amendment in 1868 had spurred more challenges. Three northern states, and two southern states under Reconstruction regimes, passed laws making it a crime for owners of public-accommodation businesses to discriminate. Most state and federal court rulings on these laws between 1865 and 1880 held in favor of Negro rights, and the rulings built up a steady pressure on owners to relax racial bars.

Nevertheless, instances of exclusion and segregation continued throughout the 1870's. To settle the issue once and for all (thereby

RIDE-IN: A CENTURY OF PROTEST BEGINS

Cartoonist Thomas Nast mocked the provision of the Civil Rights Act of 1875 that allowed Negroes to collect $500 from those who barred them from places of public accommodation.

reaping the lasting appreciation of the Negro voters), congressional Republicans led by Senator Charles Sumner pressed for a federal statute making discrimination in public accommodations a crime. Democrats and conservative Republicans warned in the congressional debates that such a law would trespass on the reserved powers of the states and reminded the Sumner supporters that recent Supreme Court decisions had taken a narrow view of federal power under the Civil War amendments.

After a series of legislative compromises, however, Sumner's forces were able to enact the statute; on March 1, 1875, "An Act to Protect all Citizens in their Civil and Legal Rights" went into effect. "It is essential to just government," the preamble stated, that the nation "recognize the equality of all men before the law, and . . . it is the duty of government in its dealings with the people to mete out equal and exact justice to all, of whatever nativity, race, color, or persuasion, religious or political . . ."

Section 1 of the act declared that "All persons within the jurisdiction of the United States shall be entitled to the full and equal enjoyment of the accommodations . . . of inns, public conveyances on land or water, theaters and other places of public amusement; subject only to the conditions and limitations established by law, and applicable alike to citizens of every race or color. . . ." Section 2 provided that any person violating the act could be sued in federal district court for a penalty of $500, could be fined $500 to $1,000, or could be imprisoned from thirty days to one year. (A separate section forbade racial discrimination in the selection of juries.)

Reaction to the law was swift. Two Negro men were admitted to the dress circle of Macauley's Theatre in Louisville and sat through the performance without incident. In Washington, Negroes were served for the first time at the bar of the Willard Hotel, and a Negro broke the color line when he was seated at McVicker's Theatre in Chicago. But in other instances, Negroes were rejected despite "Sumner's law." Several hotels in Chattanooga turned in their licenses, became private boardinghouses, and accepted whites only. Restaurants and barber shops in Richmond turned away Negro customers.

Suits challenging refusals were filed en masse throughout the country. Perhaps a hundred were decided in the federal district courts during the late 1870's and early 1880's. Federal judges in Pennsylvania, Texas, Maryland, and Kentucky, among others, held the law to be constitutional and ruled in favor of Negro complainants. In North Carolina, New Jersey, and California, however, district judges held the law invalid. And when other courts in New York, Tennessee, Missouri, and Kansas put the issue to the federal circuit judges, the judges divided on the question, and the matter was certified to the United States Supreme Court.

But the Supreme Court did not exactly rush to make its ruling. Though two cases testing the 1875 act reached it in 1876 and a third in 1877, the Justices simply held them on their docket. In 1879, the Attorney General filed a brief defending the constitutionality of the law, but still the Court reached no decisions. In 1880, three additional cases were filed, but two years elapsed before the Solicitor General presented a fresh brief supporting the statute. It was not until late in 1883 that the Supreme Court passed upon the 1875 act, in what became famous as the *Civil Rights Cases* ruling. True, the Court was badly behind in its work in this period, but clearly the Justices chose to let the civil-rights cases "ripen" for almost eight years.

When they finally came to grips with the issue, six separate test suits were involved. The most celebrated had arisen in New York City in November of 1879. Edwin Booth, the famous tragedian and brother of John Wilkes Booth, had opened a special Thanksgiving week engagement at the Grand Opera House. After playing *Hamlet, Othello*, and *Richelieu* to packed houses, he was scheduled to perform Victor Hugo's *Ruy Blas* at the Saturday matinee on November 22.

One person who had decided to see Booth that Saturday was William R. Davis, Jr., who was later described in the press as a tall, handsome, and well-spoken Negro of twenty-six. He was the business agent of the *Progressive-American,* a Negro weekly published in New York City. At 10 o'clock Saturday morning, Davis' girl friend ("a bright octoroon, almost white," as the press put it), purchased two reserved seats at the box office of the Grand Opera House. At 1:30 P.M., Davis and his lady presented themselves at the theatre, only to be told by the doorkeeper, Samuel Singleton, that "these tickets are no good." If he would step out to the box office, Singleton told Davis, his money would be refunded.

It is unlikely that Davis was surprised by Singleton's action, for this was not the first time he had encountered such difficulties. Shortly after the passage of the 1875 act, Davis had been refused a ticket to the dress circle of Booth's Theatre in New York. He had sworn out a

In this cartoon Leslie's Weekly *praised theatres that flaunted the 1875 law and refused to sell Negroes tickets.*

warrant against the ticket seller, but the failure of his witnesses to appear at the grand jury proceedings had led to a dismissal of the complaint. This earlier episode, as well as Davis' activity as a Negro journalist, made it probable that this appearance at the Opera House in 1879 was a deliberate test of the management's discriminatory policies.

Though Davis walked out of the lobby at Singleton's request, he did not turn in his tickets for a refund. Instead, he summoned a young white boy standing near the theatre, gave him a dollar (plus a dime for his trouble), and had him purchase two more tickets. When Davis and his companion presented these to Singleton, only the lady was allowed to pass. Again Davis was told that his ticket was "no good." When he now refused to move out of the doorway, Singleton called a policeman and asked that Davis be escorted off the theatre property. The officer told Davis that the Messrs. Poole and Donnelly, the managers of the Opera House, did not admit colored persons. "Perhaps the managers do not," Davis retorted, "but the laws of the country [do]."

The following Monday, November 24, Davis filed a criminal complaint; on December 9, this time with witnesses in abundance, Singleton was indicted in what the press described as the first criminal proceeding under the 1875 act to go to trial in New York. When the case opened on January 14, 1880, Singleton's counsel argued that the 1875 law was unconstitutional. "It interferes," he said, "with the right of the State of New York to provide the means under which citizens of the State have the power to control and protect their rights in respect to their private property." The assistant United States attorney replied that such a conception of states' rights had been "exploded and superseded long ago." It was unthinkable, he declared, that "the United States could not extend to one citizen of

New York a right which the State itself gave to others of its citizens—the right of admission to places of public amusement."

The presiding judge decided to take the constitutional challenge under advisement and referred it to the circuit court, for consideration at its February term. This left the decision up to Justice Samuel Blatchford of the Supreme Court, who was assigned to the circuit court for New York, and District Judge William Choate. The two judges reached opposite conclusions and certified the question to the United States Supreme Court.

Davis' case, under the title of *United States v. Singleton,* reached the Supreme Court in 1880. Already lodged on the Court's docket were four similar criminal prosecutions under the act of 1875. *U.S. v. Stanley* involved the refusal of Murray Stanley in 1875 to serve a meal at his hotel in Topeka, Kansas, to a Negro, Bird Gee. *U.S. v. Nichols* presented the refusal in 1876 of Samuel Nichols, owner of the Nichols House in Jefferson City, Missouri, to accept a Negro named W. H. R. Agee as a guest. *U.S. v. Ryan* involved the conduct of Michael Ryan, doorkeeper of Maguire's Theatre in San Francisco, in denying a Negro named George M. Tyler entry to the dress circle on January 4, 1876. In *U.S. v. Hamilton,* James Hamilton, a conductor on the Nashville, Chattanooga, and St. Louis Railroad, had on April 21, 1879, denied a Negro woman with a first-class ticket access to the ladies' car.

There was a fifth case, with a somewhat different setting. On the evening of May 22, 1879, Mrs. Sallie J. Robinson, a twenty-eight-year-old Negro, purchased two first-class tickets at Grand Junction, Tennessee, for a trip to Lynchburg, Virginia, on the Memphis and Charleston Railroad. Shortly after midnight she and her nephew, Joseph C. Robinson, described as a young Negro "of light complexion, light hair, and light blue eyes," boarded the train and started into the parlor car. The conductor, C. W. Reagin, held Mrs. Robinson back ("bruising her arm and jerking her roughly around," she alleged) and pushed her into the smoker.

A few minutes later, when Joseph informed the conductor that he was Mrs. Robinson's nephew and was a Negro, the conductor looked surprised. In that case, he said, they could go into the parlor car at the next stop. The Robinsons finished the ride in the parlor car but filed complaints with the railroad about their treatment and then sued for $500 under the 1875 act. At the trial, Reagin testified that he had thought Joseph to be a white man with a colored woman, and his experience was that such associations were "for illicit purposes."

Counsel for the Robinsons objected to Reagin's testimony, on the ground that his actions were based on race and constituted no defense. Admitting the constitutionality of the 1875 law for purposes of the trial, the railroad contended that the action of its conductor did not fall within the statute. The district judge ruled that the motive for excluding persons was the decisive issue under the act: if the jury believed that the conductor had acted because he thought Mrs. Robinson "a prostitute travelling with her paramour," whether "well or ill-founded" in that assumption, the exclusion was not because of race and the railroad was not liable. The jury found for the railroad, and the Robinsons appealed.

These, with William Davis' suit against the doorkeeper of New York's Grand Opera House, were the six cases to which the Supreme Court finally turned in 1882. The Justices were presented with a learned and eloquent brief for the United States submitted by Solicitor General Samuel F. Phillips, who reviewed the leading cases, described the history of the Civil War amendments to the Constitution, and stressed the importance to the rights of citizens of equal access to public accommodation. Four times since 1865, Phillips noted, civil-rights legislation had been enacted by a Congress filled with men who had fought in the Civil War and had written the war amendments. These men understood that "every rootlet of slavery has an individual vitality, and, to its minutest hair, should be anxiously followed and plucked up. . . ." They also knew that if the federal government allowed Negroes to be denied accommodation "by persons who notably were sensitive registers of local public opinion," then "what upon yesterday was only 'fact' will become 'doctrine' tomorrow."

The Supreme Court Justices who considered Phillips' brief and the six test cases were uncommonly talented, among them being Chief Justice Morrison R. Waite, a man underrated today; Joseph P. Bradley, that Court's most powerful intellect; and Stephen J. Field, a *laissez-faire* interpreter of American constitutional law. John Marshall Harlan, the youngest man on the Court, had already started on the course which was to mark him as the most frequent and passionate dissenter in the Gilded Age.

As a whole, the Court might have appeared to be one which would have looked favorably on the 1875 act. All were Republicans except Justice Field, and he was a Democrat appointed by Abraham Lincoln. All except Justice Harlan, who was the Court's only southerner, had made their careers primarily in the northern and western states. Without exception, all had supported the Northern cause in the war, and none had any hostility toward Negroes as a class.

Yet on the afternoon of October 15, 1883, Justice Bradley announced that the Court found Sections 1 and 2 of the Civil Rights Act of 1875 to be unconstitutional. (This disposed of five of the cases; the sixth, *U.S. v. Hamilton*, was denied review on a procedural point.) There was added irony in the fact that Bradley delivered the majority opinion for eight of the Justices. A one-time Whig, Bradley had struggled for a North-South compromise in the darkening months of 1860–61, then had swung to a strong Unionist position after the firing on Fort Sumter. He had run for Congress on the Lincoln ticket in 1862 and in 1868 headed the New Jersey electors for Grant. When the Thirteenth and Fourteenth Amendments were adopted, he had given them firm support, and his appointment to the Supreme Court by Grant in 1870 had drawn no criticism from friends of the Negro, as had the appointment of John Marshall Harlan seven years later.

Bradley's opinion had a tightly reasoned simplicity. The Thirteenth Amendment forbade slavery and involuntary servitude, he noted, but protection against the restoration of bondage could not be stretched to cover federal regulation of ''social'' discriminations such as those dealt with in the 1875 statute. As for the Fourteenth Amendment, that was addressed only to deprivations of rights by the *states;* it did not encompass *private* acts of discrimination. Thus there was no source of constitutional authority for ''Sumner's law''; it had to be regarded as an unwarranted invasion of an area under state jurisdiction. Even as a matter of policy, Bradley argued, the intention of the war amendments to aid the newly freed Negro had to have some limits. At some point, the Negro must cease to be ''the special favorite of the law'' and take on ''the rank of a mere citizen.''

At the Atlanta Opera House on the evening of the Court's decision, the end man of Haverly's Minstrels interrupted the performance to announce the ruling. The entire orchestra and dress circle audience rose and cheered. Negroes sitting in the balcony kept their seats, ''stunned,'' according to one newspaper account. A short time earlier, a Negro denied entrance to the dress circle had filed charges against the Opera House management under the 1875 act. Now his case—their case—was dead.

Of all the nine Justices, only John Marshall Harlan, a Kentuckian and a former slaveholder, announced that he dissented from the

Justice John Marshall Harlan wrote the dissenting opinion on the Civil Rights Cases.

ruling. He promised to give a full opinion soon.

Justice Harlan's progress from a supporter of slavery to a civil-rights dissenter makes a fascinating chronicle. Like Bradley, he had entered politics as a Whig and had tried to find a middle road between secessionist Democrats and antislavery Republicans. Like Bradley, he became a Unionist after the firing on Fort Sumter. But there the parallels ended. Although Harlan entered the Union Army, he was totally opposed to freeing the slaves, and his distaste for Lincoln and the Radicals was complete. Between 1863 and 1868, he led the Conservative party in Kentucky, a third-party movement which supported the war but opposed pro-Negro and civil-rights measures as "flagrant invasions of property rights and local government."

By 1868, however, Harlan had become a Republican. The resounding defeat of the Conservatives in the 1867 state elections convinced him that a third party had no future in Kentucky. His antimonopoly views and his general ideas about economic progress conflicted directly with state Democratic policies, and when the Republicans nominated his former field commander, Ulysses S. Grant, for President, in 1868, Harlan was one of the substantial number of Conservatives who joined the G.O.P.

His views on Negro rights also changed at this time. The wave of vigilante activities against white Republicans and Negroes that swept Kentucky in 1868–70, with whippings and murders by the scores, convinced Harlan that federal guarantees were essential. He watched Negroes in Kentucky moving with dignity and skill toward useful citizenship, and his devout Presbyterianism led him to adopt a "brotherhood-of-man" outlook in keeping with his church's national position. Perhaps he may have been influenced by his wife, Mallie, whose parents were New England abolitionists. As a realistic Republican politician, he was also aware that 60,000 Kentucky Negroes would become voters in 1870.

Thus a "new" John Harlan took the stump as Republican gubernatorial candidate in 1871, the year of the Louisville streetcar ride-ins. He opened his rallies by confessing that he had formerly been anti-Negro. But "I have lived long enough," he said, "to feel that the most perfect despotism that ever existed on this earth was the institution of African slavery." The war amendments were necessary "to place it beyond the power of any State to interfere with . . . the results of the war. . . ." The South should stop agitating the race issue, and should turn to rebuilding itself on progressive lines. When the Democrats laughed at "Harlan the Chameleon" and read quotations from his earlier anti-Negro speeches, Harlan replied: "Let it be said that I am right rather than consistent."

Harlan soon became an influential figure in the Republican party and, when President Rutherford B. Hayes decided to appoint a southern Republican to the Supreme Court in 1877, he was a logical choice. Even then, the Negro issue rose to shake Harlan's life again. His confirmation was held up because of doubts by some senators as to his "real" civil-rights views. Only after Harlan produced his speeches between 1871 and 1877 and party leaders supported his firmness on the question was he approved.

Once on the Supreme Court, Harlan could have swung back to a conservative position on civil rights. Instead, he became one of his generation's most intense and uncompromising defenders of the Negro. Perhaps his was the psychology of the convert who defends his new faith more passionately, even more combatively, than the born believer. Harlan liked to think that he had changed because he knew the South and realized that any relaxation of federal protection of the rights of Negroes would encourage the "white irreconcilables" first to acts of discrimination and then to violence, which would destroy all hope of accommodation between the races.

When Harlan sat down in October of 1883 to write his dissent in the *Civil Rights Cases,* he hoped to set off a cannon of protest. But he simply could not get his thoughts on paper. He worked late into the night, and even rose from half-sleep to write down ideas that he was afraid would elude him in the morning. "It was a trying time for him," his wife observed. "In point of years, he was much the youngest man on the Bench; and standing alone, as he did in regard to a decision which the whole nation was anxiously awaiting, he felt that . . . he must speak not only forcibly but wisely." After weeks of drafting and discarding, Harlan seemed to reach a dead end. The dissent would not "write." It was at this point that Mrs. Harlan contributed a dramatic touch to the history of the *Civil Rights Cases.*

When the Harlans had moved to Washington in 1877, the Justice had acquired from a collector the inkstand which Chief Justice Roger Taney had used in writing all his opinions. Harlan was fond of showing this to guests and remarking that "it was the very inkstand from which the infamous *Dred Scott* opinion was written." Early in the 1880's, however, a niece of Taney's, who was engaged in collecting her uncle's effects, visited the Harlans. When she saw the inkstand she asked Harlan for it, and the Justice agreed. The next morning Mrs. Harlan, noting her husband's reluctance to part with his most prized possession, quietly arranged to have the inkstand "lost." She hid it away, and Harlan was forced to make an embarrassed excuse to Taney's niece.

Now, on a Sunday morning, probably early in November of 1883, after Harlan had spent a sleepless night working on his dissent, Mallie Harlan remembered the inkstand. While the Justice was at church, she retrieved it from its hiding place, filled it with a fresh supply of ink and pen points, and placed it on the blotter of his desk. When her husband returned from church, she told him, with an air of mystery, that he would find something special in his study. Harlan was overjoyed to recover his symbolic antique. Mrs. Harlan's gesture was successful, for as she relates:

The memory of the historic part that Taney's inkstand had played in the Dred Scott decision, in temporarily tightening the shackles of slavery upon the negro race in those ante-bellum days, seemed, that morning, to act like magic in clarifying my husband's thoughts in regard to the law . . . intended by Sumner to protect the recently emancipated slaves in the enjoyment of equal 'civil rights.' His pen fairly flew on that day and, with the running start he then got, he soon finished his dissent.

How directly the recollection of Dred Scott pervaded Harlan's dissent is apparent to anyone who reads the opinion. He began by noting that the pre-Civil War Supreme Court had upheld congressional laws forbidding individuals to interfere with recovery of fugitive slaves. To strike down the act of 1875 meant that "the rights of freedom and American citizenship cannot receive from the Nation that efficient protection which heretofore was unhesitatingly accorded to slavery and the rights of masters."

Harlan argued that the Civil Rights Act of 1875 was constitutional on any one of several grounds. The Thirteenth Amendment had already been held to guarantee "universal civil freedom"; Harlan stated that barring Negroes from facilities licensed by the state and under legal obligation to serve all persons without discrimination restored a major disability of slavery days and violated that civil freedom. As for the Fourteenth Amendment, its central purpose had been to extend national citizenship to the Negro, reversing the precedent upheld in the Dred Scott decision; its final section gave Congress power to pass appropriate legislation to enforce that affirmative grant as well as to enforce the section barring any state action which might deny liberty or equality. Now, the Supreme Court was deciding what legislation was appropriate and necessary for those purposes, although that decision properly belonged to Congress.

Even under the "State action" clause of the Fourteenth Amendment, Harlan continued, the 1875 act was constitutional; it was well established that "railroad corporations, keepers of inns and managers of places of public accommodation are agents or instrumentalities of the State." Finally, Harlan attacked the unwillingness of the Court's majority to uphold the public-carrier section of the act under Congress' power to regulate interstate trips. That was exactly what was involved in Mrs. Robinson's case against the Memphis and Charleston Railroad, he reminded his colleagues; it had not been true before that Congress had had to cite the section of the Constitution on which it relied.

In his peroration, Harlan replied to Bradley's comment that Negroes had been made "a special favorite of the law." The war amendments had been passed not to "favor" the Negro, he declared, but to include him as "part of the people for whose welfare and happiness government is ordained."

Today, it is the colored race which is denied, by corporations and individuals wielding public authority, rights fundamental in their freedom and citizenship. At some future time, it may be that some other race will fall under the ban of race discrimination. If the constitutional amendments be enforced, according to the intent with which, as I conceive, they were adopted, there cannot be in this republic, any class of human beings in practical subjection to another class. . . .

The *Civil Rights Cases* ruling did two things. First, it destroyed the delicate balance of federal guarantee, Negro protest, and private enlightenment which was producing a steadily widening area of peacefully integrated public facilities in the North and South during the 1870's and early 1880's. Second, it had an immediate and profound effect on national and state politics as they related to the Negro. By denying Congress power to protect the Negro's rights to equal treatment, the Supreme Court wiped the issue of civil rights from the Republican party's agenda of national responsibility. At the same time, those southern political leaders who saw anti-Negro politics as the most promising avenue to power could now rally the "poor whites" to the banner of segregation.

If the Supreme Court had stopped with the *Civil Rights Cases* of 1883, the situation of Negroes would have been bad but not impossible. Even in the South, there was no immediate imposition of segregation in public facilities. During the late 1880's, Negroes could be found sharing places with whites in many southern restaurants, streetcars, and theatres. But increasingly, Democratic and Populist politicians found the Negro an irresistible target. As Solicitor General Phillips had warned the Supreme Court, what had been tolerated as the "fact" of discrimination was now being translated into "doctrine": between 1887 and 1891, eight southern states passed laws requiring railroads to separate all white and Negro passengers. The Supreme Court upheld these laws in the 1896 case of *Plessy v. Ferguson.* Then in the Berea College case of 1906, it upheld laws forbidding private schools to educate Negro and white children together. Both decisions aroused Harlan's bitter dissent. In the next fifteen or twenty years, the chalk line of Jim Crow was drawn across virtually every area of public contact in the South.

Today, as this line is slowly and painfully being erased, we may do well to reflect on what might have been in the South if the Civil Rights Act of 1875 had been upheld, in whole or in part. Perhaps everything would have been the same. Perhaps forces at work between 1883 and 1940 were too powerful for a Supreme Court to hold in check. Perhaps "Sumner's law" was greatly premature. Yet it is difficult to believe that total, state-enforced segregation was inevitable in the South after the 1880's. If in these decades the Supreme Court had taken the same *laissez-faire* attitude toward race relations as it took toward economic affairs, voluntary integration would have survived as a countertradition to Jim Crow and might have made the transition of the 1950's less painful than it was. At the very least, one cannot help thinking that Harlan was a better sociologist than his colleagues and a better southerner than the "irreconcilables." American constitutional history has a richer ring to it because of the protest that John Marshall Harlan finally put down on paper from Roger Taney's inkwell in 1883.

C. Vann Woodward

Plessy v. Ferguson

The process of eroding the constitutional gains of Negroes begun by the Civil Rights Cases of 1883 was carried a long step forward in 1896 in the case of Plessy v. Ferguson. This decision, which froze school segregation on the nation for more than half a century, roused little notice at the time, despite Justice John Marshall Harlan's famous dissent, in which he reminded the nation that the Constitution was "color-blind."

The story of the case that led to the 1896 decision is told here by Professor C. Vann Woodward of Yale University. Woodward has done more than any other contemporary historian to throw light on the history of the South and of the Negro during the late nineteenth and early twentieth centuries. His Strange Career of Jim Crow called attention to the fact that complete segregation was a relatively late development in America, not a permanent part of southern civilization. His Reunion and Reaction, a history of the Compromise of 1877 ending Reconstruction, and his Origins of the New South, a general history of the period between 1877 and World War I, are standard works.

*I*n the spring of 1885, Charles Dudley Warner, Mark Twain's friend, neighbor, and his onetime collaborator from Hartford, Connecticut, visited the International Exposition held in New Orleans. He was astonished to find that "white and colored people mingled freely, talking and looking at what was of common interest," that Negroes "took their full share of the parade and the honors," and that the two races associated "in unconscious equality of privileges." During his visit he saw "a colored clergyman in his surplice seated in the chancel of the most important white Episcopal church in New Orleans, assisting in the service."

It was a common occurrence in the 1880's for foreign travellers and northern visitors to comment, sometimes with distaste and always with surprise, on the freedom of association between white and colored people in the South. Yankees in particular were unprepared for what they found and sometimes estimated that conditions below the Potomac were better than those above. There was discrimination, to be sure, and Negroes were often excluded from first-class public accommodations— as they were in the North. But that was done on the responsibility of private owners or managers and not by requirement of law. According to the Supreme Court's decision in the Civil Rights Cases of 1883 the federal law gave no protection from such private acts.

Where discrimination existed it was often erratic and inconsistent. On trains the usual practice was to exclude Negroes from first-class or "ladies'" cars but to permit them to mix with whites in second-class or "smoking" cars. In the old seaboard states of the South, however, Negroes were as free to ride first class as whites. In no state was segregation on trains complete, and in none was it enforced by law. The age of Jim Crow was still to come.

The first genuine Jim Crow law requiring railroads to carry Negroes in separate cars or behind partitions was adopted by Florida in 1887. Mississippi followed this example in 1888; Texas in 1889; Louisiana in 1890; Alabama, Arkansas, Georgia, and Tennessee in 1891; and Kentucky in 1892. The Carolinas and Virginia did not fall into line until the last three years of the century.

Negroes watched with despair while the legal foundations for the Jim Crow system were laid and the walls of segregation mounted around them. Their disenchantment with the hopes based on the Civil War amendments and the Reconstruction laws was nearly complete by 1890. The American commitment to equality, solemnly attested by three amendments to the Constitution and by elaborate civil rights acts, was virtually repudiated. The "compromise of 1877" between the Hayes Republicans and the southern conservatives had resulted in the withdrawal of federal troops from the South and the formal end of Reconstruction. What had started then as a retreat had within a decade turned into a rout. Northern radicals and liberals had abandoned the cause: the courts had rendered the Constitution helpless; the Republican party had forsaken the cause it had sponsored. A tide of racism was mounting in the country unopposed.

The colored community of New Orleans, with its strong infusion of

French and other nationalities, was in a strategic position to furnish leadership for the resistance against segregation. Many of these people had culture, education, and some wealth, as well as a heritage of several generations of freedom. Unlike the great majority of Negroes, they were city people with an established professional class and a high degree of literacy. By ancestry as well as by residence they were associated with Latin cultures at variance with Anglo-American ideas of race relations. Their forebears had lived under the Code Noir decreed for Louisiana by Louis XIV, and their city faced out upon Latin America.

When the Jim Crow car bill was introduced in the Louisiana legislature, New Orleans Negroes organized to fight it. Negroes were still voting in large numbers, and there were sixteen colored senators and representatives in the Louisiana General Assembly. On May 24, 1890, that body received "A Protest of the American Citizens' Equal Rights Association of Louisiana Against Class Legislation." An organization of colored people, the association protested that the pending bill was "unconstitutional, unamerican, unjust, dangerous and against sound public policy." It would, declared the protest, "be a free license to the evilly-disposed that they might with impunity insult, humiliate, and otherwise maltreat inoffensive persons, and especially women and children who should happen to have a dark skin."

On July 10, 1890, the Assembly passed the bill, the governor signed it, and it became law. Entitled "An Act to promote the comfort of passengers," the new law required railroads "to provide equal but separate accommodations for the white and colored races." Two members of the Equal Rights Association, L. A. Martinet, editor of the New Orleans *Crusader,* and R. L. Desdunes, placed heavy blame on the sixteen colored members of the Assembly for the passage of the bill. According to Martinet, "they were completely the masters of the situation." They had but to withhold their support for a bill desired by the powerful Louisiana Lottery Company until the Jim Crow bill was killed. "But in an evil moment," he added, "our Representatives turned their ears to listen to the golden siren," and "did so for a 'consideration.' "

Putting aside recriminations, the *Crusader* declared: "The Bill is now a law. The next thing is what are we going to do?" The editor spoke testily of boycotting the railroads, but concluded that "the next thing is . . . to begin to gather funds to test the constitutionality of this law. We'll make a case, a test case, and bring it before the Federal Courts." On September 1, 1891, a group of eighteen men of color formed a "Citizens' Committee to Test the Constitutionality of the Separate Car Law."

Money came in slowly at first, but by October 11, Martinet could write that the committee had already collected $1,500 and that more could be expected "after we have the case well started." Even before the money was collected, Martinet had opened a correspondence about the case with Albion Winegar Tourgée of Mayville, New York, and on October 10 the Citizens' Committee formally elected Tourgée "leading

In 1832 a minstrel named "Daddy"
Rice introduced "Jim Crow" as a symbol
in a blackface act ("Weel a-bout and turn
a-bout/And . . . jump Jim Crow") based
on the antics of a slave of that name.

counsel in the case, from beginning to end, with power to choose associates."

This action called back into the stream of history a name prominent
in the annals of Reconstruction. Albion Tourgée was in 1890 probably
the most famous surviving carpetbagger. His fame was due not so
much to his achievements as a carpetbagger in North Carolina, significant though they were, as to the six novels about his Reconstruction
experiences that he had published since 1879. Born in Ohio, of French
Huguenot descent, he had served as an officer in the Union Army,
and moved to Greensboro, North Carolina, in 1865 to practice law.
He soon became a leader of the Radical Republican party, took a
prominent part in writing the Radical Constitution of North Carolina,
and served as a judge of the superior court for six years with considerable distinction. He brought to the fight against segregation in
Louisiana a combination of zeal and ability that the Citizens' Committee of New Orleans would have found it hard to duplicate. They had
reason to write him, "we know we have a friend in you & we know
your ability is beyond question." He was informed that the committee's decision was made "spontaneously, warmly, & gratefully."

Tourgée's first suggestion was that the person chosen for defendant
in the test case be "nearly white," but that proposal raised some doubts.
"It would be quite difficult," explained Martinet, "to have a lady
too nearly white refused admission to a 'white' car." He pointed out
that "people of tolerably fair complexion, even if unmistakably
colored, enjoy here a large degree of immunity from the accursed
prejudice. . . . To make this case would require some tact." He would
volunteer himself, "but I am one of those whom a fair complexion
favors. I go everywhere, in all public places, though well-known all
over the city, & never is anything said to me. On the cars it would be

New Yorker Albion Tourgée—
carpetbagger, novelist, lawyer,
and self-appointed warrior
against racial discrimination.

the same thing. In fact, color prejudice, in this respect does not affect me. But, as I have said, we can try it, with another.''

Railroad officials proved surprisingly co-operative. The first one approached, however, confessed that his road ''did not enforce the law.'' It provided the Jim Crow car and posted the required sign, but told its conductors to molest no one who ignored instructions. Officers of two other roads ''said the law was a bad and mean one; they would like to get rid of it,'' and asked for time to consult counsel. ''They want to help us,'' said Martinet, ''but dread public opinion.'' The extra expense of separate cars was one reason for railroad opposition to the Jim Crow law.

It was finally agreed that a white passenger should object to the presence of a Negro in a ''white'' coach, that the conductor should direct the colored passenger to go to the Jim Crow car, and that he should refuse to go. ''The conductor will be instructed not to use force or molest,'' reported Martinet, ''& *our* white passenger will swear out the affidavit. This will give us our *habeas corpus* case, I hope.'' On the appointed day, February 24, 1892, Daniel F. Desdunes, a young colored man, bought a ticket for Mobile, boarded the Louisville & Nashville Railroad, and took a seat in the white coach.

All went according to plan. Desdunes was committed for trial to the Criminal District Court in New Orleans and released on bail. On March 21, James C. Walker, a local attorney associated with Tourgée in the case, filed a plea protesting that his client was not guilty and attacking the constitutionality of the Jim Crow law. He wrote Tourgée that he intended to go to trial as early as he could.

Between the lawyers there was not entire agreement on procedure. Walker favored the plea that the law was void because it attempted to regulate interstate commerce, over which the Supreme Court held that

Congress had exclusive jurisdiction. Tourgée was doubtful. "What we want," he wrote Walker, "is not a verdict of not guilty, nor a defect in this law but a decision whether such a law can be legally enacted and enforced in any state and we should get everything off the track and out of the way for such a decision." Walker confessed that "it's hard for me to give up my pet hobby that the law is void as a regulation of interstate commerce," and Tourgée admitted that he "may have spoken too lightly of the interstate commerce matter."

The discussion was ended abruptly and the whole approach altered before Desdunes' case came to trial by a decision of the Louisiana Supreme Court handed down on May 25. In this case, which was of entirely independent origin, the court reversed the ruling of a lower court and upheld the Pullman Company's plea that the Jim Crow law was unconstitutional in so far as it applied to interstate passengers.

Desdunes was an interstate passenger holding a ticket to Alabama, but the decision was a rather empty victory. The law still applied to intrastate passengers, and since all states adjacent to Louisiana had by this time adopted similar or identical Jim Crow laws, the exemption of interstate passengers was of no great importance to the Negroes of Louisiana, and it left the principle against which they contended unchallenged. On June 1, Martinet wired Tourgée on behalf of the committee, saying that "Walker wants new case wholly within state limits," and asking Tourgée's opinion. Tourgée wired his agreement.

One week later, on June 7, Homer Adolph Plessy bought a ticket in New Orleans, boarded the East Louisiana Railroad bound for Covington, a destination "wholly within the state limits," and took a seat in the white coach. Since Plessy later described himself as "seven-eighths Caucasian and one-eighth African blood," and swore that "the admixture of colored blood is not discernible," it may be assumed that the railroad had been told of the plan and had agreed to co-operate. When Plessy refused to comply with the conductor's request that he move to the Jim Crow car, he was arrested by Detective Christopher C. Cain "and quietly accompanied the officer." The New Orleans Times-Democrat remarked that "It is generally believed that Plessy intends testing the law before the courts."

In due course Homer Plessy's case became Plessy v. Ferguson. The latter name belonged to John H. Ferguson, Judge of Section A of the Criminal District Court for the Parish of New Orleans, who overruled the plea of Tourgée and Walker, the defendant's counsel, that the Jim Crow law was null and void because it was in conflict with the Constitution of the United States. Plessy then applied to the State Supreme Court for a writ of prohibition and certiorari and was given a hearing in November, 1892. The court recognized that neither the interstate commerce clause nor the question of equality of accommodations was involved and held that "the sole question" was whether a law requiring "separate but equal accommodations" violated the Fourteenth Amendment. Citing numerous decisions of lower federal courts to the effect that accommodations did not have to be identical to be equal, the court as expected upheld the law.

"We have been at pains to expound this statute," added the court, "because the dissatisfaction felt with it by a portion of the people seems to us so unreasonable that we can account for it only on the ground of some misconception."

Chief Justice Francis Redding Tillou Nicholls, heading the court that handed down this decision in 1892, had signed the Jim Crow act as governor when it was passed in 1890. Previously he had served as the "Redeemer" governor who took over Louisiana from the carpet-baggers in 1877 and inaugurated a brief regime of conservative paternalism. In those days Nicholls had denounced race bigotry, appointed Negroes to office, and attracted many of them to his party.

L. A. Martinet wrote Tourgée that Nicholls in those years had been "fair & just to colored men" and had, in fact, "secured a degree of protection to the colored people not enjoyed under Republican Governors." But in November, 1892, the wave of Populist rebellion among the white farmers was reaching its crest in the South, and Judge Nicholls' change of course typified the concessions to racism that conservatives of his class made in their efforts to forestall or divert the rebellion. Nonetheless, at a further hearing Nicholls granted Plessy's petition for a writ of error that permitted him to seek redress before the Supreme Court of the United States.

The brief that Albion Tourgée submitted to the Supreme Court in behalf of Plessy breathed a spirit of equalitarianism that was more in tune with his carpetbagger days than with the prevailing spirit of the mid-nineties. At the very outset, he advanced an argument in behalf of his client that unconsciously illustrated the paradox that had from the start haunted the American attempt to reconcile strong color prejudice with deep equalitarian commitments.

Plessy, he contended, had been deprived of property without due process of law. The "property" in question was the "reputation of being white." It was "the most valuable sort of property, being the master-key that unlocks the golden door of opportunity." Intense race prejudice excluded any man suspected of having Negro blood "from the friendship and companionship of the white man," and therefore from the avenues to wealth, prestige, and opportunity. "Probably most white persons if given the choice," he held, "would prefer death to life in the United States as *colored persons.*"

Since Tourgée had proposed that a person who was "nearly white" be selected for the test case, it may be presumed that he did so with this argument in mind. But this was not a defense of the colored man against discrimination by whites, but a defense of the "nearly" white man against the penalties of color. The argument, whatever its merits, apparently did not impress the Court.

Tourgée went on to develop more relevant points. He emphasized especially the incompatibility of the segregation law with the spirit and intent of the Thirteenth and particularly the Fourteenth amendments. Segregation perpetuated distinctions "of a servile character, coincident with the institution of slavery." He held that "slavery was a caste, a legal condition of subjection to the dominant class, a bondage quite separable from the incident of ownership." He scorned the pretense of impartiality and equal protection advanced in the defense of the "separate but equal" doctrine.

"The object of such a law," he declared, "is simply to debase and distinguish against the inferior race. Its purpose has been properly interpreted by the general designation of 'Jim Crow Car' law. Its object is to separate the Negroes from the whites in public conveyances for the gratification and recognition of the sentiment of white superiority and white supremacy of right and power." He asked the members of the Court to imagine the tables turned and themselves ordered into a Jim Crow car. "What humiliation, what rage would then fill the judicial mind!" he exclaimed.

The clue to the true intent of the Louisiana statute was that it did not apply "to nurses attending the children of the other race." On this clause Tourgée shrewdly observed:

The exemption of nurses shows that the real evil lies not in the color of the skin but in the relation the colored person sustains to the white. If he is a dependent it may be endured: if he is not, his presence is insufferable. Instead of being intended to promote the *general* comfort and moral well-being, this act is plainly and evidently intended to promote the happiness of one class by asserting its supremacy and the inferiority of another class. Justice is pictured blind and her daughter, the Law, ought at least to be color-blind.

Tourgée then asked the Court to look to the future. Should the separate-car law be upheld, he inquired, "what is to prevent the application of the same principle to other relations?" Was there any limit to such laws? "Why not require all colored people to walk on one side of the street and whites on the other? . . . One side of the street may be just as good as the other. . . . The question is not as to the *equality* of the privileges enjoyed, but *the right of the State to label one citizen as white and another as colored* in the common enjoyment of a public highway."

The Supreme Court did not get around to handing down a decision on *Plessy v. Ferguson* until 1896. In the years that intervened between the passage of the Louisiana segregation law in July, 1890, and the time of the eventual decision on its constitutionality in 1896, the retreat from the commitment to equality had quickened its pace in the South and met with additional acquiescence, encouragement, and approval in the North. Two states had already disfranchised the Negro, and several others, including Louisiana, were planning to take the same course. In 1892 Congress defeated the Lodge Bill, designed to extend federal protection to elections, and in 1894 it wiped from the federal statute books a mass of Reconstruction laws for the protection of equal rights. And then, on September 18, 1895, Booker T. Washington delivered a famous speech embodying the so-called "Atlanta Compromise," which was widely interpreted as an acceptance of subordinate status for the Negro by the foremost leader of the race.

*Justice Henry B. Brown
delivered the majority opinion
in* Plessy v. Ferguson.

On May 18, 1896, Justice Henry Billings Brown, a resident of Michigan but a native of Massachusetts, delivered the opinion of the Court in the case of *Plessy v. Ferguson*. His views upholding the defendant's case—that the "separate but equal" doctrine was constitutional—were in accord with those of all his brothers, with the possible exception of Justice David Josiah Brewer, who did not participate, and the certain exception of Justice John Marshall Harlan, who vigorously dissented in phrases that often echoed Tourgée's arguments. In approving, to all intents and purposes, the principle of segregation, Justice Brown followed not only the trend of the times, but a host of state judicial precedents, which he cited at length. That there were no federal judicial precedents to the contrary only added to the technical strength of his position. Just as telling, perhaps, was Brown's mention of the action of Congress in establishing segregated schools for the District of Columbia, an action endorsed by Radical Republicans who had supported the Fourteenth Amendment, and sustained in regular congressional appropriations ever since.

Similar laws, wrote Brown, were adopted by "the legislatures of many states, and have been generally, if not uniformly, sustained by the courts." The validity of such segregation laws, he maintained, depended on their "reasonableness." And in determining reasonableness, the legislature "is at liberty to act with reference to the established usages, customs, and traditions of the people, and with a view to the promotion of their comfort, and the preservation of the public peace and good order."

In addition to judicial precedent and accepted practice, Justice Brown ventured into the more uncertain fields of sociology and psychology for support of his opinion. He wrote:

> We consider the underlying fallacy of the plaintiff's argument to consist in the assumption that the enforced separation of the two races stamps the colored race with a badge of inferiority. If this be so, it is not by reason of anything found in the act, but solely because the colored race chooses to put that construction upon it. . . . The argument also assumes that social prejudices may be overcome by legislation, and that equal rights cannot be secured by the negro except by an enforced commingling of the two races. We cannot accept this proposition. . . . Legislation is powerless to eradicate racial instincts, or to abolish distinctions based upon physical differences, and the attempt to do so can only result in accentuating the difficulties of the present situation. If the civil and political rights of both races be equal, one cannot be inferior to the other civilly or politically. If one race be inferior to the other socially, the constitution of the United States cannot put them upon the same plane.

One of the most fascinating paradoxes in American jurisprudence is that the opinion of a native son of Massachusetts, Brown, should have bridged the gap betweeen the radical equalitarian commitment of 1868 and the reactionary repudiation of that commitment in 1896; and that Harlan, a southerner, should have bridged the greater gap between the repudiation of 1896 and the radical rededication to the equalitarian idealism of 1868 in 1954. For the dissenting opinion of Justice Harlan, embodying many of the arguments of Plessy's ex-carpetbagger counsel, foreshadowed the Court's eventual repudiation of the *Plessy v. Ferguson* decision and the doctrine of "separate but equal" more than half a century later.

The elder John Marshall Harlan is correctly described by Robert Cushman as "a Southern gentleman and a slave-holder, and at heart a conservative." A Kentuckian of the Whig persuasion, Harlan had opposed secession and fought in the Union Army, but at the same time he opposed both the emancipation of the slaves and the passage of civil rights laws to protect the rights of the freedmen. Shocked by Ku Klux excesses, he experienced a sudden conversion, renounced his former views, became a Republican in 1868, and was appointed to the Supreme Court by President Hayes in 1877.

After his conversion Harlan became one of the most outspoken champions of Negro rights of his time, and during his thirty-four years on the bench he lifted his voice repeatedly against denial of those rights by the dominant opinion of the Court. His famous dissent in the Civil Rights Cases of 1883 had denounced the "subtle and ingenious verbal criticism" by which "the substance and spirit of the recent amendments of the Constitution have been sacrificed." And in 1896 he was ready to strike another blow for his adopted cause.

Harlan held the Louisiana segregation law in clear conflict with both the Thirteenth and the Fourteenth amendments. The former "not only struck down the institution of slavery," but also "any

burdens or disabilities that constitute badges of slavery or servitude,''
and segregation was just such a burden or badge. Moreover, the
Fourteenth Amendment ''added greatly to the dignity and glory of
American citizenship, and to the security of personal liberty,'' and
segregation denied to Negroes the equal protection of both dignity
and liberty. ''The arbitrary separation of citizens, on the basis of race,
while they are on a public highway,'' he said, ''is a badge of servitude
wholly inconsistent with the civil freedom and the equality before the
law established by the constitution. It cannot be justified upon any
legal grounds.''

Harlan was as scornful as Tourgée had been of the claim that the
separate-car law did not discriminate against the Negro. ''Everyone
knows,'' he declared, that its purpose was ''to exclude colored people
from coaches occupied by or assigned to white persons.'' This was
simply a poorly disguised means of asserting the supremacy of one
class of citizens over another. The Justice continued:

> But in view of the constitution, in the eye of the law, there is
> in this country no superior, dominant, ruling class of citizens.
> There is no caste here. Our constitution is color-blind, and
> neither knows nor tolerates classes among citizens. In respect
> of civil rights, all citizens are equal before the law. The hum-
> blest is the peer of the most powerful. The law regards man
> as man, and takes no account of his surroundings, or of his
> color when his civil rights as guarantied by the supreme law of
> the land are involved. . . . We boast of the freedom enjoyed
> by our people above all other peoples. But it is difficult to recon-
> cile that boast with a state of law which, practically, puts the
> brand of servitude and degradation upon a large class of our
> fellow citizens,—our equals before the law. The thin disguise
> of ''equal'' accommodations for passengers in railroad coaches
> will not mislead any one, nor atone for the wrong this day done.

''The present decision, it may well be apprehended,'' predicted
Harlan, ''will not only stimulate aggressions, more or less brutal and
irritating, upon the admitted rights of colored citizens, but will encourage the belief that it is possible, by means of state enactments,
to defeat the beneficent purposes which the people of the United States
had in view when they adopted the recent amendments of the constitution. . . .'' For if the state may so regulate the railroads, ''why
may it not so regulate the use of the streets of its cities and towns
as to compel white citizens to keep on one side of a street, and black
citizens to keep on the other,'' or, for that matter, apply the same
regulations to streetcars and other vehicles, or to courtroom, the jury
box, the legislative hall, or to any other place of public assembly?

''In my opinion,'' the Kentuckian concluded, ''the judgment this
day rendered will, in time, prove to be quite as pernicious as the
decision made by this tribunal in the Dred Scott Case.''

But Harlan was without allies on the Court, and the country as a
whole received the news of its momentous decision upholding the

"separate but equal" doctrine in relative silence and apparent indifference. Thirteen years earlier the Civil Rights Cases had precipitated pages of news reports, hundreds of editorials, indignant rallies, congressional bills, a Senate report, and much general debate. In striking contrast, the *Plessy* decision was accorded only short, inconspicuous news reports and virtually no editorial comment outside the Negro press. A great change had taken place, and the Court evidently now gave voice to the dominant mood of the country. Justice Harlan had spoken for the forgotten convictions of a bygone era.

The racial aggressions he foresaw came in a flood after the decision of 1896. Even Harlan indicated by his opinion of 1899 in *Cummings v. Board of Education* that he saw nothing unconstitutional in segregated public schools. Virginia was the last state in the South to adopt the separate-car law, and she resisted it only until 1900. Up to that year this was the only law of the type adopted by a majority of the southern states. But on January 12, 1900, the editor of the Richmond *Times* was in full accord with the new spirit when he asserted: "It is necessary that this principle be applied in every relation of Southern life. God Almighty drew the color line and it cannot be obliterated. The negro must stay on his side of the line and the white man must stay on his side, and the sooner both races recognize this fact and accept it, the better it will be for both."

With a thoroughness approaching the incredible, the color line *was* drawn and the Jim Crow principle was applied even in those areas that Tourgée and Harlan had suggested a few years before as absurd extremes. In sustaining all these new laws, courts universally and confidently cited *Plessy v. Ferguson* as their authority. They continued to do so for more than half a century.

On April 4, 1950, Justice Robert H. Jackson wrote old friends in Jamestown, New York, of his surprise in running across the name of Albion W. Tourgée, once a resident of the nearby village of Mayville, in connection with segregation decisions then pending before the Supreme Court. "The *Plessy* case arose in Louisiana," he wrote, "and how Tourgée got into it I have not learned. In any event, I have gone to his old brief, filed here, and there is no argument made today that he would not make to the Court. He says, 'Justice is pictured blind and her daughter, the Law, ought at least to be color-blind.' Whether this was original with him, it has been gotten off a number of times since as original wit. Tourgée's brief was filed April 6, 1896 and now, just fifty-four years after, the question is again being argued whether his position will be adopted and what was a defeat for him in '96 be a post-mortem victory."

Plessy v. Ferguson remained the law of the land for fifty-eight years lacking one day, from May 18, 1896, to May 17, 1954, when the Supreme Court at last renounced it in the school segregation cases of *Brown* et al. *v. Board of Education of Topeka,* et al. In that decision could indeed be found, at long last, a vindication, "a post-mortem victory"—not only for the ex-carpetbagger Tourgée, but for the ex-slaveholder Harlan as well.

Walter Lord

Mississippi: The Past That Has Not Died

The situation that southern Negroes and their white supporters had to contend with after the Civil War, a situation that had much to do with the frustration of President Johnson's policies and which helped to produce the Supreme Court decisions in the Civil Rights Cases and in Plessy v. Ferguson, *is described in the following essay by Walter Lord.*

This is a case study—a very useful historical approach that seeks, by examining one part of a subject, to throw light on the whole. The main advantages of the case study method are that it concentrates on a more easily mastered body of materials and permits the use of details and examples that in a broader treatment would have to be sacrificed to avoid excessive length. The disadvantages lie chiefly in the inevitable loss of perspective, and in the not always correct assumption that the case chosen is entirely typical. The effect is like looking at a distant landscape through a telescope or at a piece of tissue under a microscope. Elements that would be lost to the "normal" view are brought sharply into focus, but the image of the total object is lost or distorted.

Lord's essay on Mississippi after the Civil War is a fine example of the intelligent use of the case study. His selection of Mississippi, home of the most intransigent foes of Negro equality but also a region where blacks exercised considerable power during Reconstruction, produces undoubtedly a heightening effect that is somewhat at variance with the whole truth, but it brings out very clearly all the problems of the postwar South and the "solutions" found for them in the late nineteenth century. Mr. Lord is best known for his "you are there" style of history, first developed in his popular book, A Night to Remember, *the story of the sinking of the liner* Titanic. *However, he makes relatively little use of that technique in this essay, thus demonstrating that he is a sound analytical historian as well as a graphic storyteller.*

*S*plinters flew in every direction as the northern troops hacked apart the chairs and tables of Edward McGehee, one of the wealthiest cotton planters in Wilkinson County, Mississippi. It was October 5, 1864, and Colonel E. D. Osband's men were simply acting on the philosophy expressed by General Sherman when he told a group of protesting Mississippians, "It is our duty to destroy,. not build up; therefore do not look to us to help you."

Soon the work was done, the house in flames, and Edward McGehee left contemplating his only remaining possession—a gracefully carved grand piano. It was no comfort to Mr. McGehee, once the owner of hundreds of Negro slaves, that these deeds were done by a company of stern, efficient Negro soldiers.

Ruin upon ruin, the destruction continued for six more gruelling months of war. By the end, Mississippi seemed but a forest of chimneys. The whole town of Okolona could be bought for $5,000. There was not a fence left within miles of Corinth, not a clock running in Natchez. The capital, Jackson, was in ashes—the Confederate Hotel as complete a wreck as the cause it honored.

The first visitors from the North were stunned. Approaching old Charles Langworthy's home near Aberdeen, a man from Chicago recalled spending two pleasant weeks there back in 1855. Greeting the owner, the visitor quickly asked after Mr. Langworthy's five boys and two girls.

"Where is John, your oldest son?"

"Killed at Shiloh."

"Where is William?"

"Died of smallpox in the Army."

"And the other boys?"

"All were killed. . . ."

The Langworthy daughters came forward, dripping with mourning. Not only were their brothers gone; both also had lost their husbands in the service.

The incident was all too typical. Mississippi had sent 78,000 into the fight; only 28,000 came back. Whole companies were wiped out— the Vicksburg Cadets marched off 123 strong; only six returned. One legacy of this sacrifice was 10,000 orphans.

Nor were those who returned always able to play their full part. Surgery was not one of the happier aspects of the Civil War. Empty sleeves flapped everywhere. At a town meeting in Aberdeen a visitor noticed that one hundred of the three hundred men present had lost either an arm or a leg. It is not surprising that in the first year after the war Mississippi spent one fifth of its entire revenue for artificial limbs.

Painfully, the people of the state struggled to live again. Nearly everyone was wiped out. The greatest source of wealth—436,000 slaves worth over 218 million dollars—had vanished with Emancipation. The farm animals that meant so much to a rural people had been carried off—one out of every three mules gone. Most of the cotton was confiscated as Confederate property; any that escaped was mercilessly

*D. H. Euyett painted this water color of
the ruins of Jackson, Mississippi, in 1863,
shortly after Sherman took the state's capital.*

taxed by Washington. Land values crashed—on December 13, 1865,
alone, the Vicksburg *Herald* advertised forty-eight plantations for
sale or lease. After five years of war Mississippi tumbled from the
nation's fifth state in per capital wealth to the very bottom of the list.

"My children, I am a ruined man," Thomas Dabney told his
daughters one evening in November, 1866. In happier days Mr. Dabney had endorsed some notes. At the time there seemed little danger—
the risk was good and Dabney was the wealthy owner of Burleigh,
a fabulous plantation near the town of Raymond. But now times had
changed, and the sheriff was downstairs.

Ultimately, Burleigh was auctioned off, and Dabney managed to
buy it back only by consigning his cotton crop for years to come.
Meanwhile, the family had nothing—even the "loyal" Negro servants
had vanished. As the once pampered Dabney girls faced the novel
prospect of housework, it looked like a major victory for General
Sherman's perhaps apocryphal boast that he would force every southern woman to the washtub.

But this time the General had met his match. "He shall never
bring my daughters to the washtub," Dabney thundered. "I'll do
the washing myself!" And he did. Dabney was now seventy years
old, but for the next two years he scrubbed away, grimly satisfied that
here at least he was foiling the hated Yankee.

There were other consolations too, as the people of Mississippi
struggled to recover. There was relief that the war was over—whatever
their original feelings, most Mississippians were heartily sick of
destruction. There was also hope that the state could get back into
the Union rather painlessly; President Andrew Johnson had decided
to carry on Lincoln's lenient plans for restoration. Best of all, there

was the land. Mississippi's towns might lie in ruins, but her matchless asset was the soil itself. If only cotton could get going again . . .

But that was the problem. If the key to prosperity was cotton, the key to cotton had always been slaves—and there weren't any slaves any more. Over 380,000 freedmen aimlessly roamed the state, nearly all of them at loose ends, living where they chose, eating off the federal troops. The former owners had no influence. Most Negroes felt this was what freedom meant—no work. And there were plenty of people around the Union Army camps who advised them not to go back to their old masters. There were even rumors that Washington soon would be dividing up the plantations—forty acres and a mule for everyone.

Actually Washington was never more at cross-purposes. President Johnson suffered from being a states' rights Democrat from Tennessee, and as his prestige waned so did the chances for his lenient program. The Radical Republicans in Congress were winning control over national policy, but beyond a thirst for revenge, they had no clear-cut plans at all. As late as October, 1865, the Radical leader Thaddeus Stevens was asking his friend Charles Sumner if he knew of any good books on how the Russians freed their serfs.

The Negroes themselves could be of very little help in solving their problems. Over ninety-five per cent were illiterate. In the old days it had been illegal to teach the slaves to read or write, and now they were hopelessly ignorant. Few had any idea of citizenship, law, suffrage, or responsibility. Hauled before a court for stealing a bag of corn, one ex-slave happily camping on Jefferson Davis' plantation was asked if he wanted a jury trial.

"What's that?" was all he could say.

The whites felt cornered and helpless. For years they had done as they wanted with these people, and now the tables were turned. They were generally outnumbered, and in the rich cotton areas the margin seemed appalling—Bolivar County was eighty-seven per cent Negro; Issaquena County had 7,000 Negroes, only 600 whites.

But most frightening of all to white Mississippi residents were the Negro troops. When the United States Army's XVI Corps went home in August, 1865, 9,122 of the 10,193 Union soldiers still in the state were Negroes. Their mere presence seemed to invite the most hideous trouble. In Jackson, Major Barnes, commanding the 5th U.S. Colored Infantry, urged the local Negroes to defend their rights even to the "click of the pistol and at the point of the bayonet."

And incidents did happen. William Wilkinson was murdered at Lauderdale Springs by five of his former slaves for selling his plantation—they claimed it was rightfully theirs by Christmas. This sort of bloodshed was rare, but it was enough to set off the whites.

Terror bred fantastic rumors. The Natchez *Courier* warned that the county's Negroes were supposed to rise on New Year's Day. In Yazoo City the date was Christmas. The Brandon *Republican* set no date but reported, "They are evidently preparing something and it behooves us to be on the alert and prepare for the worst." There was nothing to any of these reports, but each rumor hardened the feelings of the whites.

They soon developed a fierce callousness toward the Negro, no matter how harmless he might be. On a quiet Sunday afternoon in Natchez an elderly freedman protested to a small white boy raiding his turnip patch. The boy shot him dead, and that was that. In Vicksburg the *Herald* complained that the town's children were hitting innocent bystanders when using their "nigger shooters."

Nor was it just the specter of Negro supremacy that aroused white Mississippians—Negro equality was just as bad. "God damn your soul, get off this boat!" raged the captain of the Memphis–Vicksburg packet on Christmas morning, 1865. The greeting was directed at a Negro couple who had dared ask for first-class passage. As their luggage was pitched ashore, the captain turned back to his work muttering, "They can't force their damned nigger equality on me."

Even when the principle of equality was acknowledged, the practice must have mystified the beneficiaries. "Take off your hat, you black scoundrel, or I'll cut your throat," a Mississippi state legislator yelled at his former slave; later he explained, "Sam, you've got just the same rights as a white man now, but not a bit better, and if you come into my room again without taking off your hat, I'll shoot you."

The case of Negro suffrage showed that even token equality was too much for whites to stomach. In 1865 President Johnson—already fearing for his generous Reconstruction program—urged William L. Sharkey, a former Mississippi Chief Justice whom the President had appointed as provisional governor, to make some gesture toward Negro enfranchisement. It might allay congressional doubts, for instance, if Mississippi gave the vote to those who could read the Constitution and write their names and who owned at least $250 in property—perhaps five per cent of the Negro population. Governor Sharkey couldn't have been less interested.

But the greatest anathema was Negro education. It was not so much a question of integrated schools; it was a question of any schools at all. At Oxford an angry band drove off the missionary assigned to the local freedmen's school, even though he was a southern man. At Okolona someone fired four shots at Dr. Lacy, the old Episcopal minister who was trying to teach the town's young Negroes.

"If any man from the North comes down here expecting to hold and maintain radical or abolitionist sentiments," warned the *Nation*'s correspondent, "let him expect to be shot down from *behind* the first time he leaves his home." Visitors were shocked by the sheer violence of the state's reaction. Lulled by a carefully cultivated tradition of moonlight and magnolias, they forgot that life in Mississippi had always been closer to the frontier than the Tidewater, indeed had been a true frontier as late as the 1830's.

Harder to explain was the stream of contradictory assurances that soon became so familiar. Negroes? "The southern people are really their best friends," a planter told author John T. Trowbridge in 1865. "We're the only ones that understand them," someone explained to Whitelaw Reid, another visitor. Just give the southerners time, begged the sympathetic editor of *DeBow's Review:* "If let alone to manage affairs in their own way, and with their intimate knowledge of Negro character, everything possible will be done in good time for the social, physical, and political advancement of the race."

There was also an odd element of fantasy in it all—almost as if the war hadn't been lost . . . in fact, as if Mississippi were dealing with Washington as an equal. When Whitelaw Reid doubted that Congress would seat the ex-Confederates who swept Mississippi's first postwar election of 1865, his listeners scoffed at the very thought. Of course they would be seated—"because of the tremendous pressure we can bring to bear." The Natchez *Courier* agreed: "The State of Mississippi still stands in all its grand individuality. Massachusetts has no more right to dictate to us now about our internal laws than she had five years ago nor has she half the power. . . ."

Occasionally a voice of doubt was raised, but the moderates seemed, in the *Nation's* words, "somewhat bewildered . . . bullied . . . humbugged." Usually they could be quickly silenced. When one Mississippi planter suggested in August, 1865, that the Negroes might be trained to use their rights, his companion shot back the clincher that was also getting familiar: "They'll be wanting to marry your daughters next."

And this was the heart of the matter. To the ordinary white Mississippian, political equality automatically led to social equality, which in turn automatically led to race-mixing. It was inevitable—and unthinkable. To a people brought up to believe that Negroes were genetically inferior—after all, that was why they were slaves—the mere hint of "mongrelization" was appalling. And all the more so in view of the homage paid the white southern woman. It was she who had sacrificed so much, whose purity, in fact, carried on the whole system. She was everything.

Of course there were other factors too. Cotton planters didn't want their field hands getting out of line; the red-neck farmers worried about Negroes taking their bread. Yet these were areas where something might be worked out; but there could be no compromise—not an inch—on anything that might open the door to race-mixing. Emancipation made absolutely no difference. "A monkey with his tail off," explained the Natchez *Courier*, "is a monkey still."

It didn't matter that the position was illogical. Northerners might snigger that if the Negro was so backward, why might he advance so far? Other visitors might wonder about the high percentage of Negroes with white blood—surely race-mixing must have once been all right with somebody. None of this made any difference. So in November, 1865, it was easy for the Jackson *Daily News* to lecture the state's first postwar government: "We must keep the ex-slave in a position of inferiority. We must pass such laws as will make him *feel* his inferiority."

Mississippi's new government understood. Under President Johnson's generous terms the state had freed the slaves but done little else.

A new constitution had been drafted—but it seemed pretty much along prewar lines. A new state legislature had been chosen—but it featured many old leaders. A new governor had been elected—but he was Benjamin G. Humphreys, an outstanding Confederate general who hadn't even been pardoned yet. On November 20, 1865, Governor Humphreys set the tone of things in a message to the legislature: "Under the pressure of federal bayonets, urged on by the misdirected sympathies of the world, the people of Mississippi have abolished the institution of slavery. The Negro is free, whether we like it or not; we must realize that fact now and forever. To be free, however, does not make him a citizen, or entitle him to social or political equality with the white man."

A series of laws, later known as the Black Code, swiftly put the Negro in his place. He was allowed to marry, own property, sue and be sued, even testify if he was a party—but that was all. No Negro could vote, keep firearms, rent a home outside town, ride in a first-class railroad car with whites, or "make insulting gestures." Any unemployed Negro over eighteen was declared a vagrant, fined $50, and turned over to whoever paid up. Any unsupported Negro under eighteen could be apprenticed out. If he tried to run away, "the master or mistress" (the law easily slipped back into ante-bellum language) had the right to pursue and recapture.

Reaction was not long in coming. "We tell the white men of Mississippi," exploded the Chicago *Tribune* on December 1, "that the men of the North will convert the state of Mississippi into a frog pond before they will allow any such laws to disgrace one foot of soil in which the bones of our soldiers sleep and over which the flag of freedom waves."

Northern fury grew as other southern states followed Mississippi's lead with Black Codes of their own. Finally, in 1867 Congress threw out President Johnson's Reconstruction program and launched a far harsher one of its own. The Confederate-dominated state governments were scrapped, and the South was divided into five military districts, each under martial law. Negroes were given the vote, new constitutional conventions held. No state could get back into the Union until Congress approved its new government . . . until it granted Negro suffrage . . . until it ratified the Fourteenth Amendment, guaranteeing the people of every state (among other things) "equal protection of the laws."

Mississippi eventually knuckled under, but only after three more years of rear-guard defiance. By 1870, however, the state was "reconstructed," and by 1873 the local Radical Republicans were riding high. The electorate was fifty-seven per cent Negro—mostly illiterate and easily controlled. The legislature boasted sixty-four Negroes and twenty-four carpetbaggers. The Speaker of the House, the lieutenant governor, the superintendent of education were all Negroes. The new Reconstruction governor himself was an ex-Union officer—General Adelbert Ames, a remote, tactless New Englander who stayed away from Mississippi for protracted periods.

It would later be argued that this state government turned in an impressive performance, and indeed there were many bright spots. The Negro legislators included at least fifteen well-educated, conscientious clergymen. The carpetbaggers were often solid middle westerners who had come not to loot but to farm. The Negro troops had all been withdrawn, and only a token force of federals remained—for instance, 59 at Natchez, 129 at Vicksburg, about 700 men altogether. The state debt never got out of hand. There was little stealing —the only major case involved the carpetbag treasurer of the state hospital in Natchez who took $7,251.81. And all the while important things were being accomplished—war-damaged bridges repaired, northern innovations like free hospitals established, courts expanded to take care of freedmen, and a public-school system launched.

All this was done, but it would take the perspective of a century to appreciate it. At the time the white people of Mississippi felt only bitterness. They didn't care if most of the troops were gone; one blue uniform was too many. They didn't know about worthy projects; they only knew taxes on land had soared 1,300 per cent in five years. They didn't notice that most key officials were honest; in their frayed poverty, they only saw any sign of waste: why, the state contingency fund even paid for Governor Ames' bedpan. And perhaps most important, they knew little about the conscientious work of many Negroes in top-level positions; they only knew their own county, where they were in daily contact, and that was often appalling.

Negro sheriffs, clerks, and magistrates thrashed about in confusion and ignorance. In Warren County the sheriff couldn't write a simple return. In Issaquena County not one member of the board of supervisors—responsible for handling the county's business—could read a contract. There wasn't a justice of the peace in Madison County who could write a summons.

Petty corruption spread everywhere, often induced by light-fingered whites. Hinds County ran up a bigger printing bill in nine months than the whole state paid in 1866–67. The Wilkinson County board of supervisors shelled out $1,500 for three bridges—containing four, eight, and twenty planks respectively. Vicksburg's Republican candidate for mayor staggered under twenty-three indictments. Nor were the dethroned Democrats entirely innocent. An officer in Vicksburg's clean-government group was caught charging the city $500 to move a safe from the river to the courthouse.

Little matter—it was all the same to most of white Mississippi. Reconstruction was to blame, and that meant the Negroes. Free voting and the shadow of federal bayonets might make them invulnerable to ordinary political tactics, but there were other ways. . . .

The shifting seasons merged into one long blur of desperate violence. There was the sunny October morning when Thomas Dabney's daughters heard a hail of shots and watched a Negro's riderless horse race across the Burleigh lawn . . . the starlit winter night in Monroe County when carpetbagger A. P. Huggins knelt on a lonely road as the K.K.K. delivered seventy-five lashes with a stirrup strap . . . the

Entitled Reconstruction, *or* "*A White Man's Government,*" *this 1868 Currier and Ives cartoon summed up Northern liberals' simplistic view of the Southern dilemma.*

bright March day when the Meridian courthouse erupted in rifle fire and the Radical judge fell dead on his bench. . . .

"Life is not sacred as it is in the North," wrote correspondent Charles Nordhoff:

> Everybody goes armed, and every trifling dispute is ended with the pistol. The respectable people of the State do not discourage the practice of carrying arms as they should, they are astonishingly tolerant of acts which would arouse a Northern community to the utmost, and I believe that to this may be ascribed all that is bad in Mississippi—to an almost total lack of a right opinion; a willingness to see men take the law into their own hands; and, what is still worse, to let them openly defy the laws, without losing, apparently, the respect of the community.

In this atmosphere there was no hope for a man with the "wrong" attitude, whatever his credentials. At Aberdeen the town teacher, Dr. Ebart, had an impeccable southern background, but he favored Negro schools, and that was the end of his job. The pressure was too much. The white Republicans soon melted away. Many crossed over to the Democratic fold; others fled north; only a few stood by the helpless mass of Negroes. The moderates, who might have been a third force, seemed mesmerized by the fury of the blast. "The quiet, sensible and orderly people," mused Charles Nordhoff, "seem to have almost entirely resigned the power and supremacy which belong to them."

This was the picture by 1875, when, with state and local elections scheduled, the Democrats decided that the time had come formally to recapture control. A skillfully conceived strategy—to be known as the Mississippi Plan and later to be copied throughout the South—took care of the two chief obstacles: the Negro majority and federal bayonets.

"We are determined to have an honest election if we have to stuff the ballot box to get it," shouted one Democratic leader, and this was only a small part of the plan. Newspaper notices warned Negroes that they would be thrown off their land if they voted the Republican ticket. Democratic "rifle clubs," usually sporting conspicuous red shirts, drilled endlessly near Negro sections. In Hinds, Lowndes, and other counties, cannon appeared and "salutes" were fired near Republican rallies.

The Negro voters got the message, but the Democrats still faced the danger of federal intervention. The trick here was not to let things go too far, and the Democratic campaign chairman, General J. Z. George, proved a past master at the art of intimidation by indirection. Still, it was a delicate tightrope. The embattled Governor Ames was calling Washington for help, and the slightest slip might bring in the federals. . . .

A crash of rifle fire scattered the 1,200 Negroes swarming around the Republican barbecue at the little town of Clinton on September 4, 1875. Here and there men fell—not all of them black. Two young white hecklers were cut down by return fire as they scurried from the scene. It seemed that Negroes too could feel strongly about elections. Wholesale shooting began, and for days undeclared war raged around Clinton. On September 8 Governor Ames appealed to General Grant for troops to restore peace and supervise the coming elections. The whole future of Mississippi hung in the balance. A nod from the President, and all of General George's strategy would fall apart.

Grant looked the other way. "The whole public are tired out with these annual autumnal outbreaks in the South," the President sighed, "and the great majority are ready now to condemn any interference on the part of the government." Word was passed to Governor Ames through Attorney General Pierrepont to try harder, to exhaust his own resources before calling on Washington for aid.

It was really not Grant's fault. The country was indeed tired of Reconstruction, and the President was but echoing the national mood. Most people had never been for Negro civil rights in the first place. Freedom, yes; but that didn't necessarily mean all the privileges of citizenship. At the end of the war only six northern states let Negroes vote, and in 1867 the District of Columbia rejected Negro suffrage 7,337 to 36. Nor did anyone feel the Fourteenth Amendment had much to do with education. In fact, stalwart Union states like New York, Pennsylvania, and Ohio all had segregated schools. Congress itself set up a segregated school system in Washington only weeks after approving the Fourteenth Amendment.

These feelings were rising to the surface, now that the initial exhilaration of winning the war was over. Other forces were at work too : the implacable Thaddeus Stevens had died . . . anti-Grant liberals were happy to attack everything about the Administration, including Reconstruction . . . northern investors were anxious to resume ''normal'' relations with the South . . . the nation's eyes were turning to fresh, exciting visions in the Far West.

The new mood showed itself in various ways. Congress had indeed passed the Civil Rights Act of 1875 (protecting the Negro in public places like trains and restaurants), but it was the dying gasp of a lame-duck session. Besides, it was a shaky victory. A school integration provision had been defeated; also a ''force bill'' giving the measure teeth. Even more significant, the Supreme Court was now nibbling away at the earlier Reconstruction Acts. And in the background came a steady chorus from the press, ''Let the South solve its own problems.'' The President understood and gave the nation its way.

The Silver Cornet Band led the Jackson victory parade to General George's house on election night, November 2, 1875. The returns were rolling in, and huge Democratic majorities were piling up: Morton, 233 to 17 . . . Deasonville, 181 to 0 . . . Yazoo County, 4,052 to 7. In the end the Democrats carried sixty-two of the state's seventy-four counties. In the time-honored fashion of all political leaders everywhere, General George gave full credit to the rank and file ''for the redemption of our common mother, Mississippi.'' Governor Ames was a practical man. Exactly 146 days later, in exchange for the withdrawal by Democrats of a set of impeachment charges, he resigned his office, packed his bags, and left the state forever. In the word of the times, Mississippi had been ''redeemed.''

To Mississippi's Negroes redemption meant a loss of power but not the trappings. The men now running the state came from the old cotton-planting gentry, who got along well with their former slaves. Some of these leaders, like Lucius Quintus Cincinnatus Lamar, were far more interested in corporation law than in eight-cent cotton, but they still had a tradition of *noblesse oblige* and gave the Negroes considerable leeway—as long as they were ''good.''

This arrangement was further cemented by a sort of gentlemen's agreement with Washington after the presidential election of 1876. The South accepted Hayes' dubious claims to the Presidency, and in return the Republicans adopted Grant's hands-off attitude as the new administration line. The last troops were withdrawn, and the old Confederacy was left free to work out its own problems. But at the same time it was always understood that the Negroes would retain at least their surface gains. The redemption leaders happily agreed. In fact, the Jackson *Clarion* had accepted the obligation on the very morning after the great 1875 victory. Observing that Negroes had helped make the triumph possible, the paper declared that the state must now ''carry out in good faith the pledges of equal and even justice to them and theirs in which they placed their confidence.''

So the Negroes continued to vote and often held minor offices. Nor were they barred from most public places. The two races drank at the same bars and ate at the same restaurants, though at separate tables. In Jackson, Angelo's Hall echoed with Negro laughter one week, white the next. And when life was done, both races could rest together in Greenwood Cemetery.

With the Negro's role settled, Mississippi's redemption government launched a massive economy wave. The conservative landowning leaders had been hit hardest by the staggering taxes of Reconstruction, and now they were determined to end all that. State expenditures were slashed from $1,430,000 in 1875 to $518,000 in 1876. Teachers' salaries alone fell from $55.47 a month in 1875 to $29.19 the following year.

In a way it was all justifiable. Mississippi remained wretchedly poor. In 1877 the state's per capita wealth was only $286, compared to a $1,086 average in the northern states. Even as late as 1890 there were only forty-six banks in the state, with combined cash assets of but $635,000. The war had wiped out Mississippi, and there just seemed no way to get going again. In those days the idea of federal recovery aid was unknown—between 1865 and 1875 Washington spent 21 million dollars on public works in Massachusetts and New York, only $185,000 in Mississippi and Arkansas.

Still, whatever the justification, Mississippi paid a high price for her sweeping economies. Letting roads disintegrate meant even more stagnant communities. Appropriating merely $5,392 a year for health meant the end of nearly all services. Spending only $2 a head on schoolchildren (against $20 in Massachusetts) meant mounting illiteracy and a new generation utterly untrained to advance in life.

Nor was cost-cutting a viable solution to the state's problems. Despite all the economies, conditions continued to slide. From the mid-seventies to the early nineties cotton sagged from 11 cents to 5.8 cents a pound. Field hands' pay fell from $15 to $12 a month . . . when there was any cash at all. More often there was the share-cropping system, which saw little money ever change hands. Yet the plantation owners themselves were certainly not getting rich. Under a vicious system of liens, they mortgaged their future crops for months or even years ahead to get the tools and supplies needed for tomorrow.

Everything seemed to conspire against Mississippi. While crop prices fell, the farmer's costs soared. Freight rates rigged in the East increased his shipping charges. Combinations like the jute-bagging trust raised the cost of his supplies. High tariffs added more to his burden. Creditors insisted that he plant only cotton; shackled to a one-crop system, his land quickly eroded. Even nature joined the conspiracy—a flood, freeze, or drought usually came along to spoil the few otherwise good years. Whether holding out in some paint-peeled mansion or hanging on in the squalor of a dog-trot cabin, most Mississippians knew only the bitterest poverty.

The state's landed leaders proved utterly unable to cope with the situation. They came from the lowlands—the cotton belt that had run everything in prewar days. They owed their authority to an odd combination of ante-bellum nostalgia and redemption heroics—certainly not new ideas. They easily took to the laissez-faire views of eastern business—tax concessions, hard money, railroad grabs like the Texas-Pacific. They shied away from new panaceas like government regulation and flexible currency. Their most lustrous figure, L. Q. C. Lamar, shuddered at the Greenback movement's "boundless, bottomless, and brainless schemes."

Such men neither understood nor even liked the up-country farmers who scratched away at the red clay hills to the east. Desperately these red-necks—along with a growing number of poor white tenants all over the state—turned to new and more radical sources of hope: the Farmers' Alliance and later the Populists.

And all the while they smouldered with growing hate—hatred for the Yankee banks and railroads that squeezed them so tightly . . . hatred for the Black Belt leaders who seemed to care so little . . . and, above all, hatred for the Negroes to whose level they were sinking so fast.

Jim Crow laws began to sprout . . . the first in twenty years. In 1888 Mississippi became the first state to have segregated waiting rooms. In 1890 Jackson extended the racial barrier beyond death by establishing a separate cemetery for Negroes. The rules grew ever more strict as the margin narrowed between white and colored living standards. If race was all the whites might have left, that was all the more reason to guard this sacred heritage. Woe to the Negro who flirted with crossing the line.

Lynchings multiplied at a fearful rate—nobody knows how many, for the press handled the incidents as casually as the weather. "Four Negroes were lynched at Grenada last week," remarked the Raymond *Gazette* on July 18, 1885, "also one at Oxford." That was the whole item.

With Mississippi in this mood, it certainly didn't help matters when the big landowners met the red-neck challenge with thousands of Negro votes from the black counties they controlled. A weird political duel, utterly lacking in logic or principle, developed as the eighties wore on. The old conservative leaders represented traditional white supremacy, yet relied on Negro votes to hold their power. The mass of poor whites had much in common with the Negro, yet fought him as a mortal enemy. The remaining Republicans in the state stood for the Negro's freedom, yet deserted him as a hopeless handicap. No wonder the Negro himself soon lost interest. Untrained in politics anyhow, he found Mississippi's brand far too confusing. Usually he just sold his vote to the highest bidder or was thrust aside while someone else cast it for him.

The situation proved too sordid to last. In 1890 a special convention assembled in Jackson to draw up a new state constitution. The solution, most people felt, was to take away the Negro's vote. Even the Black Belt leaders now agreed—the advantage Negro suffrage gave them was outweighed by the cost (usually a dollar a vote) and the ever-haunting possibility that the Negroes might some day decide to go back into politics for themselves. It was, of course, a little odd to keep Negroes from casting votes in order to stop white people from stealing them, but nobody worried too much about that. A far greater problem was how to do it. The Fifteenth Amendment specifically stated that the right to vote should not be abridged on account of color.

Clearly, the trick was to frame a set of qualifications that would technically apply to everybody but actually eliminate the Negro without touching the white. A poll tax alone was not enough—it might discourage more whites than Negroes. Nor would a literacy test do—there were thousands of good white voters who couldn't even write their names. In the end the convention came up with a series of devices which were, in the words of one delegate, "a monument to the resourcefulness of the human mind."

Most important were the new qualifications: all voters had to be able to read any section of the state constitution, or understand it when read to him, or give it a reasonable interpretation. This, of course, dumped the final decision into the lap of the examining registrar . . . who would know exactly what to do.

Reregistration began immediately. In 1885 over 1,600 Negroes had qualified in Panola County; by 1896 the figure stood at 114. The same thing happened everywhere: in Coahoma County only four per cent of its once-eligible Negroes now could vote; in De Soto, only five per cent; in Tunica, two per cent. Loyal Mississippians held their breath how would the nation react to this giant wink at the Fifteenth Amendment?

They need not have worried. The White House was in friendly hands—first under the conservative Grover Cleveland, later under the benign William McKinley. Congress was no threat either—in 1894 it repealed most of the remaining civil rights laws. The western Populists were bitter at the Negroes for sticking by their old masters. The southern progressives felt that white solidarity would weld all classes more closely together. Eastern liberals recalled the reactionary leaders who had engineered Reconstruction—and found it easy to sympathize with Mississippi. And above all, there was the American mood—a moment of bursting national pride and pious imperialism. As the liberal *Atlantic Monthly* noted with gentle irony: "If the stronger and cleverer race is free to impose its will upon the 'new-caught sullen peoples' on the other side of the globe, why not in South Carolina and Mississippi?"

The Supreme Court added its blessing in 1898. In *Williams v. Mississippi* the justices solemnly declared there was no reason to suppose that the state's new voting qualifications were aimed especially at Negroes. . . .

As the new century dawned, it was clear that the Negro—stripped of his gains, abandoned by the courts, and rejected by the country—was in a highly vulnerable position. And for the Negro in Mississippi —the state which had invented the Black Code in 1865, pioneered the "Mississippi Plan" in 1875, and led the way to disenfranchisement in 1890—the future looked bleak indeed. . . .

IMPACT
OF
INDUSTRIALISM

Robert L. Heilbroner

Andrew Carnegie, Captain of Industry

The driving force behind late nineteenth-century economic growth, social change, and the thousand new developments that heralded the birth of modern America was the rapid expansion of industry. Industrialization made the United States the richest nation in the world and placed some of its citizens among the world's richest men. At one and the same time it fostered the belief that individuals could rise from rags to riches in a generation and the fear that great extremes between the wealthy and the poor would destroy opportunity, even democracy. It lent credence to the idea that Americans were gross materialists, but it also produced a philanthropic outpouring of unprecedented dimensions.

The career of Andrew Carnegie reflects all these tendencies. Carnegie came to America as a poor immigrant boy and became the master of the American steel industry. He was a "robber baron" in the eyes of his critics, an "industrial statesman" in his own eyes and in those of many of his contemporaries. He accumulated material goods on an immense scale but dispensed hundreds of millions of dollars to a variety of worthy causes. He was even an intellectual of sorts, writing books and articles about the character of American society, the industrial system, and the duties and obligations of rich men like himself.

Professor Robert L. Heilbroner, an economist at the New School for Social Research, the author of this essay on Carnegie, has written extensively in the field of economic history and thought. In works such as The Worldly Philosophers, The Great Ascent, *and* The Limits of American Capitalism *he has repeatedly demonstrated that it is possible to write history that is at once popular and scholarly even when dealing with highly technical material.*

*T*oward the end of his long life, at the close of World War I, Andrew Carnegie was already something of a national legend. His meteoric rise, the scandals and successes of his industrial generalship—all this was blurred into nostalgic memory. What was left was a small, rather feeble man with a white beard and pale, penetrating eyes, who could occasionally be seen puttering around his mansion on upper Fifth Avenue, a benevolent old gentleman who still rated an annual birthday interview but was even then a venerable relic of a fast-disappearing era. Carnegie himself looked back on his career with a certain savored incredulity. "How much did you say I had given away, Poynton?" he would inquire of his private secretary; "$324,657,399" was the answer. "Good Heaven!" Carnegie would exclaim. "Where did I ever get all that money?"

Where he *had* got all that money was indeed a legendary story, for even in an age known for its acquisitive triumphs, Carnegie's touch had been an extraordinary one. He had begun, in true Horatio Alger fashion, at the bottom; he had ended, in a manner that put the wildest of Alger's novels to shame, at the very pinnacle of success. At the close of his great deal with J. P. Morgan in 1901, when the Carnegie steel empire was sold to form the core of the new United States Steel Company, the banker had extended his hand and delivered the ultimate encomium of the times: "Mr. Carnegie," he said, "I want to congratulate you on being the richest man in the world."

It was certainly as "the richest man in the world" that Carnegie attracted the attention of his contemporaries. Yet this is hardly why we look back on him with interest today. As an enormous money-maker Carnegie was a flashy, but hardly a profound, hero of the times; and the attitudes of Earnestness and Self-Assurance, so engaging in the young immigrant, become irritating when they are congealed in the millionaire. But what lifts Carnegie's life above the rut of a one-dimensional success story is an aspect of which his contemporaries were relatively unaware.

Going through his papers after his death, Carnegie's executors came across a memorandum that he had written to himself fifty years before, carefully preserved in a little yellow box of keepsakes and mementos. It brings us back to December, 1868, when Carnegie, a young man flushed with the first taste of great success, retired to his suite in the opulent Hotel St. Nicholas in New York, to tot up his profits for the year. It had been a tremendous year and the calculation must have been extremely pleasurable. Yet this is what he wrote as he reflected on the figures:

> Thirty-three and an income of $50,000 per annum! By this time two years I can so arrange all my business as to secure at least $50,000 per annum. Beyond this never earn—make no effort to increase fortune, but spend the surplus each year for benevolent purposes. Cast aside business forever, except for others.
>
> Settle in Oxford and get a thorough education, making the

acquaintance of literary men—this will take three years of active work—pay especial attention to speaking in public. Settle then in London and purchase a controlling interest in some newspaper or live review and give the general management of it attention, taking part in public matters, especially those connected with education and improvement of the poorer classes.

Man must have an idol—the amassing of wealth is one of the worst species of idolatry—no idol more debasing than the worship of money. Whatever I engage in I must push inordinately; therefore should I be careful to choose that life which will be the most elevating in its character. To continue much longer overwhelmed by business cares and with most of my thoughts wholly upon the way to make more money in the shortest time, must degrade me beyond hope of permanent recovery. I will resign business at thirty-five, but during the ensuing two years I wish to spend the afternoons in receiving instruction and in reading systematically.

It is a document which in more ways than one is Carnegie to the very life: brash, incredibly self-confident, chockablock with self-conscious virtue—and more than a little hypocritical. For the program so nobly outlined went largely unrealized. Instead of retiring in two years, Carnegie went on for thirty-three more; even then it was with considerable difficulty that he was persuaded to quit. Far from shunning further money-making, he proceeded to roll up his fortune with an uninhibited drive that led one unfriendly biographer to characterize him as "the greediest little gentleman ever created." Certainly he was one of the most aggressive profit seekers of his time. Typically, when an associate jubilantly cabled: "No. 8 furnace broke all records today," Carnegie coldly replied, "What were the other furnaces doing?"

It is this contrast between his hopes and his performance that makes Carnegie interesting. For when we review his life, what we see is more than the career of another nineteenth-century acquisitor. We see the unequal struggle between a man who loved money—loved making it, having it, spending it—and a man who, at bottom, was ashamed of himself for his acquisitive desires. All during his lifetime, the money-maker seemed to win. But what lifts Carnegie's story out of the ordinary is that the other Carnegie ultimately triumphed. At his death public speculation placed the size of his estate at about five hundred million dollars. In fact it came to $22,881,575. Carnegie *had* become the richest man in the world—but something had also driven him to give away ninety per cent of his wealth.

Actually, his contemporaries knew of Carnegie's inquietude about money. In 1889, before he was world-famous, he had written an article for the *North American Review* entitled "The Gospel of Wealth"—an article that contained the startling phrase: "The man who dies

*Andrew Carnegie,
the Steelmaster.*

thus rich dies disgraced." It was hardly surprising, however, if the world took these sentiments at a liberal discount: homiletic millionaires who preached the virtues of austerity were no novelty; Carnegie himself, returning in 1879 from a trip to the miseries of India, had been able to write with perfect sincerity, "How very little the millionaire has beyond the peasant, and how very often his additions tend not to happiness but to misery."

What the world may well have underestimated, however, was a concern more deeply rooted than these pieties revealed. For, unlike so many of his self-made peers, who also rose from poverty, Carnegie was the product of a *radical* environment. The village of Dunfermline, Scotland, when he was born there in 1835, was renowned as a center of revolutionary ferment, and Carnegie's family was itself caught up in the radical movement of the times. His father was a regular speaker at the Chartist rallies, which were an almost daily occurrence in Dunfermline in the 1840's, and his uncle was an impassioned orator for the rights of the working class to vote and strike. All this made an indelible impression on Carnegie's childhood.

"I remember as if it were yesterday," he wrote seventy years later, "being awakened during the night by a tap at the back window by men who had come to inform my parents that my uncle, Bailie Morrison, had been thrown in jail because he dared to hold a meeting which had been forbidden . . . It is not to be wondered at that, nursed amid such surroundings, I developed into a violent young Republican whose motto was 'death to privilege.' "

From another uncle, George Lauder, Carnegie absorbed a second passion that was also to reveal itself in his later career. This was his love of poetry, first that of the poet Burns, with its overtones of romantic egalitarianism, and then later, of Shakespeare. Immense quantities of both were not only committed to memory, but made into an integral—indeed, sometimes an embarrassingly evident—part of his life: on first visiting the Doge's palace in Venice he thrust a companion in the ducal throne and held him pinioned there while he orated the appropriate speeches from *Othello*. Once, seeing Vanderbilt walking on Fifth Avenue, Carnegie smugly remarked, "I would not exchange his millions for my knowledge of Shakespeare."

But it was more than just a love of poetry that remained with Carnegie. Virtually alone among his fellow acquisitors, he was driven by a genuine respect for the power of thought to seek answers for questions that never even occurred to them. Later, when he "discovered" Herbert Spencer, the English sociologist, Carnegie wrote to him, addressing him as "Master," and it was as "Master" that Spencer remained, even after Carnegie's lavishness had left Spencer very much in his debt.

But Carnegie's early life was shaped by currents more material than intellectual. The grinding process of industrial change had begun slowly but ineluctably to undermine the cottage weaving that was the traditional means of employent in Dunfermline. The Industrial Revolution, in the shape of new steam mills, was forcing out the hand weavers, and one by one the looms which constituted the entire capital of the Carnegie family had to be sold. Carnegie never forgot the shock of his father returning home to tell him, in despair, "Andra, I can get nae mair work."

A family council of war was held, and it was decided that there was only one possible course—they must try their luck in America, to which two sisters of Carnegie's mother, Margaret, had already emigrated. With the aid of a few friends the money for the crossing was scraped together, and at thirteen Andrew found himself transported to the only country in which his career would have been possible.

It hardly got off to an auspicious start, however. The family made their way to Allegheny, Pennsylvania, a raw and bustling town where Carnegie's father again sought work as an independent weaver. But it was as hopeless to compete against the great mills in America as in Scotland, and soon father and son were forced to seek work in the local cotton mills. There Andrew worked from six in the morning until six at night, making $1.20 as a bobbin boy.

After a while his father quit—factory work was impossible for the traditional small enterpriser—and Andrew got a "better" job with a new firm, tending an engine deep in a dungeon cellar and dipping newly made cotton spools in a vat of oil. Even the raise to $3 a week—and desperately conjured visions of Wallace and the Bruce—could not overcome the horrors of that lonely and foul-smelling basement. It was perhaps the only time in Carnegie's life when his self-assurance deserted him: to the end of his days the merest whiff of oil could make him deathly sick.

Yet he was certain, as he wrote home at sixteen, that "anyone could get along in this Country," and the rags-to-riches saga shortly began. The telegraph had just come to Pittsburgh, and one evening over a game of checkers, the manager of the local office informed Andrew's uncle that he was looking for a messenger. Andy got the job and, in true Alger fashion, set out to excel in it. Within a few weeks he had carefully memorized the names and the locations, not only of the main streets in Pittsburgh, but of the main firms, so that he was the quickest of all the messenger boys.

He came early and stayed late, watched the telegraphers at work, and at home at night learned the Morse code. As a result he was soon the head of the growing messenger service, and a skilled teleg rapher himself. One day he dazzled the office by taking a message "by ear" instead of by the commonly used tape printer, and since he was then only the third operator in the country able to turn the trick, citizens used to drop into the office to watch Andy take down the words "hot from the wire."

One such citizen who was especially impressed with young Carnegie's determination was Thomas A. Scott, in time to become one of the colorful railway magnates of the West, but then the local superintendent of the Pennsylvania Railroad. Soon thereafter Carnegie became "Scott's Andy"—telegrapher, secretary, and general factotum—at thirty-five dollars a month. In his *Autobiography* Carnegie recalls an instance which enabled him to begin the next stage of his career.

> One morning I reached the office and found that a serious acci-
> dent on the Eastern Division had delayed the express passenger
> train westward, and that the passenger train eastward was pro-
> ceeding with a flagman in advance at every curve. The freight
> trains in both directions were standing on the sidings. Mr.
> Scott was not to be found. Finally I could not resist the temp-
> tation to plunge in, take the responsibility, give "train orders"
> and set matters going. "Death or Westminster Abbey" flashed
> across my mind. I knew it was dismissal, disgrace, perhaps
> criminal punishment for me if I erred. On the other hand, I
> could bring in the wearied freight train men who had lain out
> all night. I knew I could. I knew just what to do, and so I began.

Signing Scott's name to the orders, Carnegie flashed out the necessary instructions to bring order out of the tangle. The trains moved; there were no mishaps. When Scott reached the office Carnegie told him what he had done. Scott said not a word but looked carefully over all that had taken place. After a little he moved away from Carnegie's desk to his own, and that was the end of it. "But I noticed," Carnegie concluded good-humoredly, "that he came in very regularly and in good time for some mornings after that."

It is hardly to be wondered at that Carnegie became Scott's favorite, his "white-haired Scotch devil." Impetuous but not rash, full of enthusiasm and good-natured charm, the small lad with his blunt, open features and his slight Scottish burr was every executive's dream of an assistant. Soon Scott repaid Andy for his services by introducing him to a new and very different kind of opportunity. He gave Carnegie the chance to subscribe to five hundred dollars' worth of Adams Express stock, a company which Scott assured Andy would prosper mightily.

Carnegie had not fifty dollars saved, much less five hundred, but it was a chance he could ill afford to miss. He reported the offer to his mother, and that pillar of the family unhesitatingly mortgaged their home to raise the necessary money. When the first dividend check came in, with its ornate Spencerian flourishes, Carnegie had something like a revelation. "I shall remember that check as long as I live," he subsequently wrote. "It gave me the first penny of revenue from capital—something that I had not worked for with the sweat of my brow. 'Eureka!' I cried, 'Here's the goose that lays the golden eggs.' " He was right; within a few years his investment in the Adams Express Company was paying annual dividends of $1,400.

It was not long thereafter that an even more propitious chance presented itself. Carnegie was riding on the Pennsylvania line one day when he was approached by a "farmer-looking" man carrying a small green bag in his hand. The other introduced himself as T. T. Woodruff and quite frankly said that he wanted a chance to talk with someone connected with the railroad. Whereupon he opened his bag and took out a small model of the first sleeping car.

Carnegie was immediately impressed with its possibilities, and he quickly arranged for Woodruff to meet Scott. When the latter agreed to give the cars a trial, Woodruff in appreciation offered Carnegie a chance to subscribe to a one-eighth interest in the new company. A local banker agreed to lend Andy the few hundred dollars needed for the initial payment—the rest being financed from dividends. Once again Andy had made a shrewd investment: within two years the Woodruff Palace Car Company was paying him a return of more than $5,000 a year.

Investments now began to play an increasingly important role in Carnegie's career. Through his railroad contacts he came to recognize the possibilities in manufacturing the heavy equipment needed by the rapidly expanding lines, and soon he was instrumental in organizing companies to meet these needs. One of them, the Keystone Bridge Company, was the first successful manufacturer of iron railway bridges. Another, the Pittsburgh Locomotive Works, made engines. And most important of all, an interest in a local iron works run by an irascible German named Andrew Kloman brought Carnegie into actual contact with the manufacture of iron itself.

None of these new ventures required any substantial outlay of cash. His interest in the Keystone Bridge Company, for instance, which was to earn him $15,000 in 1868, came to him "in return for services rendered in its promotion"—services which Carnegie, as a young railroad executive, was then in a highly strategic position to deliver. Similarly the interest in the Kloman works reflected no contribution on Carnegie's part except that of being the human catalyst and buffer between some highly excitable participants.

By 1865 his "side" activities had become so important that he decided to leave the Pennsylvania Railroad. He was by then superintendent, Scott having moved up to a vice presidency, but his salary of $2,400 was already vastly overshadowed by his income from various ventures. One purchase alone—the Storey farm in Pennsylvania oil country, which Carnegie and a few associates picked up for $40,000—was eventually to pay the group a million dollars in dividends in *one* year. About this time a friend dropped in on Carnegie and asked him how he was doing. "Oh, I'm rich, I'm rich!" he exclaimed.

He was indeed embarked on the road to riches, and determined, as he later wrote in his *Autobiography*, that "nothing could be allowed to interfere for a moment with my business career." Hence it comes as a surprise to note that it was at this very point that Carnegie retired to his suite to write his curiously introspective and troubled thoughts about the pursuit of wealth. But the momentum of events was to prove far too strong for these moralistic doubts. Moving his headquarters to New York to promote his various interests, he soon found himself swept along by a succession of irresistible opportunities for money-making.

One of these took place quite by chance. Carnegie was trying to sell the Woodruff sleeping car at the same time that a formidable rival named George Pullman was also seeking to land contracts for his sleeping car, and the railroads were naturally taking advantage of the competitive situation. One summer evening in 1869 Carnegie found himself mounting the resplendent marble stairway of the St. Nicholas Hotel side by side with his competitor.

"Good evening, Mr. Pullman," said Carnegie in his ebullient manner. Pullman was barely cordial.

"How strange we should meet here," Carnegie went on, to which the other replied nothing at all.

"Mr. Pullman," said Carnegie, after an embarrassing pause, "don't you think we are making nice fools of ourselves?" At this Pullman evinced a glimmer of interest: "What do you mean?" he inquired. Carnegie quickly pointed out that competition between the two companies was helping no one but the railroads. "Well," said Pullman, "what do you suggest we do?"

"Unite!" said Carnegie. "Let's make a joint proposition to the

Union Pacific, your company and mine. Why not organize a new company to do it?" "What would you call it?" asked Pullman suspiciously. "The Pullman Palace Car Company," said Carnegie and with this shrewd psychological stroke won his point. A new company was formed, and in time Carnegie became its largest stockholder.

Meanwhile, events pushed Carnegie into yet another lucrative field. To finance the proliferating railway systems of America, British capital was badly needed, and with his Scottish ancestry, his verve, and his excellent railroad connections Carnegie was the natural choice for a go-between. His brief case stuffed with bonds and prospectuses, Carnegie became a transatlantic commuter, soon developing intimate relations both with great bankers like Junius Morgan (the father of J. P. Morgan), and with the heads of most of the great American roads. These trips earned him not only large commissions—exceeding on occasion $100,000 for a single turn— but even more important, established connections that were later to be of immense value. He himself later testified candidly on their benefits before a group of respectfully awed senators:

> For instance, I want a great contract for rails. Sidney Dillon of the Union Pacific was a personal friend of mine. Huntington was a friend. Dear Butler Duncan, that called on me the other day, was a friend. Those and other men were presidents of railroads . . . Take Huntington; you know C. P. Huntington. He was hard up very often. He was a great man, but he had a great deal of paper out. I knew his things were good. When he wanted credit I gave it to him. If you help a man that way, what chance has any paid agent going to these men? It was absurd.

But his trips to England brought Carnegie something still more valuable. They gave him steel. It is fair to say that as late as 1872 Carnegie did not see the future that awaited him as the Steel King of the world. The still modest conglomeration of foundries and mills he was gradually assembling in the Allegheny and Monongahela valleys was but one of many business interests, and not one for which he envisioned any extraordinary future. Indeed, to repeated pleas that he lead the way in developing a steel industry for America by substituting steel for iron rails, his reply was succinct: "Pioneering don't pay."

What made him change his mind? The story goes that he was awe-struck by the volcanic, spectacular eruption of a Bessemer converter, which he saw for the first time during a visit to a British mill. It was precisely the sort of display that would have appealed to Carnegie's mind—a wild, demonic, physical process miraculously contained and controlled by the dwarfed figures of the steel men themselves. At any rate, overnight Carnegie became the perfervid prophet of steel. Jumping on the first available steamer, he rushed home with the cry, "The day of iron has passed!" To the conster-

The drama of the Bessemer Process is depicted in Aaron Bohrod's 1948 painting, The Big Blow.

nation of his colleagues, the hitherto reluctant pioneer became an advocate of the most daring technological and business expansion; he joined them enthusiastically in forming Carnegie, McCandless & Company, which was the nucleus of the empire that the next thirty years would bring forth.

The actual process of growth involved every aspect of successful business enterprise of the times: acquisition and merger, pools and commercial piracy, and even, on one occasion, an outright fraud in selling the United States government overpriced and underdone steel armor plate. But it would be as foolish to maintain that the Carnegie empire grew by trickery as to deny that sharp practice had its place. Essentially what lay behind the spectacular expansion were three facts.

The first of these was the sheer economic expansion of the industry in the first days of burgeoning steel use. Everywhere steel replaced iron or found new uses—and not only in railroads but in ships, buildings, bridges, machinery of all sorts. As Henry Frick himself once remarked, if the Carnegie group had not filled the need for steel another would have. But it must be admitted that Carnegie's company did its job superlatively well. In 1885 Great Britain led the world in the production of steel. Fourteen years later her total output was 695,000 tons less than the output of the Carnegie Steel Company alone.

Second was the brilliant assemblage of personal talent with which

Carnegie surrounded himself. Among them, three in particular stood out. One was Captain William Jones, a Homeric figure who lumbered through the glowing fires and clanging machinery of the works like a kind of Paul Bunyan of steel, skilled at handling men, inventive in handling equipment, and enough of a natural artist to produce papers for the British Iron and Steel Institute that earned him a literary as well as a technical reputation. Then there was Henry Frick, himself a self-made millionaire, whose coke empire naturally complemented Carnegie's steelworks. When the two were amalgamated, Frick took over the active management of the whole, and under his forceful hand the annual output of the Carnegie works rose tenfold. Yet another was Charles Schwab, who came out of the tiny monastic town of Loretto, Pennsylvania, to take a job as a stake driver. Six months later he had been promoted by Jones into the assistant managership of the Braddock plant.

These men, and a score like them, constituted the vital energy of the Carnegie works. As Carnegie himself said, "Take away all our money, our great works, ore mines and coke ovens, but leave our organization, and in four years I shall have re-established myself."

But the third factor in the growth of the empire was Carnegie himself. A master salesman and a skilled diplomat of business at its highest levels, Carnegie was also a ruthless driver of his men. He pitted his associates and subordinates in competition with one another until a feverish atmosphere pervaded the whole organization. "You cannot imagine the abounding sense of freedom and relief I experience as soon as I get on board a steamer and sail past Sandy Hook," he once said to Captain Jones. "My God!" replied Jones. "Think of the relief to us!"

But Carnegie could win loyalties as well. All his promising young men were given gratis ownership participations—minuscule fractions of one per cent, which were enough, however, to make them millionaires in their own right. Deeply grateful to Jones, Carnegie once offered him a similar participation. Jones hemmed and hawed and finally refused; he would be unable to work effectively with the men, he said, once he was a partner. Carnegie insisted that his contribution be recognized and asked Jones what he wanted. "Well," said the latter, "you might pay me a hell of a big salary." "We'll do it!" said Carnegie. "From this time forth you shall receive the same salary as the President of the United States." "Ah, Andy, that's the kind of talk," said Captain Bill.

Within three decades, on the flood tide of economic expansion, propelled by brilliant executive work and relentless pressure from Carnegie, the company made immense strides. "Such a magnificent aggregation of industrial power has never before been under the domination of a single man," reported a biographer in 1902, describing the Gargantuan structure of steel and coke and ore and transport. Had the writer known of the profits earned by this aggregation he might have been even more impressed: three and a half million dollars in 1889, seven million in 1897, twenty-one million in 1899, and an immense forty million in 1900. "Where is there such a business!" Carnegie had exulted, and no wonder—the majority share of all these earnings, without hindrance of income tax, went directly into his pockets.

Nevertheless, with enormous success came problems. One of these was the restiveness of certain partners, under the "Iron-Clad" agreement, which prevented any of them from selling their shares to anyone but the company itself—an arrangement which meant, of course, that the far higher valuation of an outside purchaser could not be realized. Particularly chagrined was Frick, when, as the culmination of other disagreements between them, Carnegie sought to buy him out "at the value appearing on the books." Another problem was a looming competitive struggle in the steel industry itself that presaged a period of bitter industrial warfare ahead. And last was Carnegie's own growing desire to "get out."

Already he was spending half of each year abroad, first traveling, and then, after his late marriage, in residence in the great Skibo Castle he built for his wife on Dornoch Firth, Scotland. There he ran his business enterprises with one hand while he courted the literary and creative world with the other, entertaining Kipling and Matthew Arnold, Paderewski and Lloyd George, Woodrow Wilson and Theodore Roosevelt, Gladstone, and of course, Herbert Spencer, the Master. But even his career as "Laird" of Skibo could not remove him from the worries—and triumphs—of his business: a steady flow of cables and correspondence intruded on the "serious" side of life.

It was Schwab who cut the knot. Having risen to the very summit of the Carnegie concern he was invited in December, 1900, to give a speech on the future of the steel industry at the University Club in New York. There, before eighty of the nation's top business leaders he painted a glowing picture of what could be done if a super-company of steel were formed, integrated from top to bottom, self-sufficient with regard to its raw materials, balanced in its array of final products. One of the guests was the imperious J. P. Morgan, and as the speech progressed it was noticed that his concentration grew more and more intense. After dinner Morgan rose and took the young steel man by the elbow and engaged him in private conversation for half an hour while he plied him with rapid and penetrating questions; then a few weeks later he invited him to a private meeting in the great library of his home. They talked from nine o'clock in the evening until dawn. As the sun began to stream in through the library windows, the banker finally rose. "Well," he said to Schwab, "if Andy wants to sell, I'll buy. Go and find his price."

Carnegie at first did not wish to sell. Faced with the actual prospect of a withdrawal from the business he had built into the mightiest single industrial empire in the world, he was frightened and dismayed. He sat silent before Schwab's report, brooding, loath to inquire into details. But soon his enthusiasm returned. No such opportunity was likely to present itself again. In short order a figure of $492,000,000 was agreed on for the entire enterprise, of which Carnegie himself was to receive $300,000,000 in five per cent gold bonds and preferred stock. Carnegie jotted down the terms of the transaction on a slip of paper and told Schwab to bring it to Morgan. The banker glanced only briefly at the paper. "I accept," he said.

After the formalities were in due course completed, Carnegie was in a euphoric mood. "Now, Pierpont, I am the happiest man in the world," he said. Morgan was by no means unhappy himself: his own banking company had made a direct profit of $12,500,000 in the underwriting transaction, and this was but a prelude to a stream of lucrative financings under Morgan's aegis, by which the total capitalization was rapidly raised to $1,400,000,000. A few years later, Morgan and Carnegie found themselves aboard the same steamer en route to Europe. They fell into talk and Carnegie confessed, "I made one mistake, Pierpont, when I sold out to you."

"What was that?" asked the banker.

"I should have asked you for $100,000,000 more than I did."

Morgan grinned. "Well," he said, "you would have got it if you had."

Thus was written *finis* to one stage of Carnegie's career. Now it would be seen to what extent his "radical pronouncements" were serious. For in the *Gospel of Wealth*—the famous article combined with others in book form—Carnegie had proclaimed the duty of the millionaire to administer and distribute his wealth *during his lifetime*. Though he might have "proved" his worth by his fortune, his heirs had shown no such evidence of their fitness. Carnegie bluntly concluded: "By taxing estates heavily at his death, the State marks its condemnation of the selfish millionaire's unworthy life."

Coming from the leading millionaire of the day, these had been startling sentiments. So also were his views on the "labor question" which, if patronizing, were nonetheless humane and advanced for their day. The trouble was, of course, that the sentiments were somewhat difficult to credit. As one commentator of the day remarked, "His vision of what might be done with wealth had beauty and breadth and thus serenely overlooked the means by which wealth had been acquired."

For example, the novelist Hamlin Garland visited the steel towns from which the Carnegie millions came and bore away a description of work that was ugly, brutal, and exhausting: he contrasted the lavish care expended on the plants with the callous disregard of the pigsty homes: "the streets were horrible; the buildings poor; the sidewalks sunken and full of holes . . . Everywhere the yellow mud of the streets lay kneaded into sticky masses through which groups of pale, lean men slouched in faded garments . . ." When the famous Homestead strike erupted in 1892, with its private army of Pinkerton detectives virtually at war with the workers, the Carnegie benevolence seemed revealed as shabby fakery. At Skibo Carnegie stood firmly behind the company's iron determination to break the strike. As a result, public sentiment swung sharply and suddenly against him; the St. Louis *Post-Dispatch* wrote: "Three months ago Andrew Carnegie

The Homestead Strike as it was pictured in a drawing from Harper's Weekly.

was a man to be envied. Today he is an object of mingled pity and contempt. In the estimation of nine-tenths of the thinking people on both sides of the ocean he has . . . confessed himself a moral coward.''

In an important sense the newspaper was right. For though Carnegie continued to fight against "privilege," he saw privilege only in its fading aristocratic vestments and not in the new hierarchies of wealth and power to which he himself belonged. In Skibo Castle he now played the role of the benign autocrat, awakening to the skirling of his private bagpiper and proceeding to breakfast to the sonorous accompaniment of the castle organ.

Meanwhile there had also come fame and honors in which Carnegie wallowed unashamedly. He counted the "freedoms" bestowed on him by grateful or hopeful cities and crowed. "I have fifty-two and Gladstone has only seventeen." He entertained the King of England and told him that democracy was better than monarchy, and met the German Kaiser: "Oh, yes, yes," said the latter worthy on being introduced. "I have read your books. You do not like kings." But Mark Twain, on hearing of this, was not fooled. "He says he is a scorner of kings and emperors and dukes," he wrote, "whereas he is like the rest of the human race: a slight attention from one of these

A New York World *cartoonist labeled Carnegie "The Modern Baron with the Old Methods."*

can make him drunk for a week . . .''

And yet it is not enough to conclude that Carnegie was in fact a smaller man than he conceived himself. For this judgment overlooks one immense and irrefutable fact. He did, in the end, abide by his self-imposed duty. He did give nearly all of his gigantic fortune away.

As one would suspect, the quality of the philanthropy reflected the man himself. There was, for example, a huge and sentimentally administered private pension fund to which access was to be had on the most trivial as well as the most worthy grounds: if it included a number of writers, statesmen, scientists, it also made room for two maiden ladies with whom Carnegie had once danced as a young man, a boyhood acquaintance who had once held Carnegie's books while he ran a race, a merchant to whom he had once delivered a telegram and who had subsequently fallen on hard times. And then, as one would expect, there was a benevolent autocracy in the administration of the larger philanthropies as well. "Now everybody vote Aye," was the way Carnegie typically determined the policies of the philanthropic "foundations" he established.

Yet if these flaws bore the stamp of one side of Carnegie's personality, there was also the other side—the side that, however crudely, asked important questions and however piously, concerned itself with great ideals. Of this the range and purpose of the main philanthropies gave unimpeachable testimony. There were the famous libraries—three thousand of them costing nearly sixty million dollars; there

A contrasting view, captioned "The Macmillion," from London's Punch.

were the Carnegie institutes in Pittsburgh and Washington, Carnegie Hall in New York, the Hague Peace Palace, the Carnegie Endowment for International Peace, and the precedent-making Carnegie Corporation of New York, with its original enormous endowment of $125,000,000. In his instructions to the trustees of this first great modern foundation, couched in the simplified spelling of which he was an ardent advocate, we see Carnegie at his very best:

> Conditions on erth [*sic*] inevitably change; hence, no wise man will bind Trustees forever to certain paths, causes, or institutions. I disclaim any intention of doing so . . . My chief happiness, as I write these lines lies in the thot [*sic*] that, even after I pass away, the welth [*sic*] that came to me to administer as a sacred trust for the good of my fellow men is to continue to benefit humanity . . .

If these sentiments move us—if Carnegie himself in retrospect moves us at last to grudging respect—it is not because his was the triumph of a saint or a philosopher. It is because it was the much more difficult triumph of a very human and fallible man struggling to retain his convictions in an age, and in the face of a career, which subjected them to impossible temptations. Carnegie is something of America writ large; his is the story of the Horatio Alger hero *after* he has made his million dollars. In the failures of Andrew Carnegie we see many of the failures of America itself. In his curious triumph, we see what we hope is our own steadfast core of integrity.

ANDREW CARNEGIE, CAPTAIN OF INDUSTRY

David Boroff

The Diaspora
in America:
A Study of Jewish
Immigration

Since all Americans are themselves at least the descendants of immigrants, it is perhaps not surprising that "native born" citizens have often displayed a kind of love-hate attitude toward newcomers. They recognize in these newcomers their own successes and failures, their pride in what they have accomplished and their shame at what they have forgotten or rejected in their heritage. This ambivalence has been exacerbated by the very real conflicts that immigration has caused. On the one hand, the immigrant has always been a national asset—his labor and intelligence add to the productivity and wealth of society; his culture enriches and diversifies American civilization. On the other hand, the immigrant has represented competition, strangeness, unsettling change. Most immigrants have been poor, many upon arrival have been ill adjusted to American values and habits. Social and economic problems have frequently resulted, especially when large numbers have flooded into the country in relatively short periods of time. This last point explains why the late nineteenth and early twentieth centuries produced the movement to restrict immigration, for the influx was greater then than at any other time.

In this essay the late David Boroff of New York University discusses the impact of Jewish immigrants on the United States and the impact of the nation on these immigrants. He focuses chiefly on the period after 1880, when Jewish immigration was heaviest. His account provides a vivid picture of the life of these people, and helps explain both why they, as well as other immigrants, were sometimes disliked and why they were themselves at times ambivalent in their reactions to America.

*I*t started with a tiny trickle and ended in a roaring flood. The first to come were just twenty-three Jews from Brazil who landed in New Amsterdam in 1654, in flight from a country no longer hospitable to them. They were, in origin, Spanish and Portuguese Jews (many with grandiloquent Iberian names) whose families had been wandering for a century and a half. New Amsterdam provided a chilly reception. Governor Peter Stuyvesant at first asked them to leave, but kinder hearts in the Dutch West India Company granted them the right to stay, "provided the poor among them . . . be supported by their own nation." By the end of the century, there were perhaps one hundred Jews; by the middle of the eighteenth century, there were about three hundred in New York, and smaller communities in Newport, Philadelphia, and Charleston.

Because of their literacy, zeal, and overseas connections, colonial Jews prospered as merchants, though there were artisans and laborers among them. The Jewish community was tightly knit, but there was a serious shortage of trained religious functionaries. There wasn't a single American rabbi, for example, until the nineteenth century. Jews were well regarded, particularly in New England. Puritan culture leaned heavily on the Old Testament, and Harvard students learned Hebrew; indeed, during the American Revolution, the suggestion was advanced that Hebrew replace English as the official language of the new country. The absence of an established national religion made it possible for Judaism to be regarded as merely another religion in a pluralistic society. The early days of the new republic were thus a happy time for Jews. Prosperous and productive, they were admitted to American communal life with few restrictions. It is little wonder that a Jewish spokesman asked rhetorically in 1820 : "On what spot in this habitable Globe does an Israelite enjoy more blessings, more privileges?"

The second wave of immigration during the nineteenth century is often described as German, but that is misleading. Actually, there were many East European Jews among the immigrants who came in the half century before 1870. However, the German influence was strong, and there was a powerful undercurrent of Western enlightenment at work. These Jews came because economic depression and the Industrial Revolution had made their lot as artisans and small merchants intolerable. For some there was also the threatening backwash of the failure of the Revolution of 1848. Moreover, in Germany at this time Jews were largely disfranchised and discriminated against. During this period, between 200,000 and 400,000 Jews emigrated to this country, and the Jewish population had risen to about half a million by 1870.

This was the colorful era of the peddler and his pack. Peddling was an easy way to get started—it required little capital—and it often rewarded enterprise and daring. Jewish peddlers fanned out through the young country into farmland and mining camp, frontier and Indian territory. The more successful peddlers ultimately settled in one place as storekeepers. (Some proud businesses—including that of Senator Goldwater's family—made their start this way.) Feeling somewhat alienated from the older, settled Jews, who had a reputation for declining piety, the new immigrants organized their own synagogues and community facilities, such as cemeteries and hospitals. In general, these immigrants were amiably received by native Americans, who, unsophisticated about differences that were crucial to the immigrants themselves, regarded all Central Europeans as "Germans."

Essentially, the emigration route was the same between 1820 and 1870 as it would be in the post-1880 exodus. The travellers stayed in emigration inns while awaiting their ship, and since they had all their resources with them, they were in danger of being robbed. The journey itself was hazardous and, in the days of the sailing vessels when a good wind was indispensable, almost interminable. Nor were the appointments very comfortable even for the relatively well to do. A German Jew who made the journey in 1856 reported that his cabin, little more than six feet by six feet, housed six passengers in triple-decker bunks. When a storm raged, the passengers had to retire to their cabins lest they be washed off the deck by waves. "Deprived of air," he wrote, "it soon became unbearable in the cabins in which six sea-sick persons breathed." On this particular journey, sea water began to trickle into the cabins, and the planks had to be retarred.

Still, the emigration experience was a good deal easier than it would be later. For one thing, the immigrants were better educated and better acquainted with modern political and social attitudes than the oppressed and bewildered East European multitudes who came after 1880. Fewer in number, they were treated courteously by ships' captains. (On a journey in 1839, described by David Mayer, the ship's captain turned over his own cabin to the Jewish passengers for their prayers and regularly visited those Jews who were ill.) Moreover, there was still the bloom of adventure about the overseas voyage. Ships left Europe amid the booming of cannon, while on shore ladies enthusiastically waved their handkerchiefs. On the way over, there was a holiday atmosphere despite the hazards, and there was great jubilation when land was sighted.

There were, however, rude shocks when the voyagers arrived in this country. The anguish of Castle Garden and Ellis Island was well in the future when immigration first began to swell. But New York seemed inhospitable, its pace frantic, the outlook not entirely hopeful. Isaac M. Wise, a distinguished rabbi who made the journey in 1846, was appalled. "The whole city appeared to me like a large shop," he wrote, "where everyone buys or sells, cheats or is cheated. I had never before seen a city so bare of all art and of every trace of good taste; likewise I had never witnessed anywhere such rushing, hurrying, chasing, running . . . Everything seemed so pitifully small and paltry; and I had had so exalted an idea of the land of freedom." Moreover, he no sooner landed in New York than he was abused by a German drayman whose services he had declined. "Aha! thought I," he later wrote, "you have left home and kindred in order to get away from the disgusting Judaeophobia and here the first German greeting that sounds in your ears is hep! hep!'' (The expletive was a Central European equivalent of ''Kike.'') Another German Jew who worked as a clothing salesman was affronted by the way customers were to be ''lured'' into buying (''I did not think this occupation corresponded in any way to my views of a merchant's dignity'').

After 1880, Jewish immigration into the United States was in flood tide. And the source was principally East Europe, where by 1880 three quarters of the world's 7.7 million Jews were living. In all, over two million Jews came to these shores in little more than three decades—about one third of Europe's Jewry. Some of them came, as their predecessors had come, because of shrinking economic opportunities. In Russia and in the Austro-Hungarian empire, the growth of large-scale agriculture squeezed out Jewish middlemen as it destroyed the independent peasantry, while in the cities the development of manufacturing reduced the need for Jewish artisans. Vast numbers of Jews became petty tradesmen or even *luftmenschen* (men without visible means of support who drifted from one thing to another). In Galicia, around 1900, there was a Jewish trader for

Her decks jammed with hopeful immigrants, the
S.S. Patricia *arrives at Ellis Island in 1906.*

DIASPORA IN AMERICA: A STUDY OF JEWISH IMMIGRATION

every ten peasants, and the average value of his stock came to only twenty dollars.

Savage discrimination and pogroms also incited Jews to emigrate. The Barefoot Brigades—bands of marauding Russian peasants—brought devastation and bloodshed to Jewish towns and cities. On a higher social level, there was the "cold pogrom," a government policy calculated to destroy Jewish life. The official hope was that one third of Russia's Jews would die out, one third would emigrate, and one third would be converted to the Orthodox Church. Crushing restrictions were imposed. Jews were required to live within the Pale of Settlement in western Russia, they could not Russify their names, and they were subjected to rigorous quotas for schooling and professional training. Nor could general studies be included in the curriculum of Jewish religious schools. It was a life of poverty and fear.

Nevertheless, the *shtetl*, the typical small Jewish town, was a triumph of endurance and spiritual integrity. It was a place where degradation and squalor could not wipe out dignity, where learning flourished in the face of hopelessness, and where a tough, sardonic humor provided catharsis for the tribulations of an existence that was barely endurable. The abrasions and humiliations of everyday life were healed by a rich heritage of custom and ceremony. And there was always Sabbath—"The Bride of the Sabbath," as the Jews called the day of rest—to bring repose and exaltation to a life always sorely tried.

To be sure, even this world showed signs of disintegration. Secular learning, long resisted by East European Jews and officially denied to them, began to make inroads. Piety gave way to revolutionary fervor, and Jews began to play a heroic role in Czarist Russia's bloody history of insurrection and suppression.

This was the bleak, airless milieu from which the emigrants came. A typical expression of the Jewish attitude toward emigration from Russia—both its hopefulness and the absence of remorse—was provided by Dr. George Price, who had come to this country in one of the waves of East European emigration:

> Should this Jewish emigrant regret his leave-taking of his native land which fails to appreciate him? No! A thousand times no! He must not regret fleeing the clutches of the bloodthirsty crocodile. Sympathy for this country? How ironical it sounds! Am I not despised? Am I not urged to leave? Do I not hear the word *Zhid* constantly? . . . Be thou cursed forever my wicked homeland, because you remind me of the Inquisition . . . May you rue the day when you exiled the people who worked for your welfare.

After 1880, going to America—no other country really lured—became the great drama of redemption for the masses of East European Jews. (For some, of course, Palestine had that role even in the late nineteenth century, but these were an undaunted Zionist cadre prepared to endure the severest hardships.) The assassination of Czar

Alexander II in 1881, and the subsequent pogrom, marked the beginning of the new influx. By the end of the century, 700,000 Jews had arrived, about one quarter of them totally illiterate, almost all of them impoverished. Throughout East Europe, Jews talked longingly about America as the "goldene medinah" (the golden province), and biblical imagery—"the land of milk and honey"—came easily to their lips. Those who could write were kept busy composing letters to distant kin—or even to husbands—in America. (Much of the time, the husband went first, and by abstemious living saved enough to fetch wife and children from the old country.) Children played at "emigrating games," and for the entire *shtetl* it was an exciting moment when the mail-carrier announced how many letters had arrived from America.

German steamship companies assiduously advertised the glories of the new land and provided a one-price rate from *shtetl* to New York. Emigration inns were established in Brody (in the Ukraine) and in the port cities of Bremen and Hamburg, where emigrants would gather for the trip. There were rumors that groups of prosperous German Jews would underwrite their migration to America; and in fact such people often did help their co-religionists when they were stranded without funds in the port cities of Germany. Within Russia itself, the government after 1880 more or less acquiesced in the emigration of Jews, and connived in the vast business of "stealing the border" (smuggling emigrants across). After 1892, emigration was legal—except for those of draft age—but large numbers left with forged papers, because that proved to be far easier than getting tangled in the red tape of the Czarist bureaucracy. Forged documents, to be sure, were expensive—they cost twenty-five rubles, for many Jews the equivalent of five weeks' wages. Nor was the departure from home entirely a happy event. There were the uncertainties of the new life, the fear that in America "one became a gentile." Given the Jewish aptitude for lugubriousness, a family's departure was often like a funeral, lachrymose and anguished, with the neighbors carting off the furniture that would no longer be needed.

For people who had rarely ventured beyond the boundaries of their own village, going to America was an epic adventure. They travelled with pitifully little money; the average immigrant arrived in New York with only about twenty dollars. With their domestic impedimenta—bedding, brass candlesticks, samovars—they would proceed to the port cities by rail, cart, and even on foot. At the emigration inns, they had to wait their turn. Thousands milled around, entreating officials for departure cards. There were scenes of near chaos—mothers shrieking, children crying; battered wicker trunks, bedding, utensils in wild disarray. At Hamburg, arriving emigrants were put in the "unclean" section of the *Auswandererhallen* until examined by physicians who decided whether their clothing and baggage had to be disinfected. After examination, Jews could not leave the center; other emigrants could.

The ocean voyage provided little respite. (Some elected to sail by way of Liverpool at a reduction of nine dollars from the usual rate of thirty-four dollars.) Immigrants long remembered the "smell of ship," a distillation of many putrescences. Those who went in steerage slept on mattresses filled with straw and kept their clothes on to keep warm. The berth itself was generally six feet long, two feet wide, and two and a half feet high, and it had to accommodate the passenger's luggage. Food was another problem. Many Orthodox Jews subsisted on herring, black bread, and tea which they brought because they did not trust the dietary purity of the ship's food. Some ships actually maintained a separate galley for kosher food, which was coveted by non-Jewish passengers because it was allegedly better.

Unsophisticated about travel and faced by genuine dangers, Jewish emigrants found the overseas trip a long and terrifying experience. But when land was finally sighted, the passengers often began to cheer and shout. "I looked up at the sky," an immigrant wrote years later. "It seemed much bluer and the sun much brighter than in the old country. It reminded me on [sic] the Garden of Eden."

Unhappily, the friendly reception that most immigrants envisioned in the new land rarely materialized. Castle Garden in the Battery, at the foot of Manhattan—and later Ellis Island in New York Harbor —proved to be almost as traumatic as the journey itself. "Castle Garden," an immigrant wrote, "is a large building, a Gehenna, through which all Jewish arrivals must pass to be cleansed before they are considered worthy of breathing freely the air of the land of the almighty dollar. . . . If in Brody, thousands crowded about, here tens of thousands thronged about; if there they were starving, here they were dying; if there they were crushed, here they were simply beaten."

One must make allowances for the impassioned hyperbole of the suffering immigrant, but there is little doubt that the immigration officials were harassed, overworked, and often unsympathetic. Authorized to pass on the admissibility of the newcomers, immigration officers struck terror into their hearts by asking questions designed to reveal their literacy and social attitudes. "How much is six times six?" an inspector asked a woman in the grip of nervousness, then casually asked the next man, "Have you ever been in jail?"

There were, of course, representatives of Jewish defense groups present, especially from the Hebrew Immigrant Aid Society. But by this time, the immigrants, out of patience and exhausted, tended to view them balefully. The Jewish officials tended to be highhanded, and the temporary barracks which they administered on Ward's Island for those not yet settled became notorious. Discontent culminated in a riot over food; one day the director—called The Father— had to swim ashore for his life, and the police were hastily summoned.

Most immigrants went directly from Castle Garden or Ellis Island to the teeming streets of Manhattan, where they sought relatives or landsleit (fellow townsmen) who had gone before them. Easy marks for hucksters and swindlers, they were overcharged by draymen for carrying their paltry possessions, engaged as strikebreakers, or hired at shamelessly low wages.

Immigrant women and children at Ellis Island eating their first American meal (1906).

"Greenhorn" or "greener" was their common name. A term of vilification, the source of a thousand cruel jokes, it was their shame and their destiny. On top of everything else, the immigrants had to abide the contempt of their co-religionists who had preceded them to America by forty or fifty years. By the time the heavy East European immigration set in, German Jews had achieved high mercantile status and an uneasy integration into American society. They did not want to be reminded of their kinship with these uncouth and impoverished Jews who were regarded vaguely as a kind of Oriental influx. There was a good deal of sentiment against "aiding such paupers to emigrate to these shores." One charitable organization declared: "Organized immigration from Russia, Roumania, and other semi-barbarous countries is a mistake and has proved to be a failure. It is no relief to the Jews of Russia, Poland, etc., and it jeopardizes the well-being of the American Jews."

A genuine uptown-downtown split soon developed, with condescension on one side and resentment on the other. The German Jews objected as bitterly to the rigid, old-world Orthodoxy of the immigrants as they did to their new involvement in trade unions. They were fearful, too, of the competition they would offer in the needle trades. (Indeed, the East Europeans ultimately forced the uptown Jews out of the industry.) On the other side of the barricades, Russian Jews complained that at the hands of their uptown brethren, "every man is questioned like a criminal, is looked down upon . . . just as if he were standing before a Russian official." Nevertheless, many German Jews responded to the call of conscience by providing funds for needy immigrants and setting up preparatory schools for immigrant children for whom no room was yet available in the hopelessly overcrowded public schools.

Many comfortably settled German Jews saw dispersion as the answer to the problem. Efforts were made to divert immigrants to small towns in other parts of the country, but these were largely ineffective. There were also some gallant adventures with farming in such remote places as South Dakota, Oregon, and Louisiana. Though the Jewish pioneers were brave and idealistic, drought, disease, and ineptitude conspired against them. (In Oregon, for example, they tried to raise corn in cattle country, while in Louisiana they found themselves in malarial terrain.) Only chicken farming in New Jersey proved to be successful to any great degree. Farm jobs for Jews were available, but as one immigrant said: "I have no desire to be a farm hand to an ignorant Yankee at the end of the world. I would rather work here at half the price in a factory; for then I would at least be able to spend my free evenings with my friends."

It was in New York, then, that the bulk of the immigrants settled —in the swarming, tumultuous Lower East Side—with smaller concentrations in Boston, Philadelphia, and Chicago. Far less adaptable than the German Jews who were now lording it over them, disoriented and frightened, the East European immigrants constituted a vast and exploited proletariat. According to a survey in 1890, sixty per cent of all immigrant Jews worked in the needle trades. This industry had gone through a process of decentralization in which contractors carried out the bulk of production, receiving merely the cut goods from the manufacturer. Contracting establishments were everywhere in the Lower East Side, including the contractors' homes, where pressers warmed their irons on the very stove on which the boss's wife was preparing supper. The contractors also gave out "section" work to families and *landsleit* who would struggle to meet the quotas at home. The bondage of the sewing machine was therefore extended into the tenements, with entire families enslaved by the machine's voracious demands. The Hester Street "pig market," where one could buy anything, became the labor exchange; there tailors, operators, finishers, basters, and pressers would congregate on Saturday in the hope of being hired by contractors.

Life in the sweatshops of the Lower East Side was hard, but it made immigrants employable from the start, and a weekly wage of five dollars—the equivalent of ten rubles—looked good in immigrant eyes. Moreover, they were among their own kin and kind, and the sweatshops, noisome as they were, were still the scene of lively political and even literary discussions. (In some cigar-making shops, in fact, the bosses hired "readers" to keep the minds of the workers occupied with classic and Yiddish literature as they performed their repetitive chores.) East European Jews, near the end of the century, made up a large part of the skilled labor force in New York, ranking first in twenty-six out of forty-seven trades, and serving, for example, as

*The immigrants' new home: a crowded, noisy, but
friendly street on New York's Lower East Side.*

bakers, building-trade workers, painters, furriers, jewellers, and
tinsmiths.

Almost one quarter of all the immigrants tried their hands as
tradesmen—largely as peddlers or as pushcart vendors in the mad-
house bazaar of the Lower East Side. For some it was an apprentice-
ship in low-toned commerce that would lead to more elegant careers.
For others it was merely a martyrdom that enabled them to subsist. It
was a modest enough investment—five dollars for a license, one dollar
for a basket, and four dollars for wares. They stocked up on pins and
needles, shoe laces, polish, and handkerchiefs, learned some basic expressions ("You wanna buy somethin'?"), and were on their hapless
way.

It was the professions, of course, that exerted the keenest attraction
to Jews, with their reverence for learning. For most of them it was too
late; they had to reconcile themselves to more humble callings. But
it was not too late for their children, and between 1897 and 1907, the
number of Jewish physicians in Manhattan rose from 450 to 1,000.
Of all the professions it was medicine that excited the greatest veneration. (Some of this veneration spilled over into pharmacy, and "drug-

gists'' were highly respected figures who were called upon to prescribe for minor—and even major—ills, and to serve as scribes for the letters that the immigrants were unable to read and write themselves.) There were Jewish lawyers on the Lower East Side and by 1901 over 140 Jewish policemen, recruited in part by Theodore Roosevelt, who, as police commissioner, had issued a call for ''the Maccabee or fighting Jewish type.''

The Lower East Side was the American counterpart of the ghetto for Jewish immigrants, as well as their glittering capital. At its peak, around 1910, it packed over 350,000 people into a comparatively small area—roughly from Canal Street to Fourteenth Street—with as many as 523 people per acre, so that Arnold Bennett was moved to remark that ''the architecture seemed to sweat humanity at every window and door.'' The most densely populated part of the city, it held one sixth of Manhattan's population and most of New York's office buildings and factories. ''Uptowners'' used to delight in visiting it (as a later generation would visit Harlem) to taste its exotic flavor. But the great mass of Jews lived there because the living was cheap, and there was a vital Jewish community that gave solace to the lonely and comfort to the pious.

A single man could find lodgings of a sort, including coffee morning and night, for three dollars a month. For a family, rent was about ten dollars a month, milk was four cents a quart, kosher meat twelve cents a pound, bread two cents a pound, herring a penny or two. A kitchen table could be bought for a dollar, chairs at thirty-five cents each. One managed, but the life was oppressive. Most families lived in the notorious ''dumbbell'' flats of old-law tenements (built prior to 1901). Congested, often dirty and unsanitary, these tenements were six or seven stories high and had four apartments on each floor. Only one room in each three or four room apartment received direct air and sunlight, and the families on each floor shared a toilet in the hall.

Many families not only used their flats as workshops but also took in boarders to make ends meet. Jacob Riis tells of a two-room apartment on Allen Street which housed parents, six children, and six boarders. ''Two daughters sewed clothes at home. The elevator railway passed by the window. The cantor rehearses, a train passes, the shoemaker bangs, ten brats run around like goats, the wife putters. . . . At night we all try to get some sleep in the stifling, roach-infested two rooms.'' In the summer, the tenants spilled out into fire escapes and rooftops, which were converted into bedrooms.

Nevertheless, life on the Lower East Side had surprising vitality. Despite the highest population density in the city, the Tenth Ward had one of the lowest death rates. In part, this was because of the strenuous personal cleanliness of Jews, dictated by their religion. Though only eight per cent of the East European Jews had baths, bathhouses and steam rooms on the Lower East Side did a booming business. There was, of course, a heavy incidence of tuberculosis—''the white plague.'' Those who were afflicted could be heard crying out, ''*Luft! Gib mir luft!*'' (''Air! Give me air!''). It was, in fact, this terror of "consumption" that impelled some East Side Jews to become farmers in the Catskills at the turn of the century, thus forerunning the gaudy career of the Catskill Borscht Belt resort hotels. The same fear impelled Jews on the Lower East Side to move to Washington Heights and the Bronx, where the altitude was higher, the air presumably purer.

Alcoholism, a prime affliction of most immigrant groups, was almost unknown among Jews. They drank ritualistically on holidays but almost never to excess. They were, instead, addicted to seltzer or soda water—Harry Golden's "2¢ plain"—which they viewed as "the worker's champagne." The suicide rate was relatively low, though higher than in the *shtetl,* and there was always a shudder of sympathy when the Yiddish press announced that someone had *genumen di ges* (taken gas).

The Lower East Side was from the start the scene of considerable crime. But its inhabitants became concerned when the crime rate among the young people seemed to rise steeply around 1910. There was a good deal of prostitution. The dancing academies, which achieved popularity early in this century, became recruiting centers for prostitutes. In 1908–9, of 581 foreign women arrested for prostitution, 225 were Jewish. There was the notorious Max Hochstim Association, which actively recruited girls, while the New York Independent Benevolent Association—an organization of pimps—provided sick benefits, burial privileges, bail, and protection money for prostitutes.

A New York sweatshop, photographed about 1910.

The membership was even summoned to funerals with a two-dollar fine imposed on those who did not attend. Prostitution was so taken for granted that Canal Street had stores on one side featuring sacerdotal articles, while brothels were housed on the other.

Family life on the Lower East Side was cohesive and warm, though there was an edge of shrillness and hysteria to it. Marriages were not always happy, but if wives were viewed as an affliction, children were regarded as a blessing. The kitchen was the center of the household, and food was almost always being served to either family or visitors. No matter how poor they were, Jewish families ate well—even to excess—and mothers considered their children woefully underweight unless they were well cushioned with fat.

It was a life with few conventional graces. Handkerchiefs were barely known, and the Yiddish newspapers had to propagandize for their use. Old men smelled of snuff, and in spite of bathing, children often had lice in their hair and were sent home from school by the visiting nurse for a kerosene bath. Bedbugs were considered an inevitability, and pajamas were viewed as an upper-class affectation. Parents quarrelled bitterly—with passionate and resourceful invective —in the presence of their children. Telephones were virtually unknown, and a telegram surely meant disaster from afar.

The zeal of the immigrants on behalf of their children was no less than awe-inspiring. Parents yearned for lofty careers for their offspring, with medicine at the pinnacle. In better-off homes, there was always a piano ("solid mahogany"), and parents often spent their precious reserves to arrange a "concert" for their precocious youngsters, followed by a ball in one of the Lower East Side's many halls.

To be sure, the children inspired a full measure of anxiety in their parents. "Amerikane kinder" was the rueful plaint of the elders, who could not fathom the baffling new ways of the young. Parents were nervous about their daughters' chastity, and younger brothers—often six or seven years old—would be dispatched as chaperones when the girls met their boy friends. There was uneasiness about Jewish street gangs and the growing problem of delinquency. The old folks were vexed by the new tides of secularism and political radicalism that were weaning their children from traditional pieties. But most of all, they feared that their sons would not achieve the success that would redeem their own efforts, humiliations, and failures in the harsh new land. Pressure on their children was relentless. But on the whole the children did well, astonishingly well. "The ease and rapidity with which they learn," Jacob Riis wrote, "is equalled only by their good behavior and close attention while in school. There is no whispering and no rioting at these desks." Samuel Chotzinoff, the music critic, tells a story which reveals the attitude of the Jewish schoolboy. When an altercation threatened between Chotzinoff and a classmate, his antagonist's reaction was to challenge him to spell "combustible."

The Lower East Side was a striking demonstration that financial want does not necessarily mean cultural poverty. The immigrant Jews were nearly always poor and often illiterate, but they were not culturally deprived. In fact, between 1890 and World War I, the Jewish community provides a remarkable chapter in American cultural history. Liberated from the constrictions of European captivity, immigrant Jews experienced a great surge of intellectual vitality. Yiddish, the Hebrew-German dialect which some people had casually dismissed as a barbarous ''jargon,'' became the vehicle of this cultural renascence. Between 1885 and 1914, over 150 publications of all kinds made their appearance. But the new Yiddish journalism reached its apogee with the *Jewish Daily Forward* under the long editorial reign of Abraham Cahan. The *Forward* was humanitarian, pro-labor, and socialistic. But it was also an instrument for acclimatizing immigrants in the new environment. It provided practical hints on how to deal with the new world, letters from the troubled (*Bintel Brief*), and even, at one time, a primer on baseball (''explained to non-sports''). The *Forward* also published and fostered an enormous amount of literature in Yiddish—both original works by writers of considerable talent, and translations of classic writers.

In this cultural ferment, immigrants studied English in dozens of night schools and ransacked the resources of the Aguilar Free Library on East Broadway. ''When I had [a] book in my hand,'' an immigrant wrote, ''I pressed it to my heart and wanted to kiss it.'' The Educational Alliance, also on East Broadway, had a rich program designed to make immigrant Jews more American and their sons more Jewish. And there were scores of settlement houses, debating clubs, ethical societies, and literary circles which attracted the young. In fact, courtships were carried on in a rarefied atmosphere full of lofty talk about art, politics, and philosophy. And though there was much venturesome palaver about sexual freedom, actual behavior tended to be quite strait-laced.

But the most popular cultural institution was the café or coffee house, which served as the Jewish saloon. There were about 250 of them, each with its own following. Here the litterateurs sat for hours over steaming glasses of tea; revolutionaries and Bohemians gathered to make their pronouncements or raise money for causes; actors and playwrights came to hold court. For immigrant Jews, talk was the breath of life itself. The passion for music and theatre knew no bounds. When Beethoven's Ninth Symphony was performed one summer night in 1915, mounted police had to be summoned to keep order outside Lewisohn Stadium, so heavy was the press of crowds eager for the twenty-five-cent stone seats. Theatre (in Yiddish) was to the Jewish immigrants what Shakespeare and Marlowe had been to the groundlings in Elizabethan England. Tickets were cheap—twenty-five cents to one dollar—and theatregoing was universal. It was a raucous, robust, and communal experience. Mothers brought their babies (except in some of the ''swellest'' theatres, which forbade it), and peddlers hawked their wares between the acts. There were theatre parties for trade unions and *landsmanschaften* (societies of fellow townsmen), and the audience milled around and renewed old friendships or argued the merits of the play. The stage curtain had bold advertisements of stores or blown-up portraits of stars.

There was an intense cult of personality in the Yiddish theatre and a system of claques not unlike that which exists in grand opera today. The undisputed monarch was Boris Thomashefsky, and a theatre program of his day offered this panegyric:

> Thomashefsky! Artist great!
> No praise is good enough for you!
> Of all the stars you remain the king
> You seek no tricks, no false quibbles;
> One sees truth itself playing.
> Your appearance is godly to us
> Every movement is full of grace
> Pleasing is your every gesture
> Sugar sweet your every turn
> You remain the king of the stage
> Everything falls to your feet.

Many of the plays were sentimental trash—heroic "operas" on historical themes, "greenhorn" melodramas full of cruel abandonments and tearful reunions, romantic musicals, and even topical dramas dealing with such immediate events as the Homestead Strike, the Johnstown Flood, and the Kishinev Pogrom of 1903. Adaptability and a talent for facile plagiarism were the essence of the playwright's art in those days, and "Professor" Moses Horwitz wrote 167 plays, most of them adaptations of old operas and melodramas. The plays were so predictable that an actor once admitted he didn't even have to learn his lines; he merely had to have a sense of the general situation and then adapt lines from other plays.

There was, of course, a serious Yiddish drama, introduced principally by Jacob Gordin, who adapted classical and modernist drama to the Yiddish stage. Jewish intellectuals were jubilant at this development. But the process of acculturation had its amusing and grotesque aspects. Shakespeare was a great favorite but "*verbessert and vergrossert*" (improved and enlarged). There was the Jewish *King Lear* in which Cordelia becomes Goldele. (The theme of filial ingratitude was a "natural" on the Lower East Side, where parents constantly made heroic sacrifices.) *Hamlet* was also given a Jewish coloration, the prince becoming a rabbinical student who returns from the seminary to discover treachery at home. And *A Doll's House* by Ibsen was transformed into *Minna,* in which a sensitive and intelligent young woman, married to an ignorant laborer, falls in love with her boarder and ultimately commits suicide.

Related to the Jewish love of theatre was the immigrant's adoration of the cantor, a profession which evoked as much flamboyance and egotistical preening as acting did. (In fact, actors would sometimes grow beards before the high holydays and find jobs as cantors.) Synagogues vied with each other for celebrated cantors, sometimes as a way of getting out of debt, since tickets were sold for the high-holyday services.

The Lower East Side was a vibrant community, full of color and gusto, in which the Jewish immigrant felt marvelously at home, safe from the terrors of the alien city. But it was a setting too for fierce conflict and enervating strain. There were three major influences at work, each pulling in a separate direction: Jewish Orthodoxy, assimilationism, and the new socialist gospel. The immigrants were Orthodox, but their children tended to break away. *Cheders* (Hebrew schools) were everywhere, in basements and stores and tenements, and the old custom of giving a child a taste of honey when he was beginning to learn to read—as symbolic of the sweetness of study—persisted. But the young, eager to be accepted into American society, despised the old ways and their "greenhorn" teachers. Fathers began to view their sons as "freethinkers," a term that was anathema to them. Observance of the Law declined, and the Saturday Sabbath was ignored by many Jews. A virulent antireligious tendency developed among many "enlightened" Jews, who would hold profane balls on the most sacred evening of the year—Yom Kippur—at which they would dance and eat nonkosher food. (Yom Kippur is a fast day.) And the trade-union movement also generated uneasiness among the pious elders of the Lower East Side. "Do you want us to bow down to your archaic God?" a radical newspaper asked. "Each era has its new Torah. Ours is one of freedom and justice."

But for many immigrants the basic discontent was with their American experience itself. The golden province turned out to be a place of tenements and sweatshops. A familiar cry was "*a klug af Columbus!*" ("a curse on Columbus") or, "Who ever asked him, Columbus, to discover America?" Ellis Island was called *Trernindzl* (Island of Tears), and Abraham Cahan, in his initial reaction to the horrors of immigration, thundered: "Be cursed, immigration! Cursed by those conditions which have brought you into being. How many souls have you broken, how many courageous and mighty souls have you shattered." The fact remains that most Jewish immigrants, in the long run, made a happy adjustment to their new land.

After 1910, the Lower East Side went into a decline. Its strange glory was over. New areas of Jewish settlement opened up in Brooklyn, the Bronx, and in upper Manhattan. By the mid-twenties, less than ten per cent of New York's Jews lived on the Lower East Side, although it still remained the heartland to which one returned to shop, to see Yiddish theatre, and to renew old ties. By 1924 Jewish immigration into the United States was severely reduced by new immigration laws, and the saga of mass immigration was done. But the intensities of the Jewish immigrant experience had already made an indelible mark on American culture and history that would endure for many years.

William V. Shannon

The Age
of the Bosses

The rapid industrialization of the United States after the Civil War, which produced great tycoons like Andrew Carnegie and encouraged millions of work-hungry Europeans to migrate, changed the shape of society in a variety of ways. One of the most obvious and important of these was industrialization's effect on where and how people lived. Huge industrial concerns brought together masses of workers in one place; commercial and service enterprises sprang up alongside the factories; in short, great cities rapidly developed and America was on its way to becoming an urban nation.

The advantages of urbanization were great—new wealth, better educational opportunities, a wide range of amusements; soon a more refined and complex culture emerged. But great problems also appeared—crowded, unhealthy living conditions, crime and vice, and countless others. Not the least of these was the problem of how to govern these gigantic agglomerations. More *government was essential to run a city, yet the nation had lived for the better part of a century by the motto:* "that government is best which governs least." New kinds *of government were necessary—building and sanitary codes, social services, a system of representation suited to a mass but atomized society—for which no precedents existed.*

It was this situation, as William V. Shannon explains below, that produced the big-city political machines and the bosses who ran them. Shannon shows that the bosses served a function; they filled a gap in the political system created by the changes resulting from swift industrialization and urban growth. Eventually better machinery than the "machine" was devised to perform that function, although the proper government of cities still eludes us today. As an editor of the New York Times, *Mr. Shannon brings to this subject a thorough knowledge of modern urban politics and, as the author of* The American Irish, *an equally solid understanding of the old boss system.*

*T*he big cities and the political bosses grew up together in America. Bossism, with all its color and corruption and human drama, was a natural, perhaps even a necessary accompaniment to the rapid development of cities. The new urban communities did not grow slowly and according to plan; on the contrary, huge conglomerations of people from all over the world and from widely varying backgrounds came together suddenly, and in an unplanned, unorganized fashion fumbled their way toward communal relationships and a common identity. The political bosses emerged to cope with this chaotic change and growth. Acting out of greed, a ruthless will for mastery, and an imperfect understanding of what they were about, the bosses imposed upon these conglomerations called cities a certain feudal order and direction.

By 1890 virtually every sizable city had a political boss or was in the process of developing one. By 1950, sixty years later, almost every urban political machine was in an advanced state of obsolescence and its boss in trouble. The reason is not hard to find. Some of the cities kept growing and all of them kept changing, but the bosses, natural products of a specific era, could not grow or change beyond a certain point. The cities became essentially different, and as they did, the old-style organizations, like all organisms which cannot adapt, began to die. The dates vary from city to city. The system began earlier and died sooner in New York. Here or there, an old-timer made one last comeback. In Chicago, the organization and its boss still survive. But exceptions aside, the late nineteenth century saw the beginning, and the middle twentieth, the end, of the Age of the Bosses. What follows is a brief history of how it began, flourished, and passed away.

Soft-spoken Irish farmers from County Mayo and bearded Jews from Poland, country boys from Ohio and sturdy peasants from Calabria, gangling Swedes from near the Arctic Circle and Chinese from Canton, laconic Yankees from Vermont villages and Negro freedmen putting distance between themselves and the old plantation—all these and many other varieties of human beings from every national and religious and cultural tradition poured into America's cities in the decades after the Civil War.

Rome and Alexandria in the ancient world had probably been as polyglot, but in modern times the diversity of American cities was unique. Everywhere in the Western world, cities were growing rapidly in the late nineteenth century; but the Germans from the countryside who migrated to Hamburg and Berlin, the English who moved to Birmingham and London, and the French who flocked to Paris stayed among fellow nationals. They might be mocked as country bumpkins and their clothes might be unfashionable, but everyone they met spoke the same language as themselves, observed the same religious and secular holidays, ate the same kind of food, voted—if they had the franchise at all—in the same elections, and shared the same sentiments and expectations. To move from farm or village to a big

Two of the most memorable and politically long-lived of the bosses were Jersey City's Frank Hague (left) and Boston's James M. Curley (right).

European city was an adventure, but one still remained within the reassuring circle of the known and the familiar.

In American cities, however, the newcomers had nothing in common with one another except their poverty and their hopes. They were truly "the up-rooted." The foreign-born, unless they came from the British Isles, could not speak the language of their new homeland. The food, the customs, the holidays, the politics, were alien. Native Americans migrating to the cities from the countryside experienced their own kind of cultural shock: they found themselves competing not with other Americans but with recently arrived foreigners, so that despite their native birth they, too, felt displaced, strangers in their own country.

It was natural for members of each group to come together to try to find human warmth and protection in Little Italy or Cork Hill or Chinatown or Harlem. These feelings of clannish solidarity were one basis of strength for the political bosses. A man will more readily give his vote to a candidate because he is a neighbor from the old country or has some easily identifiable relationship, if only a similar name or the same religion, than because of agreement on some impersonal issue. Voters can take vicarious satisfaction from his success: "One of our boys is making good."

With so many different races and nationalities living together, however, mutual antagonisms were present, and the opportunity for hostility to flare into open violence was never far away. Ambitious, unscrupulous politicians could have exploited these antagonisms for their own political advantage, but the bosses and the political organizations which they developed did not function that way. If a man

could vote and would "vote right," he was accepted, and that was the end of the matter. What lasting profit was there in attacking his religion or deriding his background?

Tammany early set the pattern of cultivating every bloc and faction and making an appeal as broad-based as possible. Of one precinct captain on the Lower East Side it was said: "He eats corned beef and kosher meat with equal nonchalance, and it's all the same to him whether he takes off his hat in the church or pulls it down over his ears in the synagogue."

Bosses elsewhere instinctively followed the same practice. George B. Cox, the turn-of-the-century Republican boss of Cincinnati, pasted together a coalition of Germans, Negroes, and old families like the Tafts and the Longworths. James M. Curley, who was mayor of Boston on and off for thirty-six years and was its closest approximation to a political boss, ran as well in the Lithuanian neighborhood of South Boston and the Italian section of East Boston as he did in the working-class Irish wards. In his last term in City Hall, he conferred minor patronage on the growing Negro community and joined the N.A.A.C.P.

The bosses organized neighborhoods, smoothed out antagonisms, arranged ethnically balanced tickets, and distributed patronage in accordance with voting strength as part of their effort to win and hold power. They blurred divisive issues and buried racial and religious hostility with blarney and buncombe. They were not aware that they were actually performing a mediating, pacifying function. They did not realize that by trying to please as many people as possible they were helping to hold raw new cities together, providing for inexperienced citizens a common meeting ground in politics and an experience in working together that would not have been available if the cities had been governed by apolitical bureaucracies. Bossism was usually corrupt and was decidedly inefficient, but in the 1960's, when antipoverty planners try to stimulate "community action organizations" to break through the apathy and disorganization of the slums, we can appreciate that the old-style machines had their usefulness.

When William Marcy Tweed, the first and most famous of the big-city bosses, died in jail in 1878, several hundred workingmen showed up for his funeral. The *Nation* wrote the following week:

> Let us remember that he fell without loss of reputation among the bulk of his supporters. The bulk of the poorer voters of this city today revere his memory, and look on him as the victim of rich men's malice; as, in short, a friend of the needy who applied the public funds, with as little waste as was possible under the circumstances, to the purposes to which they ought to be applied—and that is to the making of work for the working man. The odium heaped on him in the pulpits last Sunday does not exist in the lower stratum of New York society.

This split in attitude toward political bosses between the impoverished many and the prosperous middle classes lingers today and still colors historical writing. To respectable people, the boss was an exotic, even grotesque figure. They found it hard to understand why anyone would vote for him or what the sources of his popularity were. To the urban poor, those sources were self-evident. The boss ran a kind of ramshackle welfare state. He helped the unemployed find jobs, interceded in court for boys in trouble, wrote letters home to the old country for the illiterate; he provided free coal and baskets of food to tide a widow over an emergency, and organized parades, excursions to the beach, and other forms of free entertainment. Some bosses, such as Frank Hague in Jersey City and Curley in Boston, were energetic patrons of their respective city hospitals, spending public funds lavishly on new construction, providing maternity and children's clinics, and arranging medical care for the indigent. In an era when social security, Blue Cross, unemployment compensation, and other public and private arrangements to cushion life's shocks did not exist, these benefactions from a political boss were important.

In every city, the boss had his base in the poorer, older, shabbier section of town. Historians have dubbed this section the "walking city" because it developed in the eighteenth and early nineteenth centuries, when houses and businesses were jumbled together, usually near the waterfront, and businessmen and laborers alike had to live within walking distance of their work. As transportation improved, people were able to live farther and farther from their place of work. Population dispersed in rough concentric circles: the financially most successful lived in the outer ring, where land was plentiful and the air was clean; the middle classes lived in intermediate neighborhoods;

and the poorest and the latest arrivals from Europe crowded into the now-rundown neighborhoods in the center, where rents were lowest. Politics in most cities reflected a struggle between the old, boss-run wards downtown and the more prosperous neighborhoods farther out, which did not need a boss's services and which championed reform. The more skilled workingmen and the white-collar workers who lived in the intermediate neighborhoods generally held the balance of power between the machine and the reformers. A skillful boss could hold enough of these swing voters on the basis of ethnic loyalty or shared support of a particular issue. At times, he might work out alliances with business leaders who found that an understanding with a boss was literally more businesslike than dependence upon the vagaries of reform.

But always it was the poorest and most insecure who provided the boss with the base of his political power. Their only strength, as Professor Richard C. Wade of the University of Chicago has observed, was in their numbers.

These numbers were in most cases a curse; housing never caught up with demand, the job market was always flooded, the bread-winner had too many mouths to feed. Yet in politics such a liability could be turned into an asset. If the residents could be mobilized, their combined strength would be able to do what none could do alone. Soon the "boss" and the "machine" arose to organize this potential. The boss system was simply the political expression of inner city life.

At a time when many newcomers to the city were seeking unskilled work, and when many families had a precarious economic footing, the ability to dispense jobs was crucial to the bosses. First, there were jobs to be filled on the city payroll. Just as vital, and far more numerous, were jobs on municipal construction projects. When the machine controlled a city, public funds were always being spent for more schools, hospitals, libraries, courthouses, and orphanages. The growing cities had to have more sewer lines, gas lines, and water-works, more paved streets and trolley tracks. Even if these utilities were privately owned, the managers needed the goodwill of city hall and were responsive to suggestions about whom to hire.

The payrolls of these public works projects were often padded, but to those seeking a job, it was better to be on a padded payroll than on no payroll. By contrast, the municipal reformers usually cut back on public spending, stopped projects to investigate for graft, and pruned payrolls. Middle- and upper-income taxpayers welcomed these reforms, but they were distinctly unpopular in working-class wards.

Another issue that strengthened the bosses was the regulation of the sale of liquor. Most women in the nineteenth century did not drink, and with their backing, the movement to ban entirely the manufacture and sale of liquor grew steadily stronger. It had its greatest support among Protestants with a rural or small-town background.

To them the cities, with their saloons, dance halls, cheap theatres, and red-light districts, were becoming latter-day versions of Sodom and Gomorrah.

Many of the European immigrants in the cities, however, had entirely different values. Quite respectable Germans took their wives to beer gardens on Sundays. In the eyes of the Irish, keeping a "public house" was an honorable occupation. Some Irish women drank beer and saw no harm in going to the saloon or sending an older child for a bucketful—"rushing the growler," they called it. Poles, Czechs, Italians, and others also failed to share the rage of the Prohibitionists against saloons. Unable to entertain in their cramped tenements, they liked to congregate in neighborhood bars.

The machine also appealed successfully on the liquor issue to many middle-class ethnic voters who had no need of the machine's economic assistance. Thus, in New York in 1897, Tammany scored a sweeping victory over an incumbent reform administration that had tried to enforce a state law permitting only hotels to sell liquor on Sundays. As one of the city's three police commissioners, Theodore Roosevelt became famous prowling the tougher neighborhoods on the hunt for saloon violations, but on the vaudeville stage the singers were giving forth with the hit song, "I Want What I Want When I Want It!" As a character in Alfred Henry Lewis' novel *The Boss* explained it, the reformers had made a serious mistake: "They got between the people and its beer!"

In 1902, Lincoln Steffens, the muckraker who made a name for himself writing about political bossism, visited St. Louis to interview Joseph W. Folk, a crusading district attorney. "It is good businessmen that are corrupting our bad politicians," Folk told him. "It is good business that causes bad government in St. Louis." Thirty-five years later, Boss Tom Pendergast was running the entire state of Missouri on that same reciprocal relationship.

Although many factory owners could be indifferent to politics, other businessmen were dependent upon the goodwill and the efficiency of the municipal government. The railroads that wanted to build their freight terminals and extend their lines into the cities, the contractors who erected the office buildings, the banks that held mortgages on the land and loaned money for the construction, the utility and transit companies, and the department stores were all in need of licenses, franchises, rights of way, or favorable rulings from city inspectors and agencies. These were the businesses that made the big pay-offs to political bosses in cash, blocks of stock, or tips on land about to be developed.

In another sense, profound, impersonal, and not corrupt, the business community needed the boss. Because the Industrial Revolution hit this country when it was still thinly populated and most of its cities were overgrown towns, American cities expanded with astonishing speed. For example, in the single decade from 1880 to 1890, Chicago's population more than doubled, from a half million to over a million. Minneapolis and St. Paul tripled in size. New York City increased from a million to a million and a half; Detroit, Milwaukee, Columbus, and Cleveland grew by sixty to eighty per cent.

Municipal governments, however, were unprepared for this astonishing growth. Planning and budgeting were unknown arts. City charters had restrictive provisions envisaged for much smaller, simpler communities. The mayor and the important commissioners were usually amateurs serving a term or two as a civic duty. Authority was dispersed among numerous boards and special agencies. A typical city would have a board of police commissioners, a board of health, a board of tax assessors, a water board, and many others. The ostensible governing body was a city council or board of aldermen which might have thirty, fifty, or even a hundred members. Under these circumstances, it was difficult to get a prompt decision, harder still to coordinate decisions taken by different bodies acting on different premises, and easy for delays and anomalies to develop.

In theory, the cities could have met their need for increased services by municipal socialism, but the conventional wisdom condemned that as too radical, although here and there a city did experiment with publicly owned utilities. In theory also, the cities could have financed public buildings and huge projects such as water and sewer systems by frankly raising taxes or floating bonds. But both taxes and debt were no more popular then than they are now. Moreover, the laissez-faire doctrine which holds that "that government is best which governs least" was enshrined orthodoxy in America from the 1870's down to the 1930's.

As men clung to such orthodox philosophies, the structures of government became obsolete; they strained to meet unexpected demands as a swelling number of citizens in every class clamored for more services. In this climate the bosses emerged. They had no scruples about taking shortcuts through old procedures or manipulating independent boards and agencies in ways that the original city fathers had never intended. They had no inhibiting commitment to any theory of limited government. They were willing to spend, tax, and build— and to take the opprobrium along with the graft. Sometimes, like Hague in Jersey City, Curley in Boston, and Big Bill Thompson in Chicago, they got themselves elected mayor and openly assumed responsibility. More often, like Pendergast in Kansas City, Cox in Cincinnati, the leaders of Tammany, and the successive Republican bosses of Philadelphia, they held minor offices or none, stayed out of the limelight, and ran city government through their iron control of the party organization. In ruling Memphis for forty years, Ed Crump followed one pattern and then the other. Impeached on a technicality after being elected three times as mayor, Crump retreated to the back rooms and became even more powerful as the city's political boss.

What manner of men became political bosses? They were men of little education and no social background, often of immigrant parentage. A college-educated boss like Edward Flynn of The Bronx was a rarity. Bosses often began as saloonkeepers, because the saloon was a natural meeting place in poorer neighborhoods in the days before

Prohibition. They were physically strong and no strangers to violence. Seventy-five years ago, most men made their living with brawn rather than brain, and a man who expected to be a leader of men had to be tough as well as shrewd. Open violence used to be common at polling places on Election Day, and gangs of repeaters roamed from one precinct to another. Although the typical boss made his way up through that roughneck system, the logic of his career led him to suppress violence. Bloody heads make bad publicity, and it is hard for any political organization to maintain a monopoly on violence. Bosses grew to prefer quieter, more lawful, less dangerous methods of control. Ballot-box stuffing and overt intimidation never disappeared entirely, but gradually they receded to weapons of last resort.

Political bosses varied in their idiosyncrasies and styles. A few, like Curley, became polished orators; others, like the legendary Charles Murphy of Tammany Hall, never made speeches. They were temperate, businesslike types; among them a drunk was as rare as a Phi Beta Kappa. If they had a generic failing it was for horses and gambling. Essentially they were hardheaded men of executive temper and genuine organizing talents; many, in other circumstances and with more education, might have become successful businessmen.

They have disappeared now, most of them. Education has produced a more sophisticated electorate; it has also encouraged potential bosses to turn away from politics toward more secure, prestigious, and profitable careers. A young man who had the energy, persistence, and skill in 1899 to become a successful political boss would in 1969 go to college and end up in an executive suite.

The urban population has also changed. The great flood of bewildered foreigners has dwindled to a trickle. In place of the European immigrants of the past, today's cities receive an influx of Negroes from the rural South, Puerto Ricans, Mexicans, and the white poor from Appalachia. As they overcome the language barrier and widen their experience, the Puerto Ricans are making themselves felt in urban politics. New York City, where they are most heavily concentrated, may have a Puerto Rican mayor in the not too distant future.

But the other groups are too isolated from the rest of the community to put together a winning political coalition of have-nots. The Mexicans and the ex-hillbillies from Appalachia are isolated by their unique cultural backgrounds, the Negroes by the giant fact of their race. Inasmuch as they make up a quarter to a third of the population in many cities, are a cohesive group, and still have a high proportion of poor who have to look to government for direct help, the Negroes might have produced several bosses and functioning political machines had they been of white European ancestry. But until Negroes attain a clear numerical majority, they find it difficult to take political power in any city because various white factions are reluctant to coalesce with them.

Regardless of the race or background of the voters, however, there are factors which work against the old-style machines. Civil service

In this contemporary cartoon Michael Ramus has pictured Mayor Daley of Chicago as "The Last Leaf" on the blasted tree of old-style urban bossism.

regulations make it harder to create a job or pad a payroll. Federal income taxes and federal accounting requirements make it more difficult to hide the rewards of graft. Television, public relations, and polling have created a whole new set of political techniques and undermined the personal ties and neighborhood loyalties on which the old organizations depended.

The new political style has brought an increase in municipal government efficiency and probably some decline in political corruption and misrule. But the politics of the television age puts a premium on hypocrisy. Candor has gone out the window with the spoils system. There is still a lot of self-seeking in politics and always will be. But gone are the days of Tammany's Boss Richard Croker, who when asked by an investigating committee if he was "working for his own pocket," shot back: "All the time—same as you." Today's politicians are so busy tending their images that they have become incapable of even a mildly derogatory remark such as Jim Curley's: "The term 'codfish aristocracy' is a reflection on the fish."

Curley entitled his memoirs *I'd Do It Again.* But the rough-and-tumble days when two-fisted, rough-tongued politicians came roaring out of the slums to take charge of America's young cities are not to come again.

Robert L. Beisner

Two Early Critics of Industrial America

Critics, as creators have always been quick to point out, are seldom truly objective in their judgments; they tend to impose their own prejudices on the work they presume to evaluate. This has been as true of social critics as of persons who review books or theatrical productions. Robert L. Beisner's essay on E. L. Godkin and Charles Eliot Norton, two sharp critics of post-Civil War American society, proves beyond question that these men were fundamentally subjective in their attitudes. They disliked the changes that industrialization was bringing to America and, viewing their world with jaundiced eyes, exaggerated and distorted the evils they complained about. Furthermore, they sought to reverse irreversible trends, to turn back the clock of history. Since we know—actually they knew it too— that this was impossible, we tend either to scorn or laugh at critics like Godkin and Norton, to dismiss them as crabbed, selfish reactionaries. Yet their criticism was not necessarily inaccurate because it was self-serving. And, as Beisner shows, it had a constructive as well as a destructive side; dislike of what was happening to American society did not destroy their commitment to that society.

Professor Beisner, who is an associate professor of history at The American University, is a specialist in late nineteenth-century social and intellectual history. His book Twelve Against Empire: The Anti-Imperialists, 1898–1900 *won the Allan Nevins prize of the Society of American Historians.*

*I*t used to be said in Cambridge, Massachusetts, that all of the dogs in the town wailed mournfully whenever E. L. Godkin and Charles Eliot Norton got together to swap their pessimistic views on the state of the nation. In the summer of 1897 Norton wrote Godkin that he had recently been forced to put his paper aside one evening "because with each note or article the gloom deepened till it grew darker than it used to be even in my study when after an evening of talk you declared that it was enough to make Rome howl." For more than thirty years Godkin and Norton sustained and fed each other's pessimism, sorely disappointed as they both were with developments in post-Civil War America. They believed that American morality had declined precipitately since the early days of the republic. They lamented the lack of good men in politics and the domination of the public service by men of coarse and corrupt nature. They watched with jaundiced eyes as millions of immigrants poured into their country. They took in the "General Grant" architecture, read the new literature, deplored the new wealth, saw successful businessmen gain entrance to their private clubs, faced America's plunge into imperialism and the glaring headlines of the yellow press—and declared it an age of vulgarity and a nation of "chromo-civilization."

There have always been such men, convinced in the core of their being that what had been in their youth a world of gold had lately turned to dross. In the era of industrialism and mass democracy these Jeremiahs have more often than not come from the ranks of the old landed, learned, or professional elites most in danger of being superseded or ignored by a democratic and acquisitive society. The quicker the rate of change and the fresher the memory of better times, the greater the likelihood that these gentle Brahmins would deplore the life around them. The rapidly changing America which emerged from the Civil War provoked just such an outcry of genteel despair—a dismay eloquently expressed by E. L. Godkin and Charles Eliot Norton. Both men placed the blame for their unhappiness on precisely those features of American civilization which were most highly valued by the majority of their countrymen: material prosperity and democratic government.

Edwin Lawrence Godkin was born in Moyne, County Wicklow, Ireland, on October 2, 1831. His father was a Presbyterian clergyman who became a political journalist after being ejected from the pulpit for his advocacy of home rule for Ireland. Young Edwin, too, went into journalism after making an indifferent record at Queen's College, Belfast. Already the youthful author of a history of Hungary, Godkin left for the Crimea in 1853 as a war correspondent for the London *Daily News*. Upon his return two years later he resolved to emigrate to the United States. In November of 1856 he reached America, where for nearly a decade (except for a short period spent in Ireland and Europe) he occupied himself with law studies and writing letters on American affairs for the London *Daily News*. His early friends included a number of important eastern Republicans, and in 1865, when they decided to found a journal that would reflect their political and

The critics: Editor Edwin Lawrence Godkin (left) and Professor Charles Eliot Norton (right).

economic views, they established the weekly *Nation* and selected to edit it the thirty-four-year-old Godkin. One of the prime backers of the enterprise and a close friend of the new editor was Charles Eliot Norton.

Godkin's sharp and authoritative editorials quickly made the *Nation* a habit for thousands of readers (one would be hard put to recognize it in the *Nation* that is published today); later on, his work performed the same service for the daily New York *Evening Post* (equally unrecognizable in the modern *Post*), whose editor he became in 1881 while retaining his position on the *Nation*. The critical tone of the *Nation* made it seem to some a "weekly judgment day," and neither it nor the *Evening Post* attracted a large circulation. Both, however, exercised wide influence. College students adopted Godkin's opinions for their own the way later generations of students would parrot H. L. Mencken and Walter Lippmann. And other newspapermen paid close attention to Godkin's editorials. Once when New York's Democratic Governor David B. Hill was under attack by the *Evening Post* he remarked: "I don't care anything about the handful of Mugwumps who read it in New York [City]. The trouble with the damned sheet is that every editor in New York State reads it."

Yet Godkin had formidable critics. The most vehement among them was Theodore Roosevelt, who called Godkin almost every disagreeable epithet that came to his fertile mind. To him Godkin was an unpatriotic man, "a malignant and dishonest liar" who suffered from

"a species of moral myopia, complicated with intellectual strabismus."
Lincoln Steffens, who worked for a short time with Godkin, thought
that his editorials were "clever, forceful, [and] ripping" but also
"personal and not very thoughtful." The Boston banker and philan-
thropist Henry L. Higginson believed that as Godkin's career unfolded,
his words became "so twisted and stained by great conceit, arrogance,
evil temper, that they lost their fairness, their perspicacity, their
virtue and therefore their value."

Charles Eliot Norton had those qualities of gentleness and con-
templativeness that his friend Godkin lacked. He too was the son of
a clergyman, Andrews Norton, a prominent Unitarian divine. Born in
Cambridge, Massachusetts, in 1827, Norton spent his youth in the
scholarly surroundings of a home frequented by such distinguished
visitors as Francis Parkman, George Bancroft, George Ticknor, and
Henry Wadsworth Longfellow. While still a youth he developed a
great passion for rare books and art objects, thus demonstrating an
early and serious interest in the field to which he was unable to devote
his full attention until he was nearly fifty. He made Phi Beta Kappa
at Harvard, and after his graduation in 1846 spent a decade in
business The next twenty years were passed in studying, living in
Europe, writing and editing books, supervising Union propaganda
activities during the Civil War, and working both as editor and con-
tributor for the cream of American journals—the *Atlantic Monthly,*
North American Review, and the *Nation.* Finally, in 1875, he was

appointed Harvard's first professor of fine arts, a post which he retained until he retired in 1897.

As a scholar, Norton was an acknowledged master of medieval studies and a respected translator of Dante. He wrote an important volume entitled *Historical Studies of Church-Building in the Middle Ages* as well as studies of Dante, Donne, Ruskin, Gray, Michelangelo, Holbein, and Turner. In addition, he edited the letters of James Russell Lowell, the Thomas Carlyle-Ralph Waldo Emerson correspondence, the Carlyle-Goethe correspondence, and the letters he had received from John Ruskin. As a teacher, Norton's aim was to advance aesthetic values and inculcate high standards of taste. Art was not to be studied merely for its own sake. Norton believed that man had reached his greatest moral and intellectual heights in ancient Greece and medieval Italy, and he thought that this superiority could be seen in the artistic achievements of those epochs. It was his habit in class to illustrate this relationship between art and morality with frequent deprecating references to the barrenness of American art and the moral and intellectual inferiority of American life.

The story is told that Norton once began a lecture on the idea of the "gentleman" by remarking airily: "None of you, probably, has ever seen a gentleman." It was inevitable that a teacher with such a rarefied taste for the antique would become the subject of parodies and the source of much campus amusement. One story has it, for instance, that an undergraduate emerged after three meetings of Norton's Fine Arts 3 course with his total notes reading:

    (1) Greece.
    (2) Bully for Greece.
    (3) There are no flies on Greece.

Norton's general aesthetic sensibilities and his displeasure with the design of many new buildings at Harvard were parodied in a tale to the effect that he had died and was about to enter heaven when he suddenly drew back, shaded his eyes and exclaimed: "Oh! Oh! Oh! So overdone! So garish! So Renaissance!" Despite the numerous campus jokes made at his expense, Norton's encouragement of the fine arts and his efforts to direct public attention to the advancing deterioration of America's landscape and cities made him an important figure in post-Civil War America—a friend of art museums, conservation projects, parks, and schools. In the opinion of Van Wyck Brooks, "no one aroused the country more to a sense of its general ugliness and a will to create a beautiful civilization."

In politics Godkin and Norton were mugwumps—independents who refused to commit themselves to the fortunes of any particular party. Both feared that American politics had rejected the country's "good men," and hoped for a breakup of the old party organizations. As early as 1859 Godkin had complained that the "nominating conventions toss men like Clay and Webster aside, and fish out from amongst the obscurities Pierces and Buchanans as likely to prove more pliable instruments in factious hands." The political machines, he charged, put up such bad men to run for office that good men were

A Harvard student drew this caricature of Professor of Fine Arts Norton in 1901.

no longer tempted to enter public affairs.

For Godkin and Norton the decline in political morality was but one aspect of a more serious decline in the quality of American life. Each felt that the United States had once enjoyed a Golden Age of reason, simplicity, and high morality. But the push toward an industrial way of life was transforming the social and physical landscape of their once-Arcadian America, and wherever they looked they now saw deterioration and decadence. Godkin deplored the ''moral anarchy'' of modern business methods and despised those who employed them. He fought the admission of businessmen to the Century Club of New York, complaining that most of them ''rarely open a book'' and ''know no more, read no more, and have no more to say than the bricklayer and the plumber.'' For his part, Norton was particularly concerned with the aesthetic changes and the unfortunate transformation in the tone of society. The country he had known had vanished under a wave of vulgarity. The ''barren'' art and literature of the late nineteenth century depressed him:

> Nowhere in the civilized world are the practical concerns of life more engrossing; nowhere are the conditions of life more prosaic; nowhere is the poetic spirit less evident, and the love of beauty less diffused. The concern for beauty, as the highest end of work, and as the noblest expression of life, hardly exists among us, and forms no part of our character as a nation.

Norton told a friend in 1873 that America had lost its original bright promise and was ''not a pleasing child.'' Only Harvard, Yale, the *Nation,* and the *North American Review* stood firm as ''solid barriers against the invasion of modern barbarism & vulgarity." The other landmarks and manners of an earlier and better day were disappearing before his very eyes. Even Cambridge was slipping away; Norton felt himself a stranger in his birthplace. The few houses that remained from his childhood were occupied by "new people." Norton could find only "half a dozen men or women" who could converse on those general subjects once familiar to all people of education— "My fair neighbor asks, 'What are Pericles?'" Thus Norton, condemned to live in an age of industrialization and specialization, sighed under his burden of nostalgia. One of his students—young Josephine Peabody, who heard him lecture at Radcliffe in 1895, wrote:

> Professor Norton lectured in Italian 4 this afternoon. The dear old man looks so mildy happy and benignant while he regrets everything in the age and the country—so contented, while he gently tells us it were better for us had we never been born in this degenerate and unlovely age.

What had brought America to its present condition? Godkin found in the very heart of the American Experiment—in its commitment to political democracy and social equality—the cause of what he deemed to be its failure. These noble ideals simply did not work in practice. The triumph of popular rule had come to mean only that politicians catered to the lowest level of understanding. The ideal of equality, which in theory referred to an "equality of burdens," had in actuality degenerated into a contempt for the excellent and superior, a "disregard for special fitness." Could anything but disaster be expected from the masses whom this egalitarian democracy had thrown to the top? Godkin wrote in 1870:

> Their rush into the forum and into the temples and palaces and libraries is not an agreeable sight to witness, and it would be foolish to expect that under their ruthless touch many gifts and graces will not be obscured, many arts will not be lost, many a great ideal, at whose shrine the best men and women of three generations have found courage and inspiration, will not vanish from the earth . . .

Along with equality and democracy both Godkin and Norton believed that the third agent of destruction was prosperity. Norton had long maintained that there was a causal connection between great wealth and the dissolution of national character. The decline of Greece had been set off by the "increase of private luxury [and] selfishness" and the rise of "unrestrained individuality." Surely it was vanity to believe that America could be spared the disastrous effects of excessive material wealth. As early as 1853 Norton had warned that the long and uninterrupted history of prosperity enjoyed by the United States was beginning to take its toll in a declining national character. After the Civil War the blight grew worse and spread beyond the frontiers and across the ocean. Money-getting was proving the ruin of literature and was blunting the intelligence of the people; even in Europe materialism was leaving its imprint. A foolish optimism was in the air. From Florence in 1869 Norton wrote:

> Italy in losing tyrants, in becoming constitutional, in taking to trade, is doing what she can to spoil her charm. The railroad whistle just behind the church of Santa Maria Novella, or just beyond the Campo Santo at Pisa, sounds precisely as it sounds on the Back Bay or at the Fitchburg Station,—and it and the common school are Americanizing the land to a surprising degree. Happy country! Fortunate people! Before long they may hope for their Greeleys, their Beechers, and their Fisks.

Norton did not deny that democracy could "work," but as he said following the election of 1884, it appeared to work "ignobly, ignorantly, brutally." Or it could work as it had begun to in Europe, bringing about "the destruction of old shrines, the disregard of beauty, the decline in personal distinction, the falling off in manners." What was clear was that democracy did not work as Norton had hoped it would. In his view democracy was supposed to mean that everyone in society would be public-spirited. But it had turned out in practice to mean that everyone was involved in the selfish pursuit of private interests. Rather than heightening the individual's awareness of his civic responsibilities, universal suffrage had furnished "a distinct source of moral corruption." Rather than increasing the wisdom of all citizens, democracy had diminished the regard for intelligent counsel and produced a general "rejection of authority." The sense of license and the smug complacency that had been created by democracy and prosperity had made "extravagant self-confidence" and willful conduct the hallmarks of the American people. Writing in 1896, Norton declared: "It seems to me not unlikely that for a considerable time to come there will be an increase of lawlessness and of public folly."

Godkin was savage in his dislike for the many immigrants who were so rapidly being incorporated into the American political system. Their votes gave power to the corrupt urban bosses who exploited them. One could see on every hand, Godkin exclaimed, the "ignorant" foreign voter "eating away the political structure, like a white ant, with a group of natives standing over him and encouraging him." In 1891 he proposed that all immigrants be shut out unless they could read and write the English language. This would mean, he admitted, that all but a few immigrants would perforce come from the British Isles, "but why not, if the restriction be really undertaken in the interest of American civilization? We are under no obligation to see that all races and nations enjoy an equal chance of getting here." Godkin called it natural law "that the more intelligent and thoughtful of the race shall inherit the earth and have the best time, and that all others shall find life on the whole dull and unprofitable."

Godkin did not pretend to have answers to the problems of the age that he and Norton castigated. The structure of American life seemed too corrupt to save, too rotten to shore up with marginal improvements, and he eventually determined to return to England rather than witness its expected collapse. Norton had no answers either, but his pessimism was relieved by a limited belief in the worth of ameliorative action, and his distrust of acquisitiveness and democracy was mitigated by his interest in the unprecedented material and educational achievements of America's lower classes.

As an active participant in the social and political processes, Norton established a night school for the poor in 1846; he promoted better housing for the underprivileged; he was in the forefront of the campaign for female suffrage and education (with the hope that women would raise the ideals and tone of American society); and, in the interest of preserving at least the landscape of America, he fought hard and effectively to save both the Adirondacks and Niagara Falls from exploitation and desecration. In an effort to exert direct influence upon public opinion, Norton founded the Ashfield "academy dinners," held each summer from 1879 to 1903 in Ashfield, Massachusetts. On these occasions civil-service reform, tariff reduction, Negro education, and anti-imperialism, as well as many other mugwump interests, were discussed by William Dean Howells, George Washington Cable, William James, James Russell Lowell, Booker T. Washington, and many others, including Norton himself.

Norton was consoled and reassured by the knowledge that, in his country, the economic and educational level of the lower classes had been elevated to the highest point in history. When William Dean Howells inquired of him, "Well, after all, if you could change, would you rather have been an Englishman than an American?" Norton unhesitatingly replied: "No, if I could choose I would rather have been American."

But, at best, progress came at a maddeningly slow pace, and Norton succeeded only intermittently in maintaining his optimism. In 1871 he bitterly predicted that the creation of a really sound republic would take as long as the evolution from monkey to man. In 1884 he described himself as an "absolute" pessimist—a man who had learned not to hope for any good in the world and who thus lived a life free of expectations and complaints:

> Your out-and-out pessimist is cheerful, even though nature herself plays false, and uses loaded dice against him in the game. Darwinism has helped us a good deal. You expect less of men when you look at them not as a little lower than the angels, but as a little higher than the anthropoid apes.

By the mid-1890's E. L. Godkin and Charles Eliot Norton had lived for a third of a century believing that their country was in a steady decline, that its onetime promise had been largely submerged by a rising tide of corruption, immorality, tastelessness, and stupidity. Thus it was more than coincidental that, at this time, the thoughts of each man turned to the fall of Rome. In 1895 Godkin wrote Norton:

> You see I am not sanguine about the future of democracy. I think we shall have a long period of decline like that which

followed the fall of the Roman Empire, and then a recrudescence under some other form of society.

A year later Norton wrote an English friend:

It is hard to have the whole background of life grow darker as one grows old. I can understand the feeling of a Roman as he saw the Empire breaking down, and civilization dying out. It will take much longer than we once hoped, for the world to reorganize itself upon a democratic basis, and for a new and desirable social order to come into existence.

But—with the faith that never completely left him—he added: "If we set our hope far enough forward we need not lose it."

By 1895 Godkin and Norton had come to sound increasingly like men who were close to abandoning all hope for their country. From the *Nation* and from Harvard they watched the ailing American Experiment falter and fail. It was the Spanish-American War and the expansionism that accompanied it that administered the *coup de grâce*. Godkin and Norton were angry and saddened but not surprised, for they had expected all along that something of the sort would happen. The times had long been out of joint, and imperialism was but another blow—albeit the heaviest—against the America they had known. Only one question remained for them: was the blow fatal?

For thirty years Godkin had been an opponent of expansionism, hammering away against every annexation scheme that dared to raise its head. Three months before the outbreak of the Spanish-American War, when the Senate was considering the annexation of Hawaii, Godkin had summarized his objections to a policy of territorial annexation in a *Nation* editorial:

The sudden departure from our traditions; the absence from our system of any machinery for governing dependencies; the admission of alien, inferior, and mongrel races to our nationality; the opening of fresh fields to carpetbaggers, speculators, and corruptionists; the un-Americanism of governing a large body of people against their will, and by persons not responsible to them; the entrance on a policy of conquest and annexation while our own continent was still unreclaimed, our population unassimilated, and many of our most serious political problems still unsolved; and finally the danger of the endorsement of a gross fraud for the first time by a Christian nation.

At the close of the war in August, 1898, Godkin remained firmly opposed to all annexation schemes, and throughout the rest of that year and all of the next he repeatedly emphasized the difficulties the United States would face if it became an imperialist power. He believed that the establishment of a colonial administration would necessitate a drastic overhaul of the American government, "a complete change in our destiny, political, military, and naval." If the United States annexed the Philippines and had to defend them from the covetousness of other powers, it would be necessary to arm to the teeth with naval and military forces capable of being "instantly" mobilized and dispatched to any danger spot on the globe. And we would need a "permanent" colonial service:

> It will not do to vote money and build ships, simply, and drill armies and sailors. If we are going to annex and rule over countries the population of which differs from us in race, religion, language, in history and every variety of antecedent, and who will probably hate us and treat our rule as a "yoke," we shall have to get administrators ready, as well as guns and ships. We shall have to do what the other conquering and colonizing nations do, what England does, what Russia and Germany do.

In his anger Godkin railed at the expansionists for their betrayal of American principles. In the Philippines, he charged, McKinley, "drunk with glory and flattery," had substituted "keen effective slaughter for Spanish old-fashioned, clumsy slaughter." When eager missionaries began planning new translations of the Bible in the various tongues of the Filipinos, the *Nation* derisively commented that they should read: "Mow down the natives like grass and say unto them. the Syndicate has arrived." But there was no longer much heart in Godkin's protest, for he had concluded that the fight was virtually lost. In late 1898 and early 1899 he gave way to utter despair, publicly declaring that "the old American republic is in a bad way." In private letters he poured out his full sorrow:

> I am, heart and soul, an American of the *vielle roche*. American ideals were the intellectual food of my youth, and to see America converted into a senseless, Old World conqueror, embitters my age. [May, 1899]

> I came here fifty years ago with high and fond ideals about America. . . . They are now all shattered, and I have apparently to look elsewhere to keep even moderate hopes about the human race alive. [Late 1899]

> I have suffered from seeing the America of my youthful dreams vanish from my sight, and the commencement on this continent of the old story. . . . [November 13, 1899]

Godkin suffered a stroke in February of 1900. Fifteen months later he left his adopted country and returned to England. Occasionally the bitter humor of former days would return to him, as when he wrote James Bryce: "Do come over soon, and we'll lie under a tree at Dublin while you abuse Great Britain and I abuse the United States." He died in Devon on May 21, 1902, and was buried in the Hazelbeach churchyard, Northampton, to rest forever in England. In America, the country he had abandoned, the *Nation* published a fitting epitaph:

He grew old in an age he condemned
Felt the dissolving throes
Of a Social order he loved,
And, like Theban seer,
*   Died in his enemies' day.*

Charles Eliot Norton, like Godkin, interpreted the Spanish-American War and its aftermath as final proof that his early hopes for a special American destiny had been in vain. Amid the popular enthusiasm aroused by early American victories in Cuba and at Manila Bay, he advised students not to enlist (familiar note!) and declared before an audience in Cambridge that the United States had rashly:

> hurried into war, and . . . she who more than any other land was pledged to peace and goodwill on earth, unsheathes her sword, compels a weak and unwilling nation to a fight, rejecting without due consideration her earnest and repeated offers to meet every legitimate demand of the United States. It is a bitter disappointment to the lover of his country; it is a turning-back from the path of civilization to that of barbarism.

Godkin and Norton were among those nineteenth-century idealists who had hoped, like the Puritans of the seventeenth century, that America would be a city set on a hill—a state and civilization that would attract the admiration of and serve as an example to the world. Despite disappointments, these two remarkable men, schooled in the genteel tradition, were never able to resist the lingering hope that America might yet be saved, and they flattered themselves that men such as they might yet create in the distant future a superior civilization in America. In 1902—with Americans in control of Cuba, Puerto Rico, and the Philippines—Norton counselled his friends not to give up:

> While all the congregation of the children of Israel are wandering in the wilderness of Sin . . . we, the little remnant of the house of Judah that has escaped, must comfort one another as best we may. . . . we are defeated for the time; but the war is not ended, and we are enlisted for the war.

Richard Hofstadter

The Myth
of the
Happy Yeoman

The following essay, like Oliver La Farge's essay on the American
Indian in Volume I, is a study in the differences between reality
and men's view of reality. Usually the historian seeks only for the
reality and discards the myths that surround it in the records of the
past. But in some contexts the myths themselves are vitally important; if the subject is men's views, these views become the reality in
question, and thus the proper subject of historical analysis.

The concept of the yeoman farmer had, as Professor Richard
Hofstadter of Columbia University demonstrates, a solid basis in
fact in early America. Farming was for many a way of life, not
primarily a way of making a living. But national growth and
development changed this steadily, and after the rapid expansion
of industrialization the true yeoman practically disappeared. Why
the myth persisted is the subject of Hofstadter's inquiry. The tale
is part of the larger story of the impact of the industrial revolution
on American thought, a subject which Hofstadter develops at greater
length in his Pulitzer Prize history, The Age of Reform.

The United States was born in the country and has moved to the city. From the beginning its political values as well as ideas were of necessity shaped by country life. The early American politician, the country editor, who wished to address himself to the common man, had to draw upon a rhetoric that would touch the tillers of the soil; and even the spokesman of city people knew that his audience had been in very large part reared upon the farm.

But what the articulate people who talked and wrote about farmers and farming—the preachers, poets, philosophers, writers, and statesmen—liked about American farming was not, in every respect, what the typical working farmer liked. For the articulate people were drawn irresistibly to the noncommercial, non-pecuniary, self-sufficient aspect of American farm life. To them it was an ideal.

Writers like Thomas Jefferson and Hector St. John de Crèvecœur admired the yeoman farmer not for his capacity to exploit opportunities and make money but for his honest industry, his independence, his frank spirit of equality, his ability to produce and enjoy a simple abundance. The farmer himself, in most cases, was in fact inspired to make money, and such self-sufficiency as he actually had was usually forced upon him by a lack of transportation or markets, or by the necessity to save cash to expand his operations.

For while early American society was an agrarian society, it was fast becoming more commercial, and commercial goals made their way among its agricultural classes almost as rapidly as elsewhere. The more commercial this society became, however, the more reason it found to cling in imagination to the noncommercial agrarian values. The more farming as a self-sufficient way of life was abandoned for farming as a business, the more merit men found in what was being left behind. And the more rapidly the farmers' sons moved into the towns, the more nostalgic the whole culture became about its rural past. Throughout the nineteenth and even in the twentieth century, the American was taught that rural life and farming as a vocation were something sacred.

This sentimental attachment to the rural way of life is a kind of homage that Americans have paid to the fancied innocence of their origins. To call it a "myth" is not to imply that the idea is simply false. Rather the "myth" so effectively embodies men's values that it profoundly influences their way of perceiving reality and hence their behavior.

Like any complex of ideas, the agrarian myth cannot be defined in a phrase, but its component themes form a clear pattern. Its hero was the yeoman farmer, its central conception the notion that he is the ideal man and the ideal citizen. Unstinted praise of the special virtues of the farmer and the special values of rural life was coupled with the assertion that agriculture, as a calling uniquely productive and uniquely important to society, had a special right to the concern and protection of government. The yeoman, who owned a small farm and worked it with the aid of his family, was the incarnation of the simple, honest, independent, healthy, happy human being. Because he lived in close communion with beneficent nature, his life was believed to have a wholesomeness and integrity impossible for the depraved populations of cities.

His well-being was not merely physical, it was moral: it was not merely personal, it was the central source of civic virtue; it was not merely secular but religious, for God had made the land and called man to cultivate it. Since the yeoman was believed to be both happy and honest, and since he had a secure propertied stake in society in the form of his own land, he was held to be the best and most reliable sort of citizen. To this conviction Jefferson appealed when he wrote: "The small land holders are the most precious part of a state."

In origin the agrarian myth was not a popular but a literary idea, a preoccupation of the upper classes, of those who enjoyed a classical education, read pastoral poetry, experimented with breeding stock, and owned plantations or country estates. It was clearly formulated and almost universally accepted in America during the last half of the eighteenth century. As it took shape both in Europe and America, its promulgators drew heavily upon the authority and the rhetoric of classical writers—Hesiod, Xenophon, Cato, Cicero, Virgil, Horace, and others—whose works were the staples of a good education. A learned agricultural gentry, coming into conflict with the industrial classes, welcomed the moral strength that a rich classical ancestry brought to the praise of husbandry.

Chiefly through English experience, and from English and classical writers, the agrarian myth came to America, where, like so many other cultural importations, it eventually took on altogether new dimensions in its new setting. So appealing were the symbols of the myth that even an arch-opponent of the agrarian interest like Alexander Hamilton found it politic to concede in his *Report on Manufactures* that "the cultivation of the earth, as the primary and most certain source of national supply . . . has intrinsically a strong claim to pre-eminence over every other kind of industry." And Benjamin Franklin, urban cosmopolite though he was, once said that agriculture was "the only *honest way*" for a nation to acquire wealth, "wherein man receives a real increase of the seed thrown into the ground, a kind of continuous miracle, wrought by the hand of God in his favour, as a reward for his innocent life and virtuous industry."

Among the intellectual classes in the eighteenth century the agrarian myth had virtually universal appeal. Some writers used it to give simple, direct, and emotional expression to their feelings about life and nature; others linked agrarianism with a formal philosophy of natural rights. The application of the natural rights philosophy to land tenure became especially popular in America. Since the time of Locke it had been a standard argument that the land is the common stock of society to which every man has a right—what Jefferson called "the fundamental right to labour the earth"; that since the occupancy and use of land are the true criteria of valid ownership, labor expended in cultivating the earth confers title to it; that since govern-

According to this 1869 engraving from The Prairie Farmer, *each occupation has its uses, but the farmer alone foots all the bills.*

ment was created to protect property, the property of working land-holders has a special claim to be fostered and protected by the state.

At first the agrarian myth was a notion of the educated classes, but by the early nineteenth century it had become a mass creed, a part of the country's political folklore and its nationalist ideology. The roots of this change may be found as far back as the American

Revolution, which, appearing to many Americans as the victory of a band of embattled farmers over an empire, seemed to confirm the moral and civic superiority of the yeoman, made the farmer a symbol of the new nation, and wove the agrarian myth into his patriotic sentiments and idealism.

Still more important, the myth played a role in the first party battles under the Constitution. The Jeffersonians appealed again and again to the moral primacy of the yeoman farmer in their attacks on the Federalists. The family farm and American democracy became indissolubly connected in Jeffersonian thought, and by 1840 even the more conservative party, the Whigs, took over the rhetorical appeal to the common man, and elected a President in good part on the strength of the fiction that he lived in a log cabin.

The Jeffersonians, moreover, made the agrarian myth the basis of a strategy of continental development. Many of them expected that the great empty inland regions would guarantee the preponderance of the yeoman—and therefore the dominance of Jeffersonianism and the health of the state—for an unlimited future. The opening of the trans-Allegheny region, its protection from slavery, and the purchase of the Louisiana Territory were the first great steps in a continental strategy designed to establish an internal empire of small farms. Much later the Homestead Act was meant to carry to its completion the process of continental settlement by small homeowners. The failure of the Homestead Act "to enact by statute the fee-simple empire" was one of the original sources of Populist grievances, and one of the central points at which the agrarian myth was overrun by the commercial realities.

Above all, however, the myth was powerful because the United States in the first half of the nineteenth century consisted predominantly of literate and politically enfranchised farmers. Offering what seemed harmless flattery to this numerically dominant class, the myth suggested a standard vocabulary to rural editors and politicians. Although farmers may not have been much impressed by what was said about the merits of a noncommercial way of life, they could only enjoy learning about their special virtues and their unique services to the nation. Moreover, the editors and politicians who so flattered them need not in most cases have been insincere. More often than not they too were likely to have begun life in little villages or on farms, and what they had to say stirred in their own breasts, as it did in the breasts of a great many townspeople, nostalgia for their early years and perhaps relieved some residual feelings of guilt at having deserted parental homes and childhood attachments. They also had the satisfaction in the early days of knowing that in so far as it was based upon the life of the largely self-sufficient yeoman the agrarian myth was a depiction of reality as well as the assertion of an ideal.

Oddly enough, the agrarian myth came to be believed more widely and tenaciously as it became more fictional. At first it was propagated with a kind of genial candor, and only later did it acquire overtones of insincerity. There survives from the Jackson era a painting that shows Governor Joseph Ritner of Pennsylvania standing by a primitive plow at the end of a furrow. There is no pretense that the Governor has actually been plowing—he wears broadcloth pants and a silk vest, and his tall black beaver hat has been carefully laid in the grass beside him—but the picture is meant as a reminder of both his rustic origin and his present high station in life. By contrast, Calvin Coolidge posed almost a century later for a series of photographs that represented him as haying in Vermont. In one of them the President sits on the edge of a hay rig in a white shirt, collar detached, wearing highly polished black shoes and a fresh pair of overalls; in the background stands his Pierce Arrow, a secret service man on the running board, plainly waiting to hurry the President away from his bogus rural labors. That the second picture is so much more pretentious and disingenuous than the first is a measure of the increasing hollowness of the myth as it became more and more remote from the realities of agriculture.

Throughout the nineteenth century hundreds upon hundreds of thousands of farm-born youths sought their careers in the towns and cities. Particularly after 1840, which marked the beginning of a long cycle of heavy country-to-city migration, farm children repudiated their parents' way of life and took off for the cities where, in agrarian theory if not in fact, they were sure to succumb to vice and poverty.

When a correspondent of the *Prairie Farmer* in 1849 made the mistake of praising the luxuries, the "polished society," and the economic opportunities of the city, he was rebuked for overlooking the fact that city life "*crushes, enslaves*, and *ruins so many thousands of our young men* who are insensibly made the victims of *dissipation*, of *reckless speculation*, and of *ultimate crime*." Such warnings, of course, were futile. "Thousands of young men," wrote the New York agriculturist Jesse Buel, "who annually forsake the plough, and the honest profession of their fathers, if not to win the fair, at least form an opinion, too often confirmed by mistaken parents, that agriculture is not the road to wealth, to honor, nor to happiness. And such will continue to be the case, until our agriculturists become qualified to assume that rank in society to which the importance of their calling, and their numbers, entitle them, and which intelligence and self-respect can alone give them."

Rank in society! That was close to the heart of the matter, for the farmer was beginning to realize acutely not merely that the best of the world's goods were to be had in the cities and that the urban middle and upper classes had much more of them than he did but also that he was losing in status and respect as compared with them. He became aware that the official respect paid to the farmer masked a certain disdain felt by many city people. "There has . . . a certain class of individuals grown up in our land," complained a farm writer in 1835, "who treat the cultivators of the soil as an inferior caste . . . whose utmost abilities are confined to the merit of being able to discuss a boiled potato and a rasher of bacon." The city was symbolized as the home of loan sharks, dandies, fops, and aristocrats with European ideas who despised farmers as hayseeds.

The growth of the urban market intensified this antagonism. In areas like colonial New England, where an intimate connection had existed between the small town and the adjacent countryside, where a community of interests and even of occupations cut across the town line, the rural-urban hostility had not developed so sharply as in the newer areas where the township plan was never instituted and where isolated farmsteads were more common. As settlement moved west, as urban markets grew, as self-sufficient farmers became rarer, as farmers pushed into commercial production for the cities they feared and distrusted, they quite correctly thought of themselves as a vocational and economic group rather than as members of a neighborhood. In the Populist era the city was totally alien territory to many farmers, and the primacy of agriculture as a source of wealth was reasserted with much bitterness. "The great cities rest upon our broad and fertile prairies," declared Bryan in his "Cross of Gold" speech. "Burn down your cities and leave our farms, and your cities will spring up again as if by magic; but destroy our farms, and the grass will grow in the streets of every city in the country." Out of the beliefs nourished by the agrarian myth there had arisen the notion that the city was a parasitical growth on the country. Bryan spoke for a people raised for generations on the idea that the farmer was a very special creature, blessed by God, and that in a country consisting largely of farmers the voice of the farmer was the voice of democracy and of virtue itself.

The agrarian myth encouraged farmers to believe that they were not themselves an organic part of the whole order of business enterprise and speculation that flourished in the city, partaking of its character and sharing in its risks, but rather the innocent pastoral victims of a conspiracy hatched in the distance. The notion of an innocent and victimized populace colors the whole history of agrarian controversy.

For the farmer it was bewildering, and irritating too, to think of the great contrast between the verbal deference paid him by almost everyone and the real economic position in which he found himself. Improving his economic position was always possible, though this was often done too little and too late; but it was not within anyone's power to stem the decline in the rural values and pieties, the gradual rejection of the moral commitments that had been expressed in the early exaltations of agrarianism.

It was the fate of the farmer himself to contribute to this decline. Like almost all good Americans he had innocently sought progress from the very beginning, and thus hastened the decline of many of his own values. Elsewhere the rural classes had usually looked to the past, had been bearers of tradition and upholders of stability. The American farmer looked to the future alone, and the story of the American land became a study in futures.

In the very hours of its birth as a nation Crèvecœur had congratulated America for having, in effect, no feudal past and no industrial present, for having no royal, aristocratic, ecclesiastical, or monarchial power, and no manufacturing class, and had rapturously concluded: "We are the most perfect society now existing in the world." Here was the irony from which the farmer suffered above all others: the United States was the only country in the world that began with perfection and aspired to progress.

To what extent was the agrarian myth actually false? During the colonial period, and even well down into the nineteenth century, there were in fact large numbers of farmers who were very much like the yeomen idealized in the myth. They were independent and self-sufficient, and they bequeathed to their children a strong love of craftsmanlike improvisation and a firm tradition of household industry. These yeomen were all too often yeomen by force of circumstance. They could not become commercial farmers because they were too far from the rivers or the towns, because the roads were too poor for bulky traffic, because the domestic market for agricultural produce was too small and the overseas markets were out of reach. At the beginning of the nineteenth century, when the American population was still living largely in the forests and most of it was east of the Appalachians, the yeoman farmer did exist in large numbers, living much as the theorists of the agrarian myth portrayed him.

But when the yeoman practiced the self-sufficient economy that was expected of him, he usually did so not because he wanted to stay out of the market but because he wanted to get into it. "My farm," said a farmer of Jefferson's time, "gave me and my family a good living on the produce of it; and left me, one year with another, one hundred and fifty dollars, for I have never spent more than ten dollars a year, which was for salt, nails, and the like. Nothing to wear, eat, or drink was purchased, as my farm provided all. With this saving, I put money to interest, bought cattle, fatted and sold them, and made great profit." Great profit! Here was the significance of self-sufficiency for the characteristic family farmer. Commercialism had already begun to enter the American Arcadia.

For, whatever the spokesman of the agrarian myth might have told him, the farmer almost anywhere in early America knew that all around him there were examples of commercial success in agriculture—the tobacco, rice, and indigo, and later the cotton planters of the South, the grain, meat, and cattle exporters of the middle states.

The farmer knew that without cash he could never rise above the hardships and squalor of pioneering and log-cabin life. So the savings from his self-sufficiency went into improvements—into the purchase of more land, of herds and flocks, of better tools; they went into the building of barns and silos and better dwellings. Self-sufficiency, in short, was adopted for a time in order that it would eventually be unnecessary.

Between 1815 and 1860 the character of American agriculture was transformed. The rise of native industry created a home market for agriculture, while demands arose abroad for American cotton and foodstuffs, and a great network of turnpikes, canals, and railroads helped link the planter and the advancing western farmer to the new markets. As the farmer moved out of the forests onto the flat, rich prairies, he found possibilities for machinery that did not exist in the forest. Before long he was cultivating the prairies with horse-drawn mechanical reapers, steel plows, wheat and corn drills, and threshers.

The farmer was still a hardworking man, and he still owned his own land in the old tradition. But no longer did he grow or manufacture almost everything he needed. He concentrated on the cash crop, bought more and more of his supplies from the country store. To take full advantage of the possibilities of mechanization, he engrossed as much land as he could and borrowed money for his land and machinery. The shift from self-sufficient to commercial farming varied in time throughout the West and cannot be dated with precision, but it was complete in Ohio by about 1830 and twenty years later in Indiana, Illinois, and Michigan. All through the great Northwest, farmers whose fathers might have lived in isolation and self-sufficiency were surrounded by jobbers, banks, stores, middlemen, horses, and machinery.

This transformation affected not only what the farmer did but how he felt. The ideals of the agrarian myth were competing in his breast, and gradually losing ground, to another, even stronger ideal, the notion of opportunity, of career, of the self-made man. Agrarian sentiment sanctified labor in the soil and the simple life; but the prevailing Calvinist atmosphere of rural life implied that virtue was rewarded with success and material goods. Even farm boys were taught to strive for achievement in one form or another, and when this did not take them away from the farms altogether, it impelled them to follow farming not as a way of life but as a *career*—that is, as a way of achieving substantial success.

The sheer abundance of the land—that very internal empire that had been expected to insure the predominance of the yeoman in American life for centuries—gave the *coup de grâce* to the yeomanlike way of life. For it made of the farmer a speculator. Cheap land invited extensive and careless cultivation. Rising land values in areas of new settlement tempted early liquidation and frequent moves. Frequent and sensational rises in land values bred a boom psychology in the American farmer and caused him to rely for his margin of profit more on the appreciation in the value of his land than on the sale of crops. It took a strong man to resist the temptation to ride skyward on lands that might easily triple or quadruple their value in one decade and then double in the next.

What developed in America, then, was an agricultural society whose real attachment was not, like the yeoman's, to the land but to land values. The characteristic product of American rural society, as it developed on the prairies and the plains, was not a yeoman or a villager, but a harassed little country businessman who worked very hard, moved all too often, gambled with his land, and made his way alone.

While the farmer had long since ceased to act like a yeoman, he was somewhat slower in ceasing to think like one. He became a business-man in fact long before he began to regard himself in this light. As the nineteenth century drew to a close, however, various things were changing him. He was becoming increasingly an employer of labor, and though he still worked with his hands, he began to look with suspicion upon the working classes of the cities, especially those organized in trade unions, as he had once done upon the urban fops and aristocrats. Moreover, when good times returned after the Populist revolt of the 1890's, businessmen and bankers and the agricultural colleges began to woo the farmer, to make efforts to persuade him to take the businesslike view of himself that was warranted by the nature of his farm operations. "The object of farming," declared a writer in the *Cornell Countryman* in 1904, "is not primarily to make a living, but it is to make money. To this end it is to be conducted on the same business basis as any other producing industry."

The final change, which came only with a succession of changes in the twentieth century, wiped out the last traces of the yeoman of old, as the coming first of good roads and rural free delivery, and mail order catalogues, then the telephone, the automobile, and the tractor, and at length radio, movies, and television largely eliminated the difference between urban and rural experience in so many important areas of life. The city luxuries, once so derided by farmers, are now what they aspire to give to their wives and daughters.

In 1860 a farm journal satirized the imagined refinements and affectations of a city girl in the following picture:

> Slowly she rises from her couch. . . . Languidly she gains her feet, and oh! what vision of human perfection appears before us: Skinny, bony, sickly, hipless, thighless, formless, hairless, teethless. What a radiant belle! . . . The ceremony of enrobing commences. In goes the dentist's naturalization efforts; next the witching curls are fashioned to her "classically molded head." Then the womanly proportions are properly adjusted; hoops, bustles, and so forth, follow in succession, then a profuse quantity of whitewash, together with a "permanent rose tint" is applied to a sallow complexion; and lastly the "killing" wrapper is arranged on her systematical and matchless form.

But compare this with these beauty hints for farmers' wives from the *Idaho Farmer*, April, 1935:

> Hands should be soft enough to flatter the most delicate of the new fabrics. They must be carefully manicured, with none of the hot, brilliant shades of nail polish. The lighter and more delicate tones are in keeping with the spirit of freshness. Keep the tint of your fingertips friendly to the red of your lips, and check both your powder and your rouge to see that they best suit the tone of your skin in the bold light of summer.

Nothing can tell us with greater finality of the passing of the yeoman ideal than these light and delicate tones of nail polish.

*Unemployed white and Negro
workers parade in New York
City in 1909 to protest discriminatory hiring practices.*

AGE
OF
REFORM

Thurman Arnold

Economic Reform and the Sherman Antitrust Act

The growth of industry in the United States produced not only more manufactured goods but bigger manufacturing establishments, and these large organizations tended to combine with one another into huge complexes called trusts. This development roused profound anxieties in the minds of many persons. The fear of monopoly, which these trusts created, was only the surface manifestation of these anxieties; more basic was the fear that these enormous enterprises presaged the appearance of sharp cleavages between rich and poor and the development of a rigid social structure. Thus, it was thought that the trusts might undermine democracy itself. The Sherman Antitrust Act of 1890 was one result of the public distaste for these large organizations.

The Sherman act did not check the trend toward large-scale manufacturing, but over a period of time bigness itself proved less dangerous than late nineteenth-century citizens had feared. Democracy has survived despite U.S. Steel and General Motors, although there have been (and still are) those who see such giants as a threat to American institutions. Nevertheless, the Sherman act has remained on the statute books, and it has served a useful if changing function as the character of American industry has evolved. The author of this essay, Thurman Arnold, headed the federal government's antitrust division from 1938 to 1943. He has written, among other works, The Folklore of Capitalism *and* Democracy and Free Enterprise.

*E*ver since the Civil War ended there has been a continuous conflict between two opposing ideals in American economic thinking. The first of them states that business management, if relieved from the rigors of cutthroat competition, will be fair and benevolent. The age of competition is over, the theory continues, and great corporations with the power to dominate prices benefit the economy. In the field of big business, this philosophy justifies giant mergers. In the field of small business, it leads to the passage of fair trade laws and similar forms of legalized price fixing.

J. P. Morgan is the traditional hero of this philosophy. He organized United States Steel, our first billion-dollar enterprise, to make investments secure, and to eliminate cutthroat competition in steel. Andrew Carnegie, who was doing pretty well as an aggressive competitor, was paid twice what he thought his business was worth to go along. Morgan made the steel business safer for the investor but tough on the consumer, and it has been so ever since.

The opposing economic ideal says that industrial progress can best be obtained in a free market, where prices are fixed by competition and where success depends on efficiency rather than market control. Under this theory it becomes the government's function not to control or regulate but only to maintain freedom in the market place by prosecuting combinations whenever they become large enough to fix prices. Henry Ford represents this ideal. By producing cars at cut prices on a nationwide scale, he helped wreck many of the existing automobile companies. But he also revolutionized the industry.

This second ideal is also represented by a remarkable piece of legislation called the Sherman Antitrust Act, passed by Congress on July 2, 1890, which states that ''Every contract, combination in the form of trust or otherwise, or conspiracy, in restraint of trade or commerce among the several States, or with foreign nations, is hereby declared to be illegal.'' The act goes on to authorize the federal government to proceed against trusts which violate the act, and empowers federal circuit courts with jurisdiction over such violations.

If I may be permitted to say so, as one who has had some experience with enforcing it, this law is historically unique. Prior to the Second World War, no other nation had any legislation like it. It is different from any other criminal statute because it makes it a crime to violate a vaguely stated economic policy—and a policy, what is more, on which public attitudes often change. The average American citizen—and, indeed, the average court which administers the Sherman act—would like to believe simultaneously in both of the conflicting economic ideals described above. For that reason, the Supreme Court swings back and forth in Sherman act cases, in more important ones splitting five to four. The history of the Sherman act is the history of the conflicts and compromises between these two economic ideals.

But the dominant ideal in our American economic thinking has been the ideal of the Sherman act. The business pressures against its actual enforcement are great, but support of the *principle* of the act is so unanimous that no one ever suggests its repeal. Big business, labor, farmers—each economic group wants the Sherman act strictly enforced, against everyone but itself.

In meeting these pressures the Sherman act has shown extraordinary elasticity. It may bend at times, but it always bounces back. Thus it is like a constitutional provision rather than an ordinary statute, and its history tells much about our national attempt to create an economy that will be at the same time both disciplined and free.

How was this ideal born in the first place? The most improbable feature of the Sherman act is that this apparently anti-big business measure was introduced by a senator who was a high-tariff advocate and an extreme conservative, and was passed with only one dissenting vote by a big-business Republican Congress.

The initial pressure for it came from agriculture, which since the Civil War had been reduced to a fairly steady depression. Railroad monopolies were charging farmers all the traffic would bear, and sometimes a little more. Rates were rigged to favor big railroad customers and ruin small ones. As farm income fell, prices that farmers had to pay rose steadily. Monopolies kept them high. If the pressure from the agricultural states was strong, so was the rebellion against other aspects of the dog-eat-dog business ethics of the times. The necessity of some restraint on such practices came at last to be recognized even by business itself.

Big business during the latter half of the nineteenth century had come to regard competition as an unmitigated evil which could be alleviated only by combination. At first the combinations took the form of "pools" or agreements—regional rather than national—to restrain trade, to control prices, to restrict output and divide markets. But businessmen soon learned that agreements between members of an industry were too weak. Only the surrender of business independence by the units could make domination of the market certain.

Pools gave way to trusts, the first of which, established by Standard Oil in 1879, became a model for subsequent business combinations. Each party to the trust surrendered his stock-voting power to trustees, receiving trust certificates in return. Thus the nine trustees of the Standard Oil Trust, without the investment of a dollar, obtained absolute power over the nation's oil industry. The pattern set by Standard Oil was so widely followed that the name "trust" became a byword for any large industrial combination even after the trust device had been abandoned.

Prior to the Sherman act the federal government had no power to prevent predatory business activities. Therefore, the states themselves began an ineffective attack on the trusts in state courts. In 1887 Louisiana prosecuted the Cotton Oil Trust. In 1889 California prosecuted the Sugar Trust; in 1890 Nebraska prosecuted the Whiskey Trust. The attorney general of Ohio sought to repeal the charter of the Standard Oil Company of Ohio.

In 1892 the supreme court of Ohio ordered the local oil company to sever its connections with the Standard Oil Trust. The order was never effectively enforced. But these state attacks on it made the device

In 1888 Senator John Sherman introduced the resolution that two years later became the Sherman Antitrust Act.

so risky that corporate organizations looked for some other form of combination that could not be prosecuted under state law. New Jersey provided the model, by amending its incorporation statute to permit one corporation to own the stock of another. From then on it was easy.

Corporations A, B, and C would give 51 per cent of their stock to holding company X. Holding company X would in turn give 51 per cent of its stock to holding company Y. Thus holding company Y, with only about 25 per cent interest in the operating companies, controlled them completely. Y would transfer enough stock to Z, at which point Z needed only 12½ per cent to control the industry. And so on until fantastic pyramids were built up. No state could attack these pyramids because they were legal in the state of incorporation. Only Congress could interfere with this process.

In July, 1888, John Sherman, senator from Ohio, introduced the resolution that led to the passage of the Sherman act. He had been Secretary of the Treasury under President Hayes and was known as an expert in finance and taxation. He was big business-minded and an ardent advocate of high tariffs. In this important respect, he was opposed to the very interests that were demanding antimonopoly legislation. In the farm belt the tariff was called the mother of monopoly. Sherman could have no part in such radical doctrine. His resolution reconciled that contradiction very neatly. It asked the Finance Committee to report on a bill that would

> tend to preserve freedom of trade and production, the natural competition of increasing production, the lowering of prices by such competition, and the full benefit designed by and hitherto conferred by the policy of the government to protect and encourage American industries by levying duties on imported goods.

In other words, Sherman contended that the increased production by local industry protected by tariffs would more than offset the increased prices due to the tariffs, if domestic competition was free and unrestrained.

The Sherman act as it reads today was passed in the Senate 52 yeas to 1 nay, and signed by President Harrison on July 2, 1890. No votes were cast against it in the House.

The act is unexampled in economic legislation. In effect it says: "We want competition in the United States and we will leave it to the federal judiciary to determine, case by case, just what action constitutes a restraint on competition." That this law could be passed by a conservative Republican Congress whose most influential leaders were closely associated with big business is remarkable in the extreme. Many writers have argued that the act was a hypocritical piece of legislation, designed as a political sop to the farm belt, and that no one expected it to be of any consequence. For example, Senator Nelson W. Aldrich, who was known as J. P. Morgan's floor broker in the Senate, voted for it.

Such facts are sometimes cited to support the view that the original passage of the bill was only an attempt to placate western senators in exchange for votes on higher tariffs. But this interpretation has been completely refuted by Hans B. Thorelli in his recent book, *The Federal Antitrust Policy*, the most complete and objective analysis of the history of American monopoly policy. Thorelli concludes that a majority of congressmen were sincere and that the Sherman act represented for men of both parties the symbol and the image of what they sincerely desired the American economy to become.

By that I do not mean that the Republican supporters of the act would have welcomed the breakup of great American combinations into smaller units. At the same time, they would have instinctively rejected the system of domestic and international cartels that had been growing up in Germany and spreading to France from 1870 on, which would surely have become the American pattern if the Sherman act had not been passed.

The Sherman act fitted in with the American economic and legal philosophy that was religiously held in 1890 and which is still our dominant philosophy today. In 1890 Americans distrusted any form of governmental regulation. It was the tradition of the American common law that the relation between business and government should be based on some broad common-law principle which would acquire definite meaning only through a series of court decisions. The Sherman act followed that tradition. Our faith in the common law was such that Congress believed that the courts could give a better and more practical meaning to the principles of the act than Congress could possibly do by further definition or regulation.

The Sherman act was definitely on the shelf during the administrations of Presidents Harrison, Cleveland, and McKinley. Cleveland's attorney general not only instituted no proceedings but dropped the prosecution of the notorious Cash Register Trust, even though he had won a victory in the lower court. Under Cleveland the principal impact of the Sherman act was against labor in breaking the Pullman strike. McKinley was equally indifferent to the Sherman act. During his four and one half years only three suits were brought.

The first Sherman act decision by the Supreme Court was in the case of United States *v.* E. C. Knight & Co. It amounted to a virtual repeal of the act. The Supreme Court held that the Sugar Trust, in acquiring a monopoly over sugar manufacturing, affected interstate commerce only indirectly and, therefore, did not violate the act. As Justice John Marshall Harlan pointed out in his dissent: "While the opinion of the Court in this case does not declare the Act of 1890 to be unconstitutional, it defeats the main object for which it was passed." The Knight case thus emasculated the Sherman act. As a result of that decision the government became powerless to prevent the formation of a monopoly through the device of a holding company.

Yet within the short space of eight years, through the daring and ingenuity of Theodore Roosevelt, the Sherman act was transformed again from a meaningless and ineffective formula into a sharp weapon. Theodore Roosevelt was one of the few politicians of his time who had seriously studied the antitrust problem. He had his first experience with monopoly power as a New York State assemblyman during the investigation of Jay Gould. He campaigned for re-election on the antimonopoly issue in 1882. In 1899, as governor, he wrote: "I have been in a great quandary over trusts. I do not know what attitude to take. I do not intend to play a demagogue. On the other hand, I do intend, so far as in me lies, to see that the rich man is held to the same accountability as the poor man, and when the rich man is rich enough *to buy unscrupulous advice from very able lawyers, this is not always easy.*" (Italics added.)

It was the empire-building ambition of J. P. Morgan that gave Theodore Roosevelt his chance. During the last year of the McKinley Administration the Northern Securities Company had been formed as a compromise between E. H. Harriman and Morgan in their fight to control the Northern Pacific Railroad. The holding company device was used to combine under one management two of the nation's largest competing railroads, the Northern Pacific and the Great Northern. Had the scheme succeeded, it could have led to the domination of all American railroads by this group. It could have created a pattern for the cartelization of all American industry.

Roosevelt, as one of the first acts of his Administration, determined to attack this respected citadel of corporate power. This enterprise was very different from that of using the act to attack mere dishonesty in business, and Roosevelt must have realized that the legal odds were very much against him. A careful lawyer would have advised him that the Knight case exempted J. P. Morgan's ambitious plans. The decision in the Knight case stood for the principle that the acquisition of monopoly control was immune from attack because, though it affected prices "indirectly," it was not a conspiracy to fix them "directly."

The issue as Roosevelt saw it went far beyond the merger of the two railroads involved in Northern Securities. The issue was nothing less than effective national sovereignty. The federal government had been relegated to such minor roles as distributing the mail and collecting tariff duties. Big business was the real sovereign in infinitely

Joseph Keppler, the founder of Puck, captioned this 1904 cartoon of Teddy Roosevelt fighting the merger- and monopoly-minded titans of American business, "Jack and the Wall Street Giants."

more important areas. In the Northern Securities case, Theodore Roosevelt was to obtain for the federal government a magna carta limiting the power of the business princes.

Roosevelt gambled that the Supreme Court, with new faces in it since the Knight case, would repudiate or at least alter that decision. He directed Attorney General Philander C. Knox to draw up a case against the Northern Securities Company. It was to be a head-on attack on the philosophy of the Knight case decision. Fully aware of the tremendous pressures that would be exerted against him, he directed Knox to prepare the prosecution in complete secrecy. Not even his close friend and adviser, Elihu Root, the Secretary of War, was told.

When Knox finally released to the press his intention to prosecute Northern Securities, there was consternation and panic in the financial world. Root, a Wall Street lawyer, was dismayed and resentful. Morgan and his like-minded friend, Senator Chauncey Depew of New York, descended upon the White House like the emissaries of some independent sovereignty whose rights were being invaded. But by that time the prosecution was a *fait accompli*.

On this case all of Roosevelt's antitrust program depended. It came before the Supreme Court in March, 1904. By that time, Roosevelt had appointed Oliver Wendell Holmes to the Court, believing that Holmes's reputation as a liberal was an indication that he would vote against the tremendous extension of monopoly power. In this hope he was to be bitterly disappointed. Had Holmes been able to win over to his side Justice David Brewer, as he thought he had, the legitimacy of monopoly would have been established, perhaps for all time, in this country as it was in Europe.

The Court was bitterly divided, five to four. The majority held that the Sherman act was intended to prevent giant combinations formed under any device and that such exercise of congressional power over industry was not unconstitutional.

Holmes, who wrote one of the two principal dissents, made the statement, believed by many at that time, that the Sherman act was not intended to prevent combinations in restraint of trade. He said: "It was the ferocious extreme of competition with others, not the cessation of competition among the partners, that was the evil feared."

Justice Holmes had faith in the benevolence and efficiency of the rich. He believed that the Constitution should protect them in their efforts to create industrial empires. But the ideal of a dynamic competitive economy and government-maintained freedom of industrial opportunity, I believe, was beyond him. He would have approved of the system of domestic and international cartels that dominated industry and caused it to stagnate in Europe before World War II.

Roosevelt, though a rich man himself, was one of the few men of his time to realize the destiny of America as a land of economic freedom. He had the ability to infuse the public with his point of view. Senator Sherman initiated the antitrust act, but it was Teddy Roosevelt who gave it vigor and meaning, made the policy of the Sherman act an economic religion and its violation an economic sin, and, finally, made it emotionally impossible for American business to co-operate in the European cartel system.

To appraise the effect of the Sherman act on American business institutions correctly we must view it apart from particular prosecutions, or particular periods of enforcement or nonenforcement. Theodore Roosevelt's achievement was to enshrine the ideal of the act as part of our national folklore. And its influence has continued in a far more potent way than perhaps any other statute on the books. The image of the Sherman act has not prevented tremendous concentrations of economic power, but it has prevented such concentrations from obtaining legitimate status.

Only once since its passage has the principle of the act been repudiated. That was in production codes of the National Recovery Administration during Franklin D. Roosevelt's New Deal. They were designed to raise prices and restrict production, after the European model. The theory was that this would protect investments and rescue business from insolvency.

But the competitive tradition represented by the Sherman act was too strong for the NRA. The Sherman act over the years, even when it was unenforced, had built up an abiding faith that the elimination of competition in business was morally and economically wrong. Then the Supreme Court threw out the NRA, and Franklin Roosevelt turned back to the antitrust laws as a major instrument of economic policy, and placed me in charge of their enforcement.

When I took office, years of disuse of the Sherman act, culminating in its repudiation by NRA, had made violation of the antitrust laws common, almost respectable. I will never forget the amazement of the Wisconsin Alumni Research Foundation, an organization whose profits were used to support the University of Wisconsin, when the Justice Department charged it with using a vitamin patent to raise prices and restrict manufacture of important food products. It never occurred to the high-minded management of this foundation that it was doing anything wrong. The indictment was considered an attack on education itself.

Thurman Arnold, former head of the Antitrust Division of the Justice Department, testifying before the Senate Banking Committee in 1949.

I believed that my principal function was to convince American businessmen that the Sherman act represented something more than a pious platitude; second, that its enforcement was an important economic policy. But there was very little support among economists for the latter notion.

As indictments of respectable people began to pour out from the Justice Department in unprecedented numbers, cries of outrage could be heard from coast to coast. I will never forget the pain and astonishment caused when criminal charges were brought against the American Medical Association, which had established a pretty effective boycott on all forms of group health plans. I was pictured as a wild man whose sanity was in considerable doubt. One major newspaper referred to me as ''an idiot in a powder mill.'' Letters of protest poured into the White House. Adverse publicity reached its peak when the Associated Press was charged with violation of the Sherman act for refusing to sell its news service to any new newspaper that would be competing with one of its member publications. Editorials appeared from coast to coast accusing the department of destroying freedom of the press.

Yet the enforcement program of the Antitrust Division on a nationwide scale between 1938 and the outbreak of World War II survived all such attacks. This was because American businessmen did not want to repudiate the principle of the Sherman act, however much they disliked particular prosecutions. It showed that the Henry Ford tradition was still dominant.

It is difficult now to appraise the economic effect of the revival of the Sherman act at that time. Opinions differ, and my own is, of course, biased. But this at least can be said: American business learned that the Sherman act was something more than a false front to our business structure. The public gained an idea of the purpose of the act, the act itself gained renewed vitality, and American business approved this revival.

There are two principal evils of concentrated economic power in a democracy. The first is the power of concentrated industry to charge administered prices rather than prices based on competitive demand. A second is the tendency of such empires to swallow up local businesses and drain away local capital. Prior to the Depression this condition had advanced so far that our concentrated industrial groups had helped destroy their own markets by siphoning off the dollars that could have been a source of local purchasing power.

It is idle to say that periodic enforcement of the antitrust laws has solved these problems, but the laws themselves have given us an image of what our economy should be. In a cartel economy no one could question the legitimacy of the recent rises in steel—or any other—prices. In an antitrust-minded economy it seems a legitimate and natural thing for a congressional committee to call the companies to account. . . .

John A. Garraty

Robert M. La Follette: The Promise Unfulfilled

The leading figures of the Progressive Era have suffered considerably at the hands of historians in recent years. Their insensitivity to the fate of Negroes becomes ever more apparent as scholars study their attitudes toward racial minorities. Their middle-class orientation stands out in contrast to their radical rhetoric. Their inconsistent record on such questions as immigration and labor legislation, as well as their widespread support of imperialistic ventures, appears less than liberal from a contemporary point of view. Indeed, one historian, Gabriel Kolko, has titled his study of the Progressive Era The Triumph of Conservatism.

The following essay criticizes the Progressives from a different perspective and is in part an attempt to cast certain doubts on the character and motivation of all American reformers. The subject examined here, Robert M. La Follette, was one of the most vigorous and effective of the Progressives; he has often been seen as the beau idéal of the type. Yet as I have tried to show, his personal inadequacies raise serious questions about his liberalism, as well as about his judgment.

O ne day in July, 1904, Lincoln Steffens, the famous muckraking reporter of *McClure's Magazine,* appeared unannounced in Milwaukee, Wisconsin, hot on the trail of a big story. Steffens had won a well-deserved reputation as an exposer of what he called *The Shame of the Cities;* now he was studying corrupt state politics, and the Wisconsin "machine" of Governor Robert M. La Follette was next on his list. He arrived in Milwaukee convinced that despite a lot of fancy talk about "reform," La Follette was a "demagogue . . . a charlatan and a crook."

Steffens' first informant was a prominent banker. When asked for evidence of the Governor's corruption, the banker could not contain himself. La Follette was a "crooked hypocrite" and a "socialist-anarchist"; he was ruining Wisconsin. But the banker was too angry to present a reasoned indictment. Next Steffens turned to a local railroad lawyer. Though this man had better control of his temper, his detailed analysis of La Follette was studded with words like "fanatic," "boss," and "actor."

Presently, Steffens moved on to Madison to confront the Governor directly. He was met at the Capitol by a man approaching fifty, short and stocky but so brimming with vitality and enthusiasm that he appeared taller than he actually was. He had a shock of brown hair sparingly flecked with gray and a thick bull neck. His lips were sensitive, his eyes calm, his forehead noble. His strong chin and square, muscular jaw reflected a person who habitually set his teeth hard in the face of opposition. Somehow he projected an image which combined kindliness with strength, immense energy with serenity of spirit. The Governor literally ran to greet Steffens, assuming that any reformer would come as a friend. He insisted upon bringing him home to dinner, where Mrs. La Follette and the children offered a warm welcome, also taking it for granted that Steffens was on their side. But the journalist, still unconvinced, did not respond to these advances. Instead he arranged to interview La Follette at length about his whole career.

Thus it was that Lincoln Steffens learned the story of one of the most remarkable personalities of modern times, a man who, finding the state of Wisconsin a satrapy controlled by a handful of lumber barons and hack politicians, changed it into a great laboratory for democratic reform, the home of the "Wisconsin Idea." That he would also help to wreck the whole Republican party and deliver it for a long generation into the hands of its own right wing neither Steffens nor La Follette himself could possibly have known in 1904.

It was a fascinating tale that the Governor related to Steffens. Born in a log cabin at Primrose, Wisconsin, in 1855, he was accustomed to farm life and in later years prided himself on his ability with scythe and plow. He had also developed a wide assortment of other skills; for example, he was a first-class carpenter and an expert barber. As his wife, Belle, explained, Bob seemed to pick up special skills "without anybody's knowing when or how." He also had a strong intellectual bent, and had worked his way through the University of Wisconsin. As a student, he did well; also, he was so remarkably successful in campus theatricals that he seriously considered making the stage his career. But his primary ambition was to be a "statesman," and after graduation he went on to law school and then entered politics.

From the start he was a rebel. In 1880, after being admitted to the bar, he declared himself a candidate for the Republican nomination for district attorney in his home county. The local party boss, Postmaster E. W. Keyes, had other plans. He took La Follette aside and in a firm but kindly way told him that another man had already been decided upon for the job. The young lawyer had neither money nor influence, but the fighter in him was instantly roused. "I intend to go on with this canvass," he told Keyes, "and I intend to be elected district attorney. . . ." He intensified his campaign at once. "I traveled by day and by night," he later recalled. "I stayed at farm-houses, I interviewed every voter in the county whom I could reach." These tactics paid off. The boss could not control his own convention, and La Follette was nominated. In the election, although the angry Keyes supported a Democrat, La Follette carried the district.

This victory established the pattern of his career. Always within the framework of the Republican party (he became a warm admirer of William McKinley), he made his way independently and against the opposition of the Wisconsin Republican machine. Diligent campaigning at the grass roots and a reputation for honesty, courage, and faithful service to his constituents enabled him repeatedly to defy the local powers. He exposed the chairman of the party's state committee, who had been robbed while dead drunk in a Madison hotel room and had later sought to hush the case up. When various politicos tried to have minor legal cases quashed for influential friends, he refused to go along. Later, when U.S. Senator Philetus Sawyer, the powerful lumber king, offered him a "retainer" in a case where Sawyer stood to lose over $150,000, La Follette indignantly announced that the Senator had tried to bribe him.

La Follette was elected to Congress in 1884, after another battle with the Republican machine. In Washington he was a model legislator, attending sessions faithfully, caring for the needs of his constituents, and diligently seeking to master the complications of public issues upon which he felt himself inadequately informed. When he was placed on the unimportant Committee on Indian Affairs, for example, he swallowed his disappointment, bought a small library of secondhand books on Indians, and soon became an expert on the subject. One is reminded of the youthful Bryan (for a time his colleague in the House) laboring to master tariff and monetary problems.

Although by no means a radical at this period, La Follette made a name for himself as an uncompromising foe of "pork-barrel" legislation and of business interests like lumber companies and railroads seeking fat land grants and other special favors from Congress. But after three terms he was defeated in the Democratic tidal wave of 1890 and forced to resume his law practice back home.

He then began a ten-year struggle to gain control of the Wisconsin

*Robert Marion La Follette,
a photographic portrait, 1922.*

Republican party. He spoke everywhere in the state and wrote count-less letters—1,200 in a single campaign on behalf of his friend Nils P. Haugen. He conducted a "county fair crusade" to win the support of the rural people. Frustrated by the bosses in his efforts to win the gubernatorial nomination, he made the direct primary one of his chief demands, attracting national attention with a brilliant oration on "The Menace of the Political Machine," at the University of Chicago in 1897. Finally, in 1900, he could no longer be denied. He won the nomination for governor and was easily elected.

Still, for a time, the bosses managed to frustrate his program of reform. A primary bill was smothered in the state senate, and a scheme of his to increase railroad taxes failed in the lower house. Re-elected in 1902, La Follette was able to force through the primary bill (subject to popular ratification at the next election) and to obtain some revision of the railroad tax structure. His broad plan for a powerful railroad commission was defeated, however, despite a tremendous 181-page special message by the Governor explaining why the commission was needed. In 1904, sensing that their day would soon be over if La Follette were not stopped, the conservatives made a supreme effort to defeat his bid for a third term. It was at this critical point that Steffens came to Wisconsin.

Steffens was a cynic. Long experience had led him to believe that all politicians were interested primarily in power and position. "Reform" was the cry of the demagogue; Steffens personally preferred the forthright scoundrel to the hypocrite posing as a friend of "good government." But his conversations with La Follette convinced him of the Governor's honesty and good intentions. His story, published in the October *McClure's,* no doubt contributed to La Follette's re-election the following month, a victory that enabled the Governor eventually to carry out his entire program. But Steffens' help was really of minor importance: by 1904, years of struggle had made "Fighting Bob" a master politician and a brilliant public leader in his own right.

Under La Follette Wisconsin became, in the words of Russel B. Nye, "the proving ground" of twentieth-century Progressivism. "The Wisconsin Idea" became famous. Actually the "Idea" was more a practical program than a theory, but whether as theory or as example, it had a remarkable impact on other states and in time on the federal government. It made the political machinery more directly responsive to the popular will. Besides the direct primary law, Wisconsin by 1914 had a corrupt practices act and laws restricting lobbying and excessive campaign expenditures. Furthermore, much was done in the way of social legislation: pure-food, child-labor, and workingmen's-compensation laws were passed, and the educational system was greatly

The genuine effectiveness of La Follette's reform politics was the subject of this cartoon by John T. McCutcheon; from the Chicago Tribune, *1911.*

improved. New regulatory commissions were set up to protect the public against economic exploitation by "the interests." Finally, the tax structure was overhauled, and the burden of paying for these reforms distributed more equitably. A tax commission, headed by the able Nils Haugen, was established, and state income and inheritance taxes were added to the heavier levies on corporations. Small wonder that the party bosses—and even many unbossed conservative Republicans—did not go along quietly.

Not all of these programs originated in Wisconsin; indeed, some of the basic Progressive ideas, such as the initiative and referendum, were not enacted there. What really made "the Wisconsin Idea" so influential was the comprehensiveness and practicality of the program and the effective way it was administered. For this La Follette deserves most of the credit, even though much of what was done came after he left the governorship for service in the U.S. Senate.

It was in this great forum that Robert Marion La Follette was to make his mark upon America; there he would serve, through one of the country's most exciting periods, until his death. To understand this later career, in prospect so promising, in the end a promise unfulfilled, it is necessary to examine the formidable strengths—and important weaknesses—he brought with him on his return to Washington.

To begin with, he was an exceptionally fine public speaker. While only a small child he was in demand at picnics and other rural social gatherings where formal recitations were in order; at college he won an interstate oratorical contest. As a political speaker, his only fault was longwindedness: he could go on for hours at a stretch, and usually did. His performances, often staged beneath a blazing summer sun, drew heavily on his stamina; he reported upon occasion becoming so giddy from the heat that he almost lost the thread of his argument, and he suffered so from blistered feet that he finally bought himself some cool white canvas shoes. His wife, worried by the strain of such ordeals, gave him an alarm watch and made him promise to set it for two hours after he began speaking. Yet he seldom allowed the tinkling alarm to stop him. "I talked too long & beg your forgiveness," he wrote her after a speech in San Francisco. "My audience held on till 12 o'clock and would *not let* me stop!" He might talk endlessly, but always to a purpose; his speeches were solid with statistics, concrete illustrations, vivid arguments. He was militant, determined, a crusader, a doughty champion, a tribune, a standard bearer.

And if he spoke too long, his audiences were seldom bored. "After Bob began," his wife once wrote, "it seemed to me no one moved until he had finished." And an observer who heard him at the 1897 Winnebago County Fair said: "The speech made a profound and lasting impression on me. . . . I was a Democrat and always before that time I had gone away from a Republican meeting more a Democrat than ever. But here was a man who spoke to me as a citizen, not as a partisan."

Another important La Follette asset was his superb political skill. While in the House of Representatives he had had a form printed with blank spaces for recording the names of "active Republicans" and "fair-minded Democrats." These he sent to key supporters all over Wisconsin, and thus built up a large mailing list of influential voters whom he kept supplied with copies of his speeches and other political matter. And no congressman was more assiduous in attending to the needs of his constituents or in squiring visitors around Washington.

La Follette had in fact developed a mastery of every technique for influencing public opinion. In each campaign he concentrated on no more than one or two issues, hammering at them relentlessly, riveting the attention of the voters upon them. He could take advantage of defeat, occasionally even deliberately cultivating it in order to develop a campaign issue. As governor, in 1903 he had pushed a bill establishing a powerful commission to regulate Wisconsin's railroads. When, as he had expected, the legislature rejected this bill, he took the question to the people in the 1904 campaign.

And he was capable of dramatizing a controversial question. In 1898 he had caused a furor by announcing that a railroad had allowed Governor Edward Schofield to ship a cow halfway across the state without cost. It was a trivial matter, and Schofield's action was perfectly legal, but it pointed up La Follette's crusade against special favors to public officials. "Schofield's cow became famous," La Follette recalled in his *Autobiography*, "her picture appeared in the newspapers, and she came to be known in every home in the state." The next year a law outlawing such favors was passed.

But the greatest source of the new senator's strength lay in his intimate understanding of the desires, needs, and prejudices of the Wisconsin farmers. Like Bryan, he was a product of the agricultural unrest that had engulfed the Middle West after the Civil War. He was convinced that "big business" was an evil force in society, exploiting the farmer at every turn. At eighteen he had been profoundly impressed by a local orator who denounced "vast corporate combinations" and "the accumulation of individual wealth . . . greater than it ever has been since the downfall of the Roman Empire." He took up this cry himself, and half a century later he was still tilting at big corporations like U.S. Steel and "wealth [that] will not and cannot be made to bear its full share of taxation." Throughout his political life he would assail Wall Street, lobbyists, and the other standard spectres that haunted the rural imagination. Late in his Senate career he would denounce the Four-Power Pact of the Washington Arms Conference as a conspiracy of international bankers bent on protecting their investments. One may smile at his obvious prejudice, but his pronouncements were taken as gospel by many in Wisconsin and throughout the Middle West.

This rapport with the ordinary citizens of his region developed in La Follette an abiding faith in democracy, a belief that the average man could judge rightly on public issues. Of course this faith was characteristic of nearly all Progressives—men as dissimilar as Bryan, Wilson, and George Perkins shared it—but La Follette possessed it completely and acted upon it consistently. "Bob was always conscious of this native power of the plain people to grasp thought," his wife has recorded. "It never occurred to him to speak 'down' to his audiences or to consider any theme beyond their reach." Or, one might add, to wonder whether popular majorities could not be wrong, whether in installing prohibition or electing a Huey Long.

He was an energetic campaigner. To take only one example: in the 1900 gubernatorial contest he covered 6,433 miles in three weeks, making 61 speeches to a total of some 200,000 people. He believed that if he could reach the voters they would see that he was right and sweep him to victory. His espousal of the direct primary reflected his wish to take nominations away from the politicians and give them to the people.

Genuine though it was, La Follette's faith in the intelligence and good sense of farmers was neither mystical nor unrealistic. He knew that government was a complicated science and a delicate art; its effective administration called for special skills and technical knowledge that the average man did not possess. The easy Jacksonian confidence that any ordinary citizen could handle most government positions—the belief that led Bryan to pack the State Department with "deserving Democrats"—did not enchant "Fighting Bob." Instead he employed many experts, drawing especially upon the faculty of the University of Wisconsin, where, after 1903, his classmate Charles R. Van Hise was president. "The University exists for the state," La Follette said. Soon he was drafting economists and political scientists as advisers and civil servants.

"Fighting Bob" campaigning in 1900 for the governorship of Wisconsin. He won handily.

This reliance on experts and intellectuals marked La Follette as something more than a rural spellbinder. So did his emphasis on regulatory commissions to control railroads, other public utilities, and insurance companies. Here again, his faith in the people was tempered with realism: the personnel of such commissions were to be appointed rather than elected, for the best railroad commissioner, La Follette knew, might not be a good campaigner.

All these qualities had helped La Follette rise to power in Wisconsin, and his success in his home state not only took him to the Senate chamber, but made him the idol of early twentieth-century reformers. Still, success tended to obscure certain rather unfortunate aspects of his personality, certain disturbing elements in his thinking. He spoke frequently (and he was sincere enough) about his principles, but in the last analysis he cared more for ends than for means. He was too much the zealot, considering himself an infallible judge of right and wrong. This conviction served him effectively in battle, but in the long run it led many people to mistrust his judgment and resent his power.

As governor, for example, he made effective—even ruthless—use of patronage. He demanded absolute obedience from his henchmen, and rewarded their faithfulness with appointments to public office. The Wisconsin game wardens became notorious for their political activities. Instead of tracking down poachers, one editor complained, they devoted their energies to "strolling around . . . hunting for men who will vote for La Follette." Furthermore, if his speeches were effective and filled with facts, they were also often oversimplified and sometimes distorted the information he was presenting to the electorate. In his powerful attacks on the "interests," he never tried to understand the motives, methods, or accomplishments of the "villains" he assaulted. His was the hard-handed farmer's unreasoning suspicion of men who won wealth by manipulating symbols.

When La Follette talked of trusting "the people," he had, as we have seen, important if unspoken reservations. His dislike of the big cities with their teeming millions scarcely differed from that of his rural constituents. In this and other ways, without realizing what he was doing, he sometimes undermined the very precepts of democracy he was sworn to defend. He could even, upon occasion, be as much the representative of a special-interest group as any other politician. As a congressman, for example, he had assailed the meat packers as one of the evil interests; but he argued for a federal tax on oleomargarine that benefited only the dairy interests so powerful in Wisconsin.

Like many crusaders, La Follette tended to discount the possibility that others could disagree with him and still be sincere. He was wont to override even friendly critics; like Woodrow Wilson (whom he resembled in many ways) he left a trail of shattered friendships wherever he went. "I can no more compromise . . . than I could by wishing it add twenty years to my life," he once said. He took everything too seriously; he was too intent and too intense.

It is very revealing that he was prone to imagine all sorts of plots and conspiracies against him. In the governor's mansion in Wisconsin he often claimed to hear mysterious knocks on the door, and the door-bell sometimes rang in an inexplicable manner. Although a careful watch was kept, no one was ever caught thus harassing him. In later life he actually claimed that someone had tried to kill him by poisoning a glass of milk he was drinking while filibustering in Congress against a banking bill. "Bob ran constant risk of violence," his adoring wife firmly believed. But no actual attack was ever made on him. Considering his reputation for integrity and courage, it is remarkable how many people supposedly tried to bribe or threaten him. Could his enemies really have been so foolish? In his controversy with Philetus Sawyer, for example, Sawyer hotly denied that he had tried to buy La Follette's support by offering him a retainer. Probably La Follette's ingrained suspicions sometimes made him interpret in the worst possible light the efforts of practical politicians to reach agreement.

These, then, were the strengths and weaknesses, the great-hearted instincts and the narrowing limitations, which Senator La Follette brought with him to Washington. At home, where a solid majority shared his prejudices, he had been able to bend the Republican organization to his will. In the United States Senate conditions were very different, and he was less successful—but no less determined. In 1906, when he took his seat, the sands of the national arena were comparatively smooth. Theodore Roosevelt, midway in his second term, had instituted changes the significance of which people were only beginning to understand. By reviving the Sherman Antitrust Act and by moving toward stricter regulation of railroads, the protection of natural resources, a pure-food-and-drug act, and other reforms, Roosevelt had encouraged Republican liberals. At the same time he had roused conservatives to the defense of the old order typified by McKinley and Mark Hanna. Soon controversial questions like the protective tariff and the control of monopoly were to divide the liberals themselves into warring factions. Both La Follette and George Perkins, for example, considered themselves Republicans and Progressives, yet La Follette was for breaking up the trusts and lowering the tariff, while Perkins—who would be one of T. R.'s major backers in the Bull Moose revolt of 1912—wanted to keep the tariff high and regulate, rather than dismember, the trusts.

In this explosive situation, La Follette was determined (as always) to remain a Republican. But he was also (again as always) unwilling to grant quarter to fellow Republicans whose views he disliked. He would no more deal with Senator Nelson Aldrich and other G.O.P. conservatives in Washington than with Boss Keyes or Philetus Sawyer back in Wisconsin. As a result, no man had more to do with the disruption of the party than he.

In the Senate he was a maverick from the start. Tradition dictated that new senators should not take part in debates during their first year. La Follette refused to conform; on April 19, 1906, a month after taking his seat, he rose to speak on an important railroad bill. Many senators indignantly left the floor. La Follette took no notice until he had finished the first part of his speech. Then he turned coolly to the presiding officer and said:

> I cannot be wholly indifferent to the fact that Senators by their absence at this time indicate their want of interest in what I have to say upon this subject. The public is interested. Unless this important question is rightly settled seats now temporarily vacant may be permanently vacated by those who have the right to occupy them at this time.

It was no idle threat. As soon as Congress adjourned, La Follette took to the stump. In state after state he described how his bills had been sidetracked in the Senate. Everywhere he "read the roll calls" to show how local senators had voted on these proposals.

Actions like these were hardly calculated to endear the freshman to the Senate as a whole. Nevertheless, by 1909 La Follette was the leader of a small group of liberal senators who were beginning to call themselves Progressives. He also organized a magazine, *La Follette's Weekly,* in which he regularly flayed the conservatives of both parties. In the Senate he led the fight against the Republican-sponsored Payne-Aldrich tariff, and broke with Taft when the President supported it. He even accused Taft of trying to ruin him politically. He organized a National Progressive Republican League—the accent fell on the word "Progressive"—which endorsed a comprehensive reform program, including national primaries and the direct election of senators.

No one can doubt La Follette's sincerity as a reformer, but at least part of his militancy was the result of ambition. He wanted to be President and had set his sights on 1912. Taft stood in his way, and to win the Republican nomination (a third-party nomination would have had little practical value) La Follette had to make a final break with him. But the ideological split thus fostered affected others as well as himself. Theodore Roosevelt, the most distinctive political personality of the era, was also a Progressive. No liberal movement in the Republican party could succeed without his support. Yet what would his place in such a movement be?

La Follette considered Roosevelt a lukewarm reformer at best. In 1907 he had written: " [Roosevelt] will always say a lot of good things and half do a good many things—But it all ends rather disappointingly." He later wrote that T. R. disliked "the plodding investigation necessary to a solution of great economic questions," although he confessed that the former President was superb at "arousing the public conscience." When Roosevelt refused to join La Follette's League, the Senator was probably more pleased than disappointed. In any case, the League proceeded to make its main business the nomination of La Follette for the Presidency.

In the battle between Taft and La Follette, Roosevelt hoped to remain neutral. He saw little chance for either to win the election, and hoped to reassert command of the party after the expected defeat. But events soon threw him into the anti-Taft camp.

As soon as Roosevelt swung over to the Progressives, many of La Follette's most enthusiastic supporters prepared to switch their alle-

THE ONLY ADEQUATE REWARD.

In March of 1917 the New York World *printed this cartoon by Rollin Kirby taking La Follette severely to task for his outspoken opposition to American entry into World War I.*

giance to the attractive ex-President, for he seemed far more popular in the nation at large. Fear of being abandoned had much to do with La Follette's unfortunate performance in a speech before a group of magazine publishers on February 2, 1912. Tired, ill, worried, and frustrated, he lost control of himself and delivered an intemperate, confused, and repetitious harangue that caused even friendly observers to question his mental and emotional stability. Although a short rest completely restored him, many of his former backers seized the opportunity to flock to Roosevelt.

La Follette reacted characteristically: he refused to quit the race. After the Republicans had nominated Taft, and Roosevelt had organized what La Follette called the "Roosevelt-Perkins-Steel-Trust-Party," he would support neither group. Nor would he come out for the Democratic candidate, Woodrow Wilson, at least not officially. He gave Wilson indirect aid in the columns of *La Follette's Weekly* but himself cast a blank ballot in November.

During the Wilson administration La Follette was still nominally a Republican, but he pursued no fixed course. He was the only member of his party to vote for the new low Democratic tariff, and later he supported the administration's Railway Labor Act. But the Federal Reserve Act, which he might have been expected to embrace, he opposed on the ground that it gave bankers too much control over the currency. His greatest contribution in this period was the La Follette Seamen's Act—designed to protect the rights of merchant sailors and increase the safety of passengers at sea—which he pushed through Congress

ROBERT M. LA FOLLETTE: THE PROMISE UNFULFILLED 449

The aging warrior speaks on radio in 1924 as presidential candidate of the League for Progressive Political Action.

after a long fight in 1915.

He broke with Wilson over the question of American entry into the First World War. Europe's troubles were none of our own, he said; the war was the work of international bankers and profiteers. Thereafter, terrible abuse was his lot; even the faculty of his beloved alma mater turned almost unanimously against him, and an effort was made to expel him from the Senate.

But La Follette would not change his course. He opposed conscription, objected to the Espionage Act, attacked profiteering even where it did not exist. After the defeat of the Central Powers, La Follette was conspicuous in the Senate fight against the League of Nations. But he also fought consistently against all efforts to restrict civil liberties, and he urged that war costs be met by taxation rather than by borrowing.

The reaction against Wilsonian internationalism that followed the war restored La Follette's popularity. In 1922 he was re-elected to the Senate by a huge majority. But he was no more at home in the Republican party in the twenties than he had been in the time of Taft. He could not stomach Harding and Coolidge, who seemed too obviously allied to the "interests." In 1920 he had refused to head a Farmer-Labor party but by 1922 he was willing to consider running independently for the Presidency in order to "drive special privilege out of the control of the government." In 1924, with Burton K. Wheeler as his running mate, he polled nearly five million votes, although he carried only Wisconsin. Though nearly seventy, he was undaunted, and ready to continue the battle. "We have just begun to fight," he said. But a few months later, on June 18, 1925, he suffered a heart attack and died.

La Follette was certainly more "progressive" than most of the well-known politicians of his era. He fought for labor as well as for depressed farmers and businessmen, supported basic civil liberties as well as narrow political reforms. His lifelong dedication to public service and the principles of democracy entitles him to a high place in the liberal pantheon.

But his grave personal weaknesses limited his effectiveness. Despite his really remarkable talents and many virtues, there were, as we have seen, important flaws in his personality. He was headstrong, ruthless, suspicious, sometimes intellectually confused if not dishonest; and these qualities, perhaps even more than the consistent opposition of the "interests," were responsible for his repeated failure to achieve the Presidency. And if, as age came upon him, he never developed Bryan's bland, ignorant self-assurance, he remained, like most zealots, annoyingly certain that God and justice were always on his side.

Yet withal, Robert La Follette was indeed the *beau idéal* of the reformer, and hence liberals are conscious of an element of sadness, even of resentment, as they contemplate his career. For they expect more of their leaders than of ordinary men, so that their "human" failings, more tolerable in lesser men, prove preternaturally disillusioning. In the first decades of the century, Progressive leaders asked much of the voters, who, responding, flocked by the millions to the standard of Reform. But Bryan ended by insulting their intelligence, Perkins by refusing to let them help run their own party, La Follette by insisting that his was the one way to Heaven. Theodore Roosevelt spent his last years assailing pacifists and internationalists instead of fighting for the Square Deal. Even Woodrow Wilson, the greatest idealist of them all, sacrificed principle to expediency at Versailles and then arrogantly dug in his heels and refused to compromise at all when it came to seeking Senate approval of the League of Nations. The Progressive movement collapsed suddenly, but little wonder: its failure, essentially, was the failure of its leaders to measure up to their own ideals.

Anne Firor Scott

Jane Addams: Urban Crusader

As the reputations of Progressive political leaders have declined, those of some of the social reformers of the era have risen. This is particularly true of social workers like Jane Addams and other founders of the settlement-house movement, who in modern eyes seem to have had a more profound grasp of the true character of the problems of their age and to have worked more effectively and with greater dedication in trying to solve those problems than did any of the politicians.

These social workers were quite different from those of today—they were more personally involved and far less professionally oriented. Many were also, it is true, somewhat patronizing in their approach to those they sought to help and took a rather romantic and thus unrealistic view of the potentialities both of the poor and of their own capacity to help the poor. This essay by Professor Anne Firor Scott of Duke University makes clear, however, that Jane Addams of Chicago's Hull-House was neither patronizing nor a romantic. Mrs. Scott, who is engaged in writing a biography of Jane Addams, is also an authority on American urban history and the history of the South.

*I*f Alderman Johnny Powers of Chicago's teeming nineteenth ward had only been prescient, he might have foreseen trouble when two young ladies not very long out of a female seminary in Rockford, Illinois, moved into a dilapidated old house on Halsted Street in September, 1889, and announced themselves "at home" to the neighbors. The ladies, however, were not very noisy about it, and it is doubtful if Powers was aware of their existence. The nineteenth ward was well supplied with people already—growing numbers of Italians, Poles, Russians, Irish, and other immigrants—and two more would hardly be noticed.

Johnny Powers was the prototype of the ward boss who was coming to be an increasingly decisive figure on the American political scene. In the first place, he was Irish. In the second, he was, in the parlance of the time, a "boodler": his vote and influence in the Chicago Common Council were far from being beyond price. As chairman of the council's finance committee and boss of the Cook County Democratic party he occupied a strategic position. Those who understood the inner workings of Chicago politics thought that Powers had some hand in nearly every corrupt ordinance passed by the council during his years in office. In a single year, 1895, he was to help to sell six important city franchises. When the mayor vetoed Powers' measures, a silent but significant two-thirds vote appeared to override the veto.

Ray Stannard Baker, who chanced to observe Powers in the late nineties, recorded that he was shrewd and silent, letting other men make the speeches and bring upon their heads the abuse of the public. Powers was a short, stocky man, Baker said, "with a flaring gray pompadour, a smooth-shaven face [sic], rather heavy features, and a restless eye." One observer remarked that "the shadow of sympathetic gloom is always about him. He never jokes; he has forgotten how to smile . . ." Starting life as a grocery clerk, Powers had run for the city council in 1888 and joined the boodle ring headed by Alderman Billy Whalen. When Whalen died in an accident two years later, Powers moved swiftly to establish himself as successor. A few weeks before his death Whalen had collected some thirty thousand dollars—derived from the sale of a city franchise—to be divided among the party faithful. Powers alone knew that the money was in a safe in Whalen's saloon, so he promptly offered a high price for the furnishings of the saloon, retrieved the money, and divided it among the gang—at one stroke establishing himself as a shrewd operator and as one who would play the racket fairly.

From this point on he was the acknowledged head of the gang. Charles Yerkes, the Chicago traction tycoon, found in Powers an ideal tool for the purchase of city franchises. On his aldermanic salary of three dollars a week, Powers managed to acquire two large saloons of his own, a gambling establishment, a fine house, and a conspicuous collection of diamonds. When he was indicted along with two other corrupt aldermen for running a slot machine and keeping a "common gambling house," Powers was unperturbed. The three appeared before a police judge, paid each other's bonds, and that was the end of that.

Proof of their guilt was positive, but convictions were never obtained.

On the same day the Municipal Voters League published a report for the voters on the records of the members of the city council. John Powers was described as "recognized leader of the worst element in the council . . . [who] has voted uniformly for bad ordinances." The League report went on to say that he had always opposed securing any return to the city for valuable franchises, and proceeded to document the charge in detail.

To his constituents in the nineteenth ward, most of whom were getting their first initiation into American politics, Powers turned a different face. To them, he was first and last a friend. When there were celebrations, he always showed up: if the celebration happened to be a bazaar, he bought freely, murmuring piously that it would all go to the poor. In times of tragedy he was literally Johnny on the spot. If the family was too poor to provide the necessary carriage for a respectable funeral, it appeared at the doorstep—courtesy of Johnny Powers and charged to his standing account with the local undertaker. If the need was not so drastic, Powers made his presence felt with an imposing bouquet or wreath. "He has," said the Chicago *Times-Herald*, "bowed with aldermanic grief at thousands of biers."

Christmas meant literally tons of turkeys, geese, and ducks—each one handed out personally by a member of the Powers family, with good wishes and no questions asked. Johnny provided more fundamental aid, too, when a breadwinner was out of work. At one time he is said to have boasted that 2,600 men from his ward (about one third of

The antagonists: Jane Addams (left) in London in 1888 just prior to taking on Johnny Powers, Democratic ward boss, seen here (right) in a photograph taken about 1910.

the registered voters) were working in one way or another for the city of Chicago. This did not take into account those for whom the grateful holders of traction franchises had found a place. When election day rolled around, the returns reflected the appreciation of job-holders and their relatives.

The two young ladies on Halsted Street, Jane Addams and Ellen Starr, were prototypes too, but of a very different kind of figure: they were the pioneers of the social settlement, the original "social workers." They opposed everything Johnny Powers stood for.

Jane Addams' own background could hardly have been more different from that of John Powers. The treasured daughter of a well-to-do small-town businessman from Illinois, she had been raised in an atmosphere of sturdy Christian principles.

From an early age she had been an introspective child concerned with justifying her existence. Once in a childhood nightmare she had dreamed of being the only remaining person in a world desolated by some disaster, facing the responsibility for rediscovering the principle of the wheel! At Rockford she shared with some of her classmates a determination to live to "high purpose," and decided that she would become a doctor in order to "help the poor."

After graduation she went to the Woman's Medical College of Philadelphia, but her health failed and she embarked on the grand tour of Europe customary among the wealthy. During a subsequent trip to Europe in 1888, in the unlikely setting of a Spanish bull ring, an idea that had long been growing in her mind suddenly crystallized: she would rent a house "in a part of the city where many primitive and actual needs are found, in which young women who had been given over too exclusively to study, might restore a balance of activity along traditional lines and learn something of life from life itself . . ." So the American settlement-house idea was born. She and Ellen Starr, a former classmate at the Rockford seminary who had been with her in Europe, went back to Chicago to find a house among the victims of the nineteenth century's fast-growing industrial society.

The young women—Jane was twenty-nine and Ellen thirty in 1889 —had no blueprint to guide them when they decided to take up residence in Mr. Hull's decayed mansion and begin helping "the neighbors" to help themselves. No school of social work had trained them for this enterprise: Latin and Greek, art, music, and "moral philosophy" at the seminary constituted their academic preparation. Toynbee Hall in England—the world's first settlement house, founded in 1884 by Samuel A. Barnett—had inspired them. Having found the Hull house at the corner of Polk and Halsted—in what was by common consent one of Chicago's worst wards—they leased it, moved in, and began doing what came naturally.

Miss Starr, who had taught in an exclusive girls' preparatory school, inaugurated a reading party for young Italian women with George Eliot's *Romola* as the first book. Miss Addams, becoming aware of the desperate problem of working mothers, began at once to organize a kindergarten. They tried Russian parties for the Russian neighbors, organized boys' clubs for the gangs on the street, and offered to bathe all babies. The neighbors were baffled, but impressed. Very soon children and grownups of all sorts and conditions were finding their way to Hull-House—to read Shakespeare or to ask for a volunteer midwife; to learn sewing or discuss socialism; to study art or to fill an empty stomach. There were few formalities and no red tape, and the young ladies found themselves every day called upon to deal with some of the multitude of personal tragedies against which the conditions of life in the nineteenth ward offered so thin a cushion.

Before long, other young people feeling twinges of social conscience and seeking a tangible way to make their convictions count in the world of the 1890's came to live at Hull-House. These "residents," as they were called, became increasingly interested in the personal histories of the endless stream of neighbors who came to the House each week. They began to find out about the little children sewing all day long in the "sweated" garment trade, and about others who worked long hours in a candy factory. They began to ask why there were three thousand more children in the ward than there were seats in its schoolrooms, and why the death rate was higher there than in almost any other part of Chicago. They worried about youngsters whose only playground was a garbage-spattered alley that threatened the whole population with disease. (Once they traced a typhoid epidemic to its source and found the sewer line merging with the water line.) In the early days Hull-House offered bathtubs and showers, which proved so popular a form of hospitality that the residents became relentless

Chicago's old Hull mansion, refurbished and renamed Hull-House, about 1910.

lobbyists for municipal baths.

Hull-House was not the only American settlement house—indeed, Jane Addams liked to emphasize the validity of the idea by pointing out that it had developed simultaneously in several different places. But Hull-House set the pace, and in an astonishingly short time its founder began to acquire a national reputation. As early as 1893 Jane Addams wrote to a friend: "I find I am considered the grandmother of social settlements." She was being asked to speak to gatherings of learned gentlemen, sociologists and philosophers, on such subjects as "The Subjective Necessity for Social Settlements." When the Columbian Exposition attracted thousands of visitors to Chicago in 1893, Hull-House became—along with the lake front and the stockyards— one of the things a guest was advised not to miss. By the mid-nineties, distinguished Europeans were turning up regularly to visit the House and examine its workings. W. T. Stead, editor of the English *Review of Reviews,* spent much time there while he gathered material for his sensational book, *If Christ Came to Chicago.* By that time two thousand people a week were coming to Hull-House to participate in some of its multifarious activities, which ranged from philosophy classes to the Nineteenth Ward Improvement Association.

Neither her growing reputation nor the increasing demand for speeches and articles, however, distracted Jane Addams from what was to be for forty years the main focus of a many-sided life: Hull-House and the nineteenth ward. Much of her early writing was an attempt to portray the real inner lives of America's proliferating immigrants, and much of her early activity, an effort to give them a voice to speak out against injustice.

The Hull-House residents were becoming pioneers in many ways, not least in the techniques of social research. In the *Hull-House Maps and Papers,* published in 1895, they prepared some of the first careful studies of life in an urban slum, examining the details of the "home-work" system of garment making and describing tumble-down houses, overtaxed schools, rising crime rates, and other sociological problems. The book remains today an indispensable source for the social historian of Chicago in the nineties.

Jane Addams' own interest in these matters was far from academic. Her concern for the uncollected garbage led her to apply for—and receive—an appointment as garbage inspector. She rose at six every morning and in a horse-drawn buggy followed the infuriated garbage contractor on his appointed rounds, making sure that every receptacle was emptied. Such badgering incensed Alderman Powers, in whose hierarchy of values cleanliness, though next to godliness, was a good bit below patronage—and he looked upon garbage inspection as a job for one of his henchmen. By now John Powers was becoming aware of his new neighbors; they were increasingly inquisitive about things close to Johnny Powers' source of power. By implication they were raising a troublesome question: Was Johnny Powers really "taking care of the poor"?

For a while, as one resident noted, the inhabitants of the House were "passive though interested observers of their representative, declining his offers of help and co-operation, refusing politely to distribute his Christmas turkeys, but feeling too keenly the smallness of their numbers to work against him." They were learning, though, and the time for passivity would end.

In company with many other American cities, Chicago after 1895 was taking a critical look at its political life and at the close connections that had grown up between politics and big business during the explosive era of industrial expansion following the Civil War. "The sovereign people may govern Chicago in theory," Stead wrote; "as a matter of fact King Boodle is monarch of all he surveys. His domination is practically undisputed."

The Municipal Voters League, a reform organization that included many of Jane Addams' close friends, was founded in 1896 in an effort to clean up the Common Council, of whose sixty-eight aldermen fifty-eight were estimated to be corrupt. The League aimed to replace as many of the fifty-eight as possible with honest men. But it was not easy: in 1896, as part of this campaign, a member of the Hull-House Men's Club ran for the second aldermanic position in the ward and against all expectations was elected. Too late, his idealistic backers found that their hero had his price: Johnny Powers promptly bought him out.

Jane Addams was chagrined but undiscouraged. By the time Powers came up for re-election in 1898, she had had time to observe him more closely and plan her attack. Her opening gun was a speech—delivered,

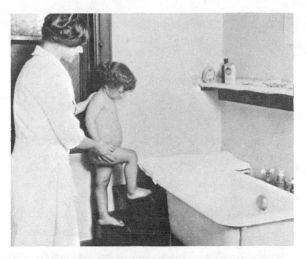

Children were Hull-House's first concern. Infants were bathed (right) and moppets put into nursery school (below).

Older boys (right) took shop lessons to prepare them to become successful artisans.

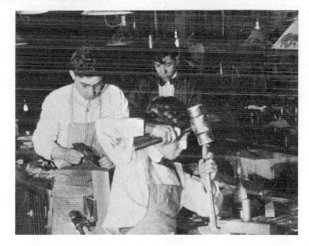

improbably enough, to the Society for Ethical Culture—with the ponderous and apparently harmless title, "Some Ethical Survivals in Municipal Corruption." But appearances were deceptive: once under way, she took the hide off Powers and was scarcely easier on his opponents among the so-called "better elements."

She began by pointing out that for the immigrants, who were getting their first initiation in self-government, ethics was largely a matter of example: the officeholder was apt to set the standard and exercise a permanent influence upon their views. An engaging politician whose standards were low and "impressed by the cynical stamp of the corporations" could debauch the political ideals of ignorant men and women, with consequences that might, she felt, take years to erase.

Ethical issues were further complicated, she said, by habits of thought brought to the New World from the Old. Many Italians and Germans had left their respective fatherlands to escape military service; the Polish and Russian Jews, to escape government persecution. In all these cases, the government had been cast in the role of oppressor. The Irish, in particular, had been conditioned by years of resentment over English rule to regard any successful effort to feed at the public crib as entirely legitimate, because it represented getting the better of their bitterest enemies.

On the other hand, Miss Addams continued, there was nothing the immigrants admired more than simple goodness. They were accustomed to helping each other out in times of trouble, sharing from their own meager store with neighbors who were even more destitute. When Alderman Powers performed on a large scale the same good deeds which they themselves were able to do only on a small scale, was it any wonder that they admired him?

Given this admiration, and their Old World resentments toward government, the immigrants' developing standards of political morality suffered when Powers made it clear that he could "fix" courts or find jobs for his friends on the city payroll. It cheapened their image of American politics when they began to suspect that the source of their benefactor's largess might be a corrupt bargain with a traction tycoon, or with others who wanted something from the city of Chicago and were willing to pay for it.

Hull-House residents, Miss Addams said, very early found evidence of the influence of the boss's standards. When the news spread around the neighborhood that the House was a source of help in time of trouble, more and more neighbors came to appeal for aid when a boy was sent to jail or reform school, and it was impossible to explain to them why Hull-House, so ready to help in other ways, was not willing to get around the law as the Alderman did.

Removing Alderman Powers from office, Jane Addams told the sober gentlemen of the Society for Ethical Culture, would be no simple task. It would require a fundamental change in the ethical standards of the community, as well as the development of a deeper insight on the part of the reformers. These latter, she pointed out, with all their zeal for well-ordered, honest politics, were not eager to undertake the responsibilities of self-government 365 days a year. They were quite willing to come into the nineteenth ward at election time to exhort the citizenry, but were they willing to make a real effort to achieve personal relationships of the kind that stood Johnny Powers in such good stead?

On this last point, Hull-House itself had some experience. As Florence Kelley—a Hull-House resident who was to become a pioneer in the Illinois social reform movement—subsequently wrote:

> The question is often asked whether all that the House undertakes could not be accomplished without the wear and tear of living on the spot. The answer, that it could not, grows more assured as time goes on. You must suffer from the dirty streets, the universal ugliness, the lack of oxygen in the air you daily breathe, the endless struggle with soot and dust and insufficient water supply, the hanging from a strap of the overcrowded street car at the end of your day's work; you must send your children to the nearest wretchedly crowded school, and see them suffer the consequences, if you are to speak as one having authority and not as the scribes . . .

By 1898, after nine years of working with their neighbors, the Hull-House residents were ready to pit their influence against that of Powers. Jane Addams' philosophical address to the Ethical Culture society was followed by others in which she explained more concretely the relationships between Yerkes, Chicago's traction czar, and the city council, relationships in which Johnny Powers played a key role. With several important deals in the making, 1898 would be a bad year for Yerkes to lose his key man in the seats of power.

The election was scheduled for April. The reformers—led by Hull-House and supported by independent Democrats, the Cook County Republicans, and the Municipal Voters League—put up a candidate of their own, Simeon Armstrong, to oppose Powers, and undertook to organize and underwrite Armstrong's campaign. By the end of January, the usually imperturbable Powers suddenly began paying attention to his political fences. The newspapers noted with some surprise that it was the first time he had felt it necessary to lift a finger more than two weeks in advance of election day.

His first move was an attack on Amanda Johnson, a Hull-House resident who had succeeded Miss Addams as garbage inspector. A graduate of the University of Wisconsin and described by the papers as blond, blue-eyed, and beautiful, she had taken the civil service examination and duly qualified for the position. Alderman Powers announced to the world that Miss Johnson, shielded by her civil service status, was telling his constituents not to vote for him. The Chicago *Record* dropped a crocodile tear at the sad picture of the martyred alderman:

General sympathy should go out to Mr. Powers in this, his

latest affliction. Heretofore he has been persecuted often by people opposed to bad franchise ordinances. He has been hounded by the upholders of civil service reform. He has suffered the shafts of criticism directed at his career by disinterested citizens. A grand jury has been cruel to him. Invidious comments have been made in his hearing as to the ethical impropriety of gambling institutions. . . . It is even believed that Miss Johnson in her relentless cruelty may go so far as to insinuate that Mr. Powers' electioneering methods are no better than those attributed to her—that, indeed, when he has votes to win, the distinctions of the civil service law do not deter him from going after those votes in many ways.

Powers' next move was to attempt a redistricting that would cut off the eastern, or Italian, end of his ward, which he took to be most seriously under Hull-House influence. It was reported that he also felt this area had been a "large source of expense to him through the necessity of assisting the poor that are crowded into that district." "These people," the Chicago *Record* reported, "formerly tied to him by his charities are said to be turning toward Hull-House and will vote solidly against him next spring."

Neither of Powers' first efforts was notably successful. A few days after his attack on Miss Johnson the *Tribune* reported:

Trouble sizzled and boiled for Alderman John Powers in his own bailiwick last night. The Nineteenth Ward Independent club raked over the Alderman's sins . . . and . . . much indignation was occasioned by Alderman Powers' opposition to Miss Amanda Johnson. One Irish speaker says Johnny is a disgrace to the Irish race now that he has descended to fighting "poor working girls."

Meantime, Powers' colleagues on the council redistricting committee had no intention of saving his skin at the expense of their own, and stood solidly against his gerrymandering effort. Now the shaken boss began to show signs of losing his temper. He told reporters that if Miss Addams didn't like the nineteenth ward she should move out. Later, still more infuriated, he announced that Hull-House should be driven out. "A year from now there will be no such institution," he said flatly, adding that the women at Hull-House were obviously jealous of his charities. The *Record* published a cartoon showing Powers pushing vainly against the wall of a very substantial house.

The news of the campaign soon spread beyond the bounds of Chicago. The New York *Tribune* commented that Powers

wouldn't mind Miss Addams saying all those things about him if he didn't begin to fear that she may succeed in making some of his well-meaning but misled constituents believe them. She is a very practical person, and has behind her a large volunteer staff of other practical persons who do not confine their efforts to "gassin' in the parlors," but are going about to prove to the plain people of the nineteenth ward that a corrupt and dishonest man does not necessarily become a saint by giving a moiety of his ill-gotten gains to the poor.

By March the campaign was waxing warm, and Powers resorted to an attempt to stir up the Catholic clergy against Miss Addams and the reform candidate. One of the Hull-House residents, a deputy factory inspector and a Catholic herself, went directly to the priests to find out why they were supporting Powers. When she reported, Jane Addams wrote to a friend:

> As nearly as I can make out, the opposition comes from the Jesuits, headed by Father Lambert, and the parish priests are not in it, and do not like it. Mary talked for a long time to Father Lambert and is sure it is jealousy of Hull-House and money obligations to Powers, that he does not believe the charges himself. She cried when she came back.

In another letter written about the same time, Miss Addams said that Powers had given a thousand dollars to the Jesuit "temperance cadets," who had returned the favor with a fine procession supporting Powers' candidacy. "There was a picture of your humble servant on a transparency and others such as 'No petticoat government for us . . .' We all went out on the corner to see it, Mr. Hinsdale carefully shielding me from the public view."

By now the battle between Hull-House and Johnny Powers was sharing headlines in Chicago newspapers with the blowing up of the *Maine* in Havana's harbor and the approach of the war with Spain. "Throughout the nineteenth ward," said the *Tribune*, "the one absorbing topic of conversation wherever men are gathered is the fight being made against Alderman Powers." It was rumored that Powers had offered a year's free rent to one of the opposition leaders if he would move out of the ward before election day, and the Hull-House group let it be known that the Alderman was spending money freely in the ward, giving his lieutenants far more cash to spread around than was his custom. "Where does the money come from?" Jane Addams asked, and answered her own question: "From Mr. Yerkes." Powers was stung, and challenged her to prove that he had ever received one dollar from any corporation.

"Driven to desperation," said the *Tribune*, "Ald. Powers has at last called to his aid the wives and daughters of his political allies." Determined to fight fire with fire, he dropped his opposition to "petticoat politicians" and gave his blessing to a Ladies Auxiliary which was instructed to counteract the work of the women of Hull-House. An enterprising reporter discovered that few of the ladies had ever seen Miss Addams or been to Hull-House, but all were obediently repeating the charge that she had "blackened and maligned the whole ward" by saying that its people were ignorant, criminal, and poor.

As the campaign became more intense, Jane Addams received numbers of violent letters, nearly all of them anonymous, from Powers' partisans, as well as various communications from lodginghouse keepers quoting prices for votes they were ready to deliver! When the Hull-House residents discovered evidence of ties between banking, ecclesiastical, and journalistic interests, with Powers at the center, they proceeded to publicize all they knew. This brought upon their heads a violent attack by the Chicago *Chronicle,* the organ of the Democratic ring.

Suddenly a number of nineteenth-ward businessmen who had signed petitions for the reform candidate came out for Powers. They were poor and in debt; Powers gave the word to a landlord here, a coal dealer there, and they were beaten. The small peddlers and fruit dealers were subjected to similar pressure, for each needed a license to ply his trade, and the mere hint of a revocation was enough to create another Powers man.

When Alderman John M. Harlan, one of the stalwarts of the Municipal Voters League, came into the ward to speak, Powers supplied a few toughs to stir up a riot. Fortunately Harlan was a sturdy character, and offered so forcefully to take on all comers in fisticuffs that no volunteers appeared. Allowed to proceed, he posed some embarrassing questions: Why did nineteenth-ward residents have to pay ten-cent trolley fares when most of the city paid five? Why, when Powers was head of the city council's free-spending committee on street paving, were the streets of the ward in execrable condition? Why were the public schools so crowded, and why had Powers suppressed a petition, circulated by Hull-House, to build more of them?

Freely admitting Powers' reputation for charity, Harlan made the interesting suggestion that the councilman's motives be put to the test: Would he be so generous as a private citizen? "Let us retire him to private life and see."

Powers was pictured by the papers as being nearly apoplectic at this attack from Miss Addams' friend. He announced that he would not be responsible for Harlan's safety if he returned to the nineteenth ward. (Since no one had asked him to assume any such responsibility, this was presumed to be an open threat.) Harlan returned at once, telling a crowd well-laced with Powers supporters that he would "rather die in my tracks than acknowledge the right of John Powers to say who should and who should not talk in this ward." Summoning up the memory of Garibaldi, he urged the Italians to live up to their tradition of freedom and not allow their votes to be "delivered."

In a quieter vein, Miss Addams too spoke at a public meeting of Italians, where, it was reported, she received profound and respectful attention. "Show that you do not intend to be governed by a boss," she told them. "It is important not only for yourselves but for your children. These things must be made plain to them."

As the campaign progressed, the reformers began to feel they had a real chance of defeating Powers. Jane Addams was persuaded to go in search of funds with which to carry out the grand finale. "I sallied forth today and got $100," she wrote, and "will have to keep it up all week; charming prospect, isn't it?" But on about the twentieth of

March she began to have serious hopes, too, and redoubled her efforts.

As election day, April 6, approached, the Chicago *Tribune* and the Chicago *Record* covered the campaign daily, freely predicting a victory for the reformers. Alas for all predictions. When election day came, Powers' assets, which Jane Addams had so cogently analyzed in that faraway speech to the Society for Ethical Culture, paid off handsomely. It was a rough day in the nineteenth ward, with ten saloons open, one man arrested for drawing a gun, and everything, as Miss Addams wrote despondently when the count began to come in, "as bad as bad can be." Too many election judges were under Powers' thumb. The reform candidate was roundly defeated. Hull-House went to court to challenge the conduct of the election, but in the halls of justice Powers also had friends. It was no use.

Even in victory, however, Powers was a bit shaken. Hull-House had forced him, for the first time, to put out a great effort for re-election. It was obviously *not* going to move out of the nineteenth ward; indeed, if the past was any portent, its influence with his constituents would increase.

Powers decided to follow an ancient maxim, "If you can't lick 'em, join 'em." Early in the 1900 aldermanic campaign, several Chicago papers carried a straight news story to the effect that Hull-House and Johnny Powers had signed a truce, and quoted various paternally benevolent statements on the Alderman's part. In the *Chronicle*, for example, he was reported to have said: "I am not an Indian when it comes to hate . . . let bygones be bygones." A day or two later another rash of stories detailed a number of favors the Alderman was supposed to have done for Hull-House.

Jane Addams was furious, and after considerable deliberation she decided to reply. It was one of the few times in her long public career when she bothered to answer anything the newspapers said about her. She knew that with his eye on the campaign, the master politician was trying to give the appearance of having taken his most vigorous enemy into camp. She had been observing him too long not to realize what he was up to, and she could not possibly let him get away with it.

On February 20, 1900, a vigorous letter from Miss Addams appeared in nearly all the Chicago papers, reaffirming the attitude of Hull-House toward Mr. Powers. "It is needless to state," she concluded, "that the protest of Hull-House against a man who continually disregards the most fundamental rights of his constituents must be permanent."

Permanent protest, yes, but as a practical matter there was no use waging another opposition campaign. Powers held too many of the cards. When all was said and done, he had proved too tough a nut to crack, though Hull-House could—and did—continue to harass him. An observer of the Municipal Voters League, celebrating its success in the *Outlook* in June, 1902, described the vast improvement in the Common Council, but was forced to admit that a few wards were "well-nigh hopeless." He cited three: those of "Blind Billy" Kent, "Bathhouse John" Coughlin, and Johnny Powers.

From a larger standpoint, however, the battle between "Saint Jane" (as the neighbors called Jane Addams when she was not around) and the Ward Boss was not without significance. It was one of numerous similar battles that would characterize the progressive era the country over, and many of them the reformers would win. Because of her firsthand experience, because she lived *with* the immigrants instead of coming into their neighborhood occasionally to tell them what to do, Jane Addams was perhaps the first of the urban reformers to grasp the real pattern of bossism, its logic, the functions it performed, and the reason it was so hard to dislodge. Years later political scientists, beginning to analyze the pattern, would add almost nothing to her speech of 1898. If copies of *The Last Hurrah* have reached the Elysian fields, Jane Addams has spent an amused evening seeing her ideas developed so well in fictional form.

The campaign of 1898 throws considerable light on Jane Addams' intensely practical approach to politics, and upon a little-known aspect of the settlement-house movement. If anyone had told her and Ellen Starr in 1889 that the logic of what they were trying to do would inevitably force them into politics, they would have hooted. But in due time politics, in many forms, became central to Hull-House activity. For Jane Addams herself, the campaign against Powers was the first in a long series of political forays, all essentially based on the same desire—to see that government met the needs of the "other half."

The regulation of child labor, for example, was one political issue in which Hull-House residents became involved because of their knowledge of the lives of the neighbors. The first juvenile court in Chicago was set up as a result of their efforts; it was a direct response to the anxious mothers who could not understand why Hull-House would not help get their boys out of jail. The first factory inspection law in Illinois was also credited to Hull-House, and Florence Kelley became the first inspector. Another Hull-House resident—Dr. Alice Hamilton— pioneered in the field of industrial medicine. Because of their intimate acquaintance with the human cost of industrialization, settlement workers became vigorous advocates of promoting social justice through law.

It was a long jump but not an illogical one from the campaign against Powers to the stage of the Chicago Coliseum in August, 1912, when Jane Addams arose to second the nomination of Teddy Roosevelt by the Progressive party on a platform of social welfare. More remarkable than the ovation—larger than that given to any other seconder—was the fact that the huge audience seemed to listen carefully to what she had to say.

Some newspapers grandly estimated her value to T.R. at a million votes. "Like the report of Mark Twain's death," she commented, "the report is greatly exaggerated." But she campaigned vigorously, in the face of criticism that this was not a proper role for a woman, and when the Bull Moose cause failed, she did not believe it had been a waste of time. It had brought about, she wrote Roosevelt, more discussion of social reform than she had dared to hope for in her lifetime.

Alderman Powers was still in office—as were many like him—but the sources of his power were being attacked at the roots.

When the 1916 campaign came around, Democrats and Republicans alike made bids for Jane Addams' support. The outbreak of war in Europe had turned her attention, however, in a different direction. As early as 1907, in a book called *Newer Ideals of Peace,* she had begun to elaborate William James's notion of a "moral equivalent of war," and had suggested that the experience of polyglot immigrant populations in learning to live together might be laying the foundations for a true international order. Like her ideals of social justice, those that she conceived on international peace had their beginning in the nineteenth ward.

To her, as to so many idealistic progressives, world war came as a profound shock. Her response was a vigorous effort to bring together American women and women from all the European countries to urge upon their governments a negotiated peace. In Europe, where she went in 1915 for a meeting of the Women's International Peace Conference, she visited prime ministers; at the end of that year she planned to sail on Henry Ford's peace ship, but illness forced her to withdraw at the last moment. At home she appealed to President Wilson. Unshaken in her pacifism, she stood firmly against the war, even after the United States entered it.

Her popularity seemed to melt overnight. Many women's clubs and social workers, who owed so much to her vision, deserted her. An Illinois judge who thought it dangerous for her to speak in wartime was widely supported in the press. For most of 1917 and 1918 she was isolated as never before or again. But she did not waver.

When the war ended she began at once to work for means to prevent another. Through the twenties she was constantly active in searching for ways in which women could cut across national lines in their work for peace. In 1931, in her seventy-first year, she received the Nobel Peace Prize—the second American to be so recognized. She died, full of honors, in 1935.

As for Johnny Powers, he had lived to a ripe old age and died in 1930, remaining alderman almost to the end, still fighting reform mayors, still protesting that he and Miss Addams were really friends, after all. From whichever department of the hereafter he ended up in, he must have looked down—or up in amazement at the final achievements of his old enemy, who had been so little troubled by his insistence that there should be "no petticoats in politics."

Gerald H. Carson

Consumer Protection: The Pure Food and Drugs Act

*If early twentieth-century reform is seen as the attempt to solve
problems resulting from industrialization and urbanization, then the
relative paucity of significant federal legislation that the Progressive
Era produced becomes easy to explain: most of the problems appeared
to the people of those days to require local, or at most, state action.
Except for regulating railroads and large corporations engaged in
interstate commerce, there seemed to be little that the national government could do about contemporary evils. The career of Jane Addams,
for example, illustrates this point. In her political battles with Boss
Powers and her broader concerns with the needs of Chicago slum
dwellers, it was to the state and the city (and to local voters) that
she turned for assistance or support.*

*One national reform that was accomplished during this period,
however, was the passage of the Pure Food and Drugs Act of 1906. The
story of this reform and of its leading advocate and technician, Dr.
Harvey W. Wiley, is told here by Gerald Carson, a former advertising executive who has won a richly deserved reputation as a social
historian. Mr. Carson's books include* The Old Country Store, *which
won the Dunning Prize of the American Historical Association, and*
The Social History of Bourbon.

On a hot humid July morning in 1902, a burly 200-pound scientist and connoisseur of good food and drink sat hunched over his desk in a red brick building in Washington, D.C., and he planned deliberately to feed twelve healthy young men a diet containing borax. Dr. Harvey W. Wiley, chief chemist of the Department of Agriculture, had in mind a double objective: first, to determine the effects upon human beings of certain chemicals then commonly used to preserve processed foods; and, more broadly, to educate the public in the need for a federal "pure food" law. Food preparation was becoming industrialized and subject to more complicated processing; products were traveling longer distances, passing through many hands. Manufacturers, facing a novel situation, turned to dubious additives to make their products appear more appetizing or to preserve them. Borax compounds, the first object of Dr. Wiley's investigations, were used to make old butter seem like new.

Volunteers for the experiment were recruited from the Department of Agriculture. They pledged themselves to obey the rules. A small kitchen and dining room were fitted out in the basement of the Bureau of Chemistry offices with the assistant surgeon-general in attendance to see to it that the subjects of the experiment did not get too much borax, and Dr. Wiley to see that they got enough. A bright reporter, George Rothwell Brown, of the Washington Post, gave the volunteers an enduring handle, "the poison squad"; and before long the public began referring to Wiley, affectionately or otherwise according to the point of view, as "Old Borax."

Six of Dr. Wiley's co-operators at the hygienic table got a normal ration plus measured doses of tasteless, odorless, invisible boracic acid. The other six also enjoyed a wholesome diet, with equally tasteless, odorless, invisible borate of soda added to their menu. The resulting chemical and physiological data was quite technical. But the meaning was clear. The effects of borax included nausea and loss of appetite, symptoms resembling those of influenza and overburdened kidneys. The feeding experiments continued over a five-year period. After the borax initiation, which made a popular sensation, the squad subsequently breakfasted, lunched, and dined on dishes containing salicylates, sulfurous acid and sulfites, benzoates, formaldehyde, sulfate of copper, and saltpeter. Seldom has a scientific experiment stirred the public imagination as did Dr. Wiley's novel procedures in, as he said, "trying it on the dog."

"My poison squad laboratory," said Dr. Wiley, "became the most highly advertised boarding-house in the world."

A popular versifier wrote a poem about it, the "Song of the Pizen Squad." Lew Dockstader introduced a topical song into his minstrel show. The chorus closed with the prediction:

> Next week he'll give them mothballs à la Newburgh or else
> plain:
> O they may get over it but they'll never look the same!

The New York Sun sourly handed Wiley the title of "chief janitor

Dr. Harvey W. Wiley (center rear) and his youthful "poison squad" in 1903.

and policeman of the people's insides," an expression of one line of attack which the opposition was to take—invasion of personal liberty.

The movement to protect the health and pocketbook of the consumer was directed no less at "the patent medicine evil" than it was at the chaotic situation in the food manufacturing field. The "cures" for cancer, tuberculosis, "female weakness," the dangerous fat reducers and "Indian" cough remedies were a bonanza for their proprietors, and many an advertising wizard who knew little enough of drugs or materia medica came to live in a jigsaw mansion and drive a spanking pair of bays because he was a skillful manipulator of hypochondria and mass psychology. Slashing exposés in the popular magazines told of babies' soothing syrups containing morphine and opium, of people who became narcotic addicts, of the use of tonics that depended upon alcohol to make the patient feel frisky.

"Gullible America," said Samuel Hopkins Adams in an angry but thoroughly documented series of articles, "will spend this year [1905] some seventy-five millions of dollars" in order to "swallow huge quantities of alcohol . . . narcotics . . . dangerous heart depressants . . . insidious liver stimulants."

The nostrum vendors at first looked upon the Food and Drugs Act as a joke. In time the manufacturers of Pink Pills for Pale People learned the hard way that they were living dangerously when they ignored the precept, "Thou shalt not lie on the label."

As public interest rose in "the food question," powerful groups took their places in the line of battle to contest the pure food and drug bills which appeared, and died, in Congress with monotonous regularity. On the one side were aligned consumer groups—the General

Federation of Women's Clubs, the National Consumers' League, the Patrons of Husbandry, and the labor unions. With them stood food chemists who had had experience in state control work, the American Medical Association, important periodicals *(Collier's Weekly,* Bok's *Ladies' Home Journal, World's Work, The Independent, Cosmopolitan),* President Theodore Roosevelt, and Dr. Wiley.

In opposition were the food manufacturers and manufacturers of articles used in the adulteration of foods and drugs such as cottonseed oil, the proprietary medicine industry, the distillers, canners, *Leslie's Weekly* (to which Dr. Wiley was anathema), newspaper publishers opposed for business reasons, Chicago meat packers, and powerful lobbyists holed up at the Willard and the Raleigh Hotel; also an obdurate Senate, responsive to pressures from big business. Wiley, as the leading personality in the fight for a food bill, achieved the uncommon distinction of acquiring almost as many enemies as did President Roosevelt himself.

When the average member of Congress, newspaper publisher, or pickle manufacturer smelled socialism and deplored the effects of the proposed legislation upon business, he was only responding normally to two powerful stimuli: self-interest and the nostalgic memory of his lost youth. Most mature Americans of the 1880–1900 period were born on farms or in rural areas and knew the conditions of life of a scattered population. The close-knit farm family was the dominant economic unit. It raised, processed, cured, and stored what it ate, and there is abundant evidence that it ate more and better food than the common man of Europe had ever dreamed of tasting. There was no problem of inspection or of deceptive labels. No "Short-weight Jim" invaded the home kitchen or smokehouse. If the preparation was unsanitary, it was no one else's business. What wasn't raised locally was obtained by barter. There were adequate forces of control over that simple transaction—face-to-face bargaining, community of interest, fear of what the neighbors would say.

As to drugs and medicines, grandma could consult the "family doctor" book and compound her home remedies from roots, herbs, and barks gathered along the edge of forest, meadow, and stream: catnip for colic, mullein leaf for asthma, the dandelion for dyspepsia, and so on through the list of simples, essences, flowers, tinctures, and infusions, whose chief merit was that they did not interfere with the tendency of the living cell to recover.

When Americans were called to the cities by the factory whistle, a dramatic change took place in their food supply. No longer was there personal contact between the producer and consumer, nor could the buyer be wary even if he would. For how could a city man candle every egg, test the milk, inquire into the handling of his meat supply, analyze the canned foods which he consumed in increasing quantities?

Since foodstuffs had to stand up in their long transit from the plant to the home, it is not surprising that unhealthy practices developed. During the "embalmed beef" scandal, for example, there was a debate as to whether a little boric acid in fresh beef was after all only an excusable extension of the ancient and accepted use of saltpeter in corning beef. Analytical chemistry was called upon increasingly to make cheap foods into expensive ones, to disguise and simulate, to arrest the processes of nature. The food manufacturers raided the pharmacopœia. But the salicylic acid that was approved in the treatment of gout or rheumatism was received with mounting indignation on the dining room table where it proved to be a depressant of the processes of metabolism. It was objectionable on another ground too—that it led to carelessness in the selection, cleansing, and processing of foodstuffs.

It is difficult to picture today the vast extent of adulteration at the beginning of this century. More than half the food samples studied in the Indiana state laboratory were sophisticated. Whole grain flour was "cut" with bran and corn meal. The food commissioner of North Dakota declared that his state alone consumed ten times as much "Vermont maple syrup" as Vermont produced. The *Grocer's Companion and Merchant's Hand-Book* (Boston, 1883), warned the food retailer, in his own interest, of the various tricks used to alter coffee and tea, bread and flour, butter and lard, mustard, spices, pepper, pickles, preserved fruits, sauces, potted meats, cocoa, vinegar, and candies. A New York sugar firm was proud to make the point in its advertising of the 1880's that its sugar contained "neither glucose, muriate of tin, muriatic acid, nor any other foreign, deleterious or fraudulent substance whatever." The canned peas looked garden-fresh after treatment with $CuSO_4$ by methods known as "copper-greening." The pork and beans contained formaldehyde, the catsup benzoic acid. As a capstone of inspired fakery, one manufacturer of flavored glucose (sold as pure honey) carefully placed a dead bee in every bottle to give verisimilitude.

The little man of 1900 found himself in a big, big world, filled with butterine and mapleine.

This is not to suggest that the pioneer food manufacturer was as rascally as his contemporaries, the swamp doctor and the lightning rod peddler. What was occurring was less a collapse of human probity than an unexpected testing of human nature in a new context. Someone has said that all morality is based upon the assumption that somebody might be watching. In the milieu of late nineteenth-century business, nobody seemed to be watching. Thus the food crusade became necessary as a means of redressing the balance in the market which had turned so cruelly against the ordinary American and, indeed, against the honest manufacturer.

The ensuing controversy was symptomatic of the passing—painful, nostalgic to many, including no doubt many a big business senator—of the old, simple life of village and farm which was doomed by the expanding national life. It was, one feels, not solely in defense of the hake (sold as genuine codfish with boric acid as a preservative) that Senator George Frisbie Hoar of Massachusetts rose in the Senate to exalt "the exquisite flavor of the codfish, salted, made into balls, and eaten on a Sunday morning by a person whose

ATHLOPHOROS.

FOR RHEUMATISM AND NEURALGIA

"NO MORE RHEUMATISM FOR ME"

The Pure Food and Drugs Act, which demanded accurate labeling, meant the end of flamboyant, misleading advertising for such products as "Athlophoros" and other nostrums.

theology is sound, and who believes in the five points of Calvinism.''

The friends of food reform needed all the courage and public discussion they could muster. Since 1879, when the first federal bill was proposed, 190 measures to protect the consumer had been introduced in Congress, of which 49 had some kind of a subsequent history, and 141 were never heard of again. Meanwhile the states did what they could. About half of them had passed pure food laws by 1895. But there was no uniformity in their regulations. Foods legal in one state might be banned in another. Some of the laws were so loosely drawn that it was quite conceivable that Beechnut Bacon might be seized by the inspectors because no beechnuts were involved in its curing. Was Grape-Nuts misbranded because the great Battle Creek ''brain food'' had only a fanciful connection with either grapes or nuts? One bill actually proposed a numerical count of the contents of a package—the grains of salt, the cherries in a jar of preserves. What if Mr. Kellogg had to count every corn flake which went into his millions of packages?

Conflicts and foolish regulations could be ironed out over a period of time. The fatal flaw was that individual states had no power to get at the real problem: interstate traffic in the ''patented'' bitters, cancer cures, and strawberry jellies made out of dyed glucose, citric acid, and timothy seed.

The act which Wiley drew up was first introduced in 1902. It was successfully sidetracked in one legislative branch or the other for four years. The provisions were simple. In essence, it was a labeling act.

''Tell the truth on the label,'' Dr. Wiley said, ''and let the consumer judge for himself.''

Some of the legislators who opposed the act were states' rights Democrats, concerned about constitutional interpretation, who in the end fortunately saw the wisdom of sacrificing principle for expediency. Others were Old Guard Republicans who were special custodians of the *status quo* and highly sensitive to the sentiments of the business community: men like Senators Aldrich of Rhode Island (wholesale groceries), Kean of New Jersey (preserving and canning), Platt of Connecticut (home of the great Kickapoo Indian remedies), Hale and Frye of Maine, along whose rock-bound coast the familiar Maine herring became "imported French sardines," packaged in boxes with French labels.

The tactic in the Senate was one of unobtrusive obstruction and lip service to the idea of regulation. Open opposition was never much of a factor. "The 'right' to use deceptive labels," observed *The Nation*, "is not one for which impassioned oratory can be readily invoked." When a serious try was made to pass a general pure food law in 1902-3, Senator Lodge was able to direct the attention of the Senate to legislation more urgently needed, such as a Philippine tariff bill. In the last session of the 59th Congress (1904-5) the food bill was considered less pressing than a proposal to award naval commissions to a couple of young men who had been expelled from the Academy for hazing but still wanted very much to become officers in the United States Navy.

President Roosevelt finally decided to push the issue. "Mr. Dooley" offered a version of how it happened. "Tiddy," he said, was reading Upton Sinclair's novel, *The Jungle*, a grisly sociological tract on "Packingtown." "Tiddy was toying with a light breakfast an' idly turnin' over th' pages iv th' new book with both hands. Suddenly he rose fr'm th' table, an' cryin': 'I'm pizened,' begun throwin' sausages out iv th' window. Th' ninth wan shtruck Sinitor Biv'ridge on th' head an' made him a blond. It bounced off, exploded, an' blew a leg off a secret-service agent, an' th' scatthred fragmints desthroyed a handsome row iv ol' oak-trees. Sinitor Biv'ridge rushed in, thinkin' that th' Prisidint was bein' assassynated be his devoted followers in th' Sinit, an' discovered Tiddy engaged in a hand-to-hand conflict with a potted ham. Th' Sinitor fr'm Injyanny, with a few well-directed wurruds, put out th' fuse an' rendered th' missile harmless. Since thin th' Prisidint, like th' rest iv us, has become a viggytaryan. . . ." At any rate, in his annual message to Congress, December 5, 1905, Roosevelt recommended in the interest of the consumer and the legitimate manufacturer "that a law be enacted to regulate interstate commerce in misbranded and adulterated foods, drinks and drugs," and the bill was re-introduced in the Senate by Senator Weldon B. Heyburn of Idaho. Pressure from the American Medical Association, the graphic exposé of revolting conditions in the Chicago packing houses, and Roosevelt's skillful use of the report of an official commission which investigated the stockyards, finally forced a favorable vote in the Senate and then the House on the Pure Food and Drugs Bill. The meat inspection problem was, actually, a different matter. But an angry public was in no mood to make fine distinctions. Meat, processed foods, and fake medicines all tapped the family pocketbook, all went into the human stomach, and all smelled to high heaven in the spring of 1906. Roosevelt signed the bill into law on June 30, 1906.

The enforcement of the law was placed in the hands of Dr. Wiley. According to the Doctor, it was after the bill became law that the real fight began. Most food and drug manufacturers and dealers adjusted their operations to the new law, and found themselves in a better position because of it, with curtailment of the activities of fly-by-night competition and re-establishment of the consumers' confidence in goods of known quality. But there were die-hards like the sugar and molasses refiners, the fruit driers, whisky rectifiers, and purveyors of wahoo bitters, Peruna and Indian Doctor wonder drugs.

The administration of the Food and Drugs Act involved the Bureau of Chemistry in thousands of court proceedings, *United States* v. *Two Barrels of Desiccated Eggs, United States* v. *One Hundred Barrels of Vinegar*; and one merciful judge noted that Section 6 extended the protection of the act to our four-footed friends. Pure food inspectors had seized 620 cases of spoiled canned cat food. When the case of the smelly tuna fish turned up in the western district court of the state of Washington, the judge cited man's experience with cats throughout recorded time: "Who will not feed cats must feed mice and rats." He confirmed the seizure and directed an order of condemnation.

The law was subsequently strengthened both by legal interpretations and by legislative action, as experience developed needs not met by the original act. Government technicians worked with private industry in the solution of specific problems such as refrigeration and the handling of food. When Dr. Wiley retired from public service in 1912, a revolution had occurred in food processing in only six years' time. Yet the food industry had hardly begun to grow.

"The conditions created by the passage of the act," said Clarence Francis, former president and chairman of the board of General Foods Corporation, "invited responsible business men to put real money into the food business."

The next 25 years saw the decline of the barrel as a food container and its replacement by the consumer unit package; the setting of official standards for the composition of basic food products; and the banning of quack therapeutic mechanical devices such as the electric belt, whose galvanic properties were once presented so vividly to the "Lost Manhood" market. We still have with us in some measure the "horse beef" butcher and the "butterlegger." Tap water remains a tempting means of "extending" many foods. But there is no question about the general integrity of our food supply, the contribution to the national well-being of the original food law, as amended, and the readiness of today's food industry leaders to accept what is now called the Food, Drug, and Cosmetic Act as a proper blueprint of their obligation to the nation's consumers.

AMERICA IN WORLD AFFAIRS:1898-1945

William E. Leuchtenburg

The Needless War with Spain

Seldom have events so pregnant with future significance occurred in an atmosphere so devoid of an understanding of their significance as in 1898 when the United States went to war with Spain. It is perhaps not quite accurate to say that the United States emerged from that war as a world power. In retrospect the nation was a world power well before the war began. But the war made Americans aware that the United States was a world power, and from that awareness flowed American imperialism, American participation in World War I, and much that followed.

As William E. Leuchtenburg explains in this essay, there was no shortage of "aggressive, expansionist, jingoistic" feeling in America during the early 1890's. But the conflict with Spain derived chiefly from the desire of Americans to help the beleaguered Cubans win their independence from Spain. Americans wanted the war (which could well have been avoided) but they had little understanding of what the results of that war would be.

Mr. Leuchtenburg, professor of history at Columbia University, is the author of Franklin D. Roosevelt and the New Deal, 1932–1940, *which won a Francis Parkman Prize, awarded each year to the book in American history that best combines sound scholarship and literary distinction. This essay also combines these two qualities.*

The United States in the 1890's became more aggressive, expansionistic, and jingoistic than it had been since the 1850's. In less than five years, we came to the brink of war with Italy, Chile, and Great Britain over three minor incidents in which no American national interest of major importance was involved. In each of these incidents, our secretary of state was highly aggressive, and the American people applauded. During these years, we completely overhauled our decrepit Navy, building fine new warships like the *Maine*. The martial virtues of Napoleon, the imperial doctrines of Rudyard Kipling, and the naval theories of Captain Alfred T. Mahan all enjoyed a considerable vogue.

There was an apparently insatiable hunger for foreign conquest. Senator Shelby M. Cullom declared in 1895: "It is time that some one woke up and realized the necessity of annexing some property. We want all this northern hemisphere, and when we begin to reach out to secure these advantages we will begin to have a nation and our lawmakers will rise above the grade of politicians and become true statesmen." When, in 1895, the United States almost became involved in a war with Great Britain over the Venezuelan boundary, Theodore Roosevelt noted: "The antics of the bankers, brokers and anglo-maniacs generally are humiliating to a degree. . . . Personally I rather hope the fight will come soon. The clamor of the peace faction has convinced me that this country needs a war." The Washington *Post* concluded: "The taste of Empire is in the mouth of the people. . . ."

In the early nineteenth century, under the leadership of men like Simon Bolivar, Spain's colonies in the New World had launched a series of successful revolutions; of the great Spanish empire that Cortes and Pizarro had built, the island of Cuba, "the Ever Faithful Isle," was the only important Spanish possession to stay loyal to the Crown. Spain exploited the economy of the island mercilessly, forcing Cubans to buy Spanish goods at prices far above the world market, and Madrid sent to Cuba as colonial officials younger sons who had no interest in the island other than making a quick killing and returning to Spain. High taxes to support Spanish officialdom crippled the island; arbitrary arrests and arbitrary trials made a mockery of justice; and every attempt at public education was stifled.

The island of Cuba had been in a state of political turbulence for years when in 1894 the American Wilson-Gorman Tariff placed duties on Cuban sugar which, coupled with a world-wide depression, brought ruin to the economy of the island. The terrible hardship of the winter was the signal for revolution; on February 24, 1895, under the leadership of a junta in New York City headed by José Martí, rebels once more took the field against Spain. At first, the American people were too absorbed with the Venezuelan crisis to pay much attention to another revolt in Cuba. Then, in September, 1895, came the event which changed the course of the Cuban rebellion: William Randolph Hearst, a young man of 32 who had been operating the San Francisco *Examiner* in a sensational fashion, purchased the New York *Morning Journal*, and immediately locked horns with Joseph Pulitzer and the

World in a circulation war that was to make newspaper history.

Hearst capitalized on the fact that the American people had only the most romantic notions of the nature of the Cuban conflict. The rebels under General Máximo Gómez, a tough Santo Domingan guerrilla fighter, embarked on a program of burning the cane fields in the hope not only of depriving the government of revenue but also of so disrupting the life of the island that the government would be forced to submit. Although there were some noble spirits in the group, much of the rebellion had an unsavory odor; one of the main financial supports for the uprising came from American property owners who feared that their sugar fields would be burned unless protection money was paid.

While Gómez was putting Cuba to the torch, American newsmen were filing reports describing the war in terms of nonexistent pitched battles between the liberty-loving Cubans and the cruel Spaniards. The war was presented, in short, as a Byronic conflict between the forces of freedom and the forces of tyranny, and the American people ate it up. When Hearst bought the *Journal* in late 1895, it had a circulation of 30,000; by 1897 it had bounded to over 400,000 daily, and during the Spanish-American War it was to go well over a million.

The sensational newspapers had influence, yet they represented no more than a minority of the press of the country; and in the South and the Middle West, where anti-Spanish feeling became most intense, the representative newspaper was much more conservative. Certainly the yellow press played a tremendous part in whipping up sentiment for intervention in Cuba, but these feelings could not be carried into action unless American political leaders of both parties were willing to assume the terrible responsibility of war.

By the beginning of 1896 the rebels had achieved such success in their guerrilla tactics that Madrid decided on firmer steps and sent General Don Valeriano Weyler y Nicolau to Cuba. When Weyler arrived in February, he found the sugar industry severely disrupted and the military at a loss to meet the rebel tactic of setting fire to the cane fields. Weyler declared martial law and announced that men guilty of incendiarism would be dealt with summarily; he was promptly dubbed "The Butcher" by American newspapermen.

By late 1896 Weyler still had not succeeded in crushing the insurrection, and his measures became more severe. On October 21 he issued his famous *reconcentrado* order, directing the "reconcentration" of the people of Pinar del Río in the garrison towns, and forbidding the export of supplies from the towns to the countryside. Reasoning that he could never suppress the rebellion so long as the rebels could draw secret assistance from people in the fields, Weyler moved the people from the estates into the towns and stripped the countryside of supplies to starve out the rebellion. Since many of the people had already fled to the towns, the *reconcentrado* policy was not as drastic as it appeared; yet the suffering produced by the policy was undeniable. Lacking proper hygienic care, thousands of Cubans, especially women and children, died like flies.

This pro-McKinley cartoon, from Puck's *April 13, 1898, issue, applauded the President's efforts to restrain war hysteria; but two days earlier McKinley had reversed his pacifistic policy.*

When William McKinley entered the White House in 1897, he had no intention of joining the War Hawks. "If I can only go out of office . . . with the knowledge that I have done what lay in my power to avert this terrible calamity," McKinley told Grover Cleveland on the eve of his inauguration, "I shall be the happiest man in the world." McKinley came to power as the "advance agent of prosperity," and business interests were almost unanimous in opposing any agitation of the Cuban question that might lead to war. Contrary to the assumptions of Leninist historians, it was Wall Street which, first and last, resisted a war which was to bring America its overseas empire.

The country had been gripped since 1893 by the deepest industrial depression in its history, a depression that was to persist until the beginning of 1897. Each time it appeared recovery might be on its way, a national crisis had cut it off: first the Venezuelan boundary war scare of December, 1895, then the bitter free silver campaign of 1896. What business groups feared more than anything else was a new crisis. As Julius Pratt writes: "To this fair prospect of a great business revival the threat of war was like a specter at the feast."

McKinley was not a strong President, and he had no intention of being one. Of all the political figures of his day, he was the man most responsive to the popular will. It was his great virtue and, his critics declared, his great weakness. Uncle Joe Cannon once remarked: "McKinley keeps his ear to the ground so close that he gets it full of grasshoppers much of the time." If McKinley was not one of our greatest Presidents, he was certainly the most representative and the most responsive. Anyone who knew the man knew that, although he was strongly opposed to war, he would not hold out against war if the popular demand for war became unmistakable. "Let the voice of the people rule"—this was McKinley's credo, and he meant it.

The threat to peace came from a new quarter, from the South and West, the strongholds of Democracy and free silver. Many Bryanite leaders were convinced that a war would create such a strain on the currency system that the opposition to free silver would collapse. Moreover, with the opposition to war strongest in Wall Street, they found it easy to believe that Administration policy was the product of a conspiracy of bankers who would deny silver to the American people, who would deny liberty to the people of Cuba, who were concerned only with the morality of the countinghouse. Moreover, Bryan was the spokesman for rural Protestantism, which was already speaking in terms of a righteous war against Spain to free the Cubans from bondage. These were forces too powerful for McKinley to ignore. McKinley desired peace, but he was above all, a Republican partisan, and he had no intention of handing the Democrats in 1900 the campaign cry of Free Cuba and Free Silver.

While McKinley attempted to search out a policy that would preserve peace without bringing disaster to the Republican party, the yellow press made his job all the more difficult by whipping up popular anger against Spain. On February 12 the *Journal* published a dispatch from Richard Harding Davis, reporting that as the American steamship *Olivette* was about to leave Havana Harbor for the United States, it was boarded by Spanish police officers who searched three young Cuban women, one of whom was suspected of carrying messages from the rebels. The *Journal* ran the story under the headline, "Does Our Flag Protect Women?" with a vivid drawing by Frederic Remington across one half a page showing Spanish plainclothes men searching a wholly nude woman. War, declared the *Journal*, "is a dreadful thing, but there are things more dreadful than even war, and one of them is dishonor." It shocked the country, and Congressman Amos Cummings immediately resolved to launch a congressional inquiry into the *Olivette* outrage. Before any steps could be taken, the true story was revealed. The *World* produced one of the young women who indignantly protested the *Journal*'s version of the incident. Pressured by the *World*, the *Journal* was forced to print a letter from Davis explaining that his article had not said that male policemen had searched the women and that, in fact, the search had been conducted quite properly by a police matron with no men present.

The *Olivette* incident was manufactured by Hearst, but by the spring of 1897 the American press had a new horror to report which was all too true. Famine was stalking the island. Cuba had been in a serious economic state when the rebellion broke out in 1895; two years of war would, under any circumstances, have been disastrous, but the deliberate policies pursued both by the insurgents and by the government forces made the situation desperate. It was a simple matter for Hearst and Pulitzer reporters to pin the full responsibility on Weyler.

By the middle of July, McKinley had formulated a policy which he set down in a letter of instructions to our new American minister

Frederic Remington's rendition of the Olivette incident was actually the work of Hearst, who had Remington exaggerate the supposed impropriety.

to Spain, General Stewart L. Woodford. The letter emphasized the need of bringing the Cuban war to an end and said that this could be done to the mutual advantage of both Spain and the Cubans by granting some kind of autonomy to Cuba. If Spain did not make an offer to the rebels and if the "measures of unparalleled severity" were not ended, the United States threatened to intervene.

On August 8 an Italian anarchist assassinated the Spanish premier; and when Woodford reached Madrid in September, a new government was about to take over headed by Señor Sagasta and the Liberals, who had repeatedly denounced the "barbarity" of the previous government's policy in Cuba. Sagasta immediately removed General Weyler, and the prospects for an agreement between the United States and Spain took a decided turn for the better.

While Woodford was carrying on skillful diplomatic negotiations for peace in Madrid, the Hearst press was creating a new sensation in this country with the Cisneros affair. Evangelina Cisneros was a young Cuban woman who had been arrested and imprisoned in the Rocojidas in Havana, guilty, according to the American press, of no other crime than protecting her virtue from an unscrupulous Spanish colonel, an aide to Butcher Weyler. The Rocojidas, Hearst's reporter told American readers, was a cage where the innocent beauty was herded with women criminals of every type, subject to the taunts and vile invitations of men who gathered outside.

When it was reported that Señorita Cisneros, whose father was a rebel leader, was to be sent for a long term to a Spanish penal colony in Africa or in the Canaries, the *Journal* launched one of the most fabulous campaigns in newspaper history. "Enlist the women of America!" was the Hearst war cry, and the women of America proved willing recruits. Mrs. Julia Ward Howe signed an appeal to Pope Leo XIII, and Mrs. Jefferson Davis, the widow of the president of the Confederacy, appealed to the queen regent of Spain to "give Evangelina Cisneros to the women of America to save her from a fate worse than death." When the *Journal* prepared a petition on behalf of Señorita Cisneros, it obtained the names of Mrs. Nancy Mc-Kinley, the mother of the President, and Mrs. John Sherman, the wife of the secretary of state, as well as such other prominent ladies as Julia Dent Grant and Mrs. Mark Hanna.

It was a startling coup for Mr. Hearst, but he had not yet even begun to display his ingenuity. On October 10, 1897, the *Journal* erupted across its front page with the banner headline: ''An American Newspaper Accomplishes at a Single Stroke What the Best Efforts of Diplomacy Failed Utterly to Bring About in Many Months.'' Hearst had sent Karl Decker, one of his most reliable correspondents, to Havana in late August with orders to rescue the Cuban Girl Martyr ''at any hazard''; and Decker had climbed to the roof of a house near the prison, broken the bar of a window of the jail, lifted Evangelina out, and, after hiding her for a few days in Havana, smuggled her onto an ·American steamer. Decker, signing his dispatch to the *Journal* ''Charles Duval,'' wrote: ''I have broken the bars of Rocojidas and have set free the beautiful captive of monster Weyler. Weyler could blind the Queen to the real character of Evangelina, but he could not build a jail that would hold against *Journal* enterprise when properly set to work.'' The Cuban Girl Martyr was met at the pier by a great throng, led up Broadway in a triumphal procession, taken to a reception at Delmonico's where 120,000 people milled about the streets surrounding the restaurant, and hailed at a monster reception in Madison Square Garden. The Bishop of London cabled his congratulations to the *Journal,* while Governor Stephens of Missouri proposed that the *Journal* send down 500 of its reporters to free the entire island.

On October 23 Sagasta announced a ''total change of immense scope'' in Spanish policy in Cuba. He promised to grant local autonomy to the Cubans immediately, reserving justice, the armed forces, and foreign relations to Spain. On November 13 Weyler's successor, Captain-General Blanco, issued a decree modifying considerably the *reconcentrado* policy, and on November 25 the queen regent signed the edicts creating an autonomous government for the island. In essence, Madrid had acceded to the American demands.

While Woodford was conducting negotiations with a conciliatory Liberal government in Madrid and while there was still hope for peace, the fatal incident occurred which made war virtually inevitable. On January 12, 1898, a riot broke out in Havana, and Spanish officers attacked newspaper offices. The nature of the riot is still not clear; it was over in an hour, and it had no anti-American aspects. If the United States now sent a naval vessel to Havana, it might be buying trouble with Spain. Yet if a riot did break out and Americans were killed, the Administration would be stoned for not having a ship there to protect them. For several days McKinley wavered; then he ordered the *Maine* to Havana, but with the explanation that this was a courtesy visit demonstrating that so nonsensical were the rumors of danger to American citizens that our ships could again resume their visits to the island.

As the *Maine* lay at anchor in Havana Harbor, the rebels, with a perfect sense of timing, released a new propaganda bombshell. In December, 1897, in a private letter, Señor Enrique Dupuy de Lôme, the Spanish minister at Washington, had set down his opinions of President McKinley's annual message to Congress: "Besides the ingrained and inevitable bluntness (*grosería*) with which it repeated all that the press and public opinion in Spain have said about Weyler," De Lôme wrote, "it once more shows what McKinley is, weak and a bidder for the admiration of the crowd, besides being a would-be politician (*politicastro*) who tries to leave a door open behind himself while keeping on good terms with the jingoes of his party." De Lôme added: "It would be very advantageous to take up, even if only for effect, the question of commercial relations, and to have a man of some prominence sent here in order that I may make use of him to carry on a propaganda among the Senators and others in opposition to the junta."

De Lôme had, to be sure, written all this in a private letter (which was stolen by an insurgent spy in the Havana post office), not in his official capacity, and his characterization of McKinley was not wholly without merit, but it was a blunder of the highest magnitude. Not only had De Lôme attacked the President, but he had gone on to suggest that the negotiations then going on over a commercial treaty were not being conducted in good faith. Throughout the letter ran precisely the tone which Hearst had been arguing expressed the Spanish temper —a cold, arrogant contempt for democratic institutions. The State Department immediately cabled Woodford to demand the recall of the Spanish minister, but Madrid had the good fortune of being able to tell Woodford that De Lôme, informed of the disaster the night before, had already resigned.

A week after the publication of the De Lôme indiscretion, at 9:40 on the night of February 15, 1898, came the terrible blow which ended all real hope for peace. In the harbor of Havana, the *Maine* was blown up by an explosion of unknown origin. In an instant, the ship was filled with the sounds of shrieking men and rushing water. The blast occurred in the forward part of the ship where, a half hour before, most of the men had turned in for the night; they were killed in their hammocks. Of the 350 officers and men on board, 260 were killed. By morning the proud *Maine* had sunk into the mud of Havana Harbor.

"Public opinion should be suspended until further report," Captain Sigsbee cabled to Washington, but even Sigsbee could not down his suspicions. The *Maine* had gone to a Spanish possession on a courtesy call, and the *Maine* now lay at the bottom of Havana Harbor. What could it mean but war? "I would give anything if President McKinley would order the fleet to Havana tomorrow," wrote Theodore Roosevelt. "The *Maine* was sunk by an act of dirty treachery on the part of the Spaniards." Volunteers lined up for war service, even though there was no one to enlist them; in New York 500 sharpshooting Westchester businessmen volunteered as a unit for the colors. The *Journal* reported: "The Whole Country Thrills With War Fever."

On February 15, 1898, the battleship Maine
exploded; with it went any chance for peace.

The cause of the explosion of the *Maine* has never been finally established. That Spain deliberately decided to blow up the *Maine* is inconceivable, although it is possible that it might have been the work of unauthorized Spanish extremists. The one group which had everything to gain from such an episode was the rebels; yet it seems unlikely that either they or Spanish hotheads could have carried out such an act and remained undetected. The most likely explanation is that it was caused by an explosion of internal origin; yet the evidence for this is not conclusive. In any event, this was the explanation that the Navy in 1898 was least willing to consider since it would reflect seriously on the care with which the Navy was operating the *Maine*.

The move toward war seemed relentless. On March 9 Congress unanimously voted $50,000,000 for war preparations. Yet the days went by and there was no war, in part because important sectors of American opinion viewed Hearst's stories of the atrocious conditions on the island with profound skepticism. Senator Redfield Proctor of Vermont decided to launch his own investigation into conditions on the island. On March 17, after a tour of Cuba, Proctor made one of the most influential speeches in the history of the United States Senate.

Proctor, who Roosevelt reported was "very ardent for the war," had not generally been regarded as a jingo, and no man in the Senate commanded greater respect for personal integrity. Proctor declared that he had gone to Cuba skeptical of reports of suffering there, and he had come back convinced. "Torn from their homes, with foul earth, foul air, foul water, and foul food or none, what wonder that one-half have died and that one-quarter of the living are so diseased that they can not be saved?" Proctor asked. "Little children are still walking about with arms and chest terribly emaciated, eyes swollen, and abdomen bloated to three times the natural size. . . . I was told by one of our consuls that they have been found dead about the markets in the morning, where they had crawled, hoping to get some stray bits of food from the early hucksters."

The question of peace or war now lay with McKinley. The Spaniards, Woodford had conceded, had gone about as far as they could go; but with the *Maine* in the mud of Havana Harbor, with the country, following Proctor's speech, crying for war, how much longer could McKinley hold out? The jingoes were treating his attempt to preserve peace with outright contempt; McKinley, Roosevelt told his friends, "has no more backbone than a chocolate éclair."

"We will have this war for the freedom of Cuba," Roosevelt shouted at a Gridiron Dinner on March 26, shaking his fist at Senator Hanna, "in spite of the timidity of the commercial interests." Nor was McKinley permitted to forget the political consequences. The Chicago *Times-Herald* warned: "Intervention in Cuba, peacefully if we can, forcibly if we must, is immediately inevitable. Our own internal political conditions will not permit its postponement. . . . Let President McKinley hesitate to rise to the just expectations of the American people, and who can doubt that 'war for Cuban liberty' will be the crown of thorns the free silver Democrats and Populists will adopt at the elections this fall?"

On March 28 the President released the report of the naval court of inquiry on the *Maine* disaster. "In the opinion of the court the *Maine* was destroyed by the explosion of a submarine mine, which caused the partial explosion of two or more of the forward magazines," the report concluded. Although no one was singled out for blame, the conclusion was inescapable that if Spain had not willfully done it, Spain had failed to provide proper protection to a friendly vessel on a courtesy visit in its waters. Overnight a slogan with the ring of a child's street chant caught the fancy of the country:

> *Remember the Maine!*
> *To hell with Spain!*

"I have no more doubt than that I am now standing in the Senate of the United States," declared Henry Cabot Lodge, "that that ship was blown up by a government mine, fired by, or with the connivance of, Spanish officials."

Desiring peace yet afraid of its consequences, McKinley embarked on a policy of attempting to gain the fruits of war without fighting. On March 29 Woodford demanded that Spain agree to an immediate armistice, revoke the reconcentration order, and co-operate with the United States to provide relief; Spain was given 48 hours to reply.

On March 31 Spain replied that it had finally revoked the reconcentration orders in the western provinces; that it had made available a credit of three million pesetas to resettle the natives; that it was willing to submit the *Maine* controversy to arbitration; and that it would grant a truce if the insurgents would ask for it. In short, Spain would yield everything we demanded, except that it would not concede defeat; the appeal for a truce would have to come from the rebels. Since the rebels would not make such an appeal, since they were confident of ultimate American intervention, the situation was hopeless; yet Spain had come a long way. Woodford cabled to Washington: "The ministry have gone as far as they dare go to-day. . . . No Spanish ministry would have dared to do one month ago what this ministry has proposed to-day."

For a week the Spaniards attempted to cling to their last shreds of dignity. On Saturday, April 9, Madrid surrendered. Driven to the wall by the American demands, the Spanish foreign minister informed Woodford that the government had decided to grant an armistice in Cuba immediately. Gratified at achieving the final concession, Woodford cabled McKinley: "I hope that nothing will now be done to humiliate Spain, as I am satisfied that the present Government is going, and is loyally ready to go, as fast and as far as it can."

It was too late. McKinley had decided on war. Spain had conceded everything, but Spain had waited too long. Up until the very last moment, Spanish officials had feared that if they yielded to American demands in Cuba, it might mean the overturn of the dynasty, and they preferred even a disastrous war to that. Proud but helpless in the face of American might, many Spanish officials appeared to prefer the dignity of being driven from the island in a heroic defensive war to meek surrender to an American ultimatum. In the end they surrendered and promised reforms. But they had promised reforms before—after the Ten Years' War which ended in 1878—and they had not kept these promises. Throughout the nineteenth century, constitutions had been made and remade, but nothing had changed. Even in the last hours of negotiations with the American minister, they had told Woodford that the President had asked the Pope to intervene, when the President had done nothing of the sort. Even if their intentions were of the best, could they carry them out? Spain had had three full years to end the war in Cuba and, with vastly superior numbers of troops, had not been able to do it. And the insurgents would accept nothing from Madrid, not even peace.

On Monday, April 11, McKinley sent his message to Congress, declaring that "the forcible intervention of the United States as a neutral to stop the war, according to the large dictates of humanity and following many historical precedents" was "justifiable on rational grounds." The fact that Spain had met everything we had asked was buried in two paragraphs of a long plea for war. It took Congress a full week to act. On Monday night, April 18, while the resolution shuttled back and forth between the two chambers and the conference room, congressmen sang "The Battle Hymn of the Republic" and

"Dixie" and shook the chamber with the refrain of "Hang General Weyler to a Sour Apple Tree." At three o'clock the next morning the two houses reached an agreement—the United States recognized the independence of Cuba, asserted that we would not acquire Cuba for ourselves, and issued an ultimatum to Spain to withdraw within three days. On April 20 President McKinley signed the resolution. War had come at last. But not quite. Although hostilities had begun, not until four days later did Congress declare war. When it did declare war, it dated it from McKinley's action in establishing a blockade four days before. To the very end, we protested our peaceful intentions as we stumbled headlong into war.

We entered a war in which no vital American interest was involved, and without any concept of its consequences. Although McKinley declared that to enter such a war for high purposes, and then annex territory, would be "criminal aggression," we acquired as a result of the war the Philippines and other parts of an overseas empire we had not intended to get and had no idea how to defend. Although we roundly attacked Spain for not recognizing the rebel government, we, in our turn, refused to recognize the rebels. Although we were shocked by Weyler's policies in Cuba, we were soon in the unhappy position of using savage methods to put down a rebel uprising in the Philippines, employing violence in a measure that easily matched what Weyler had done.

It would be easy to condemn McKinley for not holding out against war, but McKinley showed considerable courage in bucking the tide. McKinley's personal sympathy for the Cubans was sincere; only after his death was it revealed that he had contributed $5,000 anonymously for Cuban relief. It would be even easier to blame it all on Hearst; yet no newspaper can arouse a people that is not willing to be aroused. At root lay the American gullibility about foreign affairs, with the penchant for viewing politics in terms of a simple morality play; equally important were the contempt of the American people for Spain as a cruel but weak Latin nation and the desire for war and expansion which permeated the decade. The American people were not led into war; they got the war they wanted. "I think," observed Senator J. C. Spooner, "possibly the President could have worked out the business without war, but the current was too strong, the demagogues too numerous, the fall elections too near."

Harold A. Larrabee

The Enemies
of Empire

*When the war with Spain ended, the United States found itself
in control of Spain's Pacific and Caribbean colonies; what to do with
them was the first problem the new proprietor had to confront. The
controversy that developed over this issue in America was relatively
brief—by 1900 it appeared to have been settled in favor of those who
wanted to create an American empire. However, the basic issues raised
in this debate have never been settled; the history of American foreign
policy in the twentieth century is full of the repercussions and elabora-
tions of the arguments of 1898–1900. To what extent, if any, should
questions of national interest and honor take precedence over those
of morality and the national interests of other peoples? What is
"national honor"? Is colonialism always evil, no matter how administered or for what end?*

Professor Harold A. Larrabee of Union College and author of
Decision at the Chesapeake *describes below the argument as it first
developed between imperialists and anti-imperialists after the Spanish-
American War. He takes a strong anti-imperialist position, and few
today would disagree. That he is probably too favorable in his estimate
of the anti-imperialists of that day—many of them, for example,
opposed annexing colonies because they disliked bringing nonwhites
under the American flag—detracts little from the value of his essay
as a graphic re-creation of the mood of the times. Larrabee provides
fascinating glimpses into the minds of the anti-imperialists, the
defenders of expansionism, and those many sincere but somewhat
befuddled citizens who, like President McKinley, had great trouble
deciding between these two positions.*

*W*e know, to the hour and minute, when this country reached the point of no return on its way to becoming a world power. It was at exactly 5:39 A.M., Manila time, on Sunday, May 1, 1898, when Commodore George Dewey, U.S.N., commanding the Asiatic Squadron of four small cruisers and two gunboats, coolly turned from his position on the bridge of his flagship *Olympia,* and said to its captain in words that were to echo across distant America: "You may fire when you are ready, Gridley." The command loosed salvos of shells that swiftly crushed the decrepit fleet of the Spanish Admiral Montojo (two cruisers and seven small gunboats of an antiquated type), which had been huddling under the defenses of Manila. The battle was, in the words of the English historian Herbert W. Wilson, "a military execution rather than a real contest."

Its effects on American foreign policy, however, were incalculable, and the end is not yet. Hawaii was swiftly annexed as a territory on July 7, 1898; and by the ratification of the Treaty of Paris ending the war on February 6, 1899, we found ourselves the sovereign rulers of all the Spanish colonial possessions in the Philippines, there to remain for the next forty-seven years. The Pacific Ocean was thenceforth to be regarded as "an American lake." What we now often forget, however, is how many Americans were in those early days opposed to the idea of an American Empire. Sixty years ago imperialism, then defined as the raising of the flag by force over noncontiguous territory, and called by its friends "expansionism," was the burning issue of the day. It was bitterly contested, largely on abstract moral grounds as a gross betrayal of American principles, by a small but tenacious band of New England reformers.

The hard core of the anti-imperialist movement, both at the start and at the finish, was composed of conservative Boston lawyers and bankers, many of them lineal descendants of the Pilgrims. They soon gathered about them a remarkable nationwide galaxy of literary lights, college presidents, leaders of industry and labor, editors, and politicians, constituting what has been called "the first great national propaganda organization of the twentieth century." Their achievements were greater in the vigorous expression of their views than in practical politics. Yet they lost one of their major battles in the Senate by only one vote; for a time they threatened to endanger McKinley's re-election in 1900; and there can be no doubt that their tireless needling of the American conscience about colonialism, which continued until 1920, hastened the eventual independence of the Philippines.

Crusades being somewhat out of fashion nowadays, it may be difficult to recover the fervor of these heirs of Wendell Phillips and Charles Sumner as they denounced the extension of American rule by force in the Philippines, not because of what it might do to the Filipinos, but because of what they were convinced it was bound to do to American democratic ideals. They saw in the American seizure and retention of the Islands "the infamy of the doctrine that a people may be governed without their consent." At least some of the Filipinos, under Emilio Aguinaldo, were not "consenting" to their "pacification" by our

In Rufus Zogbaum's canvas, Commodore George Dewey directs the American victory at the Battle of Manila Bay from the bridge of the Olympia.

troops. A spineless administration in Washington, too much influenced by a group of jingoes in high places and by the yellow press, had liberated the Islanders from Spain only to try to enslave them again. This was rank apostasy from our professed principles in the Declaration of Independence and the Gettysburg Address. Could it be that Aguinaldo was fighting for *our* principles, while we had succumbed to the evil colonial policy of defeated Spain?

The expansionists' reply to this plea for democracy was the twin slogan: duty and destiny. It was, they said, the moral and religious duty of a civilized nation to accept the white man's burden, imposed upon us, in this instance, by our own idealistic crusade to free the Spanish possessions from centuries of misrule. As a moral aristocrat among nations, blessed with so many special advantages, America must, as a matter of *noblesse oblige,* undertake a self-sacrificing mission of political education in a world of backward peoples. In the words of the archexpansionist Theodore Roosevelt: ''Peace cannot be had until the civilized nations have expanded in some shape over the barbarous nations.'' And besides, such expansion was inevitable. What John Hay called ''cosmic tendency'' and others invoked as Manifest Destiny (now enlarged to a global scale) was irresistibly impelling the onward march of the white men who spoke what Sir Cecil Spring-Rice called ''God's language.'' Richard Croker, the boss of Tammany, remarked that ''My idea of anti-imperialism is opposition to the fashion of shooting everybody who doesn't speak English.''

What intensified and prolonged the conflict was the fact that both sides professed to want liberty for the Filipinos: the anti-imperialists believed that for us, as democrats, to deny them *immediate* liberty was to stultify our own ideals; while the expansionists maintained that the hopelessly backward Islanders were to be granted *eventual* liberty after a sufficient but indefinite period of Yankee tutelage. On both sides, then, there was an appeal to conscience by sincere but profoundly ignorant American patriots who found themselves enmeshed in the toils and tangles of historical circumstances, including domestic party politics. Since a moral issue was involved, the other side was not only wrong, but wicked, and words like "blood lust" and "murderer" were hurled at the imperialists, while the antis were denounced as "cowards" and "traitors." Nothing stirs the American people so deeply as a controversy in which both parties claim to be morally right: witness the battles over slavery, woman suffrage, and prohibition. In our day, "imperialism" has become a term battered almost beyond recognition in the cold war. But the central issue of 1898–1902—what constitutes the consent of the governed, and who is qualified to give it—has never been more alive than today, as one former colonial possession after another struggles toward a precariously independent nationhood.

"You have a wolf by the ears in the Philippines. You cannot let go of him with either dignity or safety, and he will not be easy to tame," said an anonymous American diplomat to one of our peace commissioners who was leaving for Paris in the fall of 1898. Even some of the expansionists themselves deplored our grip on the wolf in the first place, but were nevertheless extremely reluctant to let go. This was at once the strength and the weakness of the anti-imperialists' case. The imperialists had to admit, in the words of one of their leaders, Ambassador Whitelaw Reid, that "it was perfectly true that the American people did not wish for more territory, and never dreamed of distant colonies." Yet the grip on the wolf was an accomplished fact, and the practical difficulty of letting go with dignity and safety was the fatal flaw in the position into which the anti-imperialists found themselves maneuvered.

The clinching argument of the imperialists was "where once the flag goes up, it must never come down." The crucial decisions that sent Dewey to Manila in the first place, and ordered troops to his support as early as May 4, even before the news of his victory had reached Washington, were the work of a small elite group in the Republican administration who had managed to convert a pliable President. In 1897, McKinley had told Carl Schurz, "Ah, you may be sure there will be no jingo nonsense under my administration." But there was some truth in the popular conundrum: "Why is McKinley's mind like an unmade bed? Answer: Because it has to be made up for him every time he wants to use it." Theodore Roosevelt's friend Henry Adams spoke of his "alarm and horror of seeing poor weak McKinley, in gaiety . . . plunge into an inevitable war to conquer the Philippines contrary to every profession or so-called principle of our lives and history."

The ringleaders in the open conspiracy to move into the Orient via Hawaii and an isthmian canal, without ever consulting the American people, were two ardent disciples of Captain Alfred Thayer Mahan, U.S.N., the author of *The Influence of Sea Power Upon History, 1660–1783,* namely—Senator Henry Cabot Lodge of Massachusetts and the young and aggressive Assistant Secretary of the Navy, Theodore Roosevelt. It is one of the ironies of history that Captain Mahan himself was an anti-imperialist until the year 1885, and for precisely the reason most often advanced against his later followers: empire "would destroy free government." By 1890, however, a study of British sea power had converted him to the belief that the United States could take "a larger part in external affairs without risk to their institutions and with benefit to the world at large." Theodore Roosevelt, then a civil service commissioner, devoured Mahan's book, and reviewed it with enthusiasm in the *Atlantic Monthly,* later proclaiming Mahan "the only great naval expert who also possessed in international matters the mind of a statesman of the first rank."

Mahan's advice to Roosevelt in May, 1897, was: "Do nothing unrighteous; but take the [Hawaiian] islands first, and solve afterwards." The Roosevelt of 1898, described by William James as "still mentally in the *Sturm und Drang* period of early adolescence," needed little urging. He had been frustrated by President Cleveland's blocking of the annexation of Hawaii, but with the advent of a Republican administration his hopes were high. He was, however, soon indignant over the hesitancy of President McKinley, who, he said, "has no more backbone than a chocolate éclair." Behind McKinley stirred the powerful boss Mark Hanna, senator from Ohio, who flatly opposed the coming Spanish war at a Gridiron dinner on March 26, 1898, less than three weeks before it was declared. Introduced by the toastmaster at the same dinner as "At least one man connected with this administration who is not afraid to fight," Theodore Roosevelt, by that time in the Navy Department, declared: "We will have this war for the freedom of Cuba, Senator Hanna, in spite of the timidity of commercial interests." As William James put it, "Roosevelt gushes over war as the ideal condition of human society, for the manly strenuousness which it involves, and treats peace as a condition of blubberlike and swollen ignobility, fit only for huckstering weaklings, dwelling in gray twilight and heedless of the higher life. . . . One foe is as good as another, for aught he tells us."

Roosevelt's superior, Secretary John D. Long, seems to have had few inklings of what was to come, and "every time his back was turned," says David S. Barry, "Roosevelt would issue some kind of order in the line of military preparedness. . . ." On February 25, 1898, Long went home early, and as Acting Secretary of the Navy for a few hours, Roosevelt proceeded to send his momentous cable to Dewey in Hong Kong specifying "offensive operations in the Philpine [*sic*] islands." Next morning Long found that "in his precipitate way," his assistant had "come very near causing more of an explosion than happened to the *Maine* . . . He has gone at things like a bull in a china shop." Roosevelt was never again left in charge of the Navy Department for even part of a day, but his order to Dewey was not rescinded.

In this cartoon from Frank Leslie's Official History of the Spanish-American War, *captioned "Better rags with honor than patches with dishonor," Uncle Sam peers angrily over his shoulder at patches showing the* Maine *exploding and Spanish soldiers blowing off the heads of members of the Virginius' crew.*

Long seems to have thought he was dealing merely with a young subordinate who was unduly impetuous, rather than with the representative of a coterie with an elaborate imperialist philosophy and the determination to do something about it. Roosevelt was showing what a man of daring with a plan, influential associates, amenable superiors, and a little brief authority could do in the making of American foreign policy.

That the American people were unprepared for the new possessions supposedly "flung into their arms by Dewey's guns" is a gross understatement of the facts. McKinley freely confessed that, before consulting a globe, he could not have told "within two thousand miles" where the Philippines were. Incredible as it may seem to us, Dewey's staff did not include a public relations officer, and the presence of two newspapermen on board the revenue cutter *McCulloch* was a pure accident.

The public's state of bewilderment, after the first delirious celebrations of Dewey's bloodless victory had subsided, was best expressed by Finley Peter Dunne, editor of the Chicago *Journal,* whose Mr. Dooley conversed with his friend Mr. Hennessy "On the Philippines."

"I know what I'd do if I was Mack," said Mr. Hennessy, "I'd hist a flag over th' Ph'lipeens, an' I'd take in th' whole lot iv thim."

"An' yet," said Mr. Dooley, " 'tis not more thin two months since ye larned whether they were islands or canned goods . . . If yer son Packy was to ask ye where th' Ph'lipeens is, cud ye give him anny good idea whether they was in Rooshia or jus' west iv th' thracks?"

"Mebbe I cudden't," said Mr. Hennessy, haughtily, "but I'm f'r taking thim in, annyhow."

Not everyone in the country, however, went along with the bulk of the press and the expansionist-led administration. One month and one day after Dewey's triumph, the first recorded protest was made against "the insane and wicked ambition which is driving this country to ruin . . . and a slavery worse for Massachusetts, at least, than that of the Negro." It came in the form, classically correct for a proper Bostonian, of a letter to the editor of the *Evening Transcript* of June 2, 1898, entitled "A Cry for Help." It was written by Gamaliel Bradford, father of the well-known biographer. He was a seventh-generation descendant of Governor William Bradford of Plymouth, a retired banker, a Republican mugwump (he had deserted Blaine for Cleveland in 1884), and the author of several thousand letters to the newspapers in behalf of various reforms. His offer to join with any others who would help him in securing Boston's traditional Cradle of Liberty, Faneuil Hall, resulted in the first public meeting "to protest against the adoption of a so-called imperial policy by the United States."

Bradford was soon joined by another Pilgrim descendant, Erving Winslow, who was to prove the most undiscourageable of all the anti-imperialists, and by the able Boston lawyer Moorfield Storey, who was to become the acknowledged long-time champion of the movement. Presiding at the June 15 meeting that he had convened, Bradford took good care to say that its purpose was not to oppose "the vigorous prosecution of the war," but rather to check "the rush of reckless and unbridled ambition for dominion" evident in "a certain faction in Congress," which might turn "a war of liberation into a war of conquest." Storey laid down what was to be the most enduring plank in the anti-imperialist platform when he declared: "When Rome began her career of conquest, the Roman Republic began to decline . . . Let us once govern any considerable body of men without their consent, and it is a question of time how soon this republic shares the fate of Rome." The *Evening Transcript* spoke of the meeting as "a solemn warning against surrendering to the madness of the hour"; but Lodge depicted it to Roosevelt (en route to Cuba with his Rough Riders) as "a very comic incident."

The strange mixture of popular war hysteria, whipped up for their own purposes by Joseph Pulitzer of the *World* and William Randolph Hearst of the *Journal,* and the as-yet-unshaken confidence of many intellectuals in the pacific intentions of McKinley was vividly portrayed and analyzed by the philosopher William James in a letter written to his French friend François Pillon, just before James left his house in Cambridge to attend the Faneuil Hall meeting:

A curious episode of history, showing how a nation's ideals can be changed in the twinkling of an eye, by a succession of outward events partly accidental. It is quite possible that, without the explosion of the *Maine,* we should still be at peace . . . The actual declaration of war by Congress, however, was a case of *psychologie des foules,* a genuine hysteric stampede at the last moment . . . Our Executive has behaved very well. The European nations of the Continent cannot believe that our pretense of humanity, and our disclaiming of all ideas of conquest, is sincere. It has been *absolutely* sincere! The self-conscious feeling of our people has been entirely based in a sense of philanthropic duty . . . But here comes in the psychologic factor : once the excitement of action gets loose, the taxes levied, the victories achieved, etc., the old human instincts will get into play with all their old strength, and the ambition and sense of mastery which our nation has will set up new demands. We shall never take Cuba . . . But Porto Rico, and even the Philippines, are not so sure. We had supposed ourselves (with all our crudity and barbarity in certain ways) a better nation morally than the rest, safe at home, and without the old savage ambition, destined to exert great international influence by throwing in our "moral weight," etc. Dreams! Human Nature is everywhere the same, and at the least temptation all the old military passions rise, and sweep everything before them . . . It all shows by what short steps progress is made . . .

It soon became evident that William James had not overestimated the immense task facing the small band of anti-imperialists : no less than the complete reversal of public opinion in the face of easy victories, promised spoils, and a flag-waving press. For one thing, during the summer of 1898, history was being made at a furious pace. Whether one accepts the John Hay version, "a splendid little war," or "a jolly war," or the London *Saturday Review*'s estimate, "never a more shabby war," it was decidedly a short one. In less than four months it was all over but the disposition of "the waifs of the world deposited on our doorsteps." At a foreign policy conference at Saratoga Springs, New York, on August 18, 1898, just five days after the armistice, Carl Schurz, who had embarked upon a one-man crusade to impress McKinley, delivered a vigorous anti-imperialist address in which, ironically, he used against Senator Lodge and his fellow expansionists "the very principles which Lodge was to exalt so extravagantly twenty years later in the fight against the Covenant of the League of Nations." A delegation from the Sarotoga conference, with Samuel Gompers as one of its members, waited upon McKinley but was received only with suave hospitality.

To the public in the fall of 1898 the President offered the image of a sorely tried pacifist in doubt about the propriety of retaining the Philippines, even speculating that "if old Dewey had just sailed away after he had smashed the Spanish fleet, what a lot of trouble he would have saved us." But his every action was in line with what Lodge called "our large policy" of complete possession. McKinley packed the peace commission virtually four-to-one in favor of expansionism (three of them senators who would later have to vote on their own work), and gave them ever more sweeping instructions about what was to be demanded of the Spaniards, even though his Cabinet was divided on the issue. How he arrived at his final decision to tell the peace commission to demand "the whole archipelago or none" was told by the President himself on November 21, 1899, to a committee representing the General Missionary Committee of the Methodist Episcopal Church, then in session in Washington. Surely it is one of the most amazing descriptions of the workings of a Chief Executive's conscience in the field of foreign policy that has ever been recorded.

The delegation was about to leave the White House, when McKinley turned to them, and said earnestly:

> Hold a moment longer! Not quite yet, gentlemen! Before you go I would like to say just a word about the Philippine business. I have been criticized a good deal about the Philippines, but don't deserve it. The truth is I didn't want the Philippines, and when they came to us, as a gift from the gods, I did not know what to do with them. . . . I sought counsel from all sides—Democrats as well as Republicans—but got little help. I thought first we would take only Manila; then Luzon; then other islands, perhaps, also. I walked the floor of the White House night after night until midnight; and I am not ashamed to tell you, gentlemen, that I went down on my knees and prayed Almighty God for light and guidance more than one night. And one night late it came to me this way—I don't know how it was, but it came: (1) That we could not give them back to Spain—that would be cowardly and dishonorable; (2) that we could not turn them over to France or Germany—our commercial rivals in the Orient —that would be bad business and discreditable; (3) that we could not leave them to themselves—they were unfit for self-government—and they would soon have anarchy and misrule over there worse than Spain's was; and (4) that there was nothing left for us to do but take them all, and to educate the Filipinos, and uplift and civilize and Christianize them, and by God's grace do the very best we could by them, as our fellow men for whom Christ also died. And then I went to bed, and went to sleep, and slept soundly, and the next morning I sent for the chief engineer of the War Department (our map-maker), and I told him to put the Philippines on the map of the United States [pointing to a large map on the wall of his office], and there they are, and there they will stay while I am President!

The anti-imperialists' first battle, for the mind of the President as the chief architect of the nation's foreign policy, was thus lost to higher authority before it had hardly begun. But the country might still be persuaded to reject McKinley's Philippine policy. On November 19,

1898, in the Boston office of Edward Atkinson, retired textile manufacturer—later to become notorious because of the Postmaster General's
closing of the mails to his publications—the Anti-Imperialist League
was organized. Its object was: "to oppose, by every legitimate means,
the acquisition of the Philippine Islands, or of any colonies away
from our shores, by the United States."

The only thing more remarkable than the high quality of the
League's adherents was their extreme diversity. As its perpetual secretary, Erving Winslow, remarked: "We must in our organization
stand shoulder to shoulder: Republican, Democrat, Socialist, Populist,
Gold-Man, Silver-Man, and Mugwump, for the one momentous, vital,
paramount issue, Anti-Imperialism and the preservation of the Republic." Such advice, however, was not always easy to follow, since
the anti-imperialist leader in the Senate, George F. Hoar, regular
Republican, had once called the Mugwumps "the vilest set of political
assassins that ever disgraced this or any other country."

Besides every shade in the country's political spectrum, the
League's ever-lengthening list of vice presidents, many of whom lent
only their names to the movement, included every variety of American
reformer: municipal, civil service, social welfare, single-taxer, free-
trader, pacifist, and prohibitionist. Education furnished a long list of
college presidents: Eliot, Jordan, Rogers, Alderman, Stanley Hall,
Schurman, King, and Faunce, with such distinguished teachers as
Charles Eliot Norton, George Herbert Palmer, William Graham
Sumner, Felix Adler, William James, John Dewey, and Franklin H.
Giddings. From industry and finance came the extremely active donor
Andrew Carnegie, and Richard T. Crane and George Foster Peabody.
The contribution of "interest" groups (beet sugar and tobacco),
which wanted no Philippine competition, was remarkably small.

At the peak of the League's activities in 1899, it claimed thirty
thousand members and "half a million contributors" in branches
located in a dozen large cities from Boston to Portland, Oregon. One
of its conferences, in Chicago on October 17–18, 1899, attracted ten
thousand delegates; and by 1900 the League claimed to have distributed
four hundred thousand pieces of literature. This spreading of its
work enhanced its prestige, no doubt, but it proved to be a handicap
in exerting political influence. For what leader could be found who
could win and keep the confidence of quite so many kinds of followers?

The first political battle fought by the anti-imperialists was the
one in which they came the closest to victory: the heated conflict over
the ratification of the treaty of peace with Spain in January and February, 1899. The only controversial section in the document was the
article providing for the cession of the whole Philippine archipelago
to the United States. As Peace Commissioner Whitelaw Reid put it:
he and his associates were accused of "overdoing the business, looking after the interests of the country too thoroughly . . ." Since a
two-thirds vote was required for ratification in a Senate composed of
forty-six Republicans, thirty-four Democrats, and ten members of
minor parties, it was evident that a substantial number of Democratic

senators would have to be won over.

Fresh from his discharge from the Army, William Jennings Bryan announced in an interview at Savannah, Georgia, on December 13, 1898, that although he was firmly anti-imperialist, he believed that the treaty should be ratified and the issue of imperialism settled by resolution at a later date. The less politically minded anti-imperialists (Carnegie, Schurz, and Storey) regarded this as a sacrifice of principle in order to secure a campaign issue to go along with free silver (which they detested) in the election of 1900. Ten Democratic senators helped to ratify the treaty by only one vote more than the necessary two thirds, and although two or three of them may have been swayed by the outbreak of fighting, two days earlier, between Filipino and Amercian soldiers, Bryan has generally been credited with influencing the key votes. Many senators were undoubtedly influenced by Lodge's argument that failure to ratify would be a repudiation of McKinley and a continuation of the war. If there could have been a clear-cut decision regarding the retention of the Philippines, "the imperialists," says the diplomatic historian Thomas A. Bailey, "would almost certainly have failed to obtain a two-thirds majority." A few days later the Bacon amendment, pledging ultimate independence to the Filipinos, resulted in a tie vote, decided in the negative by the vote of Vice President Garret A. Hobart.

Despite this setback, the movement grew, rather than declined, as the 1900 election approached, although Bryan had created an amount of distrust in the minds of the "true" anti-imperialists, which led to talk of a third-party ticket designed to split the McKinley vote. Bryan agreed to make anti-imperialism "the paramount issue" of his campaign, and was finally endorsed by the League's Liberty Congress in Indianapolis in August, 1900. But many of the anti-imperialists refused to stomach Bryan's continued insistence upon free silver, and either voted for McKinley or held aloof from both candidates. Bryan secured fewer votes in 1900 than in 1896, and his defeat "marked the end of anti-imperialism as an important factor in American politics."

Political failure did not prevent literary success for the cause, although most of the blows struck by the pen came too late to turn the tide of public opinion. The one man whose emotional response to imperialism became enduring literature was the poet William Vaughn Moody. He risked his position as teacher of English at the University of Chicago by publishing several anti-imperialist poems in the *Atlantic Monthly*. In contrast to its noble sacrifices in the Civil War, Moody saw his country engaged in "ignoble battle," but protested:

We have not sold our loftiest heritage
The proud republic hath not stooped to cheat and scramble in the
  market place of war ...
That so our hand with better ease
May wield the driver's whip and grasp the jailer's keys.

Warning the country's leaders to "tempt not our weakness, our cupidity," the poet declares that "save we let the island men go free,"

In this 1899 cartoon from Puck, E. L. Godkin, William Jennings Bryan, and other anti-imperialists are pictured defiling the favorable image which imperial adventures had won for the United States.

our soldiers will have died in vain. In a shorter poem entitled "On a Soldier Fallen in the Philippines," (*Atlantic Monthly*, February, 1901), Moody makes use of the poignant contradiction between the honor due to the fallen and the dishonor of his cause:

Toll! Let him never guess
What work we set him to . . .
Let him never dream that his bullet's scream went wide of its island
  mark,
Home to the heart of his darling land where she slumbled and sinned
  in the dark.

Moody's language was mild and temperate compared with that of his fellow Chicagoan, the novelist Henry Blake Fuller, who became convinced that McKinley's policies were not only ignorant and stupid but actually vicious. Fuller addressed the President:

> *Thou sweating chattel slave to swine!*
> *Who dost befoul the holy shrine*
> *Of liberty with murder! . . .*

A much saner poetic approach was that of Ernest Crosby, president of the New York branch of the movement, whose Whitmanesque lines ran:

There is only one possession worth the capturing, and that is the
  hearts of men;
And these hearts can never be won by a nation of slaves.
Be free, and all mankind will flock to your standard.

Mark Twain was one literary figure who was won over from the opposition, in part by the urging of his friend William Dean Howells. "I left these shores at Vancouver [on his way to Vienna]," he wrote, "a red-hot imperialist. I wanted the American eagle to go screaming into the Pacific. It seemed tiresome and tame for it to content itself with the Rockies. Why not spread its wings over the Philippines, I asked myself? And I thought it would be a real good thing to do." But gradually Twain began to see the Philippines in a different light, for early in 1900 he wrote to Joseph Twichell: "Apparently we are not proposing to set the Filipinos free and give their islands to them . . . If these things are so, the war out there has no interest for me." From the day of Twain's triumphant return to this country in October, 1900, he joined forces with Howells in a steady barrage of articles, interviews, petitions, and pamphlets in behalf of anti-imperialism. The League made extensive use on cards of his "salutation-speech from the Nineteenth Century to the Twentieth," in which he said:

> I bring you the stately matron named Christendom, returning bedraggled, besmirched, and dishonored from pirate-raids in Kiao-Chou, Manchuria, South Africa, & the Philippines, with her soul full of meanness, her pocket full of boodle and her mouth full of pious hypocrisies. Give her soap and a towel, but hide the looking glass.

At a welcoming dinner for the young English war correspondent Winston Spencer Churchill in the Waldorf-Astoria Hotel on December 13, 1900, Mark Twain introduced the half-English, half-American speaker with these words: "I think that England sinned when she got herself into a war in South Africa which she could have avoided, just as we have sinned in getting into a similar war in the Philippines . . . yes, we are kin. And now that we are also kin in sin, there is nothing more to be desired. The harmony is complete, the blend is perfect—like Mr. Churchill himself, whom I now have the honor to present to you."

One of the most effective presentations of the case for anti-imperialism was made by the peppery Yale sociologist William Graham Sumner under the striking title, "The Conquest of the United States by Spain," but it was buried in the *Yale Law Journal* for January, 1899. Logic in terms of political theory, however, proved a poor match for the logic of events. Professor Richard Hofstadter has acutely observed that the Spanish-American War was fought because the American people wanted "not so much the freedom of Cuba as a *war* for the freedom of Cuba." Once war was under way, in the opinion of the late Vice President Charles G. Dawes, who was a close McKinley associate, "the retention of the Philippines was inevitable. . . . No man, or no party, could have prevented it." Yet in the sober judgment of Samuel Flagg Bemis, "looking back on those years of adolescent irresponsibility, we can now see the acquisition of the Philippines, the climax of American expansion, as a great national aberration."

But it was in vain that the anti-imperialists of that era cited the words of Abraham Lincoln: "No man is good enough to govern another without that other's consent." The missing premise in the arguments of both sides was the lack of adequate knowledge of the Filipinos and their capacity for solving their immediate political problems. The anti-imperialists saw them as ready and able to govern themselves democratically; the imperialists were just as convinced that they were mostly untutored barbarians. Neither side had enough facts, and as a result both substituted passion for logic.

The anti-imperialists saw the whole problem as a simple matter of political morality, which could never be settled until settled "right." By their indefatigable agitating they administered such a shock to sensitive American consciences that the burden of guilt could not be lifted. In time it came to be assumed that the pledge of Philippine independence defeated by a single vote in 1899 had, morally speaking, been given.

What the imperialists, notably Theodore Roosevelt, could never grasp was the Filipinos' yearning for *self*-government. Both sides entertained illusions: the imperialists saw a mirage of untold wealth in trade with the Orient, which did not materialize; the anti-imperialists foresaw "tyranny at home" as the sure result of "tyranny abroad." The latter were also incorrect in their belief that their opponents would never "let go" of the archipelago, although it was not until 1935 that the Commonwealth was established, with complete independence promised in 1946. The promise was kept, and the Philippines became "the first colony ever to be surrendered voluntarily."

The annual reports of the Anti-Imperialist League, which continued until its nineteenth and last meeting in 1917, make melancholy reading as the necrology lengthened and the budgets shrank. Treasurer Greene declared doggedly: "Anti-Imperialists are not quitters"; but when Erving Winslow died in 1923, Moorfield Storey wrote: "Almost everybody who belonged to the League is dead, and the young men do not take up the work. I am still its representative, but I have no followers."

One of the striking characteristics of the League in its heyday was the lack of contact between its zealous leaders in America and the Filipinos in whose behalf they were enduring a steady rain of epithets: little Americans, seditionists, cowards, and traitors. But the Filipinos had subtle ways of showing their appreciation. Long before they were allowed the privilege of self-government, they named the square directly in front of the Malacañang Palace in Manila, the official residence of the American Governor General, *La Liga Anti-Imperialistica*.

Thomas A. Bailey

Woodrow Wilson and the League of Nations

Woodrow Wilson was surely one of the most paradoxical figures in American history. He was both a great idealist and a shrewd practical politician; a man capable of enormous achievements yet physically delicate; one who concealed hot emotional fires beneath an icy exterior; a brilliant public orator but a man who could seldom persuade or inspire other individuals in private confrontations.

In this essay Thomas A. Bailey, professor emeritus of history at Stanford University, analyzes the role played by Wilson's complex personality in the great tragedy that closed his brilliant career—the defeat of his plan to enroll the United States in the League of Nations. That Wilson's personal qualities had a great deal to do with the Senate's rejection of the League goes without saying. However, as Bailey makes clear, forces far larger than those exerted by any man were also involved. Thus his discussion serves as a case study of the interaction of great men with their times. It is one of Bailey's strengths as a historian that he is able to describe the difficult and tangled events of 1918–20 briefly and simply without doing violence to truth and to carry the narrative of events along swiftly and smoothly at the same time that he is focusing the attention of the reader on the personal qualities of Wilson and the other principal actors in the drama.

Among Professor Bailey's many books are Woodrow Wilson and the Lost Peace, Woodrow Wilson and the Great Betrayal, Presidential Greatness, *and two popular textbooks,* A Diplomatic History of the American People, *and* The American Pageant.

T he story of America's rejection of the League of Nations revolves largely around the personality and character of Thomas Woodrow Wilson, the twenty-eighth President of the United States. Born in Virginia and reared in Yankee-gutted Georgia and the Carolinas, Wilson early developed a burning hatred of war and a passionate attachment to the Confederate-embraced principle of self-determination for minority peoples. From the writings of Thomas Jefferson he derived much of his democratic idealism and his invincible faith in the judgment of the masses, if properly informed. From his stiff-backed Scotch-Presbyterian forebears, he inherited a high degree of inflexibility; from his father, a dedicated Presbyterian minister, he learned a stern moral code that would tolerate no compromise with wrong, as defined by Woodrow Wilson.

As a leading academician who had first failed at law, he betrayed a contempt for "money-grubbing" lawyers, many of whom sat in the Senate, and an arrogance toward lesser intellects, including those of the "pygmy-minded" senators. As a devout Christian keenly aware of the wickedness of this world, he emerged as a fighting reformer, whether as president of Princeton, governor of New Jersey, or President of the United States.

As a war leader, Wilson was superb. Holding aloft the torch of idealism in one hand and the flaming sword of righteousness in the other, he aroused the masses to a holy crusade. We would fight a war to end wars; we would make the world safe for democracy. The phrase was not a mockery then. The American people, with an amazing display of self-sacrifice, supported the war effort unswervingly.

The noblest expression of Wilson's idealism was his Fourteen Points address to Congress in January, 1918. It compressed his war aims into punchy, placard-like paragraphs, expressly designed for propaganda purposes. It appealed tremendously to oppressed peoples everywhere by promising such goals as the end of secret treaties, freedom of the seas, the removal of economic barriers, a reduction of arms burdens, a fair adjustment of colonial claims, and self-determination for oppressed minorities. In Poland university men would meet on the streets of Warsaw, clasp hands, and soulfully utter one word, "Wilson." In remote regions of Italy peasants burned candles before poster portraits of the mighty new prophet arisen in the West.

The fourteenth and capstone point was a league of nations, designed to avert future wars. The basic idea was not original with Wilson; numerous thinkers, including Frenchmen and Britons, had been working on the concept long before he embraced it. Even Henry Cabot Lodge, the Republican senator from Massachusetts, had already spoken publicly in favor of a league of nations. But the more he heard about the Wilsonian League of Nations, the more critical of it he became.

A knowledge of the Wilson-Lodge feud is basic to an understanding of the tragedy that unfolded. Tall, slender, aristocratically bewhiskered, Dr. Henry Cabot Lodge (Ph.D., Harvard), had published a number of books and had been known as the scholar in politics before the appearance of Dr. Woodrow Wilson (Ph.D., Johns Hopkins). The Presbyterian professor had gone further in both scholarship and politics than the Boston Brahmin, whose mind was once described as resembling the soil of his native New England: "naturally barren but highly cultivated." Wilson and Lodge, two icy men, developed a mutual antipathy, which soon turned into freezing hatred.

The German armies, reeling under the blows of the Allies, were ready to give in by November, 1918. The formal armistice terms stipulated that Germany was to be guaranteed a peace based on the Fourteen Points, with two reservations concerning freedom of the seas and reparations.

Meanwhile the American people had keyed themselves up to the long-awaited march on Berlin; eager voices clamored to hang the Kaiser. Thus the sudden end of the shooting left inflamed patriots with a sense of frustration and letdown that boded ill for Wilson's policies. The red-faced Theodore Roosevelt, Lodge's intimate of long standing, cried that peace should be dictated by the chatter of machine guns and not the clicking of typewriters.

Wilson now towered at the dizzy pinnacle of his popularity and power. He had emerged as the moral arbiter of the world and the hope of all peoples for a better tomorrow. But regrettably his wartime sureness of touch began to desert him, and he made a series of costly fumbles. He was so preoccupied with reordering the world, someone has said, that he reminded one of the baseball player who knocks the ball into the bleachers and then forgets to touch home plate.

First came his brutally direct appeal for a Democratic Congress in October, 1918. The voters trooped to the polls the next month and, by a narrow margin, returned a Republican Congress. Wilson had not only goaded his partisan foes to fresh outbursts of fury, but he had unnecessarily staked his prestige on the outcome—and lost. When the Allied leaders met at the Paris peace table, he was the only one not entitled to be there, at least on the European basis of a parliamentary majority.

Wilson next announced that he was sailing for France, presumably to use his still enormous prestige to fashion an enduring peace. At this time no President had ever gone abroad, and Republicans condemned the decision as evidence of a dangerous Messiah complex—of a desire, as former President Taft put it, "to hog the whole show."

The naming of the remaining five men to the peace delegation caused partisans further anguish. Only one, Henry White, was a Republican, and he was a minor figure at that. The Republicans, now the majority party, complained that they had been good enough to die on the battlefield; they ought to have at least an equal voice at the peace table. Nor were any United States senators included, even though they would have a final whack at the treaty. Wilson did not have much respect for the "bungalow-minded" senators, and if he took one, the logical choice would be Henry Cabot Lodge. There were already enough feuds brewing at Paris without taking one along.

Doubtless some of the Big Business Republicans were out to "get" the President who had been responsible for the hated reformist legis-

Woodrow Wilson acknowledging a cheering crowd at the Waldorf-Astoria in New York.

lation of 1913–14. If he managed to put over the League of Nations, his prestige would soar to new heights. He might even arrange—unspeakable thought!—to be elected again and again and again. Much of the partisan smog that finally suffocated the League would have been cleared away if Wilson had publicly declared, as he was urged to do, that in no circumstances would he run again. But he spurned such counsel, partly because he was actually receptive to the idea of a third term.

The American President, hysterically hailed by European crowds as "Voovro Veelson," came to the Paris peace table in January, 1919, to meet with Lloyd George of Britain, Clemenceau of France, and Orlando of Italy. To his dismay, he soon discovered that they were far more interested in imperialism than in idealism. When they sought to carve up the territorial booty without regard for the colonials, contrary to the Fourteen Points, the stern-jawed Presbyterian moralist interposed a ringing veto. The end result was the mandate system— a compromise between idealism and imperialism that turned out to be more imperialistic than idealistic.

Wilson's overriding concern was the League of Nations. He feared that if he did not get it completed and embedded in the treaty, the imperialistic powers might sidetrack it. Working at an incredible pace after hours, Wilson headed the commission that drafted the League Covenant in ten meetings and some thirty hours. He then persuaded the conference not only to approve the hastily constructed Covenant but to incorporate it bodily in the peace treaty. In support of his adopted brain child he spoke so movingly on one occasion that even the hard-boiled reporters forgot to take notes.

Wilson now had to return hurriedly to the United States to sign bills and take care of other pressing business. Shortly after his arrival the mounting Republican opposition in the Senate flared up angrily. On March 4, 1919, 39 senators or senators-elect—more than enough to defeat the treaty—published a round robin to the effect that they would not approve the League in its existing form. This meant that Wilson had to return to Paris, hat in hand, and there weaken his position by having to seek modifications.

Stung to the quick, he struck back at his senatorial foes in an indiscreet speech in New York just before his departure. He boasted that when he brought the treaty back from Paris, the League Covenant would not only be tied in but so thoroughly tied in that it could not be cut out without killing the entire pact. The Senate, he assumed, would not dare to kill the treaty of peace outright.

At Paris the battle was now joined in deadly earnest. Clemenceau, the French realist, had little use for Wilson, the American idealist. "God gave us the ten commandments and we broke them," he reportedly sneered. "Wilson gave us the Fourteen Points—we shall see." Clemenceau's most disruptive demand was for the German Rhineland; but Wilson, the champion of self-determination, would never consent to handing several million Germans over to the tender mercies of the French. After a furious struggle, during which Wilson was stricken with influenza, Clemenceau was finally persuaded to yield the Rhineland and other demands in return for a security treaty. Under it, Britain and America agreed to come to the aid of France in the event of another unprovoked aggression. The United States Senate short-sightedly pigeonholed the pact, and France was left with neither the Rhineland nor security.

Two other deadlocks almost broke up the conference. Italy claimed the Adriatic port of Fiume, an area inhabited chiefly by Yugoslavs. In his battle for self-determination, Wilson dramatically appealed over the head of the Italian delegation to the Italian people, whereupon the delegates went home in a huff to receive popular endorsement. The final adjustment was a hollow victory for self-determination.

The politely bowing Japanese now stepped forward to press their economic claims to China's Shantung, which they had captured from the Germans early in the war. But to submit 30,000,000 Chinese to the influence of the Japanese would be another glaring violation of self-determination. The Japanese threatened to bolt the conference, as the Italians had already done, with consequent jeopardy to the League. In the end, Wilson reluctantly consented to a compromise that left the Japanese temporarily in possession of Shantung.

The Treaty of Versailles, as finally signed in June, 1919, included only about four of the original Fourteen Points. The Germans, with considerable justification, gave vent to loud cries of betrayal. But the iron hand of circumstance had forced Wilson to compromise away many of his points in order to salvage his fourteenth point, the League of Nations, which he hoped would iron out the injustices that had crept into the treaty. He was like the mother who throws her younger children to the pursuing wolves in order to save her sturdy first-born son.

Bitter opposition to the completed treaty had already begun to form in America. Tens of thousands of homesick and disillusioned soldiers were pouring home, determined to let Europe "stew in its own juice." The wartime idealism, inevitably doomed to slump, was now plunging to alarming depths. The beloved Allies had apparently turned out to be greedy imperialists. The war to make the world safe for democracy had obviously fallen dismally short of the goal. And at the end of the war to end wars there were about twenty conflicts of varying intensity being waged all over the globe.

The critics increased their clamor. Various foreign groups, including the Irish-Americans and the Italian-Americans, were complaining that the interests of the old country had been neglected. Professional liberals, for example the editors of the *New Republic*, were denouncing the treaty as too harsh. The illiberals, far more numerous, were denouncing it as not harsh enough. The Britain-haters, like the buzz-saw Senator James Reed of Missouri and the acid-penned William R. Hearst, were proclaiming that England had emerged with undue influence. Such ultra-nationalists as the isolationist Senator William E. Borah of Idaho were insisting that the flag of no superstate should be hoisted above the glorious Stars and Stripes.

When the treaty came back from Paris, with the League firmly riveted in, Senator Lodge despaired of stopping it.

"What are you going to do? It's hopeless," he complained to Borah. "All the newspapers in my state are for it." The best that he could hope for was to add a few reservations. The Republicans had been given little opportunity to help write the treaty in Paris; they now felt that they were entitled to do a little rewriting in Washington.

Lodge deliberately adopted the technique of delay. As chairman of the powerful Senate Committee on Foreign Relations, he consumed

Henry Cabot Lodge in 1909.

A cartoon by Bronstrup in the San Francisco Chronicle *captioned, "They Won't Dovetail" summed up the attitude of many opponents of the League.*

two weeks by reading aloud the entire pact of 264 pages, even though it had already been printed. He then held time-consuming public hearings, during which persons with unpronounceable foreign names aired their grievances against the pact.

Lodge finally adopted the strategy of tacking reservations onto the treaty, and he was able to achieve his goal because of the peculiar composition of the Senate. There were 49 Republicans and 47 Democrats. The Republicans consisted of about twenty "strong reservationists" like Lodge, about twelve "mild reservationists" like future Secretary of State Kellogg, and about a dozen "irreconcilables." This last group was headed by Senator Borah and the no less isolationist Senator Hiram Johnson of California, a fiery spellbinder.

The Lodge reservations finally broke the back of the treaty. They were all added by a simple majority vote, even though the entire pact would have to be approved by a two-thirds vote. The dozen or so Republican mild reservationists were not happy over the strong Lodge reservations, and if Wilson had deferred sufficiently to these men, he might have persuaded them to vote with the Democrats. Had they done so, the Lodge reservations could have all been voted down, and a milder version, perhaps acceptable to Wilson, could have been substituted.

As the hot summer of 1919 wore on, Wilson became increasingly impatient with the deadlock in the Senate. Finally he decided to take his case to the country, as he had so often done in response to his ingrained "appeal habit." He had never been robust, and his friends urged him not to risk breaking himself down in a strenuous barnstorming campaign. But Wilson, having made up his mind, was unyielding. He had sent American boys into battle in a war to end wars; why should he not risk his life in a battle for a League to end wars?

Wilson's spectacular tour met with limited enthusiasm in the

Middle West, the home of several million German-Americans. After him, like baying bloodhounds, trailed Senators Borah and Johnson, sometimes speaking in the same halls a day or so later, to the accompaniment of cries of "Impeach him, impeach him!" But on the Pacific Coast and in the Rocky Mountain area the enthusiasm for Wilson and the League was overwhelming. The high point—and the breaking point—of the trip came at Pueblo, Colorado, where Wilson, with tears streaming down his cheeks, pleaded for his beloved League of Nations.

That night Wilson's weary body rebelled. He was whisked back to Washington, where he suffered a stroke that paralyzed the left side of his body. For weeks he lay in bed, a desperately sick man. The Democrats, who had no first-rate leader in the Senate, were left rudderless. With the wisdom of hindsight, we may say that Wilson might better have stayed in Washington, providing the necessary leadership and compromising with the opposition, insofar as compromise was possible. A good deal of compromise had already gone into the treaty, and a little more might have saved it.

Senator Lodge, cold and decisive, was now in the driver's seat. His Fourteen Reservations, a sardonic parallel to Wilson's Fourteen Points, had been whipped into shape. Most of them now seem either irrelevant, inconsequential, or unnecessary; some of them merely reaffirmed principles and policies, including the Monroe Doctrine, already guaranteed by the treaty or by the Constitution.

But Wilson, who hated the sound of Lodge's name, would have no part of the Lodge reservations. They would, he insisted, emasculate the entire treaty. Yet the curious fact is that he had privately worked out his own set of reservations with the Democratic leader in the Senate, Gilbert M. Hitchcock, and these differed only in slight degree from those of Senator Lodge.

As the hour approached for the crucial vote in the Senate, it appeared that public opinion had veered a little. Although confused by the angry debate, it still favored the treaty—but with some safeguarding reservations. A stubborn Wilson was unwilling to accept this disheartening fact, or perhaps he was not made aware of it. Mrs. Wilson, backed by the President's personal physician, Dr. Cary Grayson, kept vigil at his bedside to warn the few visitors that disagreeable news might shock the invalid into a relapse.

In this highly unfavorable atmosphere, Senator Hitchcock had two conferences with Wilson on the eve of the Senate voting. He suggested compromise on a certain point, but Wilson shot back, "Let Lodge compromise!" Hitchcock conceded that the Senator would have to give ground but suggested that the White House might also hold out the olive branch. "Let Lodge hold out the olive branch," came the stern reply. On this inflexible note, and with Mrs. Wilson's anxiety mounting, the interview ended.

The Senate was ready for final action on November 19, 1919. At the critical moment Wilson sent a fateful letter to the Democratic minority in the Senate, urging them to vote down the treaty with the hated Lodge reservations so that a true ratification could be achieved. The Democrats, with more than the necessary one-third veto, heeded the voice of their crippled leader and rejected the treaty with reservations. The Republicans, with more than the necessary one-third veto, rejected the treaty without reservations.

The country was shocked by this exhibition of legislative paralysis. About four fifths of the senators professed to favor the treaty in some form, yet they were unable to agree on anything. An aroused public opinion forced the Senate to reconsider, and Lodge secretly entered into negotiations with the Democrats in an effort to work out acceptable reservations. He was making promising progress when Senator Borah got wind of his maneuvers through an anonymous telephone call. The leading irreconcilables hastily summoned a council of war, hauled Lodge before them, and bluntly accused him of treachery. Deeply disturbed, the Massachusetts Senator said: "Well, I suppose I'll have to resign as majority leader."

"No, by God!" burst out Borah. "You won't have a chance to resign! On Monday, I'll move for the election of a new majority leader and give the reasons for my action." Faced with an upheaval within his party such as had insured Wilson's election in 1912, Lodge agreed to drop his backstage negotiations.

The second-chance vote in the Senate came on March 19, 1920. Wilson again directed his loyal Democratic following to reject the treaty, disfigured as it was by the hateful Lodge reservations. But by this time there was no other form in which the pact could possibly be ratified. Twenty-one realistic Democrats turned their backs on Wilson and voted Yea; 23 loyal Democrats, mostly from the rock-ribbed South, joined with the irreconcilables to do the bidding of the White House. The treaty, though commanding a simple majority this time of 49 Yeas to 35 Nays, failed of the necessary two-thirds vote.

Wilson, struggling desperately against the Lodge reservation trap, had already summoned the nation in "solemn referendum" to give him a vote in favor of the League in the forthcoming presidential election of 1920. His hope was that he could then get the treaty approved without reservations. But this course was plainly futile. Even if all the anti-League senators up for re-election in 1920 had been replaced by the pro-League senators, Wilson would still have lacked the necessary two-thirds majority for an unreserved treaty.

The American people were never given a chance to express their views directly on the League of Nations. All they could do was vote either for the weak Democratic candidate, Cox, who stood for the League, and the stuffed-shirt Republican candidate, Harding, who wobbled all over the map of the League arguments. If the electorate had been given an opportunity to express itself, a powerful majority probably would have favored the world organization, with at least some reservations. But wearied of Wilsonism, idealism, and self-denial, and confused by the wordy fight over the treaty, the voters rose up and swept Harding into the White House. The winner had been more anti-League than pro-League, and his prodigious plurality of 7,000,000 votes condemned the League to death in America.

What caused this costly failure of American statesmanship?

Wilson's physical collapse intensified his native stubbornness. A judicious compromise here and there no doubt would have secured Senate approval of the treaty, though of course with modifications. Wilson believed that in any event the Allies would reject the Lodge reservations. The probabilities are that the Allies would have worked out some kind of acceptance, so dire was their need of America's economic support, but Wilson never gave them a chance to act.

Senator Lodge was also inflexible, but prior to the second rejection he was evidently trying to get the treaty through—on his own terms. As majority leader of the Republicans, his primary task was to avoid another fatal split in his party. Wilson's primary task was to get the pact approved. From a purely political point of view, the Republicans had little to gain by engineering ratification of a Democratic treaty.

The two-thirds rule in the Senate, often singled out as the culprit, is of little relevance. Wilson almost certainly would have pigeonholed the treaty if it had passed with the Lodge reservations appended.

Wilson's insistence that the League be wedded to the treaty actually contributed to the final defeat of both. Either would have had a better chance if it had not been burdened by the enemies of the other. The United Nations, one should note, was set up in 1945 independently of any peace treaty.

Finally, American public opinion in 1919-20 was not yet ready for the onerous new world responsibilities that had suddenly been forced upon it. The isolationist tradition was still potent, and it was fortified by postwar disillusionment. If the sovereign voters had spoken out for the League with one voice, they almost certainly would have had their way. A treaty without reservations, or with a few reservations acceptable to Wilson, doubtless would have slipped through the Senate. But the American people were one war short of accepting leadership in a world organization for peace.

By 1919, when this Bronstrup cartoon appeared, Wilson was sinking rapidly in a whirlpool of adverse public opinion.

Colonel T. N. Dupuy

Pearl Harbor:
Who Blundered?

The Japanese attack on Pearl Harbor, aptly characterized in this essay by the military historian Colonel Trevor N. Dupuy as "the worst disaster in the military annals of the United States," was an event so implausible, so shocking, and so enormous in its results that it has been studied exhaustively—by politicians, by military men, by plain citizens, and of course, by historians. "What happened" was never difficult to determine; why it happened—who was responsible for the unpreparedness of the American forces in Hawaii—is a question that has excited the bitterest of controversies.

Colonel Dupuy's effort to untangle the events of late November and early December, 1941, takes an unusual but interesting and effective form. Superficially his essay appears almost a chronicle. He describes day by day from November 25 to December 7 what was going on in Washington, in Hawaii, and in the western Pacific, where the Japanese attack force was steaming toward its destination. The dramatic force of this approach is considerable, but alone it would not produce a sound history of the affair. To it Dupuy adds both a prologue, setting the stage and introducing the main characters in the tragedy, and a conclusion, in which he weighs and balances the evidence and offers his own explanation of what went wrong.

Precisely at 7:55 A.M. on Sunday, December 7, 1941, a most devastating Japanese aerial attack struck the island of Oahu, Territory of Hawaii. When it was all over, the battleships of our Pacific Fleet, moored by pairs in their Pearl Harbor base, had received a mortal blow. Our army air strength in Hawaii—the Japanese found its planes ranged neatly wing to wing on airfield ramps—was a tangled mass of smoking wreckage.

The worst disaster in the military annals of the United States had ushered us into World War II. As in most wars, the political and diplomatic background was so complex and confused as to defy definitive analysis—though this has not prevented historians and others from making the attempt. But as to the disaster itself, the military record is clear.

A well-planned and brilliantly executed surprise attack by Japanese carrier-based aircraft was launched against the major American bastion in the Pacific. The United States government, its senior military leaders, and its commanders in Hawaii had had sufficient information to be adequately warned that an attack was possible, and had had time to be prepared to thwart or to blunt the blow. The information was largely ignored; the preparations were utterly inadequate.

Someone had blundered. Who? And how?

At the moment of the attack four professional military men filled posts of vital importance. In Washington, General George C. Marshall, Chief of Staff, was responsible for the entire United States Army and all of its installations. In a nearby office sat his Navy counterpart, Admiral Harold R. Stark, Chief of Naval Operations. On the Hawaiian island of Oahu, Lieutenant General Walter C. Short commanded the Hawaiian Department, the Army's most vital overseas outpost. Commanding the United States Pacific Fleet was Rear Admiral Husband E. Kimmel; his headquarters was also on Oahu, overlooking the great Navy base at Pearl Harbor.

Marshall, product of the Virginia Military Institute, had a well-deserved reputation for brilliant staff work under Pershing in France in World War I. Later he had taken a prominent part in developing the Army's Infantry School at Fort Benning, Georgia. Short, a graduate of the University of Illinois, had entered the Army from civilian life in 1901. Early in 1941 he had been chosen by Marshall to command the Hawaiian Department.

Both Stark and Kimmel had graduated from the United States Naval Academy at Annapolis—Stark in 1903, Kimmel a year later. Both had risen to their high positions in the Navy following exemplary command and staff service at sea and on shore. Close personal friends, both were highly respected by their naval colleagues.

The thinking and attitudes of these four men were shaped by two decades of unanimous opinion among American soldiers and sailors that someday Japan would clash with the United States in a struggle for predominance in the vast Pacific Ocean. All accepted without question the basic elements of U.S. doctrine for the defense of the Pacific in such a war.

The political smoke screen for Japan's surprise attack was provided by both parliamentary speeches in Tokyo and diplomatic moves in Washington. On November 17, 1941, Prime Minister Tojo (right) delivered a warlike harangue to the Japanese legislature.

The doctrine was that the United States Navy—and in particular its Pacific Fleet—was the essential element to American success in a Pacific war. Immobilization or destruction of that fleet would be the greatest damage Japan could inflict on the United States. Upon the Army lay the responsibility for furthering the offensive powers of the fleet by protecting its great Pearl Harbor base; by safeguarding the Panama Canal, the Navy's life line from the Atlantic to the Pacific; and by defending the advanced Philippine delaying position, which in military opinion was likely to be Japan's initial target.

Since 1939 the top military authorities of the nation, including President Franklin D. Roosevelt, had understood the almost inexorable logic of events that pointed to our eventual involvement either in the conflict which Hitler had begun in Europe or that in Asia between Japan and China—or both. And under Roosevelt's skillful guidance the nation, albeit grudgingly, was very slowly building up its military strength.

As 1941 rolled along, it became apparent, even to the man in the street, that the most pressing danger lay in the Far East. Our diplomatic relations with Japan were worsening; by November they appeared to be almost at the breaking point. The long-continued diplomatic bickering between the two nations on a variety of subjects had resulted in the arrival in Washington of a special envoy, Saburo Kurusu, who—with Ambassador Kichisaburo Nomura—had on November 20 presented the State Department with a document that was practically an ultimatum.

Japan would acquiesce to our government's demands that she withdraw from Indochina only upon "establishment of an equitable peace in the Pacific area" and, further, upon "supply to Japan [by the U.S. of] a required quantity of oil."

In 1940, our cipher experts had cracked the Japanese secret codes —a cryptoanalytical procedure known in the War Department as "Magic." Hence our government knew that the envoys had received instructions to press for American acceptance of this "final proposal" by November 25. The ambassadors had been warned that for reasons "beyond your ability to guess" this was essential, but that if the "signing can be completed by the 29th" the Imperial Japanese government would wait. "After that things are automatically going to happen."

It was also known through Magic radio intercepts that a large proportion of Japanese military strength—land, sea, and air—was concentrating in the Indochina and South China Sea areas. No evidence of aircraft carriers had been found, however, either in those areas or in the Japanese mandated islands. Intelligence agencies, monitoring Japanese radio traffic, considered it probable that the carriers were still in their home waters, but they were not certain.

On this basis Marshall, Stark, and their respective staffs concluded that the Japanese were preparing to strike in Southeast Asia; this threat, of course, included the Philippine Commonwealth. Accordingly our Army and Navy commanders in the Philippines and at Guam had been specifically warned. The commanders in Hawaii, Panama, Alaska, and on the West Coast were kept informed of important developments.

This was the situation as Marshall and Stark saw it early on November 25. From that time on events succeeded one another with increasing rapidity, both in Washington and in Hawaii. This is how they unfolded:

Washington, Tuesday, November 25

Marshall and Stark attended a "War Council" meeting with the President, Secretary of State Cordell Hull, Secretary of War Henry L. Stimson, and Secretary of the Navy Frank Knox. Were the Japanese bluffing? Hull thought not; rejection of their terms would mean war. "These fellows mean to fight," he told the group. "You [Marshall and Stark] will have to be prepared."

Adequate preparation could not be guaranteed by either service chief. The great draft army was still only a partly disciplined mass. The Navy, better prepared for an immediate fight, was still far from ready for an extended period of combat. Marshall urged diplomatic delay. If the State Department could hold war off for even three months, the time gained would be precious, especially in the Philippines, where Douglas MacArthur's newly raised Commonwealth Army was only partly organized and equipped.

Perhaps the State Department's formula—*modus vivendi* they called it—which had been sent by cable to our British, Chinese, Australian, and Dutch allies for comment—would gain the needed time. This was a proposal for a three-month truce in Sino-Japanese hostilities, during which the United States, in return for Japan's withdrawal from southern Indochina, would make limited economic concessions to her.

It was evident to all concerned that otherwise hostilities were almost certain to break out within a few days. The President, noting Japan's proclivity for attacking without a declaration of war, impressed on all concerned that if war came, it must result from an initial blow by Japan. How, then, asked Roosevelt, could the United States permit this without too much danger to itself?*

That evening Stark wrote a lengthy warning to Kimmel in Hawaii, informing him that neither the President nor the Secretary of State "would be surprised over a Japanese surprise attack," adding that while "an attack upon the Philippines would be the most embarrassing thing that could happen to us . . . I still rather look for an advance into Thailand, Indochina, Burma Road areas as the most likely." Marshall reviewed the incoming and outgoing messages to overseas commanders, and busied himself with the almost numberless duties of his most important task: preparing our Army for combat.

Honolulu, Tuesday, November 25

Kimmel and Short had more than a passing interest in the status

---

* The claim has been advanced—notably by Rear Admiral Robert A. Theobald in *The Final Secret of Pearl Harbor* (Devin-Adair, 1954)—that President Roosevelt abetted the Japanese surprise "by causing the Hawaiian Commanders to be denied invaluable information from decoded Japanese dispatches concerning the rapid approach of the war and the strong probability that the attack would be directed at Pearl Harbor." He did so, according to now-retired Admiral Kimmel in a recent interview with United Press International, to "induce the Japanese to attack Pearl Harbor and thus permit him to honor his secret commitments to Great Britain and the Netherlands with the full support of the American people."

The report of the Army Pearl Harbor Board, submitted to the Secretary of War on October 20, 1944, apportioned a share of the blame for the surprise to the War and Navy Departments and their top military officers in Washington. Even so, the service inquiries concluded that General Short and Admiral Kimmel had sufficient information to realize that war was imminent and had no excuse for inadequate security measures. They were not court-martialed, despite their requests, largely for political reasons. In this they were grievously wronged, for they had a right to be heard in their own defense. On the other hand, although I am not an apologist for the late President Roosevelt, it is simply ridiculous to suggest that he, who loved the Navy perhaps more than did any of our Presidents, would deliberately offer the Pacific Fleet as a sacrifice to entice Japan into war, and that this scheme was abetted by other responsible military men and statesmen. So many people would have known of such a nefarious plot that it would in fact have been impossible to muffle it.—T.N.D.

On November 17 in Washington Japanese ambassadors Kichisaburo Nomura and Saburo Kurusu (with cane), accompanied by Secretary of State Hull, arrive at the White House for talks with Roosevelt.

of our negotiations with Japan. Admiral Kimmel had been kept informed of the increasingly strained relations by frequent frank and newsy letters from Admiral Stark. One of these, dated November 7, had said in part: "Things seem to be moving steadily towards a crisis in the Pacific. . . . A month may see, literally, most anything . . . It doesn't look good."

Admiral Kimmel undoubtedly was thinking of that letter when he reread the official radio message which he had received the day before, November 24:

> Chances of favorable outcomes of negotiations with Japan very doubtful . . . A surprise aggressive movement in any direction including attack on Philippines or Guam is a possibility. Chief of Staff has seen this dispatch, concurs and requests action addressees to inform senior Army officers their areas. Utmost secrecy necessary in order not to complicate an already tense situation or precipitate Japanese action.

Admiral Kimmel promptly sent a copy of the message to General Short. He had standing instructions to show such messages to the

Army commander: the most critical messages from Washington were usually sent over Navy channels because the Army code was considered to be less secure. The Admiral saw no need for further action. After receiving a warning message on October 16 he had taken some measures for a partial alert and reported those promptly to Stark, who replied: "OK on the disposition which you made."

Admiral Kimmel and General Short had a cordial personal relationship, despite subsequent widespread but unfounded allegations to the contrary. They had frequently discussed, officially and personally, the possibility of a surprise Japanese attack and the measures to be taken to prepare for it and to thwart it if it should come. These plans had been approved in Washington. The Navy was responsible for long-range reconnaissance up to 700 miles, while the Army, with its land-based aircraft, was responsible for inshore reconnaissance for a distance up to twenty miles from shore. The Army's new radar would provide additional reconnaissance and air-warning service for a distance of up to 130 miles from Oahu. Periodically the commanders held joint maneuvers to test the plans and the readiness of their forces to carry them out.

They commanded large forces which might soon be called upon to fight, and it was essential that they maintain an intensive training schedule to assure the highest possible standard of combat efficiency. This was a formidable task, since many of their officers and men were inexperienced and untrained, having only recently been brought into our rapidly expanding armed forces. At the same time, as outpost commanders, both Short and Kimmel were well aware of their responsibilities for assuring the security of the fleet and of the island of Oahu.

Moreover, each commander assumed the other knew his business; each assumed the other's command was running on a full-time status. Each felt—as shown by later testimony—that to probe into the other's shop would be an unpardonable and resented intrusion. As a result, the liaison essential to any sort of joint or concerted operation—the daily constant and intimate exchange of details of command operations between Army and Navy staffs—was almost nonexistent. Each commander, then, was working in a partial vacuum.

On the single island of Oahu were concentrated most of the 42,857 troops that comprised the units of General Short's department. Carrying out the intensive training schedule was the bulk of two infantry divisions, less one regiment scattered in detachments on the other islands of the group. Also on Oahu were most of the antiaircraft and coast defense units of the Coast Artillery Command, and more than 250 aircraft of the Army's Hawaiian air force. Some of these aircraft, aloft on routine training exercises, were being tracked by the inexperienced crews of six Army mobile radar units newly installed at different points on the island.

There was comparable activity at the great Pearl Harbor Navy Yard, on the southern coast of the island, close by the bustling metropolis of Honolulu. Quite a few vessels of the U.S. Pacific Fleet were in port.

Here Kimmel, the fleet's commander in chief, had his headquarters, from which he and his staff closely supervised the intense training programs of their ships in Hawaiian waters. The fleet comprised eight battleships, two aircraft carriers (with a total of 180 planes), sixteen cruisers, forty-five destroyers, twelve submarines, and slightly more than 300 land-based aircraft. In addition another battleship, an aircraft carrier, four cruisers, and various smaller vessels were temporarily absent, many being in mainland yards for repairs.

The Navy Yard itself was the principal installation of the Fourteenth Naval District; both base and the district were commanded by Rear Admiral Claude C. Bloch, who was a direct subordinate of Kimmel both as base commander and as a Pacific Fleet staff officer—a setup which bred no little confusion and which was not helped by the fact that Bloch was Kimmel's senior in the service, though not in command. Kimmel properly held Bloch responsible for the functioning and local security of all the land-based installations of the fleet in Hawaii, while he himself devoted his principal attention to the readiness of the fleet to function offensively at sea. He considered Bloch to be Short's naval counterpart, so far as local protection of the fleet in Hawaii was concerned. Formal co-ordination of Army and Navy activities in Hawaii and nearby Pacific areas, however, was done at conferences—fairly frequent—between Kimmel and Short.

[*On November 25 (Washington date line), Vice Admiral Chuichi Nagumo's First Air Fleet—six aircraft carriers and 414 combat planes, escorted by two battleships, two heavy cruisers and one light, and nine destroyers—put to sea from Tankan Bay in the southern Kurile Islands. Eight tank ships trailed it. Screening the advance were twenty-eight submarines which had left Kure a few days earlier.*

This powerful naval striking force had long been preparing for a surprise attack on the United States Pacific Fleet at Pearl Harbor. It did not, however, have a final directive to carry it out. The First Air Fleet was to leave the Kurile Islands and steam slowly east into the North Pacific to await orders either to attack or, if negotiations with the United States reached a conclusion satisfactory to Japan, to return home.]

Washington, Wednesday, November 26

Before attending a meeting of the Army-Navy Joint Board, both General Marshall and Admiral Stark had learned that Secretary of State Hull, with the full approval of the President, had made a momentous decision.

During the evening of the twenty-fifth and the early hours of the twenty-sixth, the State Department received the comments of our allies on the *modus vivendi* reply to the Japanese ultimatum. The British, Australians, and Dutch gave lukewarm approval to the proposal for a three-month truce, though in a personal message to the President, Prime Minister Winston Churchill remarked pointedly, "What about Chiang Kai-shek? Is he not having a very thin diet?"

Chiang, in fact, had protested violently against the truce proposal, which, with its relaxation of economic pressure on Japan, could only work to the psychological and military disadvantage of China. The protest, as well as information gleaned from more intercepted messages indicating that the Japanese would accept nothing less than complete agreement to their demands of November 20, caused Secretary Hull to doubt the wisdom of the *modus vivendi*. Obviously, these concessions were inadequate to satisfy Japanese demands, yet, because they would seem like American appeasement they would strike a major blow to Chinese morale.

Hull therefore recommended a different reply, which the President approved. After a calm but firm restatement of the principles which had guided the American negotiations, the new note proposed, in essence: withdrawal of Japanese military forces from China and Indochina, recognition of the territorial integrity of those countries, unqualified acceptance of the National Government of China, and, finally, negotiation of a liberal U.S.-Japanese trade treaty once the other conditions had been met.

At 5 P.M. on November 26 Secretary Hull met with the two Japanese ambassadors and presented this reply to them. Special envoy Kurusu read the note, then commented that his government would "throw up its hands" and that the American position practically "put an end to the negotiations."

By frequent phone calls, Secretary Hull had kept both Stimson and Knox informed of these rapid developments, and the two service secretaries had passed on the information to their senior military subordinates. So it was that when they met at a Joint Board conference that same day, Marshall and Stark were well aware of the course of the events still in progress at the State Department. Agreeing that war was now almost certain, they both felt that it was incumbent upon them to remind the President once more of the dangerous weakness of the Army and the Navy and particularly the grave danger of disaster in the Philippines if war were to break out before further reinforcements of men and matériel could reach General MacArthur. They directed their subordinates to have ready for their signatures the next day a joint memorandum to the President which would urge avoidance of hostilities for as long as possible consistent with national policy and national honor.

Late in the afternoon General Marshall held a conference with Major General Leonard T. Gerow, Chief of the War Plans Division, to discuss what should be done the next day, November 27. Marshall had planned to be in North Carolina that day to observe the final phases of the largest maneuvers in the Army's peacetime history; he felt he should carry out that intention, despite his concern about a report that a large Japanese troop convoy had moved into the South China Sea. The two officers discussed the grave implications of the growing Japanese concentrations in the Southeast Asia region. Even though he intended to be back at his desk on the twenty-eighth, General Marshall authorized Gerow to send overseas commanders a warning in his name if further information next day—the twenty-seventh—

should point to the possibility of a surprise Japanese attack.

Honolulu, Wednesday, November 26

Admiral Kimmel received a report from the radio intelligence unit in Hawaii of a strong concentration of Japanese submarines and carrier aircraft in the Marshall Islands. This implied, but did not definitely prove, that some Japanese carriers were there as well. This information was perhaps inconsistent with a somewhat more definite report from the Philippines saying that radio traffic indicated all known Japanese carriers to be in home waters. Neither Admiral Kimmel nor members of his staff saw any need to inform General Short of these reports.

Short, meanwhile, had received an official message directing him to send two long-range B-24 bombers—due from the mainland—to photograph and observe the Japanese bases of Truk in the Caroline Islands and Jaluit in the Marshalls, reporting the number and locations of all Japanese naval vessels. He was to make sure both planes were "fully equipped with gun ammunition." But neither mission was ever flown: only one B-24 reached Short, and it was not properly equipped.

[*On the high seas, their bleak rendezvous at Tankan far astern, Nagumo's task force was steaming eastward. Radio silence was absolute. High-grade fuel kept smoke to a minimum. No waste was thrown overboard to leave telltale tracks; blackout on board was complete. Only the Admiral and a handful of his staff knew their orders; the rest of the command buzzed with speculation like so many hornets.*]

Washington, Thursday, November 27

General Gerow, summoned to Mr. Stimson's office, found Secretary Knox and Admiral Stark already there. The Secretary of War felt the time had come to alert General MacArthur in the Philippines. He told his listeners that Secretary Hull had warned him no peaceful solution was apparent. "I have washed my hands of it," Hull had said, "and it is now in the hands of you and Knox, the Army and the Navy."

Stimson added word of a telephone discussion with the President, who, agreeing that an alert order be sent out, desired all commanders to be cautioned that Japan must commit the first overt act of war. All four in Stimson's office then prepared drafts of alert messages to be sent to General MacArthur and Admiral Hart in the Philippines and to Army and Navy commanders in Hawaii, Panama, and on the West Coast.

Early in the afternoon Gerow sent out the warning:

Negotiations with Japan appear to be terminated to all practicable purposes with only the barest possibilities that the Japanese Government might . . . offer to continue.

The message then reiterated Mr. Roosevelt's desire that Japan commit the first overt act. But this, it was pointed out,

should not repeat not be construed as restricting you to a course . . . that might jeopardize your defense. *Prior to hostile Japanese action you are directed to undertake such reconnais-*

sance and other measures as you deem necessary [italics supplied], but these measures should be carried out so as not repeat not to alarm civil population or disclose intent. Report measures taken . . .

The message further directed that, should hostilities occur, commanders would undertake offensive tasks in accordance with existing war plans. It concluded with the caution that dissemination of "this highly secret information" should be limited to the essential minimum.

Stark's message to Navy commanders (as well as to our special naval observer in London, who was to advise the British) was sent at the same time; it opened bluntly: "This dispatch is to be considered a war warning." It related the end of negotiations and the expectation that "an aggressive move" might come within the next few days. Then, in contrast to the more general Army warning, it added the information that known military activities of the Japanese indicated they probably intended to launch "an amphibious expedition against either the Philippines, Thai or Kra peninsula or possibly Borneo." Like the Army warning, it directed execution of existing war plans in the event of hostilities. Naval commanders in the continental United States, Guam, and Samoa were cautioned to take antisabotage measures.

If read together, these two messages definitely pointed a finger at Southeast Asia as the expected enemy target. This, of course, in no way excuses any of the subsequent actions of our commanders in Hawaii, whose paramount responsibility was the security of their post. But it must have influenced their thinking.

Honolulu, Thursday, November 27

The official warnings from Washington confirmed to Short and Kimmel the seriousness of the international situation. Short, who noted that he was expected to report the measures he was taking, sent the following reply: "Report Department alerted to prevent sabotage. Liaison with the Navy."

The Hawaiian Department plans provided for three kinds of alert. Number 1, which was what Short had ordered, was to guard against sabotage and uprisings—long a preoccupation of all Hawaiian commanders because of the high proportion of Japanese in the Islands. Number 2 included security against possible isolated, external air or naval attacks. Number 3 was a full-scale deployment for maximum defense of the Islands, and particularly of Oahu—heart of the military organization. Only in the two higher stages of alert was ammunition to be distributed to the antiaircraft batteries; in Alert No. 1 all ammunition was to be kept stored in the dumps. Under Alert No. 1, planes would be parked closely for easy guarding; under the others they would be dispersed.

General Short felt he was confirmed in his concern over sabotage when his intelligence officer—or G-2—presented a message from the War Department G-2, warning that "subversive activities may be expected."

In obedience to the instruction to make such reconnaissance as he might "deem necessary," Short did, however, order his newly installed radar stations to operate daily from 4 A.M. to 7 A.M.; these were the dawn hours when surprise attack was most likely. Further reconnaissance, he felt, was the Navy's responsibility. He didn't know that Kimmel was having troubles of his own in attempting any sustained offshore reconnaissance. Nor was Kimmel aware that Short's radar was operating only on a curtailed basis.

Kimmel pondered over what steps he should take. Though he was already alerted to some extent, he knew that for the moment he could do little in the way of "defensive deployment" in his war plan tasks—most specifically, raids into the Japanese mandated islands. Should he then prepare for an attack against Oahu? The Washington message implied that this was not a probability. Even so, he didn't have sufficient planes for a 360 degree, distant reconnaissance from Oahu.

In compliance with instructions from Washington, Kimmel was sending some Marine planes to Wake and Midway islands. He decided that the two carrier task forces he was ordering to carry out this instruction could, en route, conduct long-range searches to the west, over the direct route from Japan to Oahu.

Task Force 8, under Vice Admiral William F. Halsey, including the carrier *Enterprise* and three cruisers, was leaving that day. In conference with Halsey before departure, Kimmel showed him the "war warning" message. Halsey asked how far he should go if he met any Japanese ships while searching. "Use your common sense," was Kimmel's reply. Halsey, it is understood, commented that these were the best orders he could receive, adding that if he found as much as one Japanese sampan, he would sink it. Kimmel, by making no further comment, apparently acquiesced.

Pending the arrival of Halsey at Wake, Kimmel sent orders to a patrol plane squadron based on Midway to proceed to Wake and return, searching ocean areas and covering a 525-mile area around Wake itself.

Kimmel felt that he had done all he could in that line without completely halting fleet training and exhausting the pilots of his relatively weak air command. But he did order immediate attack on any and all unidentified submarines discovered in the vicinity of Oahu and other fleet operating zones. Neither then nor later, apparently, did he check on the local security measures undertaken by Admiral Bloch's command, nor did he suggest any co-ordination between Bloch and Short.

[*Nagumo's force was steady on a course laid between the Aleutians and Midway Island, the carriers in two parallel rows of three each. Battleships and cruisers guarded the flanks, destroyers screened wide, and submarines were scouting far ahead.*]

Washington, Friday, November 28

General Marshall, back from his North Carolina inspection, was briefed by Gerow on the previous day's happenings. He read and approved the joint memorandum, already signed by Admiral Stark, which urged on the President the need for gaining time, particularly until troops—some already at sea and nearing Guam, others about to embark on the West Coast—could reach the Philippines. He also approved the warning message Gerow had sent to the overseas commanders.

At noon he attended the President's "War Council" meeting at the White House. The implications of a large Japanese amphibious force, known to be sailing southward through the South China Sea, were discussed. British Malaya, the Netherlands East Indies, and the Philippines were potential targets, the invasion of which would immediately involve us in war. But unless Congress should previously declare war, the United States could not attack this force. It was agreed that the President should send a message to Emperor Hirohito urging him to preserve peace, and that Mr. Roosevelt should also address Congress, explaining the dangers being created by this Japanese aggressive action. The President then left for a short vacation at Warm Springs, Georgia, directing his advisers to have the two documents prepared in his absence.

Marshall, back at his desk, thumbed through a sheaf of radio replies to the "war warning" message. Lieutenant General John L. DeWitt, commanding on the Pacific Coast, reported instituting a harbor alert at San Francisco and similar precautions in Alaska in liaison with naval authorities. He requested permission to direct air as well as ground deployment of his far-flung command. It was a long message, contrasting sharply with Short's succinct report of sabotage defense measures in Hawaii. But the Chief of Staff didn't pay much attention; it would be Gerow's job to handle any necessary responses. So Marshall initialed most of the messages and then forgot about them.

Short's message, however, was not initialed by Marshall. He would later testify he had no recollection of ever having seen it, although it bore the routine rubber stamp, "Noted by Chief of Staff."

As for Admiral Stark, he was pushing off a long message to Navy commanders on the West Coast, and to Admiral Kimmel, quoting the Army alert message of the twenty-seventh, including its admonition that Japan must commit the first "overt act."

Honolulu, Friday, November 28

Kimmel read Stark's long quote of the Army's alert message. He was particularly interested in its stress that "if hostilities cannot . . . be avoided the United States desires that Japan commit the first overt act." This appeared to confirm his decision of the previous day: limiting defensive deployment to one patrol squadron cruising from Wake to Midway and sending carrier task forces for local defense of those outposts.

Admiral Kimmel received several other interesting reports. The U.S.S. *Helena* reported contact with an unidentified submarine. An intelligence estimate based on radio intercepts indicated Japanese carriers were still in their own home waters. Another report on intercepted Japanese messages established a "winds code," by means of which Japan would notify its diplomatic and consular representatives abroad of a decision to go to war; "east wind rain" meant war with the United States; "north wind cloudy," war with Russia; "west wind clear," war with England and invasion of Thailand, Malaya, and the Dutch East Indies.

It was all very interesting. However, the Admiral never thought of mentioning any of these reports during his conference with General Short that day. They discussed mutual responsibility for security of Wake and Midway—in light of the mixed Army-Navy garrisons at both places. But neither thought of asking the other what action he had taken on the November 27 warnings, nor did either volunteer any information on matters he considered to be of interest to his own individual service only.

[*Admiral Nagumo's fleet spent the day in attempts to refuel in a plunging sea—an operation which, as it turned out, would continue for several days under almost heartbreaking conditions of bad weather.*]

Washington, Saturday, November 29

Both General Marshall and Admiral Stark received Magic copies of more intercepted Japanese messages. One of these from Premier Tojo in Tokyo to the ambassadors in Washington was quite ominous:

> The United States' . . . humiliating proposal . . . was quite unexpected and extremely regrettable. The Imperial Government can by no means use it as a basis for negotiations. Therefore . . . in two or three days the negotiations will be de facto ruptured. . . . However, I did not wish you to give the impression that the negotiations are broken off. Merely say to them that you are awaiting instructions. . . . From now on, do the best you can.

To Marshall and Stark this was clear evidence indeed that the Japanese were stalling for time only long enough to get their forces ready to attack in the Indonesia-Southeast Asia area. It seemed now only a question of time, as more reports streamed in about Japanese convoys moving into the South China Sea.

For a good part of the morning Stark and Marshall were working closely with Secretaries Knox and Stimson in preparing and revising drafts of the presidential messages to Congress and to Emperor Hirohito, in accordance with the agreement at the previous day's meeting of the War Council. Finally, about noon, the two secretaries were satisfied, and their proposed drafts were sent to Secretary Hull.

Late in the afternoon both read with considerable interest reports of a warlike speech which Premier Tojo had delivered that day (November 30, Tokyo time). The twenty-ninth had been the deadline established in the messages from Tokyo to the ambassadors. The speech, while warlike, failed to give any indication of Japanese intentions.

Honolulu, Saturday, November 29

Things were generally quiet on Oahu and in the outlying waters, as the Army and Navy both began a weekend of relaxation after five days of stenuous training. There was considerable bustle, however, at the Army's headquarters at Fort Shafter, as well as at Navy headquarters at nearby Pearl Harbor. General Short approved a message in reply to the latest sabotage warning from Washington, outlining in detail the security measures which had been taken. Admiral Kimmel received another message from Washington reminding him once more that he was to be prepared to carry out existing war plans in the event of hostilities with Japan. Thus, once again, the two commanders were reminded of the alert messages they had received on the twenty-seventh, and once again they found themselves satisfied with the actions they had then taken.

[*In the North Pacific Admiral Nagumo's fleet continued refueling.*]

Washington, Sunday, November 30

General Marshall, returning from his usual Sunday morning horseback ride at Fort Myer, found another intercepted Japanese message awaiting him; the Foreign Ministry was cautioning its envoys in Washington to keep talking and "be careful that this does not lead to anything like a breaking-off of negotiations." He agreed with G-2's conclusion that the Japanese were stalling until their South China Sea assault was ready.

Stark, at his desk, was called that morning by Secretary of State Hull, gravely concerned about Premier Tojo's warlike speech. The Secretary told him he was going to urge the President's return from Warm Springs. A later call from Hull informed Stark that President Roosevelt would be back Monday morning; Stark must see the President and report on the naval developments in the Far East.

Honolulu, Sunday, November 30

General Short, in light of his instructions "not to alarm the civil population," must have been annoyed to read the Honolulu *Advertiser* headlines that morning: "Hawaii Troops Alerted." There wasn't anything he could do about it, however; even the limited nature of his Alert No. 1 would draw newspaper attention in a critical time such as this. He also read that "Leaders Call Troops Back in Singapore—Hope Wanes as Nations Fail at Parleys" and "Kurusu Bluntly Warned Nation Ready for Battle."

Kimmel ordered a squadron of patrol planes to Midway, to replace temporarily the squadron which he had ordered to reconnoiter about Wake. He was also interested in an information copy of a Navy Department message to Admiral Hart, commanding our Asiatic Fleet at Manila, directing him to scout for information as to an intended Japanese attack on the Kra Isthmus of Thailand, just north of Malaya.

Kimmel didn't think that war could be delayed much longer. He wrote on the top of a piece of paper the words—"Steps to be taken in case of American-Japanese war within the next twenty-four hours," an *aide-mémoire* of the orders he must issue to his fleet.

[*The Japanese First Air Fleet was still engaged in the arduous refueling job, while continuing its eastward course at slow speed.*]

Washington, Monday, December 1

A busy day. Stark learned from his intelligence staff that the Japanese Navy had changed service radio frequencies and call letters for all units afloat—a normal prewar step. He went to the White House with Secretary Hull and briefed the President.

In the afternoon both Stark and Marshall digested an unusual number of important Magic intercepts of Japanese messages. Japan's Foreign Minister was urging his ambassadors to prevent the United States "from becoming unduly suspicious," emphasizing that it was important to give the impression to the Americans that "negotiations are continuing." Tokyo also had ordered its diplomatic offices in London, Hong Kong, Singapore, and Manila "to abandon the use of code machines and to dispose of them." Japan's ambassador at Bangkok reported his intrigues to maneuver Thailand into a declaration of war on Great Britain.

But most significant was an exchange between Japan's ambassador to Berlin and his foreign office. The ambassador reported that Foreign Minister von Ribbentrop had given him Hitler's unequivocal assurance that "should Japan become engaged in a war against the United States, Germany, of course, would join the war immediately." Tojo promptly told the ambassador to inform the German government that "war may suddenly break out between the Anglo-Saxon nations and Japan through some clash of arms. . . . This war may come quicker than anyone dreams."

And how quickly would that be? This was the question which sprang immediately to the minds of Admiral Stark and General Marshall, the men responsible for readying the armed forces of the United States for the coming clash of arms. They had no way of knowing that the answer lay in a brief uncoded message picked up by several American radio intelligence intercept stations just a few hours earlier. "Climb Mount Niitaka," was the message. No significance could be attached to it, so it never came to the attention of Marshall or Stark. Nor would it have meant anything to either of them.

Honolulu, Monday, December 1

Kimmel and Short held another routine conference. Presumably they discussed at some length the grave international situation. Supplementing the cryptic but alarming official intelligence reports and warnings were the headlines blazoning the Honolulu newspapers.

But neither Kimmel nor Short in their conversation discussed local security precautions or a possible threat to Oahu. Politely but inconclusively they continued discussion of the divided responsibility at Wake and Midway. Kimmel never thought to mention to Short that he had received another Washington warning about the "winds code" and that he had also been informed of the change in Japanese military frequencies and call letters. It never occurred to Kimmel that Short might not have been told about either matter.

Routine training continued in Army posts. General Short was quite pleased that his limited alert—which the War Department had apparently approved—had not interfered noticeably with training programs.

[*"Climb Mount Niitaka!"*

Admiral Nagumo sucked in his breath as the message was laid before him this day. This was it; the prearranged code which meant "Proceed with attack."

Obedient to the signal flags broken out aboard the flagship, the gray ships came foaming about to a southeasterly course, vibrating to the thrust of increased propeller speed. Inside the steel hulls the mustered crews, learning the news, cheered, quaffed sake, and burned incense to the spirits of their ancestors.]

Washington, Tuesday, December 2

Additional Magic intercepts indicated further Japanese preparations for war, with the enemy's known offensive weight still massing in Southeast Asia.

Honolulu, Tuesday, December 2

Kimmel, discussing intelligence reports with his staff, noted the change in Japanese radio frequencies as related in the Navy Department's fortnightly intelligence summary, received late the previous day. The gist of it was that Tokyo was preparing for "operations on a large scale."

Then Kimmel called for intelligence estimates on the location of Japanese aircraft carriers. Captain Edwin T. Layton, his intelligence officer, gave estimated locations for all except Divisions 1 and 2— four carriers.

"What!" exclaimed Kimmel, "you don't know where [they] are?"

"No, sir, I do not. I think they are in home waters, but—"

Sternly, but with a suspicion of a twinkle in his eyes, Kimmel delivered himself of a masterpiece of unconscious irony.

"Do you mean to say they could be rounding Diamond Head and you wouldn't know it?"

The conference ended after a discussion on the difficulty of locating a force operating under sealed orders while preserving radio silence.

Short met Kimmel that day again. They continued debate over jurisdiction at Wake and Midway.

[*Nagumo's fleet was steadily driving south toward Oahu. In prearranged code—unintelligible to American Magic interceptors— Tokyo had confirmed the target date: "X-Day will be 8 December" —December 7, Honolulu time.*]

Washington, Wednesday, December 3

Along with the other recipients of Magic information, General Marshall and Admiral Stark noted but attached no particular significance to a pair of intercepted messages made available to them that day.

One, dated November 15, was already old; its translation had been deferred for several days in order to take care of messages considered more urgent. It referred to an earlier message directing the Japanese consulate at Honolulu to make periodic reports on the location of American warships in Pearl Harbor, and requested the Honolulu consulate to step up these reports to twice a week.

No particular importance was attributed to this by Admiral Stark or his senior naval intelligence officers, since the Japanese had long been making efforts to obtain information about the activities and number of ships in harbor at other naval bases on the West Coast and at Panama. The fact that the Japanese wanted more complete data, including exact locations of specific vessels in Pearl Harbor, was assumed to be merely an indication of their thoroughness in evaluating intelligence on America's main Pacific combat force.

The other message was a reply by Prime Minister Tojo to the suggestion of his ambassadors at Washington that peace could perhaps be preserved through a high-level conference—they had proposed former Premier Prince Konoye as the Japanese envoy and Vice President Henry Wallace or Presidential Assistant Harry Hopkins for the United States—at "some midway point, such as Honolulu." Tojo's response, that "it would be inappropriate for us to propose such a meeting," seemed a less significant indication of Japan's immediate intentions than the continuing reports of her movements in and near Indochina.

Honolulu, Wednesday, December 3

Admiral Kimmel noted the continuing and surprising lack of information on Japanese carriers contained in the latest daily radio intelligence summary, which stated that "carrier traffic is at a low ebb."

That day, too, he received Admiral Stark's letter of November 25. He agreed with Stark's view that "an attack on the Philippines" might be embarrassing, but that "an advance into Thailand, Indochina, Burma Road area [was] most likely."

In the afternoon Short and Kimmel conferred. They soon got into a grim discussion of what they could do to carry out assigned war plans when and if war broke out. Both were thinking, of course, of planned naval and air raids into the Marshall Islands and of security measures for Wake and Midway. There was no mention of like measures for Oahu. Nor did Admiral Kimmel think to mention to General Short his latest intelligence reports about the burning of Japanese codes or the missing aircraft carriers.

[Nagumo's planners on the high seas were busy marking on their charts of Pearl Harbor the exact locations of six of the U.S. battle

fleet—the Pennsylvania, Arizona, California, Tennessee, Maryland, *and* West Virginia. *The data came from Honolulu, relayed by radio through Imperial Navy Headquarters in Tokyo.*]

Washington, Thursday, December 4

A mixed bag of Magic intercepts available to both Stark and Marshall gave clear indication of Japanese intentions to go to war. Instructions came to Ambassador Nomura to completely destroy one of the two special machines for secret coding, but to hold the other and its cipher key—which should be in his personal possession—"until the last minute." One intercepted message, considered to be relatively insignificant, was to the Japanese consul at Honolulu; he was to "investigate completely the fleet-bases in the neighborhood of the Hawaiian military reservation."

Stark and Marshall concerned themselves with routine activities.

Honolulu, Thursday, December 4

Admiral Kimmel conferred with two of his senior task-force commanders, scheduled to sail the next day on combined training-alert missions. One, under Vice Admiral Wilson Brown, was to proceed to Johnson Island, 700 miles southwest of Oahu, on a joint Navy-Marine bombardment and landing exercise. The other, under Rear Admiral T. H. Newton, included the carrier *Lexington*. This force was to go to Midway Island, fly off a squadron of Marine planes to reinforce the local garrison, and then rendezvous with Brown at Johnson Island. En route the *Lexington*'s planes would conduct routine scouting flights.

Kimmel's intention was that, should war break out, these forces would be available for raids into the Marshall Island group in accordance with existing war plans. Both task-force commanders understood their war-plan missions; both were aware in general of the tense international situation. Kimmel, therefore, felt he was under no obligation to inform either of Washington's November 27 "war warning" message.

The net naval situation on Oahu now was that the entire carrier force of the Pacific Fleet was either at sea or about to steam and that the approaches to the island from the west would be scouted for several days to come.

Kimmel felt that these steps would ensure a reconnaissance search of a large portion of the central Pacific Ocean, as extensive as his limited aircraft strength would permit. But, from the Hawaiian Islands north to the Aleutians, both sea and air were still bare of American reconnaissance.

Kimmel and Short did not meet that day.

[*Admiral Nagumo, watching the intermittent refueling being carried on during the day, was intrigued to learn from Honolulu, via Tokyo, that watchful Japanese eyes were "unable to ascertain whether air alert had been issued. There are no indications of sea alert. . . ."*]

Washington, Friday, December 5

Both War and Navy departments were busy compiling data for President Roosevelt on Japanese sea, land, and air strength concentrating in French Indochina and adjacent areas. In an intercepted Japanese message from Washington, Ambassador Nomura told Tokyo that in case of Japanese invasion of Thailand, joint military action by Great Britain and the United States "is a definite certainty, with or without a declaration of war." Another, from Tokyo, reiterated the previous instructions about destruction of codes and coding machines.

Admiral Stark, conferring with staff officers, decided no further warning orders need be sent to overseas naval commanders; the message of November 27 was adequate. All concurred.

Honolulu, Friday, December 5

General Short read with interest a cryptic message from G-2 in Washington to his intelligence officer, directing him to get in touch with the Navy immediately "regarding broadcasts from Tokyo reference weather." So Lieutenant Colonel George W. Bicknell, assistant G-2, gave the General all facts obtainable from his own office and from Kimmel's headquarters. Short was informed by Kimmel of the departure of the two naval task forces of Admirals Brown and Newton.

[*While pilots and squadron leaders on board Nagumo's fleet studied and restudied their coming roles, the ships—900 miles north of Midway and 1,300 miles northwest of Oahu—slid slowly down the North Pacific rollers, still far beyond the range of any American search plane.*]

Washington, Saturday, December 6

Reports of increasing Japanese concentration and movements in Indochina, South China, and the South China Sea absorbed Stark and Marshall, as well as all the other members of the War Cabinet from the President down. Mr. Roosevelt, the service chiefs were glad to learn, had decided that he would personally warn Emperor Hirohito that further aggressions might lead to war and urge the Japanese ruler that withdrawal of his forces from Indochina "would result in the assurance of peace throughout the whole of the South Pacific area."

Late in the afternoon Magic plucked out of the air thirteen parts of a fourteen-part memorandum from Tokyo to the Japanese envoys. This much of the message summarized negotiations from the Japanese viewpoint, concluding that the American note of November 26 was not "a basis of negotiations." The envoys were instructed to handle it carefully, since "the situation is extremely delicate."

Distribution of this intercept was curious. Decoding was completed after office hours. General Sherman A. Miles, Army G-2, saw no need to disturb either the Secretary of War, General Marshall, or General Gerow at their homes. (In passing it might be mentioned that one didn't disturb General Marshall at home without extremely good reason.) Some Navy people saw the message. Stark, who was at the theater, learned of it when he returned home and found that he was expected to call the White House. The President had received the intercept, as had the State Department. The details of the conversation are not known, but presumably the President told Stark, as he had earlier said to Harry Hopkins: "This means war!"

Honolulu, Saturday, December 6

In the daily radio intelligence summary received that morning from Washington, Admiral Kimmel was again struck by lack of information on the location of Japanese carriers. In other dispatches, however, there was considerable information about different kinds of Japanese activity. He received a copy of Admiral Hart's message reporting on the movement of the two convoys south of Indochina. And he received a message from Washington authorizing him, "in view of the international situation and the exposed position of our outlying Pacific Islands," to order the destruction of classified documents at these islands, "now or under later conditions of greater emergency." Neither the Admiral nor any member of his staff saw any need to pass on any information to the Army. Presumably General Short was getting it all through Army channels.

Carefully checking the reported locations of all fleet units and projecting their planned routes for the next twenty-four hours, Admiral Kimmel again made his daily revision of his personal check-list memorandum: "Steps to be taken in case of American-Japanese war within the next twenty-four hours."

Over at Fort Shafter, Army headquarters, the daily staff conference was as usual presided over by Colonel Walter C. Phillips, chief of staff. General Short did not normally attend these meetings. Bicknell, assistant G-2, who seems to have been on his toes those days, reported the Japanese consulate in Honolulu was busily burning and destroying secret papers, significant in light of similar reports throughout the world already noted in the intercepts. The chief of staff and G-2 reported this information later to General Short.

And so Oahu drifted into another weekend: a time of relaxation for both Army and Navy. Short, however, was interrupted by Bicknell early that evening at his quarters while he and his G-2—Colonel Kendall Fielder—and their wives were about to drive to a dinner dance.

Bicknell, with some sense of urgency, reported that the local FBI agent had passed to him and to Navy intelligence a transcript of a suspicious long-distance telephone message. A Japanese named Mori, talking to someone in Tokyo, mentioned flights of airplanes, searchlights, and the number of ships in Pearl Harbor, along with cryptic reference to various flowers—apparently part of some sort of code.

Both the FBI man and Bicknell were alarmed at the implications of this flower code. Neither Short nor Fielder, however, was disturbed. Short, before they hurried to the car where their wives awaited them impatiently, told Bicknell he was, perhaps, "too intelligence-conscious." In any event they could talk about it again in the morning.

The district intelligence officer of the Navy decided that the transcript should be studied further by a Japanese linguist and so put the FBI report away until Monday morning. Admiral Kimmel was not informed.

[*Nagumo's fleet, the wallowing tankers now left behind, was churning southward at twenty-four-knot speed. By 6 A.M. next day it would be 230 miles north of Oahu with its planes thrusting skyward. And at dawn, five midget two-man submarines—disgorged from five large Japanese submarines gathered offshore that night—poked their way around Diamond Head, Pearl Harbor-bound.*]

Washington, Sunday, December 7

By 8 A.M. the last part of the Japanese memorandum—Part Fourteen—had been intercepted, transcribed, and was ready for distribution. Both Army and Navy intelligence officers were slightly surprised at its mild tone: "The Japanese Government regrets . . . that it is impossible to reach an agreement through further negotiations."

Stark got it in his office. Marshall was taking his Sunday morning recreational ride at Fort Myer: the message would await his arrival —usually at about 11 A.M. All others concerned got it. Meanwhile two other messages had been intercepted by Magic, and Colonel Rufus Bratton, executive officer in G-2, was so upset by them he tried vainly to get them to the Chief of Staff.

One of the messages ordered the embassy to destroy immediately its one remaining cipher machine plus all codes and secret documents. The other read:

"Will the Ambassador please submit to the United States Government (if possible to the Secretary of State) our reply to the United States at 1 P.M. on the 7th, your time."

It will be remembered that General Marshall did not take kindly to interruptions in his off-duty hours. So, despite the limited area of his ride—an automobile or motorcycle from Fort Myer headquarters could have intercepted him in fifteen minutes at most—not until his return to his quarters at ten-thirty did Marshall learn that an important message was awaiting him. He reached his office in the Munitions Building at about 11:15, to find General Gerow, General Miles, and Colonel Bratton there. Bratton handed him the three intercepted messages—the memorandum, the instructions to destroy codes and papers, and the instruction to deliver the Japanese answer at 1 P.M. precisely. Marshall read quickly but carefully, as was usual with him. Then—

"Something is going to happen at one o'clock," he told the officers. "When they specified a day, that of course had significance, but not comparable to an hour."

He immediately called Stark, who had read all three messages. A warning should be sent at once to all Pacific commanders, Marshall felt. Stark hesitated; he felt all had already been alerted. Marshall stated that in view of the "one o'clock" item he would apprise Army commanders anyway.

Hanging up, he reached for a pencil and drafted his instruction to DeWitt, Western Defense Command; Andrews, Panama Command; Short, Hawaiian Command; and MacArthur, Philippine Command. It took him about three minutes. He read it to the group:

"The Japanese are presenting at 1 P.M. E.S.T. today, what amounts to an ultimatum. Also they are under orders to destroy their code machine immediately. Just what significance the hour set may have, we do not know, but be on alert accordingly."

As he was ordering Bratton to send it out at once, Stark telephoned back. Would Marshall please include in his dispatch the "usual expression to inform the naval officer?" Marshall quickly added the words "Inform naval authorities of this communication." He sent Bratton on his way, instructing him to return as soon as the message had been delivered to the message center.

Bratton was back in five minutes; he had delivered the message personally to the officer in charge of the message center, Colonel French.

Marshall, obviously more perturbed than any of those present had ever before seen him, asked Bratton how much time would be consumed in enciphering and dispatching the message. Bratton didn't know. So back he was rushed to find out.

Marshall, it developed, was pondering whether or not he should telephone a warning—especially to MacArthur. Time was running out; not much more than one hour remained. Marshall had a "scrambler" phone on his desk, which permitted secure long-distance conversations with similar phones in the headquarters of overseas commanders; eavesdroppers would hear only unintelligible gibberish. Marshall, however, must have had some private reservations as to the efficacy of the scrambler mechanism, and apparently feared that the Japanese might have some way of deciphering the conversation. A telephone call which could not be kept secret might precipitate Japanese action; it would almost certainly indicate we had broken their secret code. Would it be worth it?

Bratton reported back that the process would take about thirty minutes.

"Thirty minutes until it is dispatched, or thirty minutes until it is received and decoded at the other end?"

Business of rushing back to the message center again, while the big office clock ticked away. Bratton, charging back, announced that the message, decoded, would be in the hands of the addressees in thirty minutes. It was now precisely noon. In Hawaii it was only 6:30 A.M. Marshall, satisfied, made no further follow-up.

Had he done so he would have found out that Colonel French at the message center was having some troubles. To San Francisco, Panama, and Manila the warning sped without delay. But the War Department radio, so Colonel French was informed, had been out of contact with Hawaii since 10:20 that morning. French decided to use commercial facilities: Western Union to San Francisco, thence commercial radio to Honolulu. This was a normal procedure; usually it would mean but little further delay. French never dreamed of disturbing the Chief of Staff by reporting such trivia. So Marshall's warning was filed at the Army Signal Center at 12:01 P.M. (6:31 A.M. in Hawaii); teletype transmission to San Francisco was completed by 12:17 P.M. (6:47 A.M. in Hawaii), and was in the Honolulu office of RCA at 1:03 P.M. Washington time (7:33 A.M. in Hawaii). Since that was too early for teletype traffic to Fort Shafter, RCA sent it by motorcycle messenger. He would, as it turned out, be delayed through extraordinary circumstances.

Honolulu, Sunday, December 7

Extraordinary circumstances had become almost commonplace on and near Oahu as early as 3:42 A.M. At that hour the mine sweeper *Condor,* conducting a routine sweep of the harbor entrance, sighted a submarine periscope. This was a defensive area where American submarines were prohibited from operating submerged. The *Condor* flashed a report of the sighting to the destroyer *Ward,* of the inshore patrol. For two hours the *Ward* searched the harbor entrance in vain; meanwhile the *Condor* and another mine sweeper had entered the harbor at about 5 A.M.; for some reason the antisubmarine net, opened to permit the entrance of the mine sweepers, was not closed.

At 6:30 the U.S.S. *Antares*—a repair ship towing a steel barge—was approaching the harbor entrance when she sighted a suspicious object, which looked like a midget submarine. The *Antares* immediately notified the *Ward.* At 6:33 a Navy patrol plane sighted the same object and dropped two smoke pots on the spot. The *Ward* hastened to the scene, spotting the sub—her superstructure just above the surface—at 6:40, and promptly opened fire. At the same time the patrol plane dropped bombs or depth charges. The submarine keeled over and began to sink, as the *Ward* dropped more depth charges. Shortly after 6:50 the destroyer sent a coded message that it had attacked a submarine in the defensive sea area.

At about 7:40 Admiral Kimmel received a telephone call from the staff duty officer, reporting the *Ward*-submarine incident. Kimmel replied, "I will be right down." Quickly he completed dressing and left for his headquarters.

Meanwhile, the Army's six mobile radar stations on Oahu had been on the alert since 4 A.M. in compliance with General Short's Alert No. 1 instructions. At 7 A.M. five of these stations ceased operations, in accordance with these same instructions. At the remote Opana station at the northern tip of the island, Privates Joseph Lockard and George Elliott kept their set on while waiting for the truck which was to pick them up to take them to breakfast. Lockard, an experienced radar operator, planned to use this time to give Elliott a bit more instruction. At this moment an unusual formation appeared at the edge of the screen; Lockard checked the machine, found it operating properly, and at 7:02 A.M. concluded that a large number of aircraft, approximately 130 miles distant, was approaching Oahu from the north. For fifteen minutes Lockard and Elliott observed the approach of the

Left: A Zero fighter takes off from one of the Japanese carriers on December 7, 1941. The picture at right was taken from a Japanese plane during the attack. An oil slick spreads from the torpedoed ships in Battleship Row. Smoke rises from bombed installations in the Navy Yard.

formation, debating whether they should report it. Finally, at 7:20, Lockard called the radar information center. The switchboard operator informed him that the center had closed down twenty minutes before, that everyone had left except one Air Corps officer, First Lieutenant Kermet Tyler. Lockard reported the approaching flight to Tyler, who thought for a moment; the flight was undoubtedly either a naval patrol, a formation of Hickam Field bombers, or—most likely—a number of B-17's due from the mainland. "Forget it," he told Lockard.

Twenty minutes later—about 7:50—there was a bustle of activity on the decks of the ninety-four vessels of the Pacific Fleet in Pearl Harbor. It was almost time for morning colors on each vessel, and white-garbed sailors were briskly preparing for the daily flag-raising ceremony. Except for one destroyer, moving slowly toward the entrance, each ship was motionless at its moorings.

At 7:55 boatswains' whistles piped, and the preparatory signal for the colors ceremony was hoisted on each ship. At the same moment a low-flying plane, approaching over the hills to the northeast, swooped low over Ford Island, in the middle of the harbor. A bomb dropped on the seaplane ramp, close by the eight battleships moored next to the island. As the plane zoomed upward, displaying the red sun emblem of Japan, it was followed closely by others. By 9:45 some 260 Japanese planes had flashed that emblem over Oahu, and when the dreadful 110 minutes were over, 2,403 Americans—mostly sailors on the battleships—were dead or dying; 1,178 more had been wounded; the battle force of the Pacific Fleet had been destroyed, with four battleships sunk or capsized and the remaining four damaged, while several smaller vessels were sunk or damaged severely. The Japanese lost twenty-nine planes, five midget submarines, and less than a hundred men.

One small further incident is pertinent to our assessment of United States leadership in high places just before Pearl Harbor.

The Nisei RCA messenger boy carrying General Marshall's message

speedily found himself involved in trouble. Not until 11:45 could he thread his way through traffic jams, road blocks, and general confusion to reach the Fort Shafter signal office, which was itself swamped in traffic by this time.

Not until 2:58 P.M. Hawaiian time—9:58 that evening in bewildered Washington—was the message decoded and placed on Short's desk. He rushed a copy to Admiral Kimmel, who read it, remarked—perhaps unnecessarily—that it was not of the slightest interest any more, and dropped it into the wastebasket.

It had been a pretty long thirty minutes.

Who was responsible?

No disaster of the magnitude of Pearl Harbor could have occurred without the failure—somewhere and somehow—of leadership. A total of eight separate official investigations searched for scapegoats, and found them. The disaster remained a political football long after the last three of these investigations. And much confusion and argument still exist.

Yet through this welter of discord, some facts and conclusions stand out. Today, nearly thirty years later, in another time of crisis, they hold important lessons.

It makes no difference, in assessing responsibility, that exceptional Japanese military skill, shrouded by deceit and assisted by almost incredible luck, accomplished its mission. Nor, indeed, does it matter that—as adjudicated in the always brilliant light of afterthought—Japan might well have inflicted defeat upon our Pacific Fleet and our Army forces in Hawaii regardless of how well alerted they may have been on December 7, 1941.

It makes no difference, so far as responsibility for the disaster itself was concerned, whether the war could have been prevented by wiser statesmanship or more astute diplomacy—though this would have required a wholehearted and unified national determination which did not exist in America in 1941 and the years before. It makes no difference that on December 7 the President and the Secretary of State—like the civilian Secretaries of War and Navy—had their eyes fixed on the Japanese threat in Southeast Asia. They had repeatedly warned the military men that war had probably become unavoidable.

What *does* matter is that the civilian statesmen—however deft or clumsy, shrewd, or shortsighted—performed their difficult tasks of diplomacy and of administration confident that the military men would carry out their professional responsibilities by doing everything humanly possible to prepare for a war so clearly impending. They had every right to expect that—within the limits of scanty means available —the Armed Forces would be ready for any contingency.

The confidence and expectations of civilian leadership and of the nation were tragically dashed that Sunday almost thirty years ago.

Military failures were responsible for Pearl Harbor.

In Washington the most important of these were the following:

1. The War Department staff, over which General Marshall presided, was at the time a complicated but "one-man" shop, where delegation of responsibility was the exception rather than the rule. When Marshall was absent, the operational wheels tended to freeze. This situation was to some extent due to cumbersome organization, to some extent due to the personality of the Chief of Staff.

2. General Marshall, in a letter to General Short on February 7, 1941, stressed that "the risk of sabotage and the *risk involved in a surprise raid by air and submarine* [italics supplied] constitute the real perils of the [Hawaiian] situation." Yet, although definitely warning General Short on November 27 of the threat of war, and ordering him to report the measures he would take in response, Marshall did not check up on those measures; moreover, he was unaware that Short had done no more than to take routine precautions against sabotage. And General Gerow, heading the War Plans Division of General Marshall's General Staff—as he testified later in taking full responsibility for this slip—had not made any provision for following up operational orders. The net result was that both Marshall and Short remained the whole time in blissful ignorance of a vital misinterpretation of orders.

3. Marshall and Admiral Stark—and indeed all members of their staffs who knew the situation—permitted themselves to be hypnotized by the concrete evidence of the aggressive Japanese build-up in Southeast Asia which threatened our Philippines outpost. This theme, it will be remembered, ran as background to nearly all the warnings sent Hawaii. Thus succumbing to the illusory diagnosis of "enemy probable intentions," both top commanders ignored the danger implicit in our inability to locate at least four Japanese carriers.

4. Finally, on December 7, having indicated his full realization of the significance of the "one o'clock" intercept—that less than two hours now separated peace and war—and having decided not to use his "scrambler" telephone, Marshall failed to require surveillance and positive report on the delivery of his final warning.

These certainly were grave lapses in leadership. Yet in fairness, it

Her back broken by bombs and torpedoes, the battleship Arizona *rests on the bottom of the shallow harbor.*

should be noted that the consequences might not have been disastrous if all subordinate commanders had taken adequate security measures on the basis of the instructions, information, and warnings which they had received. To General Marshall's credit one must also chalk up his ability to profit by his mistakes. In less than three months after Pearl Harbor, he completely reorganized the War Department, decentralizing the mass of relatively minor administrative and executive matters that choked major strategical and tactical decisions. His newly created Operations Division of the General Staff—which he aptly termed his "command post"—ensured co-ordinated action and direction of Army activities in theaters of war all around the globe. On Oahu the situation was less ambiguous: military leadership at the top failed utterly.

Almost three decades later, with war clouds still lowering over most of the world, the story of the Pearl Harbor disaster has more significance than mere passing memorials to the brave men who lost their lives that day. If the lessons are heeded, our surviving descendants may never again have to commemorate another "day of infamy."

William Harlan Hale

The Road
to Yalta

The stormy, mercurial course of American relations with Russia over the past fifty years has been shaped primarily by great events such as the communist revolution, the Great Depression, the German invasion of Russia during World War II, and the complex of controversies that have given shape to the Cold War. However, it has also been shaped by the personal relations of individuals—not only of the great leaders (Roosevelt and Stalin; Kennedy and Khrushchev) but of ambassadors, minor diplomats, propagandists, and many others. It is the virtue of this essay by William Harlan Hale that, while paying full attention to the major events and leaders, it delves into the character and behavior of many of these lesser figures who influenced American-Soviet relations and shows how they (their strengths and their foibles) affected the course of history.

Mr. Hale draws upon personal experience as a foreign service officer as well as historical research in this essay, which appeared in American Heritage as part of a series which he edited on "America and Russia." Mr. Hale has also written Horace Greeley: Voice of the People and numerous other books.

On a wintry November day in Washington in 1933, two quite spare, tall American officials of high rank and collected demeanor emerged from under the mansards of the old State Department building to journey to Union Station and there greet a squat, rotund, grinning foreigner who in the eyes of many of their compatriots was a dangerous revolutionary. The moment itself was revolutionary, even in a sartorial sense. Protocol prescribed that when our Secretary of State and his assistants received the visiting foreign minister of another sovereign power, formal morning dress be worn. Yet on this occasion, so Under Secretary William Phillips recorded of the trip across town that he and his chief, Secretary of State Cordell Hull, undertook that day to welcome Soviet Foreign Commissar Maxim Litvinov, "None of us wore top hats because [Litvinov] came as the representative of a government not yet officially recognized by the United States."

The affable Russian, speaking excellent English and himself wearing a snap-brim felt hat, had come here to achieve exactly that recognition, and thus to restore the American-Russian relations that had been broken off in 1918 with the United States' refusal to deal with the atheistic, debt-repudiating, proselytizing new Bolshevik regime of Lenin and Trotsky. The breach had left the world's two potentially greatest powers, after more than a century of mutual cordiality, not speaking to each other for the next fifteen years. Yet now suddenly, it seemed, America's mood had changed. On the very afternoon of his arrival, Litvinov was taken in to see President Franklin D. Roosevelt, also eager to resolve what he called "this anomalous situation." After barely a week of discussions the United States—the one great nation still refusing to accept what Lenin had wrought—agreed to do business with his heir, Joseph Stalin.

In return, the Soviets agreed to mend some ways of theirs that had been particularly offensive to us. They promised to honor at least some of the debts Russia owed America and its citizens, to refrain from fomenting subversive agitation in our midst through their Communist International (or Comintern), and to protect the religious and other civil rights of American nationals in Russia. Ambassadors and a growing wealth of goods would be exchanged, and all or nearly all would now be well between our contrasting fellow republics.

Along this new route to reconciliation, however, traveling conditions were to be as subarctic as northern Russia itself: protracted deep freezes suddenly followed by brief, torrid summer; bright sunshine giving way to violent squalls and sudden darkness. The route, moreover, led over treacherous terrain, with every step along the way a challenge to the most surefooted and imaginative of explorer-diplomats.

Alas! Again, as during America's most demanding previous test —the erupting Russia of the winter of 1917–18—we had painfully few men equal to the task at hand. We had floundered then in Petrograd because we had been amateurish, indecisive, and entangled in cross-purposes. What had we learned during the intervening years about how to comport ourselves when returning to the land of the Great Bear? As in 1917–18, we now proceeded to send to Russia a series of emissaries of sharply contrasting backgrounds, commitments, and beliefs. Moreover, on occasion we again sent several simultaneously, thereby further blurring our "image."

America found itself represented in Moscow first by a millionaire, William C. Bullitt, who had been greatly taken with the Soviets at the outset and ended totally at odds with them; next by a multimillionaire, Joseph E. Davies, who became greatly taken with the Soviets and remained that way for the rest of his days; later by a crusty, retired admiral, William H. Standley, who talked back firmly to the Soviets but also to President Roosevelt, and fell out with both. And these were but a few of the contrasting American visitors to face the Russian monolith.

In the Petrograd of 1917–18 our affairs had become snarled through the presence of proliferating, independent American missions —military, Red Cross, propaganda, etc.—all bypassing our ambassador and feuding with one another. In Moscow, during a second wartime, we were to enlarge upon those precedents by establishing massive lend-lease and military-aid missions also independent of our principal envoy and, moreover, headed by successive chiefs—Generals Philip R. Faymonville and John R. Deane—of wholly diverging viewpoints. The President's personal bright star, Harry L. Hopkins, flew in briefly through the early wartime Moscow sky, as did Averell Harriman, later to return as America's able regular ambassador. Ex-Ambassador Davies oddly reappeared, too, and both a would-be President, Wendell Willkie, and an itinerant Vice President, Henry Wallace, showed up. While we spoke with multiple voices, the Kremlin talked back with one.

Clearly the President was of a divided and changing mind when confronting the heirs of Marx and Lenin. He was not alone. Our whole nation was uncertain how to deal, if deal we must, with this vexing, frightening, secretive colossus. Hence we exported to Moscow during the 1930's and the war years all our own domestic ideological differences about it—every emissary representing his own faiths or fears.

In 1933, though, when the proposal to strike up official relations with the Soviet pariahs received the new President's attention, there was widespread agreement to this much at least: let's give it a try. Times had changed radically since 1918—had been changing, so far as American estimation of Russia was concerned, for quite a number of years. For one thing, the Soviet regime had proved itself stable and responsible (save when it came to that matter of debts); it had emerged far enough from its seclusion to confer with the West at Geneva about disarmament and to ring general alarms about the new menace of militarist Japan. For another, the new, industrializing Russia had become a natural American market—an increasingly desirable and important one as the onset of world-wide depression shriveled every other.

Thus encouraged—and kept up to date on Russian affairs by

*William C. Bullitt in 1918,
when the twenty-eight-year-old
Philadelphian was an attaché
of the American Peace
Commission at Versailles. In
1933 he became America's first
ambassador to Soviet Russia.*

journalists like Walter Duranty, William Henry Chamberlin, and Vincent Sheean—Americans had become increasingly fascinated by what they called the "Soviet experiment," even while preserving varying degrees of distaste for it. No man had been more fascinated all along than the wealthy Philadelphian William C. Bullitt, who in 1919, at twenty-eight, had persuaded President Wilson to send him on an unofficial mission to the Bolsheviks to sound out possible conciliatory sentiments among them. Angered by Wilson's abrupt dismissal of his hopeful report, Bullitt had denounced what he held to be American folly, and subsequently resumed his ardent advocacy of American Soviet *rapprochement*. Intense, articulate, a polished Main Line aristocrat but also a maverick, Bullitt had at once attracted the attention of the incoming President Roosevelt—a man often drawn to such mixtures—with the result that early in 1933 he was sent to Moscow to repeat, in effect, his exploratory mission of 1919. And when this time the response brought Litvinov to Washington with powers to conclude an agreement on very broad terms, it seemed only logical to dispatch the enthusiastic Bullitt to Moscow as America's first ambassador to the Soviet Union.

He arrived there that December, bringing with him as Third Secretary a very young Foreign Service officer named George F. Kennan (soon to be joined by another named Charles E. Bohlen), and established himself across Red Square from the Kremlin in the National Hotel, the grubby capital's cavernous refuge for foreigners. Immediately Bullitt found himself receiving, over and beyond the respect due an envoy, the regime's marks of favor as a special friend. Litvinov staged for him a "tremendous" reception; and Stalin, who "until my arrival had never received any ambassador," summoned Bullitt and assured him that "At any moment, day or night, if you wish to see me you have only to ask and I will see you at once."

Yet the honeymoon begun so deliriously lasted only a very few months. By March, 1934, Bullitt was sending home flustered, disappointed cables about "misunderstandings" on matters ranging from Litvinov's debt agreement (which was not being fulfilled) to Moscow's permission for an American Embassy building to be erected there (which was now being blocked). "Oral promises of members of the Soviet government are not to be taken seriously," the veteran proponent of closer ties sourly concluded. By October, infuriated by the Kremlin's default on still another promise—that of curbing the activities of the Comintern within American borders—Bullitt reached the point of cabling Washington. "I think I might go so far as to intimate to Litvinov verbally that we might sever diplomatic relations if the Comintern should be allowed to get out of hand."

The falling out reflected underlying antagonisms between the two nations which the first genial meetings in Washington and Moscow had covered over, not resolved. It was also America's introduction to a typical Soviet tactic: demanding a foot when given an inch. Having received the accolade of recognition, the Kremlin now wanted speedy American credits and support of its drive for "collective-security" pacts against the rising threats of Nazi Germany, Fascist Italy, and Japan; America, on the other hand, insisted on settlement of at least some of Russia's debts to us before there could be talk of going further (and collective security was something that our still-isolationist republic especially did not wish to pursue). So a new freeze set in between the two capitals—coldest in Moscow as between Bullitt and Litvinov. The Kremlin had erred in assuming that its American friend Bullitt would be all-compliant. Bullitt had erred in assuming that the Russians, whom he had trusted, would live up to their word. Stalin's promised "open door" slammed shut in Bullitt's face (during a whole year, the two conferred only once), and the American who in 1933 had entered Moscow in triumph as its favored guest quit it in 1936 in frustration as one of Soviet Russia's embittered critics.

The Kremlin had learned a lesson too: never again an American liberal, with all the mercurial tendencies of the breed! Far better to have from America a hardheaded, stalwart capitalist—a "class enemy" to be sure, but at least one whose reactions you could predict. So the Soviets were relieved when President Roosevelt chose as his next envoy to them the prominent corporation lawyer Joseph E. Davies, financier, politician, and sharer—through his marriage to Mrs. Marjorie Post Close Hutton, the daughter of C. W. Post of Post Toasties— in an immense fortune. Yet Moscow was due for some surprises at Davies' hand. So was America.

A handsome, gregarious figure of many-sided accomplishment and charm, Davies had early begun moving in leading Democratic circles. He had turned down President Wilson's offer of the ambassadorship to czarist Russia in 1913, but later served Wilson as chairman of the

Federal Trade Commission and as economic adviser at the Versailles peace conference. A close friend and political backer of Franklin D. Roosevelt since Wilsonian days, he was going forth now to Moscow as the President's immediate confidant (with the result, as Secretary of State Hull was to complain, that Davies, like Bullitt before him, frequently communicated with Roosevelt directly, "over my head").

All this was impressive. But what seemed to impress the Soviets most of all was the regal state in which Ambassador and Mrs. Davies commenced their expedition to darkest Moscow. Thirty trunks, fifty smaller pieces of luggage, and six personal servants accompanied them. (" We are going to live in Moscow very quietly, very simply," explained Davies; " 'When in Rome,' you know . . .") Mistrusting Soviet produce, they also took along some two thousand pints of frozen American cream (Birds Eye process, owned by Mrs. Davies' General Foods), together with twenty-five freezers in which to store it. "Contrary to popular belief," said a Soviet spokesman in New York, "there are cows in Russia."

Half a year later, when supplies ran low, Mrs. Davies was to order another two thousand pints, along with *two tons* of frozen meats, fruits, and vegetables from home. Yet Soviet leaders, far from being affronted by this swollen self-indulgence amid Russia's lean times, were fascinated by it. Coming from below, they had tasted enough of power to like to indulge themselves, too—and the most Lucullan table to be seen in Moscow since the revolution now beckoned them. It soon appeared that the master of Spasso House (the stately mansion of a czarist grandee acquired as the American Embassy) was surprisingly hospitable to their minds as well.

The paunchy Litvinov, restored to amiability now that the demanding Bullitt was gone and this expansive capitalist was here, flattered Davies by telling him (as Davies promptly reported to Washington) that "I had acquired more information and knowledge of Russia in the three months I was here than any other ambassador had obtained in two years." He then went on to ask the new ambassador's general impressions. "I told him briefly that I was very much impressed with what they were doing, with the strength of their leadership, the difficulties they were overcoming; that I felt they were presently sincerely devoted to peace . . ." Meanwhile the colorful Mrs. Davies, to the astonishment of the British ambassador ("I have been here seven years and haven't been able to get so much as a toe in their house!"), was invited to lunch at the country *dacha* of Mme. Molotov, the Premier's consort.

It was a new thaw, evidently—passing at once into balmy summer. Then what, amid all this sweetness and light, was a secret, nocturnal Soviet agent doing in the attic of Spasso House? We come to the incident of Second Secretary Kennan and the night the Davies' cream turned sour. It is recounted by Charles W. Thayer, a young Philadelphian who had become the assistant to the gifted, Russian-speaking Kennan-Bohlen team that often had to pull ambassadorial chestnuts out of the fire.

As Thayer tells it in *Bears in the Caviar,* they had discovered that a Soviet spy was in the process of "bugging" Mr. Davies' office with a microphone run down from the attic. After several fruitless nights of vigil up there to try to observe him, they retired to more comfortable quarters below, leaving a net of cross-wire alarms to alert them at his next visit. But when the intruder returned, he got away in the night—after knocking out the entire Spasso House electrical system. Two days later, Ambassador Davies' butler reported to Thayer: "Two of the deep-freezes seem to have failed to get back into action after we reconnected the current."

"What was in them?"

"The frozen cream, and it's passed all saving."

There were indeed several hundred pints of well-publicized Davies cream rotting in the basement, and there was only one way of getting rid of them so as not to damage the Davies prestige. Since all regular Embassy employees were under close Soviet surveillance, the only thing for Thayer to do was to round up some Russian workmen to help him dump a truckload of the stuff in a deserted pine forest.

There were more hazards facing Davies than espionage and sour cream. As Kennan was to point out in a searching memorandum, "The Position of an American Ambassador in Moscow," there was Soviet evasion, double talk, secrecy, dilatoriness, and a tactic of isolating the American envoy and his staff from all but the most superficial contacts with Russians. But greatest of all (though Kennan did not bring this up) was the danger of impressionable and gullible thinking on the part of the envoy himself—and of this, Davies is one of diplomacy's classic exhibits.

In setting out, as he tells us in *Mission to Moscow* (the best-selling memoir that was to be made into one of the most debated movies of the war years), his verbal instructions from the President were to seek to persuade the Soviets to break the debt and trade impasse, meanwhile assuming a posture of "dignified friendliness" qualified by "definite reserve." Reserve, however, flew out the window at his first meeting with Soviet President Kalinin. "A fine type," Davies called him, "a kind, good man." But this was nothing compared to the Ambassador's enthusiasm on meeting Stalin himself: "His brown eye is exceedingly kindly and gentle. A child would like to sit in his lap and a dog would sidle up to him. . . . Throughout [the interview] he joked and laughed at times. He has a sly humor."

Yet there was little to laugh about during Davies' first year in Moscow. For his arrival there coincided with the start of the second and greatest of the series of "purge" trials that bewildered the world and bitterly divided those until then inclined to befriend the "Soviet experiment." A long procession of hitherto high-ranking Communist ministers, intellectuals, ideologues, and generals were quickly tried for counterrevolutionary conspiracy and duly led off to execution. Were the trials a frame-up? Had the accused been tortured in some mysterious fashion, and was this Stalin's Oriental way of disposing of his rivals?

Many observers of the macabre spectacle were torn by doubt, but Davies, watching from one of the best diplomatic seats in the Soviet Supreme Court as the "Old Bolshevik" editor Karl Radek and nearly a score of others went under, seemed untroubled. He wrote home that he accepted at face value Public Prosecutor Andrei Vishinsky's thesis of a dark terrorist plot and blandly concluded after the prisoners had been condemned: "The purge . . . cleansed the country and rid it of treason." This view he also maintained when visiting London. Dining in company with Winston Churchill, Davies was chagrined to find that it did not go down well there, "so violent is the prejudice. . . . I gave the facts as interpreted from the Soviet viewpoint."

An American ambassador handing out in London the "facts" as interpreted by Stalin: What next?

Early in 1938 President Roosevelt realized that his man in Moscow was a liability—for all his popularity there, he still had not achieved that debt settlement—and withdrew him to the safer post of Brussels. Litvinov threw Davies a great farewell dinner, and the amiable visitor left trailing such pronouncements as "I do not think that the world is in any real danger from communism for many years to come," and, later, "It is not [the Soviets'] intent to seek to project communism in the United States."

The Soviet Union was, however, embarking on a course that would once more lead to a freeze in Russo-American relations. For fully three years we would again be barely on speaking terms; for many months on end—particularly those of the Munich crisis, the height of Western humiliation and distress we were to be without an ambassador in Moscow at all.

For while the Soviets had been clamoring for joint opposition to Hitler, Mussolini, the aggressive Japanese, and then Franco, America (like its old European partners, Britain and France) had avoided doing anything effective about it—a fact that had enormously increased Communist prestige among all those aroused to resistance. Roosevelt in the fall of 1937 had tried to reverse America's position by his historic "quarantine-the-aggressors" speech, but when he was unable to prevail, it next became the turn of the Soviets to reverse their own: by the next summer they were threatening to retreat into isolation unless we came out of ours, and by the spring of 1939, in the aftermath of Munich, they did precisely that, furthermore denouncing the Western allies as "warmongers" just when these at last were arming against the general danger.

In August came Russia's second turnabout—alliance with the former enemy, in the pact that helped unleash Hitler's forces and win for Russia a share of Poland. This was followed by Russia's "dreadful rape of Finland," as Roosevelt termed it, which led us to place an embargo on many exports to this latest aggressor, while at home sentiment was rising in favor of aiding embattled France and Britain. In Moscow an appropriately chilly Foreign Service professional, Ambassador Laurence A. Steinhardt, represented us, engaged largely in delivering messages of protest over such incidents as the Soviet detention of the American freighter *City of Flint*.

Then on June 22, 1941, Hitler performed *his* fateful turnabout: he invaded Russia with 175 divisions. Overnight the whole configuration of affairs changed again: the Western "warmongers" of yesterday became in Russia's eyes partners in her "Great Patriotic War," while a hitherto lonely Britain and a defensive America set out to build with Russia the Grand Alliance. In barely a month, the President's personal adviser, Harry L. Hopkins, was on the Moscow scene with an introduction from Roosevelt asking Stalin to treat Hopkins with "the identical confidence you would feel if you were talking directly to me." Cordially welcomed at the Kremlin, he declared to Stalin "the determination of the President and our government to extend all possible aid to the Soviet Union at the earliest possible time."

It was characteristic of Roosevelt under pressure that he conveyed this vital message not through his regular ambassador on the ground or through a visit by Secretary of State Hull (with whom his own relations had become distant) but by a special emissary. Hopkins, for his part, hastened to point out to Stalin that his mission was "not a diplomatic one" in the usual sense. In title, Hopkins was Roosevelt's administrator of lend lease. In fact, he was his Colonel House and closest friend; and the skill of this extraordinary expediter, sensitive yet durable, often ill and nerve-racked yet searching and thorough, was never greater than during the crucial sessions—lasting only two days—in which he won the inscrutable Stalin's confidence, gained from him a complete picture of Soviet military strengths and weaknesses, placed Soviet-American relations upon an entirely new footing, and did all this so circumspectly as to draw from the sidetracked Hull and Steinhardt no audible murmur of criticism. As Hopkins' biographer, Robert E. Sherwood, remarks: "This was indeed the turning point in the wartime relations of Britain and the United States with the Soviet Union."

It also marked a point from which there was to be no turning back. Stalin, whose armies were reeling under German impact across the Ukraine toward Moscow, needed immediately great supplies of guns and aircraft metal. Many expert Western observers on and around the scene were pessimistic; why, asked Major Ivan Yeaton, the American military attaché at Moscow, lend aid to a doomed cause? Yet when Hopkins reported to Roosevelt, "I feel ever so confident about this front . . . There is unbounded determination to win," his word tilted the scales. Within a few days, at their seaborne conference in Newfoundland's Argentia Bay at which the Atlantic Charter was framed, Roosevelt and Churchill determined to rush all possible equipment to Stalin even at some risk to their own arsenals, and to send at once a joint supply mission to explore his needs. This was the occasion that brought Averell Harriman for the first time to Moscow, along with England's Lord Beaverbrook. Two weeks after they arrived, German spearheads had pushed to within thirty miles of the capital, government offices were being evacuated to Kuibyshev

In September of 1941 Roosevelt sent Harry Hopkins as his special emissary to Stalin.

in the rear, and Major Yeaton was reporting that the end of Russian resistance might not be far away.

Yet while Americans were concentrating on first things first—to help Russia stave off defeat—Stalin was already thinking far ahead to the shape that Europe should take after the victory. Here was the great misstep on our road to Yalta: not only did Western leaders seem to fail to realize how large the Soviets might loom in the event of victory, but they refused to discuss the future with Stalin at a time advantageous to themselves, when he was so hard-pressed and weak. Thus it happened that soon after Pearl Harbor, Roosevelt, though aware of Soviet territorial demands in Poland and the Baltic area, specifically asked Stalin to omit such questions from the treaty of alliance then being negotiated. The absence of territorial discussion now left the new alliance a one-way street—we were giving the Russians more and more aid against Hitler's onslaught, without pressing them to surrender some of their aspirations in return.

How much aid—and when? How soon are you going to open a "second front" to relieve us? When are you going to recognize our just claims in eastern Europe? These were the constant calls from Moscow, and each brought new East-West collisions. Only a few months after Hopkins' warm reception at the Kremlin, the visiting Harriman was given a brusque one: Stalin showed impatience at the slowness of Western aid and warmed only when Harriman promised him five thousand jeeps. The President, aware how tough a customer we were dealing with, now thought we had better send him as resident ambassador a markedly tough personality of our own, and so Stalin got a battleship admiral.

The President had a particular fondness for the Navy and its proven leaders—and William H. Standley had served him outstandingly as Chief of Naval Operations. A square-jawed, sharp-spoken quarter-deck disciplinarian with forty-five years in the service, Standley had no experience of Russia except for a brief ceremonial visit to Vladivostok in 1896 as a midshipman. But upon retirement he had become one of Roosevelt's staunchest supporters in the long domestic battle for aid to the Allies before Pearl Harbor; such a man might serve with insight and muscle.

His first reaction to Stalin differed noticeably from that of Davies. Standley found the Soviet dictator "a cocky, healthy-looking individual, with swarthy complexion and an Oriental cast of countenance . . ." A man of stalwart build himself, Standley carried chips on both broad shoulders: he was easily offended when Stalin kept him waiting or when Washington failed to brief him fully or when visiting firemen from home intruded. He wanted to run his Embassy as a "taut ship" in perilous waters with himself in sole command—a logical aspiration, but quixotic in view of the Rooseveltian way of conducting wartime affairs abroad. Messages passed directly between Roosevelt and Stalin, "leapfrogging over my tophatted head," Standley complained; summit conferences were arranged and second-front commitments entered into without his being the wiser; and Hopkins' and Harriman's lend-lease man on the spot, Colonel (later Brigadier General) Faymonville, pursued his own quite independent course. The old admiral finally exploded when two further visiting emissaries, Wendell Willkie and the familiar Joe Davies, arrived on the scene with powers to go over his head to the Kremlin.

Willkie, the President's 1940 electoral opponent who had subsequently been enlisted into the bipartisan war effort, touched down in Moscow during his globe-girdling "One World" tour in the fall of 1942. He delivered himself of statements declaring America's unqualified friendship for Soviet Russia, and after closeting himself alone with Stalin went so far as to remark to Standley that some of the things he had learned there were too secret for even the ambassador to know. As if this were not galling enough, Willkie made a point of telling the world that Soviet Russia had been misrepresented in the United States and that he wished to "put over a more favorable picture" of it. "Many among the democracies fear and mistrust Soviet Russia . . ." he wrote. "Such fear is weakness . . ." He issued in Moscow a call, echoing Stalin's, for the early opening of a second front.

"Mr. Willkie, I have been very patient," Standley finally exploded. "Now I feel it my duty to remind you that there is only one United States representative in the Soviet Union, and I, the American Ambassador, am that representative."

But Standley's patience was to be tried even more by the brief return engagement of Davies, who arrived the following spring on a 10,000-mile round trip from Washington—in a special plane, with a crew of nine plus his personal staff and physician—simply to deliver a letter from Roosevelt to Stalin proposing a top-level meeting. It was a message that conceivably could have been delivered to the Kremlin by Standley himself from his office four blocks away. Welcomed at the airport by Soviet dignitaries as a returning hero, Davies insisted on delivering his letter alone. He had also brought along an advance print of the Warner Brothers movie made from his *Mission to Moscow* (Stalin was flatteringly portrayed by Manart Kippen, Davies by Walter Huston), which he prevailed upon the dictator to show after dinner in the Kremlin projection room. Stalin was visibly bored by it, and diplomatic guests went up in arms over its obvious distortions of the history of the purge trials and acceptance of the Soviet line on them. Next, Davies met the American press corps, and on hearing its complaints that the Soviets were failing to show appreciation for American aid, tongue-lashed the correspondents and accused them of "non-co-operation." "His lack of knowledge regarding Russia," wrote Quentin Reynolds, "shocked us all."

The reason behind the Willkie-Davies visits was that the President had lost confidence in his newest ambassador, while Standley had taken to grumbling about the President. Standley felt himself alone in a hostile environment and at odds with Washington, which he felt was playing the game on Stalin's terms. Our policy, he snorted, was only "Do not antagonize the Russians, give them everything they want, for, after all, they are killing Germans . . ."

Increasingly suspicious, Standley fell out particularly with General Faymonville, the gifted, Russian-speaking Regular Army officer who was managing lend-lease from an office down the corridor, and whose predictions as to the staying power of the Red Army when others had given up hope in it had been amply borne out. Feeling that Faymonville was working too closely and enthusiastically with the Russians, Standley made direct representations to Roosevelt and Hopkins that the general be placed under Standley's orders. He got him reduced in size and then banished—though at the cost of any remaining White House good will toward himself.*

Standley had the ill fortune to represent us in Moscow during our hardest times there. During 1942 and most of 1943 the promised American aid never lived up to expectations, due first to enormous convoy losses and then to our own build-up for the second front that Stalin had demanded. But the Soviet chieftain kept upbraiding us

---

*A personal recollection: While at the Office of War Information in 1942, in charge of broadcasts to Germany, I was assigned by Robert E. Sherwood to go to Moscow on a mission arising from an offer made by Foreign Minister Vishinsky—that of my speaking nightly from there to eastern-front Germans in the name of the Voice of America. At that time, when American troops had not yet come to grips with Germans, it seemed a promising idea to convey in this fashion the message of Allied unity, and Vishinsky had promised that, apart from sheer military censorship, what I said over the Moscow radio would be subjected to no surveillance whatsoever. After I had waited several months with packed suitcases for travel orders, though, the mission was finally vetoed by Ambassador Standley on the ground that this, too, might lead to too-close collaboration with the Russians.

for our delays in respect to both. When Allied armies streaked across Sicily and landed on the Italian mainland, though, the Bear warmed once more; and when in October, 1943, Standley having been retired to the shades, Secretary Hull arrived in Moscow for a four-power foreign ministers' conference accompanied by a new ambassador (Harriman) and a new military-aid chief (General Deane), Stalin was genial. With enormous forces now building up for OVERLORD (the Anglo-American descent upon Normandy) and supplies flowing to Russia over several seas, broad pledges of mutual aid and confidence were exchanged. Harriman was particularly elated when, in a daring mood, he proposed a toast at the Kremlin to the day "when we would be fighting together against the Japs," and Molotov suddenly responded: "Why not—gladly—*the time will come.*"

Yet Harriman was not so elated as to lose perspective. A shrewd observer and Presidential trouble shooter, he had known all the ups and downs of American-Soviet relations, and the reassuring atmosphere of the Moscow foreign ministers' conference had not concealed from him its lack of real achievement.

Now the final stage of the road led via Teheran and Moscow to Yalta—conferences marked by increasing inter-Allied warmth as the outlines of military victory became clearer, although the ultimate political consequences remained hidden in the veil. It was as if the civil plenipotentiaries, having failed to lay a basis of searching diplomacy with each other at the start, had come to feel that the soldiers would resolve their problems for them by providing a smashing triumph that would leave everyone happy—if exhausted. Stalin was enormously impressed by the prospects of OVERLORD. Churchill was equally impressed by the avenging progress of the Red armies and supported Stalin's claim for territory to protect Russia from future German invasions, even though this meant shifting Poland several hundred miles westward. Roosevelt, though he said he wanted no part of the

In 1943 Americans cheered the wartime alliance of Roosevelt, Stalin, and Churchill. This cartoon from the Arizona Republic *questioned Stalin's intentions.*

Polish wrangle—not until after the 1944 elections, in any case—was inclined to support the Anglo-Soviet understanding reached on this point during the summit meeting at Teheran at the end of 1943.

Harriman, though a devoted admirer of Roosevelt and a believer in mobility in dealing with the Soviets, was not quite so sure. Shouldn't we, he asked, try to awaken them to the fact that we expected them to give as well as receive? In this he was supported by his top military-aid man, General Deane, a newcomer constituted very differently from his predecessor, General Faymonville. Deane demanded detailed information from the Soviets as to just what they were doing with supplies, even as Harriman kept requiring of them more specific knowledge of their political plans as Hitler's legions fell back. But then came the great convergence of Anglo-American armies upon Germany, (simultaneously with the Soviet armies' even greater one); the knowledge that the Soviets would join our hard-won march against Japan; and a profound feeling that amid so many mutual sacrifices made and joint victories won, the problems remaining between us—the fate of eastern Europe, the control of Germany, the level of reparations, the structure of the Balkans, the ratio of representation in the new United Nations—could be amicably resolved.

This was the immense agenda that faced the Big Three chiefs of government when they met at Yalta in the Crimea in February, 1945, for a week of breathless negotiating and climactic banqueting that would give new shape to the world. Time was short at Yalta—too short; the chieftains had to hurry home to direct the closing scenes of the military drama in Europe and stage its last act in Asia. Moreover, Roosevelt and Hopkins were both ailing; the new Secretary of State who accompanied them, Edward R. Stettinius, was inexperienced; and our standing representation in Russia itself had been so assorted and at times discredited that the President found himself with little in the way of a concerted body of first-hand experience there on which to draw. In our massive delegation at the Livadia Palace, the effective "Russian experts" were just two—the overburdened Harriman and young "Chip" Bohlen, serving as interpreter.

Many settlements, or what passed for settlements, were reached. The westward shift of Poland was confirmed; pledges as to the self-determination of liberated peoples were renewed; the Soviet Union, about to enter the war against Japan, was recognized as a major power in the Pacific, with legitimate aspirations there. The Soviets, in turn, recognized America's particular interest in succoring the regime of Chiang Kai-shek, gave ground on some points concerning joint occupation of Germany, and seemed willing to forego crushing reparations if it could obtain American reconstruction aid. The debate over seating at the United Nations also resulted in what both sides then regarded a fair draw; and such was Yalta's resulting mood that Prime Minister Churchill spoke in exalted terms of "the glories of future possibilities . . . before us," while Harry Hopkins reported a deep sense of accomplishment there. "We really believed in our hearts," Hopkins said, "that this was the dawn of the new day we had all been praying

The diplomats behind the Big Three at Yalta are (from left) Britain's Eden, America's Stettinius, Russia's Molotov, and (far right) Averell Harriman.

for . . . We were absolutely certain that we had won the first great victory of the peace.''

Perhaps, then, all—or almost all—would be well at last. Yet it was not to be so; and bitter blame has been heaped upon the Yalta Conference, as if it were the author of all our woes with Russia since. Yet perhaps it was culpable not so much for what it did as for what it did not do. Yalta left more matters unresolved than settled. In its headlong haste to catch up with the facts of military success, it was a political convocation that came too late. Moreover, it was one to which the warring partners came as unequals in the sense that they harbored very different political intentions, clothe them as they might. All spoke of liberation, but to the Soviets this meant also annexation of the liberated. On the other hand, the Western allies had no ulterior territorial motives: true, the British were willing to bargain with the Russians over spheres of influence so as to preserve their own, but the United States had no thought—and, it was agreed by all sides at home, no need—of aggrandizement at all.

America's position all along had been to avoid making postwar commitments until the war itself was nearly won. As late as October, 1944, Roosevelt had cabled Harriman (then sitting in on the Churchill-Stalin meetings at Moscow that prefaced Yalta), ''It is important that I retain complete freedom of action after this conference is over.'' Yet the area of such freedom was narrowing fast as Red armies swarmed over southeastern and central Europe, pushing borders westward on their own. The most that could now be done about displaced Poland was an ambiguous formula calling for ''reorganization'' of the provisional Warsaw regime—by which the West meant a new government based on democratic elections, while Moscow meant one firmly attached to itself. The West asked for free ballot boxes all over eastern Europe; Moscow promised, but at the same time began converting once-free nations into satellites.

The ailing President, returning homeward across calm seas aboard the U.S.S. *Quincy* in the trust that Yalta's promise of freedom and equity would be fulfilled, was not to be spared disillusionment in the few weeks of life remaining to him. A mere fortnight later, Ambassador Harriman in Moscow was protesting sharply against Soviet moves to make defeated Rumania a captive state, and the West flatly refused to recognize the puppet regime set up there. More trouble was in store for our ambassador when an inter-Allied commission began to work out Yalta's indecisive plan for Poland. On April 2, after wrangling sessions in which Molotov had become more and more intransigent, Harriman reported flatly, "No agreement was reached on any point." Stalin himself, on the wire to Roosevelt, concurred. Harriman, for his part, was now reaching the point of recommending to Washington that further aid to Russia be suspended until Moscow ceased violating Yalta agreements. Then Stalin, suspicious because he had not been made party to the parleys between surrendering German commanders and advancing Anglo-American troops in Italy, cabled Roosevelt to charge deception and trickery. Roosevelt, aroused to the core, expressed "bitter resentment" at such "vile misrepresentations of my actions or those of my trusted subordinates." This and Stalin's reply were the last communications that passed between the two most powerful leaders of what had briefly been a common cause.

So the bright day dimmed even when the sun seemed to stand high. Roosevelt died, and Harriman in Moscow was alone in the gathering darkness. Once again, the modern world's two titans, so different in their ways and make-up, so subject to alternating currents of mutual attraction and repulsion, drew apart. We had been by turns cordial friends over great distances (never more so than during our own Revolution and the Napoleonic wars), far-removed yet mutually amenable expansionists through the later nineteenth century, uneasy allies in two world wars, and profound ideological antagonists in the aftermath of each. Yet we had never, despite all our differences, become declared enemies on the battlefield; in fact, we were the only two great powers to have preserved peace—or what passed for it—with one another during all this long span of modern time. We did not speak one another's language; perhaps in the deepest sense we never quite would. Yet some recognition of the madness of ever making war upon one another in the name of our two immense and kindred humanities on opposite sides of the globe seemed to have been borne in upon us both. Will the time now come when, if nuclear war is unimaginable and the sheer absence of war not enough, we may proceed with firmer skill to the building of peace?

Part
Ten

MODERN
AMERICA

John Kenneth Galbraith

The Causes
of the
Great Crash

The following essay is an example of analytical history at its best. Without relying on narrative techniques, the Harvard economist John Kenneth Galbraith takes apart the economy of the 1920's and shows us how its weaknesses led to the Great Depression of the 1930's. In the course of doing so, he also "takes apart," in the colloquial sense of that expression, the Presidents of the 1920's and a number of their leading advisers.

The effectiveness and power of the essay depend upon a number of factors. One is Galbraith's mastery both of the facts he deals with and of the economic mechanisms of the society; he discusses few events that are not thoroughly familiar to students of the subject, but he has an unfailing eye for what is significant. Another is his gift for anecdote and the pithy phrase. As he says, the epigram that Elbert H. Gary of U. S. Steel "never saw a blast furnace until his death" is well known; but not everyone who writes about Gary knows enough to use it. Still a third is Galbraith's ability to state his own opinions without qualification and at the same time without passion, to make the kind of calm, reasoned judgments that are characteristic of a convinced but unprejudiced and intelligent mind. All these qualities explain why his books, such as American Capitalism, The Affluent Society, *and* The Great Crash, 1929 *(a fuller treatment of the subject of this essay), have been both popular and critical successes.*

The decade of the twenties, or more exactly the eight years between the postwar depression of 1920–21 and the sudden collapse of the stock market in October, 1929, were prosperous ones in the United States. The total output of the economy increased by more than 50 per cent. The preceding decades had brought the automobile; now came many more and also roads on which they could be driven with reasonable reliability and comfort. There was much building. The downtown section of the mid-continent city—Des Moines, Omaha, Minneapolis—dates from these years. It was then, more likely than not, that what is still the leading hotel, the tallest office building, and the biggest department store went up. Radio arrived, as of course did gin and jazz.

These years were also remarkable in another respect, for as time passed it became increasingly evident that the prosperity could not last. Contained within it were the seeds of its own destruction. The country was heading into the gravest kind of trouble. Herein lies the peculiar fascination of the period for a study in the problem of leadership. For almost no steps were taken during these years to arrest the tendencies which were obviously leading, and did lead, to disaster.

At least four things were seriously wrong, and they worsened as the decade passed. And knowledge of them does not depend on the always brilliant assistance of hindsight. At least three of these flaws were highly visible and widely discussed. In ascending order, not of importance but of visibility, they were as follows:

First, income in these prosperous years was being distributed with marked inequality. Although output per worker rose steadily during the period, wages were fairly stable, as also were prices. As a result, business profits increased rapidly and so did incomes of the wealthy and the well-to-do. This tendency was nurtured by assiduous and successful efforts of Secretary of the Treasury Andrew W. Mellon to reduce income taxes with special attention to the higher brackets. In 1929 the 5 per cent of the people with the highest incomes received perhaps a quarter of all personal income. Between 1919 and 1929 the share of the one per cent who received the highest incomes increased by approximately one seventh. This meant that the economy was heavily and increasingly dependent on the luxury consumption of the well-to-do and on their willingness to reinvest what they did not or could not spend on themselves. Anything that shocked the confidence of the rich either in their personal or in their business future would have a bad effect on total spending and hence on the behavior of the economy.

This was the least visible flaw. To be sure, farmers, who were not participating in the general advance, were making themselves heard; and twice during the period the Congress passed far-reaching relief legislation which was vetoed by Coolidge. But other groups were much less vocal. Income distribution in the United States had long been unequal. The inequality of these years did not seem exceptional. The trade-union movement was also far from strong. In the early twenties the steel industry was still working a twelve-hour day and, in some jobs, a seven-day week. (Every two weeks when the shift changed a man worked twice around the clock.) Workers lacked the organization or the power to deal with conditions like this; the twelve-hour day was, in fact, ended as the result of personal pressure by President Harding on the steel companies, particularly on Judge Elbert H. Gary, head of the United States Steel Corporation. Judge Gary's personal acquaintance with these working conditions was thought to be slight, and this gave rise to Benjamin Stolberg's now classic observation that the Judge "never saw a blast furnace until his death." In all these circumstances the increasingly lopsided income distribution did not excite much comment or alarm. Perhaps it would have been surprising if it had.

But the other three flaws in the economy were far less subtle. During World War I the United States ceased to be the world's greatest debtor country and became its greatest creditor. The consequences of this change have so often been described that they have the standing of a cliché. A debtor country could export a greater value of goods than it imported and use the difference for interest and debt repayment. This was what we did before the war. But a creditor must import a greater value than it exports if those who owe it money are to have the wherewithal to pay interest and principal. Otherwise the creditor must either forgive the debts or make new loans to pay off the old.

During the twenties the balance was maintained by making new foreign loans. Their promotion was profitable to domestic investment houses. And when the supply of honest and competent foreign borrowers ran out, dishonest, incompetent, or fanciful borrowers were invited to borrow and, on occasion, bribed to do so. In 1927 Juan Leguia, the son of the then dictator of Peru, was paid $450,000 by the National City Company and J. & W. Seligman for his services in promoting a $50,000,000 loan to Peru which these houses marketed. Americans lost and the Peruvians didn't gain appreciably. Other Latin American republics got equally dubious loans by equally dubious devices. And, for reasons that now tax the imagination, so did a large number of German cities and municipalities. Obviously, once investors awoke to the character of these loans or there was any other shock to confidence, they would no longer be made. There would be nothing with which to pay the old loans. Given this arithmetic, there would be either a sharp reduction in exports or a wholesale default on the outstanding loans, or more likely both. Wheat and cotton farmers and others who depended on exports would suffer. So would those who owned the bonds. The buying power of both would be reduced. These consequences were freely predicted at the time.

The second weakness of the economy was the large-scale corporate thimblerigging that was going on. This took a variety of forms, of which by far the most common was the organization of corporations to hold stock in yet other corporations, which in turn held stock in yet other corporations. In the case of the railroads and the utilities, the purpose of this pyramid of holding companies was to obtain control of a very large number of operating companies with a very small investment in the ultimate holding company. A $100,000,000 electric utility, of which the capitalization was represented half by bonds and half by common stock, could be controlled with an investment of a little over $25,000,000—the value of just over half the common stock. Were a company then formed with the same capital structure to hold *this* $25,000,000 worth of common stock, it could be controlled with an investment of $6,250,000. On the next round the amount required would be less than $2,000,000. That $2,000,000 would still control the entire $100,000,000 edifice. By the end of the twenties, holding-company structures six or eight tiers high were a commonplace. Some of them—the utility pyramids of Insull and Associated Gas & Electric, and the railroad pyramid of the Van Sweringens—were marvelously complex. It is unlikely that anyone fully understood them or could.

In other cases companies were organized to hold securities in other companies in order to manufacture more securities to sell to the public. This was true of the great investment trusts. During 1929 one investment house, Goldman, Sachs & Company, organized and sold nearly a billion dollars' worth of securities in three interconnected investment trusts—Goldman Sachs Trading Corporation; Shenandoah Corporation; and Blue Ridge Corporation. All eventually depreciated virtually to nothing.

This corporate insanity was also highly visible. So was the damage. The pyramids would last only so long as earnings of the company at the bottom were secure. If anything happened to the dividends of the underlying company, there would be trouble, for upstream companies had issued bonds (or in practice sometimes preferred stock) against the dividends on the stock of the downstream companies. Once the earnings stopped, the bonds would go into default or the preferred stock would take over and the pyramid would collapse. Such a collapse would have a bad effect not only on the orderly prosecution of business and investment by the operating companies but also on confidence, investment, and spending by the community at large. The likelihood was increased because in any number of cities—Cleveland, Detroit, and Chicago were notable examples—the banks were deeply committed to these pyramids or had fallen under the control of the pyramiders.

Finally, and most evident of all, there was the stock market boom. Month after month and year after year the great bull market of the twenties roared on. Sometimes there were setbacks, but more often there were fantastic forward surges. In May of 1924 the New York *Times* industrials stood at 106; by the end of the year they were 134; by the end of 1925 they were up to 181. In 1927 the advance began in earnest—to 245 by the end of that year and on to 331 by the end of 1928. There were some setbacks in early 1929, but then came the fantastic summer explosion when in a matter of three months the averages went up another 110 points. This was the most frantic summer in our financial history. By its end, stock prices had nearly quadrupled as compared with four years earlier. Transactions on the New York Stock Exchange regularly ran to 5,000,000 or more shares a day. Radio Corporation of America went to 573¾ (adjusted) without ever having paid a dividend. Only the hopelessly eccentric, so it seemed, held securities for their income. What counted was the increase in capital values.

And since capital gains were what counted, one could vastly increase his opportunities by extending his holdings with borrowed funds—by buying on margin. Margin accounts expanded enormously, and from all over the country—indeed from all over the world—money poured into New York to finance these transactions. During the summer, brokers' loans increased at the rate of $400,000,000 a month. By September they totaled more than $7,000,000,000. The rate of interest on these loans varied from 7 to 12 per cent and went as high as 15.

This boom was also inherently self-liquidating. It could last only so long as new people, or at least new money, were swarming into the market in pursuit of the capital gains. This new demand bid up the stocks and made the capital gains. Once the supply of new customers began to falter, the market would cease to rise. Once the market stopped rising, some, and perhaps a good many, would start to cash in. If you are concerned with capital gains, you must get them while the getting is good. But the getting may start the market down, and this will one day be the signal for much more selling—both by those who are trying to get out and those who are being forced to sell securities that are no longer safely margined. Thus it was certain that the market would one day go down, and far more rapidly than it went up. Down it went with a thunderous crash in October of 1929. In a series of terrible days, of which Thursday, October 24, and Tuesday, October 29, were the most terrifying, billions in values were lost, and thousands of speculators—they had been called investors—were utterly and totally ruined.

This too had far-reaching effects. Economists have always deprecated the tendency to attribute too much to the great stock market collapse of 1929: this was the drama; the causes of the subsequent depression really lay deeper. In fact, the stock market crash was very important. It exposed the other weakness of the economy. The overseas loans on which the payments balance depended came to an end. The jerry-built holding-company structures came tumbling down. The investment-trust stocks collapsed. The crash put a marked crimp on borrowing for investment and therewith on business spending. It also removed from the economy some billions of consumer spending that was either based on, sanctioned by, or encouraged by the fact that the spenders had stock market gains. The crash was an intensely damaging thing.

And this damage, too, was not only foreseeable but foreseen. For months the speculative frenzy had all but dominated American life. Many times before in history—the South Sea Bubble, John

Cartoonist Forbell titled this 1929 drawing
"Club Life in America—The Stock Brokers."

Law's speculations, the recurrent real-estate booms of the last century, the great Florida land boom earlier in the same decade—there had been similar frenzy. And the end had always come, not with a whimper but a bang. Many men, including in 1929 the President of the United States, knew it would again be so.

The increasingly perilous trade balance, the corporate buccaneering, and the Wall Street boom—along with the less visible tendencies in income distribution—were all allowed to proceed to the ultimate disaster without effective hindrance. How much blame attaches to the men who occupied the presidency?

Warren G. Harding died on August 2, 1923. This, as only death can do, exonerates him. The disorders that led eventually to such trouble had only started when the fatal blood clot destroyed this now sad and deeply disillusioned man. Some would argue that his legacy was bad. Harding had but a vague perception of the economic processes over which he presided. He died owing his broker $180,000 in a blind account—he had been speculating disastrously while he was President, and no one so inclined would have been a good bet to curb the coming boom. Two of Harding's Cabinet officers, his secretary of the interior and his attorney general, were to plead the Fifth Amendment when faced with questions concerning their official acts, and the first of these went to jail. Harding brought his fellow townsman Daniel R. Crissinger to be his comptroller of the currency, although he was qualified for this task, as Samuel Hopkins Adams has suggested, only by the fact that he and the young Harding had stolen watermelons together. When Crissinger had had an ample opportunity to demonstrate his incompetence in his first post, he was made head of the Federal Reserve System. Here he had the central responsibility for action on the ensuing boom. Jack Dempsey, Paul Whiteman, or F. Scott Fitzgerald would have been at least equally qualified.

Yet it remains that Harding was dead before the real trouble started. And while he left in office some very poor men, he also left some very competent ones. Charles Evans Hughes, his secretary of state; Herbert Hoover, his secretary of commerce; and Henry C. Wallace, his secretary of agriculture, were public servants of vigor and judgment.

The problem of Herbert Hoover's responsibility is more complicated. He became President on March 4, 1929. At first glance this seems far too late for effective action. By then the damage had been done, and while the crash might come a little sooner or a little later, it was now inevitable. Yet Hoover's involvement was deeper than this—and certainly much deeper than Harding's. This he tacitly concedes in his memoirs, for he is at great pains to explain and, in some degree, to excuse himself.

For one thing, Hoover was no newcomer to Washington. He had been secretary of commerce under Harding and Coolidge. He had also been the strongest figure (not entirely excluding the President) in both Administration and party for almost eight years. He had a clear view of what was going on. As early as 1922, in a letter to Hughes, he expressed grave concern over the quality of the foreign loans that were being floated in New York. He returned several times to the subject. He knew about the corporate excesses. In the latter twenties he wrote to his colleagues and fellow officials (including Crissinger) expressing his grave concern over the Wall Street orgy. Yet he was content to express himself—to write letters and memoranda, or at most, as in the case of the foreign loans, to make an occasional speech. He could with propriety have presented his views of the stock market more strongly to the Congress and the public. He could also have maintained a more vigorous and persistent agitation within the Administration. He did neither. His views of the market were so little known that it celebrated his election and inauguration with a great upsurge. Hoover was in the boat and, as he himself tells, he knew where it was headed. But, having warned the man at the tiller, he rode along into the reef.

And even though trouble was inevitable, by March, 1929, a truly committed leader would still have wanted to do something. Nothing else was so important. The resources of the Executive, one might expect, would have been mobilized in a search for some formula to mitigate the current frenzy and to temper the coming crash. The assistance of the bankers, congressional leaders, and the Exchange authorities would have been sought. Nothing of the sort was done. As secretary of commerce, as he subsequently explained, he had thought himself frustrated by Mellon. But he continued Mellon in office. Henry M. Robinson, a sympathetic Los Angeles banker, was commissioned to go to New York to see his colleagues there and report. He returned to say that the New York bankers regarded things as sound. Richard Whitney, the vice-president of the Stock Exchange, was summoned to the White House for a conference on how to curb speculation. Nothing came of this either. Whitney also thought things were sound.

Both Mr. Hoover and his official biographers carefully explained that the primary responsibility for the goings on in New York City rested not with Washington but with the governor of New York State. That was Franklin D. Roosevelt. It was he who failed to rise to his responsibilities. The explanation is far too formal. The future of the whole country was involved. Mr. Hoover was the President of the whole country. If he lacked authority commensurate with this responsibility, he could have requested it. This, at a later date, President Roosevelt did not hesitate to do.

Finally, while by March of 1929 the stock market collapse was inevitable, something could still be done about the other accumulating disorders. The balance of payments is an obvious case. In 1931 Mr. Hoover did request a one-year moratorium on the inter-Allied (war) debts. This was a courageous and constructive step which came directly to grips with the problem. But the year before, Mr. Hoover, though not without reluctance, had signed the Hawley-Smoot tariff. "I shall approve the Tariff Bill. . . . It was undertaken as the result of pledges given by the Republican Party at Kansas City. . . . Platform promises must not be empty gestures." Hundreds of people— from Albert H. Wiggin, the head of the Chase National Bank, to Oswald Garrison Villard, the editor of the *Nation*—felt that no step could have been more directly designed to make things worse. Countries would have even more trouble earning the dollars of which they were so desperately short. But Mr. Hoover signed the bill.

Anyone familiar with this particular race of men knows that a dour, flinty, inscrutable visage such as that of Calvin Coolidge can be the mask for a calm and acutely perceptive intellect. And he knows equally that it can conceal a mind of singular aridity. The difficulty, given the inscrutability, is in knowing which. However, in the case of Coolidge the evidence is in favor of the second. In some sense, he certainly knew what was going on. He would not have been unaware of what was called the Coolidge market. But he connected developments neither with the well-being of the country nor with his own responsibilities. In his memoirs Hoover goes to great lengths to show how closely he was in touch with events and how clearly he foresaw their consequences. In his *Autobiography*, a notably barren document, Coolidge did not refer to the accumulating troubles. He confines himself to such unequivocal truths as "Every day of Presidential life is crowded with activities" (which in his case, indeed, was not true); and "The Congress makes the laws, but it is the President who causes them to be executed."

At various times during his years in office, men called on Coolidge to warn him of the impending trouble. And in 1927, at the instigation of a former White House aide, he sent for William Z. Ripley of Harvard, the most articulate critic of the corporate machinations of the period. The President became so interested that he invited him to stay for lunch, and listened carefully while his guest outlined (as Ripley later related) the "prestidigitation, double-shuffling, honey-fugling, hornswoggling, and skulduggery" that characterized the current Wall Street scene. But Ripley made the mistake of telling Coolidge that regulation was the responsibility of the states (as was then the case). At this intelligence Coolidge's face lit up and he dismissed the entire matter from his mind. Others who warned of the impending disaster got even less far.

And on some occasions Coolidge added fuel to the fire. If the market seemed to be faltering, a timely statement from the White House—or possibly from Secretary Mellon—would often brace it up. William Allen White, by no means an unfriendly observer, noted that after one such comment the market staged a 26-point rise. He went on to say that a careful search "during these halcyon years . . . discloses this fact: Whenever the stock market showed signs of weakness, the President or the Secretary of the Treasury or some important dignitary of the administration . . . issued a statement. The statement invariably declared that business was 'fundamentally sound,' that continued prosperity had arrived, and that the slump of the moment was 'seasonal.' "

Such was the Coolidge role. Coolidge was fond of observing that "if you see ten troubles coming down the road, you can be sure that nine will run into the ditch before they reach you and you have to battle with only one of them." A critic noted that "the trouble with this philosophy was that when the tenth trouble reached him he was wholly unprepared. . . . The outstanding instance was the rising boom and orgy of mad speculation which began in 1927." The critic was Herbert Hoover.

Plainly, in these years, leadership failed. Events whose tragic

March 4, 1929: President
Coolidge (left) and President-
Elect Hoover drive from
the White House to Hoover's
inauguration at the Capitol.

culmination could be foreseen—and was foreseen—were allowed to
work themselves out to the final disaster. The country and the world
paid. For a time, indeed, the very reputation of capitalism itself was
in the balance. It survived in the years following perhaps less because
of its own power or the esteem in which it was held, than because
of the absence of an organized and plausible alternative. Yet one
important question remains. Would it have been possible even for
a strong President to arrest the plunge? Were not the opposing forces
too strong? Isn't one asking the impossible?

No one can say for sure. But the answer depends at least partly
on the political context in which the Presidency was cast. That of
Coolidge and Hoover may well have made decisive leadership impossible. These were conservative Administrations in which, in addition, the influence of the businessman was strong. At the core of
the business faith was an intuitive belief in *laissez faire*—the benign
tendency of things that are left alone. The man who wanted to
intervene was a meddler. Perhaps, indeed, he was a planner. In any
case, he was to be regarded with mistrust. And, on the businessman's
side, it must be borne in mind that high government office often nur-
tures a spurious sense of urgency. There is no more important public
function than the suppression of proposals for unneeded action. But
these should have been distinguished from action necessary to economic survival.

A bitterly criticized figure of the Harding-Coolidge Hoover era
was Secretary of the Treasury Andrew W. Mellon. He opposed all
action to curb the boom, although once in 1929 he was persuaded
to say that bonds (as distinct from stocks) were a good buy. And

when the depression came, he was against doing anything about that. Even Mr. Hoover was shocked by his insistence that the only remedy was (as Mr. Hoover characterized it) to "liquidate labor, liquidate stocks, liquidate the farmers, liquidate real estate." Yet Mellon reflected only in extreme form the conviction that things would work out, that the real enemies were those who interfered.

Outside of Washington in the twenties, the business and banking community, or at least the articulate part of it, was overwhelmingly opposed to any public intervention. The tentative and ineffective steps which the Federal Reserve did take were strongly criticized. In the spring of 1929 when the Reserve system seemed to be on the verge of taking more decisive action, there was an anticipatory tightening of money rates and a sharp drop in the market. On his own initiative Charles E. Mitchell, the head of the National City Bank, poured in new funds. He had an obligation, he said, that was "paramount to any Federal Reserve warning, or anything else" to avert a crisis in the money market. In brief, he was determined, whatever the government thought, to keep the boom going. In that same spring Paul M. Warburg, a distinguished and respected Wall Street leader, warned of the dangers of the boom and called for action to restrain it. He was deluged with criticism and even abuse and later said that the subsequent days were the most difficult of his life. There were some businessmen and bankers—like Mitchell and Albert Wiggin of the Chase National Bank—who may have vaguely sensed that the end of the boom would mean their own business demise. Many more had persuaded themselves that the dream would last. But we should not complicate things. Many others were making money and took a short-run view—or no view—either of their own survival or of the system of which they were a part. They merely wanted to be left alone to get a few more dollars.

And the opposition to government intervention would have been nonpartisan. In 1929 one of the very largest of the Wall Street operators was John J. Raskob. Raskob was also chairman of the Democratic National Committee. So far from calling for preventive measures, Raskob in 1929 was explaining how, through stock market speculation, literally anyone could be a millionaire. Nor would the press have been enthusiastic about, say, legislation to control holding companies and investment trusts or to give authority to regulate margin trading. The financial pages of many of the papers were riding the boom. And even from the speculating public, which was dreaming dreams of riches and had yet to learn that it had been fleeced, there would have been no thanks. Perhaps a President of phenomenal power and determination might have overcome the Coolidge-Hoover environment. But it is easier to argue that this context made inaction inevitable for almost any President. There were too many people who, given a choice between disaster and the measures that would have prevented it, opted for disaster without either a second or even a first thought.

On the other hand, in a different context a strong President might have taken effective preventive action. Congress in these years was becoming increasingly critical of the Wall Street speculation and corporate piggery-pokery. The liberal Republicans—the men whom Senator George H. Moses called the Sons of the Wild Jackass—were especially vehement. But conservatives like Carter Glass were also critical. These men correctly sensed that things were going wrong. A President such as Wilson or either of the Roosevelts (the case of Theodore is perhaps less certain than that of Franklin) who was surrounded in his Cabinet by such men would have been sensitive to this criticism. As a leader he could both have reinforced and drawn strength from the contemporary criticism. Thus he might have been able to arrest the destructive madness as it became recognizable. The American government works far better—perhaps it only works—when the Executive, the business power, and the press are in some degree at odds. Only then can we be sure that abuse or neglect, either private or public, will be given the notoriety that is needed.

Perhaps it is too much to hope that by effective and timely criticism and action the Great Depression might have been avoided. A lot was required in those days to make the United States in any degree depression-proof. But perhaps by preventive action the ensuing depression might have been made less severe. And certainly in the ensuing years the travail of bankers and businessmen before congressional committees, in the courts, and before the bar of public opinion would have been less severe. Here is the paradox. In the full perspective of history, American businessmen never had enemies as damaging as the men who grouped themselves around Calvin Coolidge and supported and applauded him in what William Allen White called "that masterly inactivity for which he was so splendidly equipped."

Poverty makes strange bedfellows: in Everett
Shinn's depression drawing of a breadline,
former businessmen and bums queue up.

Allan Nevins

The Place of Franklin D. Roosevelt in History

This essay, like Lewis Mumford's analysis of Emerson in Volume I, brings together a great historian and a great subject. Allan Nevins' estimation of Franklin D. Roosevelt is complicated. He says as much about Roosevelt's weaknesses as about his strengths. He looks at Roosevelt through the eyes of the President's friends and his enemies; he refers to his personal observations of the man and also makes the broadest of generalizations, based on his amazing understanding not only of the whole course of American history but of much of the history of the western world. He tells us funny stories that reveal Roosevelt in moments of relaxation and quotes from formal state papers which show him center stage at crucial points in his career. Above all, like a great conductor interpreting a symphony, he is at every stage absolute master of his subject and his materials, devoting exquisite care to every detail yet never forgetting that each separate passage contributes vitally to the total effect.

That effect is, in a word, sunny. Nevins, despite his awareness of Roosevelt's limits and defects, admires the man because of what he calls his "effective greatness," which he believes was produced by qualities of spirit rather than of intellect or even of moral fiber.

*S*eldom has an eminent man been more conscious of his special place in history than was Franklin D. Roosevelt. He thought of history as an imposing drama and himself as a conspicuous actor. Again and again he carefully staged a historic scene: as when, going before Congress on December 8, 1941, to call for a recognition of war with Japan, he took pains to see that Mrs. Woodrow Wilson accompanied Mrs. Roosevelt to the Capitol, thus linking the First and Second World Wars. As governor and as President, he adopted for the benefit of future historians the rule that every letter addressed to him, however insignificant, and copies of every document issued from his office, should be preserved. This mass of papers, mounting into the millions, soon became almost overwhelming. It might have been added, with some difficulty, to the many other official collections in the Library of Congress. But, with a strong sense of his special place in history, Roosevelt wanted a memorial all his own, a place of resort for scholars, connected uniquely with his name and his administrations. He announced the gift of his papers to the nation; his mother gave sixteen acres of land for a building at Hyde Park; some 28,000 donors subscribed $400,000 for an edifice; and Congress made the Roosevelt Library a federal institution.

In this Library at Hyde Park, as a token of his place in history, he took an almost naïve pride. I well recall the dinner he gave early in 1939 to the trustees and a select number of historians to discuss plans for its management. It took place at the Mayflower Hotel in Washington; he was wheeled up an inclined ramp to his place at a central table; he waved joyously to everyone; he enjoyed his stewed mulligatawny turtle—a favorite dish—his companions, his sense of launching another original enterprise. In a long informal speech he talked of certain predecessors: of Lincoln, of Grover Cleveland, whom he had known, and of his cousin Theodore Roosevelt; he dwelt on Woodrow Wilson's sense of history—Wilson in 1917 had forbidden young Roosevelt, then Assistant Secretary of the Navy, to bring warships up from Cuban waters to the United States lest future historians should accuse him of making a provocative gesture on the eve of our first war with Germany. I well recall, too, the still more interesting occasion when he laid the cornerstone of the Hyde Park Library on November 19, 1939. Trustees, historians, and editors lunched with him; he gaily drove his own specially equipped car to the site; he chatted blithely with everyone; and he watched the cornerstone slip into place with a gratified smile.

Today his grave lies close by that Library, and by the family home that has become a national shrine, visited by hundreds of thousands every year. To the collections there shelved, multitudes of scholars annually repair, for they are open to all. Roosevelt's own deposits, including letters, documents, books, pamphlets, films, photographs, speeches, and museum pieces, have exceeded a total of fifty million items; and to them are being added the papers of Cabinet officers and other official associates. The career of no other American President has so vast a documentation for history.

*An ebullient F.D.R. holding an outdoor press
conference at Warm Springs, Georgia, in 1939.*

Is it too soon to estimate the place of Franklin D. Roosevelt in the
stream of American and world events? It is never too soon for such a
task. History is not a remote Olympian bar of judgment, but a controversial arena in which each generation must make its own estimate of
the past. We have every right to fix the historical position of Roosevelt
as we see it today, knowing that it will be reassessed from the vantage

point of a longer perspective and fuller knowledge in 1975, and re-estimated again in 2065. That it will be a great place we may already be certain. A statue to Roosevelt has been reared in Oslo. When a statue was proposed in London, five-shilling subscriptions were opened one morning; they were closed that night with the sum oversubscribed; had they been kept open a few days money would have poured in for five statues. Streets have been named for him around the world. Fifty American historians, interrogated by Arthur M. Schlesinger, Sr., of Harvard, have all but unanimously agreed that in the roster of Presidents Lincoln stands first, Washington second, and Franklin D. Roosevelt third. Hearing of that verdict, Winston Churchill declared that in impact upon world history Roosevelt unquestionably stood first.

We have this advantage in attempting the task, that a great part of the necessary evidence is already at hand. Never before in human annals has so huge a volume of reminiscences, autobiographies, impressions, letters, official documents, and other data bearing on one man been issued within twenty years of his death. The thirteen volumes of Roosevelt's official papers edited by Judge Samuel I. Rosenman and the four volumes of personal letters edited by Elliot Roosevelt; the memoirs of Cordell Hull, Harry Hopkins, Henry Morgenthau, Harold Ickes, Henry L. Stimson, James Farley, Edward J. Flynn, Mrs. Franklin D. Roosevelt, Frances Perkins, Grace Tully, Hugh Johnson, Dwight Eisenhower, Omar Bradley, and a hundred others; the mass of comment by Washington reporters and war correspondents who watched history being made; the procession of European histories and memoirs so impressively headed by Winston Churchill's volumes —this already forms a corpus too great for one student to explore fully in a lifetime. But while we shall have immense fresh accretions of detail, it is unlikely that we shall receive any startling new "revelations," any facts that will offer a basis for sweeping revisions of judgment.

In dealing with every commanding figure of history, a fundamental question presents itself: To what extent did greatness inhere in the man, and to what degree was it a product of the situation? If great men have their stars, as Napoleon said he did, it is often because a national or world crisis favors greatness. The reason why fifty American historians did not wholly agree with Winston Churchill upon Roosevelt's rank among the nation's Presidents is, I think, simple. Washington had indisputable greatness in himself. "The first, the last, the best, the Cincinnatus of the West," as Lord Byron called him, he was great in character, great in traits of leadership, great in insight and wisdom. Lincoln had an even more manifest and appealing personal greatness. His public utterances, from the House Divided address to the Gettysburg Address, his state papers, from the First Inaugural to the final pronouncements on Reconstruction, attest a rare intellectual power. The wisdom of his principal public acts, his magnanimity toward all foes public and private, his firmness under adversity, his elevation of spirit, his power of strengthening the best purposes and suppressing the worst instincts of a broad, motley democracy, place him in the front rank of modern statesmen.

But with Franklin D. Roosevelt we feel no such assurance of transcendent personal eminence. We feel that he lacked the steadfast elevation of character exhibited by George Washington. We find in him distinctly less intellectual power than in Jefferson, Lincoln, or perhaps Woodrow Wilson. We conclude, in short, that his tremendous place in history was in lesser degree the product of his special personal endowments, and in larger degree the handiwork of his stormy times, than that occupied by George Washington or Abraham Lincoln.

That Roosevelt had remarkable intellectual gifts is plain; but these gifts fell short of the highest distinction. He possessed a quick, resourceful, and flexible mind. This fact is illustrated on an elevated level by his ability to deal with fifty important issues in a day, making shrewd decisions on each; by his power in wartime of efficiently coordinating departments, industries, and armies, of gaining the teamwork of generals, admirals, and business leaders, as no other President has ever done. He organized the national energies with unique success. His intellectual proficiency is illustrated on a lower plane by almost any of the press conferences recorded in Judge Rosenman's volumes; by his deft tact in handling two-score quick-witted newspapermen, evading some questions, dissecting the fatuity of others, using a few to touch a needed chord of publc opinion, and responding to many with concise, expert answers. Like his cousin Theodore Roosevelt, he had an insatiable curiosity about books, about men, about events. It was linked with an unquenchable zest for experience; the zest expressed in his famous wartime message to Churchill, ''It is fun to be in the same century with you.''

He had a talent for quick parliamentary hits. He could make his enemies ridiculous by a few pungent words, as in the happy rhythmical phrase about ''Martin, Barton, and Fish'' that, recited over the radio, exposed these three reactionary congressmen to a continental gale of laughter in 1940; or by a lambent flare of humor, as in his speech of 1944 picturing the Scottish unhappiness of his dog Fala over an accusation of extravagance. He had flashes of daring imagination. He had a remarkable gift of rapid improvisation, as he showed in all the recurrent crises of his twelve crowded years in office. In part this consisted of his ability to use other men's thought; ''he is the best picker of brains who ever lived,'' his intimates used to say. His power of application was remarkable even among our overworked Presidents. He had an average working day of fourteen hours (Truman later boasted of sixteen), and he told Governor James M. Cox: ''I never get tired.''

But of pre-eminent intellectual talent he had little. I recall Walter Lippmann saying in the second administration: ''He has never written a real state paper.'' In a sense that is true. No paper signed by him equals Washington's Farewell Address, Lincoln's great papers, Theodore Roosevelt's first annual message, or Woodrow Wilson's nobler productions. Nearly all his speeches were in fact largely written for him by others. Robert Sherwood describes a typical scene: Judge

As this 1938 cartoon from the Columbus Dispatch *suggests, Roosevelt was exceedingly interested in assuring himself a place among the outstanding Presidents of American history.*

Rosenman, Harry Hopkins, and Sherwood gathered about a table discussing the material for an imminent presidential address, and threshing it over and over until Judge Rosenman impatiently flung down a pencil with the words, "There comes a time in the life of every speech when it's got to be *written!*" Roosevelt wrote no books; he was probably incapable of matching such a work as Theodore Roosevelt's *The Winning of the West.* He threw out no such immortal epigrams as Churchill's sentence challenging Britons to face a future of "blood, sweat, and tears." His best phrases, like "the forgotten man" and "the new deal," were borrowed from other men.

A capacity for abstract thought was largely omitted from his equipment. The idea once current that he had a special intimacy with Maynard Keynes was obviously erroneous, for he was simply incapable of following a mind so analytical, an intellect so subtle, as that of Lord Keynes. When John Gunther asked one of Roosevelt's friends, "Just how does the President think?" he met the reply: "The President never *thinks.*" Like Theodore Roosevelt, he was primarily a man of action. His mental processes, as many friends have said, were intuitive rather than logical. He reacted rather than reflected. A President is not necessarily too busy to do abstract thinking. Newton D. Baker, who held a minor post in Grover Cleveland's administration and a major office under Woodrow Wilson, once observed to me that while Cleveland shouldered his way through difficulties like a buffalo charging a thicket, Wilson "dissolved his problems by an acid process of thought." This acid process was beyond Roosevelt. All that is told us of his reading suggests that it was rather adolescent: either escapist, like the detective stories carried on every long trip; or attached to a hobby, like naval history; or journalistic. His humor lacked the philosophic overtones of Lincoln's, or even the saltiness of Harry Truman's; it too was somewhat adolescent. It was usually the humor of the quip, as when he said to his secretary, Grace Tully, over-addicted to punctuation, "Grace, how often do I have to tell you not to waste the taxpayer's commas?" Or it was the humor of the wisecrack, as when he remarked to the six New England governors who startled him in 1933 by suddenly appearing at the White House in a body: "What, all six of you? You're not going to secede from the Union, are you?"

We all know what Lord Bacon said makes a ready man; and intellectually, the talkative Roosevelt was a ready leader—perhaps the readiest of all the world's leaders in his exigent time. This power to act quickly, shrewdly, and earnestly was a gift that served the nation and the free world with unforgettable dexterity and force. Honoring this princely capacity, we can afford to give minor weight to the fact that his mind, compared with that of Woodrow Wilson, sometimes appears superficial, and that he possessed no such intellectual versatility as Thomas Jefferson—to say nothing of Winston Churchill.

In respect to character, similarly, he had traits of an admirable kind; but we must add that even in combination, they fell short of a truly Roman weight of virtue. He held sincere religious convictions, and it was no mere gesture that led him to take his Cabinet, on the morn of his first inauguration, to divine service at St. John's. "I think," writes Mrs. Roosevelt in *This I Remember*, "he actually felt he could ask God for guidance and receive it. That was why he loved the Twenty-third Psalm, the Beatitudes, and the thirteenth chapter of First Corinthians." He was one of the unflinching optimists of his time. Having conquered a prostrating illness and horrible physical handicap, he felt an inner faith in man's power to conquer anything. When his aides made estimates of American industrial capacity, he raised them; when the Combined Chiefs of Staff set down dates for the various goals in the invasion of Europe, he revised them forward. Because of his religious faith and his ingrained optimism, he possessed an unfailing serenity. In the stormiest of hours his nerve was never shaken.

On his first day in the Presidency in 1933, with the banks of the nation closed down and the country almost prostrate with anxiety, he found his desk at six o'clock in the afternoon quite clear. He pressed a button. Four secretaries appeared at four doors to the room. "Is there anything more, boys?" he inquired. "No, Mr. President," they chorused. And Roosevelt remarked with his happy smile: "This job is a cinch!"

Equally admirable were his idealism, his consciousness of high objectives, and his frequent nobility of spirit. He was willing to sacrifice himself for the public weal. When in 1928 Alfred E. Smith, the Democratic presidential candidate, asked him to run for governor of New York, he was told by physicians that if he kept out of public life another year or two, he could regain the use of his left leg, while if he did not he would be incurably lame; but he answered the call of duty. His concern for the poor, the friendless, the unfortunate, was more keenly humane than that of any leader since Lincoln. "I see one-third of a nation," he said in his Second Inaugural, "ill-housed, ill-clad, ill-nourished''—and meant to do something about it. Moderately rich himself, he disliked those who were too rich. The steel magnate Eugene Grace, who took a bonus of a million dollars a year without the knowledge of his stockholders, aroused his bitter scorn. ''Tell Gene he'll never make a million a year again!'' was the angry message he sent the man. Frances Perkins, who had known him as a rather arrogant, snobbish young man before his seizure by infantile paralysis, and who knew him as a battler for social justice afterward, believed that this physical ordeal taught him sympathy for the afflicted and underprivileged.

Yet, we must add, these impressive virtues were flawed by certain grievous defects. He had flashes of insincerity which sometimes impaired the confidence even of close friends. Henry L. Stimson mentions in his memoirs the fact that, having found out Roosevelt in a quite needless bit of duplicity, for several years he avoided all contact with him. Henry A. Wallace committed to paper an account of Roosevelt's double-dealing (as Wallace saw it) in handling the Vice Presidential nomination in 1944. Other men have penned different stories. Even the President's defenders could not deny that his treatment of that critical problem showed a certain irresponsibility, to be excused perhaps by the fact that he was already more ill than he realized. Because of this instability, Roosevelt was ready at times to abandon principle for expediency. Cordell Hull has described how unfortunate were the results of such an abandonment in the Neutrality Acts. And Mrs. Roosevelt writes: ''While I often felt strongly on various subjects, Franklin frequently refrained from supporting causes in which he believed, because of political realities. There were times when this annoyed me very much. In the case of the Spanish Civil War, for instance, we had to remain neutral, though Franklin knew quite well he wanted the democratic government to be successful. But he also knew he could not get Congress to go along with him. To justify his action, or lack of action, he explained to me, when I complained, that the League of Nations had asked us to remain neutral. . . . He was simply trying to salve his own conscience. It was one of the many times I felt akin to a hair shirt.''

Edward J. Flynn writes flatly: ''The President did not keep his word on many appointments.'' There exists no question that he promised to make Louis Johnson Secretary of War, and broke the promise. All statesmen have to adjust principle to events and to public sentiment, and are sometimes compelled to revoke promises. But Roosevelt was at times indefensibly evasive even with intimates like Flynn and Louis Johnson, and lacked straightforwardness. It can be said, too, that he often followed a Machiavellian technique in administration. He liked, for example, to put two or three men in positions of conflicting authority, so that they worked at loggerheads, with himself as ultimate arbiter. It was in part his fault that Sumner Welles and Cordell Hull made the State Department for several years a maelstrom of rival policies and ambitions—although this is a complex story; it was in part his fault that Jesse Jones and Henry Wallace engaged at one time in a feud which sadly injured both the administration and the country.

Other unhappy traits might be copiously illustrated. Roosevelt could seem dismayingly casual about everything from a political speech to some of the issues at Yalta. He could be reprehensibly secretive; he kept the minutes of the Teheran Conference from Secretary of State Hull, and withheld from the American people the concession he made at Yalta to Russia on votes in the United Nations Assembly. He was pettily vindictive toward some opponents, as Raymond B. Moley and James Farley testify in detail, and his attempted purge of certain southern leaders in 1938 is far from the happiest chapter in his career. All in all, we must repeat our conclusion that his character lacked the symmetry, harmony, and weight found in that of Washington and of Lincoln.

Yet without the highest inner greatness Roosevelt had an effective greatness of action, in relation to his time, which will cause him to be remembered as happily as any American leader. It is significant that Churchill, intellectually so much superior, always treated him with manifest deference, as a lesser man bowing to a greater. Was this simply because Roosevelt headed the more powerful state? I think not. We must here face what seems to me a salient fact of history. A leader who puts second-rate qualities of intellect and character into first-rate application to the needs of his time may be a greater man than the leader who puts first-rate qualities into a second-rate application. Roosevelt signally illustrates this aphorism. He had, to begin with, the gift of address: a gift for doing the right thing at just the right time. He had, in the second place, the greater gift of being able to put his personal forces into harmony with the best forces of his era.

Roosevelt's effective greatness included an unrivalled power of matching the urgent crisis with the adequate act; a power of timing an impressive measure to meet a desperate need. Take the first days of 1933, after his election. Never in a period of peace—never since the days of British invasion in 1814, or Confederate victory in 1863—had the nation been in such straits. Between twelve and fifteen million men were out of work. Five million families, one seventh of the population, were supported by public relief or private charity. Since the beginning of the depression, 4,600 banks had failed. Travellers through the broad industrial belt from Chicago to New York seemed to pass nothing but closed factory gates. Half the automobile plants of Michigan had shut down. Along the Great Lakes, path of the largest marine commerce of the world, ships had almost ceased to move. In the iron beds of the Mesabi and Vermilion ranges scarcely a shovel dipped into the richest ores of the globe; in the copper mountain at Butte scarcely a drill was at work. The looms of southern textile factories were cobwebbed. On railway sidings locomotives gathered rust in long rows; behind them huddled passenger and freight cars in idle hundreds, their paint fading. Middle-western farmers gazed bitterly at crops whose market value was less than the cost of harvesting; on the high plains, ranchers turned cattle loose to graze at will because it did not pay to send them to the stockyards. In Pennsylvania and New England desperate men and women offered to work for anything, and some did work for a dollar a week.

Worst of all was the fear which gripped the nerves of the nation. To observers who travelled across the country in trains almost empty, through factory districts with hardly a wisp of smoke, the helpless populations sent up an almost audible cry of anger, bewilderment, and panic. The day before Roosevelt took office the crisis gathered to a climax. By midnight of March 3 the closing of all remaining banks had been or was being ordered in every state. Never before had a change of Presidents taken place against a background so dramatic. The people, awakening on March 4 to read that their financial system was prostrate, gathered at noon by millions about their radios to listen in anguish, in anxiety, but in hope, to the voice of their new national leader.

There ensued four of the most brilliantly successful months in the history of American government. Roosevelt's first words promised energy: "I assume unhesitatingly the leadership of this great army of our people, dedicated to a disciplined attack upon our common problems." He improvised a series of policies, and mobilized an administrative machine, with a vigor that would have done credit to any wartime executive. Within thirty-six hours he had taken absolute control of the currency and banking system, and called Congress in extraordinary session. He forthwith launched an aggressive attack along half a dozen fronts; upon banking problems, industrial prostration, farm distress, unemployment, public works, the burden of public and private debt. One reporter wrote that the change in Washington was like that from oxcart to airplane. Congress labored for ninety-nine days under the President's all-but-complete sway. Almost his every wish was obeyed by immediate votes. One staggered member said of the program: "It reads like the first chapter of Genesis."

And as Roosevelt took these steps his courage, his resourcefulness, his blithe optimism, infected the spirit of the people; he gave Americans new confidence and the *élan* of a new national unity. When he gaily signed his last bills and departed for a brief sail up the Atlantic coast as skipper of a 45-foot sailing boat, the nation realized that it had turned from stagnation to a bright adventure. As the President put it, we were "on our way."

Nor was this an isolated spasm of leadership; for each recurrent crisis found the same resourcefulness called into effective play. When France fell, when the British Commonwealth stood alone against the deadliest foe that modern civilization had known, Americans gazed at the European scene in fear, in gloom, in perpexity. With a sense of dumb helplessness, tens of millions put their intensest feeling into the hope for Britain's survival. Those tens of millions never forgot the morning of September 3, 1940, when they read the headlines announcing that Roosevelt had told a startled Congress of the transfer of fifty destroyers to embattled Britain; a defiance of Hitler, a defiance of home isolationists, a first long stride toward ranging America against the Fascist despots. Nor could lovers of world freedom ever forget the dramatic steps that followed hard upon British victory over Hitler's air force and upon Roosevelt's re-election: the Four Freedoms speech of January 6, 1941; the introduction of the Lend-Lease Bill four days later, a measure which completely transformed American foreign policy; the establishment of naval and military posts in Greenland and Iceland; the proclamation of an unlimited national emergency; the seizure of all Axis ships and Axis credits; the Atlantic Charter meeting with Churchill off Newfoundland; the establishment of convoys for American ships carrying aid to Britain; and, in the background, the stimulation of American production to an unprecedented flow of guns, tanks, shells, and airplanes, with factories roaring day and night for the defense of democracy.

These years 1940–41 were, as we see now, among the greatest crises in modern history. They were met with an imagination, boldness, and ingenuity that can hardly be overpraised. Parochialism, timidity, or fumbling might have been fatal; even a pause for too much reflection might have been fatal. We knew then that Roosevelt was determined to face the exigency with an intrepidity worthy of the republic. But his intention was even more courageous than we supposed. For we know now that Harry Hopkins told Churchill in London early in 1941: "The President is determined that we shall win the war together. Make no mistake about it. He sent me here to tell you that at all costs and by all means he will carry you through."

Roosevelt's second quality of effective greatness was his ability to vindicate the American method of pragmatic experiment, of practical *ad hoc* action, step by step. He was essentially a Jeffersonian. He belonged to the school which, following the historic Anglo-American bent of mind, is attached to facts rather than ideas, to the enlargement of precedents rather than the formulation of dazzling visions. Like all Anglo-American statesmen, he disliked sweeping generalizations of an intolerant, exclusive nature. He loved experimental advance, and was wont to say that if he were right sixty per cent of the time, he would be satisfied. Like Jefferson, he was willing to scrap a theory the moment a brute fact collided with it; he trusted experience, and distrusted flights into the empyrean. His so-called revolution, though unprecedentedly broad and swift, was like Jefferson's "revolution"; it was simply a combination of numerous practical changes, the main test of which was whether or not they worked.

The Rooseveltian changes did work. They did transform American life and the American outlook in two distinct ways. They converted a nation of aggressive individualists into a social-minded nation accepting the principles of the welfare state. They changed an isolationist or largely isolationist nation into one committed to world partnership and world leadership. The New Deal in home affairs was empirical, not ideological. The emergency program I have sketched was a stopgap affair put together to tide over a crisis, and as Mrs. Roosevelt once put it, "give us time to think." It succeeded. Taken as a whole, the New Deal passed through two phases. In the first, 1933–35, the government tried scarcity economics, reducing factory production, farm output, and hours of work, and doing what it could to cut off the American economy from the outside world. In the second and better phase, 1935–50, it tried full employment, full production, enlarged distribution of goods, and freer international trade. This led directly toward the acceptance of Cordell Hull's ideal of co-operative internationalism. American participation in world affairs after 1938 similarly passed through two phases. In the first, all the nation's energies were devoted to the defeat of the Axis. In the second, Roosevelt, Hull, Welles, and Stettinius moved step by step to construct a new world order, an enduring fabric of the United Nations. In home and foreign affairs alike action was always direct, experimental, and pragmatic.

It gave America a new social order at home, and a new orientation in global affairs. It worked; it is still working. But because it never approached a sweeping ideological revolution of the Marxist or totalitarian type, it was the despair of certain impractical theorists *pur sang*.

For example, readers of that brilliant but extraordinarily half-informed and error-streaked book, Harold Laski's *The American Democracy,* will find an almost incredible analysis of what the author regards as Mr. Roosevelt's fundamental failure. This was his failure to smash the old America completely, and build a quite new America on the theories that pleased Mr. Laski. The author draws an illuminating comparison between Lenin and Roosevelt. Lenin, it appears, made a marvelously precise and correct analysis of the maladies of modern society and economics; and he applied it with revolutionary courage. Roosevelt, on the other hand, was never converted—he never learned that "the foundations of the Americanism he inherited were really inadequate to the demands made upon its institutional expression." In particular, writes Laski, he failed to see that he should destroy "private ownership of the means of production"; that is, that the state should take over all mines, factories, transport, workshops, and farms. Roosevelt, as a result of his faulty analysis, unhappily failed to carry through a real revolution. What was the upshot? In Russia, admits Laski, life became nearly intolerable. The price of revolution proved "almost overwhelming"—starvation of millions, wholesale executions, vast concentration camps, the extinction of freedom. In America, Laski admits, life was immensely improved. Industrial production became enormous; farm output grew tremendous; the standard of living steadily rose. But theory (says Mr. Laski) is everything. Lenin with his ideology was right; Roosevelt with his practical experimentalism was a failure!

This view of the matter would be emphatically rejected by all but a handful of Americans, including those who do not admire Roosevelt. Like Jefferson, like Lincoln, like Wilson, he was innovator and conservator at once; he made daring new additions to the American fabric, but he kept the best of the old structure. While he converted

Americans to the new ideal of social security, he strengthened their old faith in individual opportunity. He proved again that America needs no ideological revolution. He vindicated our traditional method of solving problems one at a time by pragmatic trial and error. As one journalist wrote: ''One remembers him as a kind of smiling bus driver, with that cigarette holder pointed upward, listening to the uproar from behind as he took the sharp turns. They used to tell him that he had not loaded his vehicle right for all eternity. But he knew that he had stacked it well enough to round the next corner, and he knew when the yells were false, and when they were real, and he loved the passengers.''

Roosevelt's third and most important quality of effective greatness lay in his ability to imbue Americans, and to some extent even citizens of other lands, with a new spiritual strength. Well into the twentieth century, most men in the New World had shared a dream of ever-widening adventure, a sense of elated achievement. They had dared much in coming to the new continent, and still more in mastering it. They were optimistic, self-confident, exuberant. The heavy costs of the First World War, the disillusionments of its aftermath, the pressure of complex new social problems, and above all the staggering blows of the Great Depression darkened our horizons. We had entered the Shadow Belt which Bryce predicted in his book on *The American Commonwealth*. From that zone of gloom, that numbed consciousness of frustration and failure, Roosevelt lifted Americans on the wings of his great new adventures—the alphabetical adventures of the AAA, the NRA, the TVA; above all, on the wings of the greatest adventure in our history, the effort to rescue democracy from totalitarianism, and to organize the world to safeguard freedom.

For a few years Americans had felt lost, bewildered, paralyzed. Roosevelt carried them to a Moabite peak whence once more they saw promised lands. They threw off their frustrations; he gave them a feeling that they were participating in a life far wider than their everyday parochial concerns. His self-confidence, his enthusiasm, his happy faculty of obliterating old failures by bold new plans, taught them that they were not imprisoned in a dead past but were helping build a living future. In the three centuries 1607–1907 Americans had triumphantly mastered their physical environment. Just so, in the next century to come, they would master their social and economic environment at home, and join other nations in a mastery of the world environment. As the storm thickened after 1940, Roosevelt's rich voice grew more urgent—''bidding the eagles of the West fly on.'' Here at last, he seemed to say, is a task worthy of you; tyranny like Hell is not easily conquered. Lincoln had once used a phrase which haunts his countrymen. ''Thanks to all,'' he exclaimed after Gettysburg and Vicksburg, ''thanks to all: for the great republic—for the principle it lives by and keeps alive—for man's vast future—thanks to all.'' A sense of man's vast future, a hope of shaping it for the better, never left Roosevelt's cheerful heart.

It is not often realized to what a degree the spirit of adventure kindled at home under the New Deal was carried over into world affairs when the United States faced the Axis menace. The defeatism of Hoover's day was gone. A hundred and sixty million citizens had been morally prepared to undertake unprecedented tasks. They grumbled; they cursed the hard luck of their grim era; they shuddered over the mounting costs—the colossal debt, the wasted resources; but they never doubted their ability to put the job through. That change in temper was primarily Roosevelt's accomplishment. It threw open, temporarily, the portals of a wider world. The change from oxcart was a spiritual, not a material, change. Never in our history have the emotion and resolution of the American people been so completely fused as when, as the first waves of American and British troops stormed across the Normandy beaches, Roosevelt sat at the radio leading the nation in prayer.

Effective greatness—that is Roosevelt's title to a high place in the world's history. Intellect and character are not enough; to them must be added personality, energy, and an accurate sense for the proper timing of action. Roosevelt was not an intellectual giant; but what of the personality that made the Arkansas sharecropper and the Harlem Negro feel they shared all the destinies of the republic? His character did not awe men by its massive strength; but what of the gifts that made him so efficient in harmonizing labor, capital, and agriculture at home, and getting discordant nations to pool their wartime efforts? He lacked the iron traits of Cromwell—but how incomparably more successful he was! He did not have the powerful grasp of Bismarck, but how much more beneficent was his career! In time his specific achievements may be blurred, but the qualities of his spirit will be remembered. For centuries Americans will think of him as one of those spirits who ride in front; we shall see his jaunty figure, his gaily poised head, still in advance of us. We shall hear his blithe voice in his words just before his death at Warm Springs on April 12, 1945:

"The only limit to our realization of tomorrow will be our doubts of today. Let us move forward with strong and active faith."

Daniel P. Moynihan

The American City:
Continuity
and Change

*Current concerns always produce "new" history; they lead us
to reconsider the past in our search for an understanding of the
present. This essay by Daniel P. Moynihan illustrates this principle
perfectly. Moynihan has devoted most of his adult life to what may
generally be called urban problems—as a government official, as a
university professor, and as a writer. He served in the United States
Department of Labor from 1961 to 1965, rising to the post of Assistant Secretary. He then became a professor at Harvard and director of
Harvard and M.I.T.'s Joint Center for Urban Studies. He is currently
Special Assistant for Urban Affairs to President Nixon. His book*
Beyond the Melting Pot, *written with Nathan Glazer, has been a major
force in shaping liberal attitudes toward the problems of ethnic
minorities in America.*

*In the following pages Moynihan takes a hard look at American
cities today. His essay bristles with references to modern social science
studies of urban life. But in attempting to place urban problems in
perspective, he refers repeatedly to history, showing how present-day
difficulties are similar to—and different from—those of earlier times.
He ends on a note of uncertainty. Avoiding the easy tendency of many
historians to justify social evils by "proving" that they have always
existed, he concludes by admitting "we do not know" the prescription
for curing America's sick cities. But surely, if urban problems are
ever to be solved or even mitigated, it will be by considering them in
the thoughtful, learned, yet modest way that Moynihan here employs.*

*T*here is to be encountered in a Benjamin Disraeli novel a gentleman described as a person "distinguished for ignorance" as he had but one idea and that was wrong. It is by now clear that future generations will perforce reach something of the same judgment about contemporary Americans in relation to their cities, for what we do and what we say reflect such opposite poles of judgment that we shall inevitably be seen to have misjudged most extraordinarily either in what we are saying about cities or in what we are doing about them. We are, of course, doing very little, or rather, doing just about what we have been doing for the past half century or so, which can reflect a very great deal of activity but no very considerable change. Simultaneously, and far more conspicuously, we are talking of crisis. The word is everywhere: on every tongue; in every pronouncement. The President has now taken to sending an annual message to Congress on urban subjects. In 1968 it was bluntly titled *The Crisis of the Cities*. And indeed, not many weeks later, on Friday, April 5, to be exact, he was issuing a confirming proclamation of sorts:

> Whereas I have been informed that conditions of domestic violence and disorder exist in the District of Columbia and threaten the Washington metropolitan area, endangering life and property and obstructing execution of the laws, and the local police forces are unable to bring about the prompt cessation . . . of violence and restoration of law and order. . . .

The excitement is nothing if not infectious. In a recent joint publication, *Crisis: The Condition of the American City,* Urban America, Inc. and the League of Women Voters noted that during 1967 even the Secretary of Agriculture devoted most of his speeches to urban problems. At mid-1968, the president of the University of California issued a major statement entitled, "What We Must Do: The University and the Urban Crisis." The bishops of the United States Catholic Conference came forth with their own program, entitled "The Church's Response to the Urban Crisis." At its 1968 convention the Republican party, not heretofore known for an obsession with the subject, adopted a platform plank entitled "Crisis of the Cities," while in an issue featuring a stunning black coed on the cover, *Glamour* magazine, ever alert to changing fashions, asked in appropriate form the question many have posed themselves in private "The Urban Crisis: What Can One Girl Do?"

Academics who have been involved with this subject might be expected to take some satisfaction that the alarums and jeremiads of the past decades seem at last to have been heard by the populace, and yet even those of us most seized with what Norman Mailer has termed the "middle-class lust for apocalypse" are likely to have some reservations about the current enthusiasm for the subject of urban ills. It is not just a matter of the continued disparity between what we say and what we do: it is also, I suspect, a matter of *what* we are saying, and the manner of our saying it. A certain bathos comes through. One thinks of Sean O'Casey's Captain Boyle and Joxer in that far-off Dublin tenement: no doubt the whole world was even then in a "state of chassis" but precious little those two could or would do about it, save use it as an excuse to sustain their own weakness, incompetence, and submission to the death wishes of the society about them. One wonders if something not dissimilar is going on in this nation, at this time. Having persistently failed to do what it was necessary and possible to do for urban life on grounds that conditions surely were not so bad as to warrant such exertion, the nation seems suddenly to have lurched to the opposite position of declaring that things are indeed so very bad that probably nothing will work anyway. The result either way is paralysis and failure. It is time for a measure of perspective.

I take it Lewis Mumford intended to convey something of this message in his most recent book, *The Urban Prospect*, which he begins with a short preface cataloguing the ills of the modern city with a vigor and specificity that command instant assent from the reader. Exactly! one responds. That is precisely the way things are! Mumford is really "telling it like it is." (A measure of *négritude* has of late become the mark of an authentic urban-crisis watcher.) One reads on with increasing recognition, mounting umbrage, only to find at the end that this foreword was in fact written for the May, 1925, edition of *Survey Graphic*. Things have changed, but not that much, and in directions that were, in a sense, fully visible to the sensitive eye nearly a half century ago. To be sure, at a certain point a matter of imbalance becomes one of pathology, a tendency becomes a condition, and for societies as for individuals there comes a point when mistakes are no longer to be undone, transgressions no longer to be forgiven. But it is nowhere clear that we have reached such a point in our cities.

Continuity and change. These are the themes of all life, and not less that of cities. However, as in so many aspects of our national experience, Americans seem more aware of, more sensitive to modes of change than to those of continuity. This is surely a survival from the frontier experience. There has not, I believe, ever been anything to match the rapidity, nay, fury with which Americans set about founding cities in the course of the seventeenth, eighteenth, and nineteenth centuries. Only just now is the historical profession beginning to catch up with that breathless undertaking. Before long we are likely to have a much clearer idea than we do now as to how it all began. But it is still possible at this early state, as it were, to identify a half dozen or so persistent themes in the American urban experience which seem to evolve from earlier to later stages in a process that some would call growth, and others decay, but in a manner that nonetheless constitutes change.

The first theme is that of violence. Through history—the history, that is, of Europe and Asia and that great bridge area in between—cities have been, nominally at least, places of refuge, while the countryside has been the scene of insecurity and exposure to misfortune and wrongdoing. Obviously the facts permit of no generalization, but there is at least a conceptual validity, a persistence over time, of the association of the city with security. In the classical and feudal world, to be without the gates was to be in trouble. Writing of the destruction of Hiroshima and Nagasaki, the critic George Steiner evokes the ancient certainty on this point, and suggests the ways in which it lives on.

> In these two cities, the consequences have been more drastic and more specialized. Therein lies the singularity of the two Japanese communities, but also their symbolic link with a number of other cities in history and with the role such cities have played in man's consciousness of his own vulnerable condition—with Sodom and Gomorrah, visited by such fiery ruin that their very location is in doubt; with Nineveh, raked from the earth; with Rotterdam and Coventry; with Dresden, where in 1944, air raids deliberately kindled the largest, hottest pyre known to man. Already, in the "Iliad," the destruction of a city was felt to be an act of peculiar finality, a misfortune that threatens the roots of man. His city smashed, man reverts to the unhoused, wandering circumstance of the beast from which he has so uncertainly emerged. Hence the necessary presence of the gods when a city is built, the mysterious music and ceremony that often attend the elevation of its walls. When Jerusalem was laid waste, says the Haggada, God Himself wept with her.

Little of this dread is to be encountered in the United States, a society marked by the near absence of internal warfare once the major Indian conflicts were over. Warfare, that is to say, between armies. We have, on the other hand, been replete with conflict between different groups within the population, classified in terms of race, class, ethnicity, or whatever, and this conflict has occurred in our cities, which in consequence have been violent places.

An account of the draft riots in New York City in 1863 strikes a surpassingly contemporary note.

> Nothing that we could say, could add to the impressiveness of the lesson furnished by the events of the past year, as to the needs and the dangerous condition of the neglected classes in our city. Those terrible days in July—the sudden appearance, as if from the bosom of the earth, of a most infuriated and degraded mob; the helplessness of property-holders and the better classes; the boom of cannon and rattle of musketry in our streets; the skies lurid with conflagrations; the inconceivable barbarity and ferocity of the crowd toward an unfortunate and helpless race; the immense destruction of property—were the first dreadful revelations to many of our people of the existence among us of a great, ignorant, irresponsible class,

During New York's draft riots in 1863, looters did not hesitate to put homes to the torch.

who were growing up here without any permanent interest in the welfare of the community or the success of the Government— the *proletaires* of the European capitals. Of the gradual formation of this class, and the dangers to be feared from it, the agents of this Society have incessantly warned the public for the past eleven years.

—Eleventh Annual Report
Children's Aid Society, New York

In some degree this violence—or the perception of it—seems to have diminished in the course of the 1930's and 1940's. James Q. Wilson, a professor of government at Harvard, has noted the stages by which, for example, the treatment of violence as an element in American politics steadily decreased in successive editions of V. O. Key's textbook on American politics that appeared during the latter part of this period. It may be that depression at home and then war abroad combined to restrict opportunity or impulse. In any event, there was a lull, and in consequence all the more alarm when violence reappeared in the mid-1960's. But it was only that: a reappearance, not a beginning.

Yet with all this it is necessary to acknowledge a transformation howsoever subtle and tentative. The tempo of violence seems to have speeded up, the result, more or less direct, of change in the technology of communications, which now communicate not simply the fact but also the spirit of violent events, and do so instantaneously. More ominously, there appears to have been a legitimation of violence, and

Four Detroit policemen drag a handcuffed man during the riot of July 24, 1967.

a spread of its ethos to levels of society that have traditionally seen themselves, and have been, the repositories of stability and respect for, insistence upon, due process. It is one thing to loot clothing stores —Brooks Brothers was hit in 1863—to fight with the police, to seize sections of the city and hold out against them. It is another thing to seize university libraries, and that is very much part of the violence of our time, a violence that arises not only among the poor and disinherited, but also among the well-to-do and privileged, with the special fact that those elements in society which normally set standards of conduct for the society as a whole have been peculiarly unwilling, even unable, to protest the massive disorders of recent times.

A second theme is migration. The American urban experience has been singular in the degree to which our cities, especially those of the North and East, have been inundated by successive waves of what might be called rural proletarians, a dispossessed peasantry moving— driven from—other people's land in the country to other people's tene ments in the city. American cities have ever been filled with unfamiliar people, acting in unfamiliar ways, at once terrified and threatening. The great waves of Catholic Irish of the early nineteenth century began the modern phase of this process, and it has never entirely stopped, not so much culminating as manifesting itself at this time in the immense folk migration of the landless southern Negro to the northern slum. In small doses such migrations would probably have been easily enough absorbed, but the sheer mass of the successive migrations has been such as to dominate the life of the cities in their immediate aftermath. The most dramatic consequence was that popular government became immigrant government: in the course of the nineteenth century, great cities in America came to be ruled by men of the people, an event essentially without precedent in world history —and one typically deplored by those displaced from power in the course of the transformation. Let me cite to you, for example, a schoolboy exercise written in 1925 by a young Brahmin, the bearer of one of Boston's great names, on the theme "That there is no more sordid profession in the world than *Politics.*"

> The United States is one of the sad examples of the present form of government called democracy. We must first remember that America is made up of ignorant, uninterested, masses, of foreign people who follow the saying, "that the sheep are many but the shepards are few." And the shepards of our government are wolves in sheeps clothing. From Lincoln's Gettysburg address let me quote the familiar lines "a government of the people, for the people, and by the people." In the following lines I shall try and show you how much this is carried out in modern times.
>
> Let us take for example the position of our mayors. They are elected by majority vote from the population in which they live. Let us take for a case Mayor Curley of Boston. He tells the Irish who make up the people of Boston that he will lower their taxes, he will make Boston the greatest city in America. He is elected by the Irish mainly because he is an Irishman. He is a remarkable politician: he surrounds himself by Irishmen, he bribes the Chief Justice of the court, and although we know that the taxes that we pay all find a way into his own pocket we cannot prove by justice that he is not a just and good mayor.

But such distaste was not wholly groundless. The migrant peasants did and do misbehave: as much by the standards of the countryside they leave behind, as of the urban world to which they come. The process of adapting to the city has involved great dislocations in personality and manners as well as in abode. From the first, the process we call urbanization, with no greater specificity than the ancient medical diagnosis of "bellyache" or "back pain," has involved a fairly high order of personal and social disorganization, almost always manifesting itself most visibly in a breakdown of social controls, beginning with the most fundamental of controls, those of family life. The Children's Aid Society of New York was founded in response to the appearance of this phenomenon among the immigrant Irish. Let me quote from their first annual report:

> It should be remembered, that there are no dangers to the value of property or to the permanency of our institutions, so great as those from the existence of such a class of vagabond, ignorant, ungoverned children. This "dangerous class" has not begun to show itself, as it will in eight or ten years, when these

boys and girls are matured. Those who were too negligent or too selfish to notice them as children, will be fully aware of them as men. They will vote. They will have the same rights as we ourselves, though they have grown up ignorant of moral principle, as any savage or Indian. They will poison society. They will perhaps be embittered at the wealth, and the luxuries, they never share. *Then let society beware, when the outcast, vicious, reckless multitude of New York boys, swarming now in every foul alley and low street, come to know their power and use it!*

Mumford in his new book speaks of precisely the same phenomenon:

One of the most sinister features of the recent urban riots has been the presence of roaming bands of children, armed with bottles and stones, taunting and defying the police, smashing windows and looting stores. But this was only an intensification of the window-breakings, knifings, and murders that have for the past twenty years characterized "the spirit of youth in the city streets."

And note the continuity of his last phrase, which alludes, of course, to Jane Addams' book *The Spirit of Youth and the City Streets*, in which she describes just those conditions at the turn of the century in terms that William James declared "immortal" and which, we must allow, were hardly ephemeral.

Yet here, too, technology seems to have been playing us tricks, accentuating and exacerbating our recent experience. The newest migrants come upon an urban world that seems somehow to need them less, to find them even more disturbing and threatening, and to provide them even less secure a place in the scheme of things than was ever quite the case with those who preceded them. I take this to be almost wholly a function of changing employment patterns consequent upon changing technology. But this very technology has also provided an abundance of material resources—and a measure of social conscience—so that people who are not especially needed are still provided for: by 1968, after seven years of unbroken economic expansion, there were 800,000 persons living on welfare in New York City, with the number expected to reach 1,000,000 in 1969. In part this is a phenomenon of birth rates. One person in ten, but one baby in six today is Negro. The poor continue to get children, but those children no longer succumb to cholera, influenza, and tuberculosis. Thus progress more and more forces us to live with the consequences of social injustice. In a more brutal age the evidence soon disappeared!

A third theme of the American urban experience has been the great wealth of our cities. Those who have moved to them have almost invariably improved their standard of life in the not-very-long run. Nor has this been wholly a matter of the consumption of goods and services. "City air makes men free," goes the medieval saying, and this has not been less true for industrial America. The matter was settled,

Urban traffic congestion has a long history.
This is New York's Fifth Avenue in 1921.

really, in an exchange between Hennessey and Dooley at the turn of the century. The country, said that faithful if not always perceptive patron, is where the good things in life come from. To which the master responded, "Yes, but it is the city that they go to." Technology is at the base of this process. The standard of life in American cities rises steadily, and there are few persons who do not somehow benefit. And yet this same technology—wealth—takes its toll. More and more we are conscious of the price paid for affluence in the form of manmade disease, uglification, and the second- and third-order effects of innovations which seem to cancel out the initial benefits.

Nathan Keyfitz, a sociologist at the University of Chicago, has nicely evoked the paradox implicit in many of the benefits of technology. Plenty encourages freedom. It also encourages density. Density can be managed only by regulation. Regulation discourages freedom. The experienced, conditioned city dweller learns, of course, to live with density by maintaining, as Keyfitz puts it, "those standards of reserve, discretion, and respect for the rights of others" that keep the nervous system from exhausting itself from the overstimulus available on any city street. The traditional assertion of Manhattan apartment dwellers that they have never met their neighbors across the hall is not a sign of social pathology: to the contrary, it is the exercise of exemplary habits of social hygiene. Borrowing the meter from George Canning's account of the failings of the Dutch, the rule for the modern cliff dweller might be put as follows:

> *In the matter of neighbors,*
> *The sound thing to do,*
> *Is nodding to many*
> *But speaking to few.*

It may be speculated, for example, that a clue to the transformation of the roistering, brawling, Merrie England of tradition into that somber land where strangers dare not speak to one another in trains lies *in the fact of the trains*. Technology—in this case the steam engine that created the vast nineteenth-century complexes of London and Manchester—brought about urban densities which required new forms of behavior for those who wished to take advantage of technology's advances and yet retain a measure of internal balance. The British, having been first to create the densities, were first to exhibit the telltale *sang-froid* of the modern urban dweller.

It may also be speculated that the "disorganized" life of the rural immigrants of today arises in some measure at least from an inability to control the level of stimulus: to turn down the radio, turn off the television, come in off the streets, stay out of the saloons, worry less about changing styles of clothes, music, dance, whatever. Lee Rainwater, a professor of sociology at the University of Washington, has provided us with painful accounts of the feeling of helplessness of the mothers of poor urban families in the face of the incursions from the street: the feeling, literally, that one cannot simply close one's door in the housing project and refuse to allow family, friends, neighbors, and God knows who else to come and go at will. This makes for lively neighborhoods, which from a distance seem almost enviable. But also for very disturbed people.

When such groups became large enough, when densities become ominous, government regulation becomes necessary, or at least all but invariably makes its appearance, so that even for the disciplined urbanite, technology at some point begins to diminish freedom. Keyfitz writes:

> George Orwell's *1984* is inconceivable without high population density, supplemented by closed circuit television and other devices to eliminate privacy. It exhibits in extreme form an historical process by which the State has been extending its power at the expense of the Church, the Family, and the Local Community, a process extending over 150 years.

There are few bargains in life, especially in city life.

A fourth theme of the American urban experience is mobility. Cities are not only places where the standards of life improve, but also very much—and as much now as ever—they are places where men rise in social standing. Otis Dudley Duncan and Peter M. Blau in their powerful study, *The American Occupational Structure*, have made this abundantly clear. American cities are places where men improve their position, as well as their condition. Or at least have every expectation that their sons will do so. The rigidities of caste and class dissolve, and opportunity opens. Yet this has never been quite so universally agreeable an experience as one could be led to suppose from the accounts of those for whom it has worked. In the city men first, perhaps, come to know success. There also men, especially those from the most caste-ridden rural societies, first come to know failure. It seems to me that this is a neglected aspect of the urban experience. I would argue that the rural peasant life of, let us say, the Irish, the Poles, the Slavs, the Italians, the Negro Americans who have migrated over the past century and a half was characterized by a near total absence of opportunity to improve one's position in the social strata, but also it was characterized by the near impossibility of observing others improve theirs. Rarely, in either absolute or relative terms, did individuals or families of the lowest peasant classes experience decline and failure: that in a sense is the law of a non-contingent society. Only with arrival in the city does that happen, and I would argue that for those who lose out in that competition, the experience can be far more embittering than that brought on by the drab constancy of country life.

Again technology—again television, for that matter—plays its part. Stephan Thernstrom in *Poverty and Progress* has noted that the immigrant workers of nineteenth-century New England, earning $1.50 a day when they had work, nonetheless managed in surprising numbers to put aside some money and to buy a piece of property and respectability before their lives were out, despite the fact that their incomes rarely permitted them to maintain what the social workers of the time calculated to be the minimum standard of living. The difference, Thernstrom notes, was that for the migrants a minimum standard of living was potatoes. Period. So long as they did not share the expectations of those about them—even the small expectations of social workers—they were not deprived. But advertising and television, and a dozen similar phenomena, have long since broken down that isolation, and the poor and newly arrived of the American city today appear to be caught up in a near frenzy of consumer emotions: untouched by the disenchantment with consumption of those very well off, and unrestrained by the discipline of household budgets imposed on those in between. The result, as best such matters can be measured, is a mounting level of discontent, which seems to slide over from the area of consumption as such to discontent with levels of social status that do not provide for maximum levels of consumption. Thus, even those who seem to be succeeding in the new urban world feel they are not succeeding enough, while others are suffused with a sense of failure.

A fifth theme of the American urban experience relates not to the experience of the poor and the newly arrived so much as to that of the well-to-do and the comparatively well settled: the persistent, one almost says primal, distaste for the city of educated Americans. In *The Intellectual Versus the City*, Morton and Lucia White point out that "enthusiasm for the American city has not been typical or predominant in our intellectual history. Fear has been the more common reaction." Fear, distaste, animosity, ambivalence. "In the beginning was the farm." or so the Jeffersonian creed asserts. And the great symbol —or perhaps *consummation* would be the better term—of this belief was the agreement whereby in return for the Jeffersonian willingness to have the federal government accept the debts acquired by states during the Revolutionary War, the capital of the new nation would be transferred from the city of New York to a swamp on the banks of the Potomac. Do not suppose that that agreement has not affected American history. New York remains the capital of the nation, as that term is usually understood, in the sense of the first city of the land. It is the capital of finance, art, theatre, publishing, fashion, intellect, industry . . . name any serious human endeavor other than politics, and its center in the United States will be found in New York City. In years of hard-fought presidential primaries, it is even for many purposes the political capital of the nation. But the seat of government is in Washington, which is only just beginning to respond to the fact that for half a century now ours has been a predominantly urban society.

Once again technology seems to be interacting with a pre-existing tendency. As the American city came more and more to be the abode of the machine, the alarm of American intellectuals, if anything, was intensified. And to a very considerable degree legitimated, for surely machines have given a measure of reality to alarums that were previously more fantasy than otherwise. To this has been added an ever more persistent concern for social justice, so that American intellectuals of the present time now conclude their expanding catalogues of the horrors of urban life with ringing assertions that the cities must be saved. But it is to be noted that this comes almost as an afterthought: the conviction that in the cities will be found the paramount threat to the life of the Republic has changed hardly at all. But at long last what they have been saying may be beginning to be true.

A sixth theme of the American urban experience, and the last with which I shall deal, has been and continues to be the singular ugliness of the average American city. That there are great and stunning exceptions is as much a matter of accident as anything. The essential fact is that for all the efforts to sustain and assert a measure of elite concern for urban aesthetics—of the kind one associates with historical preservation societies—and for all the occasional bursts of energy within the urban planning profession, the American city remains an ugly place to live, pretty much because we like it that way. A measure, no doubt, of this persisting condition can be attributed to the business and propertied interests of the nation that have resisted municipal expenditure, notably when it passed through the hands of egalitarian city halls. But it is more than that. Somehow, somewhere, in the course of the development of democratic, or demagogic, tradition in this nation the idea arose that concern for the physical beauty of the public buildings and spaces of the city was the mark of —what?—crypto-deviationist antipeople monumentalism—and in any event an augury of defeat at the polls. The result has been a steady deterioration in the quality of public buildings and spaces, and with it a decline in the symbols of public unity and common purpose with which the citizen can identify, of which he can be proud, and by which he can know what he shares with his fellow citizens. For the past seven years, as an example, I have been involved with efforts to reconstruct the center of the city of Washington, an attempt that begins with the assertion of the validity and viability of L'Enfant's plan of the late eighteenth century. In this effort we have had the tolerant to grudging co-operation of a fairly wide range of public and private persons, but let me say that we have had at no time the enthusiasm of any. And now I fear we may have even less, since of late there has arisen the further belief that to expend resources on public amenities is in effect to divert them from needed areas of public welfare. The very persons who will be the first to demand increased expenditures for one or another form of social welfare will be the last to concede that the common good requires an uncommon standard of taste and expenditure for the physical appointments of government and the public places of the city.

This attitude was perhaps unintentionally evoked by the respected Episcopal bishop of New York who in 1967 announced that in view of the circumstances of the poor of the city he would not proceed with the completion of the Cathedral of St. John the Divine, the largest such building ever begun, situated on a magnificent site overlooking the flat expanse of Harlem. Why? Meaning no disrespect, is it the plan of the church to liquidate its assets and turn them over to the poor? How much would that come to per head? But even so, would not the completed cathedral be an asset? If men need work, could they not be given jobs in its construction? The French—*toujours gai*, as mehitabel would have it—built Sacre Coeur as an act of penance for the excesses of the Commune. Could not the Episcopalians build St. John the Divine—a perfect symbol of rebirth—as a gesture of penance for all that Brahmin disdain which, in one form or another, to use Max Ways's phrase, taught us to despise our cities until they became despicable? If the phenomenon of ugliness, the last of my urban themes, can be thought to have arisen from more or less abstract qualities of American society, in the present and foreseeable future its principal cause is visible, concrete, and ubiquitous, which is to say it is the automobile. More than any other single factor it is the automobile that has wrecked the twentieth-century American city, dissipating its strength, destroying its form, fragmenting its life. So pervasive is the influence of the automobile that it is possible almost not to notice it at all. Indeed, it is almost out of fashion to do so: the men who first sought to warn us have almost ceased trying, while those who might have followed have sought instead formulations of their own, and in that manner diverted attention from the essential fact that in the age of the automobile cities, which had been places for coming together, have increasingly become machines for moving apart, devices whereby men are increasingly insulated and isolated one from the other.

A coda of sorts that has persisted through the elaboration of the themes of this paper has been the recent role of technology in accentuating and in a sense exacerbating long-established tendencies. The impact of technology on human society—on all forms of life—is the pre-eminent experience of the modern age, and obviously of the city as well. But only of late, one feels, has any very considerable appreciation developed that a change in quantity becomes after a point a change in quality, so that a society that begins by using technology can end by being used by it, and in the process, somehow, lose such control of its destiny as past human societies can be said to have had. Technology being so outwardly rational, it has been assumed by many that those who have been concerned about its directions have not really understood it. People easily come to fear what they do not understand, and it has been suspected, not always without foundation, that a certain amount of criticism of technology has been a latter-day form of rick burning.

One begins to think that this may not be so. Take the family automobile: a simple, easily enough comprehended (or seemingly so), unthreatening, and convenient product of folk technology rather than of modern science. Who would imagine any great harm coming from the automobile? Yet consider a moment. With its advent, everyday citizens, for the first time in human history, came into possession of unexampled physical energy: the powers of the gods themselves became commonplace. And from the very outset, violence ensued. It is said, for example, that when there were only four gasoline-powered vehicles in Missouri, two of them were in St. Louis and managed to collide with such impact as to injure both drivers, one seriously. Thus was introduced a form of pathology that was to grow steadily from that year to this. Today, something between one quarter and two thirds of the automobiles manufactured in the United States end up with blood on them. Indeed so commonplace and predictable have collisions become that the U.S. Court of Appeals for the Eighth Circuit recently ruled that a crash must be considered among the "intended uses" of a motor vehicle, and the manufacturers accordingly responsible to provide for such contingency in their design.

It becomes increasingly clear that the major environment, or, if you will, vehicle, in which incidents of uncontrolled episodic violence occur within the population is that of the automobile. Whether access and exposure to this environment have increased the incidence of such episodes, or whether the urban environment now largely created and shaped by the automobile has generally increased the violence level is uncertain at best (there has, of course, been a great decline in violence directed toward animals), but with the number of deaths and injuries at the present ongoing rates, and the number of vehicles in use approaching the one-hundred-million mark, it is a matter worth pondering.

Crashes are but one form of pathology. Each year in the United States automobiles pour eighty-six million tons of carbon monoxide, oxides of nitrogen and sulfur, hydrocarbons, lead compounds and particulates into the air we breathe. Recently my younger son came home with a button that announced, "Clean air smells funny." Dr. Clare C. Patterson of the California Institute of Technology put it another way in testimony before a congressional committee: "The average resident of the United States is being subject to severe chronic lead insult," originating in lead tetraethyl. Such poisoning can lead to severe intellectual disability in children: so much that Patterson feels it is dangerous for youth to live long periods of time near freeways.

But that is only the beginning, hardly the end of the impact of this particular form of technology on the society at this time. In consequence of the management of the automobile traffic system by means of traditional rules of the road, the incidence of armed arrest of American citizens is the highest of any civilization in recorded history. In 1965, for example, the California highway patrol alone made one million arrests. Indeed so commonplace has the experience become that a misdemeanor or felony committed in a motor vehicle is no longer considered a transgression of any particular consequence, and to be arrested by an armed police officer is regarded as a commonplace. That is precisely what Orwell told us would happen, is it not?

There are some 13,600,000 accidents a year, with some thirty million citations for violations issued each twelve months. And at this point, ineluctably, technology begins to have an effect on the most fundamental of civil institutions, the legal system itself. Largely in consequence of the impact of traffic-crash litigation, it now takes an average of 32.4 months to obtain a civil jury trial for a personal injury case in the metropolitan areas of the nation. In Suffolk County, New York, it is 50 months. In the Circuit Court of Cook County, serving Chicago, it is 64 months. This past winter in Bronx County, New York, the presiding judge of the appellate division announced he was suspending civil trials altogether while he tried to catch up with criminal cases. The courts are inundated; the bar is caught up, implicated and confused; the public knows simply that somehow justice is delayed and delayed. All of which is a consequence of this simplest form of technology, working its way on the institutions of an essentially pretechnological society.

It sometimes happens that a work of art appearing at a particular moment in time somehow simultaneously epitomizes and reveals the essential truths of the time. In a most astonishing and compelling way this has happened for the American city, and it has done so, most appropriately, on Forty-second Street in Manhattan, in the persona of the Ford Foundation headquarters, designed by Kevin Roche, John Dinkeloo & Associates—a great firm, successor to Eero Saarinen & Associates whose first large commission was, of course, the General Motors Technical Center outside Detroit. Saarinen, and now Roche, have gathered a group of artist/technicians whose work, from the Dulles Airport at Chantilly, Virginia, to the Trans World Airlines Terminal at Kennedy Airport and the Columbia Broadcasting headquarters in New York City, has evoked the power and purpose of the age of technology as perhaps no other organization has.

Here in the Ford Foundation headquarters is expressed the very highest purposes of modern technological power: compassionate and potent concern for the betterment of man's lot. The building is everything a building could be: a splendid work place, a gift to the city in the form of a public park, a gift to the world simply as a work of imagination and daring. If it is a reproach of sorts to the public and private builders of the nation who by and large show little of either, it is a gentle reproach, more show than tell. In that favored form of foundation giving, it is a kind of demonstration project: an example of what can, and what therefore in an age of technology must, be done.

The exterior of the building is quiet and unassertive: it is not *that* big a building, and it seeks rather to understate both its size and importance. No-nonsense shafts of Cor-ten steel rise from the ground, here and there sheathed with a blue-brown granite and interspersed with large rectangular glass panels. Rather in the mode of a cathedral, the portals do not so much impart as suggest the experience to come. It is only on entering—Chartres, say, or Vézelay—and encountering the incomparable space, shaped and reserved for a single purpose only, that one leaves off observing the building and begins to be shaped by it: the eye rises, the mind turns to last things. So with the Ford Foundation headquarters. One passes through revolving doors to enter a garden. Truly a garden, a small park, like nothing anywhere else to be encountered, a third of an acre, lush and generous, climbing a small hill that follows the terrain of Manhattan at this point, illuminated by the now vast windows that climb nine stories toward heaven itself, and there only to be met by a glass roof. Water moves slightly in a pool—a font? Attendants move quietly, and are helpful. One notices that vegetation sprouts from beams and ledges on the third and fourth and even the fifth floors. One is awestruck by the wealth and power of the foundation, and the sheer authority of its intent to do good. Only the gray-white light is not quite what it should be: as in those French and German cathedrals whose stained glass was lost to war or revolution or Protestantism.

But this is only the entering light. As in any such edifice, there is a light within. In this case a very monstrancelike golden-brown glow that shines forth from the offices of the foundation executives, who from the floor of the park are to be seen at their work behind glass panels formed and reticulated by the same rusted beams that frame the colorless glass of two sides of the building. (Cor-ten steel seals itself by rusting and need not be painted.) At this point one perceives readily enough that the building has been built as a factory. Not precisely as a factory—any more than the Gothic Revival built office buildings precisely as medieval monasteries—but rather to evoke the style and somehow the spirit of a great plant. The huge, heavy lateral beams, from which elsewhere would be suspended the giant hoists that roam back and forth amidst the clatter and roar; the sawtooth roof; the plant managers' eyrie hung from the ceiling, keeping an eye on everything; the perfectly standardized, interchangeable fixtures in each office; the seriousness and competence of it all, even the blue-black, somehow oily granite of the cheerless rest rooms (No Loitering

*The Ford Foundation building
at night, as seen from
New York's 42nd Street.*

in the Can) magically, stunningly, triumphantly, evoke the style and spirit of the primeval capitalist factory. Cor-ten. Red. Rouge. River Rouge. Of course! And why not, for $16,000,000 of Henry Ford's money? He was that kind of man. Knew how to make automobiles and obviously liked to. Else he could hardly have done it so well. All black, just as the Ford Foundation headquarters is all brown. Same principle. So also the panopticon effect of the exposed offices wherein the presumptively interchangeable officers at their perfectly interchangeable desks labor at their good works in full view of management and public alike. (The public serving, perhaps, as the visitors to Jeremy Bentham's prospective model prison: a "promiscuous assemblage of unknown and therefore unpaid, ungarbled and incorruptible inspectors"?) Critics, at least in the first reviews, seem to have missed most of this, but no matter: the architecture needs no guidebook: the intellectual and aesthetic effect is not to be avoided, even when the intent is least perceived. All in all it is just as McGeorge Bundy proclaimed it in the 1968 annual report of the foundation: "Kevin Roche's triumph."

But it is more than that. Or rather, there is more than is to be perceived at one time. A great work of art has levels of meaning at once various and varying. Standing in the park, gazing upward, following the factory motif, the mind is of a sudden troubled. Something is missing. Noise. Factories are places of noise. Of life. Clatter. Roar.

A daytime view, looking out from the two-hundred-foot-square interior garden.

There is no noise here. Only quiet. The quiet of the . . . ? The mind oscillates. It is a factory, all right. But a *ruined* factory! The holocaust has come and gone: hence the silence. The windows have blown out, and only the gray light of the burned-out world enters. The weather has got in, and with it nature now reclaiming the ravaged union of fire and earth. The factory floor has already begun to turn to forest. Vegetation has made its way to ledges halfway up the interior. The machine tools are gone. Reparations? Vandalism? Who knows. But the big machines will no longer be making little machines. Gone too is the rational, reforming, not altogether disinterested purpose of the panopticon. One is alone in the ominous gloom of a Piranesi prison, noting the small bushes taking hold in the crevices of the vast ruined arches.

Is it the past or the future that has taken hold of the mind? Certainly the ruined steel frame is a good enough symbol of the twentieth century so far. (Where had one last seen that color? Of course. Pingree Street in Detroit after the riot. A year later there it was again, on Fourteenth Street in Washington: the fiery orange-red of the twisted steel shopping centers' framing after the looting and arson has passed.) Or is it the future? There is a *sur réal* quality that comes of standing in the ruined half of the building, watching the life going on behind the glass walls of the intact half, seemingly oblivious to the devastation without. Can ruin advance slowly like rot? No. Yes. Did the automobile start all this? No. Surely it is all this that started automobiles. One quarter to two thirds of which end up with blood on them. Blood. Red. Rouge. River Rouge.

Enough.

But then why has the American architect Joseph Stein built the Ford Foundation headquarters in New Delhi immediately adjacent the Lodi Tombs, symbols of death sensual to the point of necrophilia? Did not Bentham remark that he could legislate wisely for all India from the recesses of his study? There's a panopticon in your future.

No. Enough.

And yet it comes together in a way. "*Le siècle de la machine,*" Le Corbusier wrote in 1924, "*a réveillé l'architecte.*" Not least because the machine destroys so much of that experience of community that the architect seeks to create. A biographer describes Eero Saarinen's purpose thus: "What . . . [he] wished to renew, maintain, and improve was the organic expression of the *civitas* which he found weakened or destroyed virtually everywhere in modern civilization, with one significant exception—the university campus." And so Roche built a ruined machine-for-making-machines as the headquarters of a great philanthropic foundation whose principal concerns have been to support the universities of the nation, and to seek to strengthen the community life of its cities.

The research of James Q. Wilson and Edward C. Banfield at Harvard University is now beginning to produce results surprisingly similar to the visions of the architect/artist. As Wilson puts it, "After a decade or more of being told by various leaders that what's wrong with our large cities is inadequate transportation, or declining retail sales, or poor housing, the resident of the big city is beginning to assert his own definition of that problem—and this definition has very little to do with the conventional wisdom on the urban crisis." Wilson and his colleague asked one thousand Boston homeowners what *they* thought to be the biggest urban problem of this time.

> The "conventional" urban problems—housing, transportation, pollution, urban renewal, and the like—were a major concern of only 18 per cent of those questioned, and these were expressed disproportionally by the wealthier, better-educated respondents. Only 9 per cent mentioned jobs and employment, even though many of those interviewed had incomes at or even below what is often regarded as the poverty level. *The issue which concerned more respondents than any other was variously stated—crime, violence, rebellious youth, racial tension, public immorality, delinquency. However stated, the common theme seemed to be a concern for improper behavior in public places.*
>
> What these concerns have in common, and thus what constitutes the "urban" problem for a large percentage (perhaps a majority) of urban citizens, is *a sense of the failure of community.*

And yet cities, by definition, destroy community. Or is it only when they are too big, too unsettled, that they do this? Is it only when social conditions are allowed to arise which lead inevitably to assaults on the private communities that experienced city dwellers create for themselves, which in turn lead to more collective regulation and, in consequence, less of the self-imposed decision to behave properly and as expected, which is the essence of community?

We do not know. "Them what gets the apple gets the worm," goes an old folk saying. Is that what the Ford Foundation building represents: a shining exterior, rotting from within? A civilization whose cancerous growth has already devoured half its offspring, and is moving toward the unthinking, untroubled other half? We shall see. Hopefully, in the meantime we shall also think about it a bit. Mumford, unfailingly, has sorted out the levels of immediacy and difficulty of the current crisis.

> To go deeper into this immediate situation we must, I suggest, distinguish between three aspects, only one of which is open to immediate rectification. We must first separate out the problems that are soluble with the means we have at hand: this includes such immediate measures as vermin control, improved garbage collection, cheap public transportation, new schools and hospitals and health clinics. Second, those that require a new approach, new agencies, new methods, whose assemblage will require time, even though the earliest possible action is urgent. And finally there are those that require a reorientation in the purposes and ultimate ideals of our whole civilization—solutions that hinge on a change of mind, as far-reaching as that which characterized the change from the medieval religious mind to the modern scientific mind. Ultimately, the success of the first two changes will hinge upon this larger—and, necessarily, later—transformation. So, far from looking to a scientifically oriented technology to solve our problems, we must realize that this highly sophisticated dehumanized technology itself now produces some of our most vexatious problems, including the unemployment of the unskilled.

But something more than thinking will be required. A certain giving of ourselves with no certainty of what will come of it. It is the only known way, and imperfectly known at that.

Attend to Mrs. Boyle at the end of *Juno and the Paycock*, pleading for the return of a simpler life, a life before all things had become political, before all men were committed, before all cities somehow seemed in flames:

> Sacred Heart o' Jesus, take away our hearts o' stone, and give us hearts o' flesh! Take away this murdherin' hate, an' give us Thine own eternal love!

Martin Duberman

Harlem:
The Village That
Became a Ghetto

What Daniel P. Moynihan has done in the previous essay for the history of urban problems in general, in this article Martin Duberman does, in somewhat different fashion, for one city, New York, and one particular problem—the black ghetto. His account is both a study in microcosm of the fate of the northern Negro and a history of a particular urban neighborhood. It throws light also on many broader aspects of city life in the nineteenth and twentieth centuries: the role of urban transportation, of land speculation, of the housing problem in general (for rich and for poor). Above all it reveals the dynamic quality of the city environment and the extraordinary changes that occur one after another when a huge urban complex develops out of a cluster of villages in a relatively short span of time. The history of Harlem, "the village that became a ghetto," is, of course, entirely tragic and ignoble—a reflection of the tragedy of the black man in America and of the ignobility of the majority of white Americans in matters of race relations.

Mr. Duberman, professor of history at Princeton University, is the author of the standard biography of Charles Francis Adams and also a playwright. His In White America, *a drama based on letters and other documents dealing with Negro life, first produced in 1963, was both a commercial and critical success.*

*M*anhattan Island had Negroes almost as soon as it had settlers. They were slaves, of course, the property of the New Amsterdam Dutch; and very few of them lived in Harlem. That northeastern section of the island, although settled early, remained throughout the colonial period a distant village, a rural outpost of the metropolis. Nearly all of the seven hundred Negroes who were part of New York's population when Peter Stuyvesant surrendered his colony to the English in 1664 lived far downtown, with or near their masters. Under the Dutch, slaves received the rudiments of schooling, were allowed to own land, and in a few cases, were even permitted to obtain their freedom.

The English changed all that, developing a slave code of precise regulations and heightened restrictions. Yet by the end of the eighteenth century, the movement to abolish slavery in New York State had begun. Led by the Quakers, and given further impetus by the egalitarian ideas of the Revolution, it resulted in full emancipation through action of the state legislature on July 4, 1827.

When that date arrived, the Negro population of Manhattan and Brooklyn had grown to about fifteen thousand. The Negro citizens of New York were henceforth free but hardly equal. They had to meet higher property qualifications than their white counterparts in order to vote; they had to attend separate schools; they were barred from many public facilities; they could hold only the most menial jobs; and they were forced to live in squalid surroundings.

This does not mean that in the pre-Civil War period the Negro was confined to a single area of the city; but within a given neighborhood, segregation was usually complete. Between 1820 and 1840, Negroes were concentrated chiefly in the notorious "Five Points" district, an area that today includes City Hall and its environs. The crowded Negro section known as Stagg Town was vividly described by Charles Dickens in his *American Notes:* ". . . lanes and alleys, paved with mud knee-deep . . . hideous tenements [in] which . . . dogs would howl to lie . . . where women and men . . . slink off to sleep, forcing the dislodged rats to move away."

There was a somewhat brighter side: from 1821 to 1829 a Negro theatre existed, the African Grove, which whites were allowed to attend, but in a partitioned section at the back; the famed "old Mulberry School" produced most of the city's Negro leaders; and there was the beginning of an institutional life in the African Society of Mutual Relief and in the growing number of Negro churches.

Stability, however, was not to be the lot of New York's Negro community. By the time of the Civil War the Five Points had been taken over by the immigrant Irish, and the focus of Negro settlement had shifted to Greenwich Village. This, too, was temporary; by the turn of the century, the Negro population had become most heavily concentrated in two areas: the unsavory "Tenderloin" (today's midtown Manhattan) and "San Juan Hill" (today's west Sixties) so called because of frequent racial battles that took place in the neighborhood.

*When this lithograph was done
in 1812, Harlem was a village
of less than one hundred families.*

It was by no means only the pressure of foreign immigrant groups that kept Negroes on the move. Probably the most important factor of all was the huge increase of New York's black population itself, caused largely by the arrival of southern Negroes. By 1910 the number of blacks in Manhattan alone had jumped to over 60,000; in another twenty years the figure would more than triple.

They had to go somewhere, and where they went was determined by unpredictable factors. During a real-estate depression, for instance, the more affluent members of the Negro community would grasp at the chance to move to a better neighborhood; their advent would then lead to widespread white desertion, and the poorer Negroes would rapidly move in behind them. The curious fact is that before 1900, Harlem seemed the part of Manhattan least likely to become a black residential section, let alone a black ghetto.

For Harlem was a synonym for elegant living through a good part of the nineteenth century. As late as 1820, it had only ninety-one families, one church, one school, and one library; still a village, it was dominated by the extensive estates of the wealthy farmers known as patroons. A New York City planning commission in 1811 announced its opinion that Harlem would not be "covered with houses for centuries to come."

It is true that in the decades just before and after the Civil War, Harlem went into a temporary decline. Many of the large estates, including Alexander Hamilton's beautiful Grange, were auctioned off because of worn-out soil. Newly arriving Irish immigrants, destitute and unwanted, squatted on the village's abandoned lands, threw up flimsy shantytowns (bringing property values down still further), and thus for the first time, though not the last, turned Harlem into a slum.

But a renaissance was near at hand. The turning point came between 1878 and 1881 when the elevated railroad was extended to 129 Street, thus converting Harlem into a feasible commuting point from downtown Manhattan. Feasible soon meant fashionable, since the improved transportation came at precisely the moment when the island's population and industrial growth were necessitating new expansion—in Manhattan, that could only occur to the north.

And so by the mid-1880's, the Harlem land boom was on. Land speculators and builders seemingly overnight turned a decaying community into the city's most plush residential area. Rows of elegant brownstones (many of which are still occupied) sprang up. A stunning group of one hundred and six was designed by Stanford White; its rents started at the then-astronomical figure of eighty dollars per month (the houses are now known as Striver's Row because of their well-to-do Negro tenants). Into the new mansions moved old-line aristocrats and new-style politicians, and to tend to their needs came theatres, luxurious restaurants, Gothic-revival churches, banks, a Harlem Opera House (built by Oscar Hammerstein I in 1880), a Harlem Yacht Club, a Harlem Literary Society, and a Harlem Philharmonic Orchestra. One of America's first suburban communities had been born—and it was, for a while, one of the most elegant. "It is evident to the most superficial observer," said the *Harlem Monthly Magazine* in 1893, "that the centre of fashion, wealth, culture, and intelligence, must, in the near future, be found in the ancient and honorable village of Harlem." Twenty years later that would read like satire.

A small number of Negroes had always lived in Harlem—as slaves in the seventeenth and eighteenth centuries, and following emancipation, as small farmers or domestic servants. By the 1880's the Negro community had grown to several hundred families and was generally, though not exclusively, confined to the streets of the west 120's. It was a large enough community to provide abundant servants for fashionable white Harlem, but not large enough to create apprehension.

Then, around the turn of the century, came a substantial growth in Manhattan's Negro population and, coincidentally, the swift collapse of the Harlem land boom. Speculators had inflated real-estate values and contractors had overbuilt—the result was the bust of 1904-1905. Faced with ruin, some operators decided to rent their vacant apartments to Negroes. They had no lack of applicants, for many in the black community were eager to pay the higher Harlem rents. In 1905 there had been a brutal race riot in the ghetto of the west Sixties, and at the same time demolition on the site of the new Pennsylvania Station destroyed hundreds of Negro tenements and caused unbelievable crowding in the Negro slums of midtown. In less than a decade, at least 20,000 Negroes had come to live in central Harlem, most of them between 130 and 144 streets, bounded by Park Avenue on the

east and by Eighth Avenue on the west.

Needless to say, this new Negro influx into Harlem was protested—bitterly but futilely. Whites tried to halt the "invasion" by pressuring banks not to lend money or to renew mortgages, by forming holding companies to buy up "Negro" houses and evict their tenants, and by agreements between white property owners not to rent or sell to Negroes.

All of these efforts failed. The chief reason, apparently, was that unified action by white property owners could never be won. Some white landlords and speculators could not resist the lure of profit. Indeed, a few actively encouraged the Negro advance: they would buy a building and open it up to black tenants with the purpose of forcing neighboring whites either to sell out at a deflated price or to buy back the "Negro" building at an inflated one. By the end of World War I it became clear that the black influx could not be halted, and the white community shifted its tactics from resistance to flight. House by house, block by block, they fled the black advance. It was not Negro behavior, but white, that turned Harlem into a ghetto.

New York's pattern was hardly unique. In the early years of the twentieth century, ghettos were rising in cities all over the country. This was the result of rural southern Negroes migrating toward "freedom" and industrial opportunity, and of the subsequent decision by whites to isolate the migrants in clearly defined enclaves. New York had its Harlem, Chicago its South Side, Detroit its Paradise Valley, and almost every urban center its "Nigger Rows," "Bronze-

Harlem's fall from elegance took just about a decade. In 1908 it was still the home of fashionable ladies who rode their carriages to the races (left). By about 1918, when the photograph at right was taken, Harlem was on its way to becoming a ghetto.

villes," "Smoketowns," or "Coon Alleys."

Yet the development of city ghettos did not follow identical lines. In Chicago, for example, preexisting Negro neighborhoods simply expanded their boundaries—a pattern in contrast to the dramatic shift of New York's Negro community into a previously all-white area. Harlem, moreover, was unique in the sense that no other black ghetto arose in what recently had been a fashionable white community.

In any case, Harlem was changed in a few decades from a symbol of success to a symbol of defeat, from a gilt-edged white compound to a dilapidated black slum. The combination of high rents and low salaries had much to do with the change. By the end of the twenties, in response to the overwhelming demand by Negroes for apartments and the limited facilities available, rents in Harlem had doubled from what they had been the previous decade; the average Harlem family paid about $9.50 a room monthly compared with the $6.50 paid by the typical white working-class family elsewhere in the city. At the same time, the Negro worker, restricted to menial jobs, was earning less money than his white counterpart—roughly $1,300 a year compared with $1,600.

As a result of high rents and low incomes, families often had to take in lodgers to make ends meet, and this in turn weakened the family structure and led to more crowding and unsanitary living conditions. Another device for raising rent money in the twenties was the famed "rent party," where a twenty-five cent admission ticket bought southern barbecue and piano playing by the likes of Willie "the Lion" Smith, James P. Johnson, Willie Gant, or "Fats" Waller.

All the statistics of birth and death and disease made it clear that Harlem's health problems were the most pronounced in the city. Not all of this, however, could be laid at the door of low incomes or congested living conditions. Many Harlemites were recent arrivals from the rural South, and as "an ignorant and unsophisticated peasant people"—a description given by a Negro scholar, E. Franklin Frazier—they lacked the experience and training needed for survival in an urban environment. They tended to put their money in the hands of quack spiritualists and "healers."

Yet in the twenties, when most white New Yorkers thought of Harlem, they thought of it not as a slum community breeding disease and despair, but as the exotic locale for a night's slumming. To whites, Harlem ("Take the 'A' Train") meant bootleggers and prostitutes, jazz and chitterlings, the numbers racket and dope; it meant the little cellar cabarets and after-hours places where Jelly Roll Morton or Ethel Waters might entertain and where jam sessions might last all night; it meant the Cotton Club, where Duke Ellington's band held forth for five years; it meant the Savoy Ballroom, which took up a whole block on Lenox Avenue and where, on a two-hundred-foot dance floor under klieg lights, the Lindy Hop was born. (Malcolm X reports in his autobiography that when La Guardia closed the Savoy during World War II, Harlemites believed the real reason was to stop Negroes from dancing with white women.)

Throughout the twenties white playboys poured their money and their fantasies into Harlem. A few blacks may have profited from the money, but many more suffered from the fantasies. For most Negroes in Harlem were not swingers, were not joyous primitives or rhythmic giants. They were people struggling to adjust to a strange urban world, struggling to afford enough food and clothing, struggling to persuade the landlord to fix a leak in the ceiling or to cover up rat holes so that their babies would not be bitten at night.

A few whites were willing to face the facts of Harlem life and to try to change them, but only a few. Mary White Ovington, who in 1909 helped to found the National Association for the Advancement of Colored People, was one. John D. Rockefeller, Jr., who gave millions to Harlem charities, was another—although the Paul Laurence Dunbar Apartments, which he financed in the twenties to serve as a model housing development, were priced too high for most Negroes.

Fortunately, Harlem did not put its hopes for a better life solely on the benevolence of whites—slummers or philanthropists. The Negro community developed its own leadership and its own forms of expression. Often that leadership proved distasteful to whites—as with the black nationalist Marcus Garvey, whose Universal Negro Improvement Association flourished during the twenties, and more recently, with Malcolm X and Adam Clayton Powell, Jr. Sometimes the community's leadership, though highly acceptable to whites, was not in the best interest of Harlem itself—as when Negro political boss Ferdinand Q. Morton was recognized by Tammany throughout the

1920's and early 1930's as the head of the Harlem Democracy (often called Black Tammany) even while he dictatorially silenced opposition and used his power chiefly to promote his own rather than the community's interests. Only a few of Harlem's leaders have won and held admiration in both the white and black worlds. Foremost in this regard is A. Philip Randolph, the pioneering civil rights organizer and president of the Brotherhood of Sleeping Car Porters, whose personal integrity and devotion to the interests of the Negro community alike have been unquestionable.

It is paradoxical that the ghetto at one and the same time constricts the possibilities of Negro life and yet forms the base for such black power as has existed—not only political, but fraternal and social as well.

Harlem has changed surprisingly little since the 1920's. The Savoy Ballroom and the Cotton Club no longer exist, but in terms of basic institutional and cultural patterns, Harlem today is much what it was forty years ago. To the extent that change has come, it has often been for the worse.

Central Harlem no longer has, needless to say, a Philharmonic Orchestra or a Yacht Club, but less obvious is the fact that in the entire ghetto there is not one museum or art gallery, and only five libraries (one of which is the superb Schomburg Collection, probably the most important archive in the world devoted to Negro life and history). About all that Harlem does have more of in 1968 than it did in 1928 is churches. There are now 256 of them, the majority belonging to segregated Negro Protestant denominations; many of the rest are evangelical sects.

Economically as well as socially, Harlem is not the viable, self-contained community that it was back at the turn of the century. There are still banks, but with the exception of the Carver Federal Savings and Loan Association (with assets of more than $21,000,000), they are all branches of white-owned downtown banks. There are still thousands of stores (with an annual gross sale of nearly $350,000,000), but they, too, are mostly owned by whites who live outside the community—and who invest their profits outside. Probably the chief reason why so few of Harlem's stores are owned by Harlemites is that in a community that lives on credit, as Harlem does, future wages are already pledged, and thus there is no risk capital available for business investment. (It should be noted, though, that Jackie Robinson, the former baseball star-turned-businessman and adviser to Governor Nelson Rockefeller, recently reported that in the last two years, Negro-owned businesses in Harlem have risen from eighteen per cent to thirty-one per cent of the total.) Harlem's businesses, moreover, provide very little employment for the community's inhabitants, most of whom have to travel downtown for their daily jobs, forty-three per cent of which are in unskilled occupations due to be automated out of existence within the next decade.

In still another sense, central Harlem since World War II has been a community in decline. Many middle- or upper-income Negroes

James Reagan's 1968 drawing, Pool Hall, *expresses what Harlem looks like from the inside to an eighteen-year-old resident of the ghetto.*

have moved to Westchester or Long Island. Even the Negro masses have begun to shift to other ghettos within the city—to the lower Bronx, to Queens, and to Brooklyn's Bedford-Stuyvesant—with the result that central Harlem suffered a ten per cent population loss from 1950 to 1960, a decade in which most metropolitan ghettos were growing.

Many of the elegant brownstones still stand in Harlem and from the outside still give off an air of stability. But their interior condition is far worse than it was forty years ago. More than 230,000 people live within three and one half square miles, packed into tenements of which twenty-five per cent have been judged "overcrowded" and a full forty-nine per cent have been labelled "dilapidated." Rents, moreover, continue to be high; a single room is usually priced from $16 to $28 per month, and it is difficult to find any apartment, let alone a decent one, which rents for less than $75 per month. The city's Buildings Department averages five hundred complaints a day about rats, falling plaster, lack of heat, and unsanitary plumbing.

The disabling personal and social consequences of living under such conditions are, as Kenneth B. Clark has eloquently written in *Dark Ghetto,* beyond mere quantification. Statistics of disease, drug addiction, crime, and prostitution tell us something of these consequences, but we have heard the reports so often that they carry only limited impact. Besides, statistics cannot measure or weigh the frightful emotional costs of living in the ghetto; they cannot convey the irritability and self-alienation which results from lack of privacy, the fury which mounts at an absentee landlord's endless evasions, the anguish which comes when a fourteen-year-old child turns to prostitution or to drugs.

Expletives and activity, amid the ghetto's
boredom are all expressed in eighteen-year-old
Jeff McDonald's A Harlem Playground *(1968).*

To get some sense of the ghetto's human cost, one must look not to the statistics of the social scientists, but to the work of Negro writers for whom Harlem has been the central experience and the central metaphor. From the 1920's on, talented black poets and novelists—Langston Hughes, Countée Cullen, James Baldwin, Jean Toomer, Claude McKay, Richard Wright, Ralph Ellison—have given us insight into Harlem's special hell. Most recently of all, we have had Claude Brown's searing autobiography, *Manchild in the Promised Land*. One anecdote and one statement in Brown's book does more to sum up contemporary Harlem than any volume of statistics. The anecdote relates to Brown's experience as a young teenager hauled into court for stealing: the judge, after lecturing Brown and his friends, announces magnanimously that he is "going to give you boys another chance"; Brown takes even himself by surprise when he yells out, "Man, you not givin' us another chance. You givin' us the same chance we had before." Yet at the end of his book, Brown makes this telling statement: ". . . despite everything that Harlem did to our generation, I think it gave something to a few. It gave them a strength that couldn't be obtained anywhere else."

But finally the last word must go to Langston Hughes: Harlem "has been the subject of innumerable surveys, innumerable reports published and unpublished, innumerable official and unofficial studies, hundreds of magazine and newspaper articles, columns, radio and TV commentaries, plus an unending stream of speeches from men in pulpits, at forums and learned seminars. Seemingly all that could conceivably be written or said, has been said—and Harlem is still the same old Harlem."

Andy Logan

J. F. K.: The Stained-Glass Image

It is always difficult to evaluate recent events. Time—the perspective of history—is essential to any sound understanding of their significance. This is especially true where the careers of the main actors in recent events are concerned, and indeed the task becomes next to impossible when the subject is a man cut off in the prime of life by tragic, meaningless circumstances. The tendency to make a martyred saint of the victim, to forget his weaknesses and glorify his strengths, then becomes irresistible. This was true, as Andy Logan, staff writer for the New Yorker and author of The Man Who Robbed the Robber Barons, points out in the following essay, in the case of Abraham Lincoln and also in the recent case of John F. Kennedy.

Logan dissects with candor and critical acuity the shelves of books, many of them best sellers, which have appeared in the years since Kennedy's assassination. She exposes in detail the cant, the sentimentalism, and the obfuscations which they contain, and offers some generalizations about the genre of "Kennedy books" as well. That this essay was written in sorrow rather than anger, however, is clear. It is her own admiration of Kennedy, the belief that Kennedy's long-run reputation will only be harmed by unctuous flattery and self-serving praise, that has motivated her attack on the Kennedy biographers. The historical lesson to be learned, of course, concerns the importance of objectivity. The historian may justly admire and praise his subject; nevertheless, he must be neither an apologist nor a press agent if his work is to have any enduring value as a portrait of the man.

*I*n mid-November, 1963, according to all the major best-seller lists, by far the most popular nonfiction publication in America was a book that portrayed Jack Kennedy as "immature," "arrogant," "snobbish," "glib," "slick," "calculating," "hard as nails," "mealymouthed," "opportunistic," "Machiavellian," "intellectually shallow," "spiritually rootless," "morally pusillanimous," "passionless," "vain," "shifty-eyed," and, for every good reason, nicknamed "Jack the Knife." The book, of course, was *J.F.K.: The Man and the Myth,* by Victor Lasky. By the end of the same month there burned above the grave of the very same man an eternal flame, more often reserved in the protocol of his religion for saints of the first order. Whatever their religious or political persuasion, few Americans were protesting this instant canonization. In the horror, grief, and guilt that overwhelmed the nation following the assassination, the minor Kennedy myth that Lasky had contended against—the fine-liberal-fellow image—had expanded uncountable times, been transformed and purified, burst all mortal bonds, and soared toward the realm of the supernatural. As after the death of Lincoln nearly a hundred years earlier, the common thought of Americans was "How are the fallen mighty!" and John F. Kennedy was on his way to becoming the legendary national hero of his century.

"It is difficult now to comprehend the wave of hero-worship which swept over the country after Lincoln's assassination," Roy P. Basler wrote a generation ago in *The Lincoln Legend.* "Lincoln was suddenly lifted into the sky as the folk-hero, the deliverer, and the martyr who had come to save his people and to die for them . . . the folk mind was enraptured with the stories of how Lincoln had suffered, prayed, dreamed, and loved mankind and conquered his enemies. How he had doubted, despaired, cunningly schemed, and contrived to effect his ends, no one wanted to hear." Thousands of Americans were soon seriously arguing that Lincoln was of divine origin. (After all, in his own words he was the son of an "angel mother"; his father-of-record was a poor carpenter; and he was shot on Good Friday.) This conclusion would have astonished Lincoln only a little more than, in the view of Arthur Krock and some of John Kennedy's other friends, the lighting of the eternal flame would have embarrassed Kennedy nearly a century later. But neither man was by this time making history. It was being made for him.

Until 1872 Lincoln biography was entirely in the hands of spiritual and stylistic descendants of Parson Weems, rather than of men who had known him as he was. Then a book appeared by Ward Hill Lamon, a jovial crony of Lincoln's who had ridden the backwoods legal circuit with him in central Illinois. Lamon was "pre-eminently the Good Fellow," writes Sandburg, and the President's more punctilious associates regarded the long Lincoln-Lamon alliance as evidence of "a certain degree of . . . obtuseness" on Lincoln's part. "Sing me a little song," he often said to Lamon, who would then make him smile with some such nonsensical ballad as "Cousin Sally Downard." "I want you with me, I must have you," Lincoln told his old friend

when he was about to leave for Washington, and he arranged to have
Lamon appointed a city marshal at the capital. Lamon's biography
of Lincoln, pulled together by a ghostwriter, was based largely on
material gathered by Lincoln's onetime law partner, William H.
Herndon. A bald account of the late President's political opportunism
and his often indecorous life during his western years, it was denounced
as "shameless." "Want of delicacy and even decency," wrote a more
worshipful biographer, made its appearance "something close to a
national misfortune." The book did not even reap the traditional
reward of publications charged with indecency; it was a financial
failure. In the first years after the assassination Herndon had delivered
several lectures based on the material he had made available to Lamon,
but it wasn't until 1889 that he published his own biography, *Herndon's Lincoln,* in which Lincoln emerged as an earthy, moody, irreligious frontier hero, unrecognizable as the saintly Christian martyr
of prevailing legend. ("Why, Lamon," wrote Herndon, "if you and
I had not told the exact truth about Lincoln he would have been a
myth in a hundred years after 1865.") The Herndon book, which, of
course, launched myths of its own, such as the Ann Rutledge love
story so infuriating to Mary Todd Lincoln, brought Herndon less than

Michael Ramus' mythical cartoon pictures the Kennedy authors surrounding their hero in the White House Rose Garden. From left: Maud Shaw, Pierre Salinger, Paul Fay, Theodore Sorensen, Arthur Schlesinger, Jr., Evelyn Lincoln, Kenneth O'Donnell, David Powers, Lawrence O'Brien, and (with microphone, far right) William Manchester.

five hundred dollars in royalties in the next eight years. Their tedious, circumspect *Abraham Lincoln: A History* proved to be a more profitable venture for Lincoln's two private secretaries, John G. Nicolay and John Hay. Authorized by Robert Todd Lincoln, the President's surviving son (Nicolay and Hay, gibed Herndon, were "afraid of Bob; he gives them materials and they in their turn play *hush*"), the widely admired biography appeared in serial form in the *Century* Magazine during the eighties but was not published as a book until 1890, a quarter of a century after Lincoln's death.

The colleagues of our twentieth-century presidential martyr did not wait so long to be heard from. As we all know, among the nearly two hundred books on Kennedy issued in the thirty-six months after his death (including *The Mind of JFK, The Faith of JFK, The Kennedy Wit, More Kennedy Wit,* and other striking signs of publishers' faith in the selling power of the newly sacred name) were reports by his special counsel (Theodore Sorensen's *Kennedy*), by one of his special assistants (Arthur Schlesinger, Jr.'s *A Thousand Days*), by his chief of press relations (Pierre Salinger's *With Kennedy*), by his private secretary (Evelyn Lincoln's *My Twelve Years with John F. Kennedy*), and by his children's nurse (Maud Shaw's *White*

House Nannie). Besides these, there was *The Pleasure of His Company*, by Paul B. "Red" Fay, Jr., Kennedy's old friend from PT-boat days whom he called "Grand Old Lovable," who could always make him laugh with his uninhibited rendition of "Hooray for Hollywood!" and whom Kennedy brought to Washington by arranging his appointment as Under Secretary of the Navy.

None of these posthumous best sellers was authorized by the surviving Kennedys, of course, in the same sense that they authorized the Manchester account of the assassination. Indeed, the family tried to prevent publication of *White House Nannie*. After the attempt failed, however, they censored only a few paragraphs since it turned out to be in the inane tradition of inside stories by refined nannies who wouldn't dream of telling all ("[Mrs. Kennedy] never likes to put other people out, even the tiniest bit"). *The Pleasure of His Company* is on the family Index, although Fay submitted it for clearance and has said that he deleted 90,000 of about 180,000 words at Mrs. Kennedy's request. His publisher thinks it was not so many. He balked, he said, at removing another 30,000, which would have reduced it to a third of its original length and might have rendered it unpublishable, an outcome the Kennedys may have had in mind. No *passim* cuts could remedy its pervading indiscretion—the evidence throughout the book that Kennedy, the symbol of intellect and culture come to the White House, had chosen to spend a large share of his leisure time during the last twenty years of his life with a good-hearted end man whose mother tongue is Kiwanis Club slang and who cheerfully admits he had to be clued in on Renoir and Cézanne. ("If you have to ask a question like that, do it in a whisper," Kennedy told him. "We're trying to give this administration a semblance of class.") Rejecting Fay's three-thousand-dollar gift to the Kennedy Library, Mrs. Kennedy—for whom those long, recurrent weekends *en famille* with the Fays may have been somewhat of a trial—wrote that she regarded the contribution as "hypocritical." Of all the diarists of the Kennedy era to date, Fay, best man at the Kennedy wedding, had been closest to the Hyannisport-Hickory Hill contingent. Since the appearance of his fond but inelegant view of life with their martyred brother, he and the Kennedys have been, as the columnists say, don't-invite-'ems.

Schlesinger, Sorensen, and Salinger—the S-men—remain decidedly *grata* in the compound, however, nor have diplomatic relations apparently been severed with Mrs. Lincoln, in whose adoring book the Kennedys made no changes. She had relied almost entirely on her personal diary and her trusty notebook; but the long, intensively documented accounts of the Kennedy administration by Sorensen and Schlesinger—and, to an extent perhaps, Salinger's specialized report of those years as seen from the White House press office—could not have been written without access to information and records in Kennedy control. Only nonbelievers would suggest that the authors played "hush" in any respect just because someone named Bob gave them materials. But even before their books were stamped with

President John F. Kennedy at his desk in
the Oval Room of the White House in 1963.

approval, these men were part of the privy council, sworn to serve
the clan that the same nonbelievers have charged with assuming the
prerogatives of an American royal family in temporary exile. Members
of the council (William Manchester must now be inclined to refer
to it as another "tong," the epithet that, in *Death of a President*,
he applies to Johnson's Texas followers) are pledged to rally around
during all Kennedy campaigns, to run general interference in off-
election years, to squire the widow about on occasion, and to help
the family maintain its dominion over all insiders' published recollections of the Kennedy era—or so it appears to gawkers on the
sidelines. Of course, in the years since the White House was their
second home, they have all made other lucrative professional commit-

ments, but there doesn't seem to be much doubt about where the priorities would lie if a footman should arrive with a summons from Jackie.

During Kennedy's term of office his staff was accused of trying to manage the news. Now, of course, the charge on several fronts is that of managing history. Kennedy himself during his drive for the Presidency had no qualms about attempting to control what appeared in books written about him. In the late fifties he saw to it that some of his father's anti-Semitic remarks were removed from a biography of the family, and at about the same time, according to Sorensen, he "waged an intensive effort with his contacts in the publishing world to prevent a projected biography by a writer inaccurately representing himself to potential publishers as a Kennedy intimate—a man whom Senator Kennedy in fact regarded as uninformed, unobjective and unsound."

The authors of the certified chronicles do not pretend to be objective. Salinger notes that his inability to continue to work for Lyndon Johnson was no fault of Johnson's, whom he liked. He simply came to realize that "the memory of J.F.K. was too over-powering." "Our faith in him and in what he was trying to do was absolute," he writes of Kennedy's cadre of White House assistants, and, in retrospect, Sorensen is moved by their sense of common challenge and dedication to their leader's cause to quote Henry V at Agincourt:

> . . . we . . . shall be remembered—
> We few, we happy few, we band of brothers. . . .
> And gentlemen . . . now abed
> Shall think themselves accurs'd they were not here.

Kennedy once joked with his staff about Evelyn Lincoln's blind devotion to him. "If I had said just now, 'Mrs. Lincoln, I have cut off Jackie's head, would you please send over a box?' she still would have replied, 'That's wonderful, Mr. President, I'll send it right away. . . . Did you get your nap?' " Often, in these approved histories, when a head has been cut off, Schlesinger and company, though they don't run for a box, seem to suggest that somebody else did the dirty deed or anyhow talked Kennedy into it, or that, even if their leader did it himself, it was all, in the long run, for the best—especially if he got his nap. For example, they cite every pragmatic political excuse for Kennedy's trepid record on McCarthyism, and Sorensen himself takes full blame for not pairing him against McCarthy in the Senate vote on censure. (Since Kennedy was incommunicado in the hospital and had not heard the final debate, says his loyal assistant, Sorensen felt it would be in violation of due process to record his vote.) Kennedy, having assailed Eisenhower for failing to issue an executive order forbidding racial discrimination in federally financed housing, then sat on the same order for nearly two years after he took office, but *his* delay is treated as an instance of his shrewd sense of values— even grace under pressure—since the controversial edict would have endangered the rest of his legislative program. The excuse is not extended retroactively to his predecessor.

The band of brothers combines to portray Mrs. Roosevelt as a villainess, as indeed she appeared to Kennedy in the pre-nomination days when she held him in deep distrust and maneuvered her forces in favor of Stevenson and Humphrey. And although Kennedy did once telephone the *New York Times* and suggest a vacation for David Halberstam, whose Vietnam dispatches were rankling, he made the call, argues Salinger, knowing full well that its effect would be to insure Halberstam's continued presence in Southeast Asia. As for the Cuban invasion, some of the press at the time noted that while Kennedy at his own desk was manfully taking entire responsibility for the disaster, his staff in the outer office was plying newspapermen with evidence that the debacle was really the fault of the C.I.A., the Joint Chiefs of Staff, and the previous administration. In their books they are still at it. But then, as Sorensen writes: "This is not . . . a neutral account. An impassioned participant cannot be an objective observer."

Still, if we should not be surprised to find Kennedy's friends giving him the best of it, it's all right, perhaps, to be taken aback when Schlesinger in the *Life* serialization of *A Thousand Days* has the President crying in his wife's arms after the Cuban setback and then removes the scene from his published book, announcing that "it sounded sob-sisterish" and "didn't come off." Apparently where John Kennedy is concerned, the previous winner of the Bancroft, Parkman, and Pulitzer prizes for history thinks of historic material as something that may be tried this way, turned around and tried that way, and balled up and discarded if it doesn't seem entirely becoming to the subject. And then there is the matter of the style sheet that probably didn't need to be sent to these prospective authors since they knew the house rules. Among its apparent proscriptions:

Don't call Bobby "Bobby," as everybody else does. Salinger, Sorensen, Fay, and Mrs. Lincoln dutifully make it "Bob." Schlesinger prefers "Robert Kennedy," even in describing the celebrated occasion when, fully clothed, he jumped or fell into Robert's swimming pool. There are a few exceptions, almost unavoidable since the books are full of remarks by their President in which he used the politically awkward diminutive. Schlesinger breaks ranks all the way on the few pages that cover the events at the 1960 convention after Kennedy offered Johnson the vice-presidential nomination and, apparently to his astonishment, was accepted, and his brother then appeared in the Johnson hotel suite on what Johnson interpreted as a campaign to talk him out of it. In the farrago that followed, right out of the second act of *Three Men on a Horse*, the cast of characters included another Bobby, last name Baker. Possibly Schlesinger won a special dispensation, arguing that to play fair and also call the latter "Robert" struck him as a bit much. However, in the account of the same melee by Sorensen, now quite a formal fellow for a born-and-bred Nebraskan, it is "Robert Baker."

Pretend you always called the President's wife "Mrs. Kennedy"
or "Jacqueline," not "Jackie," as the whole world knows her. Although he complies, this stipulation must have been a particular drag to Paul Fay, a highly informal type whose own wife the President always referred to as "the Bride," who knew Kennedy for many years as "Shafty Boy," and who shared with him a fraternity of pals called, in middle age as in their youthful Navy days, by such nicknames as Bitter Bill, Dirty John, and Jim Jam Jumping Jim.

The President's father is not to be called "Joe," "Old Joe," or
"Big Joe." Refer to him as Mr. Joseph P. Kennedy or "the Ambassador"—and always respectfully. ("I would like to see Red Fay write this story if my father was not ill—I think it is an outrage," runs a notation on the Fay manuscript beside an anecdote about Kennedy, Sr., that did not appear in the book.)

Rules having to do with nomenclature need not signify much. Yet anyone reading a biography of Jack Kennedy that leaves out characters called "Jackie," "Bobby," and "Big Joe" may be entitled to wonder what else has been omitted to suit his survivors. The only matters suppressed in his book, says Sorensen, are those absent "for reasons of security or propriety." One of the men delegated by Mrs. Kennedy to help blue-pencil the Fay as well as the Salinger efforts is J. Kenneth Galbraith (who once wrote an essay on the general topic of the political build-up, which he defined as "synthesizing a public reputation as a matter of deliberate design"). Most of the deletions that were eventually made in the books in question, he wrote recently, "involved the elimination of language or anecdotes which, out of context, cast reflection on the dignity of the office of President or which might, without purpose, have injured the feelings of personal friends of President Kennedy"—a patriotic and benevolent censorship policy with built-in conveniences. Mrs. Kennedy, he added, insisted on protecting more feelings—that is, removing more material—than he thought strictly necessary. One noticeable excision from all the books, just for openers: the name of any woman Kennedy ever had the slightest interest in other than his wife, unless you count Mrs. Lincoln's passing reference to a few anonymous girls so unimportant to Kennedy in his premarital years that he usually took them to the movies once apiece and had his secretary set up the dates at that. One of Fay's unforgiven transgressions, according to rumor, is his casual mention of the presence at the inaugural festivities, presumably with Kennedy's approval, of a young actress the President is said to have admired. Other evidence in the Fay book makes it obvious that Grand Old Lovable saw a great deal of his old Navy friend in the decade between the PT-boat episode and Kennedy's marriage at the rather advanced age of thirty-six, but virtually everything that went on in that unencumbered time is apparently among the thousands of words that Fay was persuaded to sacrifice in the vain hope of staying in the family favor. His book was published by Harper and Row, which had brought out *Profiles in Courage* and at the time was hoping to publish

Manchester's *Death of a President* without legal incident. Clearly, if the present keepers of the eternal flame can prevent it, there will be no Ann Rutledge chapter in the Kennedy legend.

Lincoln once found a life of Edmund Burke "so lavish in praise of his every act that one is almost driven to believe that Burke never made a mistake or a failure in his life." Most biographies, he grumbled, "commemorate a lie, and cheat posterity out of the truth." Kennedy had a similar complaint after reading the first volume of Eisenhower's autobiography. "Apparently Ike never did anything wrong," he said. "When we come to writing the memoirs of this administration, we'll do it differently." Whatever blocking tactics Kennedy tried to use on books about himself during his long campaign for the Presidency, once that was won and then irrevocably lost, it was his remark about biography and infallibility that his personal historians tried to keep in mind. Despite all their excuses for him vis-à-vis McCarthy, they felt free to conclude that in many respects he was "insensitive" and "wrong" on this issue. After all the many alibis for the Bay of Pigs, his performance there is labelled essentially "stupid"—and, as is often the case in these books, the harsh judgment is his own.

Kennedy's part in the Vietnam war is not glossed over: it was "his great failure in foreign policy." The influence of his humor and instinct for self-mockery is consistently present, as when Sorensen points out that in his chapter on the 1960 fight for the nomination he finds that he has referred to powerful Kennedy supporters as "political leaders" while those in the opposition camp are "bosses," who are then converted to "political leaders" when they come over to the right side. And though Ambassador Kennedy gets the specified respectful treatment, his son Jack made a telling remark that is also available for balance. It came after a Georgia court had sent Dr. Martin Luther King, Jr., to jail and Kennedy had made a sympathy call to King's pregnant wife. On learning of the call, King's father announced that it had persuaded him to support Kennedy, whom he had planned to vote against on strictly religious grounds. The candidate's comment was, "Imagine Martin Luther King having a bigot for a father. . . . Well, we all have fathers, don't we?"

Soon after he took office, Kennedy directed the Voice of America to broadcast the nation's story "with all our blemishes and warts, all those things about us that may not be so immediately attractive." If certain of his own blemishes are still considered unmentionable, the authorized accounts are not without authorized warts. They don't hesitate to mention his crankiness, his scorching sarcasm and quick temper, his lack of consideration for those working for him, and his impatience with anyone, no matter how worthy, who bored him. Although only an infrequent "son of a bitch" or "kicked in the can" is quoted, there is no pretense that his language in private was in keeping with his posthumous saintlike image. Even the White House nannie tells of an occasion when Caroline left behind in Kennedy's office a large doll whose special accomplishment was that it would repeat whatever was said to it. The feat involved a tape recorder, and the next day when Caroline retrieved the doll and pressed the proper button, there emerged from its rosebud plastic lips Daddy's angriest voice, using, said Miss Shaw, "a very naughty word." Not knowing how to erase the tape, she hastily called a Secret Service agent to perform a disembowelment.*

The books by Kennedy's three White House assistants are, of course, the memoirs that will be of serious interest to future historians. Of these the gracefully written *A Thousand Days* is much the best job. After all, Schlesinger has been arranging presidential crises into orderly chapters for two decades. Moreover, most of his White House years were spent not in Kennedy's West Wing wheelhouse but in the East Wing writing voluminous memos, from which task he would be summoned now and then for advice or for a bit of political legwork. His engagement in Kennedy's program was not the roll-call-by-roll-call affair that it was to Sorensen and Salinger, and he was able to view it with some perspective against a background of what had gone before and what was happening elsewhere and was thus able to write a book that is more the history of an exhilarating national interval than the biography of one man. Sorensen's *Kennedy* is shorter than the Schlesinger book (758 pages *vs.* 1,031) but it gives the impression of being far longer, since it covers in dense detail the last eleven years of Kennedy's life (Schlesinger was involved only in the last four) from a vantage point rarely more than a centimeter from Kennedy's elbow. Salinger's *With Kennedy* is a slighter book than either of these; yet it has a certain long-range interest, especially in its accounts of the vast preparations for total war in October, 1962, the problems confronting the American press during the two Cuban crises, and his own comparative intimacy with individual Russians, including Khrushchev.

Before joining Kennedy's staff, reports Schlesinger, he was warned that he would be plunging into "a ruthless scramble for access and power." He found instead that "the Kennedy White House remained to the end remarkably free of the rancor which has so often welled up in Presidential households." Although the three members of the brotherhood whose memories of Kennedy are now in print often deal with the same event, in which each played some part, little jockeying for historical position clutters their books. Their put-downs and waspish digs are generally reserved for others, usually those not wearing a PT-boat tie clasp. Here also the influence of Kennedy as editor-*in-absentia* is apparent. "Nor would he tolerate from his

---

* Curiously, Miss Shaw's account of the day of the assassination omits Caroline's harrowing ride through the Washington streets with a Secret Service man just after the news from Dallas began to come in, the episode that *Death of a President* relates in such detail. Caroline and John, she says, had just had lunch at the White House with Teddy Kennedy's children and were about to be put down for their naps when the word came. Thus, as in so many aspects of the Kennedy saga, historians are reminded of how variable is the human memory of events even so soon after the fact.

staff the slightest disparagement of the Vice President," notes Schlesinger, and although it may have taken some self-control, there are no swipes at the Vice President by these witnesses. All three, in fact, write with sympathy of Johnson's understandable discomfort in his diminished role. Kennedy's biographers feel freer to let their disparagement show, however, in reporting the 1960 convention when the two politicians were sworn enemies and, as Schlesinger puts it with historical detachment, Johnson was "laying about with heavy saber strokes, Kennedy mastering him with an urbane and deadly rapier." As for Rusk, since Kennedy's commitment to him was no longer total by 1963, Sorensen and Schlesinger permit themselves to write of him with less than total Saint Crispin's Day loyalty. He was "almost too amiably cautious," "bland," "colorless," "Buddha-like," and so circumspect that during any given crisis "no one knew quite where he stood."

There have been complaints, of course, that it was unseemly for Kennedy confidants to rush into print—and then off to the bank—with their versions of events that were so recent and that in some cases involved men still in office. But some historians will presumably be grateful that these reports were published while the memories of the impassioned participants were fresh and feisty rather than, like the biography by Lincoln's secretaries, written decades later when the excitements of the age were measured from a stately distance. As for their lack of neutrality and occasional discreet excision, perhaps their degree of candor should be compared to that of accounts of the Eisenhower administration that Sherman Adams or George Humphrey might have written if *their* President had died in office—whether or not the testimonials had been cleared with his survivors.

History, like the news, has always been subject to some management, but the stage directions should be out of earshot. The question is how far the Kennedys and company propose to carry their by now conspicuous presumption. Only three of Kennedy's ten White House assistants and none of his Cabinet have so far been heard from. But nearly all of them, it now appears, scurried directly home from the West Wing each night to write in their diaries, and the next wave of memoirs should start rolling from the typewriters soon. The planned collaboration by the Irish Mafia—Ken O'Donnell, Dave Powers, and Larry O'Brien—will apparently be a mere tandem affair. O'Brien, unlike the rest of the old gang, is still welcomed in the redecorated West Wing where augmenting the J.F.K. mythology is not politically healthy. But doubtless O'Brien's version will not be permanently withheld from us.

Will the heirs and tenders of the Kennedy mystique continue to assert editorial rights over each new volume, and will the authors acknowledge their eminent domain? No doubt it will depend on whether the authors firmly believe that a new Saint Crispin's Day lies ahead and care to keep their place among the happy brotherhood around the new Henry V. If so, they will probably see the merit of not tampering with the legend. After all, the saintly-Lincoln myth that flourished after 1865 was of prodigious value to the then-new Republican party, whose dubious political caracoles in the next decades often took place behind a blown-up poster image of a much-loved President dead by an assassin's hand.

Kennedy's inaugural message was written after Sorensen, at the President-elect's direction, made a searching study of the Gettysburg Address, trying to discover its magic formula for immortality. To White House gratification, Sam Rayburn announced after hearing the result of this effort that Kennedy was "better than Lincoln" ("I think—I really think—he's a man of destiny"). But in *Portrait of a President,* his first book on Kennedy, published before he became a true, genuflecting believer, William Manchester wrote: "Certainly John Kennedy is not as lovable as Abe. He has a weaker grasp on the nation's heartstrings, and the reason isn't that he hasn't been shot." It was, of course, after he was shot that the two names began to be linked in an incessant litany. (The other two assassinated Presidents, Garfield and McKinley, were way out of it.) Reams were written about their common vein of humor, their similar fatalism about the danger of assassination, their century-apart (and equally gingerly) enlistment of the authority of the Presidency to help the Negro cause. Jim Bishop, who had written *The Day Lincoln Was Shot* and was soon making plans to give the same treatment to November 22, 1963, played a macabre game in the Hearst papers, listing numerous other similarities—from the fact that both men were succeeded by Vice Presidents named Johnson to the discovery that the names John Wilkes Booth and Lee Harvey Oswald had fifteen letters each. And right after the murder, Bill Mauldin's cartoon in the Chicago *Sun-Times* showed the statue in the Lincoln Memorial covering its face with its hands.

"Find out how Lincoln was buried," were Jacqueline Kennedy's words to Chief of Protocol Angier Biddle Duke a few moments after Air Force One landed at the Washington airport on the tragic flight from Dallas. It was not a precedent that was desirable to follow in all details. After the Washington rites, Lincoln's body was borne on a dead march through a dozen cities before finally being laid to rest in Springfield on May 4, nearly three harrowing weeks after the murder. The Lincoln funeral arrangements were in the hands of Secretary of War Stanton, the widow being bedfast and only half-lucid. Fortunately for the nation, Mrs. Kennedy was of a different mettle. Indeed it seems probable that the memory of her strength and heartbreaking dignity and the part she played in getting the American people through that terrible weekend will make it impossible for most of them to find serious fault with anything she does for the rest of her days (unless, as she herself shrewdly put it three years later, "I do something silly like run away with Eddie Fisher"). At her direction, Kennedy's coffin, like Lincoln's, stood in the candlelit East Room of the White House beneath chandeliers draped in black, and then in the great rotunda of the Capitol on the same catafalque, covered in black velvet, that had held Lincoln's coffin.

Following the ninety-eight-year-old scenario, six gray horses drew it down Pennsylvania Avenue to the same muffled roll of drums. Behind the wooden caisson walked, as in 1865, a riderless gelding with boots reversed in the stirrups, the military symbol of the fallen warrior. Two weeks later when Mrs. Kennedy and her children left the White House, the new tenants found that, in case anyone had missed the point, the names of the two murdered Presidents were now permanently linked in stone. The words "In this room lived John Fitzgerald Kennedy with his wife Jacqueline during the two years, ten months, and two days he was President of the United States, January 20, 1961–November 22, 1963" had been carved in the white marble fireplace of what had been Kennedy's bedroom, directly below those that had long read: "In this room Abraham Lincoln slept during his occupancy of the White House as President of the United States, March 4, 1861—April 13, 1865." It is doubtful if A. Philip Randolph, who a few days earlier had said that Kennedy's "place in history will be next to Abraham Lincoln," expected his words to be followed so literally, or so soon. But what seems most remarkable of all is that Abraham Lincoln found his place—in history, graven in stone, enshrined in legend—although at the time of his death his widow was the kind of woman no one paid any attention to, and he hadn't a father, mother, sister, or brother to his name.

Copyright Acknowledgments

Picture Credits

11, Collection of Warren Clifton Shearman. 14 (left), Culver Pictures, Inc. 14 (right), California Historical Society, San Francisco. 24, Gilcrease Institute of American History and Art. 30, *History of America*, Windsor, Vol. II, 1886. 35, *The Journal of Christopher Columbus*, 1621. 37, *Historia de Gentibus* . . . 1555. 41, The Bettmann Archive. 44, New York Public Library, Rare Book Division. 47, Culver Pictures, Inc. 51, New York Public Library, Rare Book Division. 55, Collection of Mr. and Mrs. Samuel Schwartz. 61, By Permission of the Owner, Mr. and Mrs. William Byrd. 65, Library of Congress. 68, Culver Pictures, Inc. 73, New York Public Library, Picture Collection. 81, *Abstract of Evidence on . . . Slave Trade, 1792.* 84, New Haven Colony Historical Society. 90, *Harper's Weekly*, June 2, 1860. 93, American Antiquarian Society. 97, Sinclair Hamilton Collection of American Illustrated Books, Princeton University Library. 101, Courtesy of The Henry Ford Museum, Dearborn, Michigan. 103, Library of Congress. 106, Colonial Williamsburg Collection. 107, By Permission of the Trustees of the British Museum. 111, National Maritime Museum. 118, Collection of Mrs. Carlos A. Hepp. 119, Massachusetts Historical Society. 129, Colonial Williamsburg Photo. 140, Culver Pictures, Inc. 144, Culver Pictures, Inc. 150, Free Library of Philadelphia (Picture Collection). 151, Independence National Historical Park Collection, Philadelphia. 155, National Archives. 163, Collection of Davenport West, Jr. 172, Courtesy, Henry Francis du Pont Winterthur Museum. 184, Colonial Williamsburg Photo. 188, Washington and Lee University Collection. 195, Colonial Williamsburg Photo. 202, Courtesy of The New-York Historical Society. 206, Courtesy of The New-York Historical Society. 215, Courtesy of the Museum of Fine Arts, Boston: M. and M. Karolik Collection. 219, Courtesy of The New-York Historical Society. 223, Courtesy of The New-York Historical Society. 233, Culver Pictures, Inc. 245, National Cyclopedia of American Biography (James T. White Company). 249, Rhode Island Historical Society. 255, Gibbes Art Gallery, Charleston. 256, Chicago Historical Society. 257, Library of Congress. 260, National Archives. 265, Cook Collection, Valentine Museum. 270, National Archives. 271, Collection of Frederick H. Meserve. 276, John N. Holloway, *History of Kansas*, 1868. 281, Library of Congress. 285, Courtesy of the Museum of Fine Arts, Boston: M. and M. Karolik Collection. 286, Library of Congress. 288, Cooper-Hewitt Museum of Design, Smithsonian Institution. 313, Library of Congress. 318, Free Library of Philadelphia. 323, Library of Congress. 324, *Harper's Weekly*, April 17, 1875.

326, Culver Pictures, Inc. 329, Library of Congress. 337, Library of Congress. 338, Culver Pictures, Inc. 342, Library of Congress. 348, Mississippi Department of Archives and History. 354, Harvard College Library. 361, Brown Brothers. 365, Culver Pictures, Inc. 371, National Steel Corporation, Pittsburgh, Pa. 375, Library of Congress. 376, New York *World*, July 1, 1892. 377, Culver Pictures, Inc. 381, Culver Pictures, Inc. 385, Culver Pictures, Inc. 387, Library of Congress. 389, Brown Brothers. 396, Photo by Margaret Bourke-White, *Life* Magazine, © Time Inc. 397, 1958 Time Inc. 404, Drawn by Michael Ramus for *American Heritage*. 406, Library of Congress. 407, Harvard University Library. 409, Harvard University Library. 419, Library of Congress. 427, Library of Congress. 431, Brown Brothers. 434, *Puck*, January 13, 1904. 436, Wide World Photos. 441, Library of Congress. 442, State Historical Society of Wisconsin. 445, State Historical Society of Wisconsin. 449, Library of Congress. 450, Culver Pictures, Inc. 454, Photo by Wallace Kirkland. 455, Chicago Historical Society. 457, Chicago Historical Society. 459, (top), Photo by Wallace Kirkland. 459 (middle), Photo by Wallace Kirkland. 459 (bottom), Chicago *Tribune Library*. 473, War-shaw Collection of Business Americana. 477, Official U.S. Navy Photograph. 481, Culver Pictures, Inc. 483, New York *Journal*. 486, Chicago Historical Society. 492, State of Vermont. 495, *Leslie's Official History of the Spanish-American War*. 501, *Puck*, March 22, 1899. 507, Library of Congress. 509, Garraty, *Henry Cabot Lodge*, 1953. 510, Library of Congress. 513, The San Francisco *Chronicle*. 516, Wide World Photos. 519, UPI. 538, National Archives. 539, National Archives. 541, National Archives. 545, National Archives. 551, Wide World Photos. 554, *Arizona Republic*. 556, UPI. 559, Photo by Cornell Capa, Magnum. 565, *Judge*, November, 1929. 569, Wide World Photos. 571, Collection of Rita and Daniel Fraad. 574, Wide World Photos. 577, Evans, in the Columbus *Dispatch*, November, 1938. 590, Courtesy of the New-York Historical Society. 591, Wide World Photos. 594, Ewing Galloway. 602, UPI. 603, UPI. 608, Brown Brothers. 610, Brown Brothers. 611, Brown Brothers. 614, James Reagan and HARYOU-ACT Commercial Workshop. 615, Jeff McDonald and HARYOU-ACT Commercial Workshop. 619, Drawn by Michael Ramus for *American Heritage*. 621, Photo by Fred Ward, Black Star.